U2
at the End of the World

"THIS ROLLER COASTER OF A TOUR BOOK IS REQUIRED READING . . . IT HAS A HUMAN HEART AS WELL AS AN ACADEMIC SOUL. . . . By far the best book written in recent years about the band. . . . If you want uncensored insider gossip on supermodels, famous rock stars, politicians, intraband business deals, literary giants, U2's next creative steps, and what Frank Sinatra's minder said to Bono prior to videoing their *I've Got You Under My Skin* duet, then, truly, this excellent book is the one for you."—*The Tribune Magazine* (Ireland)

"AMAZINGLY GOOD . . . FLANAGAN TREATS THE BAND AS IF THEY SET OUT ON A QUEST AS TRYING AS ANY TRADITIONAL HERO'S JOURNEY. He paces their story as fast as their globe-trotting lives and makes it as inspiring as their fans find their music. He provides a remarkable glimpse into the hearts and minds of a group that has dazzled ears and eyes throughout the world, and in doing, renders great service to U2."—*Booklist*

"HONEST AND ENGROSSING . . . Would you like to be a fly on the wall following a major rock band traveling on the road, visiting recording sessions, and sharing intimate secrets? Well, *Musician* magazine editor Bill Flanagan did just that and the proof is in the pudding with his candid and exceptional new biography *U2 at the End of the World*."—*Hard Rock*

Please turn the page for more extraordinary acclaim. . . .

"PANORAMIC AND INSIGHTFUL . . . THE BOOK U2 DESERVES . . . Flanagan is granted candor on subjects that are usually more taboo than even sex and drugs—namely business and finance."—*MOJO*

"FLANAGAN PRESENTS U2 AS RESIDING AT THE HEART OF POLITICS AND SOCIAL CHANGE. . . . His minutely detailed accounts of them also render them compellingly human."—*Publishers Weekly*

"IT READS LIKE A JAMES JOYCE MEETS HUNTER S. THOMPSON NOVEL. IT'S THE LITERARY EQUIVALENT OF THE 'ZOO TV' TOUR—A BRASH, AMBITIOUS MARATHON WITH A MOMENTUM ALL ITS OWN."—*The Boston Globe*

"CONSISTENTLY ENTERTAINING, WITTY AND REVEALING . . . Even if you're not a U2 fan—even if you're not a music fan—the view from the inside is fascinating."
—*The Orange County Register*

BILL FLANAGAN

AT THE END
OF THE WORLD

Delta
Trade Paperbacks

A Delta Book
Published by
Dell Publishing
a division of
Bantam Doubleday Dell Publishing Group, Inc.
1540 Broadway
New York, New York 10036

ISBN: 0-385-31157-5

Reprinted by arrangement with Delacorte Press

Manufactured in the United States of America
Published simultaneously in Canada

August 1996

10 9 8 7 6 5 4 3 2 1

BVG

*This book is dedicated to Susan Gallagher Flanagan
from the NoName, with love*

Author's Note

The ideas, opinions, descriptions, and conclusions in this book are all mine. Although U2 spent endless hours listening to my theories, answering my questions, and explaining their work and their workings, there are lots of things in here that some or all the members of U2 will disagree with. That's okay. I'll stand behind it all. I am as pigheaded as any of them.

Those aristocrats who fall on the floor writhing and swallowing their tongues when writers put rock & roll into the same boat as high art, poetry, philosophy, and other university subjects should get out now. You won't like it here. But if you want to understand U2, you have to understand how they draw from the highbrow stuff as well as the dumb things down in rock & roll's designated station.

And it might save a fistfight or two if I spell this out: when I talk about U2's relationship with Bill Clinton or Salman Rushdie or Wim Wenders or other cultural bigshots, it is not to suggest that U2 influenced those people; it is to show how those people influenced U2.

All right, that should shake off the whiners. Let's go.

I

Brezhnev's Bed

---

buzzing the reichstag/ bono faces eviction without his pants/ how U2 got into this mess/ the hats vs. the haircuts/ "one"/ channel surfing through the new world order

BONO WAKES up in Brezhnev's bed. He can't remember where he is. When he opens his eyes the daylight shocks his dilated brain. He tries to organize his thoughts. He is in Brezhnev's bed, in East Berlin, in the communist diplomatic guest house rented to him for a good price because the communist diplomats have fled the country. In fact, the country has fled after them. He may have gone to bed in a Soviet satellite state, but he's waking in a reunited Germany. The Cold War is over! The Wall has fallen! It's safe for Bono to go back to sleep.

He thought he heard somebody downstairs, but he must have been dreaming. He is here alone. Bono pulls himself upright, his latitude out of whack from last night's celebrating. U2 arrived in Berlin yesterday, to seek inspiration and renewal at the celebration of the end of the world they grew up in. The Berlin Wall was raised as the four members of U2 were being born. Seeing it come down shook their assumptions about the way things were and would always be. Bono told the Edge, Adam Clayton, and Larry Mullen that this was the great moment to leap into. Now was the time to go to Berlin and begin making music for the new world! They arrived on the last flight into East Germany before East Germany ceased to exist. They had the whole sky to themselves. The British pilot was so giddy with historical moment that he announced they would buzz Berlin, fly down the Strasse des Juni where the revelers were gathering, and swing over the broken wall on which the free people of eastern Europe were dancing. "On your left you see the Brandenburg Gate," the pilot announced with pip-pip and tally-ho delight as he swung his airship around. Why not? They were the only plane in the sky, the final flight to East Berlin before East Berlin was sucked into history.

As soon as they got their feet on the ground, U2 rushed to join the festivities. They leaped into the first parade they saw and waited for the contact high of liberation to intoxicate them. It was a long wait. These marchers were grim, dragging themselves along wearing dour faces and holding placards. Bono tried to muster some good Irish parading gusto, to no avail. He whispered to Adam, "These Germans really don't know how to party." Maybe, U2 thought, we've misjudged the sentiment here. Maybe the proper reaction to the end of a half-century of oppression is not celebration for what is newly won but grief for all that can never be regained. U2 looked at each other and looked at the bitter marchers and tried to fit in as they tramped along to the Wall. It was only when they got there and saw the joy everyone else was exhibiting compared with the morbidity of their company that U2 realized they were marching in an antiunification demonstration. They had hooked up with a phalanx of angry old communists, gathering one last time to show solidarity with the workers of the world and protest the fall of their Evil Empire.

"Oh, this will make a great headline," Bono said. "U2 ARRIVES IN WEST BERLIN TO PROTEST THE PULLING DOWN OF THE WALL."

In the West U2 wandered familiar streets filled with people walking as if through their dreams. The citizens of the East—not just East Germany but the newly freed Hungary, Poland, and Czechoslovakia—were still anxious, afraid that this was only a brief opening, a momentary aberration, and that if they did not find refuge quickly they would be dragged back when the communists regained their senses. For almost thirty years West Berlin had been held up to the East as a sort of capitalist Disneyland, shining with unattainable promise just over the barbed wire and gun towers. It was not just a symbol of freedom, it was the closest thing the oppressed peoples had to Oz. Their belief in its magic was not stifled by their own leaders warning them to pay no attention to that world behind the iron curtain. But in the year since people from the East began moving West, first as a trickle through Hungary and Czechoslovakia and then in a flood right through the falling Wall, the free people of West Germany have become a little less tickled with the family reunion. As Easterners looked to share in the prosperity of the west, the Westerners began to fear being saddled with the poverty of the East. *Great to see you, Cousin,* seems to be the prevailing sentiment. *When are you leaving?*

Now that U2 could walk back and forth from the East to the West, they realized that the sense of West Berlin as illuminated was not an illusion. The lights were literally brighter. The streetlamps of the East were dull, dirty yellow. The streetlights of the West were golden and white, and of higher wattage. The West had better generators. Bono was especially struck by the glow of ultraviolet lights in the windows of Eastern buildings so crowded together that little sunlight got through. Bono had associated the purple glow of UV lighting with nightclubs and raves, but to the East Germans it represented an attempt to grow flowers in the shadows.

By the sides of the streets in the West were the abandoned, burned-out carcasses of Trabants, the comically cheap automobiles manufactured in East Germany. Refugees had driven the Trabants as far as they'd go, and then left them where they died to continue their migrations on foot. Big trucks full of East German currency were rolling up to West Berlin banks to exchange bales of useless money for deutsche marks to pay the soldiers of the disintegrating communist army. The spirit of Berlin felt less rapturous, more mundane, than U2 had thought it would. They passed the one subway terminal where heavily patrolled trains had been allowed to move from East to West, and where East Germans trying to sneak aboard had been killed. They took note of its name: Zoo Station.

At 7 in the morning exhaustion dropped on their history-happy heads and U2 were led to the accommodations Dennis Sheehan, their road manager, had arranged. For Bono it was this private house where Soviet officials had lodged, and the special comfort of Brezhnev's bed.

So this morning Bono, full of emotion and alcohol, should be sleeping like Lenin but something has awakened him. He crawls out of bed hoping for a glass of water and, in his hungover state, wanders down into the basement. While standing there, naked from the waist down, dressed only in a dirty T-shirt, he thinks he hears low voices and the rattling of doorknobs. Someone is trying to get into the house. He creeps up the stairs and sees that the intruders are inside already! Bono is suddenly aware, like Adam in the Garden, that he has no pants on and his cock is hanging out. As the intruders enter the hallway where Bono is crouching he tries to cover his nuts with one hand while with the other waving and in his hoarse voice declaring, "This is my house! You do not belong here!"

Bono is unprepared for the response he gets from the ringleader, an elderly German man, who shouts back, "This is not *your* house! This is *my* house! You get out!" Bono, bent over with his balls in his hand, surveys the gang of home invaders, a middle-aged to elderly family of six filing in cautiously behind the firm father, who seems prepared to jump on Bono and wrestle him to the floor. Bono is disoriented. He feels like a kid caught trespassing by his elders, not a wealthy international figure whose accommodations have been intruded upon. "This is *my* house!" the old man repeats. And as Bono stumbles to try to find his German and sort out the confusion, it becomes apparent that the old walrus is not misdirected. This is their house. They were visiting the western side of town in 1961 when the Wall went up. Now they are home, and they want their house back.

And so it comes to pass that Bono and the rest of U2 end up checking into a particularly ugly East Berlin hotel (no rooms in the West!) while bellhops disconnect the KGB security cameras and unscrew the bedposts to check for Stasi bugs. There are prostitutes in the lobby trying to organize some currency exchanges. Bono knows well the unspoken meaning of the doleful looks he gets from Adam, Edge, and Larry. He's been getting them since they started their schoolboy band fourteen years ago. The looks say, "Another of your great ideas, Bono, another inspiration."

It is the autumn of 1990 and U2 has spent the year out of the public eye. Playing an emotional concert at home in Dublin on the last night of the 1980s, Bono told the audience, "We won't see you for a while, we have to go away and dream it all up again." It was widely speculated in the press that this meant U2 was breaking up. In fact it just meant that the band knew that the musical line they had been following had run out of track. On tour in Australia in the autumn of '89 Larry had told Bono that if this is what it meant for U2 to be superstars, he didn't like it. They were turning into the world's most expensive jukebox. They became so bored playing U2's greatest hits that one night they went out and played the whole set backward—and it didn't seem to make any difference.

It sure didn't help that the critics had turned against U2 with neck-snapping speed. Their album *U2 Rattle and Hum*—conceived as a throwaway, bargain-priced grab bag of live tracks and rootsy originals to accompany their live concert film—had been savaged in the press as a pretentious attempt to place U2 in the company of Bob Dylan, the Beatles, B. B. King, Billie Holiday, Jimi Hendrix, John Coltrane, and all the other musical seraphim the album celebrated. U2 claimed the record was meant to show that even they, the biggest band in the world, were still fans. That explanation struck critics as conceited too. U2 walked into the sucker punch with their chins stuck out and their hands in their pants. On an album dizzy with roots references, hero worship, and collaborations with rock legends, Bono was thoughtless enough to sing, "I don't believe in the sixties, in the golden age of pop/You glorify the past when the future dries up."

U2 jokes circulated in the music industry. "How many members of U2 does it take to change a lightbulb?" "Just one: Bono holds the lightbulb and the world revolves around him."

What stung more than the misunderstanding of their musical intentions was that so much of the criticism was personal. Since they began, U2 had sung about what was in their hearts and on their minds. In their music and in their public pronouncements, as in their personal lives, they were quick to share what they had just heard, just read, just figured out. They were by nature truth-tellers, and Bono was by nature a big mouth. The great thing about such openness was that fans who paid close attention to U2 really did know them, had a genuine connection to them. But in the last couple of years that was less than comforting, as it also meant that those who ridiculed the band were not just mocking the music, they were mocking the four people.

The more sensitive U2 became about being misunderstood, the more they tried to control how they presented themselves. I suggested to the Edge that maybe the band brought some of the accusations of self-seriousness on their own heads by maintaining such rigid control of their image. The film *Rattle and Hum* had been tightly supervised by U2, so if they came off as humorless and self-important, it was considered not the fault of the director, but of U2. In the same way, they were very selective about who got to interview them, and almost all the photos of the band available to the press were Anton Corbijn's moody, U2-controlled shots of stoic men standing stone-faced in deserts or snow.

"I'm all for propaganda!" Edge grinned. "It is a fine line and you're going to get it wrong sometimes. I think we're aware that maybe that is part of why we ended up being the caricature. A little bit. *Rattle and Hum,* the movie, was an example of that. We were criticized by some people for not revealing more. We actually made quite a conscious decision not to reveal more, because we didn't feel comfortable with it. It is a balance, because you have to give up so much more when you reveal all. It's like you no longer have a private life. But at the same time, if you don't reveal all, people don't really get the full picture. So it's a compromise. With *Rattle and Hum* we just didn't want to reveal ourselves. My attitude was, 'What? Do you think we're crazy? Cameras in the dressing room? What do you think we are—*stupid?*'

"I love what we do, because we control it. Because we've set it up where we're comfortable with it. That's why we *could* do it. If it was done in a way where our private lives were an open book, I don't think I could be in the band. I didn't get into the band to become a celebrity. I got into the band because I wanted to play music and write songs and tour and do all that stuff. Some people might object to that but I say, 'Well, fuck you!'" He laughed. "It's my life and this is the way it works for me."

Lately Bono likes to quote Oscar Wilde: "Man is least himself when he talks in his own person; give him a mask and he will tell you the truth." One of U2's assignments in Germany is to figure out if it's possible, ten years into their public lives, to construct masks that will allow them to say exactly what they are thinking in their songs while providing some sort of protection for their personal lives. They have realized, with the forehead-slapping regret of late bloomers, that the Rolling Stones, Bob Dylan, and Led Zeppelin figured all this stuff out *before* they got famous; by adopting public personas they could establish some space between their on-duty and off-duty lives. U2 spent their first ten years keeping nothing for themselves. They won't screw that up again.

The band assembles at the Hansa recording studio not far from the Berlin Wall. The place was once a Nazi ballroom. In the mid-seventies it was the site of some groundbreaking work by David Bowie, who in collaboration with producer Brian Eno made a trilogy of albums, *Low, Heroes,* and *Lodger,* that stretched the conventions of rock & roll into the corners of European experimental music. U2 heard about the glory of those days when Eno was coproducing the U2 albums *The Unforgettable Fire* and *The Joshua Tree.* On *Heroes,* Bowie found a grand metaphor in

Berlin's division. Bono cooked up the notion that by coming to Hansa now, U2 could tap into the spirit of reunification.

It was a nice idea, but if ideas like that worked, English professors would be successful writers. Instead U2 discovers when they get into Hansa that the studio has deteriorated since Eno and Bowie left there twelve years before. There is constant talk of the area being condemned and the building knocked down, so no one has kept Hansa humming. The two producers, Dan Lanois and Flood, will have to import their own recording equipment.

But that's not the big problem. The big problem is that the four members of U2 cannot agree on the value of the new material that Bono and Edge play for Larry and Adam, or on the sense of the new direction in which Bono and Edge want to steer the band. Edge has been swimming in experimental music, noise rock, electronics, and alternative guitar sounds. He comes in lecturing his bandmates about Insekt, Nitzer Ebb, Nine Inch Nails, KMFDM, and Front 242—stuff that sounds like walkie-talkies in washing machines.

Larry, the no-nonsense drummer, says he doesn't know any of those people. *Well,* Edge asks, *what have you been listening to?* Led Zeppelin, says Larry. Jimi Hendrix. Trying to figure out how other bands in U2's position did it and catching up on music he ignored during the postpunk era when U2 grew up.

Bono tries siding with Edge, talking about getting out of the seventies, raving about how the rappers have used high tech to make a core connection back to their souls, and saying that U2 should check out dance rhythms as the Manchester bands Stone Roses and Happy Mondays do. That is too much for Adam, who spends more time in clubs and discos than the other three combined and who thinks Bono trying to be hip just shows how out of it he really is. Manchester is over. Adam's attitude is as it has always been: *can we cut the bullshit and get to the music?* But this time there doesn't seem to be any music to get to. This time it seems less like a band than a debating society.

A division is quickly established between the Hats, Edge and Bono, and the Haircuts, Larry and Adam. Lanois, who became almost a fifth member of U2 on *Unforgettable Fire* and *Joshua Tree,* is clearly leaning toward the Haircut position, which only makes Bono and Edge more defensive. Lanois's attitude is: *You can only be what you are and we know what U2 is. Why try to pretend to be something else?*

It has never been this hard for U2 before. The band members begin to consider that they really have reached the end of the line together, that *Rattle and Hum* was the start of a downhill slide they'd be best off halting before it goes any further. They have some demos they cut at a small Dublin studio in the late summer, but Larry and Adam don't think those songs are particularly good. Their attitude is: *We tried our best to make something out of these in Dublin, now we've tried in Berlin; let's admit it's not happening.* Bono keeps trying to make something out of a track called "Who's Gonna Ride Your Wild Horses" that the others would as soon toss in the toilet. They have the outlines for songs called "Acrobat," "Real Thing," "Love Is Blindness" and "Tryin' to Throw Your Arms Around the World." Bono and Edge won't give up on one chorus—"It's alright, it's alright, it's alright/She moves in mysterious ways," even though Edge keeps changing all the music around it to try to find something worth making a song from.

Bono's attitude is that he and Edge may not have come back to the band as sharp as they should have, "but we are both a lot sharper than Larry and Adam!" Bono's wide-eyed raps about junk culture and disposable music are met with disinterest from Adam and impatience from Larry, who finally says, "What the *fuck* are you talking about?" Larry says there's a simple problem here: "You haven't written any songs! Where are the *songs*?"

That really goes up Bono's ass sideways. When Bono and Edge started abandoning the U2 tradition of all four of them writing together and brought in songs on their own, Larry was the first one to bitch that he and Adam weren't getting enough input, were being forced into a predetermined structure. But now that Bono's laying the burden on the four of them again, Larry wants the songs written for him. There's a fight brewing.

Bono and Larry represent the two poles of U2—Bono is the most open to new ideas, fads, impulses, innovation, and rationalization. Larry is the most conservative, steady, and grounded. When one of Bono's ideas leaves the realm of reality, it is Larry who calls time-out. In the past they both appreciated that balance, and everyone could laugh about their contrary traits. Now, though, it feels different. It feels less like two sides of one coin than two entirely separate currencies.

Larry accuses Bono of not knowing who he is, which Bono throws back at him, saying Larry always knows who Larry is because Larry never changes. "You haven't changed your *haircut* in ten years!" Bono says, "Yes, I sometimes fail, but at least I'm willing to experiment." Bono accuses Larry of not knowing how to improvise.

(Much later, Bono says, "I'm actually in awe of Larry for knowing exactly who he is. I don't know if I'm this or that or what. But why can't I be all of them?" Another time he says, "If I knew who I was I wouldn't be an artist, I wouldn't be in a band, I wouldn't be here screaming for a living.")

Adam's attitude is that he and Larry aren't the ones who didn't do their homework. The rhythm section put in their time on the Dublin demos. Then Bono and Edge were supposed to go off and write melodies, words, guitar hooks, and fill in any missing sections in the compositions. Adam thinks Bono's rhetoric is partly a disguise for his not having taken care of the fundamentals. "I'd really love to make a rhythmic record," Adam says. "I'm a bass player! Why wouldn't I? I don't know much about industrial music, but as long as there's a song I'll be rhythmic, and if you want to change the sounds to be industrial, fine. There's a point in the process where Larry and I have done everything we can do and we leave it to Bono and Edge to finish the songs. But those things we did in Dublin haven't really advanced."

That's not how Bono sees it. He broods that by bringing up references to dance culture—not just to current trends but even to the Rolling Stones' "Miss You" and "Emotional Rescue"—he is putting the creative obligation back on the rhythm section. "Adam knows," Bono says, "that I'm putting the weight back on *him.*"

Bono says that on this album he wants to explore the subject of sex and fidelity. "Rhythm is the sex of music," he says. "If U2 is to explore erotic themes, we have to have sexuality in the music as well as the words. The flat rhythms of white rock & roll have had their day. Rhythm is now part of the language." At the tensest moments Bono even asks Edge if he thinks Adam is deliberately dragging his ass on the bass parts in order to sabotage this new musical direction.

In the middle of one of Bono's criticisms one especially touchy afternoon Adam takes off his bass, holds it out to Bono, and says, "You tell me what to play and I'll play it. You want to play it yourself? Go ahead."

Thus the Hansa sessions crawl along, with Berlin getting darker and colder. Everyone's freezing all the time and it seems to never stop raining. They eat most nights in a gray, oppressive gruel hall. With nothing else to do short of disbanding, U2 keep plodding along, trying to figure out a way to take their music into the nineties and feeling like they're getting nowhere. Edge is getting frustrated with Lanois, who he thinks *just doesn't get it.* Larry defends Lanois.

Edge comes in one afternoon and there's Lanois in the studio, playing guitar and singing, desperately trying to make a new song called "Down All the Days" sound like the old *Joshua Tree* U2. "He's really panicking," Edge says. "I had no idea Danny was so confused by what we were doing."

Edge starts thinking that maybe the rumors that U2 was going to disband after the New Year's show were prophetic. "Maybe this *is* what we should do," he admits. "Maybe we should break up and see what happens."

It seems like every time U2 starts to get going musically something goes wrong, someone makes a mistake. When that happens Bono—not known for keeping his feelings to himself—howls his frustration. This really gets on his partners' nerves. Finally they get together and impose a band ruling: the hyped-up Bono is permanently forbidden to drink coffee.

U2 needs some objective ears. Brian Eno, producer with Lanois of their two best albums and the historic Mensa of Hansa, is drafted to come in for a few days and listen to what they've done. It turns out to be a great relief. Eno—thin, pale, and ascetic—has the patience of a university professor taking over a class of unruly freshmen. He is able to mediate between Edge's ambitions and his old partner Lanois's resistance. He goes to the board and shows how, by adding oddball vocal effects and a few jarring sounds, it's possible to bring some of the more conventional material U2 has been fiddling with into fresh sonic territory. Eno assures the frustrated band that they're doing better than they think, and that Edge's desire to get into new acoustic areas is not incompatible with Danny and Larry's desire to hold on to solid song structures.

"Eno is the person both Bono and Edge really connect with," Adam says. "Intellectually they can bounce ideas off him. Eno isn't loyal to any philosophy for very long. It's no problem for Eno to say, 'Okay, if that's the type of thing you want to do, here's how we do it.' Where Danny has been saying, 'Okay, that's what you want to do, but I'm this kind of record producer and you're that kind of band, so let's make what you're trying to do happen through what you've always done before.' So Eno's important. What Eno won't do is take responsibility. He won't let you off the hook. And that's fine."

Eno's input gives U2 encouragement to keep working, but it does not settle their stomachs. One night they are struggling with a track called "Ultra Violet" and it's going nowhere. Edge figures the song needs another section and goes to the piano in the big room to come up with a middle eight. After playing for a while he has two possible parts and isn't sure which one would be better for the song. He comes back into the control booth, picks up an acoustic guitar, and plays both of them for Lanois and Bono to see which they prefer. They say that those both sound pretty good—what would it be like if you put them together?

Edge goes back out into the studio and starts playing the two sections together, one into the other. Larry and Adam fall in behind him on the drums and bass. Bono feels the muse knocking on his head as surely as in one of those old Elvis movies where the king jumps up in the middle of a clambake and starts rocking. Bono goes out to the microphone and begins improvising words and a melody: "We're one, but we're not the same—we get to carry each other, carry each other."

U2 plays the new song for about ten minutes. "Is it getting better," Bono sings, "or do you feel the same? Is it any easier on you now that you've got someone to blame?" Edge feels that it's suddenly all jelling— the band is clicking and all four of them know. They come into the booth and listen to a playback with a relief close to joy. By the next morning they have recorded "One," as strong a song as U2 has ever written. It came to them all together and it came easily, as a gift.

"Phew," Edge jokes, "the roof for the house in the west of Ireland is looking good! I'll be able to change the car this year after all!"

There's still an enormous amount of work to do, but at least U2 knows they can still bring good music out of each other. "I suppose in the back of your mind everyone thinks that maybe one day we're going to write together and we just won't have anything to say," Edge explains. "Literally, there will be nothing more to add. You all hope that everyone knows when that time has come and you don't go on and do some completely awful album that everyone recognizes to be a disaster."

He thinks "One" represents the turning point away from that ugly proposition. U2 agrees they should get out of Berlin and pick up this thread again at home, in Dublin. They decide they will move out of Germany in January of '91. Larry feels, though, that there's an issue even bigger than the music to resolve before U2 goes forward. The band grew out of friendship between the four of them, he says, and if it's a choice between continuing the friendships or continuing the band, U2 has to go.

So during a Christmas break in Dublin the four members of U2 engage in heart-to-heart talks about what they expect from each other, as partners and as friends. Listening to the Hansa tapes again after a break, they sound a lot better than they did in Germany. There's plenty of good material there to work with and they decide that they can again trust each other enough to go through it together.

"There is a love between the members of this band that is deeper than whatever comes between us," Larry says after the armistice. "After almost fifteen years, which would be time for a divorce in almost any relationship, we looked at each other and said, 'Lay down your arms.'"

They have to go back to Berlin in January to finish some bits before setting up in Dublin. While they are packing up, war breaks out in the Middle East. It's been building up the whole time U2 has been recording—Iraq invaded Kuwait last summer and the United States began assembling an alliance to threaten them into withdrawal. It was the first test of President George Bush's New World Order, an international scheme in which the East-West, communist-capitalist schism was to be replaced by a pyramid of interconnected nations (with, needless to say, America on top). A current bestseller refers to this moment, the proposed dawning of a post–bipolar world, as "The End of History." The British techno-pop band Jesus Jones even has a big hit this week called "Right Here, Right Now," about the same subject: "Right here, right now—watching the world wake up from history."

Right here, right now, it's looking like the end of Saddam Hussein's history anyhow. Bush got the Europeans to agree to impose a deadline on Iraq, after which if they didn't pull out of Kuwait they'd be attacked. Then he convinced the Soviets to come in, the Japanese, most of the other Arab states, and even China. While waiting for Saddam to back down, the rest of the world slapped Iraq with an embargo and diplomatic sanctions.

That Saddam, Iraq's dictator, is an obvious nut with eyes on grabbing other oil-producing neighbors was a big incentive to the Middle

Eastern states to join with the U.S. (and Israel!) in this crusade. Iraq had previously invaded Iran, so there was no hope of help coming for Saddam from the Islamic fundamentalists. Feeling a bit overextended, the Iraqi ruler even tried lobbing a few missiles at Tel Aviv, hoping to unite the Arabs in a holy war against the Jews. The Arabs didn't bite.

The countdown to the U.N. deadline has been dominating the news for a couple of weeks, but still, it's a shock to hear that the war has begun and U.S. missiles are blowing up downtown Baghdad. Bono sits at the TV transfixed, amazed that CNN is broadcasting the war live twenty-four hours a day, and that he—like millions of TV viewers—finds himself watching war as if it were a football match. He turns on a movie, switches to the war for a while, over to MTV, back to the war: *Whoa, look at those missiles! That was a big one!*

Edge is struck by the fact that the young pilots returning from bombing raids and the soldiers directing the missiles from launchpads far from Baghdad often compare what they're doing to playing video games at home. It is all computer controlled, they never see any blood or destruction—children who grew up using toys to pretend they were at war end up at war pretending they're using toys. They fly off on missions with the Clash's "Rock the Casbah" blaring. Edge and Bono are watching TV together when a young American pilot is interviewed on CNN. When asked what the bombing looks like from the plane, he says, "It's so realistic." Bono and Edge look at each other, amazed.

Bono thinks that something fundamental has changed, not just in the world's political structure, but in the way media has permeated the public consciousness. In the last decade cable TV has spread through what used to be called the free world. There is no more line between news, entertainment, and home shopping. Bono says that when U2 tour behind this album, they have to figure out a way to represent this new reality.

2

Dogtown

---

*the toughest guy in the band/ why rich people have no
friends/ the wives will kill us/ U2 in nighttown/ adam exposes
himself/ springtime for bono*

EVERYTHING IS EASIER in Dublin in the spring of '91. Everything
musical anyway. One of the side effects of starting up the U2
machine again is the havoc it causes in the home lives of the
members. Adam, a swinging bachelor, has nothing to keep him from
commiting to a long stretch on the road. Larry has a longtime girlfriend
named Ann Acheson, but they have no children and she has her own life
and work.

It's different for Bono and Edge, who have both been married for
years and have young children. Edge has three daughters. Bono has a
two-year-old girl and a second on the way. Their wives have the right to
say that after putting their marriages aside for months or even years at a
time in order for U2 to conquer the world, they might have expected,
now that all the band's goals had been reached, to settle into a more
normal family life. Elvis Presley, the Beatles, and Bob Dylan all quit
touring after hitting the top and devoted themselves to making records
and living with their wives and children. U2 is now talking about
releasing the new album in the autumn of '91, touring America and
Europe in the spring of '92, going back to America in the summer and
fall of '92 if the demand is there, and then, if things go really well,
touring Europe again in '93. As the band returns to Dublin with their
unfinished album, they are looking at a work schedule that will cause
them to put their domestic lives on hold for the next three years.

There are boxes within boxes in the U2 organization, and what goes
on between the band members and their families is in the smallest box
of all. I don't know what finally sets it off and it's surely nobody's

business, but around Easter Edge moves out of his home and away from his wife, Aislinn. He settles into Adam's guest house and work on the album continues.

"I could tell stories of times each of the others has been there for me," Edge says at dinner one night. "I mean, there have been periods when Adam and I didn't particularly get along, over the years. Yet when I left Aislinn I moved into Adam's." Edge, who is rarely inarticulate or sentimental, has a little trouble getting the next words out: "I suppose that the other three are the closest friends I have."

That friendship can be tough for any outsider to penetrate. And no one's tougher to tie down about it than the hardheaded Larry Mullen.

"People say, 'Why don't you do interviews? What do you think about this? What do you think about that?' " Larry sighs. "My job in the band is to play drums, to get up on stage and hold the band together. That's what I do. At the end of the day that's all that's important. Everything else is irrelevant."

Many people on this planet say they hate horseshit, but no one hates horseshit as much as Larry Mullen, Jr., does. The possibility that he might somehow add to the rising stew of crap that threatens to submerge our civilization in hype and nonsense appalls him so much that he slaps on a scowl and shuts his mouth at the first inkling of glad-handing, backslapping, false sincerity, sucking up, ass-kissing, air-kissing, overpraise, fair-weather friendship, freeloading, hyperbole, ligging, flattery, posturing, complement chewing, ego-stroking, bootlicking, cheek-smooching, groveling, pratspeak, toadying, leg-lifting, fame-grubbing, schnoring, idol worship, starfucking, or brown-nosing.

Boy, did he pick the wrong business!

Bono says that with Larry everyone is presumed guilty until proven innocent—but if he makes up his mind that you're okay he'll not only let you into his house, he'll let you sleep in his bed.

Larry's always been tough. He can laugh heartily telling the story of how as little kids on Christmas Eve he and his sister kept pestering their father, saying, "I think I hear Santa, Dad! I think I hear Santa!" Until their annoyed old man said, "There is no Santa Claus! Now go to sleep!" When his mother told him he could not go off, underage and illegal, to play in bars with U2, he told her flat out that he *had* to do it, there was nothing to argue about. And off he went.

Larry effectively founded U2 at Mount Temple, their Dublin high school when he approached Dave Evans (Edge) about starting a band. Word got out and Paul Hewson (Bono), Adam, and a few other kids came by Larry's family's kitchen to bang on guitars and sing cover tunes. Before long membership was knocked down to the four characters who remain U2 today. Edge was a couple of months older than Larry. Adam and Bono both had more than a year on him. With his blond hair and pretty features, Larry looked younger than the others. He looked like a little kid. But Larry was always as bullheaded as a minotaur. He has joked that he gave up on being leader of the group as soon as he met Bono, but in some indefinable way he has remained the center of U2 from high school to here. It's not even that he's the band's conscience; it's more that he's the one who knows what each of them is and what each of them might or can never become, and he will never hesitate to say so to any of their faces. Somehow, by defining that, Larry defines what U2 ends up being.

"What's made U2 has always been the relationship," he says. "The relationship has not only been a personal one, it's also been a musical one. It's been an understanding. It's a cliché, but U2's biggest influences have always been each other. We've always played with each other. We've always played against each other musically. When we came to Berlin we were suddenly, musically, on different levels and that affected everything. The musical differences affected the personal differences.

"It's a very, very strange world that we live in. I was very young when the band started. I ended up doing it because of tragedy, in some ways. My mother died and I went straight into the band, that was the kick. On the road I was surrounded by people who were older than me and more experienced than I was. I was seventeen. I was a virgin. I had difficulty as any normal teenager would.

"When you're a kid and you're thrown into this, it's very hard. Some people cope with it better than others. I feel that I'm less affected now than maybe some of the other guys are because I have fallen in love with this. I loved it when I was a kid, then when I went on the road it was so difficult I just didn't know what was going on, it was very hard. Then, after a whole lot of different things happening with the band being successful, I made a very clear decision in my own mind that this is really what I want to do and I want to make a serious go of it. I don't just want to be the drummer in U2 anymore. I want to actually contribute on a different basis and do more."

When Larry says he was kicked into U2 because his mother died (she was killed in a traffic accident around his seventeenth birthday), he is tapping into a secret history of rock & roll. Losing his mother as a kid is a tragedy Larry shares with John Lennon, Paul McCartney, Jimi Hendrix, Madonna, Sinéad O'Connor, and Bono. Throw in Elvis Presley and Johnny Rotten, two singers very close to mothers who died just after they got famous, and you have a pretty good representation of the biggest blips on rock & roll's forty-year seismograph. Bono lost his mother in 1974, when he was fourteen. She collapsed from a stroke at her own father's funeral and died immediately thereafter.

Larry says having that loss in common brought Bono and him together. "There was a connection there," he explains. "He understood a little of what I felt. I was younger than him. I didn't have any brothers. My father was out of whack anyway, so Bono was the link. He said, 'Look, I understand a bit what you're going through. Maybe I can help you.' And he did. Through thick and thin he's always been there for me. Always.

"People think the band is this unit that's always together. We fight and argue all the time! But I have to say that through it all Bono has always been there. And that was where it started, that was the original connection. When I was in deep shit, he made himself available for me, he was around. Even on the road when I was going through a rough time I used to share a room with him. He just used to make sure I was okay." Suddenly Larry smiles and says, "It was a bit like baby-sitting, y'know what I mean?"

I ask Larry how his life was affected by becoming wealthy.

"It was only after *Joshua Tree* that we started to make money," he says. That's a surprise—*Joshua Tree*, which came out in 1987 and sold 14 million copies, was U2's fifth album. The world figured they were rich long before that. "After *Joshua Tree* we invested a lot of money into *Rattle and Hum.* So we *saw* a lot of money but never made any. It was put back into the movie. I remember walking away with about twenty thousand dollars. That was the money that was there when I arrived home from the *Joshua Tree* tour. There was more later on. I remember going down to Waterford. I had been saving for years and years to buy myself a Harley. That was the first real material thing I ever bought. The money came in very, very slowly. It wasn't immediate at all. It wasn't like we did the *Joshua Tree* tour and then someone gave me five million dollars and said,

'There you are, son, go with it.' It wasn't like that at all, it was a very slow thing."

What was the reaction of friends and family when they assumed, perhaps before it was true, "Oh, Larry's a millionaire now"? Does everybody wait for you to pick up the check at dinner?

"To a limited degree," he says. "It's only recently that it's become a major issue, 'cause there is publicity about it, a lot of people talk about it. What disturbs me most is that people figure, 'Hey, look, a hundred quid to me is two weeks wages. It's nothing to you!' I find that incredibly offensive. That's jumping to conclusions. It's just taking advantage. That's the biggest thing that's affected the way I feel about some people. I find there are two very distinctly different reactions. There's those people who say, 'I don't give a damn what you do, I buy my round, you buy your round. We're friends. I expect nothing from you.' And there's the other ones. It's hard because the people you grow up with are generally people who don't have any money. They work in banks or they're electricians and they don't make as much. I think they should be responsible for themselves and not take advantage. I think it's lack of respect for themselves. I certainly don't respect them."

I ask why Larry told Bono, during the last tour, that he didn't like what U2 had become.

"It had become very serious, very hard work. And just no fun. It was nothing to do with music. It was to do with getting up and going to work. Because we take care of a lot of our own business, we spend a lot of time in meetings. We've always done that. On the stage it was good, but it was very intense and was very hard work. You were *grimacing* because you were stressed. I remember coming off that tour and feeling, 'If this is what it is, I really don't want to do it anymore, I *can't* do this anymore.'

"It was just stressful on a musical level. I suppose we had realized that we weren't as capable of plugging into other people's worlds—like B. B. King's—as we'd hoped. And I certainly found it was nothing to do with where I was coming from. I'm glad to have had the experience, but that's it. I come from a different world."

Well, I say, the stretch in Berlin wasn't exactly a load of laughs.

"No," Larry says. "It was suddenly trying to unplug that different world of *Rattle and Hum* and plug into another one. That's very hard to do. When we plugged into *Rattle and Hum* we'd lost touch with where it was we had come from—which is trying to find *new* ways. Some people were quicker at finding the route than others, and it caused immense strain within the band. Because for the first time in the band there was no consensus musically. Whereas in the past, although everyone might not agree, there was some sort of understanding of what was going on. This time there was no understanding. No one knew what the fuck anyone else was talking about. That was the basis of all those problems."

All of what the band has been going through gets thrown into Bono's lyrics. It is only in the final weeks before the album is due to be delivered to the record company that most of it comes together. "We tend to spend 90 percent of the time on 30 percent of the material," Adam explains, "and the rest happens incredibly quickly."

U2 bring in their old producer Steve Lillywhite, as well as Eno, Flood, and Lanois, and get everyone mixing. Different producers mix the same songs and then present them to the band, who pick one (or worse, pick aspects of each and ask one of the exhausted producers to combine them). What emerges is a weird juxtaposition of frantic sound (influenced by techno, hip-hop, and other urban pop trends, but grounded in solid song structures) and introspective lyrics about the tension between domestic life and the lure of the outside world's adventures. The music, the sound itself, is so full of life and electricity that it's easy to understand what's seducing the lyricist away from his responsibilities at home; the music conveys how much fun there is to be had out there in the world of discos, boom boxes, rock concerts, and raves. The words may reveal the guilt and concern going through the singer's head, but the music demonstrates the fun and exuberance racing through his bloodstream.

The first song—"Zoo Station"—blasts open with a barrage of electronic sounds and distortion. Bono's voice is processed so heavily, it barely sounds human. If you strain you can make out what he's saying: "I'm ready, ready for what's next."

The music conjures up an environment like Times Square or Piccadilly Circus at 11 P.M. on a July Saturday. It's full of pushing and shoving, hip-hop samples, loud arguments, bursting images, and screaming guitars. Some of Bono's lyrics sound like they were read off the T-shirts in an all-night souvenir shop ("Don't let the bastards grind you down," "A woman needs a man like a fish needs a bicycle"), like they are being recited by a man in that late-night state of sensory overload where you babble phrases you just overheard.

The central character that emerges on this expedition through urban perdition is a man messing up his secure home life by charging out into the night's temptations. The album is full of romantic and spiritual anguish, of the bargains made between couples and the recriminations they throw at each other when those deals are breached. In this context, when Bono sings, "We're one, but we're not the same," it sounds less like a comfort than an excuse.

One good side effect of Bono's bad habit of leaving all his lyrics in flux until the last minute is that by the time he puts the final vocals on an album there is usually a narrative coherence to the whole thing. Your old English teacher might tell you that this results in a novelistic cohesiveness. Certain members of U2 who have nothing left of their fingernails might call it the result of a long intellectual constipation finally ended by a verbal diarrhea. I myself would like to point out that in this case it results in an album-long metaphor of the moon as a dark woman who seduces the singer away from his virtuous love, the sun. In the middle of Side Two the singer, lying in the gutter in a vain attempt to throw his arms around the world, looks up and sees the sun rising. He asks, "How far are you gonna go before you lose your way back home?" Then he starts crawling home, exhausted, elated, ashamed, satisfied, and nursing a bloody nose.

That would be an easy place for the album to end, and in the Andy Capp world of most rock & roll, that's usually where we fade out. U2 doesn't let their listeners off the hook so easily. The darkness of the doubts they've raised cannot be exorcised by a night on the town. The last three songs face the big issue of how couples begin to reconcile the suffering they force on each other. In "Ultra Violet" the singer pleads with his love to light his way home, only to find that "the day is as dark as the night is long." The couple crawl into bed together, unable to sleep. He marvels at his own hypocrisy: "I must be an acrobat to talk like this and act like that." They decide that if they can't sleep maybe they can speak their dreams out loud and (Bono's quoting Delmore Schwartz here) "begin responsibilities." The album fades out with the conclusion that "Love Is Blindness," the inability to distinguish day from night.

This is U2 in Nighttown, an X ray of four men who spent their teens and twenties being focused, serious, and pious and who, as they hit thirty, want to see what they missed. There was a song recorded in Berlin that didn't make the final sequence, in which Bono sang of wanting to "see and touch and taste as much as a man can before he repents." The Nighttown James Joyce created in *Ulysses* was a nocturnal urban world that promised knowledge in exchange for innocence. *Ulysses* was, among other things, a parody of Homer's *Odyssey*, with the hero battling the demons of his soul rather than mythical monsters on his long journey home to his wife. This trip U2 is intent on undertaking is just beginning. There's no way of telling how far it will bring them, or whether they'll all make it back.

"I don't think I've ever come home from a tour the same person I left," Bono says. "So there is always a moment where the people you come home to wonder if you're going to get on with them. Or if they even want you in the house. I'm an intinerant at heart. When I was fourteen my mother died. I lived with my father, and it was a house but it wasn't really a home after that. I always ended up sleeping on the floor of other people's places. And so, wherever I am I'm happy enough. I probably wouldn't come home at all if it weren't for the fact I had family." Bono thinks about that for a bit and says, "I think the real problems start when you come back, not when you go out."

The new album will be U2's first since the multinational record company Polygram, itself a division of the multinational electronics company Philips, bought Island Records, the label to which U2 is signed. Polygram paid something like $300 million dollars to get Island, which really means—given that Island has no other living superstars—they paid it to get U2. Polygram is planning a massive push behind their first album by their superstar band and they need some information to get the ball rolling for the autumn campaign—like, *Does the album have a name?*

U2 consider the title *Cruise Down Main Street*, a reference to the cruise missiles that winged with such precision through downtown Baghdad, and to the Rolling Stones' classic *Exile on Main Street*. They talk about titling the record *Fear of Women*—but reject that as sure to make the Pretentious Police reach for their revolvers. They are determined not to call attention to the seriousness of the lyrics, to keep the media's eye on the flashy surface. It is all part of erecting the mask Bono talked about, the false face that will keep U2 from the embarrassment of standing around with their dicks hanging out. Which brings up a good idea! How about this for a cover: a big photograph of Adam standing there naked. The band calls in photographer Anton Corbijn and Adam proudly hangs out his manhood for the camera. Adam thinks that if they use this as the sleeve they should call the record *Man*—the logical sequel to their first album, *Boy*. Edge thinks it might be funnier to go with the nude shot and call the album *Adam*, in tribute to both their bassist and the first mortal (who was also the first man to get kicked out of his home and into the cruel world).

There is some brow mopping at Polygram when they hear rumors about a nude album jacket. Eventually U2, unable to decide which of Anton's many possible cover concepts to use, decides to go with them all: create a big montage with everything from the Adam willie shot to portraits of the four band members squeezed into one of those little Trabants. Anton is sort of distressed at the idea, but it's not his album. As for the name, they settle on something that no critic can take seriously: *Achtung Baby*. It is a reference—used frequently in Berlin by U2 soundman Joe O'Herlihy—to *The Producers*, the Mel Brooks movie about a pair of sleazy theater swindlers who try to create the biggest Broadway flop of all time by staging a musical called *Springtime for Hitler*.

U2 figures that no critic will accuse them of pomposity with a title like that! Although this critic thinks that given the album's theme of faith and faithlessness *Achtung Baby* suggests what Elvis Costello called "emotional fascism"—the dictatorship of fidelity.

"It's a bit of a con to call it something as flip as *Achtung Baby*," Bono admits. "Because underneath that thin layer of trash it's blood and guts. It's a very heavy, loaded record. It's a dense record." He grins. "I told somebody I thought it was a dense record and word got around that we were making a *dance* record.

"I think that the real rebels of the nineties are probably not musicians but comedians. Stand-up comics. Because they have people laughing while they're telling them where they're at. If people see you coming with a placard these days they just get out of your way. U2 has got to be careful. And smart."

By the way, in *The Producers* the crooked accountant who stages *Springtime for Hitler* is named Leo Bloom. Maybe U2 has hit on the insight that he could be the same Bloom that James Joyce sent into Night-town in *Ulysses*. See, if you switch through the channels long enough, your synapses keep clicking around even after the TV is turned off.

3

Achtung Bono

---

rock and recommodification/ why keep going/ ghosts in the machines/ when def leppard shamed U2 and other lessons learned from car stereo systems/ can we order now?

NOW THAT U2's civil war is over, the album is complete, and the bandmembers have embraced each other with the quivering chins of an old couple renewing their wedding vows, Bono feels comfortable spinning out his take on where U2 has to go and why getting up to the starting gate was so tough.

"It's hard for people," Bono says over lunch one afternoon in a restaurant where a Muzak version of "Over the Rainbow" adds a special poignance to his talk of his ambitions for U2's second public decade. "If you realize that this friction makes you smarter, quicker, and tougher, then it's surely wise to stick with it. But if you want an easy life, if you're happy with your lot, if you see success as your goal, it's over. I've had this out with various members of the band, as you know, and, I'll be honest, with Ali." Ali is Bono's wife, Alison Stewart Hewson. "We thought, okay, maybe it'll take ten years to get to this place, but *when* we got there we could stop this kind of madness. But *I don't think it's mad.* I think that that's the fun of it. I think there's nothing sadder than people who feel that they've arrived. I think it might have just taken a couple more minutes for some of the other people to realize the same thing.

"When you're thirty you're just starting your creative life if you're a painter or a writer. Some don't start till they're forty, or probably shouldn't. It's just that in rock & roll terms, in the way that it used to be, a lot of people were burnt out. They were shooting stars, and of course they burned bright and they burned fast, but with a lot of great artists it's the opposite; they just got better and better. That's what I want U2 to be. I feel like we've just had a taste of it and that the success, in a way, is a distraction. That's not false modesty, it's genuinely knowing that this work was extraordinary because of what it *hinted at* more than what it was."

Bono says that after all the *Rattle and Hum* success (the album, reviled though it might have been, sold 7.5 million copies) and backlash, after Larry's complaint that U2 onstage was turning into a jukebox, after accepting that maybe embracing American roots music was a dead end for U2, Bono came home after that good-bye concert in Dublin at the end of 1989 feeling sapped and rotten.

"I had a terrible time at Christmas," he admits. "A very convenient end-of-decade depression. Y'know, I don't buy the idea that U2 reinvented itself in that moment, because I've always felt that all through our life was a process of re-creation and killing off the old and bringing on the new. It's just that this was a more spectacular murder.

"I looked back and said, 'Okay, it was wonderful and a lot of good work was done,' but I felt very unhappy. I said, 'If this is it, this is not enough.' I think that everyone else would have come to that conclusion, but it might have taken a few average albums and I don't think that was on. So there were a few simple tasks to be faced. Like: rhythm was now part of the language of even white rock & roll. There was no way back from it. How does a three-piece be polyrhythmic? You have to have another thing. On *Unforgettable Fire* Brian's contribution was to find little tape loops for us to play off. So that's how this technology thing came together. These are practical problems. So that you can focus on the personality of Adam's bass playing, rather than just the pure timekeeping of it. And you can have the sort of hammer aspect to Larry's kickdrum and still have the delicacy of a conga part. But it was very hard, and learning to adapt to that new technology created tension. It's a bit like trying to help somebody across the road who's saying, 'Hey, what are you doing? I like it here!' But they wouldn't *really.* It's just that they're not ready to cross the road yet."

U2 has now embraced sequencers that play prerecorded instrumental parts both to fatten up their sound and to allow the musicians to play embellishments and counterpoint while a machine takes care of basics. At one time U2 would have thought of that as cheating. Now they see it as a liberation. The values that inspired *Rattle and Hum*—"Let's learn about roots and how the old songwriters did it"—have been put in deep storage.

"U2 are the world's worst wedding band." Bono shrugs. "We are. Why don't we just own up to it and stop fucking about? For instance, we were always jealous of the fact that we never knew anyone else's songs. That started a lot of B sides where we did cover versions and tried to get into the structure of songwriting vicariously and then apply it. This is a band that's one of the biggest acts in the world, and we know fuck-all in terms of what most musicians would consider to be important. 'Cause all of these bands, including this new crop, have all played in bar bands, they're all well versed in rock & roll structure— which is also why they're all so well versed in rock & roll clichés.

"Imitation and creation are opposites. The imitative spirit is very different from the creative spirit, which is not to say that we all don't beg, steal, and borrow from everybody, but if the synthesis of it all is not an original spirit, it's unimportant.

"Compare white rock to the state of African American culture. The black position is so much more modern, so much more plugged in, so much more postmodern even. They're begging, stealing, and borrowing, but creating new things, using the technology that's available. The springboard for rock & roll was the technology of the electric guitar, the fuzz box, and printed circuits. I think it's fascinating that in Compton and in the Bronx, there are sixteen- and seventeen-year-olds who are part of the next century plugging into all this technology to create new sounds, while middle-class kids from Ivy League colleges are listening to music that is Neanderthal. Not Neanderthal in that it's raw and primitive screaming, but that the form and fashion of it is."

When Bono gets on a roll like this there's no shutting him up. But it's worth paying attention, 'cause after *Achtung Baby* is released U2 is going to put all this theory into practice or flame out in the attempt. And by then he may not want to spell it all out.

"I have a theory about technology, if you can stand it," Bono says, digging in. "It's long, but it's interesting. Sitting on Sunset Strip outside the recording studio, working on the *Rattle and Hum* soundtrack in 1988, on Friday nights, we used to watch the parade. It was an extraordinary sight to see these cars that were fitted out as music systems. You've seen that parade of Mexican hopping trucks, and there's a sound." Bono cups his hands over his mouth and imitates the heavy, distorted backbeat of hip-hop blasting through a beefed-up car stereo system, over which he then sings a bluesy wail.

"I thought, 'I know this music!' " He sings the bluesy wail again, this time bending the notes just a little more off the Western standard than blues notes already bend. Now Bono's hip-hop singing sounds Arabic.

"I thought, wow, this sound reminds me so much of when I was traveling in Africa, recording the kind of atonal call-and-response music that you find in North Africa. And it dawned on me that a journey had happened in black music that is so extraordinary. You take from Africa people two hundred, three hundred years ago by force to cotton plantations. You take away from them their own music, forbid the talking drums. It was often Irish slave drivers keeping them away from their native musical forms, as the Irish were the lowest rung on the white ladder. Through the Irish and Scottish slave drivers they picked up the three chords of Celtic folk music and a new format arrived: the blues, and eventually gospel.

"It all starts to get mixed up. The technology keeps it changing. The printed circuit has arrived, the electic amplification, and rock & roll is this new hybrid, which eventually goes back to Europe and hits big there with the Beatles and the Stones, and then goes back to America where Hendrix takes it further. Then it goes back into Europe, and you have in Germany a group called Kraftwerk working with pure synthesized sounds, completely electronic sounds, where you remove any original signal from a musical instrument. This is kind of interesting, this starts to influence back across America, and you have people like George Clinton and Stevie Wonder getting into electronic sounds and synthesizers. This goes back across to England, there is an invention, the sampling device, the Fairlight and Synclavier. Sampling goes back across, this dance going on between two continents continues with technology playing the music. And with this new sampling device you are able to grab and recombine bits from old records and from that a new format arrives—hip-hop.

"What's completely mind-boggling to me is that after three hundred years, the music gets back to its core through technology. You have kids in the Bronx scratching records, creating a call and response, using this technology to get back to their center. What does that say? That is so big. It's an idea that has ramifications to me beyond music.

"I suppose as an Irish person who has worked so hard to sort of musically try and reinvent what it is to be Irish, that is great for me. Because people listen to U2 and say, 'Well what you are doing *is* Irish, yet by the look of it, it's not.' It's a spirit.

"That was one of the things that to me exploded the idea of *authenticity,* which is, of course, the catchphrase of all these rock groups: 'This is *real,* because we are in control of it.' 'Disco sucks.' That's *wrong.* I started to see Kraftwerk as some sort of soul group. And all the ideas of authenticity, which we had played with in *Rattle and Hum*—'Let's write acoustic songs, let's try it like other people did, and let's be fans, and discover it.' We discovered wonderful things, learned wonderful things, wrote a few songs I ought to proud of. But that was like going down a road and then finding out, 'No.' "

Bono pauses to let the dowsing pole of my understanding touch the bottom of the deep pool of his insight. Before I can say, "Let's order," he's digging another well.

"Parallel to that," he says, "I realized that technology can facilitate freedom. In fact, what I think people don't understand about the music business is that people do not buy stereos to play their records; people buy records to play their stereos! Think about it from the consumers' point of view; the purchase of the hardware is much more expensive than the purchase of the software. If you are living in the real world, which I certainly was when I was sixteen, and you buy one of these motherfuckers, you want to buy the record that plays it well. That's why the Beatles again run parallel to technology. *Sgt. Pepper* was a *stereo* album. When the success of *Sgt. Pepper* is written about, that's just not mentioned. But this was hardware companies putting out this new device for listening to music, and here was a way you could show off the thing. This can be followed through to Pink Floyd, as it further developed, and on into CD and the success of Dire Straits."

I have to admit that Bono's onto something. In the early seventies teenagers went wild for stereo headphones, and bought albums that were mixed to swing back and forth, from right to left. Recently, new bands such as Nirvana and Nine Inch Nails have taken advantage of the wide dynamic range of CDs to make albums that jump from very soft to very loud in a way that vinyl records never could.

"And if you want to know why white people are listening to rap music," Bono says, "apart from the sort of white-guy-being-attracted-to-the-things-you're-afraid-of social thing, it's a lot to do with the hardware systems, the car systems, club systems. The bottom end has to be tight, so you can turn it up. Suddenly records that sounded great on a stereo or even on the radio—that FM rock sound—suddenly don't sound so great compared to these guys. You know, you put on a Public Enemy record, and it sounds like the end of the world!"

Bono first thought about this—and felt U2 was lacking—when he and Adam were hitchhiking in Tennessee during their *Rattle and Hum* pilgrimage to Graceland and Sun Studios. A kid picked them up and had on his car stereo an album by the pop-metal group Def Leppard, produced by South African soundmaster Mutt Lange. Bono was knocked out by how powerful the Def Leppard music—which had never meant anything to him before—sounded on a cranked-up, bottom-heavy car system. The driver got wildly goosed when he recognized his passengers, yanked off the Def Lep and stuck on a U2 tape. It didn't sound half as exciting.

"Def Leppard's 'Pour Some Sugar on Me,' to me is one of the first industrial records," Bono says, knowing that he's picking a fight. "I haven't fully realized the implications of that. I think we've got to make records that sonically make more use of the technology. That's something we have yet to do."

"All that's great," I say, waving frantically for the waiter before Bono leaves port again, "but it doesn't do the band much good if half the guys don't want to go that way."

"Yeah, but great ideas are great persuaders," Bono says. "If you're arguing a lot, it's not a clear enough idea. A great idea is clear to everybody. And the problem with what happened in *Achtung Baby* was that the ideas, the concepts, were good, but the songs early on weren't good enough to convince everybody. The reward wasn't in sight. And Danny, of course, was pulling his hair out. Brian knew what we were doing and understood the great fun we could have deconstructing—" Bono catches himself and smiles. "It was hard not to use art terms. And art terms, just because they're art terms, annoy some people. It's a hard thing to talk to a guy who is trying to get a drum sound together about *recommodification* or this idea that you have to 'take this sound and turn it on its head like one of those Christmas bubbles and see what happens.'

"It's like playing the set backwards! Let's play U2 backwards and see what happens. So it was a very hard time. I'd say if the songs had come quicker—but the reason the songs didn't come quicker is that people had lost touch. All of us had lost touch. Osmosis is the unsung hero of all rock & roll. Osmosis is the way we all pick up everything. Music is another language and you become articulate in it. If you lose it by not living it, smartness can get you by to a degree, but not really. I think we were a little out of touch. I think that was part of the problem too. We got to Berlin and realized, 'Uh-oh. It's a few years now since *Joshua Tree*, and the rest of it has been fun; doing *Rattle and Hum* was a piece of piss. We hung out in Los Angeles, learned how to drink, playacted a bit, had a lot of cigarettes and songs and hung out with some interesting people. This had been a few years! We didn't know what it was like to be in the studio and to *think* and it stunned everybody. We weren't as great as we figured we were."

4

Tech & Trabants

setting up the stage/ a journey into the eastern bloc/ U2 makes their own clothes/ the woman's perspective: tying his testicles and tugging/ shaking down philips

THE FIRST SINGLE from *Achtung Baby* will be "The Fly," a track chosen because it sounds nothing like U2. The band figures that after not having a new U2 single for a couple of years, radio will play whatever they give them—so why not give them something weird. When they go in to do a video for the track, Bono looks like a human fly in a black leather suit and big, bubble-eyed sunglasses. He decides that he should dress like this for the tour. The fly shades are almost a mask—he goes into character as soon as he puts them on. The black leather suit conjures up a pantheon of rock legends—from Jim Morrison to Iggy Pop—but is most clearly the suit Elvis Presley wore in his 1968 TV comeback special. Like Elvis, Bono dyes his brown hair black to turn himself into the personification of a rockin' cat.

Bono's ideas for staging the concerts are ambitious enough to make grown accountants weep. He wants giant TV screens across the stage, broadcasting not just U2 but commercials, CNN, whatever's in the air. He still has the televised juxtapositions of the Gulf War flipping through his head. Stage designer Willie Williams sees a chance to really go to Designer Valhalla. He wants to erect the illusion of a whole futuristic city, with the big TVs flashing and towers shooting up toward the sky. Bono will be the Fly crawling up the face of this *Blade Runner* landscape. Larry and Adam, it is agreed, should look like cops or soldiers—the future-shock troops. Edge has a different job. He's the guitarist, so he has to look flashy. The white shirts and black jeans he used to wear onstage have no place in future world. Fintan Fitzgerald, U2's wardrobe man, starts working out ways to tart up Edge like a guitar hero from the Hendrix era, with oversize knucklebuster rings, pants covered with elaborate studded patterns, and a wool stevedore's cap instead of the hats and do-rags that usually cover his receding hairline. An evil-looking thin mustache and goatee complete Edge's transformation to psychedelic thug.

The band and the inner circle of Principle, their management company, have started referring to the proposed show as "Zoo TV." It's an outgrowth of the song "Zoo Station" and in U2's imagination a visual extension of the "Morning Zoo" radio programs popular in America on which, between spinning records, wiseass disc jockeys make rude jokes, take phone calls, and play tapes of celebrities embarrassing themselves.

U2 has never accepted corporate sponsorship—the dubious institution whereby a big advertiser picks up a lot of the money for a tour in exchange for being allowed to run ads (even on the tickets) that say, "Jovan presents the Rolling Stones" or "Budweiser presents the Who." Like R.E.M., Springsteen, and some other high-class rockers, U2 has always figured that—like selling songs to be used in commercials— sponsorship takes a bite out of the music's integrity and degrades the relationship between the artist and the audience. It's like inviting someone over to your home and then trying to sell them Tupperware.

But in the spirit of irony and contradiction-kissing that they want to cook up for this tour, U2 plays with the idea of covering the whole stage with logos like the billboards on a crowded highway. Willie Williams draws sketches for a stage design splattered with the logos of Burger King, Shell, Sony, Heinz, Singer, Betty Crocker, Fruit of the Loom, and a dozen other corporations, with three house-size TVs in the middle. One shows Bono singing, one shows a man selling beer, and the third is a close-up of Edge's guitar with a potato chip slogan nudging into it. Willie labels this design "Motorway Madness." It raises a big question: if they decorate the stage with all these corporate emblems anyway, why not let the corporations pay for them? Why not just sell the whole stage to advertisers, taking their money and mocking them at the same time? U2 plays with the notion for a while and then decides that if they ironically put up the logos, and then ironically take the money, it's not ironic anymore. At that point they have sold out, and no semantic somersaults can justify it. So they scrap "Motorway Madness."

Willie has another notion that he floats to Bono and Edge separately before springing it on all the Principles. He thinks it would be hilarious to buy a bunch of Trabants, those cheap little East German cars that U2 saw abandoned along roadsides after reunification, and hang them from the ceiling as spotlights. Anton Corbijn has been drawn to the Trabants in his album cover photos. Willie says, as the band chuckles, that they could hollow out the cars, put huge spotlights inside, and make it look like the Trabants' headlights are illuminating the stage.

U2 gives Willie the go-ahead. Manager Paul McGuinness volunteers to lead an expedition into darkest Deutschland where he will buy up Trabants like a carpetbagger grabbing cut-rate southern cattle after the Civil War. "As an image of what went wrong with Communism, the Trabant is useful," McGuinness explains. "Because it is a car that makes its driver look pathetic. It's a demeaning thing to be in. It also smells like shit and it's very uncomfortable."

The drive across Germany is less jolly than McGuinness and his Zoo crew had hoped. The Soviet occupation troops who had been stationed in East Germany before reunification have no home to go back to. The Germans want them out, but the Russians are asking them to stay away —there is no housing for them, food is already scarce, and their government is on the verge of collapse. In Berlin, Soviet soldiers are selling their weapons and uniforms for whatever money they can get. The further east McGuinness and company drive, the bleaker it becomes. At one stop along the motorway they see a Russian officer in his long coat, high boots, and epaulets buying cigarettes and a bottle of booze, then slowly going back outside, sitting on the bumper of his car, and passing the bottle back and forth with his driver.

When they reach the Trabant factory in Chemnitz, on what was until recently Karl-Marx-Stadt, the place is almost deserted. No one wants to buy these cheap, partly wooden toy boxes when there is a chance of getting a Volkswagen or an Audi. The car factory had been the center of the local economy since the 1920s, when it was the Auto Union (later Audi) factory. Production switched to Trabants at the dawn of the Cold War. Now it's gone, and the people who used to work there are hungry.

"Thirty thousand people just lost their jobs," McGuinness says after nosing the situation. "No one here thinks the Trabant is funny."

McGuinness takes the factory tour. With the Trabants discontinued, the mill is now serving as a warehouse for postal vans awaiting delivery to the mail-deprived East. Asked how he feels about U2's plan to make his automobile famous in the West, the grief-stricken factory manager says, "We feel fine about it, but it is too late."

When McGuinness gets back to Dublin, U2 owns enough Trabants to swing from the rafters, shine on the stage, and drive around the dressing rooms. They bring in Catherine Owens, an artist and old friend from the days when her all-girl punk band the Boy Scoutz used to share bills with the teenage U2, to paint designs on the little cars. One of Owens's designs is what she calls "The Fertility Car," a Trabant covered with blown-up personal ads from dating columns and a sketch of a woman giving birth while holding two pieces of string tied to her husband's testicles, "so he can share the pain."

Owens pushes her opinions to the front because, she feels, U2 has men making all the creative decisions and is slipping into completely male-centered designs. "Let's get some curves in here," she says when looking at a stage design of sharp angles and boxes, while the members of U2 go: "Huh?"

Adam, who knows more about art (and, some would say, women) than the other three, pushes Owens's ideas forward and empowers her to go out and recruit visual artists to contribute to the video barrage that will be needed to fill up all those TV screens. Owens scours Europe and the U.S. (she lives in New York and is tied in with lots of artists there) for the right people. Among those whose work she brings back are video artist Mark Pellington, David Wojnarowicz—an acclaimed and touchy New York photo/conceptual artist who is dying of AIDS, and the Emergency Broadcast Network. EBN are a satirical group from Rhode Island who use computer tricks to sample images as well as sounds. One of their proudest accomplishments is a film of President Bush, looped and edited so that the President seems to be chanting the lyrics to Queen's "We Will Rock You" while pounding his podium. In the USA 1992 will be an election year, and after his quick thrashing of Iraq in the Gulf War, Bush is considered unbeatable. U2 decide that this Bush bit will open their concerts.

While Bono is running around recommodifying his imagination and cleaning out the band's bank accounts, Adam, Edge, and Larry start tour rehearsals without him. They have a lot of grunt work to do for which Bono is not needed—learning to play with the sequencers and programs that will provide sonic beds under their own instruments, working out live arrangements and endings for the new songs. It gives the singer a chance to cool down and gives the other three a break from Bono and a chance to reconnect as musicians. It is an important time for Adam, Edge, and Larry; it moves them back into position as one unit after the Bono & Edge/Larry & Adam split in the early days of the album. As with any group of equals, there are various ways in which the factions within U2 configure. When Bono finds the other three aligned against him, he tends to bring in McGuinness to back him up. For a period in the eighties when Edge, Larry, and Bono first embraced charismatic Christianity, it was Adam and McGuinness vs. the three Born Agains. As in any family, the alliances shift all the time. It is important before heading out on the road together that Edge, Adam, and Larry close ranks. Then as Bono joins rehearsals he gets drawn back into a united band.

The four band members and McGuinness share all business decisions equally, and the four band members without McGuinness make all creative decisions—not just regarding the music but concerning staging, photos, album jackets, and so on. Bono maintains that this got started at the dawn of U2 because being a struggling band in Dublin, where there was no music business, they knew no other way.

"We don't necessarily like to do everything ourselves," Bono says. "We call it 'making our own clothes.' But because of the circumstances, we had to. Paul McGuinness is just so uninterested in the details of a band's aesthetic life. It was hard to find advice. So we had to become video makers to make good videos. We had to become art directors. We made the albums, we made the album covers, we made the videos, we made the stage set. We used local Dublin people because we didn't *know* anybody else, and we collaborated with them and grew together.

"Paul got us to do everything for ourselves and I don't quite know why. He got out of the way, which takes a lot of guts. His instinct was to trust ours. And this developed this whole Gang of Four thing where you become the corporation. A gang of four musically, a corporation of five with Paul, seven with Ellen (Darst, who runs U2's U.S. operation) and Anne-Louise (Kelly, who runs Principle Dublin), eight with Ossie (Kilkenny, U2's financial advisor).

"Brian Eno said, 'Almost as extraordinary as what you're doing as artists is this organization—or organism—that seems to be evolving around you.' We had this idea that you could be creative in business, that you didn't have to divide it up into art and commerce. We'd meet these record company people on tour in the U.S., and to most punk bands coming out of the U.K., these were the enemy. And I didn't think they were the enemy. I thought they were workers who had gotten into music for probably all the right reasons, and weren't as lucky as we were, weren't able to fulfill their ambition to be musicians and were now working the music. Maybe they lost their love and I felt that part of our thing was to reignite that.

"So a lot of people got inspired and they rallied around us, creating a network, and that protected us, created this kind of cushion. Then you start to see organization in a creative light. You start to say, 'Well, these are important decisions, this artwork, and these things.' And you realize that, in fact, to be a group is the art."

As the release of *Achtung Baby* and rehearsals for the Zoo TV tour impend, U2 ideas are expanding faster than their bank accounts. They have drawn up a plan to build a giant doll of an Achtung Baby with a working penis that will pee on the audience. McGuinness suggests it's an expensive indulgence. Edge starts thinking, then, that maybe what they should do is create fake photos of, say, the giant baby on top of Tower Records and try to convince the press that it really happened: fake media events! That, too, gets nixed.

Plans for the staging are settling into something more stark and spooky than the *Jetsons* city of the initial designs. Now the band is talking about black scaffolding, like oil wells or TV towers, shooting into the air with video screens flashing across and throughout. There will be a second tier, above the band, to which Bono can ascend. There will be two wings at the front corners of the stage onto which Bono and Edge can venture. Larry's main question at each new proposition is, "What's it going to cost?"

Bono's imagination is not encumbered by such fiscal concerns. He has an inspiration: how about a small second stage stuck way out in the middle of the audience and connected to the main stage by a ramp? Then, after hitting the crowd with all this high-tech hoopla, the band can stroll out to the B stage and busk with acoustic guitars. Kind of like in Elvis's '68 comeback special when, after tearing up the joint with rock & roll, he went out and sat surrounded by the audience and strummed the old songs with his band. The designers aren't sure how to make that work, but they say they'll try it. They eventually come up with a design for a long ramp departing from Edge's side of the stage and ending in a small platform. It is like a big fist at the end of a long, thin arm.

Larry's question hangs in the air. What is it going to cost? One element essential to the whole enterprise is the purchase of a Vidiwall, a giant television screen. The bad news is, it costs four to five million dollars. The good news is, the Vidiwall is built by Philips, the company that owns Polygram, the company that just bought Island, the record label to which U2 is signed! McGuinness has been wanting the band to meet Alain Levy, the head of Polygram. The band hatch a plan to invite Levy over and really butter him up. They will invite him to dinner at Adam's house and to spend the night at Bono's—and they'll hit him with the notion that it would be great for everyone if Philips gave U2 the Zoo video gear for free—as a demonstration of corporate synergy. Here's the hardware from Philips, the album from Polygram, and the music from U2.

At dinner Levy, a Frenchman, seems neither unpleasant nor overly chummy. What he clearly is is smart. Bono figures if they try to play games with the guy they'll just insult him. After all, Philips/Polygram just paid $300 million for Island, essentially to get U2. *They must like the band.* So during dinner Bono leans over and asks: How about you asking Philips to give us the video screens? Levy looks at Bono coldly and says, "You don't even wait for dessert to ask me this?"

Bono is taken aback. Levy continues coolly: "I'm not stupid. I know why you asked me here. I'll look into it. We'll see."

To U2's disappointment (and resentment) Philips rejects Levy's proposal. U2 will have to fork out the money for their Vidiscreens like anybody else. Apparently the research scientists at the electronics company care less about U2 than they would about a longer-burning lightbulb. Levy gets Polygram to kick in a half million bucks or so in tour support, as a gesture of goodwill.

By the time U2 starts getting a fix on just how expensive their plans are going to be to execute, Larry's not the only one swallowing hard. Mounting Zoo TV could easily cost $50 million. They agree to take it one step at a time. The album is coming out in time for Christmas of 1991. In the spring they will do a tour of indoor arenas in the USA and Europe. If the album is not well received or if the shows don't sell out as quickly as they expect them to, that may be all they do. Perhaps next summer they could do some sort of TV concert as a finale. McGuinness suggests they could even broadcast such a show from the Trabant factory.

If *Achtung Baby* is a hit and the ticket demand is big enough, they will return to America to play football stadiums in the second half of the summer. But with the cost of this show, the potential profit margin is only 4 to 5 percent. If U2 commits to playing outdoors and then America has a cold, rainy summer, they could end up wiping out their savings in indulging their creative impulses.

Bono is nonetheless delighted by all the possibilities the new gear—and the new idea of U2—offers. When the big TV monitors arrive they are desposited in the Factory, the building where U2 rehearses and Bono walks between them explaining how it will all work like a kid contemplating the train set he's getting for Christmas.

He asks if I'm familiar with the headline-type aphorisms of Barbara Kruger and Jenny Holzer. I am. They are New York artists known for bold-lettered proclamations. Bono points out that the song "The Fly" is full of *new* truisms ("A liar won't believe anyone else") and when they play that song live he wants the screens to flash all sorts of epigrams, messages, and buzz words, from *Call your mother* to *Guilt is not of God* to *Pussy.*

"I really enjoy addressing the subject of rock & roll itself," Bono says, referring to the over-the-top staging, as well as his own new Fly persona. "Ask yourself, what would Dali or Picasso have done if they had video at their disposal. If they had samplers or sequencers or drum machines or electric guitars, photography, cinematography!"

I'm having a little trouble imagining it, actually. This seems like a really good way for even a wealthy band to go broke. Another line from "The Fly" is "Ambition bites the nails of success."

5

A Trip Through Edge's Wires

down at the zoo tv rehearsals/ bono's bid for monkeedom/
the entire history of U2 condensed and presented by the
edge/ how the hound of heaven almost took a bite out of the
band/ the rock & roll hall of fame

*A*CHTUNG BABY is released just before Christmas of 1991 to good
reviews and strong sales. Shortly after it hits number one on
the *Billboard* charts, the Soviet Union collapses. Coincidence?
Let history judge.

Arriving in Dublin in January, I am greeted at my hotel by a note
from Bono: "Welcome to Nighttown." When I head down to the
Factory, Zoo TV tour rehearsals have passed the point of anxiety and
are approaching frenzy.

The Factory occupies an old stone mill near the Dublin docks. To
get in you ring a buzzer in a black door in a stone wall, climb an indoor
fire escape, pass through a security door and desk, go through swinging
doors, and proceed down a very long corridor. As you walk down the
hall the music gets louder and louder. Sort of like *Get Smart.* Then you
turn a corner, open another door, and there's U2 blasting through "The
Fly." Bono's listening to the band, swaying in place at the soundboard
and making suggestions to engineer Joe O'Herlihy. Larry and Adam are
creating a fat, funky bottom. The Edge is stretching out, filling in all the
sonic colors of the album version of the song while singing the high
countervocal that Bono overdubbed on the record.

"We've been trying to work out how to get all the *Achtung Baby* sounds
live," Bono explains when the song finishes. "Basically, we can do it if
Edge plays something different with every one of his appendages."

U2's American tour begins on March 1, 1992. At this point—
January 14—Bono reckons they are one week behind schedule with one

week left to go here in Dublin before they pack up all the gear and move to the States. Bono says that the material they have worked on has been so good that he's not worried about running late. Edge, however, is. He now understands how much can go wrong on a tour this big. "In the past"—he smiles—"I didn't know. I thought it was easy."

The band picks up their instruments again and begins "Mysterious Ways." Over the opening groove Bono chants, "Who loves you? Who loves you? Who loves you?" (He calls it the Kojak Mix.) Edge establishes a thick post–wah-wah guitar groove that suggests what might have happened if the Isley Brothers had joined the Manchester rave scene.

At 7:30 rehearsal breaks up and Edge, Bono, and Adam head to Kitty O'Shea's, a nearby pub. That it is my birthday is all the excuse these Irishmen need to begin a night-long beer and blarney session. U2 recounts the usual tall stories: meeting Frank Sinatra in Las Vegas, being summoned backstage at Madison Square Garden by Michael Jackson, the compelling but at times unsettling brilliance of Bob Dylan and Van Morrison. These boys have been keeping fast company and, I think, measuring themselves against the icons they encounter.

When we get on the subject of Zoo TV and all its proposed monkey business, I ask Bono to enlighten me about how the multimedia silliness reflects, for example, the Gulf War.

"It's Guernica!" Bono responds.

Let me clean out my ears, Bono, I thought you said, "It's Guernica."

"The response has to contain the energy of the thing it is describing," Bono says. "To capture the madness of the Spanish Civil War, Picasso imbued his work with that madness, and with the surreal."

Blame it on the rotgut, but this starts making a lot of sense to me. I suppose, I suggest, that from "The Rape of the Sabine Women" on, every attempt to use beauty as a vehicle to describe brutality ends up glorifying the brutality, and more generations sign up for the next war.

"That's right." Bono nods. "That's exactly right."

So the way to represent war is as Picasso does in "Guernica," with distorted screaming horses and cubist knives, or as Zoo TV does, with a media barrage that mixes films of cruise missiles and nuclear bombs with rapid-fire video snatches of TV commercials and campy rock & roll singers in leather suits—a live and onstage re-creation of the couch-potato view of the Gulf War. Sounds great in theory; let's see how it works in the civic center!

Edge has to leave Ireland before dawn so he can fly to New York to induct the Yardbirds—Jimmy Page, Eric Clapton, and Jeff Beck among them—into the Rock & Roll Hall of Fame. Edge appreciates both the honor and the irony of a guitarist who has done more than anyone to dismantle the old myth of the *guitar hero* inducting the three men most responsible for creating it. At the pub, what started out as one or two drinks turns into one or two barrels and Tuesday has given way to Wednesday by the time Edge goes home to catch a couple of hours sleep.

I am flying with Edge so I get up to leave, too, but Bono and Adam remind me, "It's your birthday," and convince me to stay for another round. Adam was supposed to be coming with us, but there's trouble with U.S. immigration over an Irish marijuana bust a couple of years ago, so the bassist will be sitting out this trip. Which means I'm the only one still in the pub who can't sleep late tomorrow.

After the bar has closed and the other patrons leave, Bono goes looking for a guitar so he can sing me a country song he's written called "Slow Dancing." It's a beautiful tune about longing and faithlessness— typical Nashville and U2 subjects. He sent it to Willie Nelson but never got a reply.

Walking home through a dark tunnel, Bono insists we throw our arms over each other's shoulders and sing the theme from *The Monkees.* He's still upset because he was shot down in his bid to get U2 to adopt the names of the Monkees as hotel pseudonyms for this tour. Bono wanted to be Davy Jones, the short, maracas-shaking singer. Edge was to be Mike Nesmith, the serious, wool-hatted guitarist. He thought Adam might object to being the troublemaking blond bimbo Peter Tork, but Adam said no problem. The whole idea sank when Larry refused to be Mickey Dolenz.

Edge's version of the story is slightly different; he told me it wasn't Larry who shot down the plan; it was the fact that the Monkees names are more famous than the names of the members of U2. "We'd still have fans ringing the rooms," Edge protested, "but it'll be somebody else's fans!"

Bono should have learned this lesson by now. During the *Joshua Tree* tour he registered in hotels as "Tony Orlando" until one night when he ended up in the same hotel with the real Tony Orlando and chaos ensued. He then switched to a name no one else was likely to have:

"Harry Bullocks." He had to give that up when Ali refused to be Mrs. Harry Bullocks. He should learn a lesson from Adam ("Maxwell House") or Larry ("Mr. T. Bag").

Many such stupid things sound funny when you've been up all night drinking. It's even something of a knee-slapper when Bono throws himself so completely into *The Monkees* theme while parading through the auto tunnel that he doesn't see the car headlights bearing down on him until I yank him out of the way. (Imagine if I had not. People would be asking me Bono's last words and I'd have to say, " 'Hey, hey, we're the Monkees and people say we monkey around.' ")

All this hilarity seems a lot less funny forty-five minutes after I fall asleep, when the alarm goes off and I have to stagger to the airport to meet Edge. When the sun comes up we are on a plane from Ireland to England, where we will make a connection for a flight to New York.

As I stare at the greasy sausages staring back at me I calculate that this day—which thanks to changes in time zones will include twenty-nine hours—is looking far too long to be any good. A car picks us up at Heathrow to drive us from one terminal to another, where we sit in a smoky departure lounge for an hour and try to get some work done. The ambitious conceit is that Edge and I will cover the entire history of U2 between here and the Rock & Roll Hall of Fame.

"*Achtung Baby* is definitely a reaction to the myth of U2," Edge begins as he has his second cup of coffee. "We really never had any control over that myth. You could say we helped it along a bit, but the actual myth itself is a creation of the media and people's imagination. Like all myths. There is very little resemblence to the actual personalities of the band or the intentions of the band, and *Achtung Baby* balances things out a bit."

"But the myth has a *basis* in the personalities," I protest. (Hey, at this point I'd protest "Hello.") "For example, the cartoon image of Bono may be a caricature—but like all caricatures it bears some exaggerated resemblence to the real person."

"It's a caricature of one facet of his character. It's Bono as seen through the songs. But the character of Bono is totally different to that. Maybe over our career our ability to create music that shows the full range of the personalities of Bono and the other members of the band was very poor. But that's the truth—that guy is totally different to the way most people think of him. He's far funnier, takes himself far less seriously than most people think. He's wild, he's not reserved. None of the clichés that spring to mind when you think of people's perception of him.

"This is not just a problem for Bono, this is a problem for the whole band. Everyone has this sort of caricature impression of what we are like. We just decided that we were going to find out how we could allow the other aspects of ourselves to come through. We're exploring whole new avenues of music and it's great fun. I mean, we can *do* it as well, that's what's brilliant about it. That's the good news for us. It's actually something we can do! I suppose we just weren't that interested early on."

I ask Edge if, because U2 was serious and focused at a very young age, the band is now going through at thirty what most young men go through at twenty.

"I think there's a bit of that, yeah. This is actually quite an important point. Throughout our career we've been struggling and fighting for survival: to get out of Ireland in the first place, to get a deal, to just make it happen. And I think we've finally got to a stage where we realized we could relax a bit. It's still not easy, but it doesn't have to be quite so much do or die."

"Do you think that Bono was talking to you in some of the *Achtung Baby* lyrics?"

"I think that what was going on in my life had an influence on Bono and therefore on the lyrics to some of the songs," Edge says evenly. "That's for sure. A lot of people have read into the lyrics that it's the story of my marriage breaking down. I'm not denying that that has had an influence, but I think there's a lot of stories in there and it's not just my story."

I suggest to Edge that it would have been easy to end the album with "Tryin' to Throw Your Arms Around the World," letting the listener off the hook with an all-is-forgiven finale. But U2 makes us go back inside the house with him and face the consequences of his betrayals.

"Yeah, it's not a very comforting ending, is it?" Edge says, and then he considers it and adds, "But that's okay, I think. I suppose that's what we've learned. Things aren't all okay out there. But that's the way it is."

Our flight is called halfway through our second breakfast and we make our way to the boarding gate, past young Londoners who do double takes and then yell, " 'Ey, Edge! 'Ow 'bout an autograp'?" Once we sink into the nice, comfortable seats of the first-class bubble that sits like a tumor atop the plane, we turn back the clock to the birth of U2 and begin our excavation in earnest.

"I suppose it really starts with picking up the electric guitar, age fifteen, and playing a lot of cover versions," Edge says. "Knowing a few Rory Gallagher licks or whatever. Then suddenly you're in this band and there's all this fantastic music coming at you that challenges everything that you believed about what the electric guitar was for. Suddenly the question is, 'What are you *saying* with it?' Not 'Can you play this lick?' or 'What's your speed like?' It's, 'What are you saying with your instrument? What is being communicated in this song?' Suddenly guitars were not things to be waved in front of the audience but now were something you used to *reach out* to the crowd. If you were in the fourth row of the Jam concert at the Top Hat Ballroom in Dunleary in 1980, when Paul Weller hit that Rickenbacker twelve-string, it *meant* something and it said something that everyone in that building knew. There were other bands, other guitar players. They all sounded different, but they all had that thing in common which was that there was something behind what they did, which was communicating.

"I had to totally reexamine the way I played. It was such a challenging thing to hold up your style against this and say, 'Well, what are *you* saying? What is this song about? What does that note mean? Why *that* note?' So much of this bad white-blues barroom stuff that was around at the time was just guitar players running up and down the fretboard. It was just a kind of big wank. There was nothing to it, it was gymnastics. I started trying to find out what this thing around my neck could do in the context of this band. Songs were coming through and 'Well, that sort of works' and integrating the echo box, which was a means of further coloring the sound, controlling the tone of the guitar. I was not going for purity, I was going for the opposite. I was trying to fuck up the sound as much as possible, go for something that was definitely messed with, definitely tampered with, had a character that was not just the regular guitar sound.

"Then I suppose I started to see a style coming through. I started to see how notes actually *do* mean something. They have power. I think of notes as being expensive. You don't just throw them around. I find the ones that do the best job and that's what I use. I suppose I'm a minimalist instinctively. I don't like to be inefficient if I can get away with it. Like on the end of 'With or Without You.' My instinct was to go with something very simple. Everyone else said, 'Nah, you can't do that.' I won the argument and I still think it's sort of brave, because the end of 'With or Without You' could have been so much bigger, so much more of a climax, but there's this power to it which I think is even more potent because it's held back.

"I suppose ultimately I'm interested in music. I'm a musician. I'm not a gunslinger. That's the difference between what I do and what a lot of *guitar heroes* do."

Ten or twelve years into this, I remind Edge, he can look out at a lot of guitarists he's influenced.

"Yeah." He shrugs. "Unfortunately when something is distilled down to a simple style, those who copy the style basically are copying something very flat. You take what I do, bring it down to a little, short formula and try and apply it in another context, another guitar player, another song—it's going to sound terrible. I think that's probably what's happened to Jeff Beck and Eric Clapton and Jimmy Page. So many of their strong ideas have been taken up by other guitar players in other bands and the result is some pretty awful music. Heavy metal for one."

The first U2 albums were dominated by Edge's heavy use of an echo effect on his guitar. It fattened the band's sound, covering up the fact that neither the guitarist nor bassist in this band were playing very much. It also gave the early U2 songs a feeling of reverberating size and —not least—laid a coat of common personality over the material. U2 had a *sound.*

Edge says it started with Bono: "We had a song we were working on called 'A Day Without Me' and Bono kept saying, 'I hear this echo thing, like the chord repeating.' So I said, I'd better get an echo unit for this single. I got one down to rehearsal and played around with it with limited success. I didn't really like it; I thought it muddied up the sound. Then I bought my own unit, a Memory Man Deluxe made by Electro-Harmonix. I mean, Electro-Harmonix made the cheapest and trashiest guitar things, but they always had great personality. This Memory Man had this certain sound and I really loved it. I just played with it for weeks and weeks, integrating it into some of the songs we'd already written. Out of using it, a whole other set of songs started to come out."

Was there any moment when Bono said, "Oh, no, I've created a monster! Turn that echo off!"?

"When the *War* album was coming together we all—but particularly Bono—felt that we should try to get away from that echoey thing," Edge says. "It was a very conscious attempt at doing something more abrasive, less ethereal, more hard-edged. Less of that distant thing. I realized that the echo could become too much of a gimmick. There are a couple of tricks you can do with a guitar and echo that sound impressive, but I could see they were blind alleys. I've always left it and gone back to it. I don't like to use effects in an obvious way. You get sick of the same textures. Variety becomes important."

Between the first album, which established U2 as a hot underground band, and *War*, which began moving them into the mainstream, MTV, and headlining arenas, came the troubled second album, *October*. Recorded quickly, with Bono improvising words after his lyric notebooks were stolen, the album reflected the moment when U2 almost split up over Bono, Edge, and Larry's embrace of charismatic Christianity, much to the chagrin of Adam and McGuinness.

"I think *October* suffered as an album because of the lack of time we had to prepare it, but it actually is a pretty good record," Edge says. "There's some real spontaneity, some real freshness, because we didn't have time to have it any other way. I like 'Stranger in a Strange Land,' 'Tomorrow.' 'October' was a song that could have gone places but we didn't have time to do any more with it, so we said, 'Well, let's just put it out as it is.'

"*October* is a very European record because just prior to writing those songs and recording the album we spent all our time touring around Europe. We'd never been to Germany, Holland, Belgium, France. We would drive through these bleak German landscapes in winter. Those tones and colors definitely came through in the songs that we wrote.

"It was a real eye-opener. *Boy* was written and recorded in the context of Dublin. Four guys get together, decide to be a band, write some songs because they get inspired by this huge new sort of music happening across the water. There's all these albums filtering back: the Jam, Patti Smith's *Horses* was a very big album for us, Television, Richard Hell and the Voidoids. It was an incredibly exciting time. But here we are in Dublin, trying to make sense of the stuff we're hearing from out there, trying to make sense of our own life in the context of Dublin.

Then we end up in the middle of Europe in a Transit van, driving down the corridor between East and West Germany, going to Berlin. It just gave us a totally different perspective. In a weird way it was a more Irish perspective, because suddenly our Irishness became more tangible to us, much more obvious, maybe even more important.

"*October* was a struggle from beginning to end. It was an incredibly hard record to make for us because we had major problems with time. And I had been through this thing of not knowing if I should be in the band or not. It was really difficult to pull all the things together and still maintain the focus to actually finish a record in the time that we had. You could hear the desperation and confusion in some of the lyrics. 'Gloria' is really a lyric about not being able to express what's going on, not being able to put it down, not knowing where we are. Having thrown ourselves into this thing we were trying to make some sense of it. 'Why are we in this?' It was a very difficult time."

"You and Larry and Bono were having doubts about whether it was okay for you as Christians to devote your lives to a rock band."

"It was reconciling two things that seemed for us at that moment to be mutually exclusive," Edge says. "We never did resolve the contradictions. That's the truth. And probably never will. There's even more contradictions now."

Even at the time of *October* U2 resisted going public with their Christianity. I remember writing an article about U2 at the very moment when the future of the band was in doubt—a struggle everyone around them was trying hard to conceal from the outside world. I knew about U2's faith, but when I got McGuinness on the phone and asked him to go on the record about it he backpedaled like a man about to bicycle over a cliff.

"I was still very nervous about the Christian label," Edge says. "I have no trouble with Christ, but I have trouble with a lot of Christians. That was the problem. We wanted to give ourselves the chance to be viewed without that thing hanging over us. I don't think we're worried about it now. Also, at that stage we were going through our most out-there phase, spiritually. It was incredibly intense. We were just so involved with it. It was a time in our lives where we really concentrated on it more than on almost anything. Except Adam, who just wasn't interested."

Adam's distance from the rest of the band at that time was easy to spot. The guy most interested in the fun of being a rock & roller found himself in the ridiculous position of having finally seen his band get a record deal, tour internationally, and start to build a great reputation— when the other three guys began to talk about rejecting all that. Adam was not happy. A friend of mine who had just been forced out of a big band was staying at my house when I brought *October* home. He looked at the cover photo, pointed to Adam, and said, "That guy's going to get sacked. Look at how the other three are forming a circle and he's outside it."

I tell this to Edge and he's surprised. "Well, he was wrong, but he was also right," Edge says of my friend's analysis. "We never considered firing Adam. That would have been completely ridiculous. But I think Adam did feel kind of isolated, marginalized during that period. It wasn't our intention to do that, but I suppose it is inevitable he felt a little like the odd guy."

Even after Bono and Larry decided it was okay to go on with U2, there were a couple of weeks in 1981 when word spread that Edge had quit. I remember complete radio silence descending over the U2 camp, at the end of which I got a call from Ellen Darst saying the fire was out, Edge was still in.

"I didn't actually leave the band," Edge says, "but there was a two-week period where I put everything on hold and I said, 'Look, I can't continue in my conscience in this band at the moment. So hold everything. I want to go away and think about this. I just need a couple of weeks to reassess where I'm headed here and whether I can really commit to this band or whether at this point I just have to back out.' Because we were getting a lot of people in our ear saying, 'This is impossible, you guys are Christians, you can't be in a band. It's a contradiction and you have to go one way or the other.' They said a lot of worse things than that as well. So I just wanted to find out. I was sick of people not really knowing and *me* not knowing whether this was right for me. So I took two weeks. Within a day or two I just knew that all this stuff was bullshit. We were the band. Okay, it's a contradiction for some, but it's a contradiction that I'm able to live with. I just decided that I was going to live with it. I wasn't going to try to explain it because I can't. So I went forward from that point on, and it was great in a way because it did get rid of all that shit. It was like, 'That's gone. Right.

This band is going forward, there is no doubt in anyone's mind.' So we carried on.

"I remember walking down the beach and breaking the news to Bono. 'Listen, mate, I really need to find out about this. I can't go on unless I really find out.' He kind of looked at me and I thought he was really going to freak out, but he actually just said, 'Okay, fine. If you're not up for it, that's it. We're going to break up the band. There's no point going on.' I think he felt exactly like I did, just wanted to know which way to go. Then, once the decision was made, that would be it, there would be no more doubt, no more second guessing. There would be no more taking other people's advice. This was our chosen path."

You were twenty then. You're thirty now. Do you feel that the old pieties no longer work as well for you?

"I suppose we've changed our attitudes a lot since then," Edge says. "The central faith and spirit of the band is the same. But I have less and less time for *legalism* now. I just see that you live a life of faith. It's nothing to do necessarily with what clothes you wear or whether you drink or smoke or who you're seeing or not seeing."

The stewardess comes around with our third breakfast. As we fly west and the clock keeps running backward it never gets any later. I ask Edge about U2's fourth album, the first with Eno and Lanois. "Most of your albums capture a moment," I tell him. "*The Unforgettable Fire* is the only one that stands completely outside of time."

"It's interesting that you say that," Edge says, buttering up a bun and me at the same time. "We've had discussions about that very point. There is a quality to great work which is timeless. You've got to balance being relevant and commenting on something that's happening today with trying to attain that timelessness. *Unforgettable Fire* is probably less fixed to any time, more a work that will mean the same in ten years as it meant when it was released.

"On *Unforgettable Fire* probably more than our other records the music has such a strong voice that Bono's vocals are almost like another musical element. We got criticized that it was a sort of cop-out, that we weren't writing songs anymore, that this was ill-disciplined work. I could see where the reviews were coming from, based on probably a weekend listening to it, but I knew there was far more to it than just that. It was not U2 going arty, there was actually something there that was really valuable and enduring. I still listen to that record."

We take a break from the trip down memory lane while Edge writes the speech he will make tonight inducting the Yardbirds into the Rock & Roll Hall of Fame. He scribbles away, reading me bits as I grunt approval. We get into a long argument about the correct pronunciation of Chris Dreja's name. After that we try to watch the in-flight movie, *Regarding Henry*, with Harrison Ford as a mean, materialistic guy who turns sweet and understanding after getting shot in the head. If my own head was clearer I might construct a horrible metaphor here for some aspect of U2, so consider yourself lucky that Edge gives up on the movie and we start talking again. I ask him if the sheer size of the operation U2 is assembling for this tour is intimidating.

"Yeah, a bit," Edge says. "But what's actually more intimidating is the expectations. I don't really worry about *mistakes.* I've never had a problem with mistakes. There's a certain thing that happens to us onstage, a certain spark, a certain electricity. It's impossible to describe but it's sort of like that *is* the show, you know? That's what the band's always had. 'Chemistry' only describes one aspect of it. We haven't played for a while and we're assuming that spirit, that spark will still be there. I don't know whether it will. I remember shows when it *wasn't* there. It scared the shit out of me. It was like, 'Oh . . . this thing can go away!' That was an eye-opener. I suppose if I have any dark fears it's that that thing will have gone."

Did you think it was gone in Berlin at the start of the *Achtung Baby* sessions?

"There were some pretty difficult moments." Edge sighs. "It really tested everyone very severely. To get over that hump and get on with that record and finish it was not easy. We rode out that storm and I think it's a great record. I'm delighted with it. Actually I think U2 has got a lot of great records left. I think we're good for another ten years at least. I think we're getting better on almost every level, and the commitment is still there."

I ask what he thinks was missing at Hansa.

"To put it in a word, the *magic* just wasn't there. Whether it was the playing, the material, the arrangements, the direction of the material, the studio, the flute sound, who knows why? It just wasn't happening."

Perhaps to avoid blaming other members of the band, Edge tended to focus his early frustrations in Berlin on Dan Lanois. Larry warned me to be careful of buying that line, saying Danny was no more at sea than any of them. Lanois was unknown when Eno brought him along for *Unforgettable Fire*, but he has since developed a distinctive style, earthy and ethereal, that he has brought to two terrific albums of his own songs, as well as productions for Peter Gabriel, Robbie Robertson, Bob Dylan, and the Neville Brothers. Edge suggests that Lanois has to be careful that that seductive sound does not become a cliché.

"In *Achtung Baby* Danny knew he was not going back to the swamp," Edge says. "He knew this was going to be something different. I don't think he fully appreciated how different it was going to be and how difficult it was going to be for him to adjust. There were a couple of weeks where it was, 'Does Danny *get* this?' But Brian came in and Danny and Brian work off each other very well, because Brian is so clear, so opinionated, and so dead-ahead. Danny is, by comparison, instinctive. He feeds off Brian's theoretical side, but he's got all this music coming out of every pore. So Danny was kind of tuning in on what Brian was feeling and thinking, based on what we were saying and playing. Danny really started to get it then, and that was good."

In America a man accused of murdering a young TV actress named Rebecca Schaeffer claimed that he was inspired by listening to the U2 song "Exit," which takes a trip through the head of a violent man losing control. Bono has said that it sounds like a clever lawyer trying to create a novel defense, but it's something U2 doesn't like drawing attention to. When I mention it to Edge he gets cranky.

"Well, what do you want me to say?" he asks. "I think it is very heavy. It gets back to self-censorship. Should any artist hold back from putting out something because he's afraid of what somebody else might do as a result of his work? I would hate to see censorship come in, whether from the government or, from my point of view, personal."

"Exit" was from *The Joshua Tree*, U2's exploration of America, and their most popular album. I ask Edge what the band was trying to capture.

"I think that record was a great stepping-stone for Bono as a lyricist. He was going for something. Points of reference were the New Journalism, *The Executioner's Song* by Norman Mailer, Raymond Carver, the bleak American desert landscape as a metaphor. There's a definite cinematic location, a landscape of words and images and themes that made up *The Joshua Tree*. It's a subtle balance, a blend of the songs and lyrics."

The album's emotional high point was "Bullet the Blue Sky," a song that had been started in Dublin before Bono and Ali went on a trip to Central America in 1986. Bono had the very novelistic notion that if he was going to write about the United States, he had to see the worst side of the American dream, the imperialism that was manifesting itself in undeclared war in El Salvador and Nicaragua. He came back to Ireland with lyrics about what he'd experienced and a challenge for Edge: to "Put El Salvador through your amplifier."

Edge played like a bombing raid on that track, liberated by the subject matter to indulge in some of the heavy guitar rock muscle he usually avoids. Some of the success of his soloing was accidental—he didn't know the tape was rolling and did not have his headphones on, he was just playing with weird guitar noises when he looked up and saw Bono and Lanois looking through the studio glass giving him high signs and going, "Yeah! Yeah!"

I ask Edge what goes through his head when he plays "Bullet" onstage.

"Whoa." He smiles. " 'Hope I don't fuck up!' It's obviously an incredibly dark song. We used to call that part of the set 'The Heart of Darkness.' From 'Bullet' to 'Exit' was all very, very intense. Sometimes Bono would come offstage in the break and would not have left character. The darkness would still be there with him. Sometimes it was hard for him to shake it off and get into playing the next songs. That darkness has a certain kind of adrenaline."

Speaking of that, the British reviewer Mat Snow wrote in Q magazine that "Until the End of the World," on the new album, which seems to be a dialogue between a macho guy and the women he's just kissed off, is actually Judas speaking to Jesus.

"Yeah," Edge says. "There's an Irish poet named Brendan Kennelly who's written a book of poems about Judas. One of the lines is, 'If you want to serve the age, betray it.' That really set my head reeling. He's fascinated with the whole moral concept of 'Where would we be without Judas?' I do think there is some truth that in highlighting what *is* rather than what we would ideally like to be, you're on the one hand betraying a sort of unwritten rule, but you're also serving."

Bono actually wrote an enthusiastic review of Kennelly's *Book of Judas* for the Irish *Sunday Press*, enthusing, "This is poetry as base as heavy metal, as high as the Holy Spirit flies, comic and tragic, from litany to rant, roaring at times, soaring at other times. Like David in the psalms, like Robert Johnson in the blues, the poet scratches out Screwtape Letters to a God who may or may not have abandoned him and of course to anyone else who is listening." In the same paper Kennelly reviewed *Achtung Baby* with the enthusiasm of a practiced logroller but no evidence he'd played it more than once.

The plane is descending into JFK airport. I can see my bed from here! But it is not to welcome me anytime soon. Edge is whisked through a special VIP customs gate and we are shown to a waiting limousine. What makes Edge cool, though, is not that sort of Imelda Marcos treatment; what makes him cool is that he isn't carrying any other clothes. He will wear the mismatched jeans and desert coat he put on in the dark at home in Dublin onto a stage in New York, make a speech before the most powerful people in the music biz and many legends of rock, play guitar in an all-star jam session, and then probably socialize until morning and get on a plane back to Dublin, where the U2 rehearsals will continue.

On the way to the banquet, I bend Edge's captive ear with my theory about the difference between the sort of power trios Beck, Clapton, and Page formed after the Yardbirds, and U2. "The Jeff Beck Group, Cream, and Led Zeppelin grew out of the Hendrix model—a guitar hero blasting hot solos while the bassist and drummer played support," I say. "U2 seems to have more in common with the Who model, where all three pieces are equal and the guitar is the glue."

"I've always had a slight problem with the whole idea of guitar heroes and gunslinger guitar players," Edge says. "I was never really attracted to that. I think Townshend is different from the other players that you mentioned because he's primarily a songwriter. He understands the importance of guitar playing within the discipline of songwriting, as opposed to guitar playing that just justifies itself. I can appreciate, I suppose, guitar players who just get up there and improvise over bass and drums, but it's not something that interests me that much."

Edge nonetheless makes a generous speech inducting the Yardbirds into the Hall of Fame, and suggesting diplomatically that the shadow they cast was so long that players such as himself had to devote themselves to finding something left to do outside of it.

At midnight Eastern time (5 A.M. back in Dublin) he is on a stage at the Waldorf-Astoria Hotel, playing "All Along the Watchtower" and other guitar blowouts with an all-star band that includes—lined up together—Carlos Santana, Johnny Cash, John Fogerty, Jimmy Page, Neil Young, Robbie Robertson, and Keith Richards. (Beck is standing there but I'm not sure he ever actually plays.) Watching all these legendary guitar players interact I recognize, with some surprise, that Edge belongs among them. The sound he heard in his head has now been heard around the world, has been absorbed into rock & roll's vocabulary, and will continue to reverberate when he's as old and legendary as the company he's keeping tonight.

One roadie from the instrument rental company standing behind the stage can stand the proximity to greatness no longer. He slips up on the stage, plugs his guitar into a free jack in Edge's amp, and joins in—overloading the amp and blowing it out just as Neil Young points to Edge and calls for a solo. Edge is surprised when he leans in to wail and no sound comes out, but when he finds out what happened he thinks it's great—he figures there's more rock & roll spirit in that brave and sneaky roadie than in all the tuxedos in the house.

6

Treat Me Like a Girl

*a swinging models and transvestites party/ preachers who
live in glass cathedrals/ a phone call from hell/ pickup lines
of the great authors/ adam's interest in ladies' underwear*

LATER IN the winter all of U2 lands in New York and tramps
around Times Square looking urban for the video camera of
their old documenter, director Phil Joanou. After *U2 Rattle and
Hum* elevated him to the big time, Joanou directed the Hitchcockian
Final Analysis with Richard Gere and the Scorsesean *State of Grace* with
Sean Penn and Gary Oldman. He has agreed to slip down from that
high cinematic perch to rescue "One," the *Achtung Baby* track most likely
to give U2 a number one single, from its first two videos.

The first "One" video featured U2 in drag; not the sort of thing the
band imagined MTV would care to dish up to middle America. The
second "One" video was a slow-motion film of a buffalo running over a
cliff—a nice metaphor for the AIDS epidemic, perhaps, but not sizzling
promotion. Tonight's assignment is to make a "One" promo the TV
audience can love. After traipsing around Manhattan for a while, the
band, the director, and his crew decamp to Nell's, a Manhattan nightclub that was chic in the eighties, when money flowed like champagne in
New York and cocaine was laid out like loose floozies. Nell's has been
cleared for the night so that Joanou can execute his vision of "One." For
anyone not employed to be here this would be a dull enterprise if not
for (a) the lavish banquet, (b) the generous bar, and, most of all, (c) the
extras: gorgeous young female models *and* garish transvestites from the
New York demimonde.

Upstairs, lights and cameras are mounted and Bono, with a few great-
looking extras around him, is sitting at a table mouthing the song's
lyrics over and over while a tape plays. Downstairs the basement party

rooms are full of gorgeous women and cross-dressed men. Edge is being painted by a makeup woman while tray after tray of catered food is layed out. There are big plates of M&M's and Hershey's Kisses and chocolate chip cookies and Bazooka bubblegum. The bars are open and free drinks are pumped out by barmaids as striking as the models.

Upstairs Bono has to lip-synch "One" for seven hours. Downstairs the rest of the band and their staff and friends and the models and the transvestites party and wait to be called to the set and party some more.

What can one say about a soiree where all the woman are professional beauties and all the men are gay? A happy Adam Clayton explains, "If you can't pull tonight, you're hopeless." Every time the cameraman changes film Bono bounds down the stairs, trying to get into the fun. Then, just as he raises a glass to his lips, his name is shouted and he has to go back and mime under the hot lights some more.

At 10 P.M. Bono leaps into record producer Hal Willner's lap and begins telling tall stories when a series of voices, like echoes through the Grand Canyon, comes down the stairs: "Bono! Bono! Bono!" He sighs and goes back to work. A huge Divine-like drag queen leers at U2's drummer's backside and tells her friend, "I've got to get Larry Mullen's room number!"

At midnight I wander onto the set and Bono engages me in an intense discussion of what he hopes to accomplish with the Zoo TV tour. He talks about embracing irony, the stupid glamor of rock & roll, the mirror balls and limousines—without abandoning the truth at the heart of the music itself. He compares it to Elvis Presley in a jumpsuit singing "I Can't Help Falling in Love with You" to a weeping woman in Las Vegas. It might have been hopelessly kitsch, but if the woman believed in the song *and Elvis believed in the song,* it was not phony. Maybe rock & roll was at its truest in the space between those apparent contradictions.

"Basically," Bono says, "it's waking up to the fact that there's a lot of bullshit in rock & roll, but some of the bullshit is pretty cool. That's important to me, because we thought success was this big bad wolf. It seemed to compromise us, to make us look like charlatans. Getting all this money for things we'd do for free. I thought they'd shut us up finally, because how do you write about some of the stuff that I'm interested in writing about and be in big business? Suddenly I felt gagged. If I wrote a song about the Gulf War, then that would be making money out of the war! I couldn't write a song about faith and doubt anymore because that would turn me into the preacher in this glass cathedral of rock & roll. So I decided the only way was, instead of running away from the contradictions, I should run into them and wrap my arms around them and give 'em a big kiss. Actually write *about* hypocrisy, because I've never seen a righteous man that looked like one. So I wrote about that, and actually turn myself into, literally, 'a preacher stealing hearts in a traveling show.' Rather than write about the character, *become* the character. Rather than write about some sleazy psycho, become one. I didn't realize these sleazy psychos had so much fun!

"I always felt like 'The Fly' was this phone call from hell. You know, with the distorted voice and shit. It's a call from hell—but the guy likes it there! 'Honey, I know it's hot here . . . but I like it!' " We have a good laugh at that one and Bono adds, "Another subject that I'm interested in is rock & roll itself—the medium and the machine. I hope that comes through. One of the greatest contradictions of rock & roll is that it's very personal, private music made on a huge public address system."

At 1:30 in the morning Edge is seated in a chair in the middle of the downstairs room talking intently to a model. One of the drag queens has taken off her huge, heavy, helmetlike wig with ostrich feather and left it on the chair behind Edge. Hal Willner, who has been drinking beer all night and is now slightly out of focus, picks up the wig, weighs it in his hands, and studies the back of Edge's head. Hal creeps up behind the oblivious Edge like Hiawatha and starts maneuvering to drop the great hairpiece onto the guitarist's dome. Suddenly a harpielike voice cuts across the party: *"Put down my wig!"* Hal looks up to see a fierce, bald drag queen looming toward him. He drops the wig and bolts.

By 3 A.M. it is dawning on Larry, Adam, Edge, the transvestites, and the models that they may never be called to the set. "One" is quickly becoming an all-Bono video. The mood downstairs starts getting a little edgy. Nell seems to have let some of her regulars slip in. Author Jay McInerny appears, finds a drink, and tries to engage a young woman by saying, "When I wrote my first novel, *Bright Lights, Big City* . . ."

Paul McGuinness notices a Manhattan society type surreptitiously snapping photos. He corners her and she claims in vague *Vogue*-speak that she only has her camera with her because she's coming from a party at Anna Wintour's place. . . . McGuinness ain't buying it. He doesn't believe she is really the spaced-out socialite she seems to be—he figures her for an undercover newspaper photographer and tears into her. I reckon the manager is being paranoid, but the next night I see the woman again, shooting pictures of a Sting rain forest benefit for a New York tabloid. Yep, she says—her space-shot society manner replaced by a no-bullshit attitude—McGuinness had her pegged. That's why he's a big-time manager. Everybody at Nell's was pretending to be something they weren't.

It occurs to me that not only did Adam, Larry, and Edge never get into the "One" video, but neither did all the transvestites. I ask Bono why the drag queens had been assembled, filmed standing around eating and drinking, but never used in the final cut. And what was the deal with the first video, with U2 in drag? Was there a subtext to that lyric that I missed?

"Originally," Bono says, "the idea of the video was that these were men whose understanding of women was so low that they dressed up as women to try and figure them out. That was the kind of absurd, Sam Beckett point of view we had. It wasn't related to transvestism. And then we thought, 'Oh, God, this is an AIDS benefit single! After the years it's taken the gay community to finally convince people that AIDS is not a gay issue, here's U2 dressing up as women!' "

Bono explains that filming U2 in drag, "had been based on the idea that if *U2 can't do this*, we've got to do it! We were in Santa Cruz, on this island off Africa, at carnival time. I've been going to carnivals for a few years. It's an interesting concept because it means *carning*—flesh, meat-eating before Lent, and the run up to Easter. I'm interested because it's not a *denial* of the flesh, it's a celebration. We were there, Anton Corbijn was there, everything was getting a bit silly, and we couldn't get out into the carnival looking like us. So rather than just dress up in fancy masks, Anton suggested that we dress up as women. So we went for it, and . . ." Bono starts laughing, "nobody wanted to take their clothes off for about a week! And I have to say, *some* people have been doing it ever since!"

Whoa, I say, what was the initial reaction of the ultramasculine and nonsense-hating Larry Mullen, Junior, to this idea?

"Two short, clipped words," Bono answers. "The funny thing about Larry was that, okay, he got into the dress and he put on the makeup, but he was *fighting* with it. He wouldn't take off his Doc Martens and when he was sitting he'd put his feet up on the table. But as macho as he tried to be, he still looked like some extra from a skin flick. That was the irony. Whereas *Adam* was just getting people to do him up in the back and swapping makeup tips with any girl that passed. You know, suddenly he could own up to being interested in their underwear!

"The whole business of being in a rock & roll band is just so ridiculous," Bono says. "I was thinking, it's like having a sex change! Being a rock & roll star is like having a sex change! People treat you like a girl! You know? They stare at you, they follow you down the street, they hustle you. And then they try to fuck you over! It's a hard thing to talk about because it's so absurd, but actually it's valuable. When I'm with women I know what it feels like. I know what it feels like to be a *babe.*"

The third "One" video does the trick. Bono looks as cool as Camus sitting in a black-and-white cabaret amid beautiful people while crooning soulfully. The clip goes into heavy play on MTV, the song goes into heavy play on American radio, and the single raises lots of dough for AIDS charities. A common interpretation of "One" is that it is sung in the voice of a son who is HIV-positive confronting and reconciling with his conservative father. That is one of the many ways the song can be heard. "One" seems to have an infinite capacity to open up, and U2 shows no inclination to tie it down.

7

The Arms of America

the zoo tour begins/ the ghosts of martin luther king, jr., and phil ochs sit in/ picking up a belly dancer/ bruce springsteen on the quality of bigness/ axl rose invites himself aboard

O<small>N MARCH FIRST</small> the Zoo TV tour begins in Lakeland, Florida, about an hour from Tampa. The Trabants are hung from the ceiling with care, the colossal TV screens are blinking above the stage, and Bono is being shoved into his leather suit. Out in the audience Irish imp B. P. Fallon, a 1960s peace-and-love vet who has been both a rock critic and Led Zeppelin's publicist, is sitting in one of the Trabants dressed in a cape and a wide-brimmed black hat, playing deejay for the anxious audience and blasting out the soul-inspiring sounds of John Lennon, Bob Marley, and other great dead people.

As Bono, flylike in his bug-eyed sunglasses, waits backstage to step onto the makeshift elevator that will raise him up into the spotlight, he has a revelation: he doesn't actually know what he's going to do when he gets out there.

"You know," he says, "for this tour we worked for months before leaving Dublin. We designed the Fly, we got the goggles, assembled our postmodern rock star." He points to each of his limbs as if giving a tour of the temple: "We have our leg of Jim Morrison, our Elvis top, Lou Reed, Gene Vincent—we glue it all together and create it. Make the tapes, make the loops, figure out how to play polyrhythms, spend months at it. We arrive here, people are unpacking cases. I get into the suit. Now what?"

Performers like Prince and Michael Jackson spend months working with mirrors, rehearsing what they're going to do onstage, meeting with choreographers. U2 doesn't think about that. They just figure Bono will do something interesting when he gets out there.

Good thing he does! The lights dim and President Bush appears on screen to tell the audience "We will, we will rock you!" while Adam, Edge, and Larry slip onto the stage in the darkness. The intro to "Zoo Station" blasts out of the dark as the Vidiwalls fill up with blue snow and static. As the song shakes the room Bono slowly ascends to the upper level of the stage, his silhouette in profile against the blue, buzzing screen behind Edge, and twice as big as life in the video reflection of him being projected on the blue, buzzing screen behind Adam. The crowd cheers and stamps and claps and Bono figures he better do something, so he reels back each time the massive beat comes down, stumbling like a drunk, first in place and then along the catwalk across the span of the stage, singing as he goes, "I'm ready, ready for the laughing gas! I'm ready for what's next!" Bono knows what he's doing is working, but he also wonders, "What would happen if I actually *thought* about this?"

On "The Fly" Bono really plays Elvis '68, rockin' in his leather to a song that, for all its sonic modernity, strikes me as very much like an Elvis Presley song. Partly it's the epigrammatic phrases—can't you hear Elvis preaching, "A man will rise, a man will fall, from the sheer face of love like a fly on a wall"? But it's also that the song's core structure is an old time rock & roll verse going into a gospel chorus. Anyway, none of this may be apparent to the crowd, who are dazzled by the aphorisms and cuss words flipping a mile a minute across all the TV screens: *Call your mother, I'd like to teach the world to sing, Everyone's a racist except you.* As the song climaxes the slogans flash by faster and faster.

For the first forty minutes of the set U2 play only material from *Achtung Baby,* a risky move that turns out to be right. Rather than treat the unfamiliar new songs as excuses to go get popcorn between the hits, the audience is forced to put all their energy into the new material, and —abetted by the visual fireworks—they go for it.

After ripping through seven of the new songs—and at the very point when the audience might be adjusting to the sensory overload—Bono finds his way out onto the ramp between the main stage and the B stage and sings "Tryin' to Throw Your Arms Around the World" while strolling out through the crowd. It's a little touch of Engelbert intimacy after a sustained blast of Tom Jones aloofness, and the fans' pulses really speed up when Bono plucks an excited young woman from the audience, dances with her, and then shakes up and pops open an exploding bottle of champagne. He shares it with her and then hands her a handicam, a small portable palm-corder, and directs her to shoot him with it. When she presses down the button the Zoo screens fill with her close-up view of Bono singing to her. Edge then wanders down the ramp, leans into Bono's handmike, and the two of them sing together while the guest camerawoman keeps shooting. The voyeur and the subject have traded places.

When that song ends Edge and Bono wander onto the B stage as if they just noticed it there, and to the delight of the crowd signal to Adam and Larry to come out and join them. After the audiovisual barrage that some old-timers might have feared meant the end of the old U2, here are the boys up close and personal, with no special effects, strumming acoustic guitars, banging on congas, and singing old hits like "Angel of Harlem." At the end of the acoustic set Bono and Edge remain on the B stage to play a delicate version of Lou Reed's "Satellite of Love" while a Trabant covered with tiny mirrors swings slowly around over their heads, reflecting prisms around the arena, making it look like the whole place has drifted up into space.

When U2 returns to the main stage they light into their greatest hits and crowd pleasers—"Bullet the Blue Sky," "I Still Haven't Found What I'm Looking For," "Pride (In the Name of Love)," and "Where the Streets Have No Name" as even the cops tap their nightsticks and the hotdog men shake their buns.

Bono returns for the encore dressed in a suit made of mirrors, shades, and a big cowboy hat. He comes out holding a full-length mirror in which he admires himself and then kisses his reflection. He sings "Desire" as this Mirrorball Man, a proto-American hustler with a southern evangelist's accent and a TV car-salesman's demeanor. This is the character based on the lines in "Desire" about a "preacher stealing hearts in a traveling show for love or money, money, money." After finishing the song (and throwing fake dollars to the audience) the Mirrorball Man picks up a telephone and dials the White House. The audience listens in with delight as a befuddled operator tells him President Bush cannot come to the phone at this time.

This finale reminds me of a bizarre and pretty-much forgotten incident from the late sixties, when the talented, tortured protest singer Phil Ochs risked his career and lost. Ochs—held by the leftist folkies as their leader after Dylan "sold out" by going electric—announced he was going to play an important show at Carnegie Hall. He came onstage in a gold lamé suit like Elvis wore on the cover of his greatest hits album, and proceeded to try to Elvis-ize the protest crowd. The long-suffering folkies were mortified. They went back to Greenwich Village and declared that Ochs was insane. They were wrong. Ochs had decided that it did no good to be perceived as a sourpuss and preach to the converted. If you really wanted to reach a mass audience, if you really wanted to be subversive, the best way to do it would be to try to communicate as completely and as generously as Elvis Presley did. Give people the showbiz razzmatazz, but give them something solid to chew on too.

I don't know if U2 have ever even heard of Phil Ochs, but when Bono strolled onstage with the gold and silver lights reflecting off his suit and sang some of the deepest, most personal songs U2 have ever written with his hips twitching and the crowd dancing, I thought, "Geez, maybe Phil was onto something after all!" The real proof was when, in the middle of "Pride," the Vidiwalls lit up with a film of Martin Luther King giving his "I have been to the mountaintop" speech the night before his assassination. Dr. King was used as an audiovisual sample while U2 riffed under him, and when he finished with "I've seen the promised land!" the kids went as ape as if he had just sung "Stairway to Heaven."

One night I'm sitting in a bar with Bono when a guy comes up, sticks out his hand, and says, "Bono, I work with Michael Ochs, the brother of Phil Ochs?" He says the folksinger's name with a question mark, unsure if Bono will recognize it. "Don't tell me," I butt in. "He wants Phil's suit back!" Bono does a double take and says, "Good catch, Bill." It turns out he knows all about Phil Ochs' gunfight at Carnegie Hall.

Over the next couple of weeks the Zoo TV tour charges up the eastern seaboard across Florida, Georgia, Carolina, and Virginia, then north to Long Island, Philadelphia, and New England. It's a triumphant show. During rehearsals in Florida one of the crew met a woman fan in the parking lot who identified herself as a belly dancer. As a joke, the crew had her dance onstage and startle Bono during a rehearsal of "Mysterious Ways." After the first show Bono decided he liked the effect, so now the dancer, named Christina Petro, has been added to the entourage. Each night during "Mysterious Ways" she swirls around just out of reach while Bono strains to touch her.

Bono's brain is blown one night by Eunice Kennedy Shriver, the sister of JFK and mother of Bobby Shriver, a young Democratic power broker and ally of U2's friends Jimmy Iovine and Ted Fields. Eunice tells Bono that there have always been angels on U2's stage, but now they are letting in the devils too. She says she likes that; it makes for a fairer fight.

U2 plays a great set at Madison Square Garden on the last day of winter. Backstage big names from the worlds of sports (John McEnroe) music (Peter Gabriel) and movies (Gary Oldman) elbow each other to get close to the band. Bono is crowded in a corner with Bruce Springsteen, who compliments him on managing the hard feat of pulling off an arena show filled with surprise. Bono explains that throughout the concert tonight he was distracted by the thought of one obnoxious Wall Street trader who had accosted him in the hotel bar. The yuppie bragged that he and his pals had bought a string of tickets from scalpers, just the sort of thing U2 has been bending over backward to stop. "All through the show tonight," Bono says, "I kept finding this one jerk coming into my head." He mimed slapping himself. "I kept thinking of him sitting out there smirking."

Springsteen looks at Bono and says, "That's pathetic!" Bono looks hurt and Bruce laughs and says, "It's because we're such egomaniacs! We've got to win over every last person in the place!"

Bono starts laughing too.

Springsteen has been a significant figure for U2. He came backstage to see them when they were still playing in clubs, and always expressed confidence they'd reach a big audience. To U2, Springsteen was proof that it was possible for a working-class musician from nowhere to get to the top without compromising his principles or fitting into a rock-star lifestyle. This was good news to four kids from Dublin who were not nearly as fashionable as the sensations pouring out of London at the time.

Later, when U2 began to enjoy success comparable with Springsteen's, Bono had the balls to challenge Bruce to write less about fictional characters and more about himself. This was just after *Born in the USA* had made Springsteen the biggest rock star in the Milky Way, so most people would have thought Bruce had his methods successfully worked out. But for Bono—who came out of the John Lennon, "Here's another little song about *me*" tradition—Springsteen was ducking something.

Bruce told Bono that he didn't think his life was all that interesting. "I get on a bus, I get off a bus," he said. But his next album, *Tunnel of Love,* was clearly autobiographical. It was also superb. Bono doesn't have a head big enough to think that he swayed The Boss, but he was proud that his impulse was accurate.

Springsteen says that the reason he was sure from the start that U2 would be big had to do with the different ways rock & roll works in clubs, theaters, arenas, and stadiums. "My own music was sort of suited to a big place 'cause *it* was big," he says. "I think that's one reason U2 were so successful. Their music was big and echoey. The minute you heard them you could hear them in a big space. They had big emotions, big ideas. Those things tend to translate well into playing to bigger crowds, which can be a fantastic experience. I've had amazing nights in stadiums, but it does alter what you do. In a club it's much easier to focus. The audience is closer and watching whatever you do. You can tune a guitar or tell a story. A theater retains a concert feeling. In an arena you can still retain a good part of that concert feeling, but the size of the thing broadens what you do. It's *the arena* and it calls for a big gesture of some sort. You have to be able to switch gears and adjust to the context you're in. Some people are only great in a club. Some, like the Who and U2, are great in a stadium."

I tell Adam what Springsteen said and he agrees and goes further: "U2 were never any good in clubs, in small places," he says in defiance of all those *Boy* fans who tell their little brothers: *You should have seen them then.* "I think the thing that people—A & R men, journalists—who saw us in those places responded to was not what we were, but what we could become."

As Zoo TV tears across America on what is essentially a spring warm-up tour before taking to the football stadiums in the summer, Axl Rose, the mercurial singer of Guns N' Roses, shows up a couple of times. In L.A. he is one of a gaggle of stars backstage and it's impossible for Bono to get any sense of him. But when he comes to a concert in Texas they get a chance to talk. The women of Principle have no trouble reaching their assessment; they think Axl's a doll.

"Surprisingly little cant," is Bono's reaction. "It was easy enough to get a direct line. I can see why people like his music so much. There isn't much editing done in his conversation or, obviously, in his work. It's a direct line with his gut. That's what I like about it."

"They're my favorite band right now," Axl says of U2. "I'm finally getting certain songs that I never understood before or couldn't relate to. I've always listened to them, but the only song I really got into was 'With or Without You.' I couldn't relate to their other songs because I was like, 'That's great, but I just don't see that part of the world.' Things were a little too dark for me. Now I can see more of the things he's talking about.

"I bought *Achtung Baby* and I actually want to do a cover of the third song, 'One.' I want to play it on tour this summer. I think 'One' is one of the greatest songs that has ever been written. I put the song on and just broke down crying. It was such a release. It was really good for me. I was really upset that my ex-wife and I never had a chance because of the damage in our lives. We didn't have a chance and I hadn't fully accepted that. That song helped me see it. I wanted to write Bono a letter just saying, 'Your record's done a lot for me.'"

When I mention this to the different members of U2 I get a series of different reactions. Adam smiles and says not to make too big a deal out of what might be only a passing interest on Axl's part. Edge says he already knew—a limo driver told him that Axl sat in the back of his car and played "One" over and over again.

When I go tell Bono, though, he jumps right into the association. He says that every decade needs a band that will stand up and reflect the spirit of its time without any shields. U2 did that in the 1980s and they are not going to do it anymore—it's too painful. Maybe that's Guns N' Roses' role now. To be out there with all their nerve endings open, reflecting the currents passing through the collective consciousness without any irony or distance.

Bono says U2 is working in a more subtle way now. I ask him, "How can you reflect the age *and* challenge it?"

"Just *paint* it," Bono says. "To describe it is to challenge it. Isn't that really what artists are supposed to do? It's not their job to solve the problem. It's their job to describe the problem. And part of the description is to realize that this is very attractive. And to admit one's own attraction to it. It was Bertolucci who gave me that clue.

"He was talking about women's fashion magazines and he said that he had never imagined a time as ephemeral as the eighties. And yet he found himself thumbing through women's fashion magazines and enjoying the energy of them. And that these images had lost all meaning a lot of the time; it was pure surface—but there was really something in that. That was a landmark for me. Because to deny the energy is bullshit. And that's the classic rock & roll position: to belittle it. To do that is to not realize how big it is. So the job is to describe what's going on, describe the attraction, and be generous enough to not wave your finger at it as it's going by.

"Rock & roll is *folk* music now. Rock & roll has never been so uninspired, so codified. If rock & roll has to be only one thing, then you might as well say it can only be Little Richard. Which is not to say we might not make a folk album, but that can't be *all* we can do. Rock & roll is a spirit and that spirit is in Zoo TV."

8

"One" If By Land, U2 If By Sea

---

the adventures of bono's bomb squad/ adam clayton, secret
agent/ U2 eludes the police & invades england on a raft/ a
shipboard romance/ larry's nautical fashion sense

I JUST KICKED Bono in the head. He didn't notice. He's asleep at my feet and I accidently banged him with my shoe when Larry Mullen climbed across my lap to try to catch some winks on the seat at my right while the Edge, on my left, leans against the bus window, either dreaming or gazing out into the northern English night. I can't tell for sure.

It's 3 in the morning and we've been traveling for three hours. Edge, Larry, and I are on the backseat of a hired bus. Bono, dozing in the aisle, has his arm draped across his wife, Ali, who is asleep on the seat in front of ours. Further up the bus I can see Adam Clayton creeping past the unconscious Greenpeace people with another bottle of champagne. Paul McGuinness is awake up there, as is their lawyer, who warns Adam what to say and what not to say to the police if we're arrested. Adam, who has been busted before, says don't worry, he's now working on how *not* to get arrested. Then he sips his champagne with the daredevil suave of James Bond on a secret mission.

This cramped scene might be kind of cozy if we were not eluding police roadblocks on our way to hook up with a ship to sail down the Irish Sea to row ashore carrying barrels of radioactive waste to dump at the leukemia-producing door of one of what Greenpeace believes is the most dangerous plutonium plants in the world. When I climbed aboard this bus in Manchester at midnight I was asked to accept legal liability if I am arrested, drowned, or riddled with cancer as a result of joining U2 as they circumvent the British court injunction that has been issued to stop them getting near this little atomic cesspool on the English coast. Next time, I told McGuinness, let's do a phoner.

Four hours ago U2 were onstage in Manchester, playing another superb set in the series of superb sets that have marked this month-long European leg of the Zoo TV tour, a teaser amid the American shows for a longer European tour next year. Edge unleashed breathtaking Hendrix-like solos on "Bullet the Blue Sky" and "Love Is Blindness" that were beyond what I had imagined to be his ability. Lou Reed, who joined the band for "Satellite of Love," enthused backstage that Edge was now alone out in front of his guitar-playing peers. (He may never climb to the top limb of the tree of technique, but for creativity on his instrument, Edge is in the vanguard.) Also backstage was Peter Gabriel, who has been at recent U2 shows in New York and London, too, and who said that while acts such as Prince might leave him impressed, U2 truly touched his heart.

The TV screens that flash messages at the audience during U2's shows had new slogans last night. *Fallout, Plutonium, Mutant, Radiation Sickness, Chernobyl.* The concert had been planned as a rally to protest the expansion of the Sellafield nuclear plant, which dumps radioactive waste into the Irish Sea from adding to its grisly enterprise a second processing facility for the atomic by-products other countries don't want. Bad enough, Greenpeace and U2 say, that this plutonium mill sends radiation to the shores of Ireland, Scotland, England, and Wales. Bad enough, Greenpeace say, that the leukemia rate around Sellafield is three times the national average. But now they wanted to add to it a collection point for deadly waste from all over the Earth? That was the last straw. So U2, along with Public Enemy, B.A.D. II, and Kraftwerk, agreed to play a concert for Greenpeace the night before a licensed protest rally was to be held outside Sellafield. When the nuclear facility found out that a whole lot of people might show up, they went to court and got an injunction against the protest, claiming it was a *concert* that could attract thousands of rock fans who might do damage to the properties of local residents. This specious argument convinced the British court. But then, Sellafield is owned by the British government.

Onstage in Manchester Bono told the crowd, "They've cancelled a peaceful demonstration on the grounds of *public safety!* These people are responsible for the deaths of innocent children, for God's sake. Public safety doesn't come anywhere near them!" Later he added, "Don't let them gag you! We only live 130 miles from Sellafield. So do you in Manchester. It's a lot farther to Number Ten Downing Street!"

When the concert ended, U2 climbed aboard this hired holiday bus and lit out into the night. The Sellafield injunction prohibited U2 from setting foot on any of the land anywhere near the nuclear facility. So U2 and Greenpeace hatched the plan of U2 coming in by water and proceeding only as far onto the beach as the high tide line, reasoning that the injunction did not apply to the ocean. On the bus, Bono announced his intention to cross the literal line in the sand and step onto Sellafield soil, but the Greenpeace organizer insisted that any such deliberate provocation would be contempt of the injunction and could lead to the court seizing all of Greenpeace's assets. U2 should abide by the letter of the law. She went on to say that the sand we would be stepping on was irradiated sand, the water we would be wading in was irradiated water. Everybody swallowed hard but nobody chickened out.

"We heard tonight they're setting up roadblocks in a radius twenty miles around Sellafield," Edge said. "If we get stopped there may be some sort of showdown with the cops. I don't know. Right now we're guests on a Greenpeace action. We don't know what's going to happen.

"There's a fair amount of scientific evidence to suggest that pollution from Sellafield has had an effect on the health of people living on the east coast of Ireland. Impossible to prove, but connections can be made. We're members of Greenpeace, so when we heard about Sellafield 2 we got even more pissed off. The British Nuclear Fuels people have been effective at stopping the groundswell of concern and anxiety about it through huge TV campaigns presenting Sellafield as a safe, well-controlled, well-monitored, efficient, and benign installation. They will spend a few million pounds per annum on TV adverts extolling the virtues of Sellafield. They even opened a visitors' center! They've got some very slick PR people."

"The biggest advertising and publicity agency in England," Larry added. "They are also the publicity people for the government. Sellafield is owned by the government and therefore has all the protection that the government can afford it—i.e., MI6 and MI5 (British intelligence). People from Greenpeace and any other organization that opposes what's happening at places like Sellafield and elsewhere are on these lists. Then they have difficulty getting jobs because the lists go into computers and companies ring up and check out the names. It's all very underhanded and seedy. The whole thing is sick."

"There's no doubt that the Greenpeace office phones are tapped," Edge said. "You're not dealing with a private body here, you're dealing with the government. All the money British Nuclear Fuels spend is taxpayers' money, all the TV campaigns are paid for by the taxpayers, and as Larry said, they have access to all the information of covert agencies. You're not dealing with big business, you're dealing with the British government."

Larry went on: "After we did the Amnesty International tour and Live Aid and a lot of benefit concerts, Bono and I sat down and talked about how we were going to approach the future. We came to the conclusion that maybe the best thing to do was leave Amnesty—continue to support them, obviously, but doing more concerts may be a mistake for now—and let's do something for Greenpeace. We've donated to them for a long time, we've done gigs with them, but we've never actually been involved in an action. When this came up it was an opportunity.

"It would be nice if we didn't have to do this kind of shit, 'cause it's *nothing* to do with rock & roll. Absolutely nothing to do with it. This is crazy, Live Aid was crazy. That we're traveling in a bus trying to get to Sellafield is an indictment of how our government and the British government is responding to environmental problems. The fact that Sting has to go out to the Amazon! There's a guy who goes out there and puts his ass on the line. Peter Gabriel is another. And people go, 'Aw fuck, another benefit.' I have great admiration for Peter Gabriel and Sting, for the amount of work they do, because they've been *slagged* from one end of the British press to the other."

Now, with Larry and Edge asleep, I step over Bono and find a seat next to Adam. Owing either to the champagne or the risky expedition, the bass player is in a reflective mood. "People get into rock & roll for all the right reasons and then end up getting out for all the wrong reasons," Adam says quietly. "They get into it out of naïveté, and then when the naïveté runs out they think, 'This isn't what I expected,' and they want to quit. I was just thinking how lucky I am to be in a band, to be one of four and not alone. No matter what happens, at least I always know that I have three friends." I ask Adam if I should turn on my tape recorder and he says no, no, let's just talk. So we do, and the member of

U2 who most often comes across as the party guy, the funny one, the rowdy of the group, reveals himself to be a thoughtful character very aware of being caught up in a great lifetime adventure.

Dawn comes early in the hinterlands on the summer solstice, the longest day. By 4:30 the sky is light and we have crossed the Cumbrian lake country, shaken off the cars that followed us, avoided the police roadblocks, and reached the Irish Sea. Bono rouses B. P. Fallon, U2's court philosopher and deejay, crying, "B. P.! Let's have some appropriate music on the blaster!"

"Something like 'Get Up, Stand Up'?" asks B. P.

"No," Bono answers. "I was thinking more, 'Theme from Hawaii Five-O.'"

We crawl out of the bus, blinking like newborn moles, and survey the cold, cold ocean, the steep stone steps, and the orange rubber life rafts that wait to ferry us to the Greenpeace ship. We are told to trade in our shoes for high rubber boots and to zip ourselves into orange survival suits before casting off. Five minutes later we're tearing across the waves and that little ship on the horizon is getting bigger and bigger. Bono is looking professionally heroic in the ocean spray, as a second Greenpeace raft—this one bearing a film crew and photographers—chops alongside us, immortalizing his nobility. It's as if Washington had crossed the Delaware with Emanuel Leutze paddling next to him in a canoe, furiously painting.

We pull up alongside the Greenpeace ship *Solo* and the brave hippie crew gaze down from the decks and wave. The size of the Greenpeace vessel is impressive when you're bobbing next to it in a dinghy, as is the knowledge that these people spend their lives throwing themselves into peril in defense of the ecosystem. One Greenpeace ship was blown up by the French government. U2 might be, as Bono says, rock stars on a day trip, but they're day-tripping with heroes.

"Throw out your treasure and your women and you'll be fine!" Bono shouts up from our raft. Then we tie on and start scurrying up the metal stairs along the hull of the ship. The captain explains that it will take us two or three hours to sail south to Sellafield, so we might as well wiggle out of our flotation suits and have some breakfast. (I make the mistake of asking for a Coke; from the reaction of the Greenpeace health food herbivores you'd think I requested a club to beat baby seals.) The *Solo* is sort of a combination of the Staten Island ferry and a college dorm—a big functional vessel with cute notes and nicknames stuck on the doors of the individual sleeping cabins. A woman from a London newspaper who caught wind that *something* was going to happen on this trip and horned her way aboard begins interviewing any U2 member she can corner. The Greenpeace film crew shoots Adam looking at nautical charts on the bridge. A Thor-like mate who's perhaps been at sea too long quietly tries to convince Bono to hire him as a roadie.

One woman present suggests to Bono that there's an empty cabin available if he'd like to go lie down for a while. Thanks, Bono says, that would be great. She leads Bono in and stands there staring at him as he lies down on the cot. Bono is exhausted; he tries to ignore her. Then she says, "Aren't you going to take off your pants?"

Er, Bono says, no, that's okay. I'm fine. Thank you. Then she climbs onto the cot next to him. Gently but firmly Bono explains that the young woman upstairs with the brown hair is his *wife*. Ahhh. And maybe *she'd* like to take a nap with me, hmmm? That's right, okay, thank you. The woman goes off to fetch Ali and Bono lies back, relieved. A couple of minutes later the door opens again, Ali comes in and lies down next to her husband. It is the first time the two of them have been alone together in ages, what with Bono on the road, and the weary couple try to make the best of this odd circumstance. As they begin to cuddle, though, Ali lets out a yelp. Their hostess is back and has climbed into bed with them. Well, Bono says, jumping up, let's see what's going on on deck.

Adam is wandering the bowels of the ship, looking for a place to sit quietly. An emotional subtext of this operation is that Sellafield is a British facility polluting the Irish Sea, and U2 is an Irish band. Radiation recognizes no borders, but the history of British oppression and Irish resentment gives this particular action an extra edge. Adam was born in England to British parents. Does he see this as an issue of nationalism?

"There *is* a nationalism issue, but more it's an *arrogance* issue," Adam answers. "The idea that if you put something this dangerous into a part of the world that is fairly primitive like the Lake District, you can get away with it because the people are relatively unsophisticated by White-hall terms. The arrogance is much more offensive than the nationalism."

During the last six months U2 has succeeded in erecting that screen between their public image and their personal lives and convictions.

They have agreed that this will be their only public do-gooding this year. They intend to camp it up as much as possible, too, avoiding the sort of piety for which they were so berated in the eighties. Sellafield is a test of how versatile U2's new image can be.

Musically, the band has switched gears before—from the mystical moodiness of *Boy* and *October* to the straight rock of *War,* and from that rock to the Eno watercolors of *The Unforgettable Fire.* Adam sometimes embraced such turns reluctantly. Not this time.

"This is definitely a turn that couldn't have come sooner, as far as I'm concerned," the bassist declares. "I think this is something everyone in the band wanted early on but didn't know how to get to. We always wanted to be able to be just a rock & roll band, but in a way we developed the other possibilities of the band precociously, *before* being a rock & roll band. It happened that way because of the way music was in the eighties; there was a lot of surface and not much substance and we didn't feel comfortable with that surface without learning something about the substance. So we started to mine into gospel, blues, early rock & roll. We wanted to go back and find out what it was all about before we felt confident presenting a version that represented the spirit of what *we* had."

Adam is interrupted by a summons to head below deck for a briefing. I'm left thinking of a line from *Achtung Baby,* a line Bono told me applied to Adam long before the other three U2's got loose enough to join him: "Give me one more chance to slide down the surface of things."

By 7 A.M. the gruesome towers of Sellafield are looming on the horizon like Mordor. The *Solo* drops anchor about a mile out. The Greenpeace organizer announces it's time for all those who are going ashore to get into their rubber boots, face masks, and hooded radiation suits. We all look like big stuffed animals, except for the roughishly handsome Larry Mullen, who puts his radiation suit over his black motorcycle jacket and then pulls his leather lapels out through the zipper. With his sunglasses and army camouflage cap, Larry is the epitome of combat rock. "I invented cool," he drawls, "and *you're* on a boat with me."

Bono and Edge, on the other hand, look like burritos with sunglasses. They stare at each other, trying not to laugh. Bono reaches out and takes his partner's hand. "Edge," he says romantically, and they embrace as the gawking Greenpeacers giggle. "Talk about safe sex!" Bono shouts from his space suit. "You can't get much safer than this!" Adventure, radiation, and sleep deprivation have conspired to cast a goofy mood over U2. The hooded suits don't help.

The Greenpeace team are loading barrels of radioactive sand from Irish beaches into the rubber rafts. The idea is that U2 will hit the beach and deposit these barrels at Sellafield's door, a graphic example of what Sellafield is pumping out to Ireland. On the shore Greenpeace activists from England, Wales, and Scotland are lugging barrels from their own countries' beaches to the factory. Paul McGuinness watches them through binoculars. Then the manager turns his attention to a special project for his boys. Paul has with him the cover of the Beatles' album *Help* with its photograph of the Fab Four waving navy signal flags. Paul has eight red flags and a booklet of instructions on how to spell out letters. He summons U2 to the top deck and lines them up and they begin learning to spell out first "H-E-L-P" and then "F-O-A-D"—a favorite expression of Larry's that abbreviates "fuck off and die."

Great rock band though they are, choreography has never been U2's strong suit. They spend a lot of time getting their signals backward (they are following McGuinness, who is facing them, which gets confusing) and hitting each other with flags. During the difficult "Switch!" from "H-E-L-P" to "F-O-A-D," Adam pokes Bono in the eye. Eventually the entire exercise degenerates into a sword fight with semaphores. Then a great commotion comes up the stairs from the lower decks. It's time to invade England.

9

Bono, Row the Boat Ashore

---

*the band establishes a beachhead/ bono hoisted high/ edge
among the little people/ a deft segue from oral sex to w. b.
yeats/ a dubious urchin/ transcending the clusterfuck*

"I FEEL LIKE a wally in my Wellies," says Larry as he stomps around
the *Solo* in the rubber boots ("Wellingtons") we have been ordered to redon before wading in the atomic water. As U2
prepares to board their landing craft the Greenpeace organizer notices
with a start that Bono has on his feet not Wellies but his own leather
motorcycle boots. "You can't wear those!" she insists. "That water is
radioactive! Whatever you wear into it has to be discarded afterward!"

"It's okay," Bono says. "I won't get my feet wet."

"You don't understand," she says. "Weighed down by the barrels, the
rafts can't get all the way up to the shore. You're going to have to wade
in!"

"Get my feet wet!" Bono sputters, adopting a spoiled, *Spinal Tap*
accent. "Oh, no, no, no, this whole thing is off!"

A quick search finds no spare rubber boots on the *Solo.* The weary
Greenpeace leader says, "It's all right, Bono. I understand you can *walk*
on water."

As we prepare to board the two landing rafts one of the Greenpeace
organizers puts out her hand to stop me. This is as far as you go, she
says. From here on it's only members of U2 and the camera crew. I tell
her that if she thinks I came all this way to stay on the boat and wave
she should pull into port and have her bottom scraped, but she is
adamant. I sulk for a minute, and then it occurs to me that in these
hooded suits we all look alike. So I go up to one of the film crew, tap
him on the shoulder, and tell him he's got to go back and get a life
jacket. As soon as he leaves I take his place in the raft, where the

Greenpeace commissar counts our heads and orders us to cast off. Away we go.

As U2's rubber raft skims the surf toward the nuclear shoreline, the tension that ran through all the preparations for this adventure has given way to a Monty Python mood. Still, as the camera boat runs alongside them, the bandmembers and McGuinness raise themselves into serious, even heroic poses. The main purpose of this expedition is to give the newspapers and TV an image that will focus attention, if only in the second paragraph, on how dangerous the Sellafield facility is. So as they approach the shore, U2 gets focused on that objective.

Nearing land, U2 can see Greenpeace activists in white radiation suits lined up like an army of ghosts along the line where public beach turns into injuncted no-man's-land. They can see reporters and cameramen. They can see bobbies with a photographer, taking pictures of U2 with a flash camera on a sunny day from a half mile inside the Sellafield land. Behind the plant gates are paddy wagons too. (*Paddy* wagon: another great token of contempt for the Irish.)

U2's raft gets as close as it can to the shore and then, before Bono can get his shoes wet, a huge Greenpeace member splashes into the brine, lifts the singer out of the raft, and carries him to the beach. Bono holds up his arms as he's hoisted, waving V signs at the reporters who rush toward him, clicking and snapping. Bono is deposited on the sand and he turns and stares nobly back toward the *Solo*, the journalists dancing around him like a maypole. Not one reporter pays any attention to Edge and Adam, standing in the water struggling to hoist their barrel of poison sand. While cameras capture Bono from every angle, Edge and Adam grunt past unnoticed, lugging their radioactive burden.

At the high tide line U2 dumps their barrels and convenes a press conference. "I actually don't believe Sellafield 2 will go ahead," Bono tells the reporters. "Word is that at the highest levels people are very nervous about this. They just spent millions of pounds on it—nobody wants to admit it was a mistake, so they have to continue. It will be a great scandal later, when the real facts come out. That's all we can do— bring the facts out. We're a rock & roll band! It's kind of absurd we have to dress up like complete wankers to make this point."

After all the pictures have been taken and all the reporters' questions answered, McGuinness and U2 confer. The bus that brought them to the sea has managed to make its way down here. If they hike a mile or so down the beach they can get on board and drive out, rather than returning to the *Solo*. That strikes everyone as fine. They walk away from the reactor, eventually coming to a town. Local children make saucer eyes as they see this phalanx of creatures in white body suits emerging from the shore.

Edge is the first one off the beach and a waiting broadcast journalist at a pay phone ropes the guitarist into a live radio interview. The local kids start poking each other and gasping, "It's the Edge!" One little boy calls out to his even littler friend, "Richie! You want to see Bono? That's him down there!" The smaller boy runs up and stares. He sees a figure in a hooded radiation suit. "That's Bono?"

The kids start lining up for autographs. U2 peels off their protective gear and deposits it in Greenpeace bags. Bono is told he should probably throw away his motorcycle boots—even if they never touched the water, the sand at Sellafield is dangerous. He chucks them away. Then a local couple come up and start tearing into one of the Greenpeace activists. "Our child died from leukemia caused by that plant!" the husband says angrily. "You come here for a day and you go away! What do you know! We have to live with this all the time!" He storms off. His wife slaps the Greenpeace volunteer, then turns and follows her husband.

Back on the bus Bono leans his head on his wife's shoulder and waves to the children gathered around the coach. He adopts a broad American accent and brays, "Oh, look, dear. Aren't they a-*dor*-able. Oh, I'd just like to put them all in my suitcase and take them home!"

I kick the back of his seat. "Hey, quit making fun of Americans!"

Bono turns around apologetically and explains that he's mimicking the U.S. tourists he met as a child at St. Patrick's Cathedral in Dublin. "I would charge them for tours of the cathedral," he says. "I made good money."

"Oh," I say, "you were an *urchin*."

"I was!" Bono says brightly, at which Ali bursts out laughing. She knows her husband never urched.

As the bus begins to pull out, Bono glances out the window—and sees that one of the juvenile U2 fans is proudly making off with his irradiated boots. "Oh, hell! Stop the bus!" The kid refuses to give up his souvenirs until all four members of U2 give him their autographs.

As we head down the highway away from Sellafield we pass—facing the other way—a series of police roadblocks. There they are, all lined up and waiting to stop U2 or Greenpeace from approaching the plutonium mill. As we fly past the cops, Larry shouts out the window and waves.

During the long drive back to Manchester, Bono—who has become father to two children since U2 last toured—talks about readjusting to the rock star life. "Going out on the road is not difficult," he says. "The real problems start when you come home, readjustment. When you're on the road, everything is put second to the gig. You have minders who follow you out at night to make sure you come back and play the next concert. And when you come home, the *clusterfuck* mentality you bring back from the road can be very funny. Like the whole room-key thing. When you're on the road a room key is like your dog tag. It gets you home at night, it pays your bills. I've had situations where a month after a tour has ended I'll be in Dublin and I'll give some nightclub owner a key from the Ritz-Carlton in Chicago instead of cash, and he'll look at me like 'What the fuck is he on?' "

We begin talking about the selfishness most musicians, most artists, cultivate on the underside of their dedication to their art. "We're living a fairly decadent kind of selfish, art-oriented lifestyle," Bono says. "There's nothing to get in the way of you and your music when you're on the road. Real life doesn't raise its head."

I quote back at Bono his lines from "The Fly": "Every artist is a cannibal, every poet is a thief, all kill their inspiration and sing about the grief."

"Yeah," Bono sighs. "I hope I'm not like that, but I suspect I might be. And I really hate that picture. The great thing is, under the guise of 'The Fly' I can admit to all this shit."

Bono lumbers up to the front of the bus, unwinds the tour guide microphone, and starts torturing us all with his imitation of a drunken Irish lounge singer. He mumbles inebriated dedications, sings awful songs, and dares anyone to come take the microphone away from him. It's too bad that much of the public thinks of Bono as a sourpuss. He's a card. The problem is that when people get as famous as U2, other people start treating them like gods or freaks. So they have to build a protective bubble in which they can be themselves. Inside the bubble they can be as they've always been, with no rock star baloney. But from outside the bubble they look strange and distorted.

This bus ride back to Manchester from Sellafield has now lasted about three hours, and McGuinness has been promising us a breakfast stop the whole way. We pull off at a roadside tourist cafeteria and everyone pours out and starts lining up for sausage, ham, uncooked bacon, and all the other artery-hardening, cloven-hoofed delights of British cuisine. In the restaurant Bono tries to convince Edge to come outside and sit in the grass, but Edge grumbles that he's seen enough outdoors for one day.

When the bus trip resumes, Bono and I head to the backseat. As we approach Manchester I say, "Well, of course, Bono, everybody must be asking you about all the references to oral sex in your new songs. . . ."

"WHAT?" Bono sputters. "Bill, you've turned to the wrong page in your notebook, you're asking me Prince questions!"

Listen, I say, to these lines from recent U2 songs: "Surrounding me, going down on me," "You can swallow or you can spit," "Here she comes, six and nine again," "Did I leave a bad taste in your mouth." . . .

"Ahh." Bono mumbles something about sixty-nine being one of the most equal sexual positions and then strongly suggests we *get onto another subject.*

Okay, I say, in "One" you sing, "You say love is a temple, love's the higher law. You ask me to enter and then you make me crawl." That's a hell of a sacrament/sin, temple/vagina metaphor; it's like Yeats's "Love has pitched his mansion in the place of excrement."

"Yeah, whoa," Bono exhales. "That line, you really touched on something. You know, it was no accident that Jesus was born in the shit and straw. . . ." The bus comes to a halt. We're back in Manchester at last. We head into the hotel to pick up our bags and check out. U2 has a plane waiting to take them back to Dublin. Bono asks me if I want to come along. No, thanks, I say, I've left all my clothes in a laundry in London and I've got to get them back.

A few days later Bono telephones and asks if I saw our Sellafield adventure on the TV news and in the papers. He says the nuclear industry tried to counter all the coverage Greenpeace got by sending PR men out to stand on the beach in their shirtsleeves, "looking as if they were going to build a sandcastle." One nuclear spokesman really screwed up by telling reporters that U2 had no right to get involved in Britain because they were Irish and they should be home in Belfast trying to stop kids from building bombs. That mixed-up statement (aside from its bigotry, Britain considers Belfast part of the U.K.) brought angry charges of "Paddy-bashing" down on the unfortunate public relations man. Then he mentions our bus conversation.

"I think I was talking to you about Jesus being born in the shit and straw," Bono says. "I suppose the nineties equivalent of that is Las Vegas, the neon strip. I found in amongst the trash to be a great place to develop my loftier ideas, and a great disguise as well."

It's interesting to find your loftier ideas in the debris, I say.

"Yeah," Bono says. "It's the best place for them. Because they don't call themselves big ideas down here. They don't draw attention to themselves. They don't have a big sign saying 'ART.' " He pauses and sighs. "I'm desperately trying to think how I can talk about this and not sound like a complete arsehole.

"People might think that where U2 is right now is much more throwaway, but I think the stuff we're throwing away is maybe much more interesting that what you'd at first suspect. I've never been as turned on about rock & roll as I am now because there seem to be so many possibilities. Sex and music are still for me places where you glimpse God. Sex and *art*, I suppose, but unless you're going to get slain in the spirit by a Warhol or Rothko, I think for most of us art *is* music.

"We're looking for diamonds in the dirt, and the music is more in the mud now. Our heads may still be in the clouds, but our feet are definitely dragging the dirt. As dark as it gets, though, we are looking for shiny moments. Those shiny moments, for me, are the same as they've always been. There are big words for them, like *transcendence*. I'm still interested in the things of the spirit and God and the mind-boggling idea that He might be interested in us. And faith and faithfulness, sexually and spiritually speaking.

"Everybody's in a state of confusion sexually in the nineties. Love and sex are just up for grabs. Nobody knows what to make of them. Marriage looks like an act of madness, if grand madness. One thing I actually like about the drug culture, though I'm not really part of it, is that it acknowledges the other side, the fourth dimension that everybody else kind of buries. For a hundred years people have been told they don't have a spirit, and if you can't see it or can't prove it, it doesn't exist. Anyone who listens to Smokey Robinson knows that isn't true.

"We've got more contradictions on stage now than ever before. I think it's a very interesting tension that that brings about. People are made to chose between flesh and the spirit, when people are both."

Yeah, I say, on the Zoo TV tour and on the *Achtung Baby* album you're trying to balance things that are perceived as opposites, though in fact they may not be.

"Yes," Bono says. "That's an important point. What look like opposites but may not be, like plastic and soul."

Like sex and God?

"Exactly."

Where's your ethical line now? What subject would U2 refuse to sing about?

"There's none. By singing about something you make it clean. Because you bring it out into the open."

Edge told me last winter that the themes of *Achtung Baby* were, "Betrayal, love, morality, spirituality, and faith." A lot of the songs deal with the temptations that disrupt and might destroy a marriage. Was Edge's the only troubled marriage you were drawing on?

"Well, I was going down that road anyway," Bono says. "But certainly . . . I don't know which came first, to be honest. The words or what Edge went through. They're all bound up in each other. But there are a lot of other experiences that went on around the same time. It all gets back to the fact that it's an extraordinary thing to see two people holding on to each other and trying to work things out. I'm still in awe of the idea of two people against the world, and I actually believe it *is* to be against the world, because I don't think the world is about sticking together. AIDS is not the only threat, you know. AIDS is the big bad wolf at the moment, but I see all the threats. I see people's need for independence, their need to follow their own ideas down. These are all not necessarily selfish things. Everything out there is against the idea of being a couple: every ad, every TV program, every soap opera, every novel you buy in an airport. Sex is now a subject owned by corporations. It's used to sell commodities. It is itself a commodity. And the message is that if you don't have it, you're nobody.

"I've had my problems in my relationship. It's tough for everybody. I think fidelity is just against human nature. That's where we have to either engage or not engage our higher side. Certainly I'm not trying to come up with easy answers. It's like in school when they tell you about drugs. 'If you smoke drugs you'll become an addict and you'll die the next week.' They don't tell you even half the truth. I think the same is true about sex. You know, if you tell people that the best place to have sex is in the safe hands of a loving relationship, you may be telling a lie! There may be other places. If the question is, can I as a married man write about sex with a stranger, 'yes' has got to be the answer. I've got to write about that because that is part of the subject I'm writing about. You have to try and expose some myths, even if they expose *you* along the way. I don't want to talk about my own relationship, because I've too much respect for Ali to do so. What I'm saying to you is, I may or may not be writing from my own experience on some of these, but that doesn't make it any less real."

Bono and I talk on, we talk for more than two hours. He gives me a quote from Sam Shepard to sum up: "Right in the middle of a contradiction," he says, "that's the place to be."

10

Giants Stadium

_____

a history of U2 in the usa/ a tour of underworld/ bono gets hit with a hairbrush/ ellen darst, native guide/ women in the workplace/ how the author lost his objectivity/ canning the support band

KIDS GATHER for days in the parking lots of the Giants football stadium in northern New Jersey, across the river from Manhattan, while the mighty stage is erected for ZOO TV: THE OUTSIDE BROADCAST. They hunker down in wonder and confusion, like the apemen studying the monolith in *2001*. For their summer stadium tour of America, U2 has blown everything up to elephantine proportions. The stage, huge and black, looms across one end of the football field, its spires crawling up toward the sky like the steeples of postnuclear cathedrals. They are supposed to look like TV towers— black scaffolding narrowing as it ascends to a flashing red point—but the effect is creepier than that. The eleven-story stage is only the framework for the giant TV screens that flicker and crackle above and across the entire proscenium. When the stadium lights go off and all those screens flash to life it hits a lot of tribal buttons in the audience; U2 may have uncovered a subconscious link between the recent family rite of sitting around the television and more primitive ritual equivalents —such as the clan gathering to be entertained by the shaman. When U2 takes the stage even the helicopters circling overhead for a peek and the airplanes using the stadium as a landing marker seem like blinking red ornaments buzzing around the big voodoo, little mechanical sparks rising from the electric bonfire.

Underworld, the vast network of work areas behind and beneath the stage, is a beehive city. On Edge's right, in a bunker two steps down, sits guitar tech Dallas Schoo with a roomful of guitars, tuners, and spare parts. It is a fully functioning guitar shop. During the concert Dallas will break off a conversation to pump a wah-wah pedal so that Edge can get the effect while keeping his own feet free to move across the stage. Just outside Dallas's room, in a cubbyhole that gives him a clear view of the stage, sits Des Broadbery at an elaborate console of keyboards and computer screens. Des runs the sequencers that fill out U2's sound and make it possible to approximate the elaborate sonic effects of *Achtung Baby* onstage. Des has a computer file standing by with any U2 song the band might suddenly pull out of their hats, and if it needs a synth pad or second guitar, Des is ready to drop it in. When Edge is playing the solo on "Ultra Violet (Light My Way)," for example, Des is under the stage providing a sampled eight-bar guitar figure in the background.

"There's no room for human error in what I do," Des says. "You have to be sharp. There's an awful lot depending on what goes on in my area. What really matters when they're up there onstage is to make sure they're with me or I'm with them."

I ask Des what he does when the band loses their place in mid song, as a result, say, of Bono getting excited and coming in early. "What would happen," Des explains, "is I let them find out where they all are and then I go ahead of them to a chorus or verse and wait there until they catch up."

U2 first used sequencers in concert to get a handle on "Bad" from *The Unforgettable Fire.* By the *Joshua Tree* tour sequencers were beefing up eight numbers. Now it's a rare U2 song that doesn't have Des adding some sample, phrase, or backing part.

From Des and Dallas's wing you can go up a short flight to a vast backstage hall, across which sits a small dressing room with a punching bag where band members hover during the encores, and where they can switch clothes during breaks. One night Bono came in raging during Edge's guitar solo on "Bullet the Blue Sky." Everything was going wrong that night and he was furious. Before he fell into the chair where stylist Nassim Khalifa dolls him up he punched the bag, threw a chair, and kicked the wall. While Nassim was trying to brush his hair he pounded the table and screamed, "Fuck! Fuck!" So she bonked him on the top of the head with the hairbrush as if he were a bad dog. Bono was startled. *That hurt!* He looked in the mirror and saw Nassim calmly combing, saying nothing. He shut up and behaved.

Beneath that level is the brain center of the Zoo TV operation, a web of desks, control boards and television monitors usually described in the press as "an entire TV station under the stage." That is actually misleading, because when most people think of a TV station they think of something much less elaborate than this setup. What this really resembles is NASA mission control. On each screen is a different image, multiple shots of Bono, Larry, Adam, and Edge as well as different broadcast TV channels pumping out their programming, pretaped bits and pieces used during the show, the aphorisms that flash on the screens, and all the programming created for the concert, from a buffalo that runs in slow motion across the series of screens during "One" to the nuclear bombs that erupt during "Until the End of the World." There are eleven laser disc players feeding images to a total of 262 video cubes (the normal-TV-screen-size component parts of the vidiwalls) each of which can be controlled separately, if anyone were lunatic enough to want to.

Keeping this operation on the road costs U2 $125,000 a day, every day—concert or not. In the face of such expense their refusal to take on corporate sponsorship is almost heroic.

There is another music shop, this one equipped with drum gear and some bass equipment, in the bunker at Adam's left, and there is a sort of little shed hidden behind Adam, at Larry's left, where the bassist can duck for a quick swig of water or glance at a chord chart. All through Underworld there are people running around talking into headsets, driving forklifts, and throwing switches with a determination I have seen only in Scotty in the engine room when Captain Kirk is fighting the Klingons. What's most remarkable is that this megastructure must be rebuilt and razed in every city along the way—which among other burdens means that U2 has to rent a football stadium for three nights in order to play once, because it takes that long to erect the stage building.

Looking at this mighty enterprise and the eighty-five thousand people itching for U2's arrival, I have to slap myself to remember that twelve years ago it took only my dented little Dodge Dart to transport U2, myself, and Ellen Darst from the Providence, Rhode Island, Holiday Inn to lunch in Warwick to a radio interview at Brown University to soundcheck at a bar called the Center Stage across the river in East Providence. We were all a lot smaller then.

My friend Ellen seemed to know what U2 would be from the moment she first heard them. In 1980 she had just been promoted from being a field rep for Warner Brothers Records in Boston to a job in the Manhattan office. I was still living in New England then, but I'd visit her when I was in New York. One day I went in to see Ellen and she said, "You've got to hear this!" and played me "I Will Follow." Warners was distributing Island Records and Island chief Chris Blackwell had this new band, U2. I thought the single was good, but Ellen thought it was the second coming. She made me promise to come see U2 when they played the Paradise, a club in Boston.

On stage U2 were exciting, still very raw but filled with such energy and belief that the crowd got caught up and were on their feet, dancing and pushing toward the stage to reach out to Bono. My memory is that they did both "I Will Follow" and "Out of Control" twice in the short set, which was actually not uncommon in the punk days. Bands tended to start playing gigs before they had an hour's worth of songs. Later I learned that U2 had lots of tunes that preceded their recording contract, but I guess they wanted to stick to their best stuff for their first American shows.

A lot of people who bought *Boy*, the first album, when it came out and saw those early gigs like to sit around now claiming that U2 was never that good again and telling the grandchildren, "If you had seen U2 when they were teenagers, as I did, you wouldn't be impressed by all this Zoo TV junk now." It's actually not true. The young U2 were charismatic as all hell, but they were still relying on passion (and Edge's striking guitar sound) to get them over a shortage of great songs and a lack of musical tightness. When faced with an audience that wasn't interested in suspending their disbelief, the young U2 could sound pretty ordinary. Lately Larry has echoed what Adam said earlier—that the band actually wasn't that good when they first came to America. What people responded to was not what U2 were but the promise of what they could become.

I had promised Ellen Darst after the Paradise show that I would peddle a freelance article about U2 to one of the rock magazines I was then writing for. I had a hard time finding anyone interested. Finally *Output* magazine on Long Island said all right. The day U2 arrived in Rhode Island, where I lived, looking to do the interview, my pals, a local band called the Shake, were having a big cookout at their house and I didn't want to miss it. So I offered to pick up U2 at the Holiday Inn and bring them along. It was a sweltering, humid Memorial Day and when I showed up at the motel to collect them Bono, Larry, and Edge were in the pool. Adam was waiting for me at the front door. "Come on," Adam called to the others, "we're going to a burnout!"

"A cookout," I corrected. "A cookout is a barbecue, a burnout is a drug casualty."

"Ah," Edge said, "and will there be burnouts at the cookout?"

We spent the afternoon eating hot dogs with local bands and their families at the Shake's house, and at one point U2 and I went off to the rehearsal room in the basement and did a long interview in which they told me their story up to that point. Given that the oldest of them, Adam, had just turned twenty-one, it was not a very long story. I was impressed with the fact that they wrote all their songs through jamming in a room together; they seemed determined to keep everything equal between them. Bono was adamant about the fact that bands these days weren't real bands, where it's all for one and one for all. Now it was one or two leaders and hired sidemen. He made a big point of the fact that U2 would always be what they had grown up believing the Beatles and Stones were: a real band. The Shake had a color poster of the early Beatles hanging on the wall and I remember U2 staring at it, fascinated by the fact that on this poster all the Beatles had jet black hair. They were impressed by the possibility that the Beatles had dyed their hair to look more alike. (Actually, I suspect that the poster company did the tints, not Brian Epstein.)

Back upstairs at the party Edge asked me about the Shake and I said they were a real good band who played six nights a week, fifty weeks a year, hoping to get a record deal. He said that wasn't the way to do it. Edge said a single, even a homemade single, with one great song would do more for a band than five years of club dates. "I Will Follow" was the proof.

Over the next two and a half years, from the spring of 1981 to the fall of 1983, U2 played the Northeast so much that you'd have thought they lived in Seekonk. Even when they weren't on tour between Boston and Washington they kept up a strong presence with interviews in the local music papers and airplay on college radio stations. I remember running into Adam at Boston clubs between tours, lapping up America and making sure U2 had its finger on whatever was happening. Ellen Darst was always beside them. Later in 1981 Warners laid her off along with a ton of young executives in reaction to a general plummet in the postdisco record business. U2 helped Ellen land a job at Island, keeping her close. She told me the Island job would only be temporary if things worked out with the band.

Things did. Paul McGuinness and U2 had used Ellen as their guide to the American music business. As soon as U2 had enough money to do it, they set up a New York office and put Ellen in charge. Ellen hired Keryn Kaplan as her assistant. Keryn, fresh out of college, had been a secretary at Warners who was also laid off in the purge. Not long after that, Paul brought in Anne-Louise Kelly to help organize their office in Dublin, and realized that she was way too smart to waste on typing and filing. Anne-Louise was made Director of Principle Management Dublin, the same title Ellen held in New York.

I know Ellen felt strongly that women were treated badly in the U.S. record business and was determined to take advantage of all the smart women who were being ignored or underutilized by the overpaid men in the old boys' club. I have no idea if Anne-Louise felt the same way, but both the New York and Dublin offices of Principle Management were staffed almost entirely by women. They still are. I think it's one of the reasons U2's organization has an entirely different—and much more comradely—atmosphere than does most of the music business. Most management companies—and indeed, the top levels of most record labels—have the spirit of a football club or military campaign. There's a lot of Us vs. Them shouting and a lot of macho posturing—which is always obnoxious when people are engaged in an enterprise that requires no physical courage and little personal risk. People burn out fast in that sort of environment. I'm sure one of the reasons the women at Principle put in long hours for years on end is because it is, most of the time, a friendly and supportive place to work.

"Ellen taught me so much about America in the early days," McGuinness says. "If you're on the road with four or five guys and all that macho stuff that goes along with rock & roll, a very effective counterbalance is association with a lot of women. It seems like the right way to do things. There's enough maleness in rock & roll without having it in the office as well. There are a lot of women in the music business who are not recognized for what they could do and I think it's just stupid. We're not going to be stupid about that."

Once U2 had their organization functioning they worked like gophers to win new converts to their cause. Bono was unstoppable in his pursuit of audiences, jumping into crowds, dancing with fans, leaping onto outstretched arms, and—as the halls they played got bigger—climbing up into the scaffolding, hanging from wires on the walls, and swinging from the balconies. The band organized a series of courts-martial at which they chewed him out for endangering himself and any kids in the crowd who might try to imitate him. He finally got the message when Edge, Adam, and Larry threatened to break up U2 if he didn't stop making like Tarzan. Bono told me at the time that he was also influenced by a concert review written by Robert Hillburn in the *Los Angeles Times* in which the critic said that U2's music didn't need such distractions. I think Hillburn has remained Bono's conservative conscience over the years. As Zoo TV expands further and further, all sorts of possibilities for future U2 expansion into interactive video, computer networks, and cable TV are being waved in front of the band. Bono is interested in all that, as well as screenwriting and the offers of movie roles that regularly slip through Principle's transom. But he has mentioned more than once that Hillburn said to him, "If you put your entire energy into developing your music, you could be one of the all-time great songwriters. Think of what Gershwin left behind, think of Hank Williams. Should you let anything else distract you from that?" That reprimand rattles around Bono's head. He is still wrestling with it.

The first time U2 headlined at an arena in the United States was at the Worcester, Massachusetts, Centrum in the autumn of 1983, six months into the *War* tour. The Centrum was then a new hall, with a capacity of fifteen thousand and located at a population nexus about fifty minutes from Boston, to the northeast, Hartford to the southwest, and Providence to the southeast. The fans U2 had been winning in three states poured in and sold out the show. It was a big night for the band, a portent of things to come, and some overexcited kids ran onto the stage to try to hug Bono. When security came charging after one girl, Bono motioned them away, wrapped his arms around her, and waltzed with her around the lip of the stage. Then he continued singing while she slumped down and hung onto his leg. Eventually Bono came in from his emoting long enough to realize that she wasn't just hugging him. She had chained herself to his ankle. And she did not have a key. The concert had to continue with Bono attached to the fan until the roadies could get a saw and chop her off. U2's unmediated relationship with their audience was changing.

I went back into the dressing room right after U2 came offstage that night, congratulated the other guys on selling out the Centrum, and went over to say hi to Bono. He was covered with sweat, had a towel around his neck, and was talking, wide-eyed, in his fullest flights of poetry. After a couple of minutes I realized he didn't know me. It did something to his brain to try to communicate with fifteen thousand people, and his commitment wasn't an act. He couldn't switch it off the moment he left the stage. He was changing from the kid I'd met when "I Will Follow" was new into someone bigger.

A year later, after "Pride" had brought U2 to the next level of success, playing smaller halls was no longer an option. By then I had moved to New York and U2 were playing at Radio City Music Hall. It was too small a venue. The crowd was charging the stage, security guards were fighting the fans, Bono was struggling to regain control like Mick Jagger at Altamont. Bono got into fights with cops who were hitting kids. The show stopped several times while the guards tried to restore order. It was a big mess that almost ended with Bono being arrested and pretty much assured that U2 were done with playing mid-size halls in America.

In the summer of 1986 U2 agreed to headline an American fundraising tour for Amnesty International. They topped a bill that included Sting, just split from the Police, Peter Gabriel, and Lou Reed, one of their early heroes. The final night of the Amnesty tour was a show here at Giants Stadium that would be televised on MTV. Guest stars were coming out of the woodwork and tension was very high, as MTV moved in and took over command. Miles Davis played, Muhammad Ali spoke, Pete Townshend got off the plane in New York and received word his father had just died in London. He turned around and went home. Joni Mitchell, who had been scheduled to play only a couple of songs, was asked to go out unrehearsed and do a whole set to fill in for Townshend. The place was nuts with vanity, panic, threats, and brown-nosing.

The biggest ego-war was over who would close the show. It was U2's tour, always had been, but in these final days Sting's recently deceased band the Police had reunited for a grand prisoner-liberating, conscience-raising farewell. The Police were a bigger name than U2, and the fact that this was their last ever, farewell, goodbye-to-all-that performance left no doubt in the mind of their manager Miles Copeland about who should climax this prime-time spectacle. Tour promoter Bill Graham disagreed. Graham, Copeland, and Amnesty boss Jack Healy went at it about who should open for whom. There has rarely been as much angry energy expended in the service of political prisoners as there was backstage at Giants Stadium that day.

Finally a compromise worthy of Solomon was achieved. U2 went on first and played a commanding set. Bono, his hair grown long, looked like Daniel Webster and held the football stadium in his hand. People who watched it on TV told me it seemed overdone, hammy, and that may be, but in the coliseum it was mesmerizing. I was pretty ecstatic that they'd pulled it off. I ran into Ellen backstage and said, "Ellen! They were the best they've ever been! The Police don't have a chance!" and she ripped my metaphorical ass off and shoved it down my throat. "It is not a competition!" Ellen blasted. "These musicians have nothing but respect and affection for each other and it does them no good at all when people around them try to turn it into a battle of the bands!"

"Yikes!" I explained, shrinking like a cheap shirt in a hot wash. Ellen calmed down and said, sorry, it's been a tough day.

The great compromise was that U2 got off in time for the Police to have a good chunk of prime television time, before MTV's broadcast ended, and at the finale of the Police's (excellent) set they went into "Invisible Sun," their haunting song about the troubles in Northern Ireland. One by one the members of U2 emerged from the wings and took over the Police's instruments. Larry took Stewart Copeland's place behind the drums, Edge took Andy Summers's guitar, Adam took Sting's bass, and Bono stepped up to finish singing the Police's song. It was a graceful gesture, the outgoing Biggest Band in the World publicly handing off the baton to the new one.

Looking back at the Amnesty finale a year later, Sting said, "The last song we played we handed our instruments over to U2. Every band has its day. In '84 we were the biggest band in the world and I figured it was U2's turn next. And I was right. They are the biggest band in the world. A year from now it'll be their turn to hand over their instruments to someone else."

And now, seven years later, we are back at Giants Stadium with U2 onstage. Sting was wrong about one thing; they have held onto their Biggest Band in the World mantle tighter and longer than any group since the Rolling Stones. Amnesty vet Lou Reed's back in the house tonight too. He strolls out onto the B stage to join Bono on "Satellite of Love," bringing a huge roar from the eighty-five thousand people in attendance. One of the benefits of all this technology is that when U2 move on they can bring Lou Reed with them. They have prepared a video of him singing the song, which will crackle in and out of the big TV screens in duet with Bono for the rest of the tour.

In the same way, they will continue to carry a piece of their opening act, the rap group Disposable Heroes of Hiphoprisy, with them after their stint as support band ends. For the year and a half remaining in the tour Hiphoprisy's song "Television, the Drug of the Nation," will be played over the eruption of the Zoo TV screens before U2 take the stage. An update of Gil Scott-Heron's "The Revolution Will Not Be Televised," it is a Zoo perfect anthem, at once a commentary on the mass media culture and a state-of-the-art example of it. Hiphoprisy leader Michael Franti says he's having a good time with U2, especially now that he's been pulled aside and told that the guitarist's name is "Edge." Michael had been calling him "Ed."

There is a moment of poignance amid all the backstage madness. Artist David Wojnarowicz is here with his family, from whom he's been estranged for years. Wojnarowicz's image of buffalo being driven over a cliff was chosen by U2 as the cover of their "One" single, itself a benefit for AIDS research, at Adam's suggestion. Wojnarowicz is dying of AIDS; he will probably not live out the summer. His family apparently saw a story about his collaboration with U2 on television and got in touch. They have come here tonight to make up for a little lost time.

The Zoo TV spectacle loses nothing in being expanded to stadium size; it works better. The sensory explosions early in the concert make the size of the crowd irrelevant—the visual pyrotechnics yank people straight into the show, without the usual sense of straining to see the little figures onstage that sticks a wedge in most stadium concerts. The barrage of visual effects draws the audience into the music. Then when the explosions stop and U2 appear on the B stage with their acoustic guitars, the audience has readjusted its perspective so that it feels as if they are in an intimate situation, and from there on—remarkably—the impediment distance puts between performer and audience seems to be gone. When Bono sings "With or Without You" it feels as if he's performing in a small club.

All the hoopla is ultimately a means to intimacy. By first shooting off fireworks and then emerging to stand revealed in the afterglow, U2 closes the space between the stage and the upper reaches of the stadium. And once that distance is overcome, the remaining distance—between Bono's voice and the listener's ear—is easy to cross. Almost all of the appeal of U2's music comes from its intimacy, its humanness. The band writes songs out of moods and then Bono searches for a way to hang a shape on those moods with his voice and lyrics. He is the first amplifier the music is put through and it is his job to pin down the feeling the music is making without distorting it. No matter how big U2's live sound or flashy the production gets, it never imposes an effect that is not already present in the composition. When U2 blasts on "Bullet the Blue Sky," they are mimicking the human rage at the heart of the song; when U2 throbs on "With or Without You," they are evoking a heartbeat. Unlike a lot of other stadium bands, they never pull out a crowd-jolting effect—an explosion or screeching guitar solo or extreme dynamic change—just to make the audience jump. Every effect grows out of the song, which is why once the impediment of physical distance is overcome the audience can feel as close to the music in the stadium as they would in a theater. I suppose it's the live-performance equivalent of the way TV performers such as Walter Cronkite, Ronald Reagan, or Bishop Sheen developed a gift for speaking to millions of people as if each was the only one listening, as if speaker and listener were alone together in a small room.

I brought along a friend of mine tonight, a recording engineer who's been in the music business for twenty years. He's been laughing and shaking his head through the whole show, which he says is the best he's ever seen. U2 are playing here at Giants Stadium for two nights, and then doing a couple more across the river at Yankee Stadium. They will play to more people during this New York stand than they did in their first three years on the road in America.

I am very glad I saw so many U2 shows early in their career, and I have a lot of sentimentality about them. But they have never been better than this.

II

Promise in the Year of Election

---

a call from the governor of arkansas/ the same mistake made by henry ii/ the search for bono by the secret service/ two shots of happy/ a setback for irish immigration/ george b. insults b. george/ the blood in the ground cries out for vengeance

O N AUGUST 28 U2 are the guests on "Rockline," a national radio phone-in show. "Bill from Little Rock" comes on the phone. The band members glance at each other; they were warned that the Democratic presidential nominee might call to engage in a little of his post-*Arsenio* public hipness. After some initial jousting (Bono: "Should I call you governor?" Clinton: "No, call me Bill." Bono: "And you can call me Betty."), Clinton and U2 hit it off. For Clinton it means another plug on MTV News, for U2 it means one more item in the daily newspapers; both parties toss another pebble of P.R. onto the big hype candy mountain and move on to the next event.

Two weeks later U2 rolls into Chicago at 3 A.M., drunk and in their stage clothes, after a three-hour journey from a stadium concert in Madison, Wisconsin. Checking into the Ritz-Carlton Hotel, they are informed that Governor Clinton is also on the premises.

"Well, go bring him here!" Bono demands loudly, joking. "We want him!" Like Henry II asking, "Will no one rid me of this meddlesome priest?" U2 should be careful what they ask for.

While the band laughs and stumbles off to their rooms to collapse, one of their well-trained roadies snaps to attention and starts off to locate Bill Clinton and deliver him to U2. In the corridor outside the candidate's boudoir, Secret Service agents pounce on U2's poor messenger like coyotes on a moose. "It's 3 A.M.," the feds explain while restraining the roadie. "The governor is sleeping."

"You don't understand," the messenger protests. "U2 wants to see him now!"

Bono, unaware of the trouble caused by his joke, finds himself in a huge, bilevel suite with spiral staircase and chandelier. Nice bunkhouse, but he's too wired to sleep. His muse goosed by alcohol, he is flooded with fresh inspiration in his life's quest to write a new "My Way" for his pal Frank Sinatra. True, Old Blue Eyes had not seen the genius in Bono's first attempt, "Treat Me Like a Girl," But *this*, this one is perfect: "Two Shots of Happy, One Shot of Sad." Bono, still in his beetle sunglasses and crushed red velvet suit, stumbles down the corridor to Edge's suite, humming the tune to himself so he won't forget it—*"Two shots of happy, one shot of sad, you think I'm a good man, but baby I'm bad. . . ."* He's got to get this masterpiece down on tape! He finds Edge, Edge finds a guitar and a tape recorder, and they work on the song until dawn.

As the sun rises over Chicago, Edge retires. Bono works a little longer, and then, spotting a guest bedroom in Edge's suite, collapses in his clothes.

While U2 is going under, candidate Bill Clinton is waking. He glances through his messages and the Secret Service men inform him that while he was sleeping some crazy hippie came bearing an invitation from U2. Clinton's response? "Why didn't you wake me?" As the government bodyguards shrug and mutter Clinton demands, "Is it too late? Where are they now?"

Suddenly it's the Secret Service's turn to run through the corridors on the whims of their king. They wake Paul McGuinness, who jumps out of bed, clears his throat, flattens his hair, and says, "Of course Bono would like to parlay with the governor! Please tell Mr. Clinton to head straight over to Bono's suite! I'll wake him!" Then the manager hangs up and tears through his bag for a necktie.

McGuinness rings Bono's suite and *there's no answer.* Okay, fine, don't panic—he's probably just passed out. The manager hightails it down to Bono's room, gets the hotel to unlock the door, and *Bono's not here.* The bed has not been slept in, the tub has not been bathed in, the spiral staircase has not been trod. There's no Bono, but *here comes Bill Clinton!* The hotel staff are as desperately helpful as elves at the North Pole, the Clinton campaign honchos are ruthlessly friendly, the Secret Service are coldly professional, and the Next President of the United States is cheerful as he surveys Bono's fabulous suite. McGuinness, his welcoming grin frozen like rictus, says welcome, welcome, and then slips into the next room to get on the phone and wake every member of U2 to say: (1) get up, (2) get over here, and (3) *where's Bono?*

"We worked on a song here till dawn," says a bleary Edge. "Then I went to bed. I don't know where he is now." Edge hauls himself out of bed to brush his teeth and meet the candidate. On the way to the bathroom he notices a spare room and pushes open the door. There, unkempt, unshaven, and unconscious, lies Bono.

"Get up," Edge prods, "Bill Clinton's in your room."

Bono doesn't even know what time zone he is in. His mouth tastes like an ulcer and his head is swimming with *"Two shots of happy, one shot of sad, you think I'm a good man . . ."* His dyed hair is in his red eyes, and like Lazarus, he stinketh. "Clinton's in my room?" Bono tries to straighten himself. He looks in the mirror. Dorian Gray. Fine. "Okay," he mumbles, "let's see how much of a politician this guy really is."

Bono weaves through the hotel and slips into his suite through the upstairs. He hears Clinton talking in the room below. Bono puts his beetle shades back on, rubs at the wrinkles in his red velvet suit, and lights up a tiny black cigar. Elegantly wasted, Bono then descends his spiral staircase into the candidate's company with the fuck-you aplomb of Bette Davis on a bad day. Clinton stops, Clinton stares, and then Clinton falls over laughing.

"Hey," Bono thinks, "this guy's okay."

Edge and Larry have drifted in and for an hour U2 sits huddled with the candidate. The blarney-hating Larry challenges Clinton: "Look, you know the system is corrupt. Why do you even *want* to be president?"

Clinton looks at Larry. He pauses and then speaks softly: "This is going to sound corny. But I do love my country and I do want to help people. I know the system is corrupt, and I don't know if the president can change it. But I know this: no one else can."

Touchdown! Gee, Larry thinks, what an honest guy. Wow, Bono thinks, he really is like Elvis (which is the candidate's Secret Service code name—big points with Bono). Bono talks to Clinton about ideas that George Lucas, the flimmaker, has promoted about using high tech to get America's education system back on line.

"I have not met George Lucas," Bono says, "but I have from a distance sort of kept tabs on what he's doing, because he's a very interesting man. Most of his energy for the last six or seven years has been spent on developing computer software programs for schools. He believes that America can be educated, and America's educational system is the biggest problem in the United States, and that the way to solve it is through video arcade type interactive study programs. I think he is right. And it's one of the important ideas out there right now."

Adam has wandered in, amazed to see the large room now full of political operatives and Zoo TV associates, all chewing the fat and exchanging road stories. Adam did not leap to his feet like Paul Revere when he got the word that Clinton was looking for the band; he had a bath and breakfast and made his way slowly over to what looks now like a busy campaign headquarters. The bassist joins his bandmates in the corner with the candidate as Bill's inviting U2 to play at the inauguration and Bono's flipping through his foggy brain trying to think of something a socially conscious cat such as he should say to the next president while he has him buttonholed.

Ah, he's got it! One for the old folks at home. "Listen," Bono says to Clinton, "Ireland is supposed to enjoy this 'special relationship' with the United States, but it's murder for any Irish person to get a visa to come here! The British come and go as they please, but I can't even get my kids' nanny in, for God's sake. If you become president will you—"

"Aw, come on, Bono," one of U2's entourage interrupts, "you know if you let an Irishman into America he'll never leave!" Bono stares daggers at the speaker while Clinton laughs at being let off the hook. *The one time*, Bono thinks, *I have a shot at scoring a point for Ireland* . . .

After Clinton leaves, Bono reprimands his impolitic associate: "If the people back home ever find out you said that to Clinton you will be found swinging from a Dublin lamppost."

It turned out in the course of their talk that Clinton and U2 both had tickets for that night's Chicago Bears football game, so they agreed to combine their motorcades and share a single police escort (this being the royal equivalent of you or I carpooling). Now, as Adam points out on the way to the game, a band in U2's position does get a little sanguine about police escorts, but you know Clinton's playing in a different league when you look around and realize that the honor-guarded cars in this escort are the *only* cars on the highway. The Secret Service has blocked off all on-ramps until the candidate and his guests pass by. Not even Led Zeppelin had that in their riders!

Watching TV a few days later, Bono is jarred to attention by a speech President Bush is making to a campaign rally: "Governor Clinton doesn't think foreign policy's important, but he's trying to catch up," Bush tells the crowd. "You may have seen this in the news—he was in Hollywood seeking foreign policy advice from the rock grop U2!"

Bono looks up. "Rock grop?"

Bush continues: "I have nothing against U2. You may not know this, but they try to call me every night during the concert! But the next time we face a foreign policy crisis, I will work with John Major and Boris Yeltsin, and Bill Clinton can consult Boy George!" Bush goes on to declare that if Clinton is elected *you, too,* will have higher inflation, *you, too,* will have higher taxes. *You, too! You, too!*

Bono doesn't get it. "Does he think I'm Boy George?" he asks.

"Nah," I say. "He's damning Clinton by association. He probably had a team of consultants sitting up all night trying to think of a rock star they could insult without offending any potential Bush voters. Madonna's too big, Springsteen need those electoral votes in New Jersey. Boy George is foreign, gay, and no longer sells any records. He's perfect."

"Yeah," Bono sighs, standing up. "Poor George is a safe target. He's not *popular.*"

On November 3, U2 watches the election returns on CNN before going onstage in Vancouver, Canada. Their crew cheers each time another state goes for Clinton. "Jesus, isn't that just like us!" Bono says. "It's a hell of a night to have just left America."

For U2 the U.S. presidential election is slightly abstract. But Bono begins to feel its weight the Sunday after the election when he goes to services at the Glide Memorial United Methodist Church in San Francisco's Tenderloin district. When he's in the area Bono is a frequent worshipper at Glide, an inner-city church built in the 1930s by Lizzie Glide, a wealthy philanthropist, which had few parishioners left when the Reverend Cecil Williams arrived there in 1964. Rev. Williams turned it into a church devoted to embracing society's outcasts, and over three decades has made it a jumping center of worship and social action for sympathetic people from all levels of the community. "It's the only church I know where you can get HIV tests during service," Bono says. "It's amazing, the singing's great, there's queues around the block on Easter Sunday. It's just a happening, really alive place."

This Sunday the church has a special day of thanksgiving for Clinton's victory, and Bono is caught up in the passion of the congregation. The reverend's wife, a poet named Janice Mirikitani, gets up and reads a poem about what this day means for American women and when she finishes about half of the 1,200 people crammed into the church jump up singing and weeping.

"That was the moment," Bono says afterward. "That's the moment when I knew how important this small victory was. I was looking around and I was thinking, 'Wow, if you're HIV, if you're a homosexual, if you're a member of the underclass or if you're a woman or if you're an artist—and that covers just about everybody in this church—this is no small thing.' This is not like a middle-class home where people say, 'Well, it's a new chance.' There's nothing small about this! This was from 'We don't exist' to 'We do exist,' you know? Whether the actual real impact of legislation on their lives will come into being, at least they know they are included. And that brought it home to me. If by having been a part of the Rock the Vote campaign we contributed to even a tiny tiny tiny part, then we did the right thing."

It was through Glide, in 1986, that Bono hooked up with C.A.M.P., the relief group that arranged for Ali and him to travel through Nicaragua and El Salvador during the Reagan-backed war against the leftists in those countries.

"In Nicaragua I'd seen supermarkets where there was no food because of the blockade," Bono explains. "I saw a body thrown out of the back of a van onto the road, you know? We saw the blight that was the Bush-Reagan era. That didn't dawn on us when we first started getting involved with the voter registration campaign. That dawned on us at the end."

I don't know if Bono knows that Bill Clinton brought Hillary to Glide last Mother's Day, and later told associates that he felt sitting there as if he had found the America he wanted to see—an all-inclusive America. Clinton and Bono have more than loving Elvis and riding in motorcades in common.

Hopped up on the new president's victory, Bono allows himself to get carried away with the possibilities of a real new world order. Over a late dinner he indulges in a little postcocktail philosophizing with U2's agent Frank Barsalona, the big wheeler-dealer who brought the Beatles to America and has been a great silent power in rock & roll ever since.

The conversation takes a sober turn when Bono tells Barsalona that America must do penance for its sins. He quotes the Old Testament line about the blood in the ground crying out for vengeance. "You know," Bono says, "that's the reason America is so violent. There was an indigenous population that was wiped out. America just has to face that. The reason the Jews are so strong is that they record and memorialize their failures as well as their triumphs, their defeats and well as their victories. America should do the same. I truly believe in expiation. This inaugural address is important. If Clinton got up at his inaugural address and apologized for America's sins, apologized to the crack dealers, the gang bangers, the prostitutes, and junkies and said, 'I know you have not failed America; America has failed you! Forgive us and join us!' Whew! Imagine if he did that." Bono shakes his head in wonder at the possibility.

Frank Barsalona shakes his head too. "Maybe so," the agent says, cutting into his dinner, "but there's not a prayer it'll happen."

12

Vegas

---

hangin' with the chairman/ goin' to the prizefights/ ridin' in white limos/ swingin' with the lord mayor/ bikin' in hotel rooms/ feelin' like a sex machine

BONO IS intrigued by Las Vegas for all the reasons he's told us: he thinks it's the trash dump in which one finds the jewels; it is our society's consumerism and materialism with its mask off; it's the cathedral of the culture. "At least if you pray to a slot machine," I suggest to him, "you get your answer right away." But I think the real reason U2 is drawn to Las Vegas is because Vegas is where they met Frank Sinatra and were inducted into the Post-Rat Pack International Brotherhood of Big Wheels and High Rollers.

In the spring of 1987 *The Joshua Tree* had just been released and U2 was enjoying the glow of their first number one album, their first number one single, "With or Without You," and they were on the cover of *Time* magazine. At the moment of all this glory they were in Las Vegas for the first time, they went to their first prizefight and saw the brilliant middleweight Sugar Ray Leonard win with a dancer's grace. Then they were given free tickets to see Sinatra and Don Rickles at what they were told was a $25-thousand-a-table performance. They were, as U2 always was in those days, dressed like Emmett Kelly, but they were treated like royalty. Sinatra was having a good night, crooning out "One for My Baby" and other signature songs, and U2 was lapping it up. Then Frank said he wanted to introduce some special guests in the star-studded audience, a group from Ireland who have the number one record in the country, are on the cover of *Time:* U2. A spotlight hit the band and they stood, hamming it up and waving to Liz Taylor, Gregory Peck, and all the other stars in the fur-shrouded audience till Sinatra busted their bubble by cracking, "And they haven't spent a dime on clothes."

After the show U2 went backstage to say hello to Frank and ended up getting into an intense discussion with him about music, a subject they had the impression no one ever talked to him about. Buddy Rich had just died and Larry asked if it was true that in the big band days the whole group followed the drummer. "The way it should be!" Larry suggested. Rich and Sinatra had been roommates, pals, enemies, and finally kindred souls, and Sinatra jumped at the chance to talk about him, to talk about the interplay between musicians in the days of Tommy Dorsey and Glenn Miller.

Sinatra's aides kept knocking on the door with the names of other celebrities who were waiting outside for the chance to say hello: "Gene Autry, Frank." "Roger Moore, Frank." Each time Sinatra would tell them to get lost, he was talking to U2. Afterward Frank's handlers seemed amazed that the boss had spent so much time with anybody, let along a rock group. U2 was offered standing invitations to racetracks in New Jersey and other insider entertainments. The joke on the tour after that was, "Since we met Sinatra, no trouble with the unions."

Bono, a big fan anyway, now threw himself into Sinatra's music. He attended a Sinatra concert in Dublin a year or two later and thought it would be presumptuous to try to go backstage—maybe Sinatra would have forgotten him. During the show he felt a tap on his shoulder and turned to see the Lord Mayor of Dublin festooned in his ceremonial ribbons and amulet crouching in the aisle saying, "Bono! Frank was asking for ya!"

So it is with some anticipated pizzazz that U2 lands in Vegas again, flush from the Clinton victory and the Glide Memorial inspiration and full of power and glory. They ran into R.E.M. guitarist Peter Buck at their concert in Alabama and talked him into coming up when they hit Sin City. Buck says that it's great to jump into U2's world, but "I feel kind of like being Hermann Goering's assistant. You're always in a white limo rocketing somewhere real interesting and no one knows why you're there. But I really enjoy it!"

R.E.M. is the band whose position and reputation is closest to U2's. In the mid-eighties Bono got on the phone and talked R.E.M. into opening some European festival dates for U2, after R.E.M. had sworn off opening for anybody in the aftermath of some bad gigs supporting

Bow Wow Wow. A friendship between the two groups began then, confirmed when Buck and R.E.M bassist Mike Mills were pressed into performing a drunken rendition of "King of the Road" on U2's tour bus.

"We were, like, twelfth on the bill on some of the shows," Buck recalls. "And I seem to remember going on at eleven o'clock in the morning to mass indifference, generally. It's funny because we played really well. I don't think we did a bad show. No one had ever heard of us. We did okay in Dublin, but at some shows I remember just seeing a lot of the backs of peoples' heads and occasionally the soles of their feet while we were playing. It wasn't bad. We were done by two o'clock in the afternoon, then we could go get drunk and watch these other bands. It was the first time we had ever done anything like that. And after we did it we thought, well, it's not really that hard."

R.E.M. and U2 both emerged in the early 1980s, and are now almost the only bands left standing from the dozens of contenders—X, Husker Du, Gang of Four, the Replacements, the Blasters—who at the time seemed equally likely to go as far as R.E.M. and U2 have gone.

"None of the other bands from the era that we came out of, postpunk, lasted at all," Buck says. "I thought maybe there was some sort of built-in obsolescence: that when you don't acknowledge the past at all, there's only so far you can go into the future. A lot of those bands' historical perspective went back to 1975 and there's not much you can really do with that. You use your youthful energy and craziness and then what? Then it's time to learn how to write songs. A lot of those people didn't. I remember the year when U2 started to sell lots of records. All of a sudden it became sort of obvious that that was going to happen because, well, who else was there? It's either going to be Bon Jovi and those bands—which it was obvious a lot of kids weren't listening to —or it's going to be U2 and to a certain degree us. I didn't think we would specifically sell a lot of records, but I could see that there was this big gap and that U2 was definitely going to go in there.

"R.E.M. don't really care that much if we're the biggest band in the world, but I think U2 does want that to a certain degree. I talked to Larry about it and he said so. You make conscious decisions. I don't think any of their decisions have changed musically where they want to go, but I think it changes how you want to present yourself, and some of us just aren't really interested in that kind of stuff. Bill Berry (R.E.M.'s drummer) said, 'If I wanted to be famous I'd be the singer.' He'd be really happy if he just never had to have his picture taken, never had to do an interview. And I'm pretty much the same way. So our picture's not on the cover of the records and we're not in the videos a huge amount. We don't do the talk show rounds. We don't present awards. We don't go to the Rock & Roll Hall of Fame. I'd just as soon not do anything except make the records, play when I want to, and when it comes time to promote the record, do the obligatory three-week meet-and-greet and interview session."

I suggest to Buck that it's better U2 has those ambitions than to leave the field to Bon Jovi.

"Yes," Buck says. "I like ambitious people. I like people that see a goal that they want to obtain and work toward it. Our goals are just different."

Buck doesn't know it yet, but he's about to be roped into a very non-R.E.M. moment. Principle's Suzanne Doyle calls Buck's room and informs him that tonight at the U2 show he is going to be presenting a Q magazine award to U2 and accepting on behalf of R.E.M. a Q magazine award from U2. Peter tries to weasel out of it; he says, "You're not going to make me do it onstage, are you?" No, no, he's told, they'll do it all in the dressing room, with photos for the magazine and filmed acceptance speeches to be played at the awards dinner in London.

So Buck is shepherded into a backstage room decorated with potted palms and he and U2 take turns presenting each other with the same trophy (the magazine only sent one) while Bono goes in and out of the Fly character and everyone keeps laughing and asking the cameraman to stop the tape and start again.

As a reward to Buck for his efforts, Bono insists he come with U2 to the heavyweight boxing championship fight the next night between champ Evander Holyfield and younger challenger Riddick Bowe. Buck's never been to a boxing match and figures he'll go along for the ride. U2 is hoping for an experience as exciting as seeing Sugar Ray Leonard five years earlier. They're not going to get it.

At the arena Bono and Buck get into an Alphonse and Gaston argument over who's going to take the better seat. Bono insists that Buck take the up-front seats with Edge and Larry; Bono's still got a good view from a few sections up. Buck says no, no, people want to see U2 walk in together. Bono says, "Look, I'll walk with you guys down to the front, then I'm going back to the other seat—I don't want to be in front." Buck gets a little dose of the treatment U2 gains by being on all those album covers and videos as they walk down among the Hollywood VIP's and everyone says hello. Jack Nicholson looks up and says, "Hi, boys!" "Hi, Jack!" (Nicholson started coming to U2 concerts on the *Joshua Tree* tour and he and Bono have hung out in Hollywood and in France. Bono is most impressed by Nicholson's remaining in perfect Jack character even in a foreign language. He does a great impression of the actor saying, with his famous inflections, "Pardoney moi, Garson. Havey vous french fries?")

Bono greets his fellow royals and then leaves Edge, Larry, and Buck down front. Buck turns to his left and introduces himself to the man sitting next to him, who turns out to be Sugar Ray Leonard himself. As the fight begins, Leonard offers Buck a running commentary, explaining every strategy and how each point is scored. This, Peter figures, is the way to see your first boxing match.

In the second round the twenty-five-year-old Bowe slams into thirty-year-old Holyfield with a low blow that the champ thinks is illegal. Holyfield turns to catch the ref's attention and Bowe sucker punches him. Holyfield flies into a rage and abandons all strategy, pounding into the younger man with blows that sound like cannons to the musicians. The fight's turned ugly. Buck closes his eyes. Larry feels his temper rise as a famous goon behind him—Sylvester Stallone—howls, "Break his fuckin' nose!" like the school bully's weasel sidekick. Buck hears Bruce Willis baying "Kill him!" and mutters that he'd like to see Willis and Stallone beating each other bloody for the amusement of millionaires. This is nothing like the Leonard fight that seemed so scientific, so graceful. This is two heavyweights trying to blast each other's heads in with blows that would kill whole genres of rock musicians.

They call these seats "the red circle," because if you're rich enough to sit here you get sprayed with blood. "To hear the fists going into the faces," Larry says, "to see the cuts opening over the eyes and the blood pouring into the fighters' eyes, is disturbing."

At the end of the fight there is a new champion: Riddick Bowe in a unanimous decision after what the *New York Times* calls, "One of history's best heavyweight brawls." Larry, Edge, and Buck are disillusioned with the sweet science and swear off boxing. Bono, who was further back, is crushed when Buck tells him that the seat he gave up was next to Sugar Ray.

The musicians jump into their white limo and are deposited at the ringside of another great African American athlete—James Brown. Catching a late night J. B. show in Vegas would be a gas anyway, but James announces he has a special guest in the audience he wants to bring up to join him on "Sex Machine." Bono prepares his hair and Brown announces, "Magic Johnson!" The place goes nuts as Magic, the super-human basketball player who recently quit the game when he learned he was HIV-positive, climbs up and joins James in singing, "Get up! I feel like a sex machine!"

Bono thinks it's an awkward choice of song for a man battling the AIDS virus after what he has described as a life of promiscuity. "Be a sex machine," Bono says, "but for Christ's sake use a condom."

When all the star-search stuff is over, when the rockers have gone back and met Magic and James and put Stallone and Willis out of their heads and said good night to stories about Jack Nicholson and Frank Sinatra, Buck talks about how new this shoulder-rubbing between rock musicians and mainstream stars really is.

"I think partly the nature of rock & roll celebrity has changed over the last ten years," he says. "If you look at any of those old Stones' films, where they check into a Holiday Inn in 1972, they're the biggest band in the world and no one knows who they are. That doesn't happen anymore. Everyone is on videos. Rock & roll people like us were brought up to practice in a basement, and no one cared what we looked like; it was just not a celebrity thing. Then when you got really huge, *kids* knew who you were.

"There's this idea that rock & roll is rebellious music and you're not doing what society says. But nowadays the first time you have a hit record you're shaking hands with guys in offices and people want to get you a different haircut. They're offering to have a guy make you suits so that you can get that Armani look. It must be mind-blowing.

"R.E.M. didn't even sell a million records until we'd been together for nine years. So at that point you couldn't really show me anything that I hadn't seen before. And U2 was the same. They were more successful out of the box than we were; I guess by about 1985 they were really huge. But still, I bet nobody over twenty-five recognized them on the streets. And it's not that way anymore. You can literally have one video and be world famous. People in foreign countries know what you look like. Rock & roll celebrity is now much closer to what traditional showbiz used to be, where they'd write about your personal habits. The Stones used to only get written about in the mainstream press when they got arrested. Now I read the gossip columns when I'm in New York or L.A. and it will say who's eating where with who. That's a whole new thing."

Buck figures what separates the artists from the posers is the willingness to keep changing what you do that made you successful. Another thing U2 and R.E.M. have in common is that both bands created instantly identifiable sounds that were widely imitated by other bands— and then abandoned those sounds and moved on to new areas.

"There are people who are in it for a career and there are people who are in it to try and find out something about themselves," Buck says. "The only way you can find out about your life and how to live your life is to try a lot of different things and fail at some of them. Probably U2's only failure was *Rattle and Hum.* I'm sure it sold ten million records, but I don't think it did exactly what they wanted it to do. And yet that's good. It opened the door for them to do something else."

Buck was impressed by Zoo TV on several levels: "Certainly over the years they've been known as being a *sincere group,* in capital letters. It was nice that they could just take that and throw it away and start over. And just technologically the show is pretty amazing. As a musician I was thinking, 'God this would be so hard. You have to work with all these cues and all this stuff going on!' I mean, if I want to go backstage during a song and pick my nose I can; there's all kinds of dark places. This was almost like a Broadway play, it was so rigid. I really thought it was a great show. Probably the best show I've ever been to in a large arena."

The others fly out of Las Vegas to California, but Larry continues on— as he has journeyed through much of America—on his motorcycle with his biker buddy, security man David Guyer. After a ride from Florida to New Orleans Larry won his wings, a Harley-Davidson patch. David says that in the motorcycle world there's no shortage of celebrities who know more about looking cool than actually riding. He names one rock star who bought a big expensive bike and made a great show of rolling into the parking lot of a hip nightclub. Unfortunately he had not learned how to stop it and crashed.

Along the desert highway between Vegas and California, Larry and David pull into a motel for the night. Larry isn't sure why David insists to the clerk that their rooms be on the ground floor. Once they've got their keys David leads Larry back outside and tells him to get on his bike, they're not leaving these Harleys out here. David rides his motorcycle into his motel room and Larry feels obliged to do the same. "I love the smell of gasoline in the morning," Larry says.

13

Harps Over Hollywood

bono does a movie deal/ shooting with william burroughs/
oldman out the back door, winona in the front/ phil joanou
takes his lumps/ coitus interruptus in the editing room

I F YOU BELIEVED the tour itinerary you'd believe U2 have the better
part of a week off in Los Angeles after they play the L.A. Coliseum and before they fly off to Mexico City for their final concerts of 1992. You'd think they'd be lolling by the pool, philosophizing about post-neoromanticism and taking harmonica lessons. But a gap in concerts does not mean a gap in U2's work schedule, and this being Hollywood the days are filled with movie meetings and the nights with television work.

The television work is the making of a U2 TV special to be aired on the Fox network on Thanksgiving weekend in the USA, and on other carriers in other countries around the world. That is to say, this masterpiece will be broadcast in a week and a half and U2 are still excavating the mountains of film they've shot on their travels and trying to figure out what to do with it all. The band has imported top rock video director Kevin Godley to help them make sense of reels of concert footage, abstract bits starring the individual band members, and clips with such non–prime time guest stars as beat writer William Burroughs, cyberpunk author William Gibson, and LSD guru Timothy Leary. Right now the chunks of cinema verité different band members are scrutinizing in different screening and cutting rooms in an L.A. film editing facility recall the artistically ambitious incoherence of "Magical Mystery Tour," the holiday TV special that burst the Beatles' critical bubble in the aftermath of the triumph of *Sgt. Pepper*.

Some of it's pretty good, though. U2 are determined to stick a wishbone in the throat of Thanksgiving Day America with their clip of

Burroughs reading his "Thanksgiving Prayer" against a superimposed American flag. It is a thank-you to "Our father who aren't in heaven" for providing Indians to kill, land to despoil, small nations to plunder, and Africans to enslave.

To tape this soliloquy Burroughs visited U2 at their hotel when the Zoo tour passed through Kansas. Hall Willner, that record producer connected to all things underground and alternative, set up the get-together. It is not entirely clear that Burroughs knew who U2 were, but he did provide entertainment—he produced a paper bag full of hand-guns. Now Burroughs is a great and important figure in American letters, but he is almost as notorious for the legend of his killing his wife while trying to shoot an apple off her head as he is for writing *Naked Lunch*. So when U2 saw that the frail old author was packing heat, even Edge's hat flew in the air.

Buffalo Bill left U2 with an epigram as good as any in "The Fly": "When I was in prison in Mexico," he said, "one of the guards told me, 'I hate to see a man in jail because of a woman.' "

Back at Burroughs's house the author and Willner armed themselves and took to blasting away at targets in the nip of the Kansas afternoon. Willner, another man whose grievances one would not wish to see augmented by firearms, managed to score three bull's-eyes, after each of which Burroughs cried, "Lethal hits!" All, unfortunately, were in the target next to the one at which he was aiming. Afterward Burroughs collected the pistols, reloaded them, dropped them back into the bag, and shuffled up the hill home.

Looking at the Burroughs footage now, Bono asks what—as an American—I think the reaction will be. The Irish band and English director turn and stare at me. I tell them that the prayer, the litany of historic abuses, is great, and Burroughs's nicotine-whinging reading is hilarious. But you've got to be real careful about mocking the U.S. flag. People from other countries don't attach the totemlike voodoo to their flags that Americans do; making fun of Old Glory is like making fun of crosses or Stars of David—it may be a symbol and not the thing itself, but plenty of people are devoted to the symbol. U2 listen, look at each other, and say, "Leave in the flag."

The nights this week are devoted to assembling the TV special; during the days Bono is hustling like a Hollywood honky to close the deal to begin production on his screenplay, *The Million Dollar Hotel*. Bono wrote the story with a Hollywood scriptwriter named Nicholas Klein and Bono holds the copyright. The story was inspired by a cheap L.A. hotel full of bizarre characters that U2 discovered during the long incubation of *Rattle and Hum.* The script was finished, offered for sale, and optioned by Mel Gibson's production company. Quite a success for a young scriptwriter with another job! Now Bono is meeting with Mel and his people in the afternoons while also shuffling the actor he hopes will play the male lead—Gary Oldman—out of his hotel suite before the proposed female lead—Winona Ryder—shuffles in. See, Oldman and Ryder just made another movie together, Francis Coppola's misnamed *Bram Stoker's Dracula.* It is the number one film in America this week! Oldman is poised to suck Ryder's neck on the covers of magazines at the newsstand in the hotel lobby! Yet *Dracula* generated bad blood between the two young movie stars, so Bono has Winona cooling her heels down in the lobby of the Sunset Marquis while he shows Oldman how much quicker it is to leave by the back.

"Winona's my guide to all this movie stuff," Bono explains. "She's given me hours of good advice." After *Rattle and Hum* Bono and Winona kicked around the idea of trying to make a western about Calamity Jane and Wild Bill Hickock, a film about the struggle between love and independence. Eventually Bono got distracted with recording *Achtung Baby* and making tour plans, Winona got involved in putting together *Dracula,* and the cowboy idea got put aside. For her twenty-first birthday Bono gave the actress a .38 Magnum with the inscription, "Happy Birthday, Winona—You've made my day."

Bono very much appreciates Mel Gibson's patronage and is grateful for the doors Gibson's box office name opens in the film industry. But he must wonder if it would be a mistake for the macho sex symbol to play the starring role in this film. The hero of Bono's screenplay is Tom-Tom, a scrawny, semiretarded hotel janitor who no one—least of all the pretty girl to be played by Winona—looks at twice. Quite a stretch for Mel! Gibson's done Hamlet to demonstrate that he's not just a *Mad Max–Lethal Weapon* action bimbo. Now he's considering playing the ugly imbecile to further stretch his range.

Gary Oldman, on the other hand, is the name at the very top of the scrawny, imbecile actor A-list. From *Sid & Nancy* to *Track 29* to *State of Grace* to *Rosencrantz & Guildenstern Are Dead,* Oldman has cornered the market on dopes, goons, and mouth-breathers. In movie industry parlance, when you're talkin' dimwits and sickos, you're talkin' Oldman.

Winona is perfect for the ghostly girl in tragic black who hides from life in the fleabag hotel. It's a natural continuation of the gifted actress's pale-faced *Beetlejuice/Mermaids/Edward Scissorhands* oeuvre. What a cast! Gibson for the women, Ryder for the men, Oldman for the critics! All Bono has to do is get them to see the greater glory.

Bono floats the notion of Mel giving the lead to Oldman and sliding over into the role of the pinhead (literally) police detective who shakes down the denizens of the Million Dollar Hotel and bullys the moron custodian hero. Gibson might not be wild about the lack of actorly challenge in playing another tough cop, but Bono hopes to impress on him that while he may have played tough cops before, he has never played a tough cop with a pointed head.

There's one other role to fill. Who's going to direct? Bono's first choice would be Roman Polanski, but, as he's exiled from America, it would mean recreating L.A. in Europe. He thinks Coppola's a great painter, a brilliant visualist, but wonders if he would stick to the story. Of course he dreams of Scorsese, and of course he'd never get him. I suggest Barry Levinson: *Diner* proved he's great with multiple character comedy/drama—and *Rain Man* showed he's a poet of nitwits. I keep throwing out names as if I (like Bono) really knew these people, and as we walk through the hotel lobby Bono sees waiting for him Phil Joanou, who directed *U2 Rattle and Hum* and then *State of Grace* with Oldman and Sean Penn and *Final Analysis* with Richard Gere. *State of Grace* was considered derivative but promising; *Final Analysis* was a disaster. Together with the box office failure of *Rattle and Hum,* that puts Joanou in a tough spot. In the time U2 spent making *Achtung Baby* the young director's gone from Boy Wonder to Next Big Thing to Has-Been. He needs a break, and a chance to work with Mel Gibson would be just the ticket.

Bono likes Joanou and believes he will eventually prove himself to be a great filmmaker—but he is afraid that if *Million Dollar Hotel* is directed by the man who made U2's tour film as well as the "One" video it will look like a U2 vanity project, like Bono wrote a script and hired U2's personal director to film it. The jittery director corners Bono and asks if there's been any word yet on setting up a meeting with Mel.

Bono says, absolutely, it's going to happen.

Joanou asks Bono if he really is in consideration for this job or is this just a polite brush-off—'cause if it is, tell him now and save him looking like a jerk. No, Bono says, he is absolutely in favor of Phil directing—*if* he can sell Mel on it.

At midnight, during a break from the TV editing, Bono hooks up for dinner with Oldman and Joanou, who worked together on *State of Grace* and on an episode of a pay-TV series called *Fallen Angels*. Joanou also directed Oldman's wife, Uma Thurman, in *Final Analysis*. The director and actor are well acquainted. Joanou is explaining in great detail the differences between himself and Francis Coppola; how Coppola never says "Print," but Joanou always yells "Print!" real loud so that the cast and crew know they've done a good job. Bono perks things up by doing a loud and grotesque imitation of Oldman's performance in *Dracula*. Everyone at the table has a good laugh at that, although Oldman, as uncomfortable as any actor with some amateur chewing his scenery, jumps in and says now he'll do an impression: Phil Joanou directing a scene.

Oldman leans forward nervously, starts chewing rapidly on imaginary gum, and pushes his hair behind his ears over and over while shouting, "Print! Print!" Everyone laughs hard, but it strikes me as a junior high school one-upsmanship.

Both Bono and McGuinness have told me repeatedly that Oldman is a big fan of Joanou's, thinks he is a real actor's director with whom people like Oldman and Penn feel safe pushing themselves to the limit. Is that true, I wonder, or is Joanou a director Oldman thinks he can dominate? McGuinness, who spent a lot of time in Hollywood as the producer of *U2 Rattle and Hum*, says there is a game of savage ball-busting that is carried on between top actors and directors that looks brutal to an outsider, but they have to respect you to let you into the game.

Joanou looks across to another table and then turns back and says, "That girl over there looking at us, she's on *Twin Peaks*, but I can't remember her name." We all steal glances. "Oh, yeah, is she . . . ?" and everybody starts listing different actresses from the cult TV series. Joanou says he's going to go get her. He does, plucking her from her own TV-level company and depositing her among the rock and movie stars. She nods and everyone else nods at her and goes back to their discussion as if she wasn't here. So the actress starts talking about this new film that would be perfect for Joanou to direct and she can set it up and there's a role for Oldman and all of a sudden Joanou yells, "Bullshit! That is just fuckin' Hollywood bullshit!" The actress is taken aback but Oldman looks up, impressed. He says to Joanou sincerely, "Fair play to you, mate."

Bono says it's time to go back to the TV studio and invites everyone to come along. He walks into the editing room, where Godley has been up for days, trailing Oldman, Joanou, and the *Twin Peaks* actress. Godley looks up as if considering the career ramifications of wrapping his fingers around Bono's throat. Bono leads his procession to a screening room to look at some finished footage. Oldman jumps into an oversize, vibrating, cocoonlike superchair and starts doing imitations as he hits the buttons on the armrest: "You cannot escape, Mr. Bond." "Uhura!"

The movie screen in the room lights up with a concert version of "Until the End of the World." On the screen Bono is walking down the ramp to the B stage, through what looks like a wheat field of out-stretched arms. The conceit of this TV production is that, in true Zoo TV style, the show will reach for the channel changer before the viewer can, so while Bono is emoting, the shot suddenly switches to a ditsy blonde from the ramp-side being asked if she got close to Bono: "Not close enough!" then cuts to an overhead shot of Bono lifting his hand in the air and singing, "I reached out to the one I tried to destroy," and then—*zap*—a despairing peasant woman in black and white and—*zap*—a tidal wave and—*zap*—Edge rocking out, and under all this Bono singing, "You said you'd wait until the end of the world." There's no doubt that all this fancy editing breaks the spell of the music.

Bono turns to his guests, who are sprawled around the room flirting and chatting and asks if they don't agree that cutting away from him during the climax of the song ruins the whole effect. Of course everyone says, "Yeah, um, right, I was thinking the same thing." Thus fortified, Bono leads his troops back into the editing room where the exhausted Godley, his wife, Sue, and his producer, Rocky Oldham, are slaving away. It's 3 A.M.; they don't look anxious for any more input.

Bono says that the strangest thing just happened: he was watching the footage with his guests here and every single one of them said they thought the power of "Until the End of the World" was ruined by all those cutaways at the climax. Godley looks up sadly. Bono's guests all nod and grunt and say, "Um, yeah. Right. I thought so too."

Bono's in an awkward position: by bringing a bunch of outsiders into the studio he knows he's breached etiquette, but the film editing really is sabotaging the music and he and Godley are going to have to argue about it in front of company.

"It breaks the *spell*," Bono explains. "All I do is create a spell. I don't paint pictures. I don't write novels. All we really do is create a spell and even watching this I find myself going under. . . . Then that pulls me out. That ruins it. I don't mind a slap in the head to wake me when it's over—that's fine—but this is coitus interruptus."

"Fine," says Godley. "I understand. But if you keep taking all these bits out you'll end up with a straight concert film."

Godley suggests Bono and his panel of judges listen to the new audio mix of "Until the End of the World" before he makes up his mind. He cues it up on a monitor in the editing room. David Saltz, a producer of rock TV shows, has been drafted by the band to add running commentary—like a sports announcer—to the concert. Last night Bono was busting with ideas and feeding Saltz lines like, "It's a dictionary on fast forward!" Bono watches "Until the End of the World" again, this time with Saltz's voice overdubbed hyperventilating a mangled play-by-play as, on the screen, Bono walks up the ramp: "Bono exorcising the Edge! Exorcising the audience! Exorcising himself!"

"It's completely, completely wrong," Bono announces gravely. "It ruins it. It's like in school when you write a paper, 'He stabbed her a hundred times and then he cut her and then he chopped her head off and then he woke up.' "

The director and Bono stare at each other. The producer breaks the silence: "Actually, I never wrote that in school."

Bono suddenly laughs and says, "Then put down the knife!"

They fiddle with the edits for another hour while Oldman, the actress, and Joanou all drift off. Finally Bono says good night and heads to the door. The director and producer steal a glance at each other and mumble, *"Coitus interruptus."*

14

The Last Tycoon

---

jumping off the million-dollar hotel/ an existential moment in a war zone/ t-bone searches l.a. for his breakfast/ mel gibson says nothing/ beep confounds the establishment/ the security system is tested

T-BONE BURNETT is a fine singer/songwriter with a number of critically acclaimed albums that don't sell very well. So he makes his fortune as a record producer, having done that duty with Elvis Costello, Los Lobos, Roy Orbison, and many, many others. He is a cynic with a heart of gold, a man who knows the inside skinny on everything from the *real* meaning of "Rosebud" in *Citizen Kane* (It was, swears T-Bone, William Randolph Hearst's nickname for his penis) to who killed JFK (T-Bone, a Texan, knows the son of one of the oilmen who says he paid for the hit). T-Bone knows where all the bodies are buried, which is one of the reasons Bono likes hanging out with him so much. The first time they met, at London's Portobello Hotel in 1985, they went right upstairs and wrote a song together: "Having a Wonderful Time, Wish You Were Her."

Since then they've recorded together, Ellen Darst did a stint as T-Bone's manager, and he's been a regular source of advice for the band both when they've asked for it and when they haven't. I remember T-Bone telling me in 1986, "Have you heard this song U2's written called 'I Still Haven't Found What I'm Looking For'? It's tremendous, it's going to be a big hit, it's like an Elvis Presley song."

Today T-Bone and Bono are putting all their talent and intelligence together to try to locate a place to eat breakfast in Los Angeles at 2 in the afternoon. Bono is still trying to manage *The Million Dollar Hotel*.

A new wrinkle has come up. With time running out before Mel Gibson's option expires and the financing collapses, Gary Oldman has announced his condition for playing Tom-Tom: the film must be directed by his great friend Phil Joanou. Sean Penn has weighed in, too, with the opinion that no one has ever given a bad performance in a Joanou film. Bono's balancing act is getting more and more difficult. Winona says she is willing to work with Oldman again, putting aside whatever tension developed over *Dracula,* but now Gibson must agree to use Joanou. And Gibson didn't even want to hear Joanou's name.

The stink made by the flop of *Final Analysis* has really soured Hollywood on Phil. But there may be subterranean forces at work too. Rightly or wrongly, Joanou believes that Richard Gere, the star of that movie, has unfairly blamed him all over town for its failure and told people throughout his powerful circle not to work with the director. Phil says that half the things that are now cited as reasons the movie failed are things Gere asked for, but now the actor has put all the blame on him. Joanou's afraid that the fix is in, but that's impossible to prove in the town of "You scratch my back and I'll stab yours." This much, though, is clear: Mel Gibson has the same agent as Richard Gere, and Gibson has said that if Phil is in, he is out.

Phil's position has been, "Just get me a lunch with Mel and let me talk to him, just let me make my case." Bono has prevailed on Gibson to meet Joanou for lunch and give him a chance to talk. If Phil can't convince Mel to give him a shot, Bono's only option would be to convince Oldman to drop Phil—which would be ugly. Bono is hoping hard that Phil charms Mel into submission.

After striking out in our quest for eggs in restaurants from East Hollywood to Beverly Hills, we end up in the coffee shop of the Beverly Hills Hotel. Bono hesitates before going in. He reminds T-Bone of the time they were ejected from the hotel restaurant, along with Edge and Kris Kristofferson, because of their shabby clothes. Bono said, "Look, how about if you ignore the jeans and we ignore the bad fake impressionist paintings?" A minute later the four of them landed on the sidewalk.

Once in the coffee shop, Bono launches into a dialogue with T-Bone —another Christian intellectual in the Thomas Merton/C. S. Lewis/ Billy Sol Estes tradition—about art, faith, and the nature of knowledge. (Hey—don't let me keep you; skip ahead to Mexico if you want.) Bono says that when U2 hooked up with Eno they were modernists because they wanted to write songs and make records no one had ever made before. With *Achtung Baby* they have entered their postmodern phase because they are combining new with old, grabbing references from other rock eras, while trying to move the whole thing forward. Bono says that he had to stop and ask himself after *Rattle and Hum* why he had wanted to be in a band to begin with. "Was it to save the world? I don't think so. To be honest it was probably because I saw Mark Bolan on *Top of the Pops.*" So he began trying to get back to that essence while experimenting with new sounds.

Bono is quick to admit that many of his ideas are instinctive, not intellectual—he does not have the time to be rigorous in researching or testing them. One of the theories that gets him into great arguments is that he believes that modernism started with Luther, with the Reformation, with the dismantling of the iconography of the culture and insistence on simplicity and function. Bono says he initially followed the modernist trail back to the Shakers. Then he got Frank Barsalona, who had a collection of Shaker furniture, to put him in touch with an authority who confirmed Bono's guess that the Shakers were influenced by European ideas and the Bauhaus movement was in turn influenced by the Shakers. Bono is convinced that all this stripping down and directness goes back to the Protestant impulse, back to Luther, and that the modernists made the great mistake of taking on the antireligion of the existentialists and lost that thread. (It's one of the wonders of Bono's considerable intellect that he can construct a unified field theory of all his interests—even when they have nothing to do with each other.)

Bono's collaborator on *The Million Dollar Hotel*, Nicholas Klein, is a metaphysicist who uses logic vigorously applied to map out the future. Bono finds a scriptural colloquy for every equation his friend comes up with. For example, Klein offered the proposition: "Independence is the opposite of love." Bono was taken aback by that idea but followed it through and decided it was the essence of God's problem with Satan. Isn't it the desire for independence that pulls marriages apart? Doesn't a parent's overwhelming love for a dependent child often sour at the moment that child becomes independent?

Like an old Jesuit, Bono believes God can be found through pure logic. Look at the word for "The Word" in St. John's gospel: *Logos.* In the beginning was the Word. In the beginning was Logos. In the beginning was Logic.

I point out that he may have his etymology backward—the development of our language may have followed the religion and philosophy of the people, creating these connections after the fact.

"I believe instinctively," Bono says, "that if we follow logic all the way to the smallest point we will find God."

"In every grain of sand?" I ask.

"Exactly," Bono says as we settle the check. "As the seed has all the genetic information for the tree. As a cell contains more information than any computer chip."

Driving back through town, this Reli.Stu. seminar gets onto the topic of liberation theology, the radical brand of Catholicism practiced in some parts of Latin America that encouraged victims of dictatorship to take up arms against their oppressors. Bono says that when he and Ali were in Central America they journeyed one day into an area where they could feel the earth shaking from nearby artillery and at one point had shots fired over their heads. Ali is fearless; she insisted on forging ahead. Finally they came to a town. One the side of a building someone had spray-painted "Fuck Jesus."

Bono recoiled. So here on the front lines, this is what they think of liberation theology, here is how they have despaired of God's mercy, here is how they lost faith in the savior of their fathers. He expressed all that to his guide and showed him the blasphemy.

"Not Jesus Christ!" The guide told him. "Fuck Hey-zoos—he lives around the corner!"

We land back at the Sunset Marquis, where four kids are waiting outside with cameras and U2 albums. Bono walks over and says he appreciates their support and he's happy to sign autographs and pose for pictures after gigs, but he'd appreciate it if they didn't hang around for days on end outside his hotel, because it makes him feel like a celebrity and he's *not* a celebrity: he's a rock & roller.

"That sounds good, Bono," I say, "but if you're not a celebrity how do you explain these eight teenage girls charging down the street toward you?" Bono looks up just before he's engulfed in squeals and giggles.

I go back up to my room and find a notice to show up in a special Zoo medical room for my pre-Mexico injections. I drag myself up to the appointed suite where a dubious-looking doctor is instructing a line of Zoo people to bend over and drop their pants and roll up their sleeves. A long needle in the ass for hepatitis and a short needle in the arm for tetanus.

There are all sorts of horror stories floated about the dysentery in Mexico. People say don't drink the water, don't even eat fruit or vegetables washed in water. Edge says he's been warned not to shower. "Of course," he concedes, "that could add to the problem."

At suppertime I go off to visit T-Bone in a rented mansion where he's producing the first album for a San Francisco band called Counting Crows. I got a self-produced demo tape from them about a year ago and unlike every other such self-made demo, it was really good. I knew the A & R man who signed them and I knew he had wanted to put them in a house to make their first album rather than a studio. I was surprised to find out that's what T-Bone was working on and was happy for the chance to go by and eavesdrop. The mansion they've rented is one of those white elephants built for millions during the eighties gold rush to sell for millions more, but not made for people to live in. The pool is cracking and water is running down the side of the mountain, and there're low-hanging objects on which the band members bang their heads as they walk around. I have the good timing to arrive at suppertime, hang around up there for a while, and break the key off in the door of my rental car. By the time I get it replaced and make it back to the Marquis, Bono, Adam, and Larry have left for work.

No one can find the Edge, but progress at the TV studio continues cranking along. There are three rooms working now, in two different buildings. Larry and Adam are in one, overseeing nuances of the sound mix that no TV speaker will ever detect. They're listening to the moment before the band begins, separating and assigning levels to the white noise from the Zoo TV screens, the ambient crowd noise and the direct crowd noise. "There are three loud bursts of applause," Larry says. "The first when the lights go down, the second when people see the band, the third when they see Bono's silhouette."

During a quick coffee break Larry mentions Clinton's victory. "I'm excited," he says. "I think he has a chance to restore balance. That's my philosophy for this year: Balance." He then goes back to balancing the sound.

Bono is in the other room arguing with the producer, who to Bono's horror showed a rough cut of the program to Fox TV executives, who objected to the burning crosses in "Bullet the Blue Sky" and to the use of the words *nigger* and *queer* in Burroughs's monologue.

"This is one of America's greatest living writers!" Bono says. "If they're going to censor him there's going to be real trouble! I'll pull the show. I thought this was being broadcast direct by satellite, I thought Fox was going to have no control over it."

Wearily, the producer explains to Bono that the show is being broadcast by satellite in the rest of the world, but not in the U.S.; that Fox has every right, contractual and moral, to see the show before they air it; and they may yet exercise their right not to show it at all.

Bono walks out in the parking lot where he is delighted to see his long lost friend, the Edge. "Reg!" he cries in a loud, goofy voice as kids hanging on the corner do triple takes. "Where have you been?"

Edge says he went off to see Ronnie Wood play at a local club and ended up hanging with an actress who goes out with Ben Stiller, a TV comedian who does a nasty impersonation of Bono. "Tell him to stop making fun of me, Edge!" Bono cries. "Tell him glamorous people have feelings too!"

They go back inside, where Larry is objecting to a sampled bit from a news broadcast that refers to a serial killer striking again. "It's obviously being played for a joke," Larry says, "and I don't feel right about that."

Edge reaches over and grabs Larry's arm and says, "It's true, he doesn't feel right."

The producer—really turning on the Hollywood hyperbole, leans forward and insists, "The important thing is it makes you feel *something!*"

Larry smiles and sits back, but I'll bet when the film is finished the serial killer will be gone. Larry's instincts are more tenacious than other people's intellectualizations.

The band works till about 4 A.M. and then Bono says he's going to bed. I get in his rented two-seater next to him. As we're pulling away Edge comes out, asks for a lift, and climbs in the jump seat behind us. Bono drives as he always drives, too fast and often on the wrong side of the road.

"Slow down, Bono, I don't want to die!" Edge shouts from his cockpit behind the seat.

"Don't worry, Edge," I tell him, crouching into a fetal position in the passenger seat, "you're in a safe spot, you'll be pulled from the wreckage! I'll be dead and all the papers will say is BONO KILLED and then at the bottom of the page, *Also another man.*"

✳   ✳   ✳

Toward the end of the L.A. week Bono pulls up at a traffic light, looks over at the driver next to him, and sees Axl Rose waving. "I knew it was you," Axl's girlfriend calls. "I recognized your earring!" Bono wishes he weren't driving a Mercedes—not very rock & roll.

Friday morning the Zoo crew get set to depart for Mexico City while the band stays behind to finish the damn TV special. Organizing the travel plans is Dennis Sheehan, U2's longtime road manager. Disorganizing them is B. P. Fallon, the viber/deejay/guru who sits in his Trabant on the B stage every night before U2 comes on and spins records and tells the crowd to love each other while wearing a cape and big floppy hat. There are no two more dissimilar persons north of the equator than Dennis and Beep, and they go back a long way. In the seventies they were also on the road together, when Dennis was Led Zeppelin's assistant tour manager and Beep was their publicist. When Bono insisted Beep be drafted for the Zoo tour, Dennis warned, in his quiet manner, that Beep was not at his best on the road. Dennis likes to run his operation like the army, and Beep is the Furry Freak Brother model of a conscientious objector.

In the lobby this morning Beep, who weighs about as much as a canary, is straining under the great weight of a wooden cart laden with a pile of suitcases, trunks, and stereo gear literally taller than the pixielike hippie. Apparently he didn't have his stuff together in time for the luggage pickup, so they left without him. Lately Beep's been on probation. He has a tendency to skip out on the incidental charges on his hotel bills, and to pile his trunks and suitcases onto staggering bellboys whom he never tips. There was so much complaining about "Freebie Fallon" from hotel staff that Dennis resorted to the heaviest penalty: B. P.'s case was handed over to Larry "the Hanging Judge" Mullen, who has agreed to let B. P. finish out the rest of the 1992 dates if he stays out of trouble. (A new deejay will be brought in for the '93 shows.)

Since then Larry has been chasing Beep up and down the inns and restaurants of America making sure he coughs up his share of the bills. Larry also ordered him to stop complaining that every room he checks into is unacceptable, and to quit calling ahead to the next hotel and saying, "This is Mr. Fallon, I'll be arriving on Tuesday and I have a list of specifications for my room." The relationship between the up-and-up Larry and the crafty leprechaun Beep is very much like that between Superman and Mr. Mxyzptlk, the mischievous imp from the fifth dimension who used to fly around Metropolis turning the *Daily Planet* globe into a giant balloon and Jimmy Olsen into Turtle-boy until Superman would trick him into saying his name backward, which would cause him to vanish back to his own dimension. Lately I think I've heard Larry mumbling, "Nollaf P. B., Nollaf P. B."

I leave B. P. hauling his luggage through the lobby like Sisyphus and head out to the airport with Dennis to watch him do the security rounds. It's part of his regular ritual. Before U2 goes to any airport or hotel Dennis has scouted it, gotten the layout, looked for trouble spots, and explained to the staff what will be likely to happen when U2 arrives (fans running toward them, congestion building up in check-in lines or at metal detectors) and trying to get their cooperation to make sure things run as smoothly as possible. Before a tour begins Dennis starts his mornings at 5 A.M. and flies to three cities a day, spending a couple of hours in each scouting out the airport, hotel, and venue. Now Dennis and two LAX staffers run through tomorrow's band departure. They walk through where the cars will let U2 off, where they'll pass through airport security, the stairs to the first-class lounge, the layout of that lounge, the special VIP holding rooms. The whole time he's memorizing this mental map Dennis is also picking up calls from the four band members on his portable phone, relaying to Suzanne Doyle or the hotel that Bono wants a car to go to lunch in half an hour or Edge wants to go to a particular club tonight.

As the airport staff escorts us through one area on our way to another I see a ball of confusion across the lobby. Alarm bells are ringing and airport security and redcaps are running after a little hippie man dragging a huge pile of luggage on a gurney behind him—he has just gone the wrong way through a metal detector and is rolling his trunks in through an "out" door.

If Dennis sees Beep spreading chaos like Johnny Appleseed, he does not let on. He continues his reconnaissance.

Dennis has spent his adult life on the road; he missed most of his children's growing up. With U2 he fought for concessions for the crew that had only been dreamed of over years of hard living. For example, each crew member has his own hotel room—an expensive luxury when 200 people are traveling, but one, Dennis insists, that allows the workers to feel like human beings. "You don't have to share with a smoker, you don't need to take a shower and find no towels." Dennis started in the early seventies with bands such as Stone the Crows. Before joining U2 in 1987 he'd been working with punk bands, and did a stint behind a desk at Arista Records working with Patti Smith and Lou Reed. But his early career was dominated by Led Zeppelin. U2 is not his first ride at the top.

In the Zeppelin days Dennis was second-in-command to Richard Cole, a notorious rock & roll wildman who grew more infamous after being the primary source for the Led Zep exposé *Hammer of the Gods,* and topped that with his own tell-all memoir. Dennis once found Cole, naked and out of his head, about to fly off the ledge of a hotel room. He wrestled him inside, surely saving his life. He says he wishes Cole the best with his books, but he could never do that, never kiss and tell. "There were nine good things with Led Zeppelin that no one knows about for every one bad thing," Dennis says. "But only the bad sells books."

We check into the first-class lounge, where the Principles are being boarded on the flight to Mexico. A panicky airport rep with a mustache runs up to Dennis and says there is a problem: "We've lost Mr. Fallon!"

"Fuck 'im," Dennis suggests.

The airport rep runs off, talking excitedly into a walkie-talkie of his own. They are holding the departure of the plane as long as they can while security is alerted to search for the missing VIP. Ten minutes later the mustached man returns to Dennis, mopping his brow and smiling triumphantly. "We found him, we got him on the plane, and they've taken off." Dennis nods and the man adds, "Whatever that guy's smoking, I don't want any."

"He's our resident leprechaun," Dennis explains.

Back in Hollywood I find U2 eating dinner near the editing studio, at a place called the Formosa that they discovered during the *Rattle and Hum* days. An older waitress comes up to Larry and says, "Aren't you growing into a fine figure of a man," while he looks embarrassed.

Bono offers me a lift back to the studio. On the way we start telling can-you-top-this stories about our fathers. We both lost our mothers as teenagers and then went through the sit-com experience of living with our widowed dads as young men. "My father's a funny old guy," Bono smiles. "He never gave me a compliment in my life. Not from the day I beat him at chess when I was five years old and not in the twenty years after. I remember when I brought him to America for the first time to see us play. It was a very emotional night. I introduced him from the stage, shined a spotlight on him. A very emotional performance. On that tour I was the first one off stage and no one followed me into the dressing room. It always takes me a few minutes after a show. Well, I came off stage and my father was right behind me. I got in the dressing room, turned around, and he was staring in my eyes. He reached out, took my hand in his, and I thought, 'Oh, my God, here it comes, after all these years . . .' And still holding my hand, he said, 'Son—that was very professional.' "

Bono pulls into the studio parking lot laughing and shaking his head. He joins the others inside and they look at a rough edit of the TV special. It is set to be broadcast on Thursday. It is 2 A.M. Saturday. They shake their heads and say, no, it's not ready yet. They sit down and get back to work.

Oh, you probably want to know what happened when Phil Joanou went off to have his lunch with Mel Gibson. Well, Mel stuck to the letter of his deal with Bono—he said he'd have lunch with Phil and let him talk. Mel never said he'd talk back to him. Phil went to the Beverly Hills Hotel, sat down with one of Mel's people, Mel showed up, chatted with the other guy, gave no sign of hearing anything Phil said, got up, and left. Gibson then told Bono his position was unchanged: Mel Gibson will not make *Million Dollar Hotel* with Phil Joanou. Gary Oldman reiterates that his position is unchanged too. He will not make *Million Dollar Hotel* without Phil Joanou. Furthermore, Oldman needs a firm commitment quickly or he's going to have to accept another offer. Bono sees his big Hollywood package disappearing in front of him. Without Gibson's production company he cannot get the financing together to pay Oldman before he drops out, but Oldman won't come in without Joanou, which knocks out Gibson. *The Million Dollar Hotel* is shelved. Oldman takes on a thriller called *Romeo Is Bleeding.* Gibson will do a movie adaption of the TV western *Maverick.* Ryder goes off to do *Reality Bites* with first-time director Ben Stiller—that TV comedian who makes fun of Bono.

Welcome to Hollywood, boyo.

15

The Conquest of Mexico

---

bono and edge perplexed by the channel changer/ larry resents his bikes & babes image/ the hidden kingdom/ the power brokers appear/ love among the latins/ every limo a getaway car

THERE IS nothing as ugly as an 8 A.M. walkup call. U2 worked on their TV special until 4 and then slouched back to the hotel. Now, five hours later, the frazzled musicians are grumbling into their coffee cups in the Sunset Marquis breakfast room, their eyes swollen shut and their chins nicked from shaving in their sleep. They nibble at muffins and drink only decaf so they can sleep on the plane to Mexico City. Adam, his blond mohawk beginning to grow out on the sides, is wearing a bright red suit "in honor of Mexico." Dennis Sheehan has gone on ahead to LAX to make ready the airport. A limo waits outside. They stare at the walls and mutter and nod off and shake their heads and sit back up and mutter more.

Finally Bono organizes his thoughts enough to demand to know why they have been made to sit here waiting to depart.

"Dennis said we *had* to leave by nine or we'd miss the gig," Larry says bitterly. "Now look! It's nine-thirty."

They all snort and nod. "And he wonders why we don't believe him," Bono says. They all grunt and agree.

Suddenly Edge opens one of his eyes. "Where *is* Dennis?" he asks.

"He's gone to the airport." Larry shrugs.

There's an old New England expression that applies here: *Dawn breaks on Marblehead.* The four members of U2 look at each other stupidly. Finally Bono speaks: "Are we waiting for a phone call that will never come?" They stare at one another. Finally Bono gets up and goes over to the limo driver. The driver has been waiting for U2 while U2, used to being transported like very expensive pandas, have been waiting for someone to move them. They are now in danger of missing the only flight that can get them to Mexico City in time for their concert tonight. They jump up and hurry to the car.

I think there should be music playing and I think it should go, (baDump) *Here we come, walkin' down the street* . . .

In the car Bono struggles to get the TV to switch channels, but it stays stuck on one of those half-hour self-help commercials. Finally, in exasperation, Bono says, "Edge, you're the scientist, can you get this to work?" Edge leans over and tries to change the station. Each time he does, it clicks back to the self-help ad. This is very strange. Edge gets down and fiddles the switches with the furrow-browed dedication of Louis Pasteur at his Bunsen burner, oblivious as Bono to the fact that Larry is sitting with a remote control by his leg, clicking the channel back each time Edge tries to change it.

At last they give up and accept the infotainment. "Too bad you can't get cable in a car," Larry says. Then the drummer asks if anyone else has ever seen the Fishing Channel. "Lots of talk about rods and hooks and the one that got away."

Bono says, "I prefer the 'Rides bikes, likes boats, and lives with girlfriend for twelve years channel.' "

Larry groans and rolls his eyes. Edge asks what they're talking about. Larry explains that Bono's recapping the thumbnail description of him in the new *Vogue* cover story on U2. Once again a journalist who was given access to the whole band went home and wrote a story that was chock-full of Bono, had a few wise parables from the Edge, and devoted to Adam and Larry roughly the same number of words that go on the back of a bubblegum card. Bono says euphemistically, "She painted Larry in bold strokes."

Adam smiles and says to the sullen Mullen, "At least you're not the one she called, 'handsome in an ugly way.' "

At the airport Dennis Sheehan greets U2 in front of a squadron of the sort of saluting, waving, pointing security agents not seen since Ferdinand Marcos hitched his wagon to a star. U2 is rushed through the metal detectors, up a private elevator, into the first-class lounge, and from there into the sort of superexclusive private white waiting rooms known only to superstars and tortured spies. There they are reunited with their manager (who in these circumstances is referred to only as "M").

It's not a long wait—that plane to Mexico is all boarded and ready to fly. The woman in charge of shipping celebrities through LAX comes in to escort the band to the first-class cabin. She tells Bono that she went to Florida to see the first show, she stood on her chair through the Los Angeles concert, "I guess you could say I'm a fan." In the elevator Bono realizes he's left his fly shades behind. The woman whips out a walkie-talkie and gets her security squad combing the holding room, the bathroom, the lounge to find them. Now, bear in mind that Bono loses everything. In the last hour Edge grabbed the book that Bono left in the car, and just now McGuinness found the same book left on the table upstairs. So when Bono says of losing his glasses, "This is unbelievable!" his bandmates correct him.

"No, Bono," Larry says, "it's not unbelievable."

Adam claims, "It's not uncommon."

Edge adds, "It's not unusual."

Larry points out, "It's not surprising at all."

U2 is loaded into first class and Bono sits in the plane on the runway, lamenting his lost fly shades. There is a buzzing between the pilot and the cabin crew and then the airplane door opens and the U2-loving airport lady rushes aboard, Bono's goggles held high. He kisses her hand and she says, "I *told* you about St. Anthony!"

On the flight McGuinness explains that this is not only U2's first-ever gig in Mexico, it's their first show in any Third World country. The local promoter is an American tied to the entertainment giant MCA/Winterland who is trying to open Mexico City to regular rock concerts. He lobbied Paul hard to do these shows. U2 was turned down for an outdoor stadium—the Mexican authorities were scared of that. Instead they'll play two nights in an indoor arena.

There's a lot of sleeping on the journey. When my watch says it's almost landing time I assume something's wrong: there are no suburbs or outskirts, no life at all in the barren expanse below us. I figure we must be at least an hour away. Then we pass over an abrupt eruption of high mountains, skirt through the clouds, and *holy smoke,* there is in the basin of the mountains an apparently endless crater filled with the biggest urban area I have ever seen. And we fly over it and fly over it and fly over it; it seems to have no end. Even the biggest metropolis—New

York, London, Hong Kong—covers only a small area from the air. You fly over satellite towns and half-developed areas for a while before the big city looms up. Not this place! Mexico City is, by population, the biggest city in the world. Ringed by rugged mountains, it has no outskirts. You are in wilderness and then you are in urbania, and urbania seems to go on forever.

Some of the vastness comes from the lack of skyscrapers. It is as if God lined up New York, Chicago, Houston, and Toronto, lopped all the tall buildings down to three- and four-story structures, and then flung them across the horizon. The population here is estimated at twenty million, but no one pretends to have any real idea; it's uncountable. Aside from being the capital of Mexico, it is the magnet for refugees fleeing political and economic hardship all over Latin America. Mexico City is the cultural center of all the nations between Texas and the South Pole.

The scene at the airport is like *A Hard Day's Night.* There are fans pressed against the glass of the terminal overlooking the runway, and about twenty-five or thirty screaming girls—the children of bigwigs who pulled strings—screeching for U2 on the tarmac. The screaming gets louder when U2 descends the stairs to the runway. There are two secondhand-looking limos waiting. Adam and Larry, as is their habit, get right in the cars while Edge and Bono, as is their wont, go over and pose for photos and sign autographs while the blessed swoon in ecstatic proximity. (Larry once accused Bono of getting an ego boost out of signing autographs, which annoyed Bono to no end. "Yeah, I really *enjoy* signing autographs and posing for pictures after traveling for seven hours," Bono snapped. He said to me, "I just find it impossible to ignore people who have been waiting for you and then drive past them in a limo.")

Hey, no passports checked or luggage examined around here! An honor guard of local cops on ancient motorcycles pulls up to escort the two oversize limos down the runway and out of the airport. The first car zooms off and the second follows—despite the fact that Paul McGuinness is standing with one foot in the car and one foot out, hanging on to the door for dear life and hopping along while Principle's Sheila Roche screams at the driver to stop. The cars are too low and heavy to make it over the speed bumps that pop up every few hundred feet, so at every bump the motorcycle cops dismount, blow their whistles, stop all traffic in each direction, and wait while the limos torturously turn twenty-two degrees and ease over the tar impediments one wheel at a time. I daresay we could walk to wherever we're going faster than this, although that would deprive those of us in the second car of the fun of watching the trunk flap open and shut on the first car as various U2 luggage bags bounce in the air like happy appaloosas. McGuinness sighs and says, "Welcome to the Third World."

Time demands that U2 haul ass straight to the Palacio de los Deportes—the sports palace—and tonight's show. The cars part the cheering fans, slip through a gate secured by many alert guards, roll into a quickly opened and closed garage door and disgorge U2 into the dusty belly of the rickety arena. From the outside, the place looks like an enormous armadillo shell. Inside it's dirty, ugly, and rusty. The audience on the floor are crammed together on cheap red plastic chairs, the sort you'd find at a PTA slide show in a poor school. B.A.D., U2's opening act, are rocking the casbah when we arrive. The narrow aisles are littered with cigarette butts, ice cream wrappers, and gum. Hawkers walk through the crowd yelling "ice cream" and "soda" in Spanish, above the music.

I wander the upper reaches of the hall while B. P., splendid in his cape and Zorro hat, stokes up "Be My Baby" for the cheering audience. The seats that climb up the sides of the arena are shaky and old. The bathrooms are dirty. It seems like a place where someone could get hurt. I go back down to the floor, to a seat not far from the soundboard, just before U2 comes on. When the lights dim, the audience, already wildly excited, climbs up on their chairs. I do too. I remember this sort of intense, overcramped energy from the punk days and I have my mean face on and my elbows pointed out, set for two hours of shoving, insults, and dirty looks.

And let me tell you something—I am full of gringo crap. U2 comes on and while the energy level is as high and wild as at an early Clash show, the gentleness and shared openness of the audience reminds me of the heyday of Joni Mitchell. It is really something to feel. The fans' pulses must be doing triplets, they are frantically enthusiastic—yet they are so careful and considerate of each other than I feel like the greatest cynic since doubting Thomas. I should be ashamed of myself. It's a good thing I found the backstage kitchen crew filling up Evian bottles with local water or I would think I'd misjudged human nature completely.

Flipping around the Zoo TV screens Bono hauls in a soccer match and announces the score: "Mexico dos, Costa Rica uno!" The crowd explodes and begins chanting a football cheer: "Méjico! Méjico! Méjico!" When Larry gets up and takes off his shirt he gets plenty of applause. When he then puts on a Mexican football jersey it turns into an ovation.

Out on the B stage Bono is so excited he launches into "La Bamba" while Edge follows and Larry and Adam just stare at him. When Lou Reed's face appears on the big screen during "Satellite of Love," Bono and Edge look up at him like worshippers on the road to Damascus. I love this film of Reed because it shows his real face, not young and quite gentle. Lou works so hard at projecting a tough-guy image that to see his private side displayed in public is a pleasure.

"Bob Marley was from Mexico, right?" Bono cries as the audience cheers. "Well, he could have been." Bono plays "Redemption Song" as thousands of lighters flash on and off together in perfect time. Then, during "Sunday Bloody Sunday" a big owl flies through the hall and lights on a rafter looking down at the spectacle like the Paraclete Himself. I overhear several evil crew members making plans to catch a mouse tomorrow and attach it to B. P.'s hat just before he goes out to deejay. They want to see if the owl will carry him away.

After the concert Bono is delighted. "I felt I was completely empty before I went out there," he says, "but it's a funny thing. That audience washed over me and we rode their energy as if we were surfing on a wave. I've been told that the shows here will get better every night, but I don't see how that's possible."

Bono's new rockish persona extends to the aftershow meet-and-greets where he dons a hideous crushed-plush smoking jacket to mingle with the music-biz insiders waiting to eat potato chips and shake his hand. Tonight there are a lot of guest stars from the States, flown in for the end of the 1992 tour and U2's first visit to Mexico. Hanging in the anteroom is Chris Blackwell, the founder of Island Records, U2's label. Blackwell is a legendary character in the music business, a blond Brit who fell in love with Jamaican music and built an English label on reggae, brought Bob Marley to the world, and in the late sixties and seventies raised an empire beyond reggae with such acts as Traffic, Free, and Cat Stevens. Also along this evening are Frank Barsalona, U2's American agent and his partner Barbara Skydel. And here comes Rick Dobbis, president of PLG, the new multilabel umbrella company formed by Polygram, the multinational that bought Island from Blackwell a few years ago. Why, there is enough music business power in this room to revive Milli Vanilli and make Kajagoogoo the next Led Zeppelin, should that power ever be turned to evil.

These topcats have every reason to line up to light Bono's little cigar tonight. With one more show to go before the Christmas break, U2's statistics for the first ten months of 1992 look like this: more than 10 million copies of *Achtung Baby* sold, 5 hit singles, 2.9 million tickets sold for the Zoo TV tour (106 shows in 84 cities in 12 countries), 54,615 miles traveled so far. The frequent-flyer miles alone will pay for this expedition. After the requisite palm pumping and nyuk-nyuking with the power brokers and local dignitaries, Bono and Edge split off to go outside to the fence where fans are waiting and sign autographs and have their pictures taken. Then it's into the limos and into the night.

We make a twenty-minute pit stop before regrouping for a night on the town. The Hotel Nikko is posh and tall, with panoramic views of the illuminated city from the upper floors, a spiderweb of lights spinning out in every direction. There is a whole secret world that the famous and powerful travel in, demarked by the special holding rooms and escorts at airports and even more by the private floors of ritzy hotels. In a place like this there are special elevators that carry the privileged to their privacy on restricted levels with their own check-in desks, their own lounges, their own butlers—so that the famous and powerful don't have to associate with the merely rich.

I have no time to trifle over such observations! I gotta brush my teeth, change my shirt, and get back downstairs without even breaking the seal on my toilet seat. I grab my key from the secret desk clerk and find my room where I share a tearful reunion with my luggage. The great thing about traveling with high rollers like U2 is that your bags disappear from your hotel room in one country and reappear in your room in the next without your ever seeing them move. The bad thing is that sometimes, as happened to me this week, my suitcase was grabbed and shipped with the bags of the Principles and crew, who came down to Mexico two days ahead of the band with whom I was loitering. I returned to my room at the Sunset Marquis to find myself with nothing but the shirt on my back. I hiked to the only clothing store within walking distance that was open at night, an athletic shop that specialized in sweatsuits emblazoned with images of Charles Barkley. I'm happy to get my real clothes back; I'm sick of slapping five with B-boys.

Back downstairs everyone piles into cars and vans to head to some hotspot that the Principles have already scoped. Our driver takes off with the back door open and one crew member halfway out and screaming.

"I'm very impressed with Mexico City, I must say," Edge declares as we cruise, and he's said a mouthful. You always hear about the terrible poverty, the awful pollution and ugliness of this place—and no doubt there's plenty of all that in this eternal (kilometer-wise) city. But nobody tells you about the parts of town we're riding through, which looks like what Washington D.C. could be if it swiped ten or twenty of Rome's best buildings. There are beautiful parks and boulevards separating great white stone monuments and museums. There are illuminated fountains and statues and immaculate city squares. There is also a lot of Moorish influence in the architecture, a suggestion of minarets. I can't believe we're in North America.

I suppose that most of the reports about the grimness and griminess of Mexico City come from tourists who have been communing with nature in the deserts or seashore and then drive in here through miles of slums, or who only see the area around the airport on their way to the resorts. Or maybe it's just the northern European prejudices against Spanish culture that were handed down from the Old World to the New. I don't know. I do know that Mexico City is beautiful.

We are eventually deposited at a fancy, multilevel restaurant/disco in what seems to be the happening part of town. Adam, Bono, Edge, and Larry grab a table together and sit laughing and talking for a couple of hours. McGuinness, at the next table, points out that one of the most unusual things about U2 is that the four of them still prefer each others' company to anyone else's, and after so many years stuck together they still have no shortage of things to philosophize, laugh, and bust each other's balls about.

U2 are seated in front of an elaborate (and dare I say, *mental*) strobe-lit Santería spin on a manger scene. Populating the life-size tableau are very large sculptures of the Holy Family accompanied by the usual angels and wisemen, but augmented here by a cowboy among the shepherds, an elephant among the sheep, and a grotesque, bat-winged flying devil sticking out his tongue at the Christ child. Now wouldn't it be a drag to learn that when William Butler Yeats wrote "The Second Coming" he was not carving out a great prophetic metaphor for the twentieth century but was simply drinking in a Mexican restaurant like this and describing a sculpture like that? Unlikely? Perhaps, but probably worth credit toward an advanced degree at any number of tweedy little universities. The four members of U2 sit laughing, oblivious to the tableau in front of which they are posed. I'll tell you, though, if the center cannot hold, that flying devil on his flimsy string is going to land right on Adam's head. He'll be picking himself up off the floor, asking, "What rough beast is this?"

The rest of the Principles and Zoo crew spread out through the rooms, some eating, some dancing, most drinking. Sheila Roche, an Irish wetback who has been working under Ellen Darst in New York, is feeling blue because Ellen has handed in her notice. The woman who guided U2 through club gigs and radio interviews when they first came to America, who tutored Paul McGuinness about the U.S. music business, and who has for the last eight years been in charge of Principle's American operation, has gotten tired of the road and accepted a job with Elektra Records. She put off the move until the American tour was finished, but now Ellen's saying good-bye and Sheila, who moved from Dublin to New York to work with Ellen, is going to miss her. Ellen's longtime second-in-command, Keryn Kaplan, will take over. One of Ellen's legacies is the number of women in power. "In the New York office we have only one man," Sheila smiles. "The receptionist."

For all the credit given to U2 and McGuinness for employing so many women, though, I have run across a minority opinion that, as all the women are in support roles, nurturing roles, and all the creative decisions are made by men, Principle is really maintaining patriarchal values under a sheen of being progressive and nonsexist. It's hard to resolve that; it's so much in the eye of the beholder. I would not deny that many of the women around U2 are nurturing, gentle types, *but so is U2.* There are people in the music business who will tell you that Ellen Darst and/or Anne-Louise Kelly is the real brains of that outfit and McGuinness rides their coattails. No doubt there are other people who assume that Paul, the man, must do all the brainwork and the women in power are glorified secretaries. People see what they want to see. If the rap against the Principle women is that they are too nurturing or gentle, then maybe they have made more genuine progress by feminizing U2's perceptions than they would have by adopting so-called *masculine* values themselves.

Suzanne Doyle, the deputy tour manager, comes tearing by looking for Larry. It seems he scolded a crew member for something that was not, Suzanne says, the guy's fault and she wants to ask him to apologize. It is an unusual hierarchy U2 has set up, where the people who work for them are allowed to tell them they're full of bull and bring them down to earth when their big heads start to interfere with operations or morale. I'm always amazed that, far from treating me like the new kid in school, crew members I've barely met greet me by name, pat me on the back, and invite me to join in when they're looking for fun. That sort of generosity is rare on rock tours.

"It comes from the top down," Sheila says. "Bono has told me that if any big shot who comes backstage ever gives me a bad time, I can tell him to fuck off. Do you know what a relief that is? Some people—L.A. is the worst for this—are so rude, so demanding and ungrateful. They get complimentary tickets and if they see somebody they know with better complimentary tickets they get upset with us. Their prestige is determined by how good their free seats are!"

In the next room Joe O'Herlihy, the band's soundman, is shaking the disco music out of his ears. Joe has been with U2 since 1979, before they had a record deal. Easygoing, likable, and possessed of whiskers that make ZZ Top's beards look like baby bibs, Joe launches into the tale of how he made it home to Dublin for the birth of his fourth child. Joe had missed the arrival of his first three kids years earlier, because he was always on the road with rock bands. He vowed to his wife that he'd be at her side when this late baby was born. U2 was filming a concert in Virginia for *Rattle and Hum* when word came that his wife back in Ireland had gone into labor. Joe flipped, but U2 had prepared for such a sudden evacuation. Joe was rushed to an airport and flown to New York. He called from JFK and heard, "It's coming!" over the phone. He ran for the Concorde and spent the four-hour supersonic flight pacing the aisles, watching the posted speed click around, and praying, "Faster, faster, faster!" Landing in London he ran to another phone. "She's at the hospital! Hurry, Joe!" He ran to the Irish flight gate and got on the next plane to Dublin, raced to the hospital, was given a sanitary robe to throw over his smelly clothes, and charged into the delivery room, pushed the attendant aside, and told his wife he was there. Ten minutes later he was holding his new daughter in his arms, weeping and weeping. Two days after that he was behind his sound desk in Tempe, Arizona, mixing U2.

"That was the first time on the whole tour the band's had a chance to sit down and tell each other our road stories," Bono says as the party starts breaking up. "We give each other space on the road, and when we get back to Dublin we won't see that much of each other."

"The only time we get to do this is when the four of us go away on a little vacation without anyone else," Adam agrees. "Then we revert to type: Edge makes all the plans, Larry handles the money, and Bono is the greeter—he interacts with other people." I don't ask, but I assume Adam's job is picking up the girls.

Adam is not one for leaving a bar while the drinks are still flowing, but at 3:40 A.M. the other three U2's are ready to call it a night. When they step outside, the street is filled with kids screaming, waving autograph pads, shoving toward the band, and pounding on the limo. Bono jumps into the car first and the driver floors it, scattering fans and leaving Edge and Larry behind, in the mob. Bono shouts at the driver to slow down and back up. Edge and Larry fall into the car with the fans tugging at them.

Larry is wiping at his cheek.

Bono says, "Someone kissed you, Larry?"

"Yeah." Larry is annoyed. Kids outside are screaming, "I love you!" Larry repeats it sarcastically and adds, "You don't *know* me."

Bono tells Larry to lighten up. Larry says *love* is a powerful word.

"You're so pedantic." Bono smiles. Bono starts to roll down the window to shake hands with some of the kids.

"No, Bono, no!" Edge commands, as to a dog. "Somebody will get hurt!"

I recognize this whole scene from traveling with U2 on a tour in the south of France in 1984. Larry climbed on the bus then bugged because some self-professed witches among the kids outside the hall had made a voodoo doll of him, which he did not consider funny. Bono was waving out the window to the French U2 fans as the bus pulled away, and he kept waving to confused pedestrians and sidewalk diners as we drove slowly through Toulouse. I remember Edge admonishing him: "Bono! Stop waving to innocent bystanders!" Everything in U2's world has changed since then except their relations with each other.

Another thing that will apparently never change is this Mexican driver thinking he's Mario Andretti. As U2's crew is opening the trunk to toss in the band's hand luggage, our driver slams on the gas again, taking off with the trunk open and the Zoo crew waving the bags, chasing the car down the street.

16

Border Radio

---

*the arena catches fire/ dignitaries' daughters are presented
to the band/ a trip to the purported red-light district/ who is
the new rolling stones with commentary by mr. jagger/ U2
among the jews*

A S IN EVERY city there's a crowd of kids waiting at all hours
outside U2's hotel. As in every city, Bono and Edge go over
and pose and sign for them before leaving for the concert hall.
I had a cultural afternoon, doing the Inca/Aztec/Mayan museums with
the soon-to-be-departed Ellen Darst and Morleigh Steinberg, a dancer/
choreographer who took over the belly-dancing slot when the Zoo tour
moved outdoors. A Californian who travels the world with the Iso dance
company, Morleigh met U2 in L.A. in the late 80s. They talked her into
doing the summer dates, and she gave the band advice about how to
move onstage to get their intentions across to the back rows. Far more
self-contained and independent than most of the Zoo people, Morleigh
has real reservations about putting her career on hold to join their
European tour next spring and summer. Tonight may be her last belly
dance.

All the members of the band are enjoying Mexico and looking
forward to another gig like last night's. Grabbing dinner with the crew
backstage, Adam says, "It's been so good, it makes you think about the
possibility of doing a Latin American tour."

U2 comes out flying tonight. They light into "Zoo Station" with all
flags billowing and Bono sidestepping across the stage like James
Brown's paler nephew. I am standing with B. P. Fallon on the side of the
stage when I see what appears to be a great new special effect out in the
audience—two lines of red flame converging in the dark at the back of
the hall. B. P. grabs my arm and points frantically as I realize *that's no*

special effect! That's a fire! The seats are too close together and they are not flame retardant. Neither is the WELCOME U2 banner someone in the balcony has made out of a bedsheet. The sheet dangled into the flame of a lighter a kid down below was holding aloft, and now the sheet's igniting, breaking into burning shards that are floating into the crowd and landing on the seats and—oh, hell—the seats are bursting into flame. I look at the band—the front three are oblivious, caught up in their song. Only Larry, drumming away, is staring with grim concentration at the spreading fire and panicking people in the back of the hall .

A figure bolts by me, running full out from the back of the stage into the crowd. It's Jerry Mele, U2's head of security. He flies across the length of the crowded hall, through the jam-packed kids dancing to the band, and disappears under the bleachers at the back. I've never seen anyone move so fast, but the fire is moving faster. Edge sees it now; he is watching intently. People in the back of the arena are shoving and running for the exits. Jerry is suddenly up there among them—he must have rocketed up the outside stairs. He is ordering the scared concert-goers into neat lines with one hand while shoving something—a coat or towel—onto the flames and stamping with his feet. Local ushers and security hands are following his orders, doing the same. All the fires are out before the song ends. When he's sure it's safe Jerry directs the shaken fans back to their blackened seats. Bono is emoting in high gusto, oblivious, while Adam is standing by his bass amp, paying no attention to anything beyond the spotlights.

Larry saw it all, though. When he gets a break the drummer says, "I thought, 'This is it.' I figured the whole place was going up." Jerry Mele moved so fast and established control so quickly that the fire becomes nothing more than a "by the way" after the show. The people with decent seats were paying attention to the band and didn't notice. But if Jerry hadn't been there, U2's big trip to Mexico City could have turned into a tragedy. It's funny that rock stars are routinely called heroes, while characters like Jerry Mele hold the door for them.

After the show U2 has reserved tables for dinner at the same restaurant they haunted last night. This time when they arrive—at a little after 1 A.M.—the band and their guests have the whole three-level place to themselves, except for a few children of VIPs waiting at the bar to be presented to U2. Bono has taken command of a table with the band, the agents, Blackwell, and other big shots when McGuinness comes over and says with half-joking gravity, "You are about to be introduced to a longstanding Third World custom—the police chief's daughters are here. They want to meet you and they *will* get autographs."

The chief's daughters (or maybe it's one daughter and one friend of the daughter—no one's certain) are lovely. Bono has been talking about trying to check out the part of town the tourists don't see, and when his attention is grabbed and pointed toward the chief's daughters he innocently asks them for details about the red-light district. Where are the best places to go there? How late is it jumping?

Bono has no sinful intentions, but that may not be apparent in the translation. Edge, realizing that one doesn't introduce oneself to policemen's daughters in Latin nations by asking about the brothels, brings the two young women over to another table and charms them for some time. Finally they say good night and he comes back to Bono's side, saying, "They told me if I'm ever arrested in Mexico City, no problem!"

Throughout the meal other such well-connected young people are escorted up to meet the band and then shuffled off again. The fellow in charge, I assume the owner, of the restaurant comes by frequently to remind U2 that in honor of them he has closed his entire club tonight, forgoing all the money he would make so that U2 could dine and drink undisturbed. After the fourth or fifth time he makes this announcement a concerned Larry leans over to Bono and says, "I wonder how much money he'll lose, closing the whole restaurant?"

"It's all jive," Bono whispers back. "By law the place has to close by one A.M. on Sunday night." Larry laughs hard at that one.

Larry talks a bit over dinner about his plans for the Christmas break. He was asked if he'd be interested in auditioning for the role of Pete Best, the deposed Beatles drummer, in a movie about the Fab Four's Hamburg days, but he had to turn it down because it conflicted with the band's work schedule.

Edge tells me to try these delicious bar nuts and gets me to eat a handful of friend grasshoppers.

Larry is a vegetarian; he asks me to taste those nachos and see if there's any meat in them. I get nothing but cheese and beans and tell him it's all clear. Larry takes a bite, swallows, and says, "Chicken! First time I've had chicken in four years and it's your fault! I'll never forget this!"

"What am I, the royal food taster?" I say. "There was no chicken in the piece I ate."

"You see, Larry," Adam says, "you let an *outsider* taste your food for you. I'm not jealous, but if you need someone to eat off your plate you should always go to your bass player."

Bono has one big problem with the impending return to Dublin. His wife doesn't want him back. Bono admits that, eight months out, tour life seems completely normal to him. If he's supposed to be getting it out of his system, it ain't working. "Because of this my lovely wife has suggested I not come right home."

"Adam is going to check into a hotel for a week," McGuinness says.

"So am I." Bono nods.

"In Dublin?"

"Yeah," Bono admits. "I don't want to, but Ali says it's better. A couple of days after I get back to Dublin we've got to be on a TV special. It will just confuse the kids if I come home and start working again right away, and she says they'll be hurt if they talk to me and I don't hear them. So I guess I'll spend my first week at home in a hotel."

I suggest that Bono go home but stay in the basement for a week. His kids could come to the top of the stairs and throw food down to him. But, of course, then they might keep doing that after he left on tour again, which would be pathetic.

"It's funny," Bono says. "I really don't feel like stopping."

"Well," I say, "maybe this is your five years to work nonstop, do everything you have to do, and then quit and become a shepherd or something."

"I already am a shepherd, Bill," he says, smiling beatifically. "Didn't you know?" He spreads out his arms to his assembled disciples, apostles, and money changers, and says, "And these are my sheep."

Stray crew members go *baaaaah*.

After a great meal and lots of handshaking and a few more reminders from the boss that he closed the whole restaurant for U2 tonight, the band heads across town to what we've been promised is the red-light district. I dunno. Where they dump us is loud and fun and there're lots of bars and the sort of women one sees in bars, but I don't think it's really a red-light district. Paul McGuinness walks around soaking up the atmosphere and periodically pulling out a portable oxygen mask from which he inhales deeply. Quite the *Blue Velvet* figure he cuts doing so, too! We settle in a mariachi bar where many of the Principles dance (some claim they have never seen Larry Mullen dance before—I guess I'd describe it as a combination of the young Fred Astaire and the old Jerry Lewis). While everyone's drinking, Bono vanishes for about half an hour and returns claiming he stumbled across a genuine brothel. I am certain it's a lie made up to torture me.

As the night threatens to turn into morning, Adam and I wander out and walk around the Plaza Garibaldi. There are bars set up and selling drinks outside, strolling bands of caballeros playing requests, and swingers stumbling out of every doorway. Adam, who has been drinking enough that whatever he says should be taken with a grain of salt (and several glasses of tequila), strolls around the square and says—not that one usually thinks in these terms about oneself—that U2 now is in the position the Stones filled in 1972.

I can truthfully tell him that I have been thinking exactly the same thing. The Rolling Stones 1972 tour was, it will always seem to me and those my age, the hottest rock tour ever. The sixties were over, the Beatles broken up, Bob Dylan had all but retired, Hendrix was dead— and the Stones had just capped their *Beggar's Banquet, Let It Bleed, Sticky Fingers* hot streak with the monumental, head-splitting *Exile on Main Street.* When they went out on their first tour in three years, every kid—male and female—in every high school lunch room wanted to look like Keith Richards. These were the Stones' second generation of fans. The older brothers who'd liked all the sixties singles—"Satisfaction," "Ruby Tuesday," "Paint It Black"—might not have cared for the new, harder, grungier Stones, but then, the older brothers always lumped the band in with a whole raft of sixties British groups. The teenagers in 1972 didn't know or care about that history; this was *their* Rolling Stones, reborn outside the shadow of the Beatles as the Biggest Band in the World.

It is telling that U2 talked seriously about calling *Achtung Baby, Cruise Down Main Street,* and the album's chaotic, multiimage cover clearly evoked the jacket of *Exile.* I tell Adam that I'm right with him on the Stones '72 comparison: one decade of hit singles and screaming girls down, now let's get past that and get heavy.

"*Joshua Tree* was a pop album." Adam nods. "This is rock."

He mentions that there are no longer many real bands around, bands of four equal members, all aboard since the start, all working together. I say, "Well, R.E.M."

"That's a different thing," Adam says, still using the vocabulary of 1972. "U2 are the Rolling Stones, R.E.M. are CSN&Y."

When I get back to New York, who should I be talking to but Mick Jagger. And what do you think Mick's bending my ear about? All these new bands that are trying to sound like the old Stones, even dress like the old Stones. He clearly means the Black Crowes and that crowd. He says that at least U2 seems to be doing something new. He liked *Achtung Baby* a lot and while he hasn't seen Zoo TV yet, from all descriptions that's one band who isn't just looking back at what someone else did twenty years ago.

Actually, I say, I was having some drinks with one of the guys in U2 and—understand this is just talk in a bar after a few pops—he was comparing U2's position today to the Stones twenty years ago.

"That's really odd." Jagger laughs. "I know that's said after a lot of tequilas or whatever, but it's rather peculiar. Things were so different then, with those little bitty amps and stuff. When we did it in 1972 there'd been nothing like it before. Though I never actually saw the Zoo TV tour, that was nothing like anything that came before, which is good. It isn't 1972, it's 1992, and I wish people would realize that. I don't remember ever saying, 'I feel like I'm Buddy Holly!' "

Ouch! There's the putdown. I think I'm onto something, though. I'll just take U2 comments and quotes from late-night drinking sessions and run them by other musicians. I call Peter Buck and ask him if he feels R.E.M. are the new CSN&Y: "Anything but that!" he cries.

One night in Mexico City Edge, Bono, and I got into a strange and winding discussion born of one of the black jokes in the *Million Dollar Hotel* script: "Jews don't commit suicide; they never had to." Bono went on to say that the Jews in Hollywood invented the myth of an America where everyone was equal and religion didn't matter, and then sold that myth back to the country. Bono sees this as a great accomplishment.

Edge picked up on that and said, "In rock, Jews are the best lyricists because of their merciless intellectual rigor."

Bono amplified the point: he said that the Jewish intellectual tradition is to dig for the truth no matter where it takes you. It is not concerned, as so many other traditions are, with proving that the virtuous win or the collective triumphs or might makes right or God is on our side or our country did the right thing: the Jews follow the truth wherever it takes them, and that is why Jews are the best lyricists.

Okay, I said, Bob Dylan, Paul Simon. Who else?

Bono and Edge started reeling off an impressive list: "Dylan, Simon, Leonard Cohen, Lou Reed," then Bono blew it by saying, "Even Neil Diamond here and there . . ."

"Hold it right there," I said. " 'Longfellow Serenade'? 'Song Sung Blue'? Did you ever hear about when Dylan met Diamond on the beach at Malibu and said, 'Didn't I hear you singin' something about "Forever in Blue Jeans"?' and Diamond denied it."

Bono looked down his nose at my sarcasm and asked, "Do you know what 'I Am, I Said' is all about?"

"Yeah, as a matter of fact I do. Diamond was in Hollywood making his acting debut as Lenny Bruce in the first attempt to film Bruce's story. *Wonder why that one went wrong.* He was having a terrible time, the picture was falling apart, and he sat down in the dressing room and wrote that song about feeling out of place in L.A. but no longer part of the Brooklyn he came from."

Bono clearly meant his question to be rhetorical; he was not expecting me to actually know the gestation of "I Am, I Said." But now we were into the sort of mutual nut-busting in which neither opponent can concede an inch, so he tried a different approach: "How does Yahweh identify himself in Genesis?"

I saw where this was leading. " 'I am who am,' " I quoted. "That's actually an interesting grammatical construction, you know, because—"

Bono cut me off: "*I am.* God is described as the great *I am.* So in that song Diamond is calling out to Jehovah. '*I am,* I said' means, 'God, I said.' To who? To no one there! And no one heard at all, not even the chair! Do you see? It is a song of despair and lost faith by a man calling out to a God who isn't interested!"

Boy, Bono will go a long way to weasel out of admitting that Neil Diamond is not one of rock's greatest lyricists. Perhaps right now some of you readers are wondering if this book has petered out altogether, but bear with me. If I wanted to I could fill up hundreds of pages with this sort of three-sheets-to-the-wind, navel-gazing dialogue between U2 and me. For the most part I have left such guff in the bars, figuring it's an Irish thing, you wouldn't understand. I include this example, though, because I've gotten really interested in this politically volatile notion that Jews make the best lyricists. I try it out on Aimee Mann, a songwriter I admire very much, and she bangs the table and says, "Yes, yes! Absolutely! I'm so glad to hear somebody else say that! Randy Newman! Jules Shear! Steely Dan!" and then she goes into a diatribe about the same virtues of intellectual scrupulosity, not going for the soft cliché, and chasing the fleet hare of truth down into the rabbit hole of disappointment and anguish cited by Bono and Edge.

Boy, I figure, I'm onto something here. The hell with U2, I'm going to be writing think pieces for *Tikkun* and going on the *Dick Cavett Show*. Then I stop and consider that the only people I have supporting this proposition are goyim like me. I need to get a rigorous Jew in here and bounce this provocative theoretical handball against the rigid wall of his scrupulous intellect. So I try to think which Jewish lyricist to call and I figure the best one must be Randy Newman, that cynical Californian who was widely quoted at the height of *Rattle and Hum* fever declaring that he never knew apartheid was wrong until he heard it from U2, "Then the scales just fell from my eyes!"

"You know, Randy," I say while he tries to remember who I am, "U2 say that all the best rock lyricists are Jews, and Aimee Mann does too."

"Jeez," Newman says. "Did they really? I'm looking for a defense. Neil Young and, um, there's plenty of others. I don't know about that. Two different people said that? That's odd. Dylan at his best was probably as good as it got, and Simon's been as consistent as anyone has been. There's no doubt about that. You know what it is about us? Jews want to be Americans so badly! Think of Irving Berlin writing," Newman starts singing like Al Jolson, " '*I'm Alabammy bound!*' He'd never been to Alabama and if he was, they chased him right out! Maybe he was there during a bond drive. And my stuff is so American that it worries me. It's like I *want* to be. I grasp these five years I spent in New Orleans as a baby and hang onto them for dear life as some sort of proof that I'm American."

That's interesting, I say. If it's the unfulfilled aspiration to sound like a real American that makes for a good rock lyricist, that would explain the Canadians—Cohen, Young, Robbie Robertson, Joni Mitchell. It would explain everyone who came out of England and Ireland. . . .

"Neil Young and Joni Mitchell are top ten of all time for sure," Newman says. "They're real interested and looking in from the outside.

Look at Prince, one of the best of all time. There's one that they forgot. Prince's lyrics are *very* good."

Well, we bravely followed that thread to its bitter denouement. Apparently it's not that Jews make the best rock lyricists. It's that white Christian Americans make the worst.

17

Home Fires

U2 insults phil collins and their parents/ the origins of adam/ spearing the penultimate potato/ the virgin prunes reunite without instruments/ legends of mannix/ an audience with edge's ancestors

U2 ARRIVE BACK in Dublin for the winter in time to do a TV satellite hookup with Los Angeles, where Phil Collins is hosting the televised Billboard Music Awards show. When Collins announces that U2 has won the award for 1991 *Billboard* Number One Rock Artist, he goes to a live satellite feed from a Dublin pub called the Docker, where Adam, Bono, and Edge are drinking Guinness and looking lubricated.

"Well done, lads!" Collins shouts across the waters.

"Hi, Phil," U2 mumbles. It's 1:30 in the morning in Dublin and the locals are still doing double takes at seeing a forty-foot trailer and a twenty-foot satellite dish parked outside the tiny pub.

"Your song 'One' has won the Number One Modern Rock Tracks Artist Award," Collins announces. "Bono, everybody always says you talk. I wonder where's Larry. Is Larry there? Let's give the drummer something."

"Larry isn't here, Phil," Edge tells the drummer-turned-singer. "He's acting a bit funny these days. You know how drummers get weird when they start singing."

"I understand," Collins says, plowing ahead. "The Zoo TV tour is also *Billboard*'s Number One Concert Tour of the Year, meaning more people spent more money to see you guys than anybody else. So if you need an opening act, I'm here, guys. I believe the barman, Paddy, is going to give you the awards."

The white-haired bartender slams down a trophy in front of Adam, who says to the camera, "Phil, Paddy's a very big fan of your music. And so are all our parents."

"I'm not *that* old," Paddy mumbles, causing much of the bar to break up laughing. Collins starts to make a crack about the band being drunk, but Bono interrupts him to smile and say, "It's really great to be home and we've had a great year and everybody spoiled us rotten. So thanks very much, we really appreciate all this."

"We anticipated that you may not be sober at this time of night," Collins says, "so we put together—"

Bono, feeling bad about Adam's insult, interrupts Collins again, this time to answer a ringing phone. "Sorry, Phil, I've George Bush on the phone here. I haven't had a wink's sleep, he's been calling me ever since I got home. We'll find a job for him somewhere."

"Let's roll the clip," Collins says, and a montage of highlights from the Zoo TV tour appears. Along with statistics ("The Zoo TV utilized 4 mega video screens, 4 Philips Vidiwalls, 36 video monitors, 18 projectors, 12 laser disk players . . . 1 satellite dish, 1 channel changer, 1 video confessional, 7 miles of cable. The Zoo TV stage was 248 feet wide and over 80 feet deep with the ramp to the B stage approximately 150 feet long. The set included 11 Trabant cars used as spotlights. The P.A. system included 176 speaker cabinets and the sound system used over a million watts of power and weighed over 30 tons. Zoo TV was seen live by over 3,000,000 people who between them bought over 600,000 T-shirts.") and concert footage, there are snatches of an MTV interview U2 did with Kurt Loder in a studio talking to the four band members on TV monitors.

"One thing about rock & roll stars is they're bigger than life, bigger than the audience, they're almost intimidating," Loder says to the video projections of the band. "Well, this whole set is like that. Isn't that off-putting? Doesn't it kill intimacy?"

"It does, absolutely," Bono agrees. "But you look great."

That cuts to a shot of the Mirrorball Man shouting, "Put your hands on the screen!" There's more concert footage and then back to Loder asking, "Do you think the audience is getting something out of this?"

"Yeah," Larry says. "They're coming to a rock & roll gig *and* watching television. What more can you ask for?"

The people watching the Billboard Awards at home see the people on TV applauding this montage that they just watched on TV. Larry wanted no part of such foolishness. He's taken a seasonal powder. Adam is glad to get home to his mansion on the hill. He lives in a huge house on twenty acres in Rathfarnham, south of Dublin, overlooking the snotty boarding school that expelled him as a teenager. Neil Young reportedly said upon seeing Adam's castle, "That's the *bass* player's house?!" The bass player collects art and sometimes makes his palace available to artist friends to use as a studio. Although he's U2's heartiest partier, Adam has a bucolic side; he doesn't mind being the Laird of Manse Clayton.

"Adam's actually a really down-to-earth, homey guy," his younger brother Sebastian observes. "That's his main fight or disadvantage. He loves rock & roll and living the whole rock star thing, but then again he likes planting an oak tree by himself on a sunny Sunday morning. He's been trying really hard to come to terms with that contradiction. Especially in the last year or two, I think he finds it really hard."

Adam's British family moved to Ireland when his father, a pilot, took a job with Aer Lingus when Adam was five. They settled in Malahide, a beautiful Dublin suburb that still looks and feels like a 1940s village. The Claytons became friendly with another family of U. K. settlers in the town, the Evanses. Young Adam went to primary school with little Dave Evans before he was the Edge. Then the boys were torn apart by the cruel cleaver of boarding school. After Adam was booted out for not giving a rat's ass, he landed back with Dave at Mount Temple school, where he met Larry and Bono.

Bono tells a funny story of going on the bus with sixteen-year-old Adam to break into the boarding school, St. Columba's, after Adam was expelled. Being Protestant, Bono had met some posh people—there were even some at Mount Temple—but not like *this:* he couldn't believe it. They went over the wall and Adam's friend invited them into the dorm. A very proper fellow named Spike reached into the breast pocket of his jacket and produced a brick of hashish. The room was decorated with Hendrix posters and they were saying things like, "Have you heard the new Beck album?" Then they all picked up guitars and strummed through their blissed-out hippie stupor. This, Bono realized listening to them, was where Adam picked up all the technical terms—"gig," "fret," "jamming"—that had so impressed Bono, Edge, and Larry that they figured he was some kind of musical genius and they'd better get him in their band. Bono was stunned to realize that everybody at this place talked like that!

The headmaster found out about Adam's nocturnal reappearance and sent to his parents a polite but subtly threatening letter, which now sits framed above the toilet in Adam's mansion, the mansion that looks down on St. Columba's and whose walks and garden abut the school property and that stands as a glorious middle finger to the faculty that expelled him and a stirring example to all the kids stuck there of at least one alternative to the perpetuation of the British class system that the school by its policies espouses.

The brand St. Columba's left on Adam, his bandmates claim, was the pitiful boarding school habit of standing by the dirty plate bin with a fork waiting to salvage other people's leftovers. Edge says Adam will wait for a spare potato with the vigilance of a hawk and spear it from the garbage. "Even now," Edge insists, "if Adam's walking down a hotel corridor and he sees something sitting on one of the room service trays left outside someone's door, he'll reach down and grab it."

"I've seen him salvage half a hamburger," Bono claims, the air hot with hyperbole, "with another guest's false teeth still in it!"

Among the painters who have used Adam's house as a studio are three artists with an imminent exhibition: Paul Hewson, Fionan Hanvey, and Derek Rowan, who in their teenage years bestowed on each other the names Bono, Gavin Friday, and Guggi. Guggi is an artist by profession and singers Bono and Gavin certainly fancy themselves men of vision worth sharing. They have committed to a joint show at a Dublin gallery in the spring and now they have to slap down some masterpieces to fill it.

In their teens and early twenties Guggi and Gavin led the Virgin Prunes, a theatrical, glitter-inspired experimental rock band that sometimes also drafted Adam, Edge, and Larry into sideman duty, and which featured Edge's older brother Dick Evans on guitar. They often played shows with U2 at Dublin's Project Arts Centre, a gallery/theatrical space run by Jim Sheridan (who has since become a world-class filmmaker with movies such as *My Left Foot*). The confrontation-goosed Prunes wore makeup and dresses and risked getting their heads busted by bottles every time they walked onstage.

It's sometimes been hard for Bono's teenage friends to stay pals with him as U2 have ascended—not because Bono and Ali don't work at it but because the buddies have to put up with the knocks of other nonrich people calling them freeloaders and asking why they're hanging around with that rock star. It takes effort from both sides not to let fame and wealth come between friendships.

Gavin is commanding, outgoing, and always fully awake. He is U2's closest advisor who is not on the Principle payroll. When the band is too buried in work to decide something for themselves they say, "Send it to Gavin."

In his own concerts Gavin uses a thirties cabaret style as a jumping-off point for music that is ironic, assuring, and confrontational, often in the same song. Gavin can puncture his onstage in-your-faceness by suddenly smiling broadly and sticking his mitt out to shake hands with the people down front, but even that sort of jolly gesture takes on an air of threat after he's been howling and pouncing for a while. On his albums (sometimes produced by the recurring Hal Willner) Gavin alternates the irony and playacting with tenderness.

Together now, Gavin, Guggi, and Bono fall into the easy patter of friends who communicate with nods, grunts, and gestures no outsider can fathom. Guggi (who speaks softly and now wears the sort of shoulder-length hippie hair the Prunes died to defeat) allows Bono to wax extensively about his recent meeting with artist Jeff Koons, a post-Warhol provocateur best known for ceramic sculptures of Michael Jackson and his monkey, and heroic busts of himself looking toward heaven with swollen nipples. Once they called it camp, then they called it kitsch, then they stopped calling it. Bono says that Koons is up for getting involved with the second year of Zoo TV and told Bono that U2 was being far more generous in these shows than they were in the past. Bono was surprised by that and wanted to know how the surface-obsessed Zoo TV was more generous than the heart-on-our sleeves U2 shows of old. "He said that in the past we were dictating emotions to the audience, now we're leaving it open for them to decide for themselves what they feel."

Koons's philosophy suggests that with so much of contemporary culture devoted to trying to con some emotional response from people, the most honest art is a glass sculpture of a puppy, or one of those paintings of little waifs with big eyes—because that obvious, corny, simpleminded art that wears its intentions on its sleeve is the only art attempting no subliminal manipulation. After describing Koons's rap

Bono waits for a reaction from Guggi, but all that comes out of his mouth is a stream of smoke. Finally Bono says, "You don't buy that."

Guggi says, "No." Bono and Guggi have been having this argument for years. Bono says art is about ideas and Guggi says no, art is about paint.

It strikes me that as much as Bono brings his "art is about ideas" philosophy to U2, particularly in the band's recent work, all those ideas would mean nothing if the band's art weren't also there *in the paint,* in the music. The emotional directness, the simplicity, that rock & roll got from blues and country is always at the heart of the music's appeal. It only took a few years for people to get used to the sound of basic rock & roll, before its directness began to seem clichéd. So new angles had to be found that surprised the ear and kept the music fresh without corrupting rock's directness. That's how we got the Beatles, who used unusual harmonies to make old rock clichés vivid again. Dylan did it with his lyrics—"Subterranean Homesick Blues" revitalized Chuck Berry and "Like a Rolling Stone," as Phil Spector pointed out, gave a whole new paint job to "La Bamba." From Hendrix to country rock to reggae to the Sex Pistols to *Achtung Baby,* rock & roll has come up with sonic innovations that allow us to hear a simple song as if we have never heard it before. But always, if the song itself is not worth singing, no one will listen. "One" and "Until the End of the World" and "Love Is Blindness" are great songs—the art is in the paint. The *ideas* that make them innovative records are finally important only because they allow us to hear the songs with fresh ears.

Down at the Factory one night Edge and Bono are fiddling with some new music. Ali did let Bono back into the house after Mexico, and gave him until January to normal up. It's no easy assignment. He compared notes with Edge, who had no home to go back to and was anxious for a distraction. They're kicking around ideas for new songs, making cassettes, and getting ambitious about mid-winter recording sessions.

I suggest to Bono one afternoon that if Edge wanted to work because he had no home to go to, it's lucky he had you to call on—the man who never goes home.

"But coming from a very different position," Bono says sharply. "I can leave *my* house because I know it will still be there."

I ask Bono if the journey away from his marriage is what's been motivating Edge to keep working. "I don't know," Bono says uncomfortably. "I think he's trying to figure out what he wants. And I can't imagine what it's like to . . ." Bono pauses and looks at my tape recorder. Then he says, "This is a hard thing to say to a civilian, and to the great outdoors. I hate this idea of hard work. If you asked Edge or any of the others, we don't think we work hard, really. Not compared to a lot of people. But we have a kind of tenacity. We'll hold on to the ankle of something, we won't give in.

"But let's say for the sake of this that it is hard work. To do all that stuff and not have support at home is unfathomable. I don't know how, with the relationship ending, Edge managed to find any energy. And it's fair to say that there were times when he certainly didn't and that wasn't easy for us either. There's definitely periods when people go AWOL and it can last a year. It can last a long time. But by and large I think he managed to keep it together."

One evening Dick Evans, visiting from London where he's finishing his Ph.D., stops by the Factory to collect his brother Edge for dinner and runs into Gavin and Guggi, who are there with Bono. The Virgin Prunes' reunion does not elicit any hugs or handstands. Watching them make small talk it's hard to imagine that this long-haired artist, confident nightclub performer, and quiet academic were ever in a rock band together—but then that's what the folks in Liverpool might be saying today about John, Paul, and George if Brian Epstein hadn't come along.

The reminiscences they share are not of the Prunes or the fledgling U2, but of the colorful characters they recall hanging around the Dublin club scene in the 1970s. They all tell awestruck tales of a tough character we'll call "F," who took the boys under his wing. Described by different witnesses here as a "poet" and an "actor," "F" also looms large in these legends for settling arguments by throwing tables through restaurant windows. Bono and Edge say he won their friendship in the early days when a punk band called the Black Catholics who used to throw bottles at U2 tried to break up a U2 show at the Project Arts Centre. "F" was working the door, and fought to keep the troublemakers out as they tried to push in. Finally from the stage U2 saw "F" vanish outside with the Black Catholics, and heard the sounds of screaming and smashing. (How did they hear the sounds over their amps? I've heard this anecdote more than once and each time the details become more vivid.) Then "F" walked back in happy as a lark. U2 asked him what happened and he produced a long knife and explained, "I acquainted them with the reality of violence."

I ask if this was the same "F" with whom Bono, Edge, and Gavin studied mime. "It was." Edge laughs. " 'F' in tights was something to see."

Dick says he's seen "F" more recently. According to this story Dick and some friends ran into "F," who invited them to drop by his room at the posh Shelbourne Hotel on St. Stephen's Green. They got upstairs and were amazed to see that "F" had a grand penthouse suite on the top floor. The poet must have either sold a sonnet or won the sweepstakes. "F" implored his guests to stay and enjoy some room service. Then he started sending down for champagne. When, after hours of celebration, the guests were tired and tipsy, "F" insisted they all sleep there, plenty of room. Dick woke up the next day feeling a little shaky and went into the bathroom. On the mirror "F" had written, "I'll see you before you see me—'F.' " Dick realized he'd been set up. "F" had left the hotel and told the desk the gentlemen upstairs would settle the bill. Dick and his friends had to sneak out through the service elevator.

"It's funny," Edge's father says. "About twice a year you read in the papers, 'U2 are about to split up.' This makes me laugh, because the people who write that obviously know nothing about them. They did grow up together. They have their differences sometimes, sure, just like any family would. But the rough edges have rubbed off against each other. They are an extended family to each other now and I must say they've stuck to it very well. And they're easy guys to get on with too. They're not all the same; they complement each other. They're a good team."

I've made it out to Malahide to have tea with Garvin and Gwenda Evans, two people who radiate decency and kindness, in spite of having generated both a U2 and a Virgin Prune.

"I don't think I ever did see them," Gwenda says of the Prunes. "They wouldn't tell me where their shows were."

"They'd direct us to the wrong place," Garvin explains.

They paid closer attention to Dave's band. Garvin went down and had a meeting with Paul McGuinness to make sure he was a decent fellow before U2 signed with the manager. (Bono warned his dad not to try doing the same thing.) When Edge finished Mount Temple he asked his parents' permission to delay starting university for one year in order to give U2 a chance. They said okay, and when that year was up U2 had a record deal. At that point Edge told his dad not to worry—even if their first album flopped he could always find work as a session musician.

"I think they were really fortunate to have Island Records and Chris Blackwell," Gwenda says. "He let them develop in their own way. I don't think he put too much pressure on them. The pressure came from their self-motivation. And they have always been hard workers, Dave especially. He was always working on the music."

The downside of this, his parents say, is that when the music stops it's harder on Edge than on the other three.

"It leaves more of a vacuum in Dave," his mother says. "He's perhaps been more wrapped up in it than the others. When Garvin gets very involved in anything he really gets into the nitty-gritty. The very first time we went skiing he bought a book on how to ski, he wanted to know how to distribute the weight. I'm much more instinctive, but I fell down a few times. Garvin really wants to get down and know how everything works, and Dave's the same. I think he does get very involved mentally and he finds it hard to come back down to normal living, for want of a better word. It would be good if he could find a fulfilling hobby or even start playing golf." Mrs. Evans realizes that sounds silly and she laughs.

Mr. Evans, a golfer, doesn't think it's a bad idea: "Why not?"

"I don't think he's reached that stage." She smiles. "But you see, that is one of the snags for the four boys. They have no . . ."

"Anonymity," Mr. Evans says.

"Yes. He's quite good at painting, actually; he likes to sketch. But that's quite a lonely hobby, really. They have to be careful what they choose to do because they are much more well known now."

"I've noticed being in Dave's company that their fame has gone up a quantum jump lately," Mr. Evans says.

"Beforehand they were known to everyone who was involved in rock & roll, fans and young people," Mrs. Evans explains. "But I think it's dawned on the general public as well now. They read all this rubbish in the papers about all the millions they're meant to have."

"We watch things like *Top of the Pops*," Edge's dad says, and he laughs: "No wonder they think U2 is so good!"

*   *   *

After Christmas U2 is polished up and sent off to England to accept a trophy at the Brit Awards. Adam says that it would seem ungrateful not to show up, but they always have to try to impress on this particular ceremony that U2 is not British. This year they are nominated in "international" categories and win the Most Successful Live Act Award.

"When you're in the business of television," Edge says in accepting, "and that is the business we're in at Zoo TV, it all comes down to ratings. Thank you very much."

Bono, splendid in his red crushed-plush suit and goggles, announces, "Never in the history of rock & roll touring has so much bullshit been created for so many by so few. Thank you to the Zoo TV crew and remember, children, taste is the enemy of art."

Adam steps up and says, "We used to think in the eighties that 'less is more.' I think in the nineties we've discovered that more is even more."

"Just one last thing," Larry says, cutting through the guff. "I'd just like to congratulate Greenpeace and its supporters for finally, finally getting Sellafield and putting them on the run. Thank you."

That's not just the wrap-up for 1992. It's the opening bell for 1993.

18

The Saints Are Coming Through

bob dylan on U2/ van morrison on bob dylan/ U2 on van
morrison/ bob dylan on van morrison/ van morrison on U2/
bob dylan plays with van morrison & U2/ van morrison plays
with bob dylan & U2/ dinner & drinks with bob dylan, van
morrison, & U2

WINTER MAY BE long in Ireland, but this one is lit up by the back-to-back arrival of two luminaries. Bob Dylan is playing Dublin's Point Theatre on Friday night and Van Morrison on Saturday. Old hippies are arriving from the hinterlands and aspiring poet mystics are clogging up the pubs. Bono has known both of these legends since 1984 when Dylan played at Dublin's Slane Castle, Van showed up to sit in, and Bono (invited to the show by Dylan) was given the assignment by the crafty editors of *Hot Press*, Dublin's rock magazine, to use his pull to try and score a joint interview with them. The good news was that Bono got the two tight-lipped laureates to actually sit down together in front of the tape recorder. The bad news was that Bono was not interested in playing the prepared reporter and ended up winging it by talking about recording studios while Dylan threw in good-natured comments along the order of: "You got your producer, you got your engineer, you got your assistant engineer, usually your assistant producer, you got a guy carrying the tapes around," and Van sat thinking about Yeats and Lady Gregory and offering no more than an occasional, "I think all the same they'll go back to two-track eventually."

Journalism's loss was the Dublin audience's gain, though, as Dylan invited Bono to join him onstage where, faced with the embarrassing fact that he did not know the words to "Blowin' in the Wind," Bono just made up his own. Dylan got a kick out of that, and if Van did not register enthusiasm, at least he could no longer claim when asked about U2 that he had never heard them.

Later Bono asked Dylan if he played chess. It turned out to be a passion the two singers shared. They sent out for a board but never got a game up. Dylan asked Bono if he knew the music of the McPeaks, an Irish folk group. Bono admitted he'd never paid any attention to traditional music, and Dylan told him that was a mistake: "You've gotta go back." Bono took the advice seriously enough to start checking out Irish folk music, which he later said was the first step on the road to *Rattle and Hum.*

Among musicians Dylan and Morrison continue to be the top birds on that branch of rock that shoots toward the same values the great poets and painters shot for. That branch is certainly literate, somewhat intellectual, but by no means without a foot in the raw and instinctive. Those who perch so high are well aware of who else is up there with them. I once asked Dylan if he felt a special connection with Morrison, and Dylan said, "Oh, yeah! Ever since Them, really. There's been nothing Van's done that hasn't knocked me out." I once asked Morrison to rank Dylan. Morrison—who rhapsodizes in his lyrics about Blake, Donne, Pound, Eliot, and enough other versifiers to sink a syllabus—said, "Dylan is the greatest living poet."

Both Dylan and Morrison are students of old folk, gospel, and blues, both have been through sometimes unsettling spiritual quests, and both have expressed disdain for attempts by their audience to hold them to one style or image. They also both achieved great success while still in their early twenties and then settled young into marriage, family, and periods of semiretirement, only to eventually return to lives of bachelorhood, road work, and travel. Both Dylan and Morrison have written classic rock songs and recorded classic rock records, but neither's career can remotely be contained by even the most generous definition of rock music. They are bigger than the genre, which is pretty big. When Bono met them, they probably represented what he hoped to become.

Around that time Bono told me, "There's got to be a spiritual link between U2 and Van Morrison. I'm sure it's not just that we're both Irish. I think it's something else. He probably wouldn't want to associate himself with our music, 'cause I know he's plugged into a tradition of soul music and gospel. As we're slightly more removed from that tradition, he may not connect with us." Bono went on to say that Van is a soul singer, "And I would aspire to being a soul singer."

I have to add that when I went on to talk to Edge about Van he listened for a while and then asked if I could recommend a good Morrison album for him to start with, his polite way of letting me know that this was not music U2 had grown up with and I should not assume that Morrison had influenced them.

In the decade since that Slane Castle summit U2 has scaled the heights of rock stardom, to the point where putting Bono in a room next to Bob and Van no longer begs someone asking what's wrong with this picture. Bono gets a big kick out of their company. He once watched them get into a friendly contest over who knew the most words to obscure old folk ballads. ("They were impressing the young man with their knowledge," Bono says.) Van would name a song and Bob would recite the lyric. Then Bob would name a song and Van recite it. Finally Van pulled out a ball-buster. He called for "The Banks of the Grand Canal" by Brendan Behan. Dylan stood up and reeled off a dozen verses. Van folded. Bono sat there gob-smacked.

Hanging around artists such as Dylan and Morrison gave U2 the misimpression that they should get as close to country, blues, and R & B roots as those older artists get. Since *Rattle and Hum* U2 have learned that their job is not to go back over ground someone else has already covered but to carry the music to the next place, where some other young band will eventually pick it up and carry it further.

Rattle and Hum contained one song written by Dylan and U2 ("Love Rescue Me"), a second song on which Dylan played organ ("Hawkmoon 269") and a U2 cover of an old Dylan song ("All Along the Watchtower"). I asked Dylan what drew him to U2 that he did not hear in other young bands and he said, "Just more of a thread back to the music that got me inspired and into it. Something which still exists which a group like U2 holds on to. They hold on to a certain tradition. They are actually rooted someplace and they respect that tradition. They work within a certain boundary which has a history to it, and then can do their own thing on top of that. Unless you start someplace you're just kind of inventing something which maybe need not be invented.

"But that's what would draw me to U2. You can tell what groups are seriously connected and"—he laughed—"seriously disconnected. There is a tradition to the whole thing. You're either part of that or not. If you're not, you're just not, but I don't know how anybody can do anything and not be connected someplace back there. You do have to have a commitment. Not just anybody can get up and do it. It takes a lot of time and work and belief."

One night Van and his sidekick Georgie Fame were visiting Bono's house when Van leaned over and with a wink accused Bono of ripping off one of his old hits for the biggest hit on *Rattle and Hum.* "That song of yours, 'Desire,' was just 'Gloria' backwards, wasn't it?"

"No." Bono smiled. "I think it was Bo Diddley, actually."

"Ah, yeah," Van said. "Georgie, remember when that Bo Diddley beat first came over here? Everybody was using it but nobody got it right!" Implying strongly that U2 hadn't either. Bono teased Van back, asking if Van's own much-imitated style might not owe just a bit to Ray Charles.

Lately I've seen Van holding forth in the bar of the Shelbourne Hotel like Marshall Dillon in Dodge City. Somebody should come up and hang a medal on him: Greatest Living Irishman. Morrison left his Belfast home when he was a teenager and has since lived in London, New York, Boston, San Francisco, and London again, slowly working his way back home. Van's been living in Dublin lately, carousing around the town with the Chieftans, Shane McGowan of the Pogues, and another new arrival, tax-exile Jerry Lee Lewis. A motlier crew of musical brigands is hard to imagine.

I think I made Bono feel bad one night while we were contemplating the great men by suggesting that both Dylan and Van might have been drawn to faith in God because after losing their families and after being worshipped like gods themselves, it was the last thing bigger than them that they could turn to. I was indulging in idle speculation, but it really seemed to bother Bono. He's a firm believer in grace and a man with few enough stars to steer by in his own life. After many drinks Bono suggested, "It is a funny thing that even though they're believers, they seem to see God in very much an Old Testament light. There seems to be a lot of judgment there, and maybe not a lot of mercy."

At the Point on Friday night Dylan plays a countryish set with a standup bassist, drummer, and second guitarist. It's a sort of Hank Williams persona for Dylan, after years of wailing electric shows. He performs songs he rarely sings in concert—"She Belongs to Me,"

"Lenny Bruce," "Tangled Up in Blue," and "Everything Is Broken"—as well as the expected "All Along the Watchtower" and "Maggie's Farm." After the concert Bono, McGuinness, and some other local celebrities —Elvis Costello, his wife Cait O'Riordan, country singer Nanci Griffith, and honorary Dubliner Chrissie Hynde—go with Dylan and his entourage to Tosca, Bono's brother Norman's restaurant. Chrissie wants to know what Dylan thinks of heavyweight champ Mike Tyson going to prison for rape. "I think it's a dirty shame, but what do I know?" says Dylan. "There's lots of guys in the joint." This leads to comparisons to Muhammad Ali being stripped of his title because he refused to go into the army during the Vietnam War. Chrissie asks Dylan how he avoided being drafted back in his protest days. "I was in New York," Dylan says. "Nobody bothered about the draft in New York."

Word comes that Morrison's court is in session around the corner at Lillie's Bordello. Dylan sends word inviting Van to come join him here; Van sends back word that Dylan should come join him there. The two kings never do confer.

The next night, though, everyone including Dylan goes to see Van put on an electrifying show, inspired, perhaps, by having Dylan in the house. He goes back to the sixties for "Sweet Thing" and up to the nineties for "Enlightenment" and makes plenty of stops in the decades in between. For the encore Van summons Bono to join him on "Gloria." Bono isn't sure of all the words, but he is annoyed that the audience is sitting in their seats reverently, so he improvises a gospel rant on the theme, "This is not a church—but this is holy ground!" That gets the crowd on their feet and jumping. Van looks over at Bono, impressed.

Van starts summoning the other famous guests from the wings. Edge, having visions of himself banging a tambourine, refuses to go, but Hynde and Costello are there in a flash. Dylan is still looming offstage, hidden under several layers of hooded shirts and coats. Bono goes back and hauls him out, recruiting Elvis and Chrissie to help peel the layers of clothing off Dylan while Van leads them through "It's All Over Now, Baby Blue," a Dylan song that Van recorded in 1966. Celebrities are climbing out of knotholes onto the stage around Morrison now. Who knew Kris Kristofferson was in Dublin? How did Steve Winwood get behind the organ? It is a surreal finale to a remarkable pair of evenings.

Van throws his arm around Bono's shoulder and tells him he did well on "Gloria" with the paternal pride of a dad who's let his sixteen-year-old borrow the family car for the first time and has seen it returned to the garage undented.

There are many beautiful women in the room and Bono is approached by former Miss Ireland Michelle Rocca. Van comes up and tells Bono, "That's *my* girl!" Van starts pointing to all the best-looking women in the room and saying, "And that's my girl, and that's my girl and that's . . ."

Bono is happily drunk, as are most of the other people bellying up to Van's bar tonight, but through the haze he wonders just how important alcohol is to the pursuit of the muse. Most people are delighted when Van has a few drinks, loosening up and shaking off the angry Morrison persona that usually keeps even well-wishers at bay. Who's to say he shouldn't indulge that social impulse? Yet Morrison and Dylan's pursuit of art and faith seems to have taken them up some strange and painful roads. Bono is trying to keep his balance while exploring those roads—trying to get a taste of the journey without falling off the edge of a trail on which the map is always changing. He often dwells on something Dylan told him: "There's only two kinds of music: death music and healing music." Dylan and Van are two decades farther along the road than Bono, and perhaps that much farther away from healing themselves. Maybe Bono is more blessed than they are. Maybe he has less genius. Or maybe we should wait and see where he is in twenty years before making any assumptions.

19

Changing Horses

*death in the family/ the clinton inauguration/ adam and larry
solicit a new singer/ everything don henley doesn't like/
bono and edge at the thalia theatre/ unbuttoning fascism's
fly/ what the president said to the prime minister*

THERE ARE two momentous events set to take place in America
in late January of 1993. Bill Clinton is being sworn in as
president in Washington and U2's farewell dinner for Ellen
Darst is taking place in New York.

Although U2 doesn't feel comfortable accepting as a band an invitation to Clinton's swearing-in, Paul McGuinness and his wife Kathy go
along. At the last minute Adam and Larry decide to join them. They
arrive in Washington and jump into a buzz of parties and get-togethers
between all the guests, entertainers, and dignitaries piling into town for
the ceremony and the balls that follow it. Paul hooks up with some of
his Democratic connections and is having a real good time being a
power broker among power brokers when word reaches him that his
younger brother has died suddenly of heart failure.

Paul, stunned, begins arranging for a flight back to Ireland. It is a
terrible reenactment of a past tragedy. Thirteen years before, when U2
was making their debut album, the young manager flew to America for
his first meeting with Frank Barsalona to discuss the agent taking on
U2. When his plane landed in New York that time, Paul was met with
news that his father had just died of a heart attack. He had to cancel the
meeting with Barsalona and get right back on a plane for Ireland then
too. Both times his family members died, he was off in America attending to business. And to have both die the same way—his younger
brother now, not even forty—must inevitably make Paul wonder if he is
black-marked by heredity. He goes and packs his bag and heads to the

airport. He will miss the presidential inauguration; Ellen's farewell dinner will have to be rescheduled. He will go home to the funeral, and to grieve privately.

Adam and Larry are left on their own, but their celebrity is their pass to various parties. Wherever they go people come up and introduce themselves and invite them someplace else. At one club they run into Michael Stipe and Mike Mills of R.E.M., another half of a band that was involved in voter registration and is here for the inauguration. Stipe tells Adam and Larry that he is going to sing with 10,000 Maniacs at MTV's televised inaugural ball, and he and Mills are thinking of doing an acoustic version of "One"—would Larry and Adam like to play it with them?

Larry and Adam look at each other, hem and haw a little, and explain that they didn't really come to perform. But after about two hours of socializing and celebrating their resistance is worn away and they agree to do it. After all, it's a U2 song. They have Michael to sing, Larry to drum—and two bassists. Mills offers to play guitar. It also seems logistically easier if Larry plays congas rather than a full drum kit. "Make it simple, don't complicate it," Larry says. "There's a large chance we could come across badly, whereas if I have the congas there it won't be too loud, we could get a good mix on the TV." They will get together the next afternoon and rehearse. Now all they need is a name. They combine the title of R.E.M.'s latest album, *Automatic for the People*, with U2's latest to come up with Automatic Baby.

The next morning is beautiful in Washington—sunny and clear. The security is so tight it looks like a war zone, but the mood is so festive—and there are so many souvenir hawkers in the streets—that it feels like a carnival. I make the mistake of waiting a little too long to cross the road to the Capitol for the start of the ceremony and have to elude a cop who tells everyone to hold it, step back behind the ropes, here comes the presidential motorcade. Well, no way am I going to risk being locked out, so I go under the rope and run around the cop and across the street. When I get to the tents that hold the metal detectors you have to pass through on the way into the lawn where the inauguration takes place, I turn around to see if I'm being chased, and instead see rolling past me the side of the presidential limos that the crowd doesn't see. The people gathered behind the rope see Bill Clinton waving out the left rear window of the limo. I see George Bush in the right. The people behind the rope see Al Gore smiling and giving them the thumbs up. I see a dejected Dan Quayle leaning his head against the window, staring sadly into space.

The ceremony is genuinely moving. A podium crowded with the top officials of the U.S. government and visiting dignitaries sits beneath the Capitol dome, which is itself illuminated by a bright winter sun. Maybe it's just the pageantry, maybe it's associations with childhood, but I am more choked up than when they shot Old Yeller.

Bono, watching on TV, is taken with the Reverend Billy Graham's invocation and with the poem read by Maya Angelou in which the ground of America cries out for the people standing on it to study war no more and learn the song the Creator taught the land "before cynicism was a bloody sear across your brow."

Bono had actually summoned the nerve to send Clinton a letter elucidating his theory about the need for the new president to make a speech of expiation. Clinton's aides called and said that Bill had loved the letter and might want to quote from it, but that doesn't happen. Bono supposed it was not possible for the president to make the sort of public act of contrition Bono suggested; it would just lead to people saying, "You want to make it up to the Indian? Okay, give back the land." But watching the speeches on TV in Europe, Bono feels that Graham and Angelou make the important points.

Graham says in his invocation, "We cannot say we are a righteous people, for we are not. We have sinned against You. We have sown to the wind and are now reaping the whirlwind of crime, drug abuse, racism, immorality, and social injustice. We need to repent of our sins and to turn by faith to You."

After taking his oath of office Clinton gives an address that deals with the end of the old world ("I thank the millions of men and women whose steadfastness and sacrifice triumphed over depression, fascism, and communism. Today a generation raised in the shadows of the Cold War assumes new responsibilities in a world warmed by the sunshine of freedom but threatened still by ancient hatreds and new plagues") and the birth of the new ("Communications and commerce are global, investment is mobile, technology is almost magical, and ambition for a better life is now universal. . . . Profound and powerful forces are shaking and remaking our world. And the urgent question of our time is whether we can make change our friend and not our enemy.")

When the inauguration ends there is a lot of milling about on the lawn, as if people aren't quite prepared to leave the field. "What struck me about it," the usually cynical Larry says, "and I think it happens at all inaugurations, was that there was a great deal of emotion. I think particularly this time around because there was a very large black presence. There was a real sense of change. I noticed a lot of older people were incredibly emotional, there were tears. I'm not used to it. I know nothing about how the systems work. But from an observer's point of view it was something I won't forget. There are people here who really believe that this is going to change things. When he was sworn in there were tears running down people's faces. It was quite touching." He pauses and says, "There was something there. I really felt that."

Larry still has ambiguous feelings, though, about U2's strange embrace of Clinton during the campaign, and mocking of George Bush during the American concerts.

"I wasn't sure if it was something we should be involved with," he says. "There were differing opinions in the band about being involved at all, about using George Bush. I was a little concerned about that. I'm naturally cautious. I'm still unsure whether it was the right thing to do. I enjoyed the ride, it was very interesting to see it from a different perspective. Meeting Bill Clinton was good. He came across like he still comes across. He seems to be an all right guy. But I'm not living in America. I don't have to live under his administration's policies. That's why I was worried about it. *We don't live here.* Are we endorsing him? What exactly are we doing? And the truth is, it was an ambiguous gesture. We weren't officially endorsing him and yet on the other hand we were saying, *Yeah, he's all right.*"

"And making fun of Bush," I remind him.

"Yeah," Larry says. "It was all a bit odd."

"I'm very suspicious of a U.S. president who hangs out with rock stars," Adam says. "But at the time Clinton didn't *know* he was going to be president. It's great he could do that and be elected. The old men of Russia and England and China never could. The colorful leaders of Europe always did and always will."

Walking around the Capitol as the crowd disperses, there is a sudden whoosh of wind as a marine helicopter rises up into the air. There in the window, looking down and waving, is George Bush being carried away.

As the day progresses the festivities devolve from the profound to the silly. My two favorites are watching inaugural guests go wild over actor Henry Winkler ("Fonzie! Hi, Fonzie! Sign this for me, Fonzie!") and the chanting that accompanies the President and Mrs. Clinton as they walk the last leg of their long parade route from the Capitol to their reviewing stand across from the White House. When the people in the exclusive bleachers set up just beyond the president's stand realize that he is going to take his seat without greeting them, they all chant, "One more block! One more block!" Bill and Hillary hear them and come over to do the big wave and smile and Presidential Point. They have this last one down; Bill touches Hillary's shoulder, whispers in her ear and points toward different spots in the guest stands and then she lights up and waves to that spot, as if they have just noticed the Most Important Guest of All. They do this about every thirty seconds.

After the parade the Clintons get dolled up for the inaugural balls. By the time they arrive and greet the crowd at the MTV party Adam, Larry, Mike, and Michael have "One" down so tight that Bono had better be careful he's not put out to pasture. The MTV people are mighty excited by this coup, and it is clear that this one-night-only, half-and-half supergroup should close the evening with their single song. The only unpleasant question that is raised is, who's going to tell Don Henley, the announced show-closer, that someone else is going to follow him? It's like the Amnesty tour all over again!

Now, you might think this is not a big deal. You might say: *So Henley does his whole inaugural set as planned and then the other guys come out as a little encore and sing "One"—what's the problem?* The problem is that Don Henley may be a great singer and a fine songwriter and a good-looking drummer, but Don Henley is not an easygoing guy. He has been known to fume and fester because the hotel maid hung the toilet paper with the flap out instead of in. He is, to put it politely, a perfectionist. He does not, to put it gently, suffer fools gladly. He was, to put in karmically, in another life the high school gym teacher who made the whole class stay after until the fat kid climbed to the top of the rope.

Tonight Henley, the former voice of the Eagles, seems to be taking his gig so seriously that one suspects he may be under the impression that his performance at the MTV inaugural ball will determine whether or not Clinton appoints him Chief Justice. He has prepared a sort of musical social studies lecture for the young people, climaxing with a performance of Leonard Cohen's "Democracy." Tom Freston, MTV's likable CEO, is told by his minions that as the boss he has the ugly job of telling Henley that this R.E.M./U2 supergroup is going to close the show.

I wouldn't want to be in Freston's shoes! A few years ago I drove with Henley from Cincinnati to Detroit and I remember him shaking his head about some of the new things in the music world that he *just didn't get* (by which I think he really meant he *just didn't like*): one of them was U2 and another was R.E.M. and a third was MTV.

Freston goes up to Henley and says, look, Don. You do your whole set, close the show, then after the applause ends these other guys'll come out and do "One" as a sign-off.

Henley goes pale—he looks shaken. He reminds Freston that *he* is supposed to close the show. Then he turns, goes into his dressing room, and shuts the door. Freston is left staring at the closed door wondering if he should knock, when someone comes up, hands him a portable phone, and says he has a call. Freston says hello and gets an earful of Irving Azoff, Henley's powerful manager, telling him he's made a big mistake and now Don's not going to go on. While Freston is saying *Oh, come on* and trying to deal with this he hears a voice announcing, "The Vice President of the United States and Mrs. Gore!" and suddenly MTV employees are tugging at Freston's coat shouting that *He has to go up and greet the Gores right now.* Freston is trying to explain his situation to Azoff, saying, "Irving, I gotta call you back, the Vice President is here," and Azoff is demanding to know who's more important, the Vice President or Irving, and the MTV staffers are yanking Freston toward the grinning Gores and *click* Freston hears Azoff hanging up on him.

So Automatic Baby go on before Don Henley, and perform "One" as beautifully as it's ever been done. When that song appeared in the studio in Berlin it seemed almost like a gift telling the struggling members of U2 that they could trust each other and lay down their arms. Later, it became the centerpiece of an album about the struggles within a marriage. As an AIDS benefit single, it spoke of the possibility of conciliation between those who hate gays and the victims of that hatred. It was the song that led Axl Rose to U2's perspective and that reunited David Wojnarowicz with his family just before his death.

During the making of the video at Nell's in New York, "One" was a source of silliness and laughter. But tonight, at the televised inaugural ball, when Stipe sings, "We're one but we're not the same, we get to carry each other," he is using the song to try—however hopelessly—to plead a case and make a promise to this whole country.

That's a lot of weight for a song to carry! "One" is a pretty strong song.

While one half of U2 is playing it to celebrate democracy in America, the other half is playing it to ward off fascism in Europe. Bono and Edge, accompanied by the Indian violinist Shankar, are singing "One" at the Thalia Theatre in Hamburg, Germany.

They have been invited by Vanessa Redgrave, the actress and activist, to perform in an antifascist evening at the Thalia. Also there is author Günter Grass, actor Harvey Keitel, Native American poet/activist John Trudell (who declares, "As far as I'm concerned, when Christopher Columbus came to America he was wearing a Nazi uniform"), old pal Kris Kristofferson, and director Robert Wilson, who is in Hamburg staging a new version of *The Black Rider* with book by William Burroughs and songs by Tom Waits.

Bono goes to see *The Black Rider*, also at the Thalia, and for all the effort of following the German translations of American writers, the creepiness of the supernatural German folktale comes across. In the story a young man must pass a marksmanship test in order to marry the head forrester's daughter. The devil offers to help the kid out by giving him magic bullets guaranteed to hit anything he aims at—except for one bullet, which will hit the devil's secret target. The young man makes the deal, and the devil's bullet kills his fiancée (what black heart decided Burroughs should adapt this story?). Actor Dominique Horwitz plays the devil—called Pegleg—as a grinning, cloven-hoofed smoothie, more like a German cabaret performer than a traditional Mephistopheles. The show ends with Pegleg alone onstage in a tuxedo, singing Waits's sentimental "The Last Rose of Summer" like a nightclub entertainer.

A different sort of devil haunts the Thalia's antifascist evening, where Bono makes a speech about the dangers of creeping Nazism in the new Europe: "We are united not just because we are antifascist, not just because mostly we're Europeans, but because as artists, filmmakers, writers, we all work in the realm of imagination and know that is our best weapon. I suggest that it is our failure to imagine both in art and other spheres that has allowed this latest movement to the far right to take place.

"The inability to put ourselves in another's shoes is the core of intolerance. In his novel *The Book of Evidence*, Irish author John Banville's narrator and murderer confesses to the unforgivable crime of having failed to imagine what it was like to be his victim. 'I could kill her,' he says, 'because for me she was not alive.' If we want to challenge hatred, emphatic imagination is central.

"As survivors of the Holocaust both Hannah Arendt and Primo Levi implored us 'to tell our stories.' And we must, not just to make real the oppressed and the oppressor. Not just to break down the idea of separateness, that we understand each other better. Not just so we don't forget! We tell our stories to put flesh and blood on *new* ideas—and to play them out, as the company of the Thalia Theatre has done for one hundred fifty years now with such wit and style. To them I would like to say thank you.

"We need to paint pictures and see them move. I think of the still frames of Helmut Hartzfeld, who changed his name to John Hartfield in protest against the original Nazis. I think of Berlin dadaists whose movement unzipped the starched trousers of the fascists, exposing them as serious—painfully serious—dickheads. Close to the poison you'll find the cure. As well as an antidote, humor, laughter is the evidence of freedom. I think of Günter Grass's black, black comedy *The Call of the Toad*, or Volker Schlondorff's film of Grass's novel *The Tin Drum*. It was from a Mel Brooks movie called *The Producers* that U2 took the name of their last album. In the bizarre musical an S.S. officer is met with the greeting, 'Achtung, baby!' to which he replies, 'Ze führer would never say *baby!*' Quite right. The führer would never say *baby*. We are writers, artists, actors, scientists. I wish we were comedians. We would probably have more effect. 'Mock the devil and he will flee from thee.' 'Fear of the devil leads to devil worship.' Anyway, for all this: imagination. To tell our stories, to play them out, to paint pictures, moving and still, but above all *to glimpse another way of being*. Because as much as we need to describe the kind of world we do live in, we need to *dream up the kind of world we want to live in*. In the case of a rock & roll band that is to dream out loud, at high volume, to turn it up to eleven. Because we have fallen asleep in the comfort of our freedom.

"Rock & roll is for some of us a kind of alarm clock. It wakes us up to dream! It has stopped me from becoming cynical in cynical times. Surely it is the inherited cynicism of our political and economic thinking that contributes so much to the despair of the 1990s.

"The fascists at least recognize the void, their pseudostrong leadership a reaction to what feels like *no* leadership, their simplistic rascist analysis as to what ails the economy and why there is so much unemployment a reaction to our government's gobbledygook, which even the smartest among us cannot understand. . . .

"Fascism is about control. They know what we won't admit: that things are out of control. We started this century with so many competing ideas as to how we should live together. We end it with so few.

"The machismo—and it is machismo—of the New Right has much to do with the impotence of an electorate who feel they have only one real choice anyway. It has much to do with a consumer society that equates manhood with spending power. *Maleness* is an elusive notion, distorted but made accessible and concrete by the Nazis. We shouldn't underestimate this. The fascists feed off youth culture and if we are to overcome them we must understand their sex appeal. And what is our appeal? The neo-Nazis have a perverted idealism, but do we have any idealism left? What is the ground we stand on politically? Economically? Spiritually?

"I don't know, but I know that in the history books democracy is the oddity.

"Democracy is a fragile thing and though the Greeks invented it, they never could live it. The Judeo-Christian idea that all men are equal in God's eyes has been suppressed everywhere. It has raised its peculiar head. Obviously this is not a German problem. In fact, we look to a people who have survived not one but two totalitarian regimes in the last sixty years. The hundreds and thousands who took part in the candlelight marches all over this country last month sent a signal to the rest of us that Germany 'will not let it happen again.' But for that you need our support, because while it is fine to fight darkness with light, it is better to make the light brighter.

"I would like to thank Vanessa Redgrave and thank you for listening. Good night."

Back in Ireland, the newspapers report that when Prime Minister Albert Reynolds was introduced to President Clinton, the President told him that "that wonderful group U2" played a big part in getting him elected. Bono is startled when he hears this. Either Clinton is giving the band more credit than they deserve, or he's using U2 as shorthand for the whole Rock the Vote registration drive, or he's taking his introduction to the Irish leader as an occasion to demonstrate an ability to speak in blarney. The newspapers say Clinton told Reynolds that he had been trying to figure out Bono's last name. "After an hour with him I realized he didn't have one, but it didn't matter."

20

Approaching Naomi

the darst dinner/ bono hosts the dating game/ love in the air/ the grammy awards/ two good reasons to resent eric clapton/ a quaker wedding

THE RESCHEDULED Ellen Darst farewell dinner is held at the Water Club, a restaurant on New York's East River, in February, one month after the original was canceled because of the death in Paul's family. Adam says he reckons it will be a year before Paul can get over the shock of his brother's death, but the manager is being a sociable host during the cocktail hour this evening. Adam's here and Larry's here. Edge cannot attend—he is deep into a recording project that is being called an EP but may expand to become a film soundtrack, part of a U2 interactive project, or anything else one can do with the music Edge hears running through his hatted head.

That means, as everyone sits down to eat, that the only person missing is Bono. Word has come that the well-organized singer missed his flight and will be along eventually. Meanwhile the guests find seats and tie on the feed bags. Adam recalls what Ellen brought to the infant U2 when they set foot in America for the first time. "Ellen was always a great communicator," Adam says. "She'd explain to us *why* we were going to this radio station, why that record shop, why we were meeting this person. She brought that influence to the organization and it continues." Adam points out that a big part of the bad feelings in Berlin making *Achtung Baby* came from forgetting Ellen's rule.

As mentioned earlier, Ellen also brought to U2 an inclination to put women in charge of running their operations. I ask Adam if there is a specific reason they stick to that and he says, "They're the only women we get to meet!" When we get done laughing he says, "I suppose we've always felt very uncomfortable around men who are part of that rock &

roll culture, that macho thing. A lot of men in rock & roll tend to be overdramatic. They act like queens, regardless of their heterosexuality. They seem to be hysterical, rather than just happy to work away at something. And I think it's a need for female contact within our world. It's a very male-dominated world and we don't feel comfortable with that."

As I scrape my soup bowl it occurs to me that Ellen's greatest gift to U2 was to make every disc jockey, journalist, and rack jobber feel that he or she had discovered the band. She is the proof that there's no limit to what you can accomplish if you don't care who gets the credit. Paul announces that like all such U2 functions this will be conducted as "a Quaker wedding," which means anyone might be called on at any time to get up and make a speech.

The soup is just being cleared when a great commotion starts hub-bubing back at the door and rolling through the room like one of those cartoon balls of dust, shoes, and mayhem. It's Bono, racing through the restaurant, dragging behind him Naomi Campbell, the twenty-two-year-old top fashion model in the world and icon of Adam Clayton's dreams. Bono is grinning like a maniac as he hauls the somewhat confused-looking Naomi up to the head table, kisses Ellen on the cheek, and plops into a chair while dropping his surprise date into the seat next to him.

Adam looks like an adolescent boy would if the pinup on his bed-room wall had just come to life. His unrequited crush on Naomi is a running joke around Principle. In the U2 tour program each member of the band is asked what he wishes for that he doesn't have. Adam's listed choice is "Naomi Campbell." He has been inviting her to U2 concerts as long as he's known about her. She actually showed up at Giants Stadium last summer but Adam was tongue-tied and she seemed disinterested. Later, after Bono did the Vogue cover shoot with her pal and fellow famous model Christy Turlington, Christy brought Naomi along to a post-Brit Awards get-together at McGuinness's London apartment. Adam was flabbergasted when Christy brought Naomi over to say hi to him, but he says he chatted so blandly that they lost interest and walked away. I doubt that's quite what happened, but the way he tells it makes clear this woman's ability to raise in Adam the sunken hull of a thirteen-year-old.

After making chitchat for a few minutes Bono asks Adam if he'd mind swapping seats so that Bono and Larry can finish a private discussion. Before Larry can say, "*What* private . . . ?" Bono is finishing Adam's dinner and Adam is next to Naomi.

As the new couple chat Bono leans over, wet with glee and perspiration, and says in a low voice, "I almost couldn't get on a plane to come here! I got scared about the flight, I don't know what it was. So unlike me, I must say. I've been so relaxed lately, so happy with my family. It was very, very hard to get on that plane today and step back into it all. I think maybe that's why I got the anxiety about the flight. Maybe that's what was really going on.

"But I got it together and went to London to get a later flight. And on this flight I met Naomi Campbell! Now Adam's got a thing for her. So I said to myself, 'I must get her here for Adam!' "

I'm getting nostalgic for the night ten years ago when Bono and Adam did the same sort of musical chairs routine in order to make sure that the woman I had a crush on (also a Ford model just in from London on the Concorde, come to think of it; also with Keryn Kaplan sitting across from us winking like she's winking now) had to sit next to me all evening. The next night as I was walking home from my first date with her, U2 pulled up in their tour bus to ask me how it went! It went great. We got married and she's here with me tonight as Adam takes a turn with the glass slipper. If this singing thing ever runs out of steam Bono could certainly host *The Dating Game.*

Paul gets up to begin the speeches. A presidential seal, probably swiped from the inauguration, is hung on the podium, altered to read IN E.D. WE TRUST. McGuinness makes a generous toast in which he says he learned all about the music business from Ellen Darst and he envies Elektra Records the talent they've gained. Then he asks Bono to come up and say a few words.

"Bow your heads," Bono begins. "The reason I don't have a speech," he explains, "is 'cause I spent the whole plane ride trying to set up a date for the bass player." Everyone laughs and Bono points to the two empty seats where Adam and Naomi have disappeared. "And it must have worked—he's split the party!"

Bono goes on to give a beautiful speech in which he refers to the death of Paul's brother and how last month what was to have been an occasion for celebration instead became a time of mourning. He says that whenever you go to a wedding you relive your own wedding, and whenever you go to a funeral you bury your own people again. Bono says his own dad didn't encourage him much, maybe to save him from being disappointed. And his way of rebelling has been to prove he can go out and win the love of the whole world. But it's a funny need for compensation, Bono says, that makes you need fifty thousand screaming people telling you they love you in order for you to feel normal. Through the years the approval he's sought most has been the approval of the band, and the approval of Paul and Ellen. He felt from his first days traveling in America with Ellen that if he had that he really had something.

Adam, meanwhile, is out in the moonlight pitching woo (and if you've ever gotten hit with a faceful of woo out there by the FDR Drive you know how romantic that can be). It turns out that he and Naomi are both flying to L.A. for the Grammy Awards the next day. Bad news is, they're on different flights. Worse news is, they both have dates; Adam's going with Larry, Naomi's going with a prominent guitar player.

They spend the whole night talking. In the early hours Adam drops her off at her door with a peck on the cheek and, he notes, no "Come in for coffee." The next afternoon Adam picks up his hotel phone messages and there's one from Naomi Campbell: "Ring me; I've missed my flight. I'm on the same flight as you." Adam leaps to the phone like a hyena on a gazelle and calls his dream girl.

"I'm going to be on your flight," Naomi tells him. "If you get to the airport before me, will you save a seat for me? And I'll do the same for you."

Hubba, as the poet said, hubba. Adam says okay and then spends more energy than a nervous dervish trying to get the deliberate Larry Mullen moving so they can get to the airport on time. (I'll bet I don't have to tell you that they end up arriving late, wondering if they're even going to make the plane.)

When they walk into the flight lounge Adam is surprised to find a bunch of airline personnel making the sort of fuss over him that usually ends with his hands cuffed behind his back.

"Are you Mr. Clayton?"

"Yeah."

"Miss Campbell's on the plane! She has a seat for you! She wants us to bring you straight down!"

"This is pretty strange." Adam smiles as he's escorted off while Larry stares after him with a look that asks, *What's he got that I haven't got?*

Adam is whisked down the shute and into the first-class cabin where the couple are reunited like Rhett and Scarlett. On the flight to California Adam and Naomi chat and hold hands and fall asleep on each other's shoulders. And when they wake up, they kiss.

Dropping into L.A. they say their sad good-byes—they won't meet again this trip; she has to stick with her date. The U2's get to their hotel and get about their business, representing the band at the Grammy Awards where *Achtung Baby* is nominated in several categories, including Album of the Year.

As soon as they get to the Grammys Adam and Larry regret coming. They'd forgotten how uncomfortable they were with the frenzied showbiz schmoozing at the Grammys when *Joshua Tree* won. Adam had actually slipped out of that ceremony early, after being blindsided by the haste with which the winners were shuffled from their acceptance speech to a series of backstage promotional duties and photo opportunities. Adam bolted and went back to his hotel. Tonight he remembers why.

"I don't have a problem with awards of merit going to whomever they are deeming whatever it is worthy of recognition," Adam says. "But there is so much puffing up of the chest that the Grammys are in some way a significant artistic achievement, which I find offensive. It's stupid to deny the effect of a good performance at the Grammys, but you're not really going along as an artist—you're going along as a performer, as a press item, as a piece of television. And that's really the worst way in which to receive something that is about the merit of your work. For us the balance is the wrong way."

You know that if an occasion like this is annoying the easygoing Adam, it's wreaking havoc with the bullshit-hating Larry. His verdict is, he will not only never go to the Grammys again, he will never *vote* in the Grammys again.

Arrested Development go up to collect an award that, Adam notes, was great when it happened last year, but why must they win again for the same album? Producer of the year goes to Daniel Lanois for *Achtung Baby*. There's an ironic postscript to that prolonged tooth-pull of a recording project. Those are about the only awards tonight that are *not* going to Eric Clapton, who wins a pile of trophies for "Tears in Heaven," his moving tribute to his five-year-old son who died. Clapton is visibly embarrassed that the Hollywood community seems to be trying to assuage his grief by giving him the Grammy in every category for which he's eligible. By the time the biggest award, Album of the Year comes up, Clapton has already won six others.

The envelope please—the Album of the Year Grammy goes not to *Achtung Baby* but to Eric Clapton's *Unplugged.* Clapton himself, staggering under the weight of his seven trophies, is generous enough to say in his acceptance that *Unplugged* was not the best album of the year. That's not news to Larry Mullen, who can't wait to wash the stain of this outhouse off the seat of his pants.

Adam doesn't care. He only has eyes for Clapton's date. Naomi Campbell.

When he gets back to Dublin Adam inaugurates a series of long, late-night telephone calls to Naomi. Their friendship grows without their ever seeing each other. Were he free to do so, Adam would be flying to her side like Jonathan Seagull, but that maniacal Mitch Miller lookalike, the Edge, has the whole band chained to the makeshift studio set up in the Factory and isn't letting anyone out. Phone calls are all the young romantics have.

Bono has a theory about all this; he figures fashion models are the 1990s equivalent of silent movie stars. We see them but never hear them, so we can project onto them whatever qualities we want. Adam is having the opposite problem—he hears his but never sees her.

Naomi is a very famous woman, and she's famous in all the places U2 knows little about—the tabloid press and scandal sheets and super-market checkout papers. There are always stories about her stormy relationship with Robert De Niro or Mike Tyson or whoever they've decided she's seeing this week, and true or not, these papers need to keep the stories coming. So inevitably, rumors begin to appear in print that the British bombshell has taken up with the bass player in U2, having met him at the Grammy Awards while she was supposed to be comforting the grieving Eric Clapton.

21

Elixir Vitae!

---

*adam rumbles the rafters/ the album that dares not speak its
name/ suzy doyle dreams of walkie-talkies/ abba vs. the bee
gees/ prof. eno's philosophy lesson*

A T THE FACTORY in Dublin there is a little alcove with a couch, a
desk, and a refrigerator in the corridor between the big room
where U2 rehearses and the sitting room where U2 relaxes,
holds meetings, and goes through their mail. Today that alcove is shuddering to the deep vibrations coming from Adam Clayton's bass amp,
which due to some trick of acoustics rumbles in here far louder than it
does in the rehearsal room where Adam is actually playing it.

Suzanne Doyle, the striking young woman who coordinates U2's
transportation on the road, has set up a makeshift office and is trying to
juggle schedules, phones, and faxes while the big bass notes shake her
nerves and rattle her brains.

"Is your head floating?" Suzanne calls to me over the throb as I come
in and hang up my raincoat.

"Yeah!"

"Well, you ain't seen nothin' yet!"

Someone has torn out a newspaper headline and stuck it on the wall:
WHY ARE YOU ALWAYS FEELING SO TIRED? The subhead contains a
misprint for the word *sun:* "It's all to do with the time of year and lack
of sin."

Suzanne goes back to her work only to have a particularly strong
musical statement shake the wall and her chair. "I'll probably never have
children," she sighs. Suzanne was a Dublin teenager when she went to
work for Anne-Louise Kelly at Principle during the *Joshua Tree* tour in
1987. She looked like the pretty blond colleen in some Irish fairytale,
but quickly showed herself to be quick and competent and ended up on

the road with the band as assistant to tour manager Dennis Sheehan. She left the U2 organization after the Love Town tour in 1989, staying on in Australia for a year. She eventually returned to Ireland to go to college. When the Zoo TV tour began U2 talked her into coming back with expanded authority.

On the road with U2 it is always a kick to see the reaction of the police and security agents of different countries when Suzanne climbs out of the tour bus with her walkie-talkie and starts giving orders for this airport gate to be opened or that row of cars to be moved. It is a culture shock for some of them to realize that this little girl is really in charge of moving this big operation, and that she knows exactly what she's doing and expects the people she deals with to perform up to her standards. Watching Suzanne deal with border guards or customs agents, you sometimes see condescension turn to confusion turn to surprised respect with remarkable speed. You also see airport gates swing open and rows of cars get moved.

Not that exerting all that authority takes no toll. When Suzanne returned to Ireland from Mexico at the end of the first half of the tour she went to stay with her mother for a few days. The first night Mrs. Doyle was startled to find her daughter sleepwalking around the house, holding her right hand to her cheek and mumbling orders into an imaginary walkie-talkie.

Suzanne's walls stop shaking and a minute later Adam comes through the door. He heads to the refrigerator and pulls out a squat little bottle of a health food drink called Purdey's Elixir Vitae. Adam claims it tastes likes roots and bark, but is better than drinking Coke all day. Edge thinks they should call U2's next album *Elixir Vitae*. Adam goes into the sitting room where he has another bass amp set up and begins rumbling again, this time more quietly, as he tries to come up with a part. His playing starts slowly and awkwardly, but keeps shifting around until it falls into a hypnotic throb, a sort of staggered heartbeat.

Edge's guitar comes through the wall on the other side. He cannot hear Adam; he is playing in the control room that overlooks the big rehearsal hall. Edge is strumming trance music, trying out some elec-tronic effects. In the alcove between the two rooms where Adam and Edge are playing, the two sounds begin to weave around each other. They are in tune, nearly in time. Hearing Adam's thick, dub-inflected bass cross over with Edge's shimmering guitar I realize that even when these two players cannot hear each other, the combination of their musical inclinations produces the sound of U2.

Before long Edge and Adam have found what they were looking for. Bono arrives in the alcove and U2 are ready to get to work. They send someone to round up Larry, who has wandered off. A few minutes later Larry strolls in in a cocky mood, asking, "What's so important you had to interrupt a perfectly good crap?"

"We need you to do some drumming," Bono answers.

Larry says, "Call my manager."

"We sent a letter to Mr. Paul McGuinness," Edge says, "requesting your services this week to play some drums."

"It's the song we were playing last night," Bono says. "Apparently you did a tremendous job, but the rest of us . . ."

Adam says, "Amazingly enough, *you* were fine."

"We face a problem we have faced in the past," Bono explains. "The song has no chorus."

"Aha!" Larry says.

"So," Bono continues, "we have to go in now and come up with one."

The four members of U2 go into the big room, pick up their instruments, and start playing. Producer Brian Eno stands near them swigging Elixir Vitae. The song they are working on is called (at least for today) "Big City, Bright Lights." As they jam on it, Bono makes up lyrics about coffee stains, ghosts, and streets.

At the mixing console in the control room a little red light goes off in the head of the man called Flood, another producer of this project. *Streets* is one of the words on Flood's list of forbidden rock song clichés, along with, for example *night, magic,* and *secret.* Flood figures fresh thinking starts with the little things. While Eno, Bono, and Edge will debate musical and lyrical ideas endlessly, Flood scores his points by attrition. He sits quietly while the others talk themselves out and then does what he had planned to do all along and waits to see if they notice.

Bono stops the song and suggests a chord change to Edge. U2 begins playing again. Bono tries pushing his voice two octaves higher, which makes the performance edgier. He improvises lyrics: "Think about forever . . . think about the rain . . . desperate sea. Jacob's ladder rescue me."

There is a great deal of speculation afoot in the outside world about just what U2 is doing in here. What was supposed to be a four-month break between tour '92 and tour '93 has turned into a marathon recording session. There has been vague talk of coming up with an EP, four or five songs to release with the summer tour of Europe. But everyone's working much too hard for that. There has been a lot of suggestion that they are recording a film soundtrack, though there is no actual film. Nobody wants to say out loud that U2 might be making their next album here, because there is only a small amount of time and nobody wants to put more pressure on the band. Ask Edge why no one will say the "A" word and he'll give you a lot of double-talk about the subtle distinctions between albums and soundtracks and projects, between songs and tracks and "vibes." Ask Adam and he'll be more straightforward: "I don't know if what we're doing here is the next U2 album or a bunch of rough sketches that in two years will turn into the demos for the next U2 album."

The idea of working through their vacation time seems to have taken hold when Edge got antsy coming home to face an empty house and the reality of the end of his marriage. He needed something to do to maintain the energy he had built up making *Achtung Baby* and touring for a year—and to keep his mind off his personal loss. Bono was going nuts hanging around his home while still in full tourhead. As he knew U2 had almost a whole other year of roadwork ahead of them, he was not prepared to begin the psychological downshifting that usually allows him to ease back into domestic life.

So when Edge wanted to get into the studio and do some recording, Bono was quick to sign on. Eno and Flood agreed to come in and see what U2 could come up with this time. The band is back to their original method of songwriting—the four of them getting into a room and jamming until a song emerges. Eno or Edge then go through the tapes, finding sections they like and editing them together into proper song form. Then the band listens, suggests alterations, and tries coming up with words and melodies to go on top of the edited tracks. Bono or Edge will then sing these lyrical and melodic ideas into a Walkman while the track plays. When a song has taken shape that way, U2 listens to the tape, goes back into the studio, and tries to play it.

Eno has, with professorial organization, set up an eraseable poster board on a tripod in the studio. On it is written, along with the musical symbols for sharps and flats:

CYCLE

HOLD
STOP
CHANGE
CHANGE BACK

A B C D E F G

Sometimes Eno likes to stand at this board with a pointer while U2 plays, directing when he wants them to go to the next section or change to a different chord. It's actually a workable system, but watching the thin, bald Eno use his board and pointer to direct a rock band is hilarious, like Ichabod Crane conducting the Rolling Stones. I am reminded of the old Three Stooges episode in which Curly is mistaken for a professor at a women's college. He puts on a mortarboard and black robe, grabs a pointer, and teaches the coeds to sing "B-I-bee, B-O-Bo" while he dances around the classroom. I keep expecting Eno to drop his pedagogical demeanor and yell, "Swing it!"

U2 start another song. Sam O'Sullivan, Larry's drum tech, runs into the control room to ask Flood what this one's called. "If God Will Send His Angels," Flood says. Sam rapidly flips through a stack of papers and says, "We don't have a tempo for this!"

"It used to be called 'Wake Up, Dead Man,'" Flood says calmly. "One twenty-eight will do fine. One-twenty-eight or one twenty-seven." Each song U2 plays has its tempo set by an electronic timekeeper, a click track, that not only holds the rhythm steady but allows the group to go back later and edit together sections from different parts of the song, or even from different takes. When they perform the songs on-stage Larry has the option of using those clicks to find his place or set the pace. He decided years ago that he hated having a *tick tick tick* coming through his headphones on stage, so he instead had the sound of a metronomic shaker or maraca fed softly through his monitor. It sounds more musical, it's unobtrusive, and if a bit of it gets picked up by the microphones it actually adds a subtle color to the sound. In the studio, though, he has to use the headphones and click track—which after eight or nine hours leaves him with a blinding headache.

The band is not sure if the tempo Flood called for is the best speed for "If God Will Send His Angels." They try playing it slowly, they try it faster, they try it too fast. "If God Will Send His Angels" goes from the stately pace of U2's "Walk to the Water" to the energetic plod of Iron Butterfly's "In a Gada Da Vida" to the stumble-footed stampede of the Doors' "Break on Through." This is not progress.

Edge adapts his guitar playing to every different tempo, finding some inspired alternatives along the way, from low, funky wah-wah to high, Ernie Isley phase-shifting to something that sounds like a mosquito pumped up to the volume of a buzz saw. Finally he lands back on the ringing dream tones that a generation of young guitarists calls "the Edge."

Eno is hitting buttons on a synthesizer, searching through the files. Bono addresses the booth through his vocal mike: "We're looking for Brian's 'Dead Man' sounds on the keyboard."

While they're looking, Larry begins playing another song. Bono picks up on it and joins in. This whole jam/tape/edit method encourages the musicians to keep their creative juices flowing—as quick as they get bored with one song they move on to another. The sorting will be done later. Edge comes in with a psychedelic guitar. Bono starts singing about climbing the highest hill, then he repeats a phrase from one of his literary inspirations, Charles Bukowski: "These days run away like horses over a hill."

"Dirty Day" emerges as the title of the song, though Bono also tries out some of the words he's using on another track, "Some Days Are Better Than Others." The lyrics to these two songs might sound abstract (a cynic would say nonsensical) outside this room, but given Bono's current state of mind they make perfect sense: "Some days you wake up with her complaining," "Some days you wake up in the army," "Some days you feel like a bit of a baby," "Some days you can't stand the sight of a puppy."

It's a pretty fair peek into Bono's current state of mind as he prowls around his house, trying not to trip over his children, his brain still filled with the smoke and mirrors of the Zoo TV tour. He is in that strange mental neighborhood where life on the road seems vibrant and natural and home life, real life, feels claustrophobic and flat.

Bono was rambling on earlier about trying in these recordings to capture the feeling you get when you're lying in bed in the morning trying to sleep and the music from your kids' cartoons is coming through the wall. Without the pictures, Bono said, the soundtracks are amazing. They are disjointed, cut up to follow the action in a way that defies the rules of music, and you never know when the violins and trumpets are going to be augmented with a sudden scream, freight train, or shotgun blast.

His divided mental state is affecting Bono's songwriting. A song called "Daddy's Gonna Pay for Your Crashed Car" begins "You're a precious stone/ You're out on your own/ You know everyone in the world but you feel alone." Sounds like a good description of U2 on tour in America to me. Bono tries handing me a line about the song as a religious metaphor ("Daddy may be God," he says, "but he could be the devil too.") and I say, "Ah, come on, Bono. Daddy is Paul McGuinness. Daddy is the organization that provides you with all these cars and planes and fancy meals and settles the bill after you leave, pays off the posse if you break something."

Bono says, yes, that's right—but he would probably say that even if it had never occurred to him before. He may very well have in mind for these songs bigger metaphors and deeper meanings than life as a rock star, but the fact that he is so deep in a tour mentality while he's writing means that they are completely informed by that strange perspective.

The new lyrics are full of U2's inability to slip out of the clusterfuck mentality and back into what's supposed to be normal life. And I hear both trepidation and excitement at the prospect. *Achtung Baby* was about being tempted away from conventional commitments by the excitement of Nighttown, but the character on *Achtung Baby* always knew where home was—he was testing how far away he could step and still get back. The character in these new songs has lost his map. He can barely remember how he used to think or who he used to be.

The music, meanwhile, has a slightly drunken feeling. Eno and Flood are getting a sound like conventional pop music underwater. It conjures up the way that, when you're in a strange country and a little drunk, the crappiest disco or pop music can sound weirdly attractive. It's not that you don't know it's stupid—it's that you don't care. It may have something to do with your being, at that moment and by the standards of that place, a little stupid yourself. (At dinner last night Bono held forth on the brilliance of the Bee Gees: "Equal to Abba, perhaps even superior. 'Tragedy' is genius.")

"Crashed Car" begins with a beat like an anvil—harsh, loud, hammering—which as the song takes off is replaced by a sound like a bass drum heard from the bottom of a swimming pool. It takes me a minute to figure out what that switch in tone reminds me of: pushing through an excited crowd into a waiting car and then rolling up the window, sealing all the adrenaline panic outside your glass-enclosed luxury.

Structurally, the songs on *Achtung Baby* were conventional—"One" or "Who's Gonna Ride Your Wild Horses" could have fit on *The Joshua Tree.* What was radical was the production—submerging Bono's vocal in distortion on "Zoo Station," for example. On the new material, though, the song structures go off in all sorts of bizarre directions. It is up to Bono and the others to come up with lyrics and melodies that impose some sense of order on these wandering tracks. On *Achtung Baby* U2 took conventional tracks and radicalized them; on this material U2 is taking radical tracks and covering them with a veneer of convention.

U2 returns to working on "If God Will Send His Angels." It is upbeat, a little Doorsy but clearly in the U2 Big Music tradition, which may make it hard to fit with the more disjointed new songs. This song, too, needs a chorus, and Bono has a plan for how to get one. He wants the band to break down at a certain point and beat out one phrase over and over while he chants the title line on top of it. Bono asks Larry to just ride his cowbell to affect this big dynamic shift. Edge and Adam are puzzling over what they should play to make the dramatic gesture Bono wants while still providing the energy lift necessary for the chorus to pick the listener up—not drop him through a sudden sonic trapdoor.

"It doesn't have to be a big deal," Eno says. "You could just hold the E for another two hours."

"Larry," Bono says, "try one of your rolls at the end of this sequence." Bono mimicks the beat he wants *rat-ta-tat-ta-tat* and then sings, "OO-OOH, GO-OOOOOH"

They try it a couple of times. Flood says it works. They play it again. Flood says they're losing it—the chorus is now a drop-off, "Not the uplift I imagine you want."

Bono suggests they come into the control room and listen to the different versions. Sitting on the couch during the playback, the band agrees that the song isn't working. Bono says that a circular progression such as this needs a great guitar part to raise it up as the chords go around and around. (In other words, let Edge solve the problem.)

Eno says that the problem may be Bono. He's pushing against the top of his range. He has to climb too high for the chorus, "Squeaking." Eno observes that the song is in E, a tough key for Bono.

"Yeah," Bono says, "E's tough, but guitar and bass players love it, and unfortunately U2 starts with the music. It's a discussion we often have." Bono says he's good in G, A, and B, but Edge and Adam don't like playing in those keys. Edge is impassive. He's not going to let Bono snake out of dealing with the vocal problem by changing the subject.

After listening to several versions of the song, Eno and Bono agree that a ragged early take is better than the later ones where everyone knew exactly where they were going and the shifts between verses and chorus were sharply defined. As the early version plays again, Eno praises it, saying, "See, that's tense without being *thuggish.* The way you're doing it now is lowbrow."

I'm impressed with Eno's use of semantics to sway musical judgment. A different producer might listen to the same version and say, "See, that's nervous without being *ballsy.* The way you're doing it now has guts."

With the backing track thus selected, Eno begins pushing Bono to figure out how he's going to get over his problem with the key and register and find "a real vocal character" for the song. Bono ducks the issue, which gives Eno an opening for his own agenda. While experimenting in the studio earlier today Eno ganged together several effects and came up with "a great new vocal sound—thin and hard." He thinks it's just what Bono needs for "If God Will Send His Angels." The cynic in me suspects that excited as he is by today's discovery, Eno would find it the perfect sound for "What's New, Pussycat," "Nights in White Satin," or any other song that Bono happened to be singing tonight.

Bono asks suspiciously if this new sound of Eno's has anything to do with the Vocoder (a device for altering vocals electronically). Eno assures him it does not. Bono tries to slip away from the subject by suggesting that he belt out the refrain, "If God will send his angels," like one of those American TV evangelists, like the Mirrorball Man, "instead of how I'm doing it now, like a bad rock singer." Bono tries it, sounding like Foghorn Leghorn. It is a slippery attempt to use a caricature to avoid his responsibility to actually hit the notes.

Eno, sensing his opponent's weakness, comes back with a semantic uppercut: "This new vocal sound I've found is like a . . . a . . ." he pretends to search for an exact description but he knows damn well what he's going to say, "a psychotic evangelist!"

Bono's eyes light up. "That's what I want!" First round to Brian Eno.

As Eno's setting up his sound, Bono tells Edge that he thinks the guitar should stop altogether during this new cowbell breakdown chorus. "It doesn't matter if you're playing different chords," Bono says, "if you're just playing them the same way."

"The chords are just the canvas," Edge says, Zen-like. "What shape canvas do you want?"

While Larry wanders off to shoot pool and Adam to go home, I sit on the couch between Edge and Bono marveling at the complex higher reasoning function of U2, the bisected hemispheres of the band brain— Edge on the left, Bono on the right—seated high and proud atop the long backbone of bass and drums. Eno washes over both sides like a superego. (Tim Booth of the British group James, who Eno also produces, has pointed out that Brian Eno's name is an anagram for "One Brain." Heavy.) It's great to watch each of these three smart, articulate men try to get his own way by bringing different forms of rhetoric to what are, finally, just matters of taste.

Eno comes on like a philosophy professor, using apparent logic to win his case. Under close scrutiny, though, Eno's syllogisms are a little shaky. He does not proceed from fact to fact to conclusion. Rather he hits on a conclusion first (based on taste or instinct or expediency) and then bends a few facts to make them fit that conclusion. So when Bono mentions that he wants to sing like a TV preacher, Eno tells him that his new vocal sound is like "a psychotic evangelist." I'll bet if Bono had said he wanted to sing like King Kong, Eno would have described his new vocal sound as "evocative of gigantic monkeys."

Bono, equally clever, tries to win arguments by couching them in moral terms. Even with Eno's new effect Bono does a bad job on his crazed-evangelist vocal. He wants to leave it and go on to something else. Eno keeps after him to redo it, until Bono, pushed into a corner, declares, "I am actually ashamed of that vocal. It embarrasses me." He pauses for effect before coming around with the left hook: "And maybe it is *right* that I should be ashamed at that moment. Maybe shame is what that lyric demands!"

Here is a bit of rhetoric any schoolboy late with his term paper could appreciate! Bono makes a *moral imperative* out of his desire to avoid resinging the song, and suggests that as he is being brave enough to charge into the machine-gun nest of public humiliation for his art, the least Eno could do is provide cover.

Edge tends to listen quietly, scrutinizing these arguments between Eno's professor and Bono's martyr, and then punctures their balloons with his own talmudic logic. Edge analyzes the conflicting propositions like a rabbi and bides his time before zeroing in on the weak spot where Eno's circumlocution or Bono's manifesto can be shattered.

Flood listens to it all and says nothing. When everyone else is talked out, exhausted, and home in bed, he will still be here, making it sound the way he wants.

"A lot of the time I'm like the junior partner," Flood says when the others are gone. "It's almost like you go around with the broom afterwards."

22

Making Sausages

*songwriting by accident/ the movie critic/ one from column
b/ a camera tour of adam's nakedness/ gavin's dirty duty/
the year of the french*

WHILE U2 IS dredging their psyches and adrenaline to make
it through these recording sessions, the hysteria of tour
preparation is going on all around them. There are a
hundred decisions to be made, and everyone wants U2's attention. In
the sitting room at the Factory, illustrations of various designs for
Edge's wool hats are laid out for his inspection. There is a check mark
next to a drawing of a snake eating its tail, along with a quotation from
a mythology text: "Ouroboros: A gnostic name for the great world
serpent." Fintan Fitzgerald, the wardrobe captain, has so despaired of
ever getting the band to sit still long enough to have their butts mea-
sured that he has convinced Suzanne to grab pairs of their jeans to send
overnight to the tailor in London standing by to cut his clothes. The
tailor will just have to base his work on these swiped trousers.

There are piles of faxes with handwritten messages across them,
things like "Needs Answer *Today!*" Suzanne tells the band members they
have to agree on the aliases they are going to use for their hotel reservations. They decide to take the names of Irish fashion models. "I want to
be Mr. Doody!" Bono declares. "You can't," Suzanne says, "Edge already has it." Edge says he will be "Mr. Rocca" in honor of the former
Miss Ireland now dating Van Morrison. Bono can be Doody.

U2 wants to focus their attention on the big stuff. They want the
Zooropa tour, the European stadium shows, to be different from what
they did in America. Bono is sure that they can push the boundaries of
taste further in Europe than in the USA. They convene in the sitting
room to look at the video footage that will play on the great Zoo TV

screens during the concerts. The men responsible for assembling this are Ned O'Hanlon and Maurice Linnane, the Rosencrantz and Guildenstern of the mighty U2 enterprise. Ned and Maurice run Dreamchaser, a Dublin video company that, while dependent on U2 for much of its revenue, is not actually a U2 subsidiary. In other words, although U2 are Ned and Maurice's biggest clients, although Ned and Maurice are very close to the center of all Zoo tour action, Ned and Maurice are not U2's employees. (Ned's wife is, though—she is Anne-Louise Kelly, the director of Principle Management Dublin.) This independence manifests itself in small ways, such as Ned and Maurice not having to sign the confidentiality agreements Principle employees sign, and in the bemused demeanor the two men affect as they deal with translating and executing U2's endless ideas about their video image.

As Ned and Maurice roll in a big TV and prepare their latest video presentation, Adam is in a chair getting his hair done for the impending tour. His head is wrapped in a towel and his hair is piled high with some horrible purple goop. Adam looks up from under his turban and asks Maurice if he went on holiday during his recent break.

"Yeah, to a Greek island."

"The gay one?"

"No."

Bono comes into the room saying, "Larry went there once. He couldn't believe it. The nightmare of his life. Everything that's happened to him since he was twelve years old times a thousand."

Edge and Larry come in. Ned and Maurice put up the film montage that will open the concert. There's an opera singer cutting to a 1950s dancer cutting to African tribesmen cutting to Bono in his fly shades speaking in a jumble of European languages.

Bono says hold it. He doesn't want himself in there. "It's not good enough, there's no content." He objects to the *jokiness* of the image of himself. Ned and Maurice won't let that go by.

"This from the man who came out on stage and said, 'Bend over, San Francisco!'?" asks Maurice.

"The man who said, 'Seig heil, Berlin!'?" asks Ned.

Bono will not be moved. He also wants the African tribesmen put somewhere else—the way the film is cut now they come right after a series of ridiculous images. Bono thinks it will look like U2 are mocking them.

Ned and Maurice groan and note the changes. Next up is the video that will run across the screens while U2 plays "With or Without You," a long, slow mood-lit pan across the mountains and valleys of Adam Clayton's naked body. "Uh-oh," Adam says while unwrapping his head to reveal hair of phosphorescent blondeness. "Maybe I should see this one alone first."

"It's going to be seen by thousands, Adam." Bono laughs. "This is no time for modesty."

The film rolls. On the screen a nude Adam, standing at attention, is bathed in deep shadows and red light as the camera pans slowly around him. The cinematography is artsy, the focus fuzzy. It is tasteful to a fault. "There's no narcissism in this," Bono explains to me as we watch. "The idea is to eroticize the male body instead of the female. You're not sure at first which it is."

The film was a reaction to an objection raised by Catherine Owens, the band's artist pal, Trabant painter, and Zoo TV board member, who insisted that the tour needed some male eros to balance the belly dancer and the pulling-women-from-the-audience-to-dance-with-Bono bits. As usual, Adam "Body Double" Clayton was drafted for the buff shot.

When the band finishes watching the clip Bono observes that there is no full frontal nudity.

"We can arrange a personal appearance," Adam offers.

The touchiest decision U2 has made is to go into Europe with snatches from German filmmaker Leni Riefenstahl's Nazi propaganda films *Triumph of the Will* and *Olympia*. It's partly a commentary on the rumblings of a fascist resurgence in Europe now, partly a comment on the ambience of giant stadium rock shows, and partly just to fry people's brains. Bono figures that by the time U2 projects *Triumph of the Will* up on giant video screens in Berlin's Olympic Stadium, the cultural tension will be stretched close to snapping. Europe is at a turning point. The Cold War order we grew up with has disappeared. The European peoples will either continue down the road toward economic and cultural unification or break apart into the ethnic tribalism where fascism breeds. U2 wants to hit their European audience over the head with their idea of how extreme those choices are.

The TV pumps out what sounds like an African tribal beat and the screen fills up with a shot from *Olympia* of a little German boy in what might be a Hitler Youth uniform beating furiously on a marching-band drum. That image desolves into Joseph Stalin into Margaret Thatcher into the Romanian dictator Nicolae Ceaușescu.

"It's too much!" Bono protests. "The only song that could follow that is 'The End of the World.' You can't go from that into 'Zoo Station.' It's too hard a cut. If I were in an arena and I saw that and then a *rock band* came out I'd riot!"

So it goes. Ned and Maurice have been working day and night to have these images ready and now they suffer the death of a thousand cuts as Bono ticks off his objections and orders changes. In years of working with U2 Ned and Maurice have memorized a long list of taboos. No shots of Edge without his hat. Avoid showing Bono's feet—he thinks they're too small ("I have no feet—my legs just end!"). If you can ever manage to get a shot of Adam on stage without his chin in the air, savor it.

One time the band okayed a U2 TV commercial Ned and Maurice had made. A week after it went out, Larry decided there was one shot of him he didn't like. Which caused Adam to mention that if they were going to reedit it anyway, there was a shot of him he'd like changed too. The discussion escalated until Bono announced of the clip, "I actually hate that."

"But you said you loved it last week," Ned protested.

They swear that Bono's reply was, "When I said I loved it, what I meant was, I hate it." Ned and Maurice are used to being sent back to the drawing board.

Right now U2 has to go back to the mixing board. The band members convene in the control booth with Eno, Flood, and engineer Robbie Adams. They have pads and pencils. It is time to listen to a number of the edited jams and assign them grades. Maybe this way they can figure out which damn songs to finish before the luggage has to leave. The first track plays. Bono (who Eno once described as "the Mother Teresa of abandoned songs") thinks it has a lot of potential. The others give it the bum's rush.

"I give that one two out of five," says Flood.

"Four out of ten," says Eno.

"But the mood is so unusual," Bono protests. "It's at least five out of ten!"

They listen to another track. Eno says it's a great jam but the guitar going *cha-chaaang* on the third beat makes it too reggae. He wants to move the bass and kick drum over one beat to compensate—have the bass land on the one instead of the two. Adam smiles and says, "And I worked so hard to not play on the one." Everybody remembers that the last reggae song they decided to try playing straight turned into "I Still Haven't Found What I'm Looking For," one of their biggest hits. Eno says that the band should plan on jamming some more tonight from 7 till 9.

Robbie protests that at this late date more jamming seems like a waste of time. Eno says, "It's actually time efficient." Edge, Adam, and Larry can keep jamming, coming up with new stuff—while Eno and Flood mix the best jams and Bono goes off and finishes the lyrics and melodies.

Bono calls it "songwriting by accident," and tells Robbie that what they have to decide now is if this is going to be a song record (see *The Joshua Tree*) or a vibe record (see *The Unforgettable Fire*). And how is U2 to address this decision? Roll out the blackboard!

Soon the band and their producers are studying a catalog of their options that looks like a Chinese menu:

Songs:	Vibes:	Soundtrack:
Babyface	Numb	Piano: Poem
Wandering	If God Will	Landscape
Sinatra	Crashed Car	Lemon
Zooropa	Jesus Drove Me	Sinatra
Wake Up, Dead Man	Cry Baby	
First Time	Indian Jam	
Kiss Me, Kill Me	Sponge	
Velvet Dress	Lose Control	
Wandering I.	Nose Job	

Bono wonders aloud if they should edit short bits of many of the different tracks together, creating a montage. He raves about the latest Beastie Boys album. He hated their raps but loved the way their songs jumped in and out of each other. Flood says that's because they couldn't play their instruments well enough to keep a groove going for a whole song, but Bono says that doesn't matter. "It's applying a deejay mentality to rock & roll. And about time."

He says that rappers make records at superspeed: "De La Soul made an album in a week! Everybody's on the floor doing everything, including writing the lyrics. These guys don't have degrees in electronics, but they know how much studio time costs. We need some of that."

As the band goes in to start jamming again, Bono apologizes to me for the tedium: "Making records is like making sausages," he says. "You'll probably enjoy them more if you don't see how it's done."

U2 falls into a jam around a bass figure similar to that of "This Is Radio Clash." Edge stays on one chord, hitting his pedals to try out different tones while Eno, at the synth, drops in little electronic accents that float around the groove like musical satellites. When they finish playing Eno says he really likes that one.

"Yeah," Edge says, "you like it 'cause nobody ever changes their part!"

"Nothing changes," Eno says. "My dream! I listened to a blank twenty-four track today. It was bliss. Turn up that hiss!" Everyone laughs.

At dinnertime Adam has to leave; he's going to appear on the Irish Recorded Music Industry's TV awards show to make a presentation to R.E.M. Edge and I go into the Factory's lunchroom to eat some Indian takeout. He turns his attention to one subject that has all the members of U2 feeling blue: they have looked at their financial prospects for the coming year. The monumental cost of keeping the Zoo TV tour on the road through the spring and summer in Europe and the autumn in Australia and Japan will eat up almost all the profits, *if* the tour is a smash and sells out most of the dates. If Europe should have a rainy summer, U2 could lose millions. A year ago, when the band was sitting here dreaming up the most extravagant rock show ever, money seemed to be made to burn. But twelve months into a twenty-four-month haul, the excitement of breaking new ground doesn't seem quite as valuable.

"We've painted ourselves into a corner," Edge says. "I can't figure how we can work for a year and earn nothing." I ask if that's literally true. "It's so close," Edge says. "The budget is so tight that if one big thing goes wrong, there goes the profit."

On the TV in the corner Adam is handing an award to Mike Mills of R.E.M. (and Automatic Baby).

Bono is in the other room suffering through a bad interview. A journalist from a French magazine has arrived. He is smart and full of insightful questions. Unfortunately he's not getting to ask many of them because the magazine's publisher (or some equivalent boss—U2's not sure exactly who he is) has accompanied him and is dominating the conversation with obnoxious non sequiturs delivered in what seems to be a parody of Gallic rudeness.

"Rock een roll!" he says to Bono. "Ees all bullsheet, non?" Then he snorts though his long nose and lets out a braying *haw haw haw.* Every time Bono tries to talk about U2's intentions this potbellied Frenchman makes a face and interrupts, usually to say something like "Stop right there, you little bastard!" and then guffaw. It occurs to Bono that this might be a technique—a good cop/bad cop routine to get him to drop his guard in the interview. Or maybe this guy is just a goon. "I like you," the bigmouth says. "I'm saying nothing against you, but rock een roll is bullsheet, haw haw haw." He lets Bono know that U2 is too hung up by their Catholic upbringing, oblivious to the fact that Bono, Edge, and Adam were raised Protestant. Bono has a way of getting out of situations like this, and his name is Gavin Friday. Gavin is supposed to be coming by for dinner with Bono, Eno, and the writer. Gavin susses the situation and steps in to take the journalists off Bono's hands. Gavin has been through the routine a hundred times. This will be another one Bono owes him.

Standing in the sitting room, waiting to depart, the Gaul with the gall tells Gavin he doesn't want to "go to any trendy sheet! We go to real Irish pub!"

Gavin says he knows just the place. The Frenchman asks, "Weel there be peegs on the floor?"

Gavin is startled, but he tries to keep a straight face. "No, there won't be pigs there. Dubliners are not farmers. Dublin is something else."

The Frenchman tells Gavin how poor Ireland is. "There are no tall buildings!"

"There's two reasons for that," Gavin says. "First, the British took all the money out and put nothing back in. Second, religion. The church wanted the steeples and crosses to be the highest points."

They head off to dinner with the Frenchman throwing out insults and idiocies (he is thrilled to be in the land of the great Irish writer Dylan Thomas) until Gavin is ready to choke him. He marches him all over Dublin, the Frenchman huffing and puffing and pleading for a cab while Gavin is saying, no, no, we poor Irish peasants walk everywhere.

Finally Gavin leads his two continental guests to a private club he knows, a British royalist bar with pictures of the Queen on the wall and Orangemen drinking to the Empire. This, Gavin tells the Parisian, is a real Dublin pub!

23

In Cold Blood

---

adam rallies the caravan/ a serbian social studies lesson/ bono recites his latest poem/ the author's uncle has an audience with the blessed mother/ waiting for the end of the world

I'M BUYING my groceries in a shop on Baggot Street one morning, paying no attention to the small talk of the Dublin housewives and little more to the radio playing quietly on the shelf of the man behind the counter. The news is on, saying something about a group of Irish relief workers in association with Amnesty International who are going to try to drive a caravan of food and medical supplies through the Serbian military lines besieging Muslim, Croatian, and secular enclaves in Bosnia, in what used to be Yugoslavia. Boy, I think, those relief workers must be saints! And like saints they are going to be martyred. The nationalists who have seized control of Serbia want blood. They have been carving their way across Croatian, Muslim, and multiethnic territory since the moment Communism lifted from Eastern Europe. The Serbs have the remnants of the Yugoslavian military machine (the Croats claim the Serbs are simply the communists trying to hold on to their power by raising the flag of ancient nationalism; the Serbs respond, "Oh, yeah? Well, your daddy was a Nazi!") and the West has refused to get involved, except to pass U.N. resolutions refusing to allow arms shipments to either side. As the Serbs are already heavily armed, this has had the effect of leaving the Croats (who at least were part of the establishment of the country that disappeared under them) at a disadvantage and the Muslims (a religious minority within the officially godless former nation) defenseless.

It is a horrible example of diplomatic malpractice, but the unspoken attitude of the West is, "You don't make an omelette without breaking a few eggs. We have seen simultaneous peaceful revolutions on a scale undreamed of as the dictatorships in Poland, Czechoslovakia, the Baltics, East Germany and—who could have imagined—the Soviet Union itself have been swept aside. Political change that might have cost as much blood as World War II has happened with peace and speed. Now, if the people of, say, Romania, want to drag their dictator and his wife before a kangaroo court and shoot them, that's ugly—but it is far less ugly than World War III would have been. So, sure, there are going to be power struggles and ethnic infighting popping up here and there as the new nations settle themselves. It's sad, but it's inevitable, and all we can do is deny them any more weapons so it does not drag on too long."

Maybe no one in the West expected the Croatians to fight back. More likely, no one expected the Bosnian Serbs to be so bloodthirsty. They do not want to conquer the Croats and Muslims, they want to destroy them. They, too, have seen the execution of the dictators of Romania and the lesson they learned was to exterminate your rivals before they can exterminate you. The Irish have been leading the efforts to raise money for relief of the besieged cities and "safe areas" of what was Yugoslavia. The English and French have been hiding under their tables, hoping it will go away; the U.S. has been oblivious—most Americans could not find Bosnia on a map. Pretty soon that won't be a problem 'cause the way things are going it won't be on the map. But what causes me to drop my groceries on the floor of this market is when I hear on the radio what sounds like talk about U2 leading this humanitarian effort to run the Serb blockade. I couldn't have heard right, could I? I just have U2 on the brain, surely the announcer said "U.N.," not "U2."

I lean over the counter, trying to catch the news above the noise of the store and, yes, that is Adam Clayton speaking about the need to take the risk of getting these supplies past the Serbian guns: "It is unacceptable in the world that we live in that these things can still be allowed to go on without being challenged!" I can't believe it. I walk back toward the Factory in a daze. Are we really going to Bosnia? Are we really going to war? Does U2 think their backstage passes will get them safely through the Serbian artillery?

As the Serbian atrocities mounted this spring there was a moment when President Clinton was pushing NATO to send in troops, but at that point the Croatians suddenly turned and started attacking the

Muslim population, too, as if to say to the conquering Serbs, "Never mind us, let's team up on the new kid!" When that happened, outside confusion about which side was the victims reached a peak, and Clinton was unable to muster support for Western intervention.

There has been speculation (not only from Muslim groups but from, for instance, Richard Nixon) that the West is not willing to defend Muslims from genocide as it would Christians and Jews.

Adam's already at the studio when I arrive. "I half heard you on the radio just now," I say to him in the sitting room. "Tell me we're not going to Bosnia."

"No, no," Adam says. "We can't, we've got this tour! We're involved in funding this caravan of supplies that's going in, but we're not going ourselves. They asked me to come down and speak this morning, to help them get publicity for it. That's all."

"That's a relief," I say. "I checked my airport travel insurance. It's void in a war zone."

Adam says very seriously, "I think, though, if we didn't have the tour I would go along. We all sit and watch this stuff on television and say, 'Why doesn't somebody do something?' I think if you have the chance to check it out, you must."

When you read that in a book it might sound like hot air, but when Adam says it to me in a room in Dublin it's not, it's entirely sincere. If he were free of his obligations to the others I believe Adam would be willing to risk his life not out of the sort of religious passion Bono musters but out of an old British sense that this is simply the proper thing for a man to do. There is something contradictory in Adam, who, as Bono says, has been thinking that he's now middle-aged since he was twenty, but who is also like a little boy determined to show that he will not be afraid, he will not be denied, he will do whatever must be done and make no fuss about it. When you first meet U2 you think that Adam has the most understandable personality of any of them, but eventually you realize that he is the most complicated. He registers everything; I think he feels everything. But he shows almost nothing.

Contrast that with Bono, who shows what he's feeling in his face, what he's thinking in his words, and what he had for breakfast on his shirt. Bono does not disguise his complexities. I go into the control room and Bono is hammering at the Powerbook personal computer that has become his salvation after a lifetime of losing his lyrics.

"So hard to watch the news from Bosnia," Bono says. "It was hard not to feel accused. A relief worker was looking at me, at each of us, saying, 'You are a *jerk* for doing nothing.' It made it very hard for me to consider working on this"—he gestures at the studio around him—"important."

He reads me what he has been writing:

> I read a book once, called "In Cold Blood"
> About a murder in the neighborhood
> Pages of facts did me no good
> I read it like a blind man, in cold blood
> So the story of a three-year-old child
> Raped by soldiers though she'd already died
> Made the mother watch as they fucked her in the mud
> I'm reading the story now in cold blood
> More now coming off the wire
> City surrounded, funeral pyre
> Life is cheaper than talking about it
> People choke on their politician's vomit
> On cable television I saw a woman weep
> Live by satellite from a flood-ridden street
> Boy mistaken for a wastepaper bin
> Body that a child used to live in
> I saw plastic explosives and an alarm clock
> And the wrong men sitting in the dock
> Karma is a word I never understood
> How God could take a four-year-old in cold blood
> I live by a beach but it feels like New York
> I hear about ten murders before I get to work
> What's it going to be, Lord, fire or flood
> An act of mercy or in cold blood?

"I'm thinking of reciting it on the album with just a drum," Bono says. "Bring in a note of brutal reality. Do you think that's too much?"

I suggest that describing soldiers raping a child is going to overpower everything that comes after it—it will disrupt the album in a way from which it might not be able to recover.

Bono says perhaps he should do it on stage—a blast of ugly truth amid all the camp, postmodernism, and irony. He goes into the other room to do an interview with Joe Jackson from the Irish music paper *Hot Press*, in which he continues to talk about Bosnia and how small U2's concerns seem when stacked up next to that.

He reads "In Cold Blood" to Jackson and then says, "Sometimes, in the middle of all the kitsch you have to stick the boot in. But that lyric, too, is about overload and I want to use it live, though it may only be samples or lines I like. But it's not so much about the cold blood involved in the various acts I describe. It's about the way we respond to those things."

The symbol of the terror in what was Yugoslavia is the ongoing seige of Sarajevo, a great cultural center quite Western in its ways and now ringed by Serbian guns. Sarajevo represents what is at stake in this war because it is not an ethnic enclave, it is a modern city. The Muslims there are not fundamentalists, they are as secular as British Christians or American Jews. Sarajevo is a city—like New York or London—where ethnic background is not a big subject among the citizens. It is important to understand that the Serbian nationalists who are firing mortars into Sarajevo are not only shooting at Muslims, they are shooting at Croatians and Serbians too. The Muslims, Croats, Jews, and Serbs of the city are huddling together trying to figure out why these backward fanatics are trying to kill them and why the outside world doesn't care. Imagine if your own hometown were set upon by bands of lunatic fundamentalist Christians and you'll get a sense of what they are going through. In fact, it is this intermingling of different tribes, the erasing of ethnic lines, that the reactionary *Chetniks* in the Serbian army most want to punish and destroy.

I suspect that the Western reluctance to defend Sarajevo has roots so deep neither Sigmund Freud nor Big Bad John could ever excavate them. Sarajevo, after all, is the exact spot where the twentieth century went off the tracks. It was in Sarajevo in 1914 that the Bosnian nationalist Gavrilo Princip managed in spite of Chaplinesque incompetence to assassinate Archduke Ferdinand on the third try, setting off World War I, which in turn set off like dominoes the Russian Revolution and the spread of Communism, the rise of Nazism in Germany, World War II and the development and deployment of the nuclear bomb, and from which all the horrors and more than a few of the marvels of our century descend. Every statesman making decisions now learned as a kid in history class that the world went wrong because of *entangling alliances*—because all the countries of Europe were nuts enough to allow themselves to be drawn into a dispute in far-off Sarajevo.

It feels these days as if this entire century-spanning sequence of events was a big historical aberration and that as the 1900s come to a close all of those mistakes are being untangled so that the next century can begin normally. The last few years have played like a videotape of the twentieth century running backward, undoing all the detours of the decades since the Archduke got plugged: *zip*, there goes liberalism, *zoom*, there goes the sexual revolution, *holy smoke*, the Berlin Wall just got unbuilt, Eastern Europe is free, oh, there're those rotten Nazis, Communism evaporates, *wow*, there goes the USSR itself, the Dickensian underclass returns, and here we are, back to war in the Balkans and the whole world trying to avoid being sucked into a mess in Sarajevo. *Yikes*, says the battered old twentieth century, *this is where I took that wrong turn!* The "widening gyre" Yeats described in "The Second Coming" turns out to have a rewind switch.

Further back, behind all the historical and political baggage, I think there's another reason the West is so frightened to stick their collective nose into Bosnia. Superstition. Anyone with even a childhood memory of the book of Revelations has to get a little twitch of millennialist dread when thinking about the impending approach of the year 2000. Certainly Ronald Reagan made no secret of his belief in a coming apocalyptic confrontation between the forces of divine justice and Satan's evil empire. He happily talked about it until his advisers warned him to shut up, he was scaring the horses. Bill Clinton claims to have that old-time American Baptist religion too. As Jimmy Carter did. Despite what the sophisticates in the middlebrow media think, this stuff isn't just the province of yahoos and hucksters. God or His impostors lurks in the back of brains from Washington to Teheran, from Waco to Jonestown, and whenever a century ends He starts humming loudly and clearing His throat. When a millennium ends? Even Castro checks his Holy Water.

There are only two places where God (alive or dead) is not considered a factor in human events—England and academia. Elsewhere He figures into most equations right alongside money, sex, property, and power. In the West during this century the principle End of the World myth has been the legend of the Third Secret of Fatima. According to the popular story (which flattens out or ignores a lot of ambiguities in the actual reports), the Blessed Mother appeared to three Portuguese peasant children during World War I and predicted (1) that the current war would soon end but an even bigger one would follow and (2) unless Russia was converted it would plunge the world into Armageddon in the second half of the century.

A third prediction was sealed and was supposed to be made public in 1960. It never was—one apocryphal story had it that Pope John XXIII opened it, read it, and fell over dead. (Maybe it was a metaphysical practical joke, maybe it said, "Pope John will die when he reads this.") There has been all sorts of speculation about what the Third Secret of Fatima is. The most common rumor is that it gives the date of the end of the world, and the Church is afraid that if they tell the public, despairing people will go out and lose themselves in orgies and abandon. Which actually makes no sense at all, because anyone who believed in an end of the world prediction given by the Virgin Mary to the Pope would obviously be someone who would spend all his or her remaining time going to confession and collecting plenary indulgences—not partying like it's 1999. From the Church's reaction it seems more likely that the third letter of Fatima predicted the ordination of women or the end of clerical tax breaks or something else that would *really* spook the curia.

Just as the Fatima visitations followed closely on the first Sarajevo crisis, the current crisis has been accompanied by reported sightings of Mary in Medugorje, a Yugoslavian village in the mountains about a hundred miles from Sarajevo. The Blessed Mother is said to have begun appearing to children there in 1981. Word spread quickly and the faithful started flooding to Yugoslavia in trains, planes, and automobiles.

I got the lowdown on Medugorje from my uncle Gus, who journeyed there with a planeload of American pilgrims. When he got back I asked Gus how holy his *hejira* was. He said it was hard to get past the attitude of his fellow faithful. "When we arrived there one fella began cursing all the local citizens who didn't speak English. He yelled, 'This place is full of foreigners!' Then we got to go into the room where the children were kneeling. We all stood there watching for a while. All at once they began smiling. Their eyes moved together across the room. 'The Blessed

Mother is here,' our translator said. The children would speak, carrying on half of a conversation with someone we couldn't see. Then they asked if any of us American visitors had any questions we wanted to ask the Virgin Mary."

"Gee, Gus," I said, "that's quite an opportunity. I hope you didn't waste it asking about the dog races."

"No, at first no one knew what to ask her. Then one lady raised her hand and said, 'Are there cats in heaven?' The translator explained to us that that was really not the sort of question with which the children wanted to pester the Mother of God and did we have anything really important to ask. So then one man raised his hand and asked, 'Are there black people in heaven?' "

The translator gave up then and Gus considered that maybe large portions of humanity had good reason to worry about being cast into hell. I guess the Black Madonna of Czestochowa was not on this group's itinerary.

Even though the country around the shrine has been destroyed by the war, pilgrims continue to arrive in Medugorje, and the children who say they've seen Mary have been given secret errands to run. To prepare for what, no one knows—maybe they're picking up groceries for the next Last Supper.

Don't think this search for end-signs is only the province of Roman Catholics, either! Protestant fundamentalists began genuflecting like Jesuits after the accident at Chernobyl, the Ukrainian nuclear power plant, in April of 1986. The Chernobyl disaster was in many ways the first public evidence of the coming collapse of the Soviet empire. Radiation levels shot up as far away as Norway, where the reindeer were irradiated. Bible readers freaked at the news that *Chernobyl* translated into English was "wormwood." The book of Revelations predicts that one of the signs of the end of the world will be the pollution of rivers and springs by a great flaming star: "The name of the star was Wormwood; and a third of the water turned to wormwood, and men in great numbers died of the water because it was poisoned."

Next Monday Bono's wife Ali is going to Chernobyl for three weeks with a Greenpeace group to make a documentary about the effects of the radiation there. She brushed off Bono's concerns about the danger by telling him that he will be exposed to more radiation standing at the center of all the electrical fields on the Zoo TV stage every night than she will be at Chernobyl.

Eno attempts to calm Bono's anxieties by telling him that according to one theory the disaster at Chernobyl was exaggerated by the Ukrainians in order to embarrass the Soviet authorities and speed up Ukraine's secession from the USSR. It's a nice theory, but it doesn't explain why Rudolph is no longer the only reindeer who glows.

Since the fall of Communism there has been all sorts of hoodoo in the air. While U2 is struggling to capture on tape the contradictory moods of relief and trepidation, the nations of Western Europe are opening their borders and debating intermingling their currencies. The whole Zoo TV enterprise is taking place as the Channel Tunnel that will connect England to France is being scooped out. Cables are being laid, satellites are going up, walls are coming down. It is certainly the end of one world. The anxiety buzzing through the culture is about what will come after it.

It occurs to me that we might learn something if we figure out when this temporal bulge crested. Let's see, 1914 to 1994 is a nice, neat eighty years. Cut it in half and it means that the pinnacle of this cacophonous century occurred in . . . 1954. Well, of course it did! You know and I know the only important thing that happened in 1954, don't we? It was the year that truck driver Elvis Presley went into Sun Studios for the first time and mixed together hillbilly music with rhythm and blues. That year was the beginning of rock & roll! The halfway marker between Sarajevo and Sarajevo is "Milk Cow Blues Boogie." *Whoot,* as the scholars say, *there it is.*

24

Do Not Enter When Red Light
Is Flashing

*a song for squidgy/ the salt in nero's supper/ a bag of
money in the back of a taxicab/ adam experiences a mood
swing/ the edge in his element*

U2 ARE JAMMING again, coming up with enough songs to insure boxed sets for years after their plane crashes. Watching them work this way, it is really striking how much of the U2 sound frequently credited to Edge alone depends on Adam and Larry. Adam often plays with the swollen, vibrating bottom sound of a Jamaican dub bassist, covering the most sonic space with the smallest number of notes. Larry, who taught himself to drum and consequently got some things technically *wrong*, plays with a martial rigidity but uses his kit in a way a properly trained drummer would not. He has tom-toms on either side of him, and has a habit of coming off the snare onto them that is contrary to how most percussionists use those drums. We're not talking about huge technical innovations here; we're talking about personal idiosyncrasies that have over fifteen years solidified into a big part of what makes U2 always sound like U2, no matter what style of music they are playing. It is also why bands that imitate U2 never get it right, and why all the guitarists who try to play like Edge end up sounding so lame; their rhythm section never sounds like Adam and Larry.

The great joke is that Adam's and Larry's playing so perfectly reflects their personalities. Larry is right on top of the beat, a bit ahead—as you'd expect from a man who's so ordered and punctual in his life. Adam plays a little behind the beat, waiting till the last moment to slip in, which fits Adam's casual, don't-sweat-it personality. The great bassist and composer Charles Mingus said that musicians should not think of the beat as a dot that has to be landed on precisely, but as a circle in which one has to land *somewhere*. Adam and Larry, who have learned their instruments together since they were schoolboys, are working illustrations of Mingus's point. They've played together so long that they seem to spread the beat out between them. And they create a blanket on which Edge's chord layers rest.

Flood says, "Larry and Adam are constantly pushing and pulling, but because they know each other so well they can work within that. And you get this weird tension in the rhythm tracks. It's such a great backbone that it allows Edge a sort of freedom to manuever in the foreground."

The band finishes playing a slippery jam and then parleys with the producers in the control room to listen to it. Edge grabs a felt-tipped marker so he can add it to the list on the drawing board. "What shall we call it?" Edge asks.

"Slidey," Bono suggests.

Edge starts to write it and Eno, smiling, says, "Squidgy."

Everyone laughs at that. "Yes!" Bono says. " 'Squidgy!' " Edge writes it. Squidgy is the pet name that Princess Diana is called by her alleged lover in an alleged tape of one of their alleged phone conversations that the British tabloids (and in fact, newspapers all over the alleged world) got hold of and printed. Bono wants to know, "Can we get the tapes?"

Edge says that actors portraying the princess and her paramour read the transcripts on TV last week. "Great!" Bono says. "Get those!" The idea is quickly hatched to have the dialogue between Di and her boyfriend be the vocal over this track. U2 and their sidekicks are turning somersaults in ecstasy at the malevolent brilliance of the idea. "Our *je t'aime* to the royal family!" Bono says.

Edge says he agreed with Prince Charles for the first time when he told *his* mistress, in another taped phone call, that he wished he could be reincarnated as a pair of women's trousers. Bono announces that this "Squidgy" track should be seen as a statement of support for Charles. People roll their eyes and cough loudly at that one.

Finally U2's genetic Englishman speaks up. "You realize," Adam says, "that if we go through with this my mother will never forgive me. 'Pop star or no pop star you're not coming in this house!' "

"She's a royalist?" Edge asks.

"Yes. She's beyond logic."

"Who does she like?"

"Charles. She thinks Diana's lost it. 'Of course, she'll lose the children. . . .' "

"Anne has become the popular one now," Edge says. "She's the Bruce Springsteen of the royals. 'Got to give her credit, she's hung in!' Whereas Charles is now *Sting.*"

"I guess," Larry says, "that makes Fergie Madonna."

It's time to try playing the track again. Eno summons Larry and Adam back to their instruments by calling, "Send for the plumbers!" Adam—making a horrible mistake—wonders aloud where the word *plumber* comes from. This sends Eno into an hour-long tutorial on the root of the word *plumber* deriving from the same Latin root as *lead,* which leads him to the entwined histories of plumbing and lead poisoning, back to ancient Rome. Eno theorizes that the fall of the Roman Empire may be attributable to lead poisoning (Larry and Adam put down their instruments and pick up the phone to order Indian food) from bad plumbing adversely affecting ancient Italian sanity.

Pretty soon we're in the pub room opening bags of tandoori as Eno continues his exegesis and Edge throws in the occasional question. Over the takeout Eno explains that a modern historian re-created a meal served to Nero from an excavated recipe and found the resulting supper to be so full of salt as to be literally inedible. "Now," Eno says, his index finger rising as triumphant as a battle flag, "what disease has as one of its symptoms the loss of the ability to taste salt?" A hush falls over the table. "Lead poisoning!"

There is little salt shaken at U2's table tonight! As we finish eating, Bono looks around the lunchroom and says, "This is like where we played our early gigs, but those places were smaller."

Larry asks if the others remember the place where Bono had to sing standing on the pool table. He says he was thinking the other day about all of them driving to some gig in the south in Paul McGuinness's car. . . . Bono jumps in: "You kept kicking him in the back through the seat with your knees—and he thought you were doing it on purpose!"

Larry is laughing hard now: "He thought I didn't like him! There's a great book to be written about the early days of U2!"

Edge looks at me and says, "Oh, no, there isn't."

Bono tells the story of when Barry Mead, U2's first road manager, first came to America. He was nervously carrying $10,000 in earnings in the back of a New York cab stuck in traffic when a robber fleeing from a $70 stickup jumped into the taxi, put his gun to the driver's head, and shouted, "Take off!"

"We can't take off!" the driver said. "We're stuck in traffic!"

Before the argument could continue the cops ran up and blasted the robber dead. They then dragged the shaken road manager off to the station to explain the paper bag filled with money.

The band returns to work. Bono is still trying to find a vocal approach for "If God Will Send His Angels" and still getting nowhere. He is trying out different melodies, singing a newspaper article about a scandal involving a movie star, looking for lyrics as he goes. Suddenly Bono jumps to his feet, his tandoori takeout demanding evacuation. "I'll be right back!" he yelps. "An Indian is after me!"

While he's gone Larry, who listened silently while Bono improvised, says he has an idea for a melody. He sings it and Eno, Edge, and Flood think it's good. When Bono returns Larry sings it for him, and he tries working with it. He's distracted. Bono has promised to spend time at home with Ali before she departs for Chernobyl and so far this week he's been a big liar. Soon he is gone. Eno decamps with engineer Robbie Adams to Windmill Lane studio, around the corner, where they have set up a second shop in order to keep the assembly line humming.

While Edge plays with more of the tapes, Adam and I head into the sitting room to talk. I ask Adam if he was as shook as Bono at the bad reaction to *Rattle and Hum* and the dead end that trail hit.

"Everyone understood what had happened over the movie," Adam says. "I don't think deep down it really hurt Larry, myself, and Edge that much. I think we felt, 'Okay, fair enough.' But the band made a lot of effort to make new music for the soundtrack album and worked very hard to make it sound good in the movie and to make the sound good on the record. Edge was doing all sorts of different mixes: there was one for the movie in stereo, one for the video cassette in mono, a third for the album, and on top of this, producing some great new tracks, some good quality work. Everyone was pretty pissed off at being kicked after going through a lot of effort to make something we were all proud of and was good value for our fans."

So the band was in bad spirits and feeling under intense pressure going to Germany to begin *Achtung Baby*. I remind Adam of Larry's insisting that the four of them lay down their arms before finishing the album in Dublin.

"More than finishing the record," Adam says, "that had to do with being able to be on the road together for the next two years. Certainly the spirit with which we went out on the road was much healthier.

"In Berlin we were dependent on each others' company and we had to decide how much we *liked* each other. I'm not saying that was easily resolved. It probably took the whole of that record to resolve all those issues. I just remember everyone was leaning on everyone else to solve their problems. Whatever went wrong was always someone else's fault.

"The problems came because the vision wasn't clear. Dan as a producer was rooted in the old way of what we did, adding atmospheres and textures to what we played. That was very frustrating for Bono because it wasn't giving him the inspiration he needed. So he was kind of fighting on all fronts. Bono was trying to invade Leningrad and secure Europe at the same time.

"There was a general problem with communication between everyone. There was a misunderstanding about the amount of effort and cohesion needed to see the project through. Whereas with this project there are probably less songs than there had been starting *Achtung Baby,* but the communication is very clear and we don't have much time. On *Achtung Baby* we had time and that was a two-edged sword. It enabled us to not face the problem, to just continue to be frustrated. When in doubt, Edge would do another guitar overdub. He'll do anything to keep the *feeling* of momentum going. Doing guitar overdubs for a week will do that.

"When Edge gets on a roll he gets on a roll. He's always been happy to keep going. I think his process of *keeping going,* although damaging on a personal front, has allowed him to make great strides, has been the right thing for his career. He's made tremendous progress, he's a great guitar player."

Did you think in the last days in Berlin that the band might break up?

"It's hard to talk after the event but I felt optimistic. I felt it was there if we could only let it happen. I didn't feel we were as far away from it as Bono felt. It just lacked a few ballsy decisions made with everyone contributing to the consensus. And Bono, through his own frustration and anger and alienation from everyone, had actually got to a point where he wasn't prepared to listen to anyone else's point of view. Maybe he was so under pressure that his own point of view had become so eroded that he needed to overstate it to get it across."

The new U2 that emerged out of all that tension is wide enough to contain a lot of contradictions. For all the confusion about what they were trying to pull off with *Achtung Baby,* in retrospect the album probably saved U2's career. Although no one predicted it at the time, all of U2's 1980s peers who recently released albums in their usual styles— Springsteen, Dire Straits, INXS, Gabriel, Petty—suffered big drops in sales. It turned out that there was a cultural shift going on in pop music that would have sunk a *Joshua Tree 2* as surely as it hit those other artists. A whole new crowd of bands from Pearl Jam to Smashing Pumpkins has taken over radio, MTV, and record sales. By changing just one minute ahead of the culture, U2 set themselves up as the first of the new groups rather than the last of the old.

"We've been lucky to have been a young band," Adam reminds me. "I'm the eldest and I'm thirty-two. A lot of our contemporaries were still struggling at this age. By the time they're in their forties maybe it's just a little too late for them to be able to go back to the drawing board. The early mistakes we made—not understanding cool, not understanding attitude, clothes, and haircuts—were because we were seventeen and eighteen and our idols like the Clash and the Jam and the Police, who had all that shit down, were making their first records at twenty-seven or twenty-eight. We were making our first record when we were twenty! So, yeah, they had their image together. It's taken us fifteen years to get an image together, or indeed to realize that image is important." Adam smiles. "And not important."

Eventually Edge comes in with a cassette of a U2 jam on a boom box, sits in on the stand-up piano, and starts playing piano chords along with it. Adam gets up and wanders back to the control room. It's after 11 P.M. and Flood's the last crewman on deck. Adam and Flood trade faces about the state of the sessions. One of the strangest aspects of this method of working is that when the four members of U2 jam together they naturally come up with songs that sound like every era of the band —from *Boy* to *The Joshua Tree.* But the rules of the new U2 demand that any such familiar sounds be scrapped or subverted. For Adam, it is sometimes an exercise in intellectualization that does not necessarily produce the best possible music.

He tells Flood that he won't be in tomorrow—he is going to an old friend's wedding and really looking forward to the break. Adam says he remembers the "black hole" U2 went into after *The Joshua Tree.* "Recording *The Joshua Tree* was relaxed, great fun," Adam says. "Then it all exploded. That tour was a piece of shit. *Rattle and Hum* was a piece of shit. Making *Achtung Baby* was a piece of shit." Adam is talking about the working atmosphere, by the way, not the work.

Flood commiserates, "I remember one meeting about scheduling a meeting to decide about making a decision."

"It was only on the Zoo TV tour that it really came together again," Adam says sadly. "And now here we are, back in the studio doing it to ourselves again."

"But you accomplished what you set out to," Flood says. "When a band's reinventing itself, as U2 has, there has to be a lot of theorizing. From now on you're going to have to carry that extra burden."

It's not hard to understand Adam's frustration with the Socratic approach to record-making. When there's a disagreement about which way to go with a song the argument is as likely to be won by who scores the most debating points as which music sounds the best. Of course, if everyone agreed on which one sounded the best, there'd be no debate.

Adam says that making the first three U2 albums was joyful. They were done in weeks. "*October* was a bit of a slog, waiting for the lyrics. For *War* we had all the songs and it was easy. *Unforgettable Fire* was tough. Same black holes, waiting for the lyrics on that one. We had six songs, then Brian came up with 'Elvis Presley and America' and '4th of July' and gave us something to tie it together." He sits sadly, blue about the amount of baggage that has been tied to a band that used to just get in a room and play.

Edge sticks his head in the door. "Phone for you, Adam. I think it's Naomi."

Adam goes off to the alcove to pick up his call and Edge comes in to play Flood the piano part he's just recorded on the boom box. Flood loves it. "Let's find a backing track with no chords," Edge says, "and put it down. We'll play Bono something he's never heard and just hand him a microphone."

Adam comes back in with a canary-scaring smile across his face. "Guess who I've got as house guests for the weekend," he announces. "Naomi Campbell and Christy Turlington! They just decided! They're going straight to the airport."

The two supermodels are stuck in Paris, too late to get a plane out, so Adam just offered to hire a plane and send it to fetch them to his castle.

Flood looks at Adam, whose black mood has been transformed, and says, "Tough life."

Adam takes off to prepare his bachelor pad for visitors. This is the time of night when Edge and Flood go to work like shoemaking elves, cranking through the small hours so that when the others return tomorrow they will be amazed at the creations laid out before them.

Edge's guitar tech, Dallas, points to his boss and smiles, "That guy never goes home." Dallas has worked for a lot of top dogs in the business, from the Eagles to Prince, but U2, he says, is something else. He says they often come into the studio without a song, jam away and you think nothing's going on, and all of a sudden—wham—a song will appear. And they'll change anything. Most bands get locked into playing a song a certain way. U2 will work and work at something, get it almost finished, and then one of the guys will suddenly change the part he's playing and they'll all follow him off in a whole different direction, Bono will start singing a different melody, and you'll think, "What are they doing? It was almost done! Wrap it up!" But often, Dallas, says, that new part will lead them into something better than what they had.

It seems to me that U2 has more faith in the strength of the song itself than many bands do. A lot of artists treat their songs as fragile things that can easily be destroyed. U2 knows that if an experiment fails, the original is still there to be returned to.

Edge puts up his new demo and listens to it. He asks if Larry is still in the building. No, Flood says, Larry went home. Edge gets up and goes out to the big room, takes a seat at Larry's drums and starts whacking out a raggedy beat while his demo plays. He spots a roadie packing a flight case and asks him to come over and just keep doing this. The roadie does, and Edge moves over to a keyboard, adding another part.

Flood records the whole thing and then Edge listens to it play back. He thinks there's a song there but would really like to hear it with a different structure—use this part as an intro, repeat the verse twice the second time through, repeat the intro going into the final chorus. He thinks about it for a while and then asks Flood if it would be possible to sample each section of the song onto a keyboard, so that hitting one key would play just the chorus, another key just the intro, another key the verse. Flood says sure. He digs out a sampler and sets about doing it.

Forty-five minutes later Edge is in Edge heaven, sitting on the studio couch with a keyboard in front of him, masking tape on the keys labeling the different parts of his song. He can play a dozen variations of the track with one finger. Flood rolls tape to capture the different versions as Edge tries a chorus at the top, using the intro as a coda, and every other structural rearrangement he can think of. He's not thinking about deadlines or record releases or tour rehearsals or family problems now. Edge is lost in his music, and he will happily stay here all night.

25

Stay

_____

*watching bono write a song/ typical drummer's critique/ the
big decision to go for an album/ flood's perspective/ bono
the baby-sitter/ the great wanderer debate*

B ONO AND Edge are standing at the drawing board, studying their
long list of song titles and making possible album sequences.
There are dots of different color next to each title, denoting
how far along each track is. A red dot means the music is there, a green
dot means the melody is finished, a blue dot means the lyric is ready. An
X means "mix the bastard." They are discussing with Larry a track they
have been listening to that is titled "Sinatra." As that title suggests, the
music was written by Edge in an attempt to emulate the classic structures of Tin Pan Alley pop songs. At one point Bono was even singing
words about "the wee small hours" over it. Bono has been trying to
come up with new lyrics and Larry is throwing in his two cents. Larry
says there are too many passing words, lines stuffed with useless *and*s
and *the*s. Bono should make those lines shorter. Larry also thinks there's
something off in the rhythm.

"Percussion?" Edge asks.

"No," Larry says, "the bass." They all laugh. Adam's off with Naomi
and he'd better watch out if he wants his bits here when he gets back.
Actually, Larry says, he loves Adam's bass part but hates a ghostly
effects-altered bass track that the producers have echoing it.

"So basically," Edge says, "your criticism is, *too much bass, too many
words, not enough drums.*" Everyone cracks up at the typical drummer's
review. Bono says that Larry really wishes he were the singer, Bono
wants to be the guitarist, and Edge is a frustrated drummer. "Adam only
wants to play the bass."

Edge and Larry go off to make some tour rulings and Bono returns his attention to the track-in-progress. A TV monitor has been rolled in and he switches on a sequence from Wim Wenders's film-in-progress, a sequel to *Wings of Desire* to be called *Far Away, So Close!* The scene is of an angel high above Berlin, looking down and contemplating earth. The angel leaps from his perch, trading divinity for mortality. As we watch, Flood plays back "Sinatra," a moody instrumental track. Bono starts singing along: "Green light, 7-eleven/You stop in for a pack of cigarettes/You don't smoke, don't even want 'em/Check your change."

It's haunting, unfixed and floating. Bono asks what I think and I tell him I think it's real good. He tries out some more lines. He sings, "And if you hit me, I don't mind/'Cause when you hurt me I feel alive." Then he says it might be better if he changed the perspective to: "And if he hits you, you don't mind."

Yeah, I say, that's a lot more concrete. Conversationally the *you* in the first version sounds like *one*. Changing it to *he* hits *you* makes it vivid. Together with a line that says this victim is "dressed up like a car crash" you're creating a real character. I tell Bono that it makes me think of the only gay kid in a small town. He says he's imagining a woman, not a homosexual, but it's great if it can be read in different ways. He sits on a couch in the control room and sings into a hand-held microphone, leaning forward to put all his emotion into it, squeezing his eyes shut, raising his arm on key lines. Bono singing on the studio couch does not act very different from Bono singing to a football stadium. He tries recording it twice, over two different versions of the backing track, one slow and moody, the other faster and more forceful.

Singing to the harder backing track, he decides that the song is no longer about Wenders's angel, so he should change one line of the chorus, which is now, "Stay—as the angel hits the ground." What's a bigger line? He solicits suggestions, stopping on "Stay and the night will be enough." He says the song is now strong enough to carry that. He sings the chorus with that phrase, trying it in different spots, from the first line of the chorus to the last. When he sings it as the conclusion, he really makes it a big declaration, raising his right hand in the air and wailing, "Stayyy—and the night will be *enough.*"

Flood is wary of melodrama; it's getting a bit romantic for his tastes. When Bono tries singing, "Stay—with your secrets sleeping rough," Flood puts his foot down. *Secrets* is one of the words that causes his bathos detector to vibrate. As the song takes on a more grand character

Bono makes small adjustments in other lyrics. In order to get in Wenders's title he has the line, "Far away, so close, up with the static and the radio waves." He had said "radio waves" in order to be deliberately unromantic, but now that the song's heading the other way, he will drop the word *waves* and sing the more Van Moorisonish, "Up with the static and the radio."

Bono is supposed to be where Ali is, where Adam is, at a friend's wedding. He told his wife to go on, he'd meet her there after a quick stop at the studio. That was hours ago. When Flood says, "How 'bout another take?" Bono says, "How 'bout a divorce?"

Edge comes in to hear what Bono's accomplished on "Sinatra." He listens, approves, and they fool around with a fade-out melody, *ba ba ba-*ing it over the ending. I say it sounds like "My Chérie Amour" and Bono assures me with a dirty look that he's not familiar with that song but he will make sure he buys a copy tomorrow and checks.

"It is getting pretty Californian," Flood says.

"Yeah," Bono says. "It sounds like . . . who's that songwriter who lives on the beach in Malibu and writes all the songs that sound like that?"

Edge: "Sting?"

Burt Bacharach is the name Bono is looking for.

Edge leaves and Bono keeps putting down tracks, changing the lyrics slightly each time. He tells Flood to change the listed title of the song to "Stay," from "Sinatra." Although, he considers, he ought to try to get some reference to Wim's film in there. He decides to call it "Stay (Faraway, So Close!)." Speaking of Sinatra, Bono says, he's heard that Frank is going to cut his first new album in almost ten years. Sinatra told Quincy Jones, "It's time to shake up the citizens." Bono is still dreaming of getting the Chairman a copy of "Two Shots of Happy."

He does not want to repeat the mistake he made in getting "Slow Dancing" to Willie Nelson. He was so excited about the song that the day after he wrote it he told a TV interviewer that he had just written a song for Willie Nelson. Before he had made any contact with Nelson. MTV picked up the item and broadcast it.

"Can you imagine?" Bono says. "Willie Nelson, one of the greatest songwriters alive, hearing me on TV saying I've written a song for him. Without his asking for it! He probably thought, 'Well, fuck you.'" Bono shudders at the thought. Then he says, "Johnny Cash said Willie probably never got the tape. He said, 'Well, Bono, Willie's had a lot of trouble.' "

Yeah, I say, some IRS agent is probably grooving to your song right now. Bono strums his acoustic guitar and I ask him to sing "Slow Dancing." I haven't heard it since my birthday at Kitty O'Shea's more than a year ago. He sings the song beautifully. Despite its country simplicity "Slow Dancing" addresses all the same conflicts as U2's *Achtung Baby* songs:

> And I don't know why a man search for himself in his lover's eye
> And I don't know why a man sees the truth but needs the lie

When Bono finishes I say, "Wouldn't that sound great coming out of all these Eno-esque vibes and distorted structures."

"That's a great idea," Bono says, then he addresses Flood: "You want to record it?"

Flood says, "You think I didn't?" He points to the vocal microphone lying in front of Bono and then to the recording console. Bono does it once more, his guitar in his lap and his lips brushing the microphone. Then he says he has to go catch up with his wife.

Outside the Factory he sees that he left Ali's car unlocked. He reaches for her car phone to call ahead and it's gone. He's in trouble again. A couple of English girls who flew to Dublin hoping to meet him come up with autograph pads while Bono struggles to remember if he left her phone somewhere—or has it been stolen?

He insists on driving me home, as he does every night. It is very gracious of him, but because Bono always gets distracted and forgets where he's going, a lift from him makes the trip twice as long as walking. As we cruise around Dublin running red lights and going the wrong way on one-way streets, Bono says, "Adam's walking around with two supermodels on his arm! Naomi and Christy Turlington, the girl I was with on the cover of *Vogue*. Adam's having a good weekend."

"Yeah," I say. "You really did him a favor when you hijacked Naomi to Ellen's party."

"They're going out now!" Bono says, wide-eyed. "They're in *love!*"

"He owes you big time."

"I'd say so."

"Bono! That was my street!"

The next day, Saturday, everyone is supposed to be off duty except Flood, who has taken on the weekend job of putting the finished songs together in a running order to prove that there is an album amid all these experiments. He talks about the evolution of "Sinatra" into "Stay."

"I think Bono would be the first to admit that lyric writing doesn't come easily," Flood says, "because it's so much to do with the baring of his soul. It doesn't matter whether it's to one or fifty thousand. When he's writing a lyric he might have three or four ideas on the boil. That song was particularly difficult because he had tried three or four times. The first and foremost thing is, he has to understand where this song is coming from. Until it has something concrete he'll continue to search. That is the first thing that has to be dealt with. You came in last night and you heard it and your point of view was quite different from the way we'd been hearing it. That gave him a spur. Then he goes one stage further and chips away here, chips away there, until he's ninety percent done. Then, okay, there's a couple of couplets that aren't quite right, he can go away and I'll let him off the hook. He can leave that till tomorrow. And obviously a lot of times Bono will worry about his actual performance as well as his lyric."

I ask how this little recording project during the tour break turned into such a high-pressure situation.

"Edge spoke to me a couple of times on the tour last year about doing an album very quickly," Flood says. "There was the assumption that we'd come into the studio, they'd have the songs ready, and we'd just record it with no overdubs. Anyway, they came in here to make not a *throwaway* album, but a quick album. And by their nature they are now finding it hard to make something that is ultimately disposable. Which is good. I think it's good that they're pushing themselves.

"Let's say *Joshua Tree* was peak number one. Had a bit of a dip on *Rattle and Hum*. Fine, you learn by your mistakes. So then a positive decision is made: 'We have to do something different.' The eventual outcome of that is: 'We've reinvented ourselves.' So now they're in a situation where I think it must be quite difficult to challenge themselves. They've been big, they've gone down, they've come back up as something different and now—they've got to do it all over again?"

I don't actually know if they do, I say. I think once they've successfully reinvented themselves the first time, they are given a free pass from that point on. No band ever had a tougher image to cast off than when the Beatles decided to bury the four Mop Tops with *Sgt. Pepper.* But once they did it, once they all grew mustaches and put on the psychedelic uniforms and sang about LSD, they were forever after free to do what they wanted. I think U2's now in the same boat.

"One of the things that appeals to me about U2 is the fact that they never rest on their laurels," Flood says. "It's brilliant that a band in their position are prepared to try anything, but on the other hand I think people now expect change. People's threshold of boredom is getting smaller and smaller. It's very strange times. So I can see it being hard if they *can't* do a record that's just a throwaway."

Well, I say, one thing's for sure—the big risk of reinventing themselves with *Achtung Baby* turned out to be their commercial salvation. It's a good thing U2 changed when they did.

"Definitely," Flood says. "Also, though, *Achtung Baby* very much came from their soul. The soul had decided to be different."

As for deciding whether or not to make this project an album, Flood thinks that yesterday U2 passed the point of no return. "If you don't have a definite point to focus on, then what are you doing? You're essentially making a selection of demos or you're rehearsing to try out some ideas. A single/EP is an underchallenging area. So why not say, 'We're going for an album'? You just have to say, well, if you don't make it it's not the end of the world. But we *could* get an album! Yesterday a decision was made; we're definitely going for an album."

Who should come wandering into the studio but Bono, the man who cannot stay home. In a concession to domesticity he is accompanied by his little daughter Jordan. I wonder if he told Ali they were going to the park. "Ali doesn't need me," Bono says. "She's packing, she's quite happy. She's completely self-sufficient. It's very disheartening." At least he found her car phone. He'd left it under the seat. He sings "Stay" a few more times, reading different lines off a yellow legal pad. His pal Guggi shows up and sits quietly listening. Eventually Ali arrives to collect Jordan.

"You're going to Chernobyl Monday?" Guggi says to her.

"Yep." Ali smiles. "Off to get some rays."

Bono works till late Saturday night. Sunday he does manage to stay home, leaving Flood to work up an album sequence.

Monday morning Suzanne Doyle is, as usual, the first one in. She is putting fresh flowers around the studio ("I'm like the ladies from the Rosary and Altar Society") while the band members and producers arrive and settle into the Factory sitting room to listen for the first time to a version of their new album. They smile, they frown, they scribble notes. At the end of Side One the sonic experiments give way to an acoustic guitar. Bono's version of "Slow Dancing" comes out of the speakers, surprising Eno, Edge, Larry, and Adam, who did not know he had recorded it. "What do you think?" Bono asks.

"I like it," Eno says, "but I'm afraid it will be a big hit. We must tamper with it somehow to prevent that."

Bono continues, looking for approval: "You don't mind that it changes the whole mood of the album?"

"Nah," Adam says. "Nothing wrong with a bit of 'obla-di obla-da.' " Edge and Larry laugh and groan at the put-down. "Obla-di" is the famously facile McCartney song that some people skip over when playing that side of the Beatles' white album. "Slow Dancing" may not make the cut.

Neither, if Flood and Eno have anything to say about it, will the version of a song called "The Wanderer" that Bono wants to use. Flood has put on this tape the version he prefers, with Bono singing his song about a man who turns his back on his family and goes off to search for God amid the worldly and sinful. Bono's version of the song is, the producers feel, the centerpiece of the album, a new direction for U2 still rooted in their past.

The trouble is that Bono wants to use a version of the song sung by Johnny Cash, recorded here when the Man in Black passed through Dublin two weeks ago. The argument has been going on ever since. Eno and Flood feel that, the merits of the track by itself aside, Johnny Cash's presence and persona is so strong and full of such vivid associations for listeners that it throws the whole album off balance. As soon as that baritone comes booming in, all the ambience and ambiguity U2 have achieved goes out the window. The Bono version of the song, in contrast, ties all the other themes together.

Bono argues strongly the other way; that hearing Johnny Cash sing over a trippy, distorted track about wandering through a wasteland "under an atomic sky" is as bizarre as it gets, and far more appropriate for this song, which is about a sort of *Wise Blood* character, a self-righteous pilgrim who reveals himself, over the course of the lyric, to be pretty much deranged.

There's a lot of merit in both arguments, but I suspect that neither one tells the real story. I think that the real reason Bono does not want to sing "The Wanderer" (the title is a conscious shot at the macho swagger of Dion's "The Wanderer") is because when Bono sings the song it comes off as a mea culpa for all the glitz and surface that U2 has spent the last two years creating. When Bono sings "The Wanderer" it seems like a public confession that beneath the fly shades he is hoping to find God by searching through the glitter and trash.

The character in the song has used Jesus' exhortation to leave your wife and children and follow Him as an excuse to skip out on his responsibilities. He is playing with the ancient antinomian heresy that you can sin your way to salvation ("I went out there in search of experience/ To taste and to touch and to feel as much as a man can before he repents"). By having Johnny Cash sing the song, Bono erects another false face. The part of the audience that shares his spiritual side (as well as the part that understands how serious a figure Johnny Cash really is) will understand the deeper message, and those who want to think it's camp will just get a kick out of U2 casting Johnny Cash as Hazel Motes.

So Flood and Eno can argue all day about how disruptive it is to have the Boy Named Sue come strolling into the finale of U2's most European, most avant-garde, most systematically disordered album. They're not going to win this one. Bono has another agenda.

26

Macphisto

---

larry injects bull's blood/ eno proposes a library sytem/ fintan goes shopping for shoes/ songs are cobbled together/ bono paints his face/ the zooropa tour begins/ hope for rich men to get into heaven

BONO GETS a sandwich from the studio pub and slips off into the sitting room to wolf it down. A minute later a howl comes through the door. Bono emerges holding his cheek. Yesterday he went to the dentist with an abscessed tooth and thought he'd gotten it under control, but it just went off again. He's reeling from the pain. Suzanne digs up some painkillers, which he swallows. By the time Bono raises his dentist on the phone the pills are dulling the discomfort, so he decides to tough it out. He will do his vocals today with a toothache. Last week he was working with a damaged leg, hurt while jogging on the rocky beach outside his house. There are bound to be wounds in an operation this size.

Bono doesn't want Larry to know he's hurt or he'll get a lecture and prescription. Larry takes a great interest in people's medical problems. He's been known to carry bags of vitamins, powders, and pills—a portable cure for any malady. Larry pays careful attention to his health but has still had some real problems—trouble in the tendons of his hands once threatened his drumming career. After overcoming that he was cursed with a disk protruding from his spine that screwed up his back terribly. Bono says Larry tried different doctors without success until he went to a German who brought in a holistic healer who started giving Larry shots of bull's blood. That did the trick! Larry's Irish doctor refuses to accept it—he looks at X rays of Larry's crooked spine and says it's impossible, but Larry feels fine. He flies to Germany for shots of bull's blood regularly.

Suzanne looks up from her desk. "Larry is full of bull's blood?" she asks. "That explains so much."

Later, when I ask Larry about this miracle cure, he puts less emphasis on the injections than on a series of exercises he does to build up the muscles around his damaged disks. The stronger muscles relieve the pressure on the spine. Typically, Larry says his problem was solved through discipline, while Bono prefers a supernatural explanation.

Back in the control room there's a discussion under way about security. Each of the four band members is taking home cassettes of Flood's rough sequence, and both Edge and Robbie Adams are worried about bootlegs. Rehearsal tapes and songwriting sessions from *Achtung Baby* were in stores before the album was, and it caused U2 all kinds of aggravation. Edge says there has to be a penalty so severe that no band member will dare lose his tape. "Everyone should have to sign something saying if you lose your tape you lose your house. Or a finger!"

Eno suggests instituting a library card system where "one of your trusty men" holds all cassettes and any band member who wants one must sign it out. That suggestion is much scoffed at.

The looming deadline imposed by the start of the European tour is giving U2's creativity a solid kick. Bono has been unable to finish the lyrics for a track called "Lemon," his attempt to write a Prince song. Faced with such a block, Eno and Edge dig up and sing an alternative melody and lyric ("A man makes a picture/ a moving picture/ through light projected he can see himself up close") that had been rejected for being too much like the Talking Heads. This second lyric is about filmmaking and quotes the director John Boorman, who once employed the young Paul McGuinness as a production manager and who used to say he made his living "turning money into light." Edge and Eno put the movie song together with Bono's Prince tribute and the result sounds nothing like Prince, Talking Heads, or U2.

The same sort of juxtaposition turns out to be the salvation of "Numb," a Kraftwerk-style track Edge has been keeping alive since the *Achtung Baby* sessions in Berlin. Bono had tried to find a way into "Numb" by singing in the high Eartha Kitt voice he used for the background vocals of "The Fly," but it didn't lead anywhere, no one could come up with a strong enough melody to carry the song, and "Numb" was almost put aside again. Then Edge suggested that maybe it didn't need a melody as much as it needed a rhythm. Maybe the words of the song could be used like percussion, like a conga. So he came up with a list of orders ("Don't grab. Don't clutch. Don't hope for too much. Don't breathe. Don't achieve. Don't grieve without leave.") and delivered them in a monotone while Bono's Fat Black Lady voice was dropped in behind it, and the two contrary approaches together created something weird and interesting. Larry came up with a melody for a hook line ("I feel numb") and sang that as a punctuation. "Numb" is the first U2 track with three different members of the band singing different parts. Bono's assessment: "I can't believe it works!"

"The First Time" is a gospel song U2 comes up with very quickly and starts to put aside as inappropriate. Eno surprises them by saying, "I love that song; it must go on the album." Bono figures the song—about a prodigal son who wanders off into a life of sin and then returns to his father's forgiveness—seems more like something from *Rattle and Hum* than this project. But the band trusts Eno's instincts, so they try playing it in a real disjointed way that disguises its gospel form. Bono sings about a lover who teaches him to sing, a brother who is always there for him, and then a father who "gave me the keys to his kingdom coming, gave me a cup of gold. He said I have many mansions, and there are many rooms to see. . . ." Suddenly Bono cannot bring himself to sing the lines he has written about returning to his father's house. Instead he finishes the verse, "I left by the back door and I threw away the key."

The questions raised in *Achtung Baby* have still not been settled. Bono is not ready to promise that he will return from this journey into Nighttown that he's only halfway through. I ask him if he's familiar with the heresy about sinning your way to salvation. "Yeah," Bono says. "Finding God through indulging the flesh." He then says that when Jesus said it was more difficult for a rich man to enter heaven than for a camel to pass through the eye of a needle, he was not—as most people assume—saying it was impossible. He was referring to a tight gate into Jerusalem that was called the Needle's Eye. "To get through it," Bono says, "you had to *stoop*."

They're down to the last days before the European shows. Tour rehearsals are going on simultaneously with the recording sessions. U2 realize with some unease that they will not be able to work out live versions of any of these new songs to perform onstage as the new album is being released. Hopefully they will get the chance to practice them at soundchecks and add them in as the tour progresses, but the Zooropa tour will begin without any songs from the new album they have decided to call *Zooropa*.

The extramusical aspects of the show will be quite different from last year's tour. Just as Ned and Maurice have updated the on-screen videos to reflect the current confused situation in Europe, Bono is constructing a new character to play on-stage during the encores. The Mirrorball Man who closed the 1992 shows was an American TV evangelist/used car salesman/game show host in a cowboy hat throwing dollars around. There is no sense using that character in Europe. So Bono sets about trying to construct a European equivalent and starts singing "Desire" in a voice that sounds like an aging British music hall entertainer, or a faded Shakespearean actor touring the provinces.

Fintan Fitzgerald has been looking for the right costume for this old ham and comes in one day with a hilarious pair of 1970s platform boots, spray-painted glittering gold. Bono starts free-associating. Maybe this old guy is the last rock star, dragging himself around some years in the future, re-creating the joys of that great music of the twentieth century for other senior citizens. But of course, that's not all he is. Bono remembers how knocked out he was by Steven Burkoff's performance of Oscar Wilde's *Salomé,* in which the actor slowed all the speeches down to half-speed. Bono tries talking like Quentin Crisp with his batteries running out and it creates a weird poignancy. "Oooh. Iii've boughhht sommmme newwww shoesssss. Doooo youuuu like them?" It feels like an old man trying to hold himself together.

But it's Gavin Friday who comes in and supplies the unifying metaphor. He demands to know—all allegory aside—who is this character really representing? Who was the Mirrorball Man really supposed to be? Bono says, "Well, the devil."

"Then," Gavin says, "he should wear horns."

Bono thinks that's ridiculous, it's too blatant. But Fintan secures some red horns and when Bono tries them on with whiteface and lipstick and platform shoes and aged British voice, he likes what he sees: he sees Mr. Macphisto—the devil as the last rock star.

Bono pulls in all sorts of orbiting signals to finish creating Macphisto's character. He takes from a magician he saw in Madrid abrupt, almost comical movements—like a senile karate expert suddenly trying to snap into his old positions. He takes from the devil character in *The Black Rider* a ringmaster's demeanor and the stiff-shinned walk of someone hiding a cloven hoof. He uses Joel Grey's character in *Cabaret* as a touchstone for the decadence from which European fascism bloomed. Macphisto is Satan as a cross between Elvis, Sinatra, and a thirties Berlin cabaret star. He is, of course, also Goethe's Mephistopheles, that proto-European symbol of great art and temptation. Like Bloom in Nighttown (or for that matter Eve in the garden) Goethe's Faust risked his immortal soul for knowledge. That's a trade-off that fascinates U2.

Macphisto's public debut is at the first concert of the European tour, in Rotterdam. Backstage Bono looks through several suits Fintan brought for his selection and chooses a gold one, to match the shoes. He paints his face, puts on the lipstick, and then goes into the band's dressing room to see Adam, Edge, and Larry's reaction. They are startled. This is a lot creepier than they expected.

Macphisto lurches out at the encore to sing "Desire" and then introduces himself to the audience, crying, "Look what you've done to me!" The crowd hoots and cheers at this satanic Bono. "You've made me very famous." They laugh. "And I thank you for it. I know you like your pop stars to be exciting, so I've bought these." He hoists up one leg and displays his platform shoes. Big footwear close-ups on the Zoo TV screens. The audience loves it. During the rest of the encore (which is in effect the fourth set, after the *Achtung*/Fly set, the B stage acoustic set, and the U2 greatest hits set) Macphisto loses his horns ("Off with the horns, on with the show!") but not his diabolical persona. Though by the time he performs "Love Is Blindness" from the lip of the B stage with the white makeup running down his face, the line between Macphisto and Bono has become blurred. He ends by singing "I Can't Help Falling in Love with You" alone, after the other members of U2 have gone. Then Elvis Presley's original version of that song comes out of the loudspeakers, drowning out the last rock star with the first, and Macphisto walks slowly down the long ramp through the audience, back to the main stage, and disappears.

"From the introduction of Macphisto on, it's all cabaret," Bono says. "Macphisto is the Fly down the line. When he goes into falsetto on 'Can't Help Falling in Love,' it's the little boy inside the corrupt man breaking through for a moment. Just like in that awful tape of fat Elvis slurring that song, there's a moment when he sings a bit of it right, and you hear Elvis's *spirit* coming through. That's what I'm shooting for."

"It was really a bizarre, kind of chilling feeling seeing him," Edge says. "It was everything we discussed. It was very disturbing, very unreasonable, and nothing to do with entertainment. It was something much heavier. I thought the idea of the horns was over the top, I thought it was spelling it all out, but in fact it really works."

U2 doesn't have much chance to appreciate how well Macphisto comes off. They are still commuting by their private Zoo plane back to Dublin to finish the album. Flood and Eno are working away, mixing and editing so that the band's work when they drag themselves back into the studio is minimized. They finally make a decision that confers an unexpected unity on the whole project: They throw off all the rock songs, all the guitar-based tracks like "Wake Up, Dead Man" and "If God Will Send His Angels" and make *Zooropa* entirely an album of disjointed, experimental pop. Now the whole enterprise is of one piece. Sonically, ironically, the finished album is much closer to the work Eno and Bowie did at Hansa in Berlin in the late seventies than *Achtung Baby* turned out to be.

"Realizing, 'Oh, this is not a *rock* album,' is a big relief," Bono says. "The world is sick of macho, sick of grunge. We need to get a female perspective in."

Edge shares the producer credit with Eno and Flood, not only because he earned it with all the extra work he put in, but because, Bono rationalizes, with the conspicuous lack of rock guitar people will otherwise wonder where Edge went.

When final mixes are complete and cassettes are run off, Des Broadbery, the keyboard tech, is delighted to hear some ideas he threw in—a little chant loop on "Baby Face," some samples on "Numb"—have made it to the finished album. Larry Mullen takes a certain subtle pride in the fact that a bass part he came up with one night when Edge was working on guitar ideas has remained on the title song; Larry is the bassist on the intro to "Zooropa."

I suggest that *Zooropa* conjures up the madness and disorientation of touring in a way that will make a special impact on musicians. "I suppose that's true," Adam says with a half-hidden smile. "It does seem to have a lot of songs musicians will identify with. But I'd hate to think we've made a nineties *Running on Empty*."

May 10 is Bono's 33rd birthday. He is now as old as Christ was at his death, as old—according to Church tradition—as all our resurrected bodies will be after the end of the world. Bono goes into his room on his birthday to find Gavin Friday has left a large gift in his bed: under the inscription, "Hail Bono, King of the Zoos" is a ten-foot cross, painted blue and big enough for Bono to hang on.

27

Business Week

the end of the record industry and other good news/ how U2 ended up owning everything by being nice guys/ ossie kilkenny's virtual reality/ U2's new deal/ mcguinness to prs: take your hand out of my pocket

FINISHING THE *Zooropa* album has a secondary benefit for U2. It completes their contractual obligations to Island Records (and to Polygram, the multinational that now owns Island). Paul McGuinness and Island have been working away at a new contract, but having an unexpected deal-finishing album to drop on the desk puts McGuinness in an even more powerful position than he was in already. Here's the carrot—a new record by your biggest act two years before you expected it. Here's the stick—U2 is now free to go anywhere we want.

Not that anyone thinks that's going to happen. Polygram chief Alain Levy talked to McGuinness about U2's intentions before Polygram bought Island, and McGuinness told him U2 and Island were great friends and Polygram had no reason to fear that U2 would leave anytime soon.

Chris Blackwell, who owned Island, always treated U2 very well. As naive kids U2 assumed that this was how all record companies behaved toward well-intentioned acts, but as they got older the band came to understand how rare Blackwell's decency was. Island never tried to force U2 to make artistic compromises. They even gave them complete control over album artwork. The only two times Island ever argued with a band decision was (1) when U2 said they wanted Brian Eno to produce them and (2) when the label sent an unfortunate emissary to Dublin to suggest to the group that the photo they had chosen for the cover of their second album, *October*, was not very good. U2 and McGuinness chewed the poor guy's tail off. How dare he, a mere businessman, try to interfere with a decision made by artists! The Island rep was sent packing and Blackwell let U2 have their cover. Which, the band agrees today, was a terrible cover. Island was absolutely right.

In August of 1986 U2 was finishing *The Joshua Tree,* the album that they knew had a good shot at making them superstars, when McGuinness and Ossie Kilkenny, U2's accountant, were told that Island Records was in big trouble. The label was close to bankruptcy. They could not even pay U2 the money they already owed them—which was five million dollars.

McGuinness and Kilkenny were stunned. They sat in a room and cursed themselves for losing all U2's money by being dumb enough to think that the record company was like a bank—you could leave the dough sitting there and pick it up anytime. And all that loss aside, if Island went under now, what would happen to *The Joshua Tree?* Would the album that U2 was counting on to carry them over the top be a victim of poor distribution and lack of promotion? Would the stores even be able to order it?

Here was the worst part of all: if Island went under, some big company could come along and buy it up, along with U2's contract. What if the band ended up working for someone they hated?

Thank goodness U2 had gotten back from Island, in a renegotiation the year before, title to their song publishing, which Island had gotten in U2's first contract, when the band was in no position to argue (and—frankly—did not understand what they were giving away). Before that any new people who bought Island could have sold "I Will Follow" for a Toyota commercial or "Sunday Bloody Sunday" as a Band Aid jingle and U2 would have had no way to stop it. They knew Chris Blackwell would never do something like that, but by now U2 had come to understand that Chris Blackwell might not always be the man across the table.

They wanted to keep him there for as long as they could, though, so after one day of panic and recriminations, U2 agreed to bail out Island by delivering *The Joshua Tree* anyway, declining to demand the money owed them, and even loaning Island some more money to get over the hump. It was generous, and typical of U2's approach to business—which valued personal relationships and obligations above dollars and cents. As soon as he was back on his feet Chris Blackwell responded in kind. Over two different negotiations (the first during this Island crisis in August of '86, and the second six months later) U2 got two things that meant more than the cash they were owed.

First was the eventual reverting of all masters of their recordings to U2. This meant that Island was now just *leasing* the rights to release U2's albums for a fixed number of years, but that if U2 someday left the label, their albums would go with them. This is the sort of deal the Rolling Stones have had since 1971, which is why every seven or eight years the Stones post-1971 catalog is reissued on a new label. It's also why the Stones are still able to get gigantic advances in their old age; when a label signs the Rolling Stones it doesn't just get the albums the band will make in the years to come; it gets "Brown Sugar," *Exile on Main Street,* and another twenty years worth of hits too. U2 would never again be in the position of worrying that their life's work might be sold out from under them.

The other provision they got for saving Island, though, was the real reason that McGuinness would not have discouraged Polygram from paying a fortune for the label: U2 got a sizable chunk of equity in Island. The amount usually reported was 10 per cent, although it was probably a bit more. Ossie Kilkenny says that a tenth was what Blackwell thought U2 had coming if he owed them five million dollars, 'cause Blackwell figured the company was worth $50 million. Ossie and Paul thought Island was probably worth something closer to $34 million (which would have entitled U2 to a seventh of the company). Whatever figure they settled on in 1987, it became the bargain of the century when Polygram bought Island for more than $300 million less than two years later. It was one more time (like choosing to go with the artsy Eno to produce *The Unforgettable Fire*) when U2 elected to do something financially suspect for personal reasons, and ended up breaking the bank anyway.

So when McGuinness drops *Zooropa* on Island/Polygram's coffee table, he comes from a position of supreme power. There is no question that Polygram will cough up a fortune to keep the jewel in their crown. The only debate is over *how much.* McGuinness did entertain a pitch from his old pal Jimmy Iovine to sign U2 to Iovine's successful new Interscope label for the USA, but never seriously considered doing it. That discussion may have been simply a courtesy to one of U2's closest allies in the business, the man who produced *Rattle and Hum,* but I'd bet that McGuinness wanted to cause Polygram to sweat a little by making it look as if U2 were shopping around.

As was the case in the renegotiation with Island seven years ago, the provisions of this deal may mean more to U2 than the money. Because although virtually no one outside the music business understands it in the spring of '93, the rapid changes going on in technology will, within the next decade, completely redefine how music is delivered to the public and what record companies do.

The end of the old world is as apparent in the entertainment industry as it is on the map of Europe. The technology for delivering music —and indeed television, films, computer information, mail, and telephone services—is all coalescing into a single home delivery system that will revolutionize the information industries, and perhaps a big chunk of the international economy along with them.

Articles being written in popular magazines about the coming "Information Superhighway" focus on what it will be like from a consumer standpoint to have all sorts of home entertainment options at your fingertips. But no one is talking about how such a revolution will shake the companies that are now in the business of delivering information and entertainment the old-fashioned ways. The record labels are scared that the effect on them of the new methods of home delivery will be like the effect the rise of the automobile had on the buggy business.

Record stores could become obsolete as music is delivered over cable, telephone wires, or satellite transmission directly into consumers' homes. This raises amazing possibilities. One is that in the next century top acts such as U2 will no longer need record companies; they will be able to make their albums and sell them directly to their audience by direct transmission. Both Bellcore (the Bell Telephone research company in Livingston, New Jersey) and Philips (the company that owns Polygram, U2's label) have set up crude working prototypes of home music delivery systems by hooking up recordable CD players to fiber-optic telephone lines. Imagine a future in which U2 finishes making an album at the Factory, and then just walks over to the computer, puts it on-line, and waits for their fans to punch in credit-card numbers and download it into their homes. No record store, no record company, no one to grab that other 80 percent of the profit.

This is why there is suddenly a rash of mergers between entertainment companies and delivery systems (such as telephone, cable TV, and satellite) companies. As in Bosnia, no one's sure who is going to eventually control this landscape, so everybody's grabbing as much property as they can. Unless governments decide to step in and limit access to the cable, phone, and satellite systems (which could place all the power in the hands of the hardware-makers) it seems likely that, as Bono says, this new contract will be the last record deal U2 ever has to make.

There is an intellectual landgrab on as real as any past gold rush. U2 knows that this race will be won by the hardware that plays the software consumers want most. And U2 is, in this game, precious software.

"We think," McGuinness says of U2's new contract negotiations, "we've provided for a future in which the sound carrier has disappeared."

How close is this revolution? Pete Townshend is rumored to be negotiating a new deal—with the British phone company. Prince has announced that he will no longer make records—from now on all his work will be audiovisual. (Of course, Prince makes apocalyptic announcements regularly and rarely sticks to them.) U2 played with the notion of making *Zooropa* an interactive audiovideo presentation, skipping CD and audiocassette altogether, but the impending deadline imposed by the tour led them to abandon that ambition and release it as an album in the traditional sense.

Kilkenny sees the future of entertainment as an audiovisual environment, in which music is less likely to be a work complete in itself as it is to be half of a sound-and-picture presentation or even a minor component in the background of a video game or a virtual reality display. After all, if one unit in your living room can play either music with pictures or music without pictures, how many people will choose "without"? So in their new contract U2 is offering the record company the right to sell the *sounds* they make, but reserving to themselves the right to sell any pictures that go with them. This, the band figures, will give them ultimate control over any evolution of their work into future media—as well as a huge chunk of the money any such future media (passive or interactive) might generate.

What Kilkenny thinks is very unlikely to be won in these negotiations is a concession from the record company that would limit Polygram's right to sell U2 albums to hard copies (CDs, cassettes, records, minidiscs) only—leaving U2 free to sell their music through cable or satellite transmission. Kilkenny says that there is not a major record company in the world that would agree to sign U2 for anything less than the total right to sell their musical product through any means available—because to limit themselves to hard copies in the face of this coming revolution would be to conspire in their own extinction.

I tell Kilkenny that if I were he, negotiating for U2, I would offer the record company the right to manufacture CDs, tapes, and other hard copies of U2's music—but reserve to the band the right to transmit and market that same music by direct electronic delivery. He shoots back, "If I were in the record business I would say, 'I won't do a deal with you! Because I am in the audio business and I believe I will always be in the audio business.' You can't deny people in the record business the right to promote that which they've got rights for in *any* new audio medium. Then you would have two competing operations marketing the same product! It wouldn't make any sense. And those companies—the Polygrams, Sonys, Virgins, Warners—that's the business they're going to be in. They're going to be in the exploitation of audio rights in whatever form.

"If you want to be businesslike," Kilkenny continues, "you can't deny a person the right to market your records. If records are an audio means, then you must give that person the right to audio use in whatever form audio use is available. We're used to formats—whether it's discs or tape—that are physical. The great uncertainty out there is, what are the new technologies? Will it be cable? Satellite? Your phone? We don't know whether it will be transaction-based or pay-for-play. So in that uncertainty all you can say to a person is, 'Okay, we grant you the audio rights, so you must have the right to sell records *or their replacement* in audio form.' What we don't know is, what should we get paid?"

What U2 has done in this new deal with Island/Polygram is to leave the division of profits from future transmissions systems flexible, to say in effect, *here's the split on a U2 compact disc, but we agree to leave the split on satellite transmission of U2's music unresolved until such time as both parties can assess the fair market value of such delivery systems.*

By thus postponing the division of monies earned by systems that do not yet exist, U2 hopes to avoid the sort of kick in the teeth that they and almost every other artist took when CDs replaced vinyl, and the bands discovered that a "new technology" clause standard in recording contracts gave artists only half royalties on new "experimental" formats. For a few years in the 1980s the labels really raked it in, charging the consumers twice as much for a compact disc as they had for records while paying the artists only half as much. Every artist and manager in the world cried, "Never again!"

While all this record negotiation and technological speculation is going on, McGuinness is also trying to prepare the ground for the Brave New World by waging war on the European performance rights organizations, an old and archaic network of agencies charged with collecting performance royalties on songs played on TV, radio, and in concert and distributing the monies to the songwriters.

See, every time anyone performs a song for money—whether it's U2 in a football stadium or a hit record played on the radio or a lounge singer crooning "Tie a Yellow Ribbon" at the bowling alley bar—the promoter or bar owner or station is supposed to pay a small royalty to the author of that song. Performing rights societies collect fees from stations, clubs, and concert halls and then pay the appropriate music publishers, who pay the writers. No one pretends that the system is remotely accurate, but at least in America the fact that there is competition between two private collection agencies has kept them somewhat responsible. ASCAP and BMI put all the money they bring in into a hat and, using a formula based on record sales, radio play, and spot-checking of venues, compute an approximation of how often different writers' songs are being played and pay them accordingly.

In Europe, by contrast, a network of national collection societies has a functional monopoly. And McGuinness contends that while that may have been a sad necessity in the old world, in this new post–Cold War, post–Treaty of Rome, post–Maastricht Europe of unified economies, U2 should have the right to collect their own money for their own performances of their own damn songs. In February McGuinness and U2 issued a writ in the High Court in London declaring that the British Performing Rights Society's rules are unenforceable under the laws of the European Union.

"There's an appalling system of collections through organizations like the Performing Rights Society and its national equivalents in each European country," McGuinness says. "Those organizations, sometimes commercial, sometimes statutory, collect on behalf of rights owners, producers, performers, and writers from television, radio, concert promoters, and so on. The whole system is incredibly haphazard and inconsistent country by country, and the European community is not making any serious effort to tackle the issue. We're in the middle of a lawsuit against the Performing Rights Society in Britain where we're basically saying to them, 'You claimed you could collect money on our behalf. It now seems that you are utterly incapable of collecting it but did not admit that.' We expect to make a lot of money from the Performing Rights Society because of that.

"Underlying that case is as well a British attitude which is that the PRS exercises some sort of benevolent function by collecting and distributing a lot of money to songwriters who otherwise wouldn't get any money. Now, sadly, if you have written a song and no one is performing it or listening to it, you're not *entitled* to any money! And on my clients' behalf I'm not prepared to accept a situation where the PRS appears to collect on our behalf *inefficiently* and then distributes our money to a load of losers and no-hopers! If they need money they should be getting it from a genuine benevolent society or the state or somewhere else. I don't see why they should be taking it out of our pockets."

McGuinness may be chasing the PRS through the European courts for a long time, but in the end he will probably help to shatter an outmoded system—and clear the way for U2 to track and collect their own money (or hand that job over to their record company—who will have to do *something* if they aren't going to physically make and ship albums anymore). The middlemen are finding their power bases disappearing in the new world. This must be how it felt a hundred years ago, when no one was sure if the future was going to be with the internal combustion engine, electric motors, or steam—but it was clear that horses were in trouble.

While U2 is starting their European tour McGuinness, Keryn Kaplan, head of Principle's New York office, and Anne-Louise Kelly, head of the Dublin office, fly to the Polygram's managing director's conference in Miami, Florida, to tell the assembled record company that they have two happy announcements for them: U2 has resigned to Island/Polygram for a long-term, six-album deal, and U2 has just delivered a new studio album, *Zooropa*, which the label can release immediately.

The Polygram executives cheer the news, which probably means their Christmas bonuses are in the bag. Business and music trade publications around the world jump on the story. The *New York Post* estimates that the deal is worth $200 million for U2.

Newsweek runs a photo of Bono onstage as Macphisto and reports:

"There's yet another hyper-deal in the music biz, this time between Irish rockers U2 and Island Records. In what may be the priciest handshake since Michael Jackson's with Sony in 1991 U2 is guaranteed $10 million a record and a sky-high 25 percent royalty rate. 'U2 has sold more than 50 million records for us,' says a company spokesperson. 'I think that speaks for itself.' True enough, but will it drown out the voices of smaller bands? *Achtung,* baby."

McGuinness won't confirm the figures, on the grounds that it is bad taste for people who have a lot of money to brag about it in a world where so many people have none. The thing to bear in mind, though, is that all the big figures that record companies love to throw out when they sign superstars are baloney, 'cause all the deals are based on performance and most advances are recoupable. It's great hype to say that Virgin paid $50 million for Janet Jackson or Elektra paid $25 million for Mötley Crüe (no one's that stupid, are they?), but it doesn't mean those artists ever banked that money. The height of such nonsense was when Michael Jackson resigned with Sony a few years ago and Sony Music chief Tommy Mottola said the deal could be worth *a billion dollars,* and the press ran out and printed it! They missed the key word: *could.* That would be like my saying I got a deal worth a billion dollars for this book. I did . . . if it sells 500 million copies.

28

Dada's a Comfort

---

*the alertness of U2 security/ neo-nazis stink up germany/
larry descends into underworld/ macphisto scares the
bellboy/ a theology monograph from cyndi lauper*

BONO IS sitting at a table in the private lounge of the private floor of a Cologne hotel when Larry comes up and sees the eggs, toast, and potatoes that Principle's Sheila Roche ordered and had to abandon when duty buzzed her walkie-talkie. "Great!" Larry says, pulling up a chair. "I was just wondering how I'd get breakfast!" Larry no sooner has the first forkful to his mouth than a waiter steps up holding the bill for all the breakfasts eaten at this table while Larry was sleeping. Bono motions to the waiter to give the check to Larry, who looks at the sum, raises an eyebrow, and signs. Then I ask for an Evian and begin to sign for it and Bono says, "No, Bill, no, no!"

That's too much for Larry. "Let him buy the *water*, Bono! I paid for all your breakfasts!" I sign and Larry says, "I'm sure the advance will cover it."

Adam comes in, sweating from a workout in the hotel gym, and pulls up a seat. McGuinness appears a moment later and asks Adam if he and Naomi are really getting married on September 15.

"Bullshit," Adam says. "Absolute bullshit."

"But I'm reading it *everywhere*," the manager says.

"You're probably telling them," Adam replies.

Bono goes off to dress and comes back a few minutes later in the black clothes, slicked-back hair, and bug-eyed shades of the Fly. His whole demeanor changes when he's dressed like this. He stands and walks with the straight back and rigid shoulders of a colonel inspecting his troops.

When everyone is assembled we ride an elevator to the lobby, and

Edge and Bono do their ritual signing of autographs for the kids waiting outside the hotel while Larry and Adam do their ritual waiting for Bono and Edge. Eventually the procession of black cars pulls out. Larry's riding his motorcycle to the gig today, which jacks up the sense that we're in a diplomatic motorcade. McGuinness stares out the car window, studying the strange architectural mix of Cologne, a city with some magnificent ancient structures surrounded by modern buildings— the result of most of the old city being destroyed by Allied bombers. Paul's father was an RAF pilot who bombed Cologne.

At the Mugersdorfer Stadium U2 settles in their dressing room and Edge tries playing "11 O'clock Tick Tock," an early song they have not performed in ten years. Adam asks what key it's in and Edge suddenly laments, "I can't remember the solo."

Bono says, "That might be good." Bono says that although you'd never know it, "11 O'clock Tick Tock" was conceived as the sort of cabaret song sung in the last days of the Weimar Republic, but Martin Hannet, U2's first producer, could not accept it that way, and so it was given the early U2 rock & roll treatment. Now Bono's interested in resurrecting the embryonic version. In Macphisto, they finally have a *Cabaret* character to sing it. (Edge, by the way, says this story is complete crap and he has the first—rock & roll—demo of "11 O'clock Tick Tock" to prove it. Well, I suggest, perhaps it was Weimer in Bono's mind.)

At soundcheck, in a light rain, U2 plays "I Will Follow" for the first time on the tour, and decides to throw it into the set tonight. As soon as they finish their run-through the crowd begins pouring into the stadium and the first of the opening acts go on. Between warm-up bands, U2 has invited a theatrical group called Macnas (Irish for "madness") to stir up the crowd by strutting out in giant U2 heads and doing a miming parody of the four band members, as if U2 had joined Mickey and Donald at Euro-Disney. The giant Edge head is especially grotesque— it looks like the Merchant of Venice. The fellow playing Larry mimics Larry's upright, macho posture, the one doing Adam imitates Adam's haughty, nose-in-the-air stance, and the actor portraying Bono minces and overemotes like a bad Hamlet hanging off the balcony. There is a real element of the jesters mocking the kings. The audience loves it. A funny thing about German crowds, though—they cheer in *low* voices, making a friendly outpouring sound sort of ominous.

Backstage U2's bodyguards are speaking into their walkie-talkies, sharing signals. Adam passes by two of the security men on his way to the catering tent and they transmit to their agent downstairs, "Number three coming down!"

Adam joins Larry in catering to do a TV interview. Edge and Bono are still up in the dressing room. Outside the tent one crew member approaches Willie Williams and asks if the band is around. "Haircuts down here, hats up there."

"How's Bono's mood?"

"Good, still not great. Lifting from yesterday."

Geez, I say, it sounds like you guys are issuing weather reports: *Number one partly cloudy, clearing expected later. Number three overcast.*

"Believe me," the crew member says. "It pays to know."

Another roadie is heckling one of the security guys, holding up an imaginary walkie-talkie and saying, "Number one is going to the toilet! Number one is doing a number two!"

Adam and most of the crew who aren't working head out front to watch the support set by Stereo MC's, whose song "Connected" seems to be playing in every disco, boutique, and café in Europe. Everybody on the tour loves the Stereo MC's—which was not the case with the opening act U2 fired last week. Einsguzende Neubauten, a German industrial band who "plays" tools and pile drivers, was thrown off the tour after one of them threw a steel bar at a Dutch audience that was pelting them with vegetables. It hit a girl who had to go to the hospital. Willie Williams observed, "Angry German performance art doesn't go over well in football stadiums in midafternoon."

This season, Germans who display too much belligerence are particularly liable to be hit with produce by hypersensitive Europeans. The neighbors are edgy about the old fatherland regaining its superpower status. In the year and a half since reunification Germany has been struggling with tremendous social adjustments. One and a half million immigrants have poured into the country since the collapse of Communism, and last week the parliament decided to impose some limits. West Germany had had a wide-open asylum policy since World War II, a reparation demanded by the countries that had absorbed waves of refugees from the Nazis. Of course, in the years right after World War II there was not a widespread desire by people to move to Germany. Now Deutschland is the promised land for immigrants from the collapsed Communist countries and the Third World. In shutting down the gates now, the German government may be simply trying to protect its economy, already strained from having to absorb all of broken East Germany in a single swallow. But the effect is to apparently ratify a growing German xenophobia.

It may be unfair that other countries think they see the specter of fascism behind any display of German nationalism, but there has been great attention focused on recent violence against non-Aryans in Germany, particularly the Turkish population. Neo-Nazis are in the news this week in Solingen for burning a Turkish family's home and painting swastikas on it. Two Turkish women and three girls were killed in the attack. Last November a grandmother and two girls were killed in Molln in identical fashion. In response to last week's murders, Turks overturned cars and smashed store windows across Germany. What is hard for people from other countries to comprehend is that German citizenship is not conferred by birth, but by ethnicity. So a person of Turkish heritage born in Germany is not considered a German, though a person of German heritage born in another country will easily be granted German citizenship. Chancellor Helmut Kohl has been widely accused of appeasing rather than resisting the bigots. He did not attend any of the funerals of the Turkish murder victims, and declared that "Germany is not a country of immigration."

Onstage tonight Bono introduces "One" by saying, in German, "This song is for the immigrants to Deutschland." He gets solid, not heavy applause. "Until the End of the World" takes on a political charge in this atmosphere, which is doubled by the insertion after it of "New Year's Day," a song at least partly inspired by and associated with the rise of Solidarity in Poland ten years ago. During the acoustic set on the B stage, Bono sings Bob Marley's "Redemption Song" as a lead-in to an unexpected—and passionate—version of "Sunday Bloody Sunday," a song about the Northern Irish troubles. That hangs in the air while the band returns to the main stage for "Bullet the Blue Sky," their exploding evocation of the wars in Central America. U2 are as political as the Clash tonight. The climax of it all comes when Bono, as Macphisto, picks up the telephone to make his nightly celebrity call.

"Around this time I usually make a phone call," he says in the lilting voice of a Profumo pimp. "Often to the president of the United States. But not tonight. Tonight I will call the chancellor, Mr. Kohl." The crowd cheers as Bono punches the numbers and explains, "When you get very famous, people give you their telephone numbers." A secretary answers and Bono says, "Hello, I'd like to speak to the Chancellor, Mr. Kohl, please." He is asked for his name. "This is Mr. Macphisto." Then, playing to the audience, the video screens lit up with his leering devil face, he says to the phone, "He's an old friend of mine, a close friend!"

"Do you know what time it is?" the voice demands.

"I know many things," Macphisto snarls, playing up the Satan side of his horned persona. "Could I leave a message for him then?"

"What is it?"

"Could you just thank the Chancellor for *letting me back into the country?*" The crowd lets out a gasp and the devil continues, cackling, "I'm baaaack! I'm *baaaack!*"

U2 is living up to their promise to push the envelope in Europe. If you give them a chance, Bono and Edge will talk your ear sore about the dadaists, the nonsense-art movement that popped up in Europe after World War I. U2's take on the dadaists is that they sought to deflate the rising fascists through mockery, that by refusing to accept the vocabulary being used to subordinate them they erected a moral defense under the pretense of anarchic silliness. U2 see Zoo TV in general and Mr. Macphisto in particular as owing a debt to dada. That the Nazis set out to wipe the floor with the dadaists is seen by Bono as proof of their potency. (Though the fact that the Nazis succeeded in stomping them may suggest a pretty good case for their long-term impotence too. Remember Woody Allen's observation that against Nazis biting satire is less useful than baseball bats).

Not that all the silliness going on around the show has such serious undertones. While Bono was doing his solo opening of "One" tonight, Larry slipped into the vast underworld beneath the stage to stretch his legs. One of the crew took off his phone operator's headset and handed it to Larry, who put it on and listened in to the video directors talking to each other, calling shots, ordering close-ups, and generally making sure the giant TV screens were jumping. Larry dialed up Monica

Caston, the live video director, and said in an American drawl like one of the security crew, "Monica, ah don't like this shot of Bono."

Her flustered voice came back, "What do you mean you don't like it? What's wrong with it?"

"Ah don't know, ah jest don't like it. Why don't you change it?"

"Blow me!"

"Monica," Larry said, switching back to his own stern voice, "this is Larry." Her scream almost blew out a few headsets. Laughing, Larry slipped back behind his drums.

At the hotel after the show everyone congregates in Bono's suite in the hope of finding something to eat. Room service seems to have disappeared. The road crew are, as one of them describes it, lumbering around searching for food like a herd of migrating cattle. By 3 A.M. everyone's holding their bellys and groaning. Sheila Roche, Suzanne Doyle, and publicist Regine Moylett have taken up seats on a couch by the phone and are calling the kitchen every half hour or so. Every time they get the same answer: "Ten minutes."

Finally Bono decides to step in. He grandly picks up the receiver and purrs, "Hello! This is Mr. Macphisto. I ordered french fries and sand-wiches an hour and a half ago and if I don't get them immediately I will . . ." and here he degenerates into a string of incomprehensible mumbles that must sound even more threatening in the translating imagination of German room service than they do in their native gibber-ish. Anyway, it works. Within minutes tray after tray of french fries is wheeled in by frightened-looking bellboys and the entire touring party falls on them famished. I whisper to Bono as he sticks a chip in his mouth, "They probably spit on them."

Somehow our party has been joined by the pop singer Cyndi Lauper, who is also staying in this hotel, and a couple of her Cyndiesque gal pals. Cyndi starts discoursing to Bono and Larry in her broad Queens accent about the shortcomings of their religion (and, in fact, everybody else's too). Cyndi lectures Bono that all the major religions are "patri-article." She loves the word, she says it more than once. She says she herself was a Hare Krishna as a kid until she realized that *they expected to sit on their fat asses while the women did all the work, and the women were supposed to wait until the men had finished to eat and then were only allowed to eat in the kitchen like dogs!* There's a word, Cyndi says, for that kind of behavior: "Patri-article!"

Sheila Roche sits quietly on the couch and says to Suzanne and Regine, "*Someone's* been reading Camille Paglia. . . ."

I go to bed before dawn but I can't find a switch to shut off the Muzak pumping through my room. I'm not kidding—it's "Girls Just Want to Have Fun."

29

Innocents Abroad

U2 drives deep into germany/ the manager finds his manger/ fly the friendly skies/ larry brings down the berlin wall/ a video shoot is planned/ bono goes ton ton/ a guest editorial by johnny rotten

P AUL MCGUINNESS elects not to fly to Berlin on the Zoo plane. The autobahn presents him with a rare opportunity to let his Jaguar rip, and he intends to take it. There is a secondary motive for the manager's intention to split off from the tour in Germany; he wants to find the place where he was born. Yes, the cat's out of the bag. Like Colonel Tom Parker, that alleged Southern gentleman who turned out later to be an illegal immigrant, Paul McGuinness was born in the Rhineland. Unlike Colonel Tom there was nothing surreptitious about Paul's nativity—his father was stationed in Germany with the occupation forces when the future mogul made his first grand entrance on June 16, 1951. Paul follows his directions to the town of Rinteln, where he pulls into a gas station and asks another customer if he can direct him to the British Military Hospital. The other customer knows exactly where the hospital is; he's an obstetrician. The doctor points out the way to the hospital and then notices the license plates on Paul's Jaguar. With some embarrassment the doctor tells Paul that he will have to report him, as those are Irish plates and, well, the IRA has taken a couple of cracks at this military installation. Paul hands the doctor his card and says, "Here's my name and number, do what you have to."

The rest of the tour party is passing overhead in the luxury of the Zoo plane, a 727 with a big "Z" painted on the tail fin. All the seats on the plane are first-class size, and arranged in rows of two, facing each other with aisles wide enough for horse racing. The PA plays Prince,

Guns N' Roses, and Luka Bloom. The Sunday papers are laid out, the flight attendants are piling on the food, and the drinks come in crystal flutes and goblets. Traveling like this makes you realize how little the usual tension of air travel has to do with the actual flying. If you take away the traffic, bag checking, flight delays, hectic terminals, and cramped on-board conditions, the up in the air part is kind of fun. It would be worth *driving* the Zoo plane to Berlin.

Coming into the city the mood darkens considerably. U2's caravan of cars swings around a park filled with white wooden crosses, a hasty memorial to the victims of AIDS. Thirteen thousand experts are convening here this week for the Ninth International Conference on AIDS, and their view is pessimistic. The more they learn about this new plague the farther off a cure seems to be.

Like Parisians and New Yorkers, Berliners have a superficial gruffness that can be startling when you've gotten used to the friendliness of the outlying areas. Right now Berlin is going through an identity crisis and the streets crackle with the feeling of a collective psyche on the edge of a nervous breakdown. The city has probably had to endure more symbolic weight in the last half century than any place could bear, and the cracks are showing. After Hitler, after destruction, invasion, and conquest, Berlin woke up to find itself the split symbol of the clash between communism and capitalism. East Berlin was subdued by the Soviet-sponsored police state. West Berlin was colonized less brutally but no less totally. The NATO countries were faced with the dilemma of how to keep West Berliners from deserting the city in the face of impending Soviet invasion and the thousand inconveniences of being isolated from the rest of the free world. Many families could not be enticed to stay under any circumstances—parents want their children to be safe, not symbols. To hold the rest of the population, Berlin offered government-subsidized apartments and other official enticements. Young men who chose to live in Berlin were exempted from national service. That drew the young and single, artists and free spirits, who in turn transformed Berlin into a bastion of twenty-four hour a day excitement, entertainment, and stimulation. West Berlin became the most progressive city in Europe, a constant reminder to the gray dominion in the east how much fun they were missing.

Cold War West Berlin was the Left Bank crossed with Las Vegas, which is a hard act to keep up now that the Wall has fallen and all those gray people are pouring in to buy some Nikes and try the food at McDonald's. Out of resentment, the idiot children of old nihilists and nationalists start waving Nazi flags. They may not be Nazis in any sense Hitler would recognize—except that they are racist thugs. They may be out less for any ideology than to rage and break things. But that can't make much difference to the Turkish Germans who've been terrorized or the foreigners who've been threatened. For the past year and a half black American soldiers in Germany have been the targets of hate campaigns. If it were all American soldiers you could write it off to nationalist resentment, but the fact that blacks have been specifically picked out stinks of something uglier.

Berlin, a liberal, progressive city, is being asked to absorb a conservative, stifled culture. Berlin, a wild, hedonistic city, is being asked to be a moral exemplar. Berlin, a youthful city that lives only in the present, is being asked to oppose the resurgent Nazi past. Berlin, defined for fifty years by its division, is being asked to embody unity. No wonder the Berlin U2 arrives in seems to be cracking from the strain.

Larry, Morleigh (the dancer signed up for another tour of duty after all), and I decide to take a drive along the jagged cement teeth that are the remains of the Wall. We visit the Hansa recording studio, cross to the miserable East German hotel where U2 saw KBG agents under every bed, and then head down to Checkpoint Charlie, which was the armed border crossing between East and West and is now being transformed into a tourist attraction, its horror receding into history. Larry points out that the East German gun towers that overlooked this place just eighteen months ago have been torn down. We drive past a recently opened secret police building where, our driver tells us, both the Nazis and the Stasi tortured political prisoners. We come to one of the sections of the Wall still standing and Larry says to stop the car. He gets out and tries chipping off a bit with a stone but comes up with only the smallest of fragments. He looks around and sees a big piece of the Wall, a pipe sticking out of a concrete chunk, lying nearby. He grabs it, hauls back, and with a mighty howl starts swinging his makeshift sledgehammer into the standing wall with a fury usually reserved for his tom-toms. It would be really easy for him to damage his drumming hands this way, but the adrenaline of freedom has Larry pumped up like Keith Moon in a Holiday Inn. He smashes his concrete club into the cement edifice again and again, shouting and laughing, sending big hunks of the Berlin Wall flying all over the sidewalk.

Back at the hotel, McGuinness has arrived and U2 are meeting in the bar with Kevin Godley, who directed their Thanksgiving TV special last fall in Los Angeles. The band asked Godley to fly in on short notice to film a video for "Numb," the unlikely choice for the first track being released to radio from *Zooropa.* Edge is the lead vocalist on the song; it will be his first starring role in a video. Too bad for Edge that the band can spare only one day to film the clip, and that day is tomorrow. U2 racked their imaginations to come up with a concept that would be striking, original, and—most important—would require only one setup. The idea they've come up with was partly inspired by an old Elvis Costello video ("I Want to Be Loved") set in a photo booth: what if we sit Edge facing the camera as if he's staring at a TV, and he remains impassive, lip-synching the words, while all sorts of funny things happen to him. It requires one shot, no real set, and some good ideas of things to be done to the deadpan Edge.

The members of the band all grab pieces of paper and make lists of what they'd like to see happen to Edge in a chair. Edge's list is full of suggestions like, "Beautiful women kiss Edge." The guitarist is taken aback when his bandmates ideas are read out: "Edge gets punched in face," "Cigarette pushed up Edge's nose," "Break egg on Edge's head." Bono sees the sick look on his pal's mug and whispers that Edge may be a little nervous about having to be a video star. I don't think that's what Edge is nervous about.

Everyone's hungry, so it's ruled that the planning of the next day's shoot should be moved to a restaurant. Due to some insane nostalgia, the place picked is the same smoky pub in East Berlin where U2 masticated during the making of *Achtung Baby.* No one seems to remember till we get there how miserable that experience was. It is quite late, nearly midnight, and the waiters hand out the menus with all the enthusiasm of men's room attendants handing towels to drunks. I try to order some fish and the waiter huffs and puffs and says, "No. Weiner schnitzel! Is easier on the chef." Well, I don't want weiner schnitzel, how about the chicken? "Weiner schnitzel!" he insists again, as if I'm hard of hearing. "Is easy on chef!" No matter what anyone wants to order, they are getting weiner schnitzel. Which wouldn't even be that bad if, when it finally arrived an hour later, it resembled any schnitzel, weiner or otherwise. The boiled ball of beef on my plate—and indeed the boiled balls of beef on the plates of my companions—does not look edible at all. It looks like a tennis ball left out all winter.

By this point the drinks on the plane and the drinks at the hotel have been supplemented by drink after drink after drink at this monkey house and nobody feels like eating anymore anyway. There are, however, some suggestions for new tortures to inflict on Edge tomorrow that seem to all assembled like the funniest ideas since the Inquisition. One of the Principles decides that the waiters are selling us watered-down vodka, and so grabs the bottle from the angry server's hand and swigs from it. Trouble is, it is way past the point where anyone can taste the difference between vodka and water anyway. It is time to adjourn the video meeting and move onto another venue. Someone has the name and address of a reggae/African music club. Suzanne Doyle, the ever-efficient transportation chief, starts summoning cars and assigning seats. When she's barking orders to a roomful of drunks like this some call Suzanne "Nurse Ratched." McGuinness calls her "Big Bird." I think they should call her "Elle Duce," 'cause she sure makes the trains run on time.

On the way across Berlin to the reggae club, Regine Moylett recalls visiting friends in East Berlin before the Wall came down. She says that obnoxious neighbors would immediately show up and insist on coming in and listening to the conversation. The neighbors would try to pro- voke some political comment from the visitor or point at Regine's rock T-shirt and demand to know how she could defend decadent pop music. She doubted these muttonheads were secret police, but guessed that many East Germans filed reports on their neighbors for the Stasi. It was a way of getting some extra favors or getting on someone's good side. The whole culture was riddled with mistrust and paranoia. It gives me a fix on the lines in "The Wanderer": "I went drifting through the capitals of tin, where men can't walk or freely talk and sons turn their fathers in."

We arrive at the African club, called Ton-Ton, commandeer a bunch of tables, and order more drinks. Bono asks who wants to dance, and one of the women of Principle volunteers. When they get out on the floor, though, the club's black patrons clear off. Bono is startled. Luck- ily the disc jockey steps in and announces that Ton-Ton has some special guests tonight and does a little rap welcoming U2. The tension dissipates and the Africans start dancing again.

Paul McGuinness and I are slumped in a corner solving the world's problems when he comes out with what I consider a remarkable insight. He says that ten years ago, he and the group never expected U2 to become the biggest band in the world—they thought they would be *one* of the biggest bands along with the Clash, Talking Heads, the Police, and the Pretenders. "We expected those bands to be with us all the way," Paul says. To U2's amazement, all the groups ahead of them in line broke up, leaving them to gather the accumulated energy and run with it. Paul says Tina Weymouth, Talking Heads bassist, came to a U2 concert and said, "Bono is everything I hoped David [Byrne] would become."

I once talked to John Lydon, the former Johnny Rotten, about the influence his group P.I.L. had on the early U2. The guitar and bass on the track "Public Image," for example, could have been the prototype for half of U2's early records.

"They've hardly been appreciative of the fact," Lydon said. "They haven't been very honest about where their influences have come from, have they? A great deal of U2 has to do with early P.I.L. It's the Edge all over, isn't it? That's fine, that's not an insult. He liked it and he took it someplace else. Made it his own. Well, good luck to him. It just gets irritating when people tell me, 'Oh, you're not as good as U2.' Don't you know where they came from?"

There's no question that U2 did come from P.I.L. And from the Clash, Jam, Patti Smith, Skids, Lou Reed, Bowie, and fifty other places. What sets them apart from their early rivals and influences is where they ended up.

30

Numb
___

the big video shoot/ whose foot is on edge's face/ more tall tales of the emerald isle/ post-chernobyl marriage shock/ hemingway's advice to rock stars/ a toast to reg, the star of the show

WHEN ADAM and Larry arrive for the "Numb" shoot at the film studio in Spandau—a big warehouse, really—Edge has already been working for five hours. He is sitting on a stool in a black sleeveless T-shirt with three sexy women on the floor around him like the cover of *Electric Ladyland*.

"Tough work, Edge?" Larry asks.

A claustrophobic little corral has been set up around Edge in the middle of the huge factory room, with screens all around and hot klieg lights overhead. A posse of young German models—boys and girls—stands around the periphery looking sunken-cheeked and existentially bored. Their job is to mill in the background, out of focus, imbuing the scene with a vague air of nihilistic ennui. Seems like typecasting to me. These kids look like they were yanked from an undergraduate Sartre seminar.

Director Godley is in the middle of coaching a little girl, about five, on how to beat on Edge's chest. "Harder! Hit harder!" he tells her.

Larry steps forward: "I'll do it!"

"Get in line," comes Maurice's voice from behind the cameraman.

The tape operator rolls "Numb" and Edge starts mouthing the words, reading them off a big board right under the camera. He recited them out of a notebook when he made the record and he's never had to memorize the litany. His unblinking intensity as he tries not to screw up the lyrics helps with the illusion that he is staring into a TV screen, oblivious to all the stimuli around him.

On cue, Maurice leans in and blows smoke in Edge's face. Then Andrea Groves, one of the singers from Stereo MC's, reaches up from the floor behind him and massages his shoulder. Two German models dressed as bimbos lean in and stick their tongues in his ears. A spoon of ice cream is stuck in his mouth. The little girl beats on his chest. Maurice come up behind him, loops a length of string over his head, and starts tying up his face. Edge cracks up laughing and everything stops.

There is an instrumental break in the middle of the song and they've decided it's a good idea to have Edge drop out of the picture during it. This decision is less aesthetic than practical; it means Godley can film two two-minute sequences rather than one four-minute shot. Given the amount of time they have to complete this clip—one day—and the number of different actions that have to be coordinated (twenty-four) and the chance of Edge blowing a lip-synch in the steady stream of lyrics, that is a great blessing. But how to get Edge out of the shot?

The director has an inspiration. He asks an assistant to throw a bunch of couch cushions on the floor behind Edge. Then he tells Larry to come over, put his hand on Edge's face, and push him straight over backward, stool and all. Larry says, great! Edge says, "Should we try it first with somebody expendable?"

They give it a shot. Larry comes up fiercely, grabs a handful of Edge's face, and sends him reeling over backward, both feet straight up in the air like a cartoon. Everybody laughs and claps. But looking at it played back on the video screen the director reluctantly concludes that it's *too* funny—the pratfall kills the numbed-out mood.

Godley suggests that maybe it should be Bono who comes up and binds Edge with the string.

"Bono?" Edge says with mock alarm. "Bono is going to tie ropes around my neck? Wait a minute . . ."

Maurice says the twine is just for rehearsal, in the actual shoot it'll be barbed wire.

Dennis Sheehan is off in the corner shouting into a walkie-talkie that Morleigh, the belly dancer, was told she was on hold for this shoot today and now no one can find her. I keep it to myself that I saw Morleigh leaving the hotel five hours ago. She said that she'd been vaguely told that she might be needed for the video today, but she sat in her room all morning and heard nothing, so she was going to go out and see Berlin. Unlike practically everyone else on the tour, Morleigh does not wait on the whims of the kings. She has her own dance company; she is a pro. If there's a call she'll be there on time and ready to work, but if no one remembers to call her she will go about her business. Luckily there will be no need to make Maurice put on breastplates and substitute for her. With his usual magical gift for finding women, Bono strolls in a minute later with Morleigh in tow. He was staring out the car window on the way through Berlin, saw her walking down a side street, and called to her to jump in and go see what was going on at the "Numb" set. Dennis Sheehan seems equally relieved that she's here and exasperated at the haphazard method of her deliverance.

The two tough-looking tongue models, their big bosoms squeezed into black bustiers, are practicing snipping the shoulder straps of Edge's sleeveless T-shirt with scissors. Each time they do, an assistant runs out and tapes the shirt back together. Adam takes over the job of blowing smoke in Edge's face. As the backward pratfall is out, Larry tries shoving Edge sideways out of the frame. That works.

The whole ballet is coming together now. The funniest thing is watching the dozen different people with walk-on roles huddle, squat, and lean to stay out of the shot when they're not doing their bits. They all have to be within arm's length of Edge so they can pop into the frame and lick, slap, spoon, or shove, and it takes a lot of deft stepping to keep them from colliding with each other as they go in and out. One assistant's job is to wiggle a strip of black cardboard in front of the klieg light shining down on Edge's forehead, to create the effect of TV screen light rippling across his face.

Finally they film the entire first sequence. It starts with a faucet dripping in time to the mechanical beat of "Numb." As the guitar comes in the camera pans down to the drops hitting the head of the passive Edge. He stares into the camera dully and intones, "Don't move, don't talk out of time, don't think, don't worry, everything's just fine . . ." while off camera a grip swings the pipe and faucet away and hauls it out of the shot. Adam leans in and blows smoke in Edge's face. Andrea's hands crawl over his shoulders and massage him. Fingers push in Edge's cheeks. The two models drag their tongues across his cheeks ("More tongue!" cries the director. "Now bite his ear! Harder! Lick his face!"), a spoonful of ice cream is stuck in his mouth, the little girl beats on his chest, the two models slice his shirt, Adam wraps the clothesline around his face, Larry sticks his face in from the right and sings, "I feel numb," Bono sticks his face in from the left and sings his Fat Lady parts, Larry pushes Edge over sideways as Bono steps back, out of the way.

After a few passes, the director announces that the first half of the clip is done. A supper break is called, and while chowing down, the band and Godley try to finalize what the second sequence will be. The director reads off the list of options: "Do you want Morleigh's legs around your neck or her foot in your face?"

Bono, Adam, and Larry say together, "The foot in the face!"

Edge: "I prefer the legs around the neck."

Godley says if Edge really wants to, they can do it without film in the camera.

Bono says it would be good if, when the solo ends, Larry comes in and puts his face in front of Edge as if he's checking out what's on the imaginary TV, but that creates a problem, "Then how do we get rid of Larry?"

Godley repeats the question. "Yeah, how do we get rid of Larry?"

Larry says, "Usually you get the manager to do it."

Guggi, whose wife is German, arrives in time for supper. Godley accepts that they are not going to be able to use two extras they imported for this shoot. He gestures to a large flight case. I open it and meet two very large pythons. Guggi reaches in and hauls out one of the snakes, petting it. This leads to a reverie between Guggi and U2 about his old snake in Dublin, and the time it escaped and wrapped itself around his flatmate.

Bono asks if I've seen *Into the West,* a new film written by Jim Sheridan about two kids growing up in the Dublin projects. I have. "Guggi and I grew up in the houses behind those buildings," Bono says. "Those were the 'seven towers' in 'Running to Stand Still.' That movie was no exaggeration. They did have kids tearing around on horseback, horses in the lifts."

Larry asks Guggi how one of the neighborhood characters is doing and Guggi says bad, he just finished a prison term for murder and his brother's body was just fished out of the canal. He's had a bad run of luck. "But, of course, he was one of twenty-two children." U2 go on to recount with great amusement inviting a movie star acquaintance of theirs who happened to be in Dublin to go along with them to a wedding, where the actor ended up drinking and having a great time with this particular hardcase. The two of them bonded and made plans to go off together later in the week. The band wondered how much trouble the Hollywood star might have ended up in before he realized that he was keeping company with the sort of bad guy you don't find in movie scripts.

Back on the set, Edge returns to his seat while Morleigh and Andrea climb up on card tables on either side of him and start rubbing their bare feet all over his face. Edge, his eyes closed, is enjoying it very much. Larry sneaks up, takes his shoe off, and adds his smelly, socked foot to the facial, ruining Edge's fun. The director encourages Morleigh to try to get her little toe into Edge's nostril.

Bono, assuming a certain directorial prerogative, walks around the set making suggestions and vetoing ideas like Cecile B. DeMille. A man leads a poodle into the room; Bono has it sent back. I whisper to him that it would be funny if someone lifted Edge's ever-present hat off— and he had another one underneath. Bono's eyes light up and he goes over and whispers the idea to Godley, who laughs. They call over Edge, who shoots it down faster than a slow duck on the first day of hunting season. Edge keeps his lid on.

The choreography continues: Ian Brown, Godley's Scottish producer, is drafted to gently caress the Edge's cheek with his big, burly hand. Morleigh in her belly dancing costume hunches beneath the camera and then rises up, wiggles in front of Edge, and spins away. One of the cameramen struts up and flashes Edge's photo, then two teenage extras run up and do the same.

With the second sequence pretty much worked out, they just need an ending. It presents itself when Paul McGuinness strolls in with some friends with whom he's just had dinner. U2 insists that the video end with Paul coming up to Edge, leaning into his ear, and saying, "I have someone I'd like you to meet."

To the band members those are the eight most dreaded words in the language. It means the manager is about to stick them with some awful radio consultant, journalist, or royal relative. U2 swears with passionate hyperbole that McGuinness saves these requests for when they are in the depths of either exhaustion, depression, or conversation with fascinating women. "It's the line," Bono says, "that puts the fear of God in all of us."

Paul has had some wine with dinner, so he's agreeable. Edge gets into position, on the floor where Larry shoved him at the end of the first half. Lights, camera, and action are called and: Larry is staring at Edge's unseen TV; Adam comes by, takes a look over Larry's shoulder, and leaves; Larry leaves; Edge regains his seat, slipping on a jacket; Morleigh's foot caresses Edge's left cheek; Andrea's foot caresses Edge's right cheek ("More pressure with feet now!" shouts Godley. "Feet out!"); Morleigh, off camera, slides off the card table and hunches under the camera; a bouquet of flowers is thrown at Edge; Morleigh shimmies in and out of the frame; boy snaps photo with flash camera; girl snaps photo and kisses Edge on cheek; cameraman snaps photo of himself with his arm around Edge; Paul McGuinness walks up and says the dreaded words and Edge sadly gets up and goes off with him.

"Numb" is shot. It is 1:15 in the morning. The filming took about thirteen hours. Everyone relaxes, gabbing and laughing and looking at videotape. Bono comes over and pulls up a chair and I ask how Ali's Chernobyl trip went. It turns out to be a touchy subject. He says that she has had an experience such as he has on tour; she went off with a group of people to a strange place, they saw some mind-blowing things, they ate and traveled and slept together as a small, tight community— and now that she's back she's taking a little time to get readjusted to domestic life. The U2 tour has a week off after Berlin, and Ali's been telling Bono not to worry about hurrying right home if he has other things to do.

This scares Bono to death. He is the one who strays in and out of the family, not she! It occurs to him with some horror that the only reason they are able to function so well is that while he changes personalities, Ali is constant. He knows she has the right to go out and experience everything he has, but if she does, will they never both be at home mentally at the same time?

In the interests of shoring up the domestic dam, Bono has arranged for Ali and the kids to meet him in Paris as soon as the Berlin concert is over. From there they'll go spend a week at their house in the south of France and he will woo her like a teenager. Bono knows very well that he is able to have everything—a wild life in the world and a secure life at home—because of Ali. He would, in every respect, be lost without her.

I keep giving Bono copies of Hemingway's *Garden of Eden* and he keeps losing them. I've told him he'll recognize himself. Occasionally he'll say to me, out of the blue, "I misplaced that last copy of *Garden of Eden* you gave me but I will get another and I will read it."

It's an amazing novel for anyone who supports himself doing anything creative, and for anyone wrestling with celebrity. It begins with a young writer on his honeymoon. He has married a wealthy young woman and they are on a romantic tour of the Mediterranean. In the early part of the book the writer is living completely in the real world—he devotes great attention to the taste of food, the feeling of sun and swimming and bicycling, and the joy of sex with his new bride. His work, writing his next novel, is simply something he goes off and does for a few hours every day; it is one aspect of his life but not in any way the center of his attention. But as the story progresses his devotion becomes divided between the real world and the world of his creation—not just his fiction but his emerging public image as a tough-talking macho man. That image is not exactly accurate—the writer is actually less sure of himself and far more emotionally complex than this cartoon persona, but he is flattered by the praise and kind of likes the notion of himself as a literary cowboy. It hurts his feelings when his wife brings him down to earth.

Over the course of the novel the writer becomes increasingly confused by the real world in which his authority comes and goes, his wife's sexual courage begins to intimidate him, and he is unsure where he stands from day to day. He is more and more drawn to the world of his fiction, where he has absolute authority, and to the life of his public image, which is simple, black and white, and wins him the applause of strangers. When *The Garden of Eden* begins, the writer's attention is focused on the real world and his work is just a pleasant job. By the end of the book he is living completely inside his fiction, and the real world is just where he goes to eat and sleep.

Bono is hung halfway between the two ends of that book. He has one foot in his home life and knows he's *really* Paul Hewson, husband, son, and father—and his other foot in Zoo World and knows he's *really* Bono, rock star, musician, and Fly. *Achtung Baby* was all about being at home and tempted by the buzz and bright lights of Nighttown. *Zooropa* is all about being out the door, on the plane, in the cabarets—and trying to remember who you used to be. The character in *Achtung Baby* is still closer to the guy at the beginning of the *Garden of Eden* than the guy at the end; he still tastes and smells the real world. The character in *Zooropa* is over the hump and picking up speed on the descent.

Once I was shopping with Bono and he pulled out a credit card to pay for a gift. As he signed I asked what name was on the card—Paul Hewson or Bono. It turned out it was neither, it was his initials. He said, in a surprisingly aloof tone, "I don't want people in shops calling me Paul. It suggests an unwarranted familiarity." I gave him a *la-di-da* look. He grinned and announced, "Paul is dead!"

The *Garden of Eden* scenario is a real threat to successful rock musicians. No doubt it's a threat to celebrities and successful artists high and low, which is why Hemingway was able to nail it. Faced with the ugly equality of marriage, it's tempting for the acclaimed artist to say to his wife, "Look, I work hard, I give you everything, and in spite of what you might think of me *all these thousands of people love me!*" So the artist looks for his audience to give him the ego-boosting affection his wife or family is withholding or saddling with conditions. The uncritical love of the audience gives him the guts to keep going along on his self-centered way, even as his marriage dissolves. The trouble is, when the day comes that the fans no longer respond, the artist is left bitter and alone.

Does that sound like *Dr. Joyce Brothers's Advice for Lonely Rock Stars and Other Big Babies?* Well, being a rock star is a rare and goofy thing to be. It's hard to hang on to any thread of normal behavior when normalcy has vanished from your life. The same part of Bono that can genuinely laugh at his own posturing and vanity keeps him conscious of how important his marriage is. He loves being a rock star because he only has to be one sometimes. I suspect that if Bono ever thought he had to be that all the time, he would quit being a rock star at all.

When we get back to the hotel I find all the others in the bar reliving the day's glories. Considering that Kevin Godley first heard of this video concept—in California—less than a week ago, its swift completion is pretty remarkable. He has no intention of going to sleep tonight—he will catch an early plane back to L.A. in the morning, and by the time he next goes to bed in California "Numb" will seem like a dream.

Adam says there is not going to be any use denying that the two pair of women's feet on Edge's face—one black, one white—are Naomi Campbell and Christy Turlington. As the sun comes up outside the hotel Larry raises a glass to Edge, star of the shoot. "To Reg!" Larry toasts, using the nickname insiders have given his famous nickname.

"To Reg!" the room replies.

Someone asks where Bono's gone.

"He's upstairs," Godley says, "furiously practicing his lead guitar."

31

The Olympic Stadium

deciphering the führer's charisma/ calling down the ugly ghosts/ bono does the goose step/ the architecture of sociopathology/ racing for the last plane home/ an ariel surprise party

ENTERING THE Olympic Stadium Hitler built to strut the master race's stuff effectively shuts the mouths of everyone in the U2 organization. It looks like the world has opened a gaping maw to reveal endless rows of concrete molars. I hail Bono on the grand stone steps as "Kaiser Hewson," but he just stares at the stadium, which spins down into the earth away from the light. The design is like an enormously inflated Athenian theater, but the sense of imposing dread is closer to what the Roman Colosseum could have been if Nero had had cement mixers. A ballpark such as this was built to function through a thousand-year reich and then serve as a tourist attraction for a couple of millenia more.

The stadium has more vibes than a xylophone factory. As we survey the grounds, everyone has the same observation: "Hitler was *nuts!*" You might suggest that this is not a fresh insight, but it sometimes takes a little firsthand scrutiny to fully appreciate the depth of even a world-famous maniac's eccentricities. Wandering between the giant statues of naked deutschmen holding back mighty stallions, looking across the vast expanse of manicured fields overhung by looming stone stadia, startled by the cement swastikas only slightly obscured by cosmetic glops of plaster, U2 realizes why Hitler, in the middle of a war with England, was cocky enough to turn around and invade Russia with his free hand while declaring war on the USA with his only gonad: *sheer lunatic audacity.* No offense to Neville Chamberlain, but one look at der Führer's taste in architecture should have been the tip-off that this dictator was a few schnitzel short of a smorgasbord. In his mind Hitler was not competing with Churchill, Roosevelt, or Stalin; in his mind he was competing with Caesar and the pharaohs.

After we've drunk it in, Bono asks what I think. "The scale's pretty inflated," I say. "It makes you think that Hitler had real problems of overcompensation. Maybe he wouldn't have needed to conquer Europe if he'd just been a little taller and had both balls."

Bono pulls himself up to his full five-foot-eight, glances nervously at his zipper and says, "Um, Bill . . . there's something else about myself I've been meaning to tell you. . . ."

A gaggle of guilty-looking crew members shuffle by giggling. They proudly announce that they have filled the Olympic torch with explosives for the finale of "Desire."

Ian Brown, the "Numb" video producer, walks by drinking it in. "It's a lovely stadium, isn't it?" he says.

"Yeah," I say, "kind of makes you want to reconsider that whole anti-Nazi attitude."

Ah, I'm just being snotty. I think of this place as scary because of what we now know about the Nazis, but think how it must have felt to Germans, humiliated after World War I, frightened by the fall of the kaiser, and broken by the Depression. What to us is an almost lunatic massiveness must have seemed to them majestic. It's easy to understand wanting to be part of it.

"Oh yeah, yeah," Bono says. "*I* feel it. As I said at that peace conference, 'You must not underestimate the sex appeal in a Hitler.' That's what so much of this is all about."

U2 has been warned of stern penalties for breaking curfew in Berlin, but they have secretly decided to do it anyway. They want this show, above all others, to have the full force of all their technology right from the first song, and that means waiting till after dark to begin. As we are in Berlin and as this is the summer solstice, that means delaying U2's kickoff until 10 o'clock. The band announces, falsely, that the delays are due to technical difficulties. Then a great debate ensues in the dressing room about whether they want to make their usual entrance in front of the Zoo TV screens, or whether they want a spotlight to hit them descending the huge stone steps into the stadium. They go back and forth, radioing each *yes, no, yes, no,* to the increasingly nervous lighting desk. They finally decide, just before going out, not to have the spotlight. They walk to the top of the steps in the new darkness and look down into the enormous well of buzzing Berliners—and a spotlight hits them. Uh-oh. They are illuminated like Nordic gods. A cheer rises up from the throng. They descend the stone stairs to the back of the stage, slowly sinking beneath the crowd's vision.

Looks impressive to the world, but in underworld there's panic. The elevator that raises Bono onto the stage is broken. A crew member is desperately trying to get it working. A signal is sent to the video crew to keep the intro tapes playing. The video guys flip—these opening montage tapes don't last too long! Okay, the elevator's fixed! Tell the vid crew the band's going on! *Where the fuck is the band?* They are still standing at the foot of the steps, admiring what a good job they did walking down. The intro tape is about to run out! *Get them onstage now!*

The audience's attention is held by the Zoo TV screens, which are lit with the gigantic images from Leni Riefensthal's *Triumph of the Will* and *Olympia.* The crowd—the vast majority of whom could not recognize these images, which have been banned in Germany—cheer as the drummer boy bangs out a beat and the German bathing beauties sweep their arms in the air and a Hitler Youth (here some of the crowd may be getting the vibe that this is toxic history) pumps a baton. Beethoven's "Ode to Joy" (See, there were good Germans too) blasts louder and louder as the Nazi images give way to a cascade of symbols of Europe in the last fifty years—from the hammer and sickle to the shroud of Turin to the little sketch of a sad astronaut that is the symbol of this tour (it is basically last year's *Achtung Baby* baby with a space helmet drawn around his face—it represents the Soviet cosmonaut who was in orbit when the USSR fell, and who was left floating up there for weeks until the new government figured out who was responsible for getting him down). The images come faster and faster, the music swells higher and higher—and then it is broken by Edge's guitar slashing out the first chords of "Zoo Station" as the video screens all turn to blue static.

As always, this drives the crowd apeshit, and climaxes with Bono rising slowly up in silhouette in front of the screen behind Edge. Bono always struts across the whole row of screens, from the left side of the stage to the right, and descends singing to take his place with the band. Tonight, though, he is not just strutting across the screens. Maurice yelps and Joe O'Herlihy shakes his head. Bono is goose-stepping. His right arm keeps trying to shoot up in a Nazi salute, like Dr. Strangelove, and his left hand keeps grabbing it and slapping it down. One of the slogans that flashes on the screens is "Taste is the enemy of art." If that's true, Bono is da Vinci tonight.

The band is playing like dervishes, opening on full throttle. Edge is standing with his feet far apart, holding his guitar out in front of him while he plays. Bono is singing in some strange accent, at the very edge of his throat, roaring the words. This is for them the most important show of the tour. This is where they have to get it right. Subtlety is not even in the repertoire.

Bono again dedicates "One" to the Turks. This time there is very little cheering; in fact, the crowd noise seems to drop when he says it. By the time the band gets out to the B stage for the acoustic set it's after 10:30 and the temperature is dropping fast. It's freezing. Bono seems to be losing his voice. But the climax is ahead.

It is illegal to display the swastika in Germany—that's why those in the walls of this building have been patched in with plaster. During the height of "Bullet the Blue Sky" the stage is bathed in bloodred light. On last year's tour, when Bono sang, "See the burning crosses, see the flames higher and higher," huge crosses filled with fire rose on the video screens. They do now, too—but when they reach the apex of their ascent the crosses tilt to the right and turn into flaming swastikas. There is no single reaction from the crowd—there are audible gasps and there is titillation, anger, embarrassment, excitement. Young Germans are particularly sensitive to the insult of foreigners linking them to the Nazis, so there is considerable tension in the pause before Bono says, in German, "This will never happen again!"

Then there is an explosion of applause and cheering. The German audience has been invited to identify fascism as the sin of the other, not of themselves. They are relieved and anxious to do so. Bono figures that saying those five words, spelling out U2's message, is completely contrary to the spirit of Zoo TV—where there is supposed to be no moralizing, where symbols are held up to raise questions and examine contradictions. But at the same time U2 is aware that some things are more important than art theories, and opposition to fascism is way up on that list. The band decided that if they were going to use the swastika—the most potent semiotic of all—they had to break character and be absolutely clear that they regarded this as evil. They wanted to offer the audience, especially the audience in places where neo-Nazis are rooting around, an opportunity to celebrate being opposed to fascism. They could not stand to risk some moron thinking they were celebrating Nazism, but even more they didn't want German kids to think U2 was pushing them into a corner where they had to defend anything corrupt out of misguided national loyalty. Bono told the crowd when speaking of the Turks, that by standing for justice in the face of evil, "You have the chance to be heroes." That is, finally, all they came to Berlin to say.

After all this tension and catharsis, "Pride," complete with its Martin Luther King samples, is a celebration. Hitler must be turning in his bunker. McGuinness makes his way to the soundboard to tell Joe O'Herlihy that *Mix* magazine has nominated him as Sound Reinforcement Engineer of the Year. "This'll make you goose-step quicker," the manager says. Joe decides to celebrate by cranking up the sound to a house-shaking level. It's now too loud to talk. McGuinness passes Joe a note—a drawing of the Zoo plane with the scribble, "After 'Love Is Blindness,' " meaning, as soon as the last song is over, run for the cars— we're racing to the airport and anyone left behind can walk back to Ireland.

Joe, sensitive to the fact that he is breaking the decibel barrier, passes a note back to Paul: "They are taking me into custody after the show tonight. Yes. Arrested."

Paul scribbles on the paper and passes it back: "Can I still vote for you if you're in jail?"

Macphisto is raving mad tonight. Pointing to his platform shoes, he cries, "The last time you saw me I was five feet eight, but now look at me! I'm gigantic! Do you know who Helmut Kohl is?" There is a negative murmur, some booing. "He's becoming a friend of mine." A few cheers. "Shall I give him a telephone call?" Lots of cheers. Macphisto gestures to the stadium around him and cackles, "I love this place!" There is some applause. "All the pomp and ceremonial marching . . ." the crowd quiets down. "Don't you love that?"

He dials the chancellor's number and gets a busy signal. "I think I might have offended the chancellor." The devil sighs. Then he starts shouting, "Hello? Can you hear me, Helmut Kohl? I don't need the telephone lines! You know who I am! And I want to thank you for letting me back into the country! I'M BACK! I'M BAAACK!!"

The moment the encore is over the band is rushed to waiting cars with a police escort and sped out of the grounds ahead of the traffic. Bono is burning rubber toward Paris to hook up with Ali and charm his way back into her affections. I am sticking with Edge and McGuinness who are hauling toward the Zoo plane, which is gassed up and waiting at an airfield in East Berlin. As soon as we cross over into what was the Soviet zone the trees give way to barren soil. (I don't mean to sound like Dan Quayle; I know photosynthesis still functioned under Communism. I'm just boggled every time I consider that East Germany was *the jewel in the Soviet crown,* the most economically successful of all communist states. Yet this landscape looks like the landfill in back of Love Canal. Lucky for me my father's dead or I'd have to listen to him saying, "I told you so" about every dinner table political argument we had between the coming of the Beatles and the fall of Saigon.)

Edge says, "That was a good show. It was a tough one. To face down the ghosts in that place. Did you hear the evil in Bono's voice when he called Kohl? *I'm baaack!*" Edge shakes his head. "You know, when Bono and I went to that peace conference in January, it seemed to us that the issue we should address on this tour was xenophobia. I had doubts about using the swastika because if it wasn't absolutely clear why we were using it, it could be seen as appropriating this image for other reasons, for shock value. But as things have worked out, everything that's been going on in Germany has been international news. Everyone gets the point."

At 2:15 A.M., way up in the air over Europe, Edge and Suzanne sneak into the Zoo plane galley and organize a surprise birthday cake for Paul McGuinness, who turned forty-two at midnight. Suzanne presents him with a wrapped gift and Edge says, "We're the ones who *really* love you, Paul." Everyone has inscribed a tour book to the manager. Edge has written, "To Paul—the best manager I ever had."

"Well," Paul says, "you're all invited to my house this afternoon for my other party."

"Do I have to bring another present?" Suzanne asks.

As Edge's onstage adrenaline starts to drain, a bit of weariness crosses his face and he becomes reflective. We go to the back of the plane to talk. "I was just realizing," he says, gesturing toward the birthday candles, "next year I'll have been in U2 half my life."

I ask about delaying the start of the concert till after sunset.

"The thinking was that of all nights, we needed to feel that we were walking on firing on all cylinders. In that situation, playing in that venue, back in Berlin. Whether the eyes of the world were there or not, we felt they were. If you feel you're playing in a situation that's less than the best possible way to present yourselves, you can feel very vulnerable.

"Coming from Ireland we're quite superstitious, and I think we all quite generally were very aware of the ghosts running around that building tonight. And with the Leni Riefenstahl opening, you know those drums are summoning up some demons, some spirits, and you'd just better make sure it's the right spirit or it could have been a very different show."

I ask if there was any moment when Edge thought U2 had bitten off more than they could chew by bringing Nazi imagery back into that place.

"How 'bout *the whole time I was onstage*! Every split second!" Edge laughs. "Quite genuinely, I was going, What the *fuck* is this? It's essentially doing"—he gives the bum's rush—"to the whole radical right wing and that was a good thing, but y'know, it's a fairly heavy presence that you're mocking. I was a bit intimidated by that tonight. The only way to deal with being intimidated is to launch at it full force, and I think that's why there was such energy."

I mention that Edge's guitar solo on "Bullet the Blue Sky" tonight went off into uncharted waters—it was an acid rock solo.

"Well, I could almost feel those swastikas coming up," Edge says. "That's the funny thing: Bono delivers the line, they come up, and then he fucks off and I'm left there! And I've got to somehow communicate with the music something that makes sense of that. Sometimes it happens, sometimes it doesn't. Tonight there was a lot of energy there."

"It was an emotional moment," I say.

"Yeah, it was for me," Edge answers. "Apart from being scared fucking shitless about it! With this show there's a lot of risk, especially for Bono, who's out there a lot of the time living or dying based on what he can drag out of himself that night. Macphisto is an example. There's a certain amount of it that he's worked out, but he's got to work with the audience and bring it to life every evening without a script, and that's hard."

I decide to hit the exhausted Edge with something Bono said to me the other day—that U2 have six good songs left over from the Dublin sessions, so there's no reason not to do another U2 album at the end of 1994. Edge looks appalled.

"That's definitely pushing it," he says. "We could release 'Wake Up, Dead Man,' no problem, it's sounding great. There's another few songs that need a little bit more work but not that much. But to make a full album. . . . See, an album's not just about a few songs you might have hanging around. For us in particular it's a collection that adds up to something more than just a few songs. It needs to have an overall logic that connects and complements and maybe not *resolves*, but has a beginning, middle, and end. I'm not sure we would have right now enough tracks to produce an album we would be happy with. We could probably do it, but I'm not sure it's the right thing."

"You've been working nonstop two and a half years, Edge," I say. "How hard is it going to be for you to stop?"

"Yeah," he says quietly. "I don't know. I'm scared. I'm purposely leaving '94 blank. I know there's a lot of things I could do—soundtracks, producing. But right now I feel the right thing to do is take some time and put things together. I'm sure it will be very hard but I know it's a really good idea."

"You've not had to really go home since the breakup of your marriage."

"Yeah. That's true. Yeah. That's been an incredible refuge in one sense. Work is fairly absolute, you've got stuff to do and you've got to get on with it. But I'm a naturally gifted procrastinator and avoider of things that are not absolute. This next year will be a good opportunity for me to start to actually deal with all that shit. Get the other parts of my life back onto an even keel."

Edge wonders how he can even *meet* women with whom he might have a chance of getting involved. He sincerely has no idea. That might sound ludicrous coming from a wealthy and successful rock star—I have seen sexy movie actresses coming around to flirt with Edge—but to him, that's the problem. He wouldn't want to get involved with someone who was interested in him because he was famous or rich, but the band is so big now that he's worried that it will be impossible to meet anyone whose perceptions of him won't be influenced by U2. Bear in mind that Edge married young, moving right from his parents' house to the home of his marriage. He has never been alone. As long as he keeps writing songs, making albums, and playing concerts, he doesn't have to be.

Paul comes down the aisle with a fax forwarded by the Italian promoter, who is dealing with local concerns about sound levels at U2's upcoming show in Rome. The final paragraph reads: "It should be said, however, that the U2 concert in Rome in 1987 created a panic situation where hundreds of residents evacuated their homes as they believed there was an earthquake. I can assure you of this incident as I have friends who live near to the stadium that suffered minor damage (broken vases and glasses) caused by sound vibrations from the concert."

Ah, Italy is only a week away. There is a lot more noise to be made and a lot more demons to drown out before Edge has to go home and hear silence.

32

Jam

italian gridlock/ pearl jam introduces stage-diving to verona/ the trouble with grunge/ news from the front/ a high-tech marriage proposal/ the wheel's still in spin

O N THE HIGHWAY to U2's concert in Verona the band's local bus driver pulls up to the wooden barrier the *policia* have stuck in front of the highway entrance to control the traffic to the U2 concert, sticks his head out the window, and exchanges shouts, curses, and hand gestures with the local cops, who finally move the barrier and let us drive through. When we get to the next barrier the whole routine is repeated. This goes on at regular intervals all the way to the show. As we drive parallel to the bumper-to-bumper traffic on the main road, we see that many concert-goers have pulled over on the side of the highway or along the median, locked their cars, and left them there, a Watkins Glen approach to concert-going quite unusual on a major highway in a big city. But then, this is Italy, where it is easier to ask forgiveness than permission.

It is the afternoon of July third. It is very hot in Verona. People in the stadium are wearing as few clothes as possible. Onstage Pearl Jam, who have with their first album become very big stars in America, are trying to connect to a large audience who don't know who they are. Eddie Vedder, the band's passionate lead singer, is not going to go down without a fight. He is telling the crowd, "This is a big place for such a little thing like music. I can't wait till we can come back and play in a place where we can see you."

The band then plays a new song called "Daughter," a slow tune with a powerful lyric—"she holds the hand that holds her down"—that like many of Vedder's songs seems to be about the grief children suffer at the hands of incompetent or oblivious parents. It means nothing to

most of the chatting, laughing, drinking crowd, but it clearly means a lot
to Eddie. When it's done he stands at the edge of the stage looking out
at the disinterested audience and sings, quietly, the first lines of U2's "I
Will Follow." It is hard to tell if he is trying to mock the public's
hunger for the headliners or make a connection. In a lot of ways Vedder
seems like a fan who has found his way onto U2's stage by mistake and
figures that as long as he's up there he'll see what singing their song feels
like. Behind him the band starts playing a very slow version of "Sympathy for the Devil" and Vedder makes up new lyrics to fit his circumstance: "I got here through twenty-nine stadiums." He holds up a devil
mask and the crowd is mildly amused. Vedder tries on his devil mask,
then tries on a fly-head mask. I wonder if he's mocking Bono's onstage
personas—devilish Macphisto and the Fly.

"I got a question," Vedder says softly, taking off the mask. "How do
you spell 1-2-3-4!" and with that Pearl Jam rips into a screaming
version of Neil Young's "Rockin' in the Free World." Vedder charges
down the ramp to U2's B stage and throws himself off, into the pogoing
part of the audience. I don't think Verona has ever seen stage-diving
before. The crowd in the grandstands is still fairly disinterested, but the
people on the ground in front of the stage go nuts. I see Vedder
bobbing up on the arms of the crowd, then disappearing under them,
then popping up, like a swimmer fighting an undertow. Finally he
scampers back up onto the ramp, most of his clothes torn to rags. He
has made contact with the audience with the same sort of recklessness
that almost got Bono kicked out of U2 a decade ago.

Pearl Jam, like their Seattle rivals Nirvana, has dominated the imagination of American rock for the last year and a half. U2 has been
guarded in their reaction to grunge, the nickname the media has given to
the music these bands make, a sort of postmainstream rock influenced
by both punk and heavy metal, those opposite poles of seventies rock
culture. Both Pearl Jam and Nirvana tend toward lyrics about the inarticulate anger of kids growing up feeling abandoned and abused. That
merciless rock critic Elvis Costello refers to the style as "Mummy, I've
wet myself again" music. Nirvana works hard at being *alternative,* in spite
of the Beatles-like melodic gifts of songwriter Kurt Cobain. Pearl Jam is
much more open about its debt to mainstream rock—as Vedder's quick
evocation of U2, the Rolling Stones, and Neil Young demonstrates.

U2 has been vaguely supportive of the new movement, though it's not hard to sense in Bono and company a subtle resentment that Seattle bands who are essentially re-creating styles of the 1970s are being hailed by critics as progressive, while U2—who has worked so hard on their last two albums to take rock into fresh territory—is often lumped in with the established superstar acts against whom the grunge bands are supposed to be rebelling.

In my conversations with them, Bono and Edge have both expressed enthusiasm for the experimental industrial pop of Nine Inch Nails, while maintaining a sort of polite skepticism about the Seattle bands. Bono often repeats his observation that poor black kids have no trouble staying on the cutting edge of technology and art, figuring out ways to make new music with computers and samplers, abandoning one style to innovate another, while middle-class white kids regurgitate the same musical clichés over and over and think they've discovered the lightbulb.

David Grohl, Nirvana's drummer, came to a U2 show during the first leg of the Zoo tour to visit the opening act, the Pixies. Bono invited him in for a talk. Bono mimicks Grohl chewing gum and saying, "Hey, man, nothing against you, but I don't know why the Pixies would do this." Bono asked if Grohl didn't think it was brave of the Pixies to try opening for U2 in arenas. Grohl didn't buy it. "We'll never play big places," he said of Nirvana. "We're just a punk band. All this success is a fluke. Tomorrow I could be somewhere else."

Bono told him to never say never: "You don't know what you'll want to do in five or ten years. It was all new to us, we had to learn it too. Why paint yourself into a corner?"

"Nah, man," Grohl said. "We're just a punk band." The next thing Bono knew Grohl was quoted in *NME* saying that Bono tried to convince Nirvana to change but they wouldn't do it. "Definitely not the brains of the group," Bono mutters.

"Recently I saw them on TV. Now they're playing big places. And the interviewer said, 'You told me a year ago you'd never do that,' and Kurt Cobain said, 'I changed my mind.' " Bono laughs. "See, that's the gift Kurt has, Sinéad has. To declare one thing one day and the next day announce the exact opposite with no self-consciousness at all. I think Eddie Vedder is a bit more honest than that. He can remember what he said the day before. He's a very soulful guy and very troubled by it. He talks about how he only wants to play clubs." Bono thinks about it and then adds, "But he's not actually *playing* clubs, is he?"

What he really wants, I say, is to be as happy and excited as he was when he was playing clubs, when he'd just quit his job in the gas station to join Pearl Jam and was suddenly singing to packed bars and the audience loved it and the record companies were coming around. That's what he really misses—not the clubs but the happiness.

"It's a terrible thing," Bono says, "to get something before you desire it. We've been lucky. We've generally desired something just before we got it. But then, it's also a mind-fuck to get everything you want."

"Rather than what you need," Edge says.

Anyway, all these media-hyped notions of Us vs. Them, Mainstream vs. Underground, Hip vs. Square are a vestige of Cold War "generation gap" thinking. Cultural polarities were important to the World War II generation and to their baby boom offspring, who in middle age have become their parents' mirror image. One of the big confusions for the baby boomers is that the next generation doesn't want to play that game. ("Okay, now *I'll* say how much better things were twenty years ago and *you* rebel. Okay? All right? Hey, where are you going?") These days such polarities are projected as marketing hooks. The publisher of an alternative rock magazine told me recently that he had cracked the Detroit auto market and now Madison Avenue advertising would be rolling into his bank account. I asked how he did it and he said by hiring "the marketing woman who discovered Generation X."

Zooropa is being released this weekend and the early reviews are ecstatic, the best of U2's career. That goes a way toward assuaging any sore feelings that U2 might have about being lumped on the wrong side of musical progress.

"The scene that they come out of has a lot of *rules,* actually," Bono says of Pearl Jam. "There's quite a code. Like with a lot of clubs, that can be quite rigid. If you try to break out of it, even if you just want to see what's across the road or around the corner, you can't do it. I do think that Pearl Jam are transcendant of their scene, but their scene is to me incredibly old-fashioned. It's an aftertaste of the sixties counterculture, which suits a certain white middle-class collegiate lifestyle. But I don't want to dis it because in Pearl Jam's case it's a place of conviction and a place where they put the music first. Who am I to comment on it? As a fan of rock & roll I have to say what I think, but in the end if the music's great it doesn't matter."

Of Vedder, Bono says, "He's not a rock & roll animal, he's come up from a different place, a place that I prefer. But he's in a rock & roll band and has to protect himself. He probably doesn't think he's got a mask, and so he might not have figured the various masks of Zoo TV. But he has a mask, and that's okay, because the important place not to be wearing masks is in the songs. That's where I live, and I think that's where he lives. Maybe they're going through what we went through in the eighties, which is running away from the bullshit. I'm sure they'll find their own way of doing it. Exactly what I *didn't* like about our position in the eighties was that we were running away rather than just kind of laughing in its face, which is more where we're at right now." Bono thinks about it and decides, "He [Eddie] is an odd character. I like him a lot, actually."

When I walk into Paul McGuinness's backstage hospitality room, two scraggly-looking visitors jump up from the couch and come toward me with eyes wide and mouths moving. There are TV lights set up, and a portable camera on a tripod. I've come to the wrong place—I was looking for the cold cuts. It turns out I've walked into two visitors from Bosnia who have crossed the war zone, the Adriatic Sea, and the concert security apparatus in the hope of interviewing Bono for Sarajevo television. Bill Carter is a Californian, long-haired and good-looking, who is trying to make a documentary about how people in Sarajevo are coping with the Serbian seige. Jason Aplon, dark and brooding, is a friend of Carter's who runs the International Rescue Committee's office in Split, in Bosnia.

Last week U2 got a fax on the stationery of Radio Televizija Bosne I Hercegovina that read, "Bosnian television, based in Sarajevo, is very interested in doing an interview with the members of U2. We understand that the group will be in Verona, Italy, July 3, and think this is the perfect opportunity to do this interview. Verona is the one concert in Europe that will have the largest ex-Yugoslavia crowd due to the fact that it is the only concert tickets are being sold for. . . . Sarajevo, in former Yugoslavia, was the center of its art and rock and roll culture. It still has an art scene trying to survive, but it lacks creative input due to obvious physical and information restraints."

The letter went on to say that they understood that U2 had helped raise money for Bosnian relief, and perhaps the band would agree to an interview exclusively for Bosnian TV to be shown "when the electricity comes back on." It further explained that no Bosnian citizens would be able to make it through the Serbian checkpoints, so if U2 agreed they would send to Verona "our foreign associate Bill Carter."

Principle sent a message back that Bono would be happy to give them an interview before going onstage in Verona. Carter and his friend Aplon journeyed for two days, crossing the sea that divides Italy and Yugoslavia on a boat crowded with refugees and U2 fans. When they arrived at the venue, the ticket office said it had no passes for them or any information about them, and security tried to throw them out. But Carter was persistent and finally snuck backstage, where he was made welcome and given a place to set up his camera. Now he is nervous about meeting Bono—a nervousness that seems inappropriate to me in a man who's been ducking bullets for several months.

Bono arrives, decked out in his leather stage suit, shakes hands with the visitors, and takes a seat on the couch. After some initial questions about Zoo TV, Carter asks Bono why, in spite of the lessons of history, people keep returning to the barbarism of war.

"It's the subject of a lot of our songs," Bono says a little awkwardly. "I come from Ireland. Ireland is also divided. Again, they say it's religion, but you know it's not religion. See, the human heart is very greedy. It seeks many excuses for that. Religion is a convenient one, color is a convenient one. I've been through various different stages in working this out. One must be political at times, but sometimes you have to look beyond that to just the state of the human spirit. I guess that's where I'm at right now. I'm examining my own hypocrisy, I'm examining my own greed. I've stopped even pointing at politicians." He laughs. "I've found there's enough subject matter in my heart to keep me going.

"I was very inspired by Martin Luther King. He was a character in the middle of a very dangerous situation—civil rights for African Americans in the sixties. It could have gone very wrong. . . . The word *peace* is like bullshit a lot of the time, it's like flowers-in-the-hair hippie talk, but he held on to a much stronger idea, a much more concrete idea about peace and respect, and he just kept on to it, he just kept pummeling it. The idea was that he'd live for his country but he didn't want to die for it and he would never kill for it. And he did die for it. It's a hard thing to hold on to. There must be an incredible urge . . . People deserve the right to defend themselves against evil and they must decide how to do that. But if there's any other alternative, obviously you've got to seek it. I know that's what you guys have been trying and you haven't been allowed, and I'm really, really sorry to hear about that. And I understand any reaction. But I just hope that even in the middle of that you don't have to become like the animals attacking you. Dignity. Self-respect. These are things that people can't take away. And humor. Humor is the evidence of freedom."

Carter tells Bono that Sarajevo is the world capital of black humor. Someone's mother will be killed in front of him and the next day he'll have a joke.

"That's when you're winning in one respect," Bono says. "If they can't take that away."

The interview wraps up and Carter suggests that Bono might consider visiting Sarajevo. The city has been imploring artists of all kinds to come see for themselves what is going on there.

"I think I would," Bono says. "I'd love to get there."

"We could arrange that," Carter answers.

Bono returns to U2's dressing room shaken. Onstage that night he talks to the audience about Bosnia and then says, "Somebody said courage is grace under pressure. I'd like to dedicate this song to the people of Sarajevo." U2 plays "One."

While he's singing "New Year's Day" Bono leaves the main stage and starts walking slowly down the darkened ramp to the B stage. Partway there he is startled to bump into a big, bare-chested Italian fan who climbed up onto the ramp while security was distracted elsewhere and has been watching the show from a particularly good vantage. Bono sizes up the grinning fellow's muscles and, still singing, jumps into his arms. Bono points toward the band and the jolly intruder carries him back up the ramp and onto the main stage, Bono singing the whole way. He hops out of the Italian's arms in front of Larry's drums, still singing the song, and the visitor is lead off by U2 security.

Back at the soundboard Naomi Campbell and Christy Turlington are soaking up the show, next to members of Pearl Jam, the two Bosnian relief workers, and a record company guest named Charlene whose friends know she's in for a big surprise. During the break between the time U2 leaves the stage and Macphisto appears for the encores, the audience is kept amused by films from the Zoo Confessional, a sort of video outhouse set up in the stadium in the hours before U2 comes on in which audience members can tape messages, jokes, football cheers, or lists of their sins. The funniest of these are shown each evening on the big TV screens. Suddenly Charlene is shocked to see her boyfriend talking to her from the huge Vidiwall. "Hi, Charlene . . . I want to know if you'll marry me." Charlene shakes visibly as her friends laugh and slap her back. She stands frozen for about sixty seconds and then looks around to see her boyfriend standing across the platform. She runs over, hugs him, and says yes. They slow dance through U2's encores. Even while Macphisto is trying to phone the pope.

33

The Masque of the Red MuuMuu

---

moonlight in verona/ planning the invasion of bosnia/ ping-pong with the supermodels/ an apostate is granted absolution/ pearl jam gets a sound check/ a dissertation on the value of men wearing dresses

T HERE IS a blue Olympic-size pool glistening in the Verona moonlight while corks pop and steaks sizzle and waiters run up and down balancing trays. U2 sits around the pool while their guests emerge from between the high hedges. Here comes Tom Freston, the head of MTV and the picture of the tall, laughing American cowboy entrepreneur. Here comes Jeff Pollack, quiet, almost melancholy, a superpower consultant behind radio playlists from the USA to the Far East. Here comes Pearl Jam, the hottest American band, followed by An Emotional Fish, an Irish group several notches further down the concert poster. Here comes Naomi Campbell, Christy Turlington, and several more fashion models from the high end of the gene pool.

And here, strangest of all, come our two visitors from Sarajevo. Bill Carter and Jason Aplon wander into the party tentatively and hang back from the buffet table like Siberians in a supermarket. Having completed their unlikely mission of getting out of Bosnia, making it to Italy, conning their way past security, and interviewing Bono, Carter and Jason have been invited to join the superstar revels tonight, before going back into the war zone tomorrow. They both look a little shell-shocked at the luxury laid out before them, but that may have less to do with the opulence than with the fact that they have, until two days ago, been dodging shells.

In the spacious two-room pool house sits a serving table laden with delicacies. Pearl Jam take up pool cues and begin the billiards. Larry

Credit: Anton Corbijn

The end of the tour at the end of the world—Japan, December 1993

Credit: Anton Corbijn

Adam and Bono in the tea room overlooking Alta Square, Tokyo

Mr. Macphisto in all his debauched glory

Credit: Anton Corbijn

The toughest guy in the band, Larry Mullen, Jr.

Credit: Anton Corbijn

Credit: Anton Corbijn

Larry leans out of Edge's shadow in a Tokyo alley.

Credit: Anton Corbijn

The invasion of Sellafield—U2 cleave the Irish Sea
on a rubber raft, June 1992.

Credit: Anton Corbijn

A live Lou Reed subs for the usual grainy video projection on
"Satellite of Love."

Credit: Anton Corbijn

Slicked down for the Zooropa tour—Macphisto and his cronies

Credit: Anton Corbijn

Adam alone, scraping the bottom of the bowl
at a curbside sushi bar

Credit: Andrew MacPherson

Brian Eno, second from left, constructing another syllogism.

Credit: Andrew MacPherson

Bono and Gavin Friday in the middle of turning
into each other

Credit: Andrew MacPherson

Flood recording *Zooropa* at the Factory, Dublin, April 1993.
Bono is on the couch behind him typing lyrics on his Powerbook.

Credit: Andrew MacPherson

Security chief Jerry Mele paying attention to everything
in the middle of a U2 concert

Credit: Andrew MacPherson

Adam Clayton, musician

Paul McGuinness, the father of
our feast

Maurice (call me
Guildenstern) Linnane,
dreaming of a year's
sleep

Suzanne Doyle, smiling on the outside, in Mexico 1992

Dreamchaser producer Ned
O'Hanlon (Rosencrantz to you)

Credit: B. P. Fallon

Sheila Roche shows the tour bus what a real singer can do.

Ellen Darst, the woman who taught U2 about the USA, contemplates getting off the road.

Credit: Stephane Sednaoui

comes over and asks how their show went tonight. "A lot better than yesterday," they say, "because today we got a half-song sound check. Of course, the arena was half full at the time, but still . . ."

"That should never happen!" Larry says, putting on his sheriff's hat. In Rome Pearl Jam will get a full sound check before the doors open! Larry *guarantees* it! He will personally make sure that U2 gets to the venue early, finishes their sound check promptly, and leaves Pearl Jam plenty of time! Leave it to Larry to walk into paradise and search out an injustice to battle.

One of U2's celebrity guests seems to have quit the hotel. Axl Rose arrived here yesterday between Italian Guns N' Roses shows, checked in and came to the U2 concert. Now the rumor is that Axl didn't like the accommodations and split. No fan of continental cuisine, Axl sent one of his lackeys out to find a McDonald's.

Adam holds court with his harem in the Ping-Pong room. He is improbably dressed in sandals and a sharp black dinner jacket over a long red dress, a sort of kimono. The babes, the feast, and the toga conspire to give Adam the bearing of a Caesar (one of the late, inbred, lunatic Caesars, perhaps, but a Caesar nonetheless).

"I don't wear it lightly," Adam says when he sees me gawking, and at first I think he means some imagined laurel wreath. He tugs at the fabric of his muumuu. "I feel that in a hot climate like this the only sort of clothing that makes any sense is a light piece of material wrapped around you." Then, taking the broader philosophical view we expect of the enrobed, he announces, "Men should not be forced to wear pants when it's not cold."

Sheila Roche, trained by years with U2 to betray no emotion beyond slight bemusement or feigned interest, joins us and lends an ear to Adam's oration. She asks if he has ever worn his frock onstage. Just once, Adam says. "It was great because I wore no underwear! I kept teasing the front row. It added a whole other dimension to the show."

"You're rock's own Sharon Stone!" I say.

"I'll tell you," Adam declares. "You learn a lot about women from dressing up in women's clothes! You learn that when a woman asks you, 'Do I look all right?' what she's really saying is, 'I have just spent a lot of time making myself uncomfortable. If I go out in this condition will I look foolish, or is it worth it?'"

"Sheila," I say, "you're a woman. Is that true?"

"There is a lot of truth in it," Sheila says. "High heels are murder."

"Sure," Adam says. "When you ask a woman to go out to dinner it's not like asking one of your mates. She has to stop and think, 'Hmm, dinner. That will be four hours of being uncomfortable.' And if she says yes and then after four hours you say, 'Let's go dancing, let's go to a club,' and she says, 'No, I want to go home,' it's because she has figured on four hours and now those four hours are up and she can only think of getting home and out of those clothes!"

"Ah," I say, "so that's why women take their clothes off after you buy them a fancy dinner!"

Adam smiles the wise smile of Archimedes overflowing the bathtub and says, "Let me go get some more wine and I'll give you some more insights into the female psychology."

He sashays off in his sarong and I say to Sheila, "I've got a new name for Adam Clayton."

"What?"

"Madame Clayton."

Bono and Edge are pulled from the poolside to go talk to Carter Alan, a disc jockey from Boston radio station WBCN. This hotel is set up like Zorro's hacienda, and Alan is sitting under an arched roof in an old stone grotto waiting to tape-record an interview with U2 for American radio. For the disc jockey it is quite a big deal; Alan is an old friend of the band who was cast out of Paradise for breaches of etiquette. This interview represents his formal readmittance to favor.

Alan's sin was turning his proximity to U2 into a book: *Outside It's America, U2 in the U.S.* To Larry Mullen this was treason; Alan had always presented himself to U2 as a friend, not a journalist, and Larry considered that Alan had cashed in on that friendship. The other members of U2 seemed less bothered about it, but they don't break ranks over matters of policy, so Alan was out. That the book was entirely complimentary was irrelevent.

I've known Alan for years, and while I would not presume to look into his soul or motives, I know he's always loved U2 and I suspect that if any member of the band had, early on in his project, picked up the phone and asked him not to write the book, he would have killed it. Edge once told me that they just assumed that as Alan was not a writer, the book he talked about would never really happen, so they ducked his messages and ignored it. By the time they realized that his book was actually being written, it was too late.

I once suggested this version of events to Larry and he cut me off at the throat. He said that Alan was specifically told by Paul McGuinness that U2 did not want him to write the book and he went ahead and did it anyway. Now, I'd bet you my Romanian royalties that that call from McGuinness came after Alan had already signed a contract, accepted an advance, and started writing. By then he was bound to deliver his book. But everyone involved has a slightly different story. What matters tonight is that when U2 was asked to talk to the big American radio syndicate Westwood One, Bono requested that Carter Alan be the interviewer.

"I don't think Carter was being malicious," Larry says of the book that caused all the trouble. "Carter is a nice guy. But if he was getting conflicting reports that the band might go along with his book it was his responsibility to find out what was going on. I think he took a chance and made a mistake. There's no doubt that he knew the band was unhappy with the situation, but he thought he could do a really great book and we would be happy with it. I don't blame him for thinking that, but I blame him for blowing the friendship with U2. I am genuinely sorry about that. And I hope that in the future we can fix that relationship."

Bono and Edge seat themselves across a wooden table from Alan in the grotto, creating a tableau like an Italian fresco: the penitent prostrating himself at the shrine of Our Lady of the Rock Stars.

"I don't like flags," Bono tells Alan once the tape starts rolling. He is still full of Sarajevo. "I don't like any of them. I'm sick and tired of the idea of flags. Europe at the moment is completely disintegrating over this issue. We had some people today from Sarajevo. They took the boat across to Italy to see this rock & roll show, to see Zoo TV. He was telling me that in the middle of the war in the former Yugoslavia they go down three nights of the week into this shelter under the ground and they listen to rock & roll. They dance and they listen to rock & roll.

"Why? Because when rock & roll is playing they don't hear the shells exploding above them. Their nerves are shot, they're fucked up, and they're into rock & roll like a lifeline. . . .

"There's another instance of flags. What is it? What do people have with flags? It's like football teams. It's great if it's a game, but if you really believe in this shit, you're fucked up. You know, we need each other. We're not very different. Human beings are very similar."

Partway through the interview the hotel loses its electricity, shutting down the tape recorder. Alan, who is jet-lagged and fighting food poisoning, struggles to maintain his professional composure. The echoes in the grotto are distorting everyone's voice, which could make the tapes useless for broadcast. It would have been easier to wear a hair shirt, get a tonsure, and flagellate himself with a stick than it is to do penance for sins against U2.

Bill Carter and Jason Aplon, our Bosnian envoys, are looming over the pool party like the Red Death at Poe's masque, grim reminders of the misery outside these well-guarded walls. Not that they are behaving like grim reminders: Bill and Jason are gingerly enjoying the celebrity soiree like slightly guilty altar boys having a hot dog on Good Friday. Bono, though, is grim enough for both of them and most of Croatia too. When he and Edge rejoin the banquet, Bono is shamefully aware that while the models, rock stars, and media moguls will all be swinging at other soirees tomorrow, these two emissaries will be back to being starved and shot at. How can Bono justify this extravagance in the face of such bottomless brutality? Our hero is clearly cooking up a little penance of his own.

"Bill Carter asked me, 'Why do people do this?' " Bono says. "I didn't know what to say. I said the human heart is greedy, it will use religion or color or any other excuse to justify its greed. Blame the human heart."

It's after 2 in the morning and Bono can't get Bosnia out of his head. He approaches Larry, who's having a tough time negotiating the oversize (but small-pocketed) billiards table and whispers an insane idea. Carter said that he and his friends gather in a bunker and play U2 records to drown out the sound of the shelling. Bono thinks the band should go into Sarajevo and play in this bunker. Larry listens, thinks, and says all right. Then he goes back to his pool game.

"Larry's the most conservative," Bono whispers. "If I've got him there's a good chance I'll get the others." Bono's evangelical charisma is getting to me; I tell him I'll go too.

He goes and puts the arm on Adam, who is sitting like a sultan, supervising a Ping-Pong match between four fashion models. Bono pulls up a chair next to him, and while the models giggle, swat, and swing, whispers, "Larry and I think the band should go and play at this disco in Bosnia. Bill says he'll come too. What do you think?"

Adam continues to watch the table tennis match, absorbing Bono's proposal as casually as if it were a suggestion that they send out for Mexican food instead of Chinese. He draws on his cigarette, exhales, and says, "I think that's a good idea. If you believe in a cause you must be willing to put yourself on the line for that cause."

And that's about all it takes for Adam Clayton to agree to risk his life. He turns his attention back to the models. 007.

Bono heads back outside to continue his recruiting drive. "I'm involved with a group," he says, "that sends food and supplies in there. And you know, this guy Bill Carter got to me tonight. He said, 'That's all right, but you're feeding a graveyard.' As a pacifist it is hard for me to justify sending arms to anybody, but God, if these people are being slaughtered you have to at least let them defend themselves."

Bill Carter explained to us earlier that the Bosnian situation has completely fallen apart since May, when Europe rejected U.S. efforts to organize NATO intervention. "It's just wholesale murder now," Carter said. "They know no one's coming to the rescue."

That image is driving Bono to distraction. "For once the U.S. had it right," Bono declares, "and Europe fucked it up! The U.S. wanted to go in and the English wouldn't agree with the French and the French couldn't agree—"

"Bono," I interrupt. "What good can a rock & roll band do in there?"

"The only thing a rock & roll band is good for," he says. "We can make a lot of noise!"

Bono sets his radar on the Edge, who is having dinner at a poolside table with Tom Freston, the MTV boss, and Jeff Pollack, the radio kingpin. He is grabbed en route by the couple who got engaged at the concert tonight. Bono signs an autograph, shakes hands, and then takes a seat by Edge's ear.

Edge is sleepy, having a few drinks, enjoying the relaxed conversation. Bono whispers to him. Edge's smile drops and he says, *"What?"* Bono keeps whispering, Freston and Pollack keep talking and laughing. Edge's face grows pale and quietly he says, "Okay, I'll do it." Bono gets up and slides away as the party chatter carries on uninterrupted, the guests oblivious to the subtle change in the demeanor of Edge, who is still sipping wine and smiling at the stories but whose eyes are now distant.

At the next pause in the conversation he looks at his watch and says, "Three-thirty, time for me to go to bed."

Bono is at another table, hovering over Paul McGuinness, pulling the manager away from his guests to let him know that U2 has made a band decision to go to Sarajevo as soon as possible, preferably right after Rome. McGuinness's mouth turns hard and Bono moves away.

Now the conspirators, filled with great intentions and wine, are exchanging knowing glances while the ignorant revel on. What looked like bourgeois luxury when this bash began is now the twilight reward for those about to risk all on a commando mission for brotherhood. "Even if all we get is some extra attention for Bosnia on MTV," Bono says, "that's something."

"Even if we all get killed," I say, really feeling my kamikaze oats, "the death of U2 would probably do more to mobilize pro-Bosnian sentiment in the *People* magazine population than all the previous killing in Serbo-Croatia has done."

Bono agrees, which is Adam's signal to pull the emergency brake. "It is probably not necessary for us to *die*," Adam says evenly, "to make this worthwhile."

The party breaks up just before dawn. As Bono and I cross the lawns toward the hotel he grabs me and whispers, "We're lookin' good!"

I see that Adam and the models have decamped to the grass outside their rooms. They are dancing barefoot to a reggae tape as the first red edge of sunlight sneaks into the lazy purple sky.

34

Four Horsemen

---

four ways of approaching the eternal city/ a surprise cameo by robert plant/ the cowboys of U2 security/ a vietnam flashback/ naomi campbell vs. the kitchen staff/ a view from the roman balcony

THERE ARE a few days off between Verona and Rome and all the members of U2 travel by routes as different as their temperaments. Edge flies in on the Zoo plane for a big family reunion with his wife, Aislinn, their daughters, and his parents, Garvin and Gwenda. Although their marriage is over, Edge and Aislinn are still united by their devotion to their kids. They play mom and dad together like the Waltons. When they pull up to the hotel in Rome there are only about ten U2 fans waiting outside, but as soon as the cops see the Evans family they fly into full alert, blowing whistles, forming cordons and running around the car until they have succeeded in making sure the whole downtown area knows that a celebrity has arrived. Pretty soon tourists are rushing up to ask for photos and autographs and Aislinn is hugging the frightened kids. The overalert Roman police have turned a completely anonymous entrance into a media event. U2 security man Eric Hausch shakes his head and mutters, "These guys aren't cops— they're mailmen with guns."

The Evans family is ushered into the hotel. Edge's parents are in great spirits—always chuckling, always warm. You get the idea that if Genghis Khan invaded with his Mongol horde Gwenda would make them all tea and Garvin would suggest a better way to shoe the horses.

Italy may derive less warmth from Larry's journey. He and David Guyer, his bike-buddy bodyguard, are hitting every pothole and screaming at every bad driver down the whole length of the Italian peninsula. Ann, Larry's girlfriend, is hanging on to his waist and trying to tilt in the right direction to keep them from crashing. They have seen three small cars squeeze together in a single lane, they have been nearly waylayed by autos slamming on their brakes in front of them and zigzagging around them. They have even had morons try to drive into the little space between the two bikes. More than a few reckless cars have had new dents kicked in them today by these uneasy riders. When a driver really pisses them off David has a dangerous trick: he sticks his leg straight out, roars alongside the jerk's car, and kicks off the rearview mirror. If you don't do it just right, you crash and die. A mirror or two has gone to Valhalla on this trip, and David's still kicking.

Bono has kidnapped three beautiful women, Morleigh, Suzanne, and Principle's Eileen Long, and let them drive him through the Italian countryside, stopping along the way to savor the wine, the food, and—oddly enough—Robert Plant, who they bump into in Florence. The former Led Zeppelin singer has known U2 for a long time, through Dennis Sheehan, who has prepared the road for both of them. Years ago Dennis drove a car in which U2 was sleeping up to Plant's house in the early morning. The confused band woke to find the hammer of the gods staring down at them. Bono refers to Plant as "the Tall, Cool One." Plant in turn refers to Bono as "the Short, Fat One." There are no grapes as sour as those sucked on by fading rock legends.

Adam is, of course, cruising down the highway having grapes fed to him by the most beautiful models in the world. The mob gathered outside U2's hotel goes nuts when Adam, Naomi, and Christy pull up and begin wading through them. They scream, they cheer, they tear at Adam's jacket as both U2 security and local cops try to part the tide. This crowd has been standing out there singing and chanting in the hot summer sun ever since word spread that Edge was in the hotel, burning up brain cells until all that is left is a primordial remnant of consciousness fixed on one goal: "U2! U2! U2!" The security men are having a tough time yanking Adam out of their clutches. The bassist is finally shoved into the revolving door and spun into the small, ornate lobby with the *you-mortals-will-never-understand* smile of the young Hugh Hefner. "Fucking hell!" He laughs.

Larry, Ann and David, dusty, exhausted and annoyed, arrive at the back of the hotel and sneak in through the garage. Pretty soon they are sitting with Adam, Naomi and Christy on the lobby stairs, studying the baying mob outside. Eric Hausch storms inside furious with the Roman police. "These guys are incredible!" Eric declares. "They wait until the moment of highest tension and then turn to you and say, 'Can you get me a U2 T-shirt?' "

The U2 security team could have been cast by Hollywood. Eric, blond and blue-eyed, is the good guy. A former fireman, county sheriff, and rescue worker, he can describe the horror of sorting through a plane crash in a way that will make you take trains forever, but he looks like the boy next door all the cheerleaders have crushes on. He is usually assigned to Bono. If Eric's the white hat, then David Guyer, Larry's man, is the black hat. Tall, dark, bearded, and moody, David came up on the wrong side of the law and still carries himself with the quiet menace of a bad-ass who knows he is always the toughest guy in the saloon. Scott Nichols, who covers Edge, is a young law-enforcement student getting some experience in security before going on to a career in police work. Scott is as handsome as a movie star, with slicked-back Elvis hair and a pumped-up body. Women on the tour try to angle to sit next to Scott in the van. All the bodyguards are American. In cowboy short-hand, Eric is Kevin Costner, David is the young Clint Eastwood, and Scott is Little Joe Cartwright. (Adam usually ducks having security.)

They were hand-picked by Jerry Mele, the security chief and a character worthy of his own book. Mele grew up in New York and served in an elite unit in Vietnam doing the most dangerous work—going behind enemy lines to bring terror to the Vietcong, sleeping tied upright to a tree, waging war close-up. After his first tour he volunteered for a second, but halfway through that round he had some sort of spiritual awakening and decided what he was doing was wrong. He came home with a drug and drink habit that he kicked by tying himself to a bed and telling his mother that no matter how much he screamed or begged, she was not to untie him. This is a tough guy.

"I've seen both Jerry and David have to take somebody out when they were forced to," Larry says. "It's not a pretty sight. Their power and authority comes from knowing they can kill someone, and not wanting to ever have to prove it."

Yet Jerry is evangelical about transforming the currency of rock concert security from what it's always been—bullying, beating, and intimidation—into something gentle and instructive. He hires men who share that philosophy to work with him and puts them through three months of training and classroom work before letting them begin.

Before U2 plays a venue Jerry has meetings with the local police and security that go on for hours, explaining his philosophy. "I've been to security meetings where they tell me, 'We've got these people trained,'" Jerry says with contempt. "Bullshit! One person can start a riot! You don't *train* people! You ask people for help. For the oddball, we ask him to go home. All these little marks on my face are stitches. I'll take the punch and say, 'You didn't knock me down yet. Now either you can walk away or I'm gonna take you down, and I can promise you, you will go to jail on assault charges. Can you afford fifty grand in lawyers' fees?' Always give 'em the option to walk away. Always give a drunk an out. I let him walk away saying, 'I didn't lose my manhood, I told him off!'"

Jerry comes out before the show and talks to the kids in the line outside the venue, brings them coffee and water, explains how things are going to be so that everybody has a good time, all but deputizes them. "I make 'em realize, 'I'm not telling you, I'm asking you.' We've done things on this tour that nobody's ever seen. Picture nine thousand people *walking* onto a field, not one person running."

Bono does a very funny impression of Jerry pulling a violent kid backstage and lecturing him like Ward Cleaver until the kid begs for a beating instead. But Jerry also gave Bono the idea for one of the strongest parts of U2's concert: Bono performs "Bullet the Blue Sky" in the voice, attitude, and clothes of a U.S. soldier leading a combat mission in the Third World, and then stays in that persona for "Running to Stand Still," a song written about Dubliners who use heroin to escape their poverty. Bono is playing Jerry Mele when he performs those songs; it was knowing Jerry that made him understand that those two characters could be the same person. At the end of that sequence every night red and yellow smoke flares go off and billow up around Bono. He took that from Jerry's stories about the chaos on the ground during a jungle firefight; one color meant it was safe for the rescue copters to come in and pick up the wounded, the other color meant stay away. The Vietcong figured out the code and started shooting up flares of their own, luring pilots to their death or keeping rescue helicopters from landing.

When I mention to Jerry that Bono is playing him onstage during those songs, his eyes fill with tears. "I didn't know that," he says softly. "God bless him for it. I didn't have a clue." He looks away. "Phew. That's heavy. Nobody's ever done . . ." He swallows and says, "I'm not here to do anything but what I think is right. My heart tells me we're not put here to hurt anybody. My mind tells me we've become corrupt."

Jerry got into concert security twelve years ago, when he was running a limousine service. One night someone attacked a celebrity who was renting one of his cars and the star's bodyguard froze. Jerry stepped in and handled the situation. The star fired his own man on the spot and insisted Jerry come to work for him. Since then he's provided security for a string of big names, none of whom he wants listed on the record, except for the heavy metal band Slayer, who have asked Jerry to use their name. That band's crowd included skinheads, neo-Nazis, the worst of the worst. His first night with them, Jerry told the crowd that he was not there to challenge their beliefs or change them—he was only there to make sure they all had a good time and forgot their troubles for a couple of hours. So in that spirit he was going to hand out tags. He wanted them to tag their weapons and pass them in to be checked. After the show was over they could pick them up again. He collected 300 knives and 56 handguns.

"We're gonna win in the end," Jerry says. "I promise you, we are gonna win."

The small car bearing Bono and the Principle women drives up to the hotel and they see the mob throbbing outside the door. Bono asks who the hell could be staying here that's drawn such a crowd. After a couple of days of Italian country living, Bono has divorced himself from his rock star persona. Then the throng spots him in the car watching them and charges. "Oh, no!" he says. He'd forgotten he was famous, a dangerous thing to do. The U2 security squad comes tearing out of the hotel and cuts through the fans like a hot phalanx through Macedonians. They haul Bono from the car and carry him across the sidewalk and into the hotel as if they were the Green Bay Packers and he were a football.

At 2 A.M. everyone's settled in and had a shower, and U2 congregates on a high piazza from which they can look down on the crowd, who are finally dispersing, and drink wine. There's Edge and Aislinn, Larry and Ann, Adam and Naomi, Ned and Maurice, Christy, Chanty—a Dublin friend of Edge's— Sheila, Eileen, Dennis, and Bono.

Naomi decides she's going to get some food and goes off to find the hotel kitchen. Officially it's shut down, but she implies that if she can get at a stove she'll whip up something herself. Maybe that's a threat designed to stir sleeping chefs to action, maybe it's sincere. I don't know, I don't care. Everyone here is just enjoying the moon and the night and the company. After a while, though, Adam begins to wonder where his fiancée's gone. Christy (who often seems to act as Naomi's conscience—or at least social governor) says she'll go check. She comes back a few minutes later with news that Naomi is in the middle of a full-pitched screaming battle downstairs.

Adam looks half concerned. "Is she fighting with anyone employed by me?"

"No," Christy says. "She's fighting with the chef."

"Oh." Adam relaxes. "That's fine."

Naomi Campbell is a difficult fit in U2's world. She is one of the most famous women in Britain and well recognized everywhere else. She is celebrated for being imperial, acting like a diva, causing a ruckus. Adam says one of the things that first made him think highly of her, before they met, was when she got headlines for belting a paparazzo at Heathrow who pursued her for a picture after an overnight flight. Adam got a kick out of that. And you know, the fashion world is so insulting, the models are treated so much like meat, that a big mouth and a thick skin can be as useful to a model as are all the other physical attributes on which she depends.

But U2's organization functions in a completely different way. It is by far the most considerate operation of its size I have ever seen in the rock world. The sort of back stabbing and dirty fighting that is routine in most comparable outfits is almost absent. Most of the people who work with U2, including the band members, really don't have a clue how unusual it is. The Principles are often hugging and holding hands and having earnest discussions about subjects personal and universal. Even the tensions and fights tend to be like the arguments in a family. Of course, those who've known nothing else don't always see it that way. One of the Principles might get his feelings hurt and think, "Boy, beneath this tranquil surface the U2 organization is a snake pit!" But the only people who could believe that are people who've never worked or traveled with other bands—or for that matter spent much time at a record company, promoter's office, or rock magazine. Compared to such rat holes U2 is paradise—a halfway house between the hippie ideal and the Boy Scouts.

Which is why Naomi's no-nonsense air of entitlement rubs some of these people the wrong way. Adam's fiancée is graceful and full of style, but she occasionally seems to think *employee* is another name for *servant*. One spoiled crew member whispered to me that Naomi was the person on the tour most likely to have a flight case dropped on her head.

Naomi returns to our company, stretches languidly across the back of Adam's chair, and pouts that the chef, who refused to cook, would not stand aside and let her at the stove. She is upset and she is going to bed. She kisses Adam good night, kisses Christy good night, waves to everyone else, and then walks straight into the glass door with a shuddering crash. Everyone jumps up, but Naomi just reels back, laughs, and tries again, this time passing through the open side and back into the hotel.

"That'll straighten her out," says the gallant Adam.

35

Words From the Front

---

tension runs high over bono and bosnia/ paying off the city inspectors/ why we weigh our tickets/ the pursuit of nancy wilson by concert security/ a dispatch arrives from the battle zone

ONCE EVERYONE'S assembled in Rome the campaign that dares not speak its name—Bono's plan to invade Bosnia—is filling the Principles with tension. It's not doing wonders for my digestion, either. The first thing Bono wanted to know when we got to Rome was if I was still committed to going with him to Sarajevo. I said sure, but good luck making it happen. I got the impression he was disappointed that I didn't leap up shouting, "You bet! Let's go!" He suspects that people are deliberately dragging their feet to prevent it from happening. "Well, *I'm* going," Bono said sharply. "I hope Paul's been working on it!"

I don't know how hard Paul's been working on it. I do know what his attitude is: "I think it's foolhardy. I think it's vain. I don't like it at any level. It's dangerous and uninsurable and seems to contradict something I thought we had all thought through. We came to the conclusion that the duty of the artist is to illustrate contradictions and point a finger at things that are wrong and terrible without the responsibility of having to resolve them. U2's effort to discuss any humanitarian issue have sometimes been accompanied by a false instinct that U2 is also obliged to resolve that issue. Going to Sarajevo seems to me to fall into that category. I think it would endanger the people we go with, endanger the tour, and endanger the band. I think it's grandstanding."

I approach Dennis Sheehan in the hotel corridor and say, "Tell me as soon as you know if Yugoslavia is on for Thursday. I've got a couple of things I've got to change before I go—my plane ticket and my will."

Dennis looks at me with the blank face of a soldier playing dumb and says, "Yugoslavia? Why are you going to Yugoslavia, Bill?"

"If U2 goes I go, Dennis."

Dennis's expression turns cold and he says, "Oh, yeah? I haven't heard about it. As far as I'm concerned it will interfere with other plans. *Like the rest of our lives!* If people talk about this Bono will be forced to do it, to fulfill everyone's expectations. And it will accomplish *nothing* except to draw all those people into one place where they will be easy targets. There's not even any power to play! Bono's an extremist and he has done some extreme things, but Sarajevo isn't Central America, Sarajevo isn't Ethiopia. As far as I'm concerned this should not happen and it will not happen unless so many people talk about it that Bono feels he has to do it. So don't talk about it!"

By the next day the unspoken tension is leaking out all over. One of the Zoo TV cameramen says he just ran into a friend, a newsman who usually covers the troubles in Belfast newly returned from Sarajevo, who says he was scared shitless the whole time: it's horrible, don't go. This news sweeps through the hotel, along with reminders of one of the stories Bill Carter told us in Verona—of how he was sitting talking to a friend not long ago and suddenly the friend fell over dead from a sniper's bullet.

Nonetheless, under Bono's orders Regine Moylett is maintaining contact with Bill Carter, who's now back in Sarajevo, and it seems that some progress is being made in trying to secure several seats on a U.N. or Red Cross transport plane to carry us in. There is a notion that it might be possible for U2 to fly in early in the morning, get to Sarajevo, play, and fly out that night. But aside from the fact that it is proving to be very hard to get seats on the relief flights, everyone the Principles talk to makes it clear that once you get into Bosnia you have to be prepared for the possiblity that you might not get out. When the airport comes under attack all flights are canceled. Or there could be a major evacuation of wounded, in which case the healthy get bumped. I write a letter for my wife to give to my kids in case we get stuck there and can't get out, trying to explain what happened to Daddy.

Leaks are springing up too. MTV's Tom Freston stops me in the hall and asks if I'm going to Bosnia. He says Bono has promised MTV footage. "It would be an amazing gesture," he says. Then with a big smile he adds, "You tell me what it's like, Bill! I'll be back in New York!"

This is becoming like a political convention—all of the arguments and intrigues are taking place in the corridors and corners of this hotel. Regine follows Bono down the hallway, trying to give the latest reasons he shouldn't go while Bono does his best to ignore her: "I spoke to Bill Carter. He says a thousand shells fell on Sarajevo yesterday and anything that gathers people together in a large group is dangerous. We can put information about Sarajevo on the Zoo TV screens, we can give Bill Carter editing facilities in Dublin so he can get his film footage out to the world. There are many, many things the band can do that will be more useful than going there and entertaining two hundred people."

Regine continues chasing Bono, throwing out bribes and petitions, while he tries to get away: "The U.N. probably won't let you in, and if you do get in you probably won't get out for at least a week. . . ."

Her summation is cut off as the elevator door opens and the people inside see Bono. Several teenage girls scream. He steps in with them, leaving Regine behind as the door closes.

"He's still determined to go," I say.

"Yes," she sighs. "And I will go with him."

Bono talks on the phone with an Irish journalist named Maggie O'Kane who reports on the Bosnian war for the London *Guardian*. Her reporting has at times reflected her fury at what she's seen in Sarajevo. Bono was impressed when she lost her temper with a Serb leader she was interviewing for the BBC; when he denied that the Bosnian Serbs were using rape as a weapon she called him a liar to his face. O'Kane's advice to Bono is, "The best possible thing you can do is to go there."

U2 plays an early soundcheck—1 P.M.—so that Pearl Jam will have plenty of time to get their levels set before the audience comes in. Every manager I know has horror stories about the comedy of concert promoting in Italy. It is just assumed that acts playing here will be bamboozled out of their fair share of the gate receipts. I have sat with the great rock impressarios of England and heard hilarious *Can you top this?* tales of bribery, corruption, and threats in the Italian concert industry. Paul McGuinness, ever diplomatic, says that he doesn't find it so bad here— it just bugs him that Italy allows bootleg T-shirts and tour merchandise to be sold around the shows, so U2's profit in that area vanishes in this country. U2 has come up with one great innovation to combat the likelihood of counterfeit or miscounted tickets giving them a false report of how many people are in any venue; they provide the tickets the promoters have to use and then they *weigh* the collected stubs at each show. U2 know exactly how many of their specially made tickets are in a pound, and any monkey business literally tips the scales.

Still, you cannot come up with a contingency for every possible perfidy. I have to laugh when 4 o'clock—the official time for the gates to open—arrives and the gates stay shut. A delegation of municipal officials has shown up and demanded proof from the local concert promoter that certain safety repairs promised to be made to the stadium after previous rock shows have been made. They have picked this particular moment to make an inspection of the entire stadium. The poor promoter is having convulsions.

Curfew time here is strict and imposed with an iron hand. U2 has been warned that the last time Springsteen played here the cops walked up to his soundboard at 11 o'clock and pulled down all the faders, shutting him right off. So every minute these local inspectors spend tut-tutting and tapping the walls is more time that cannot be made up at the other end. Big beads of sweat are rolling down the poor promoter's brow.

The inspectors murmur that this building may have to be condemned. Suddenly someone produces a substantial contribution to the building preservation fund. Or call it a fine. Call it a gesture of solidarity between fellow lovers or architecture and musical punctuality. Anyway, the cash is pocketed and the structure is declared sound. The gates are thrown open two hours late.

Exactly who paid off whom is not entirely clear. McGuinness says he knows nothing about it, I'm probably misinterpreting a legitimate civic exchange. Edge just laughs about the whole charade and says, "We were condemned and we got uncondemned." The crew have no doubts it was flat-out blackmail, but they are more pissed about another incident—when they finished erecting the stage in the boiling sun they found the doors to the showers locked. A local paisan was sitting in a chair dangling the keys in one hand while holding out his other hand for a bribe.

The crowd is in a rotten mood from having to stand outside so long and they take it out on Pearl Jam, who play a roaring set (they thanked

Larry excessively for their sound check) that is greeted with a bevy of plastic bottles and "Fuck you"s.

"Fuck me?" Eddie Vedder says. "Okay, you fuck me and then Bono will come out and fuck you." That gets some more boos. The funny thing is, Pearl Jam sounds great. I don't doubt that in five years the same people who are heckling them today will be bragging that they saw them way back when.

Backstage I run into Cameron Crowe, a legend among rock critics. Cameron was writing for *Rolling Stone* at fifteen, was made a contributing editor for his eighteenth birthday, quit to pose as a high school student for a year so he could write the book *Fast Times at Ridgemont High*, parlayed that into a job writing the script for the successful film of his book, which he in turn used as a launch pad for writing and directing his own movies. His films include the critically lauded *Say Anything* and the new *Singles*, a movie set in Seattle that features members of Pearl Jam in supporting roles and on the soundtrack. Aside from being distinguished from most of his rock critic peers by his ability to become a successful artist in his own right, Crowe is also freakish among the fraternity because (1) in a field full of sniping egomaniacs he is always gracious and generous and (2) because he married musician and video heartthrob Nancy Wilson of Heart. I don't know of any music critic who has inspired as much petty jealousy as Cameron, or in whom such pettiness is so absent.

Rolling Stone has hornswoggled Crowe into returning to his teenage vocation to write a cover story about Pearl Jam. He introduces me to Eddie Vedder and we fall into a conversation about songwriting. Eddie, who has a reputation for being touchy and reclusive, is warm and friendly as all get-out. Cameron is warm and friendly as all get-out. I can fake being warm and friendly with the best of them. We all stand around being convivial until Eddie suggests we go out to the soundboard and watch U2. When we get there Naomi and Christy are in their spots, as are Freston and Pollack. Edge's family have folding chairs set up and whenever the Zoo TV walls cut to a shot of Daddy his little girls wave at the screens. Perhaps because his kids are in the house, Edge does a rare solo song, an acoustic guitar version of "Van Diemen's Land" from *Rattle and Hum*. (Because "Numb" is now all over MTV a lot of people think it's Edge's first lead vocal on a U2 song. It's not, nor was "Van Diemen's Land." Edge sang "Seconds" on *War*, which always sent a shock through the house when U2 did it live. People assumed from the record that it was Bono.) On the side of the stage, Adam is watching Edge and Bono is trying to give Adam a hot foot.

There is a cool breeze and a magnificent moon. U2 are playing great. During an uproarious "New Year's Day" Bono, walking toward the B stage through a field of outstretched arms, turns and shouts, "I love you, Adam Clayton!"

Tom Freston says, "This is the best show I've ever seen; it should never end." He asks Christy and Naomi if they don't agree that this is the best concert they've ever seen. Yep, it is. Jeff Pollack says it might be the best concert he's ever seen too. Tom asks Eddie Vedder, who is unreconciled to all the technology and stage gimmicks, if it's the best concert he's ever seen. Eddie says he'd prefer Henry Rollins in a small club.

Some of the guards are chasing a blond woman through the crowd, trying to confiscate a video camera. She's pretty quick. She's giving them a good run for their money. Uh-oh, she is also Cameron Crowe's wife. I go tell the bouncers that the woman they just chased and shook down is Nancy Wilson of Heart, a real rock star in her own right and a legitimate laminated all-access part of the Pearl Jam's entourage.

"I guess we should give back her camera then," says one of the bouncers.

"Can we keep her film?" says another.

Onstage Bono is raging about Bosnia. "For the first time in about twenty-five years America gets it right, wants to help out the people over there across the water in Bosnia-Herzegovina. So what happens? The EEC gets together and fucks it up!"

Driving back to the hotel, Regine shows me a fax that has arrived for Bono from Bill Carter in Sarajevo. It is three single-spaced pages withdrawing the invitation for U2 to come to Bosnia, and what they might do instead:

> Yesterday hundreds of shells hit Sarajevo, which I can assure you is enough to either lose your life or worse, lose your mind. Bearing this kind of warfare in mind I think coming to Sarajevo as a group would be very dangerous. Believe me there would be nothing I would want more than to have that happen, but there are serious problems with the concept. . . .

Sarajevo is very likely the most dangerous city in modern history. The attacks are random and on the town, not exclusively on the soldiers. Thus moving around is difficult. As individuals I would say yes, let's make it happen, but as U2 the danger would be very high for the people of Sarajevo. They are beyond caring about snipers and shells, and they would gather to feel the power of U2 and there's a real possibility that people would be killed. Example: four weeks ago there was a big football match in a village in Sarajevo, and the Serbs shelled it and killed 30 people and injured 125. Third, if you made it into Sarajevo the airport could be shelled, as it is quite often, and then the airport shuts down and you would be stuck in here anywhere from 3 to 7 or 8 days. Personally I think U2 could be more powerful making aware the situation with the audience it speaks to every night.

Carter goes on to suggest that U2 allow a satellite linkup between the Zoo TV concerts and Sarajevo:

The idea is to show the insanity, the surrealness, the survival. The audience if anything would realize, Jesus, lucky I'm here enjoying this concert and not in Sarajevo. Maybe they will think about not letting it happen in their country, their city, their house. . . .

He explains that the notion of Bosnia is of a united nation of Serbs, Croats, and Muslims:

Sarajevo, the only place where your name won't get you killed, raped or put in jail. It is a war of last names. . . . Why is Sarajevo under siege? Sarajevo represents the soul of Bosnia. If the Serbs can destroy the spirit and nerves of Sarajevo they can easily start to carve up what remains of Bosnia (not much: 70% is occupied).

I finish reading the letter:

(Let me know if the idea with the satellite link is in the right direction.)

and hand it back to Regine.

When we get to the hotel people gather in a dining room where a buffet dinner has been laid out. McGuinness is explaining to Tom Freston how the Zoo TV sensibility and concept can be made into an ongoing television network, and MTV would be natural partners in this venture.

Freston is interested. He is enjoying the exquisite panorama into which we have all been dumped. The lights of Rome, the lovely guests, the wine, the feast. "This is like *La Dolce Vita!*" Freston says. Which leads McGuinness to repeat a rumor that *Dolce Vita* director Federico Fellini once wondered why he had not been asked to direct a U2 video. It might not be true, but everyone would like to believe it is.

Maurice looks up sleepy-eyed and says, "Isn't Fellini coming to the show tomorrow night?"

Everyone stops talking and looks at him. *What?*

"Naomi said Fellini's coming to the show."

"He is," Edge says quietly. He pauses a beat while everyone turns to him and then adds, "*Morris* Fellini."

The models, meanwhile, are asking Adam why Bono announced he loved him in the middle of "New Year's Day." Adam smiles and says, "You only come up with a bassline as good as that three or four times in your life."

Bono is in a dark mood. "I just talked to Bill Carter," he tells me. "The people of Sarajevo don't want us there. He says there are things we can do to help but coming there now is not one of them."

Victory for the forces of Principle. U2 is going to try to do what Carter has suggested instead: set up broadcasts from Sarajevo onto the Zoo TV video walls, bring Bosnia to thousands of Western Europeans rather than bring four Irishmen to Bosnia. It isn't going to be easy. Such a public act of do-gooding plays into all the old stereotypes of the self-righteous U2 using the rock stage to conduct social studies lectures. It will undo a great deal of what U2 has spent the last two years trying to achieve—building a wall of surface and glamour between the public masks and the four individuals. U2 doesn't have any illusions about what's more important—their image or the world ignoring a massacre. But it is still tough to know that they are going to open the door to all the old crap that they have worked so hard to bury.

"You know," Bono says seriously, "so far all the press has been great, the best of our career. You could get the impression that everybody loves what we're doing. But you watch what happens next. Watch what happens when we get to England. And wait for Dublin. Come home with us and get another perspective. Come home for our beheading."

36

The Bosnia Broadcasts

*U2 establishes a satellite beachhead/ bill carter picks up
some bullet holes/ an excruciating moment for larry mullen/
the english press eat U2 for breakfast/ salman rushdie
emerges from hiding*

IN MARSEILLES, France, on July 14 Bono makes his first attempt to
bring Sarajevo onto the Zoo TV stage. They have not yet been
able to hook up a television transmission with Bosnia, but so far
this summer Macphisto's telephone has been good enough for reaching
everyone from Pavarotti ("You're slimming down for the nineties!") to
Mussolini's granddaughter ("I think you're doing a marvelous job of
filling the old man's shoes!") so Bono will try to phone Bill Carter in
Sarajevo tonight. After Morleigh has belly danced off stage at the end of
"Mysterious Ways" Bono addresses the crowd.

"*Liberté! Égalité! Fraternité!*" he says to applause. "But not in Sarajevo!
Not in Bosnia-Herzegovina. I want to call a friend I have there." Bono
goes to the onstage phone and hits a long series of numbers slowly and
carefully. "I'm trying to get through here, hold on," he tells the audience. He holds up crossed fingers. There's a ringing and then an American voice comes on the line.

"Hello."

"Hello," Bono says, "is that Sarajevo? Is that my man, Bill Carter?"

"Hey! Hello, Bono! How are you?"

"I'm here in Marseilles," Bono says as the audience applauds, "in
France, and we are calling to tell you that we love you!"

"Hey, that feels good in Sarajevo! Thank you very much!"

"Tell us what's been happening today."

"Well, as you know, the situation is a little desperate with the basics of water, food, and electricity, but everybody is holding up, trying to stick in there."

"You have no water?"

"A little water came to the city today, but we still have no power and there's no food. Old people are starting to die 'cause there's no food."

"They die because there's no food. How do the people of Sarajevo feel about Europe? Do you feel we have let you down?"

"Yeah. There's a bit of a feeling in Sarajevo that Europe has forgotten that Sarajevo is in Europe, and the problems in Sarajevo will eventually become Europe's problems."

"Well, I just want to say one thing to you tonight, Bill. We are ashamed tonight to be Europeans and to turn our backs on you and your people." The crowd claps at this. "We wish you well, we wish you safety, and we will call again. God bless you."

With that U2 goes into "One," and back at the Holiday Inn in Sarajevo where he went to wait for the call, Bill Carter feels all hopped up at having spoken to a stadium full of people. Now he's just got to get back to his apartment in the city without getting shot. Night is a bad time to be out around here. Bill had to run across an open field to get to this hotel where Reuters News Service is headquartered and borrow their phone. Now he has to run back.

Three days later he has to take a bigger risk for a bigger payoff. Carter has managed to convince the European Broadcast Union—a satellite pool used by the news services covering the war in Bosnia—that he is not a lunatic, that he really has the wherewithal to make nightly broadcasts to stadiums full of people if the EBU will let him get on their satellite for ten or fifteen minutes. To tell you the truth, I think the EBU is more convinced by the checks Principle sends to their Geneva headquarters than by Bill's entreaties. The bad news is that Carter has to drive across dangerous terrain to get to the Sarajevo TV station and hook up with the satellite. He enlists two Bosnian pals, Darko and Vlado, to run the gauntlet with him. (Darko and Vlado are Serbian, by the way—which demonstrates that Sarajevo includes Serbs who would rather risk death for a multiethnic Bosnia than join the "ethnic cleansing," the Serbian nationalists' euphemism for wiping out other ethnic groups.)

The three drive like madmen through the open area called "Sniper's Alley" and make it inside the dark TV station with flashlights. They use portable batteries for power and get set up to go live to Bologna. At about 9:45 Carter can hear in his earpiece distant applause and Bono talking to the Italian audience: *"Grazie.* We're about 500 kilometers here from a city very different to this city. We're going to try to get through to the people of Sarajevo. We're using our high-tech shit. We got them on the phone last week, but tonight for the first time we'll try to get my friend Bill in Sarajevo. Are you there, Bill? We got you on the line?"

Bill looks into the camera and speaks into a hand microphone: "Yeah, I'm here. Can you hear me, Bono?"

"Yeah, we got ya." Bill's nervous face is lighting up the Zoo Vidiwalls. "What's happening today in Sarajevo?" Bono asks. "Where are you?"

"I'm in the TV station downtown in Sarajevo. It's about ten o'clock here. Outside the window about an hour and a half ago there were two grenades and one child was killed and five people were injured. So the situation's kind of bad. The food supply is gone, there's no water, there's no electricity. People are eating the grass. To get to water you have to walk two to three hours. Some people faint on the way to get the water. They have no energy.

"Just today I went to the hospital and saw a friend of mine who has a grenade shell in his head here." Bill points to his temple. "He went to get water, about a two-hour walk, and a grenade fell and hit him in the head. He has two daughters who are now probably going to have to get their own water. They probably won't make it. You know, if I got on a plane right now I could be at your concert before it's over. I'm less than an hour away from Bologna. And yet thanks to the EBU and satellite connections we can talk."

Bill hears applause in his earpiece. Then he hears Bono's voice again: "Well, the truth is we don't have anything that we can say to you. We are dumb. We just wanted you to know that here in Bologna, Italy, at this moment we're thinking about you and we pray for an end to your troubles and we pray that Europe will take the people of Sarajevo more seriously than they are right now. They are leaving you, they are ignoring you, we are betraying you. It's only a fucking rock & roll song, but this song is for you. Whatever that means. Good night. God bless you. Love to everybody. Thanks, Bill."

U2 plays "One." Later in the concert, after they perform "When Love Comes to Town" on the B stage, Bono says, "There's something obscene about having to beam in pictures from across the waters in Sarajevo to a rock & roll concert. It doesn't quite fit. This is a Bob Marley song. It might say things a whole lot better." And he sings "Redemption Song."

U2 agrees after the concert that the Sarajevo hookup came too early in the show, it threw off the mood before the mood had even been established. The next night they wait until the end of the B stage segment, after Bono's interstellar duet with Lou Reed's electronic ecto-plasm on "Satellite of Love." This time Bono also gets the physical distance between Bologna and Bosnia right. "We're 200 miles, 330 kilometers from Sarajevo," he says to the audience. "These are our next-door neighbors." There is plenty of supportive applause.

"I suppose the thing is with TV you don't know if what you're seeing is real," Bono tells the crowd, spelling out publicly the original motivation for the Zoo TV concept. "You can't tell the difference anymore between the adverts, and what's happening on CNN, or what's coming in on satellite. You can't ask the television some questions. We sent a satellite dish into the city of Sarajevo. We've got a friend there, a cool guy named Bill Carter, a rock & roll fan! Let's see if we can get him on the line. Is it working? Are you there, Bill?"

Carter's haggard face fills up the screens in the Bologna stadium. "Yeah, I hear you, Bono."

"Well, you got fifty thousand people here and we just wanted to say to you that it might not be on the news as much as we'd like, it might not be on the TV as much as we'd like, but you are with us here and you're in our hearts tonight." There are cheers.

"Thank you. It's about eleven o'clock here in Sarajevo. Today the fighting is very little but there's a general fear the town's getting smaller. The perimeter of the town is being fought over and the people are having to come to the center of town, so supplies of food and water and gas are becoming more of a problem. Also tonight about twelve kilometers from here about ten to fifteen thousand people, refugees, are being attacked by artillery and they have nowhere to go. On a personal note my friend that had the piece of grenade in his head died this morning."

Bono is staring blankly at the screen now, as if he's forgotten he's on a stage in a stadium full of people. Carter continues, "But tonight I have some friends with me from Sarajevo. This is Darko, who I asked earlier today what is the hardest part of the war for him."

Darko comes on and speaks in broken English: "First, I want to say hello to all the people in Bologna. Thanks to Bill, U2, and all you people we don't feel alone this night as we usually do, especially within the last few months. Anyway, answering this question: the hardest thing for me. Although we all in Sarajevo have to live with all this death, the hardest thing for me on my personal level is being separated from my family, my wife and kids. They live and they grow up somewhere without me, with no opportunity to contact them. Even more shocked is the fact that my parents live just four kilometers from this place and I'm not able to contact them—maybe, except using such satellite connection. I'm not able to contact them for a year. Those are things that are hardest for me during this eighteen months. Once again, thank you all in Bologna."

Bill Carter introduces another guest to the audience, saying, "I have another friend, Vlado, who has been separated from his wife for seventeen months. She lives in Bologna and there's a good chance she could be here tonight."

Vlado steps up. "I have a small message for my wife, *mia cara*, Mirita. My darling Mirita, I love you and I miss you. I feel alive and I feel good. Thank you. Thank you, Billy. Thank you, U2. And *grazie*, Bologna. Ciao."

In Bologna U2 goes into "Bad" and in Sarajevo, Carter, Vlado, and Darko get into their car and drive as fast as they can through Sniper's Alley. Bullets fly around them, hitting the car. They have to floor the accelerator and at the same time kill the headlights. There is almost as much chance of dying in an auto wreck as there is of being hit by the Chetnik gunfire. Finally they pull out of the exposed area and come to rest in the relative safety of a narrow street. They climb out and count the new bullet holes in the auto body.

Bill has gotten so used to the horror of life in Sarajevo that he no longer looks twice at such surreal characters as the head of the local Mafia, who promises safe passage out of the city for the right price and has taken to riding around the town on a horse, pistols dangling from his belt.

Over the next three weeks, U2 does ten more hookups with Bill Carter and his neighbors in Sarajevo. During that time U2 crosses into the U.K. and begins Zooropa's final leg: Glasgow, Leeds, Cardiff, and four nights at the huge Wembley Stadium in London. Over 400,000 tickets have been sold for these U.K. concerts. Meanwhile Bill Carter finds that both he and Bono are becoming heroes to the people of Sarajevo. The in-concert conversations are being broadcast on local radio, and provide for the Bosnians a slender bit of evidence that the outside world has not abandoned them completely. The satellite transmissions themselves become more angry, with Carter taking on a slightly messianic edge and the Bosnians he brings on camera accusing the U2 audiences of *sitting there doing nothing while we are being murdered.* It makes it hard for U2 to regain emotional control of their concerts afterward.

Much of the British press heads up to Glasgow for the first U.K. show and are slapped with an on-screen lecture from a Bosnian woman who tells them, "We would like to hear the music, too, but we only hear the screams of wounded and tortured people and raped women!"

Adam wants to put down his bass, walk offstage, get in his car, and go somewhere where he can bury his head in the sand and not think about what the next song is or who he has to shake hands with after the show.

Larry, sitting on his drum stool under the video screen, listening to this and looking out at Bono standing alone on the B stage, thinks, *This is the most excruciating thing U2 has ever been through.* He is literally squirming with discomfort. Larry is the band member who was uncomfortable using a bit of video that made fun of George Bush. For him, the Bosnia broadcasts are pure torture.

It ain't a picnic for the audience, either. There is nothing like having genocide shoved in your face to ruin a crowd's partying mood. Bono has certainly achieved his early goal of illustrating onstage the obscenity of idly flipping from a war on CNN to rock videos on MTV. The audience at the U2 concerts may be appalled, and are as likely to be angry with U2 as with the Serbians, but they are not numb. The audience is so shaken that the music can hardly recapture their enthusiasm.

In August U2 decide they will end the Bosnia broadcasts after their four-night stand in London. They rationalize that, by coincidence or indirect effect, Sarajevo has gone from being virtually unmentioned in the press three weeks earlier to dominating the front pages of the British papers every day. They will bring Bill Carter out of Sarajevo to Ireland for the final three Zooropa concerts.

As Bono predicted, by the time the tour gets to London the press is savage. They treat U2's reversion to world-saving form as a drunk's wife treats her husband's falling off the wagon. Larry says that with the Sarajevo linkup U2 has set its image back five years—but what is a rock band's image worth when put up against the genocide in Bosnia?

"I like that confusion," Bono says of the blow to U2's new persona. "When I go to the theater I need to know that the actor is not so comfortable on that stage, I need to know that he might be in my face or in my life. There's a script at a U2 show, but you need to know that the script might get ripped up and you might be out there. So occasionally when that happens and you think, 'Well, this isn't what I was told this would be! I thought they were all removed now and here they are laying this on me,' that's our job!"

A long anti-U2 tirade in London's *New Musical Express* says, in part, "The Bosnian linkup was beyond bad taste. It was insulting. Faced with the horrific description of the situation in Sarajevo, Bono was reduced to a stumbling incoherence that was probably the result of genuine concern, but came across as bog-standard celeb banality. What does the band who have virtually everything buy with their millions? The one thing they've never had—credibility. Shame it's not for sale."

In Sarajevo, though, U2 are becoming saints. People grab Bill Carter in the street, telling him how important it is that *someone* in Europe is protesting the slaughter. There's a new joke making the rounds in Bosnia: "What's the difference between Sarajevo and Auschwitz? At least in Auschwitz they had gas." During one satellite link a Muslim tells Bono that U2 has given Sarajevo a window into the world, and they pray that some light shines through it.

At Wembley U2 are exhausted, running on fumes, but are determined to shove their Irish attitude down the British gullet. At the end of the run, Bono comes out as Macphisto and makes his nightly celebrity telephone call, this time to fugitive author Salman Rushdie. For four years Rushdie has been eluding a *fatwa*, a death sentence placed on him by the Ayatollah Khomeini for offending Islam with his novel *The Satanic Verses*. The Wembley audience is astonished when Rushdie not only answers Bono's phone call, but comes out of hiding and walks onto the stage. Waving a finger in Macphisto's face Rushdie says, "I'm not afraid of you! Real devils don't wear horns!"

This is one blow too many for the *Sunday Independent*, which declares,

"Bono has made a holy joke of both Islamic affairs (of which he knows nothing) and the war in Bosnia (of which he seems to know even less)."

Seeing Rushdie onstage with U2 strikes the news media as an almost incomprehensible juxtaposition of cultural incompatibles. What in the holy hell is a fugitive intellectual doing with a leather-bottomed pop band? Who left the academic gate open? Allan Bloom must be spinning in his tomb!

When I mention that reaction to Rushdie, he says the suggestion that U2 was in any way exploiting his situation is ridiculous. "I think I was in a way exploiting *their* global audience," Rushdie says, "to get people to pay attention to another kind of important message. I think the Sarajevo linkup was the same thing. It's true that there is a very painful aspect to it, because these people are living in a very stark, life-and-death situation, and it sat very awkwardly in the middle of a rock show. One woman on the screen said, 'You're not doing anything for us!' and the next stage is—you sing another song. That's very jagged. But it's exactly what I thought was valuable in it. The fact that it felt so awkward, that the thing sat so badly in the show, is a way of saying to this huge audience, 'There are things that can't be accommodated easily and that are difficult and painful and awkward and you can't just homogenize them into the rest of the world.'

"I thought exactly the awkwardness of it, the ill-fittingness, was what made it memorable. I've never been made, in a rock & roll show, to feel the pain of the world before. It's very easy to knock that stuff, and journalists by and large cultivate the kind of cynicism from which it becomes very easy to say it is done crassly. But I didn't feel that.

"We live in an age when people want to reinvent a whole bunch of demarcation lines and say, 'If you're a rock band don't step across the line into news coverage. We reporters do that! If you're a highbrow writer don't write about popular culture, we have popular-culture writers who do that!' I think all creative activity, in fact, is a process of *destroying* frontiers. You take your voice into a place where it hasn't been before and the friction is the interesting thing. And the sparks are the work.

"We live in an age when the people who mediate the work of creative artists to the public actually don't understand something that the public and the artists both understand. So in the middle there is this block.

There are these customs officials saying, 'Don't go through the green channel!' and making it difficult.

"I haven't responded to a rock group as strongly as this for a very long time, because I think people have been so cautious. And here's a rock group taking a fantastic risk of itself. I like when people go over the edge and invite you to go with them. In this case, people have."

37

The Old Man

---

*bono's toughest critic/ his mother christened him paul, and
paul he will remain/ when gavin almost got his ass kicked/
the myth of the chess master deflated/ advice for the groom*

I 'LL TELL you one harsh critic of the London concerts in particular
and U2's Zoo TV direction in general: Bobby Hewson, Bono's
silver-haired father.

"There was an incident at the London concert where a girl got up
onstage," Mr. Hewson says sternly. "Paul lies down" —he still calls
Bono Paul. "She got on top of him and there was a simulation of sex.
That was, I think, completely uncalled for, unnecessary and objection-
able. As well as that on the same occasion he said *fuck* a few times. Now
one *fuck* is permissible, but when you continue on using the word not
only is it not permissible, but it loses its impact."

Sitting in Mr. Hewson's living room in Howth, Ireland, I feel like I'm
back in high school trying to talk one of my buddy's dads out of
grounding him.

"You know, Mr. Hewson," I say, "Bono mentioned that girl who
climbed up on him from the audience during 'Babyface.' He was as
shocked as you were!"

"Yeah, well" —Bob looks at me through narrow eyes—"the first time
it was unexpected, but the *second* time it wasn't."

He's got me there. I ask about his reaction to the whole Zoo TV
spectacle.

"You mean this particular tour? I must admit I don't particularly like
this thing of sunglasses and cigars. In fact I've several times dressed him
down over presenting a bad image. Kids follow, and every time I see him
now he has a cigar in his mouth. He maintains it's an image. He swears
he doesn't inhale! I gave up smoking twenty years ago and neither

Norman nor Paul ever smoked until now, I don't agree with that at all. I know that my view is a narrow view and we're a different generation, and I know that people onstage have to adopt certain personas. Maybe it's necessary. Personally, I don't think it is.

"As regards the 'Zooropa thing,' I think that they've lost . . ." Mr. Hewson hesitates and then explains why he's being so blunt: "When he asks for my opinion about anything I always give him the truth. I figure they've enough yes-men around them, somebody should tell them the truth." (Bono once said of his dad, "He thinks I've got too many yes-men because he is the no-man.")

Mr. Hewson gives his opinion of post-Zoo U2: "I think that the thing has got out of hand. Somebody was saying, 'What are we going to do for the next tour? It can't get any bigger.' My view is that it should go back to being four fellas with guitars and forget all of that stuff. I think something's lost in the transition from the original format that they had. Maybe these things are necessary to a certain extent, but . . ." He laughs and his face softens. "I'm only—to use an Irish expression—a goballoon, I don't know what I'm talking about."

"Well, Mr. Hewson," I suggest, "they feel that U2's fame has gotten so big and intrusive that the only way to maintain any semblance of private life is erect a bit of a facade."

"Well, I don't mind that so much," he says. "That's understandable. You can't be a public figure *all* the time. But they started off and they because successful as sort of a good, clean-living band. In America this was particularly so. Somebody in one of the American newspapers wrote, 'Most rock & roll bands start off with drink and drugs and then end up seeing the light. U2 have done it the reverse way!' I don't agree with it, I don't agree with this image of decadence they've gotten into. God, I'm going to get into trouble for saying it."

"But there's not much actual decadence," I protest. "It's more *If I'm going to be a rock star, let me really play the role of a rock star.* But I take your point, a fourteen-year-old kid may not make the distinction."

"And in changing that way they have become like any other old rock & roll band," Bobby says firmly. "I may be wrong with this, but I think in America one of the reasons for their success—apart from their music—is that they presented a new image, a clean image, God-fearing, Christian. Now, I'm not saying you can be that all the time, but at the same time I think—God, I'll get shot—the deliberate decision to alter that image I don't agree with." He smiles and throws up his hands. "I'll probably never be asked to a rock concert again."

"I think a version of that same argument went on within the band," I say, "before they headed in this new direction."

"Yeah." Bobby nods. "I don't know who was responsible. I have an idea it was my young fella, however. Wouldn't surprise me with regard to him."

"I think Bono and Edge were pushing for the band to change," I say. "Larry may have said—"

"'Why?' A very solid man, Larry. Very solid man. I remember talking to Larry in the foyer of a hotel in Paris. There was a crowd outside. Paul was with me and couldn't get away. I said to Larry, 'Aren't you the cute man now!' He says, 'Why?' I said, 'You never have to do interviews!' 'Listen, pal,' he said to me, 'I did one interview for the band and it was the last interview I've ever done!' I said, 'You're a wise man.' Larry's a very practical guy. Very likable guy too." Larry told me once that he gets along well with Bono's father. When Bobby shows up at a gig he and Larry often go off and shoot pool together.

It would be a big mistake to misunderstand a Dublin father's insistence on keeping his famous boy from getting too big a head. Mr. Hewson's pride in his son is evident from the platinum U2 albums on the wall (though his own CD shelf is filled with classical music), the photos taken by Bono in Africa that appoint his dining room, and one particularly great photograph hanging above me now, of Bobby running toward the camera with a wild expression on his face—equal parts amused, panicked, and embarrassed—with Bono and Adam laughing in the background. It turns out it was taken on stage at a big outdoor concert in Dublin. Bobby was standing in front of the stage when Bono reached down his arm to him. He thought this son was trying to shake his hand, so he reached back—and a moment later found himself hauled up on the stage and Bono dancing with him to the cheers of the crowd. He shook himself loose and got out of there as fast as he could, a photographer catching his escape as he came off. The large framed photograph—and the prominent place it has in Mr. Hewson's home— says that beneath his gruffness he takes a lot of pride in his son's accomplishments.

Which is not to say there isn't plenty of gruff. Mention that most people refer to Paul as "Bono" and Bobby says, "That used to drive me mad! I still never will call him that. I call him Paul. I've said to him on more than one occasion, 'Your mother christened you Paul and Paul you're going to remain!' In fact, I think he gets annoyed if people outside call him Paul. I think that's for family. He started off being called Bonovox or some stupid thing Derek—Guggi—or some of his pals had christened him. I think it stuck. I must say it never went down right with me."

I ask what he figured when Gavin and Guggi started coming around in makeup.

Bobby lets out a sigh, as if he's going to have to tell me some bad news for my own good. "Now, Gavin's a very nice fella," he says. "I'm very fond of Gavin. When I knew them they were in this Virgin whatever-the-hell-they-were-called. They used to come down. I remember once Gavin came down in a dress! I almost gave him a kick in the arse. And on another occasion Guggi showed up at the door with lipstick on and I said to him, 'Derek, your mouth is bleeding!' I must admit I frowned very much on the association. I'm very old-fashioned in that respect."

Gavin told me that the day he went to the Hewson house in his dress Bobby answered the door, looked at him with disgust, and said, "I'm opening the door to you now, but I never will again! Coming to get my boy looking like that!"

You're a Catholic, I say to Mr. Hewson, but Bono was raised Protestant.

"I was Roman Catholic and my wife was Church of Ireland," he explains. "Which in those days was unusual, it wasn't readily accepted. Both the boys were brought up as Church of Ireland. 'Cause I thought, well, the mother has to raise the children. When does the father see them? Only at nighttime. The responsibility is more or less hers, she should have it her way.

"Then he became mixed up with—I don't know what they called themselves, but they were some kind of a Bible group. I've always been a little bit cagey of those people who say they have all the answers. We never had rows but we used to debate the Bible for hours and hours on end. Because he seemed to think he knew all about the Bible. We used to have great arguments, go on for hours. We still do sometimes." He laughs. "I was a little skeptical. But then as he grew older it seemed to be working all right with him, so I didn't object."

"Bono told me that growing up he was allowed to find his own way."

"Spiritually? Well, that's true, because his mother died and there was only the three of us there—Norman, Paul, and me. He was a very exasperating child; he wasn't a bad child but bloody exasperating. My God, he really was. I'll give you an example that sticks in my mind and his brother Norman could confirm this. I remember one night we were having supper and we were sitting down beside the fire. My wife was alive at the time and we were having some kind of cakes. Paul took a bite and instead of putting it down on the plate he put it down on the shelf. 'You've got a plate, use it.'

"You wouldn't believe it, but we could not get him to admit that he should put the cake on the plate. The three of us—Norman was arguing with him too! I said, 'We're not going to bed until we resolve this thing once and for all!' My wife actually went to bed crying at one o'clock in the morning. At two o'clock he finally said, 'Yes, I was wrong,' and went to bed. Next morning he got up and he said, 'I only agreed because I wanted to go to bed.' He must have been twelve or thirteen. He lived in a different world even then. You'd say, 'Paul, will you slip upstairs and get me a hairbrush from the bedroom?' He'd come back and you'd say, 'Where is it?' 'Where's what?' 'Why did you go upstairs, Paul?' 'To go to the toilet.'

"And he's still the same! I warned Ali when she was marrying him. To this day I say, 'I told you and you wouldn't believe me! You were too much in love!'

"I remember on one occasion we had an awful row. I gave him a few thumps and threw him out in the hall and closed the door. I opened the door and I heard this sniggering. I looked and there was a banana skin and he was sitting on the stairs waiting for me. . . ." Suddenly Bobby laughs hard for a long time. Then he sighs and says, "Ah, he was exasperating, he really was. But there was nothing bad in him. He was living in his own world and we were sort of superfluous to it. And it still applies today. He was an extraordinary kid. He was very hard to nail down. We couldn't get him to study when he was in school, just could not get him to study. He'd go off to study and the next thing you'd hear him strummin' the guitar."

How has being the father of Bono of U2 affected your life?

"There are pros and cons," he says. "Sometimes it can be a bit of a nuisance. Particularly around concert time when all my pals, friends, and relatives are looking for tickets. Because he's a millionaire people think that I'm a millionaire, or at least half a millionaire. And that has its disadvantages. If I leave my car in for servicing and they know who it is, I'm quite sure an extra few quid is put on the bill. My standard of living, I suppose, has improved, that's an obvious advantage.

"There's disadvantages, too. They go off on tour, they live a different kind of lifestyle, and I don't get to see his children as often as I would my other grandchildren. But we've had some great times on tour with them. We've been to the States and Canada and around Europe. I see things I wouldn't normally have seen.

"They lead—to my mind anyway—a completely artificial life. We were in New York, my older son, Norman, and his wife and my brother-in-law and his wife, and we were all going out to see *Cats*, and Paul was stuck in the hotel and couldn't get out. He said to me, 'My God, I'd love to be able to go to a show with you.' It's like living in a fishbowl. His life isn't his own. He's restricted in where he can go and what he can do. You only life your life once. There are obviously tremendous financial advantages, but it's a fairly high price. He doesn't see his own children as often as he might if he lived a normal kind of life. And I think kids, particularly young children, need both parents around all the time. Not just flying visits now and then. I think it's a high price to pay. Soon his children will be fifteen and talking about leaving home. That goes by very quickly."

Mr. Hewson gets up and insists I have some tea and biscuits. We move into the kitchen. His apartment is a neat, modern place with spectacular views of the ocean. Bono brought him here for the first time on the pretense that he was considering buying it for himself and Ali. His father told him it was beautiful but it made no sense for them to move in—there was no room for children. Ah, Bono smiled, then will you have it? Now Bobby, a retired civil servant with pals in the post office, gets mail from around the world addressed only to "Bono, Ireland." Not long ago a friend of his, a cabdriver, showed up with a seventeen-year-old American girl who had gotten into the taxi at the airport and said she had come to Ireland to find U2. The driver said, well, would you settle for Bono's dad?

Bobby was taken aback but he invited the girl in and answered all her questions while his cabbie friend sat there smiling. Finally Bobby figured out the scam—the driver had his meter running the whole time! He was charging the girl a high price for this introduction.

Lately the newspapers have been carrying stories of McGuinness purchasing for Bono at a charity auction a match with Russian chess champion Gary Kasparov. The reports all explain that Bono was a child chess prodigy. One even quoted Bono as saying, "I reckon I have a good shot at beating him." Now, aside from its value as another example of the inability of some newspapers to spot a tongue in a cheek, there is some historic basis for claims of Bono's chess-playing skill. He's told me that as a kid he was crazy about the game, and at a young age he beat the local chess teacher to the wonder of all. He always downplayed this enthusiasm because chess is so un–rock & roll. Later this was a source of common ground with Bob Dylan, who had hidden his bishops under a basket for the same reason. I asked Mr. Hewson to tell me about young Bono's gift for chess.

"I think that's been blown up," he says with a tolerant smile. "The press got it and blew it up. I taught him how to play chess, though I haven't played in donkeys' years now. He did join a chess club and he won a couple of medals. He beat the chairman of the club and I think in order to maintain the chairman's reputation he more or less exaggerated Paul's prowess." We both start laughing and Mr. Hewson adds, "I think that's the real story!" (Bono once pointed out that the fact that he was a child in a club full of adults would not impress his father one bit: if Paul won the chess contest it must mean the fella he played against was no good.)

When I leave I tell Mr. Hewson I'm going to grab a cab back to central Dublin and he says that's a ridiculous waste of money, I can get the DART (Dublin Area Rapid Transit) train right down the road. I say, Oh, okay, and I think he can tell I'm planning to get a taxi anyway, so he insists on driving me to the train station. We go out and get in his car and Mr. Hewson immediately announces we can save some time by driving the wrong way down a one-way street. A curving, downhill, one-way street where you wouldn't see a truck coming around the bend until you were pasted to the grillework. I see where Bono inherited his driving skills.

I ask what, if U2 ended tomorrow, Bobby would wish for his son for the rest of his life.

"I would hope that he would readily readjust to ordinary life," he says. "That he would be happy with his wife and kids, because he has a lovely wife and lovely children. And he would maintain a normal, happy life. Wealth doesn't bring happiness."

"Ali has set up a situation that allows him to come and go," I point out. "The house functions without him."

"Oh, absolutely!" Mr. Hewson laughs. "The house functions better without him, I think! You've no idea what he's like. He hasn't changed. He's still the same as he always was. He's cute in his own way. It's the old story. I have a brother who was never any good at jobs, couldn't do anything, never even rode a bicycle. And everybody felt sorry for him. On one occasion the fella next door came in and painted his house. Once you get the name of being like that nobody asks you to do anything!

"When I was getting married there was an old chap who called me up one day and he said, 'Bobby, I'm going to give you two words of advice and remember them: the first time the wife asks you to go to the supermarket don't say no. Go to the supermarket but bring back all the wrong things. You'll never be asked to go again!' His second word of advice was, 'If the kitchen tap leaks don't send for a plumber, get a bloody big spanner and flood the kitchen. You'll never be asked to do any more jobs again.' And that's true! Perfectly true. And Paul has pursued that policy."

38

Cork Popping

---

praise from some well-known presidents/ dodging the taoiseach/ sebastian clayton's observations/ the last flight of the zoo plane/ the man who could never go home/ edge on the value of heresy

I'VE SEEN Beatlemania and I've seen Madonna fever, I've seen the whole United States trying to get tickets for Dylan's '74 tour, and screaming teenagers baying at Michael Jackson's window. But I have never seen the sort of media overload around a rock act that Ireland is experiencing during this week of U2's first local shows since 1989. There is a concert in Cork on Tuesday, and two in Dublin on Friday and Saturday. From the newspapers you'd think that U2 was on a triple bill with D-Day and the moon landing.

Some of the press is positive to the point of sycophancy, some is negative to the border of slander, but all of it is everywhere. It is beyond the Arts & Entertainment sections, past the gossip and personality pages, over and above the news reports. There are caricatures of Bono in the political cartoons, speculations about McGuinness's latest moves in the financial pages, and sermons about U2 in the churches.

Something has changed for U2 in Ireland. When they walk down the street now, tourists run up and take their pictures, or kids crowd around looking for autographs. It used to be that Dubliners gave the band a wide berth, either out of respect or out of refusal to admit they were a big deal. There seemed to be a certain local pride in not paying much attention to U2, and that suited U2 fine. But now it's different. Maybe it's because in their second decade, with the great success of *Achtung Baby* and the Zoo tours, U2 has emerged as one of the few superstar acts to make the transition into the nineties without stumbling. Maybe it's because they now come home trailing Naomi Campbell and Salman Rushdie behind them.

Or maybe it's because Dublin itself has become more cosmopolitan; the international success of filmmakers Jim Sheridan (*My Left Foot*) and Neil Jordan (*The Crying Game*), writer Roddy Doyle (*The Commitments, The Snapper*), and playwright Brian Friel (*Dancing at Lughnasa*) the rise of Sinéad O'Connor and return of Van Morrison, and the migration of rock musicians such as Elvis Costello, Def Leppard, Mick Scott, and Jerry Lee Lewis have made Dublin buzz. That buzzing has attracted to the city the sort of people who get excited by seeing celebrities. It is good for a town that was down and out just a decade ago to now be full of life and excitement, but it makes Dublin less of a refuge for its four most famous citizens.

"Dublin's like the Village in *The Prisoner*," Adam's brother Sebastian observes. "Everyone knows what everyone else is doing and thinking. Very little questioning goes on around here. People go along with what everyone else thinks. U2's always asking questions or trying to start something new. There's not a large group of people here like that. They've always held that they're Irish and Ireland is their home. I think everything is still going to be based here, but I think they've come to a stage where they can't fully have what they're doing judged by people here anymore. They've got to get out and feel and be felt by other people."

Adam's twenty-three-year-old brother is looking forward to getting out himself. Another Clayton bassist, Sebastian's band Moby Dick just broke up on the verge of getting signed to Sony. Sebastian's been living at Adam's house since he finished school three years ago. It was Adam's idea—it got Sebastian out from under his parents and gave Adam a family member to keep an eye on his castle when he was away. Now Sebastian's going to hitch a ride with U2 through the Pacific, and then go off to hook up with his parents in Malaysia, where Mr. Clayton, an airline pilot, is stationed for two years.

"I'm the wrong person to ask about Dublin." Sebastian smiles. "It's probably due to the fact that I grew up with Adam in U2, but I find the people here narrow-minded. Not in Ireland, just in Dublin. I know this guy who always says, 'Oh, U2 are crap, really bad.' Then you see him at midnight queuing to buy their new album the first day of release! That happens a lot in Dublin toward U2. Adam might be talking to someone in a pub and they'll go, 'Love the album!' Then after Adam walks away they say, 'Ah, stupid idiot! I hate that band.' But then they go buy all the records. Strange.

"I wouldn't be surprised if there are people right now on the other side of the city saying, 'Oh, you know Sebastian and the American writer are over in the bar of the Conrad having a chat.' That's how scary it is. I'm looking forward to going to Malaysia."

On the Zoo plane flying down to the concert in Cork I read today's *Irish Times,* which includes a special twenty-four page supplement called "Zoo Times," full of articles about U2, their history, finances, associates, and their upcoming concerts. There is a greeting from Irish president Mary Robinson ("The contribution of U2 to the international music scene has been of the greatest significance and has brought great honour to them and Ireland.") and one from U.S. president Clinton: "I want to congratulate U2 on the successful completion of their recent European tour. I had the opportunity to speak with and meet the band members during my campaign and found them passionate in their beliefs, dynamic and extremely hardworking. I applaud their many achievements and look forward to further contributions to an already illustrious career. U2's hard work is a bright example of determination and I wish them nothing but success in the future."

The most insightful of all the tributes and articles in this section is one by David Bowie that zooms right in on how *Achtung Baby* and *Zooropa* picked up the thread of his own Berlin trilogy.

"Throughout the twentieth century," Bowie writes, "Berlin has reemerged time and again as both corpse and artery of Europe. Come the nineties the Wall and its heroes and anti-heroes came crashing down. East German artifacts and West German rubble are strewn upon the road through millenium's end." Bowie goes on at some length and then says of U2, "They might be all shamrocks and deutsche marks to some, but I feel that they are one of the few rock bands even attempting to hint at a world which will continue past the next great wall—the year 2000."

You'd think that such a supplement would take care of the public's need for U2 news, but leafing through the *other* sections of the paper I find a long anti-U2 diatribe by columnist George Byrne, an editorial praising U2, a page 3 piece on the profits from the Zoo tour, *another* blast by George Byrne in the entertainment section, an article on how the city of Cork is preparing for the coming of U2, and an item in "What's On" mentioning, in case you missed it, that there's going to be a U2 concert. It's not like you can get away from all this stuff by turning on the radio. All you hear on the radio is U2. I don't know if I can stand to hear any more about U2. I don't know if I can stand to write this book about U2. Good God, look who's sitting all around me —it's U2! This must be how Negativland feels.

When we land in Cork the airport looks like Mexico City again: there are VIP's lined up on the runway to shake hands with U2, children of VIP's with cameras ready to rush the band when they step onto the tarmac, and a police motorcade set to ram them through the traffic fanning out from the stadium where they will perform.

It's all getting to be too much for Larry, the least public member of the band. He says it's no longer comfortable for him to go out to a restaurant in Dublin; he feels as if the press are watching them all every minute, just waiting for one of them to screw up. "It's been like this for Bono for a long time," Larry says when we arrive at the gig. "And there's a part of Bono that enjoys it. I don't. I've always been able to ignore it before, but now I can't. I love Dublin, I have a beautiful home. But this is too much. It can really mess up the way you see the world. Because this is *not* real life."

With his usual discipline, Larry is trying to convince himself to move to New York for a while, study music, learn about recording rap and hip-hop, and play with other musicians. "It's not going to get any easier for us," he explains. "I mean, it'd be easy to keep doing the same thing, but for U2 to keep breaking new ground is going to require hard work and sacrifices. I'm scared to go to New York. My girlfriend, Ann, wouldn't come with me, she's got her own life. So that's scary. But I feel right now like I should do it. I don't know. At this point in the tour I'm feeling very weird. I can't make any big decisions in this state. But that's what I'm thinking right now.

"It's a good thing the tour is ending in Australia and Japan, because if it were ending in Ireland it would just be too much. All I want to do right now is get out of here."

Meanwhile Irish Prime Minister Albert Reynolds and his entourage of ribboned dignitaries are making the handshaking rounds while Bono stays hidden in his dressing room, avoiding the photo-op. He's always wary of being roped into a campaign picture. A few years ago when the notorious former Prime Minister Charlie Haughey was running for election U2 was at some function when Bono saw him sweeping in. He called Adam, Edge, and Larry into a huddle and said, *Look, he's going to try to have his picture taken with me for the papers, so you guys make sure you stand between us at all times.* They said, *Right, we'll be there.* Everyone went back to socializing and sure enough, Bono saw Charlie coming his way with a big grin and an outstretched hand. He looked to his left—Adam had gone to the bar. He looked to his right—Larry had gone to the bathroom. He looked to his rear—Edge had gone to the buffet. He was trapped. Okay, he figured, I can't get out of having my picture taken with him but I'll make sure that no matter what happens I won't smile —I'll look grim and unhappy. Charlie came up laughing, smiling, and Bono kept a face like a constipated Tonto. No matter how great the inclination to smile politely or return a grin, his expression remained dour. So Charlie leaned over in his ear and with a wide smile whispered a string of obscenities startling from so old and public a man. Bono popped his eyes and laughed in shock—and all the flashbulbs went off. Next day's paper: two great mates yukking it up—as good as an endorsement.

Bono's learned his lesson. He lays low. Maybe it's a blessing for the politicians, anyway. They are visibly appalled when Macphisto gets onstage and starts throwing condoms to the Catholics in violation of the strict rules of the Gaelic Athletic Association, who control the stadium. "Rock & roll!" Macphisto cries. "They call it the devil's music! It is my music! Can't you feel it burning? Civilization's wobbling! Who can take you back from the brink? The GAA, that's who! There'll be no sales of condoms in here tonight! The young people will not be delivered to the gates of hell in a latex jacket! Contraception? Safe sex? AIDS? It's not their problem! No homos here tonight! Not a willie in sight! Just abstentious, castrated, happily married families here tonight!"

Another sort of energy is being produced by Bill Carter, U2's Sarajevo correspondent, who arrived in Ireland two days ago to edit his Bosnian film footage at U2's expense. After six months of running through bullets and seeing his friends shot in front of him, Bill is twitching like a man who's just had a radio dropped in his bathtub. He is happy, he is relieved, and he is so hyper that I have to go lie down after talking to him for five minutes. Ned O'Hanlon said that he always assumed that when Bill spoke through the satellite linkups, the connection was breaking up. Now he's learned that's just Bill. Carter says he still can't sleep for more than short periods. He went over and saw the editing facilities at Windmill Lane yesterday, put on his film, and when the sound of bullets came out of the speakers he dove under a table.

Everyone beats a quick retreat to the Cork airport after the show, and with some sentimentality strap in for the last flight of the Zoo plane. I'll miss this battered old bird. From now on I'll have to carry my own luggage. Suzanne comes around and asks who has passports with them. Only about half the people do, which turns out to be a real shame. It scotches a band plan to swing down to Paris for a late dinner. Instead we are dumped back in Dublin.

Most of the entourage congregates at Lillie's Bordello, a disco designed to look like a good Catholic's idea of a whorehouse—red walls and a couple of pictures of nude women. We are shown into the Library, Lillie's VIP room, which Bono swears up and down is one of the most historic rooms in Dublin. He claims, above the sound of Prince singing "Get Off," that there are frescoes on the walls behind these bookshelves from the days when this was the Jamais club where Yeats, Joyce, and Beckett used to dine. I look around the room trying to imagine those giants hanging here. Once James Joyce sat in that chair against the wall, and now it's Lisa Stansfield.

After 3 A.M. some of us are ready to go back to the hotel and hit the hay. Bono has a nice big house he hasn't been to in a long time, and it is waiting for him (even if Ali and the kids, still in the south of France, are not). I get into a car with Bill Carter, Sharon Blankson (a childhood friend of Bono's who now does publicity with Regine), Eileen Long from Principle, and travel agent Theresa Alexander. Bono decides to hitch a ride back to the hotel with us, and from there—he promises—he will go home.

As we make our way slowly across Dublin, stopping at every intersection to wait for the signal to change, Bono announces that Dublin has the most traffic lights in the world, because the municipal clerk in charge of securing the first ones made an error and added an extra digit to the order. The city ended up with ten times as many traffic signals as they needed, and couldn't let them go to waste. All the other passengers groan and tell Bono he's full of bull, but the driver volunteers that he's heard the same story.

"Look!" Bono says, pointing to a man digging a hole on the sidewalk across from the red light at which our car is waiting. "Not only are there *four* separate traffic signals here, but that man is installing a fifth!"

The spooky thing is, he's right. Bill Carter gazes happily at the changing signals and says with a sigh, "I really like Dublin."

"You just got out of Sarajevo, Bill," I say. "Worcester would look like Paris to you."

Bono announces that before we go back to the hotel we should all go out to breakfast. He claims to know a place called the Anhattan (The *M* fell off) where they will serve us, in spite of it being 3:30 in the morning on a Wednesday in Ireland. He directs the driver down narrow lanes and across great expanses until we come to a dark, locked, empty restaurant. Bono says, "Don't worry, they might open up." But no matter how long or loud he knocks, no sign of life flickers within. He gets back in the car and eventually we do spot a small eatery that's opened. We seat ourselves between framed photographs of Jim Kerr and Wendy James. The waitress comes up and Bono says, "I won't order until you put up one of me!"

She just rolls her eyes as if to say, *What an asshole.* Chastened, Bono makes his selection and she leaves. Eileen laughs and says, "You forgot, you're back in Ireland. They don't *care.*"

I excuse myself to go the bathroom and discover the U2 poster—over the urinal.

At 4:30 the driver drops us at our hotel, we all say good night to Bono and head up the steps. As we get to the door we hear the car stop and Bono's voice calling, "Are you all going to have one drink?"

We turn and look back. Bono looks like a kid anxious to stay outside playing a little longer. "Sure," I say, and he bounds out of the car and up the hotel steps. Bono, Carter, and I head to my room where I open the minibar and Bono flops onto the bed and turns on CNN. Most of the news is about Michael Jackson, who is racing around the world fleeing from child molestation charges at home. This story has been brewing for months. I remember talking about it with Paul McGuinness at Clive Davis's 1992 Grammy party, more than a year and a half ago. The big scandal that night was that some father in California was rumored to have a Polaroid of Michael in a compromising position with the man's young son. Sony Music, the Grammy gossips whispered, was going nuts for fear it would come out. The rumor stayed a rumor for a whole year, and then exploded in the headlines with nothing as concrete as a photograph, just allegations. Whether Jackson is guilty or the innocent victim of a shakedown scheme is something no one knows—but everyone has an opinion about.

Bono feels really bad for Jackson and hopes none of the accusations are true. (I feel really bad for my kids who, like millions of other children, think Michael is the greatest man since Peter Pan and don't understand why bad people are trying to hurt him.) Bono figures that if you shut out his lyrics and pretend he's singing in another language, listening to Michael Jackson is one of pop music's most sublime pleasures.

Bono empties one of the little bottles from the minibar and says, well, no sense going home now, it's almost morning. He calls downstairs and has his driver sent away.

The next item on the news is Sarajevo. Bill Carter is horrified that the reporters are saying the situation there is now under control—the U.N. has things in hand. Carter says that every time the world's attention focuses on what the Serbs are doing, they back off for a little while. The media says the storm has passed, the media goes away, and then the Serbs go right back to the slaughter.

Carter lobbies Bono to go with him to Sarajevo next week. After another round Bono begins agreeing with the idea. When Bill goes to the bathroom I suggest to Bono that he ought to slow down: in the goosed-up state Bill Carter's in right now he would—if someone offered him a stick of dynamite—jump onto a bucket and try to blow himself to the moon.

Bono calls the front desk to ask for a room. There are none. U2's employees and guests have the hotel booked solid. So Bono starts calling the crew rooms, looking for an empty bed. He finally finds one —a roadie who won't be back till mid-morning. He'll take it!

By 5:30 the minibar has nothing left but the little ice tray. Bono, Carter, and I are bonding like derelicts under a lamppost and cooking up plans to continue through the Far East after the Zoo tour ends in Japan the week before Christmas. I say we go to Hong Kong. Bono says no, Thailand. He's never taken LSD, I've never taken LSD—we should go to the jungles of Thailand and take LSD for the first time. In our current mental condition, this seems like a top-notch holiday plan.

Then Carter says, "No . . . SUMATRA."

Bono and I look at him as impressed as if he just discovered fire. Carter says he went to Sumatra once and it was *great*, it was *fantastic:* "Every night before we went to sleep we'd have to burn the leeches off our legs with torches!"

Bono and I look at each other: Hong Kong it is!

Finally the party breaks up. I'm collecting bottles and emptying ashtrays when the morning paper slides under the door. It is full of pictures of the Cork concert and articles about U2 and reaction to the scandal of the rubbers Bono rained on the crowd. Geez, I think, my head says we're still in the aftershow and here comes the news of the concert. I should get some sleep. So I lie down on the bed and close my eyes and sink straight into Rapid Eye Movement when I hear a knocking. I pry my eyes open. The clock says I've been out for a few hours. I open the door and there's Bono, still dressed in last night's clothes and pushing a vacuum cleaner. "Want to go to breakfast?" He says.

We go down to the hotel restaurant. Bono looks at the morning papers. "I look fat in these pictures," he says. "Am I?"

"No, you're not," I say. Suzanne, Morleigh, and Edge drift in and join us. There's trouble with the "Numb" video in Japan, Edge says. Apparently the bare feet on the face bit is obscene there.

"You can take out your willie and piss in the street in Japan," Bono says while scrutinizing his sausages. "But bare feet—woooo!"

It seems the feet may cause a problem in some Arab countries too. But not as much of a problem as bringing Salman Rushdie onstage in London has. Photos of that have gone out all over the world and radio stations in several Islamic nations have canceled plans to broadcast the Dublin concert. In related news, Edge is pleased to note an item in the paper reporting that the Joshua Trio, a Dublin group who make their living parodying U2, have announced a suspension of their *fatwa* against U2 biographer Eamon Dunphy for the duration of the band's Irish shows.

"Rushdie said something great about being branded a heretic," Edge says. "He said look at the three greatest heresy trials in history: Socrates, Jesus, and Galileo. The first gave the Western world its philosophy, the second its religion, and the third its science. The West should value heretics!"

Edge reminds Bono that there is a band meeting in a couple of hours at the Clarence Hotel, a local landmark U2 has bought and are in the process of restoring.

"Ah, well then," Bono says. "I guess there's no point in my going home."

39

Under My Skin

---

the walking tour enters its third day/ how edge lost the secret of the universe/ bono dubs a sinatra duet/ the old fool controversy/ secondhand smokers/ a pub crawl with gavin/ michael jackson loses face

Y OU KNOW, just because I have to hang on Bono's coattail through every gin mill, juke joint, pool hall, and pub in Dublin doesn't mean I have to drag you along with me. Let's skip ahead twenty four hours, to Thursday of the week of the Dublin concerts. You haven't missed anything. Bono's still coming up with excuses not to go home, he's still in the same clothes he's had on since he got offstage in Cork on Tuesday. We're both still awake and engaged in one of the greatest walking talkathons since Johnson jabbered to Boswell.

"Do you know the story of how Edge lost the Secret of the Universe?" Bono asks. Oh boy, a Hibernian folktale! "No, Bono, tell me."

"It started when Edge got a jar of psychedelic mushrooms," Bono begins, as wise as Uncle Remus. The legend, in summary, goes like this: Being very scientific, Edge decided that if he was going to sample any psychedelic mushrooms at all, he might as well eat the whole jar. Apparently those were potent fungi. Edge's eyes spun around and his hat flew off his head. He figured he'd better not take a chance on any impressionable members of the U2 Fan Club seeing him like this, so he went upstairs and got into his bed. He lay there for a while and then imagined he heard his wife calling him. He went to the door. No one was there. He went back to bed. And then, amid kaleidoscopes of spinning dimensions like an old Dr. Strange comic, Edge was given the Secret of the Universe.

"Wow!" he thought. "The Secret of the Universe! I'm no fool, I better get this down on tape!" See, Edge reckoned that he was not the first traveler on the astral plane to grok the S.O.T.U., but that others might in their altered state just assume they would remember it. That's where they goofed! Edge would take no such chance. He swam over to his shoulder bag and found his Walkman. He turned it on—and began laughing hysterically at the little red light. Finally the scientist within got control, he regained his composure, and spoke the Secret of the Universe into the recorder.

His duty done, he put down the Walkman and exited Earth altogether.

Upon returning the next day, Edge got out of bed, went down to the kitchen for something to eat, and when he opened the refrigerator more than one light went on. "Hey!" Edge said. "I learned the Secret of the Universe and I got it down on tape!" He ran upstairs and found his tape recorder, played it back and heard himself saying, "Gn@rjβ ®δå´βxr! Kt~rçg†βing fr^âzzp!"

Complete gibberish. Badly recorded gibberish, too, as he seemed to have been holding the Walkman upside down when he taped it.

Early in the afternoon Bono heads to STS, a small recording studio in Dublin's Temple Bar district, a sort of student/hippie section, where U2 makes many of their demos. STS is up a narrow flight of stairs, over a record shop. The first floor is the kitchen and dining room, the second floor is the recording studio. Open windows look out over shingled roofs and brick chimneys.

Bono goes into the small engineer's booth, where he is introduced to record producer Phil Ramone and EMI Records executive Don Rubin. They have come from America for this meeting with a tape recording of Frank Sinatra singing "I've Got You Under My Skin." Bono's here to overdub another vocal alongside Frank's, creating a duet for Sinatra's big comeback album. Ramone sent Bono a cassette of Frank's version so he could get familiar with the arrangement. The producer had helpfully dubbed onto that tape an American session singer doing a Bono imitation to give our hero a hint of how he might approach the song.

Bono, however, managed to lose the tape before listening to it. When it arrived he stuck it in the glove compartment of his car, and then immediately loaned the car to George Regis, one of U2's American lawyers, to take on a fishing trip to the west of Ireland. George got back last night—we ran into him at Tosca's, Norman Hewson's restaurant, where he told Bono how much he enjoyed the Sinatra tape. Oh, Bono said, that's where that went!

So Bono shows up today unprepared but undeterred. He's ready to sing with Frank. Ramone is a sort of old school New York hipster. In the seventies he produced Paul Simon, Billy Joel, and Barbra Streisand. As he puts up the track and plays Bono the guide vocal he assures him, "Just to give you a suggestion—there's no script here." Ramone has had the session singer pitch his vocal high, to stay clear of the Chairman's ever descending range. Bono says that's fine, he has no problem with flying above Frank's airspace.

The Sinatra project is a bit of a gimmick. Old Blue Eyes hasn't made a new album in the last nine years. He has no interest in doing so. He says there are no new songs out there he wants to sing (which lends a depth of tragedy to Bono's inability to get "Two Shots of Happy" to him—at least to Bono) although that may mean there are no new songs out there he wants to have to learn. Sinatra continues to tour regularly. Some nights he has extended stretches where he's fantastic, making up in phrasing, acting, and originality what he's lost in range. On a good night he proves why he is considered the greatest popular singer of his era. During those shows even Sinatra's corny moments are fun and his famous rudeness (introducing the orchestra leader as his son, Frank, Jr., and then, as soon as the applause dies down, saying, "His mother made me give him the job, nobody else would hire him.") forgivable. Also, it's great to see the old blue-haired ladies squealing like bobbie-soxers and yelling, "Oh, Frankie, you've still got it!" On a bad night Sinatra's barely there. He runs through the songs distractedly and reads his lyrics from a TelePrompTer. There's a lot to recommend Sinatra's attitude that there is no reason for him to make any more albums. If people want to buy a Frank Sinatra record, he has dozens still in print. And he is certainly not —in his seventies—going to do anything as good as the introspective masterpieces he recorded in his thirties. Why dilute the legacy?

Well, to make a lot of money, for one thing. EMI—which owns Capitol, the label for which Sinatra did his best work in the 1950s— stepped in after Sinatra let his long association with Reprise Records lapse and suggested this easy way to return to recording. All Frank had to do was go into a studio and sing the songs he did every night onstage. Ramone would take the tapes and dub in other famous people singing along with him. A great marketing hook! A way to reach all the baby boomers who would like to own one Frank Sinatra CD but don't know which one to buy. (A similar kind of marketing strategy seems to be driving a planned Johnny Cash album for which every happening cat in current rock is being asked to write a song. In a single twenty-four hour period last month Bono, Elvis Costello, and Mark Knopfler all told me, "Guess what—I'm writing a song for Johnny Cash.") Bono told the Sinatra producers at the outset that he did not want to be just "a wheeled-on celebrity." And the other guest stars—Carly Simon, Barbra Steisand, Kenny G—are not cutting edge. Madonna apparently backed out when she learned hers was not going to be the only duet on the album.

When they got Sinatra down to the studio to do his do-be-do's he had the same reaction many music critics had to the idea: "What is this? Why should I record songs I've already recorded?" Ramone and Rubin pleaded and cajoled and Sinatra gave it a try, but the first night ended badly. The singer left early in a rotten mood, leaving Ramone in a worse one. They talked him into coming down again and promised they would not ask him to sing any song more than twice. Sinatra, insecure beneath his tough-guy pose about the diminishing of his chops and the public's interest, turned in some fine work. Ramone plays us a haunted version of "One for My Baby (And One More for the Road)." Bono points out that when Sinatra first cut that song in the 1950s he was looking out at the road ahead. Now he's looking back at the road he's traveled.

"I'm thirty-three," Bono tells Ramone, "and I'm beginning to get an idea of what that road is. Frank knows."

Bono sits down on a small couch in the control room, picks up a mike, and says, "Let's make a map." Over the next hour he sings the song five different ways. One time he does it all in falsetto, on another he mumbles and flutters, as he did on U2's 1990 version of Cole Porter's "Night and Day." The third time he sings all his lines late, so that they echo Sinatra's. The fourth time through, when the instrumental break comes up, Bono unleashes a high, blaring scat solo, sounding like I imagine Margaret Dumont would if she swallowed a trumpet. Don Rubin almost jumps off his chair in surprise.

I'll bet Bono's thinking of Miles Davis. After three days wearing his Miles T-shirt I suspect the jazzman's style has sunk under Bono's skin. Miles once told Bono that Sinatra's phrasing with his voice influenced

Davis's phrasing with his horn. This might be Bono's way of reconnecting with that influence, of returning the favor. (When Miles was dying, by the way, he sometimes asked to hear *Unforgettable Fire*. There's the sort of tribute that makes up for any hundred insults.)

Ramone likes the first half of Bono's mouth trumpet solo, but thinks he loses the thread toward the end. The producer asks the singer to rethink the resolution and Bono tells them to roll back the tape and listen to this: Bono proceeds to turn into Gavin Friday, bleating Brechtian *la la la*'s like a homesick storm trooper swinging a stein in Bogart's *Casablanca*. It's so campy that it's dangerous; it would be easy for a listener not familiar with Bono's frame of reference to think he was just goofing, caterwauling like a Vegas drunk at a Dean Martin show.

Ramone and Rubin break up laughing. They seem so delighted and impressed that I wonder if they're for real. Ramone is a big, gray-bearded beatnik bear. Rubin is slight and meticulous, impeccably dressed for summer in pale pants, pale sweater, pale socks, and pale shoes. (He explained that he used to produce Bobby Darin with a historical gravity lost on Bono.) If these two go off and put together a final mix that includes some of Bono's eccentricities, this will be a weird and interesting track—a little pop music meta-text with Bono's voice serving as the contrast that comments and puts attention on Sinatra's. But the two old record men could just as easily be indulging the rock star so that they can go home and cobble together a conventional duet.

Ramone suggests that Bono go to lunch while he assembles a rough mix. Bono heads off to meet McGuinness at a restaurant a few blocks away. Walking through Dublin with Bono these days is like walking through the Magic Kingdom with Mickey Mouse. Everywhere he goes people do double takes, follow him down the street, whip out cameras, and beg for autographs. He generally says okay.

During lunch Bono and Paul ask me about the poetry slams in New York. An increasingly popular entertainment in the East Village is for poets to get up and recite their verse in clubs while audience volunteers judge them on a scale of one to ten, a sort of Olympic Pentameter.

"You hear some good stuff and a lot of bad stuff," I say. "The obnoxious thing is that a lot of them are desperate to prove that just 'cause they're poets doesn't mean they're *sissies*. They try to act punk, they try to dress tough. It's like those classical violinists who think dying their hair green will make them connect to the kids. It's hard to listen to spoken word by people who are so horny to convince you that they're macho."

"Like Henry Rollins," Paul says.

"Ah, no," I say. "Henry Rollins is good." And I immediately wonder if I've put my foot in my mouth. Rollins has a monologue on one of his spoken word albums in which he mocks U2's fans, rags on the band, and rants, "They could never fool me! We always had to see over and over again on any television channel that shithead climbing up and down the P.A. at Redrocks! That guy with the bubble butt waving a white flag! A white flag says, *Aim your crosshair sights over here! Kill ME! The one with the flag.* Pop that guy. And Edge doing that fucking fake-ass pilgrim gig like, *I'm so pious and low-key with my millions. I'll just play this one Enoesque chord.* They've been milking that same bassline and the same guitar change for like five albums and the world kisses their ass and it is the biggest pile of shite I have ever heard!"

The air hangs heavy over our lunch table for a moment and then Bono says casually, "Henry Rollins—is that the vegetarian?"

Walking back to the studio Bono and Paul run into Bill Graham, the smart Irish rock critic who introduced them when U2 was a teenage band and McGuinness was an aspiring wheeler-dealer. If this were America, Graham would be trying to shake out a finder's fee, but as it's Dublin he just grins and suggests a couple of local musicians Bono and Paul should check out.

When Bono returns to the control booth Ramone plays him the comp he's assembled—and it's great. He's used the first half of the mouth trumpet solo and finished with the Octoberfest *la-la*s. He's made smart choices all the way through. These old guys are okay! As Phil has turned out to be so cool about that, Bono decides to hit him with this: "Since Frank is singing, 'Don't you know, little fool, you never can win,' " Bono says with a huge smile, trying to slip in the stinger, "How would it be if the second time through I say, 'Don't you know, *old* fool, you never can win?' "

Ramone and Rubin stare at him.

"Like this," Bono says, and he slaps on a big, toothy smile and emotes like a Methodist minister: *"Don't you know, old fooooool."*

Ramone and Rubin stare at him.

"Like a father and son," Bono says. "But not so much fighting over the car as fighting over the same girl."

Ramone and Rubin stare at each other. They stare back at Bono. Finally Ramone says, "Okay, we'll try it. And if the old man doesn't like it, what kind of boots do you like better? Rubber or cement?"

There's a pregnant pause and then Bono smiles and says, "I want the kind of boots *Nancy* wears!" Everybody laughs. (Nancy Sinatra's boots, you younger readers may not know, were made for walkin'.)

Bono tries singing the Old Fool line and everybody gets itchy. It sounds nasty. So he tries: *"Don't you know, Blue Eyes, you never can win."* That gets a much warmer reception from the record men.

On the next pass Bono sings the whole song through, without hearing Sinatra's vocal. The first time the line comes up he sings "Blue Eyes," the second time he breaks out in a smile so wide it should carry through the microphone and sings, *"Don't ye know y'auld fool, ye never can win!"* like a happy Irish grandma teasing her beloved husband. When Ramone plays it back everybody breaks up laughing. Bono is delighted. He's proud of the way the track is turning out.

By suppertime Bono's done. Ramone will be working for a while yet. Bono invites Don Rubin and his wife—who's been out seeing Dublin— to join him for dinner. At the restaurant the waitress brings a little battery-powered phone over to the table and tells Bono he has a call. It's Gavin. Bono asks him to come over while puffing on one of his little cigars.

"Bono," I say, "how could you, Larry, and Edge go without smoking until you were *thirty* and then all start? That's nuts."

"I don't smoke," Bono says, utterly sincere. I point out that there is a lit cigar hanging out of his mouth. "Well," he says, backtracking, "I don't inhale."

He says that it started as a camp affectation and then he got to enjoy it. The members of U2 probably all liked smoking as teenagers and then Bono, Larry, and Edge went into their ascetic spiritual period and denied themselves. Edge's smoking picked up when his marriage broke up. Larry's girlfriend, Ann, is very much against it, but there is some suspicion that Larry may have been sneaking smokes when she wasn't looking.

"When people are staring at you all the time," Bono says, "smoking a cigarette can give you something to do. Otherwise you just . . ." He grins self-consciously, fiddles with his fork, messes with his hair. I never would have thought of that, but I look around the restaurant and, sure enough, from behind menus, columns, and raised cups, eyes are glanc-ing, studying, peeking, staring, and looking sideways at Bono. It's a constant ocular flutter that moves from person to person like fireflies flickering across a meadow. Fame is a bizarre thing to have happen to you. Bono exhales a stream of smoke. It occurs to me who else smoked those little cigars. Elvis.

Gavin shows up, is introduced to the Rubins, and everyone has a fine supper. After dinner Bono and Gavin decide to head out to the pubs. As he's leaving, Bono is stopped by the waitress, who asks if she can have her phone back. Bono has lost it. How embarrassing. It's not in his pocket, it's not on the table, it's not under the table. Gavin rolls his eyes. Bono starts lifting tablecloths, poking under chairs. He combs the joint like Inspector Clousseau, finally emerging—waving the phone over his head—from the men's room. He had gone off during dinner to pee and left it on the toilet. The waitress says thank you.

Out on the sidewalk, after saying good night to the Rubins, Gavin lets loose his amusement. "Lost the *telephone!* It's always been like this. I sussed very early on that you didn't lend Bono anything valuable. I loaned you my *Ziggy Stardust* album and you made a big point of the fact that you did return it to me. And I looked inside the jacket and it was some Best of Classics record! *And* you'd given the lyric sheet to some girl you were trying to impress."

Bono starts to object. Then he mumbles, "Actually, that's completely accurate."

Bono, Gavin and I visit quite a number of saloons over the next few hours. Sometimes there are musicians performing, generally folkies sit-ting on stools. Bono and Gavin offer the opinion that Dublin is too soft on such performers for their own good. We walk into one place where a young woman is singing traditional songs and the crowd is clapping promiscuously. Bono accurately observes that if she got up and did that same thing in London she'd be bottled off the stage. Which would mean that if she really wanted to be a musician she would be forced to get good fast to survive. She would get an electric guitar, develop an attitude, and figure out how to blow that crowd away. Dublin is not so demanding, with the effect that most musicians who achieve Irish suc-cess can't grab the imagination of listeners in other places. "That's the bad thing about Dublin," Bono says as we leave. "It's too *easy* here."

The later it gets the more drunk people in pubs are, and the drunker they are the pushier they get when Bono walks in. After being pestered out of one bar, Bono notices a small bed and breakfast on a second floor and says to Gavin, "Let's try this."

We climb the stairs and head toward the little lounge, where a middle-aged American couple is watching TV. A woman behind the desk says, "Stop, please, this room is for guests only." Gavin and Bono turn on the charm like Hope and Crosby wooing Dorothy Lamour and she relents. They sit down at a little bar next to the television and even talk her into serving some drinks. The tourists never raise their eyes from the television.

Sitting on the bar is today's paper, with banner headlines about the escalating Michael Jackson scandal. Jackson is staying out of the USA, racing from country to country ahead of these child molestation allegations. Yesterday Los Angeles cops went into his house with a court order seizing videotapes and photos from a "secret room." Other kids are coming forward claiming they were fondled or abused by Michael. The singer himself has canceled a concert in Thailand, claiming dehydration.

U2 once had a close encounter with Michael, and they've never forgotten it. In 1988 *The Joshua Tree* had sold fourteen million copies and won the Grammy for album of the year—beating Jackson's *Bad.* It may have startled Jackson, who did an elaborate production number at the show before the award was announced. (Adam had nipped out to go to the men's room and had to convince the guard on the door to let him back in—they had just called his band's name and he was supposed to be up at the podium.) After that Jackson got curious about U2. He invited them to one of his Madison Square Garden shows and to come backstage to meet him. They went—but when they were introduced to Michael they were startled to find he had a cameraman on hand to film the conversation. That was too weird for U2, who turned around and left.

When they got back to Dublin they got a message: Michael wanted to send a crew over to follow them around and film them working, playing, presumably eating and sleeping—so he could study them. That spooked our heroes even more.

Staring at the tabloid headlines now, Bono remembers the first indication that Jackson was interested in U2: over a decade ago there was a big blowup of U2's *War* album cover on display at the Hollywood

Tower Records. Word got back to the band that Michael Jackson had asked the store if he could have it when Tower was done with it. (The cover of *War* is a photo of a little boy, actually Guggi's younger brother.) Bono really hopes that the accusations against Jackson are not true. "If this is an innocent man being destroyed by the media, it's like *The Crucible*," he says. Bono is scared that Jackson will kill himself. I say that's a huge thing to speculate about. We can't begin to guess what's in his mind—no one knows what would make which person commit suicide.

"He's someone who has devoted his whole life to trying to win the love of the public," Bono says. "He has changed his face to win the love of the public. I think something like this could make him kill himself." Bono takes a drink and says quietly, "If you're one who gets down on your knees, I'd suggest you say a prayer for Michael tonight."

When I finally get back to my hotel—at breakfast time—I pick up the new day's paper. It says that rumors are spreading that Jackson is suicidal. I still believe no one can imagine what goes on in Michael Jackson's head, but I'll concede that Bono is in a position to have more insight than the rest of us.

40

Men of Wealth & Taste

*the three levels of ligging/ salman rushdie, rock critic/ mick
jagger sizes up the competition/ adam & naomi's public
statement/ bill carter learns to schmooze*

BACKSTAGE AT the RDS stadium U2 has set up a white tent
worthy of the greatest pasha of Persia. There is a spacious, airy
dressing room for the band, a wardrobe and makeup room
where they can be made beautiful, and large sitting room for their most
esteemed guests. This is not to be confused with the suite under the
grandstands where several dozen merely honored guests are knocking
back McGuinness's Guinness and sucking little meatballs off the ends
of toothpicks. Nor is that stateroom to be in any way mixed up with the
big mess hall across the grounds where at least two hundred more
common guests are eating grub off paper plates and drinking out of
cans. That third level is for all the people in Dublin who have no real
reason to be backstage, but who'd get their feelings hurt if they weren't
asked. The room is full of the bands' old teachers, second cousins,
former employees, friends of friends, relatives of relatives—basically,
everybody in Dublin. The second level are movers and shakers, and their
official host is Paul McGuinness. These include luminaries such as Bob
Geldof, Jim Kerr, and Patsy Kensit, as well as Tom Freston, the MTV
CEO who has just arrived from New York for the gig with a small
squad of American media heavyweights, including MTV president Judy
McGrath, EMI bigwig John Sykes, *Esquire* magazine editor Terry Mc-
Donell, and Jane and Jann Wenner, the editor/publisher of *Rolling Stone*
and the man upon whose private jet they all just crossed the ocean.

Now you must be wondering, if these VIP's are in the second level—
who rates the first? Well, Adam Clayton's parents just came in, sniffed
around for a minute, and left. Wim Wenders sat in the corner for a bit,

looking so desolate you'd think Ted Turner had just colorized *Wings of Desire.* But at the moment there's really only two guests whose wigs are so big that they need the special privacy afforded by this sheik's tepee. One is Mick Jagger. The other is Salman Rushdie.

And I, looking for a way to get the conversation started again after a Sahara-like pause, think I've found just the suggestion: "Mick, Salman —what do you fellas say the three of us slip out of here and go bowling?"

"Yeah!" Jagger says. "Fuck it! Be like those people who miss the gig, stay in the back, eat all the food, and then say 'GREAT gig, man, you were FANTASTIC.' "

Behind the walls of drapery, wardrobe coordinator Helen Campbell walks down the hanging hall and comes upon a young man she has never seen before, sitting in a folding chair drinking a beer, just outside the band's room. Helen is startled. She asks who he is. "I'm Larry's brother," he says nonchalantly.

"Oh," Helen says. She turns back down the corridor confused. Outside she asks publicist Sharon Blankson if she knew Larry's brother was here. "Larry doesn't have a brother," Sharon says. Uh-oh. Sharon tells Helen to call security and runs back into the tent where the intruder is still drinking his beer, nonchalant as a stoned donkey.

"You have to leave!" Sharon says, preparing for a fight. The False Mullen shrugs and stands. One of the security men appears and says, "Leave the bottle and go out the way you came in!" The intruder puts down the beer, lifts the bottom of the tent, and slides out on his belly. Sharon, shaken, goes into the next room and tells U2 what happened. Larry thinks it's hilarious. His attitude is, *that guy earned a drink!*

Back in the secure room, Salman Rushdie explains to me that every music lover must decide if he is a Beatles or Stones man, just as every literature lover must decide if he is a Tolstoy or Dostoyevski man. U2, he reckons, are the rarest of rock bands, because they embody both of those conflicted poles. "I myself," Salman says, cocking his famous pointed eyebrow, "was always a Dostoyevski-Stones man."

Outside someone in the starstruck Zoo crew has put "Sympathy for the Devil" on the public address system as if to remind us that Mick was writing satanic verses when Rushdie was still reading Dante.

Salman says that he thinks the only place in which U2 have not yet gone as far as they could is in Bono's lyrics: "They have not yet matched the Beatles. Bono is so bright, so full of ideas that he certainly has the potential to do so, but lyrically he has not written an 'Eleanor Rigby" or 'I Am the Walrus.' "

I don't know about that. I would take "You say love is a temple, love the higher law / you ask me to enter and then you make me crawl" over "Yellow matter custard dripping from a dead dog's eye." But then, Rushdie is older than I am. He was digging "Walrus" in his dorm when I was singing it on the schoolbus.

When it's time to head out to watch the show, Rushdie shrugs toward the big security men looming just outside the tent and says, "I can't go out there, they're afraid of taking me through the crowd." I guess he'll watch from somewhere in the wings. One thing with Salman: you don't ask details.

Out at the soundboard Adam's parents and Edge's parents are chatting like any moms and dads going to see the kids perform at the school variety show. Bobby Hewson's there, too, looking like he's keeping score. One of the moms whispers to the other, "I'm surprised to see Mick Jagger here with Jerry Hall—I thought they'd split up." Then she puts her hand over a nervous smile and says, "I should know not to believe the papers."

Those in the Irish throng who do believe the papers have lately been reading a lot of rumors that Adam and Naomi are on the skids. U2 has a public way of refuting that. Every night during "Tryin' to Throw Your Arms Around the World" Bono brings a young woman up from the audience. Tonight the woman he plucks from the crowd is Naomi, which drives the audience bonkers. Naomi glides up onto the ramp between the stages, takes the handi-cam from Bono, and struts right past him as if she were strolling a fashion show catwalk. While the singer cries, "Naomi, baby!" she continues down the ramp, up onto the main stage, past Edge, and over to Adam, with whose noble face she fills the TV screens. Bono is left playing the rejected suiter, crying, "What about me?"

When the song ends the crowd gives Adam and Naomi a big hand while Bono, the ringmaster, calls, "Naomi Campbell! Adam Clayton! What can I say?" He then hums the wedding march.

I'm standing next to Jagger for a lot of the concert. He seems remotely interested most of the time. He does not bat an eye when Bono slips various Stones quotes into the show, even at one point singing a few lines of "Fool to Cry." But when U2 comes out to the B stage and kicks into "Angel of Harlem" Mick suddenly starts really cutting loose, dancing as if this were Madison Square Garden and Charlie had just hit the cowbell for "Honky Tonk Woman." You can stand around with Jagger all evening and almost think he's a regular guy, but when he suddenly starts dancing right next to you and turns into MICK JAGGER, the eleventh grader inside has got to go, "Holy Cow!"

After the show I make it back to the tent early. Bono's still onstage singing "I Can't Help Falling in Love with You" but Adam's already got his bathrobe on, a drink in his mitt, and he's chatting with Jagger. Adam excuses himself to get dressed and I ask Mick if it's possible for him to watch the concert without analyzing it.

"No," he says. "No, I can't. I'm watching it and saying to myself, 'That bit I saw in 1984,' and 'Oh, that's good,' and 'Oh, yeah, I remember when so-and-so did that one,' 'Ah, that bit's quite nice.' " He says there were *moments* when he'd stop analyzing and get into the music, like when the band came down to the B stage. His brain switches back and forth. He says a lot of people involved in this tour worked on the last Stones tour, Steel Wheels, and he spotted some ideas that the Stones considered and rejected—because they were too expensive!

McGuinness comes out and says hi to Jagger. They discuss how they both investigated using a single enormous video screen that would cover the entire stage end of a football stadium. Jagger says the Stones went as far as having diagrams drawn up. "It looked great, but it was so expensive!"

"Yes," McGuinness says, "we came to the same conclusion." Then, as if sharing a state secret, McGuinness whispers, "Seventeen million dollars!" Jagger nods.

McGuinness tells Jagger that he insisted U2 fly with him to Turin to see the last Rolling Stones tour. "We realized you had raised the stakes of stadium shows forever. If U2 were going to play football stadiums we had to try and match it."

Jagger laughs and says, "Yeah, it's like Star Wars, isn't it? It keeps escalating!"

McGuinness looks up and sees Rushdie. "Did you know," Paul asks, "that tonight's show was broadcast around the world on radio to 300 million people? It was going to be 310 million, but several Islamic countries canceled after we brought you onstage."

"Oh." Salman shrugs. "Sorry."

By now a host of beautiful people and their plus-ones have poured into U2's tent to sip, munch, and confabulate. Bill Carter wanders in, hanging on the outside as if he's not sure he should be here. I've spent some time over at Windmill Lane this week, watching Bill edit his Sarajevo footage. It's pretty sad stuff.

At one point in Bill's documentary two Sarajevo girls talk about a crazy woman who wanders through the city, ignoring the gunfire. They say she's been that way since Serbian Chetniks burst into her kitchen, took her infant from her arms, and held her down while they roasted her baby in the oven. It cried louder and louder, the girls said, and then it didn't cry at all. That was about as much inhumanity as I could handle. Of course, we have emotional defenses; we tell ourselves that maybe it's just a story made up by the girls to try to enlist help from the West against the Serbs. I don't believe that, but sometimes I will have to tell myself that to get to sleep. The Chetniks are the real monsters of the Bosnian war. They are centered around World War II veterans who have been waiting fifty years to get back their royal Serbia. It almost makes you wish that Communism had lasted another decade, until these old villains and their ethnic hatreds were dead.

I finally asked Bill Carter what the hell he was doing in Sarajevo. I can't buy his story that an easygoing California kid who'd worked around the movie business goes bumming through Europe, hooks up with a hippie relief caravan going into Bosnia *and stays there for six months.* It's great to be a humanitarian, but I told Bill he had to have some other motivation. For the first time since I met him in Verona, Bill Carter got quiet. Then he said that back in California he and his girlfriend had packed all their belongings into a van and were getting ready to move to Mexico. Just as they were about to take off, he got a call about a possible job in L.A. So he flew down, and while he was gone his girlfriend Corrina took the van out and got into a wreck. She was killed.

So when Bill set out from California to wander across America and Europe, he felt his life was over too. Everything had vanished in an instant. He wouldn't have minded dying. Then he found himself in Sarajevo, and he found a place where he fit in. He found a place as full of pain as he was and a grief bigger than his own.

Bill wants to be a filmmaker. This party is a good chance to start making connections. "There are a lot of important people here," he says, looking around the tent. "I ought to try meeting some of them. Try schmoozing, make conversation."

"Yeah, Bill," I say. "There's Neil Jordan. He wrote and directed *The Crying Game*. He's as hot as can be. Go."

Bill just stands there. I pat him on the back. He stands there. I give him a push, he bounces back. Bill ain't going.

I ask him what's the matter.

"How can I just start talking to him? What do I say?"

"You need a lesson in hobnobbing, pal," I tell him. Making like Jiminy Cricket, I put my hand on Carter's shoulder and I explain softly, "You go up to him and you say, 'Mr. Jordan, I need your advice. I'm finishing this film Bono's producing and I'm getting all sorts of offers from all these different big shots and I don't know how to handle it. How should I decide who my agent should be?' Now, that'll probably be enough to get him going. The worst that can happen is he'll pull a conversation stopper: 'I'm with William Morris,' or 'CAA's the best.' If that happens you say, 'but couldn't a little guy like me get lost at such a big place? Would it be better to go with a small agency where I'll be a big priority?' Believe me, that will get him talking."

"Okay," Bill says, and then he continues to stand there frozen like a greyhound waiting for the wooden rabbit. I feel like Ratso Rizzo trying to explain life to the Midnight Cowboy.

"Bill," I say. "I just dug you out a big hobnobbing tunnel. Now drive through!" I put my hand on his back and push him toward Jordan. I watch as he goes over to the director and they start talking. Jordan says something brief, Bill says something long, and then Jordan's off and running. Eventually other big shots come up to meet Jordan and he introduces them to Bill. The editor of *Esquire* tells Carter his magazine will do a story on his adventures in Sarajevo. Jordan invites Bill down to New Orleans, where he's going to film *Interview with the Vampire* with Tom Cruise and River Phoenix. Liam Neeson and Natasha Richardson are moving into Bill's orbit now. (She's in Dublin making a movie called *Widow's Peak*. Most of the cast came down, although no one has seen Mia Farrow, who called to ask for tickets. Apparently Woody Allen has checked into the Shelbourne to stay in touch with their kids. Given the public feud those two have been engaged in lately, Mia may be holed up in her room with a rifle.)

When he can grab a surreptitious moment, Bill gives me a wink and a high sign. The MTV folks talk with him about hosting a special. Jann Wenner comes over and pulls me aside and says, "Hey, tell me about this guy Bill Carter."

"Sean Flynn type, Jann," I say.

"Ah, a danger junkie!" Wenner goes off to introduce himself to Bill and talk about a possible *Rolling Stone* article. Meanwhile Jordan is telling Bill that when he writes to these various Hollywood contacts he's recommending, be sure to put your letter in a U2 envelope.

McGuinness comes up to me holding a drink and stands surveying the room. "How's Bill Carter making out?" he asks.

"Hobbing his knob off," I reply.

41

Dubliners

---

why joyce had to leave ireland to write ulysses/ the surrey with gavin friday on top/ U2 turns into the virgin prunes/ wherefore wim wenders/ sunday in the tent with bono

BONO MET Salman Rushdie through their shared interest in the Reagan administration-backed war against the Marxist government of Nicaragua. They visited that country at the same time in the summer of '86. They did not meet then but kept hearing about each other as they traveled.

Rushdie's interpreter came in breathless one day and told him, "You'll never guess who's coming? You know who's coming? Bono's coming!" Then she calmed down and said, "Excuse me—who's Bono?" Later Bono read Rushdie's book about his Central American trip, *The Jaguar Smile,* and was impressed enough to invite the writer to a U2 concert.

I tell Rushdie that on the plane to Italy last month I was reading his collection *Imaginary Homelands.* When I came to his essay on Raymond Carver, I was struck by a line from Carver's poem "Suspenders" that Rushdie quoted about the "quiet that comes to a house where nobody can sleep." It clearly inspired Bono's line in "Ultra Violet (Light My Way)": "There is a silence that comes to our house when no one can sleep."

Carver was an inspiration for the lyrics of *The Joshua Tree,* so it wasn't a big surprise that U2 would quote him. But when I mentioned the reference to Bono he said, "*Ah, shit!* I didn't realize that! I must have read it and forgotten it. I thought that was my line." He grumbled for a minute and then said with mock sadness, "I thought *I* was the genius."

"Subconscious plagiarism." Rushdie smiles. "Happens to all of us all the time. I had a phone conversation with Bono the day after I was onstage at Wembley in which he talked very interestingly, I thought, about the place of the writer in a rock band. He said, the trouble is, unless you're from a kind of folkie tradition, a Dylan-like tradition, the words have very low status. He said the writer is there to feel what's in the air of the band, what the mood is, and smash it down very quickly. And if the words don't work then you throw it away and something else can be put there.

"That's what they've done and they've of course made great songs out of that. But I got the sense that he was looking to move into a different kind of songwriting, where maybe the words had more status. I think that would be very interesting. The thing about U2—and it was the same thing with the Beatles—is they never do the same thing twice. Once the Beatles had done *Sgt. Pepper* they didn't do it again. That's what interests me about this band. It seems to me they have that capacity to constantly reinvent itself that the great bands of the sixties did. I haven't seen a band since that did that.

"This is the third time I've seen the show. I was it at Earl's Court last year when it was smaller and I saw it at Wembley, which is twice this size. Tonight I thought the show found its right shape and right size and it worked. Suddenly tonight I could see right onstage all the things I've heard Bono say about the ideas of the show. I didn't need to have it explained to me. I thought, 'This is a fantastic closing act.'

"The gamble the artist—whether it's rock music or movies or novels —always makes is to say, 'This is what's happening to me at the moment and here's the language I found to say it. I say this because I don't have any choice.' Then the risk you take is that you want people to like it. If they don't like it, that's your failure. If they do like it, you're lucky. But what you learn is that the thing must always be generated by what's happening inside you. To try and respond to what the audience wants, what you think the market needs, what the people buy today—if you do that, you're dead, man."

The room is becoming more and more crowded. The same security guards who earlier tried to stop Edge's children from coming in now seem to have thrown caution to the wind. Bono is freaking out as person after person lunges into his face to talk at him. "It's like an Irish wedding," he groans. I ask if he wants to head out somewhere and he says, no, no, he's *got* to go home tonight. He's got to.

"Bono's empty," Gavin Friday says. "There's nothing left."

At about 1:30 A.M. I grab a ride back to the hotel. Salman's still in the tent having a good time. I suppose I shouldn't be surprised. How often does he get to go out to a party? Back in the hotel bar I run into Gavin, who is still fuming over a ticket screwup that stuck him and his mother in the highest bleachers, where the ushers told him that if he were the hotshot he thought he was he wouldn't be up there. It is pretty amazing that literally hundreds of liggers were enjoying U2 hospitality while the single person closest to the band—Bono's own Simon of Cyrene—was getting the bum's rush.

The bar starts filling up with Principles, when who should crawl in but Bono. Perhaps, he reckons, there's time for one drink before going home. By 3 A.M. the hotel bar seems to have filled up with every ligger from the aftershow. Gavin starts organizing a movement toward Lillie's Bordello. There's his fiancée Renee, B. P. Fallon (who has spent much of the night trying to hook up with Bono while hiding from Larry, who cast him off the tour months ago with a threat of "Either Beep goes or I do"), Christy Turlington, and Fightin' Fintan Fitzgerald.

Christy has a driver waiting outside, but he refuses to take six passengers. Gavin, B. P. and I tell the other three to go ahead and we'll grab a cab. The hotel taxi stand's empty. A carload of Italian girls screeches up. They scream "Gavin! Gavin!" snap a bunch of flash pictures, and then drive off giggling. Still no cabs. We're walking down the middle of the street when what we do spot, off in the distance, but one of the horse-drawn carriages that promenade around St. Stephen's Green. We ask the driver if he'd consider departing from the usual route to take us to Lillie's. We negotiate a fair fare and then cross Dublin as Joyce used to do it, in a horse-drawn shay. It's like being in *The Dead*.

Lillie's is hopping of a Friday night. Gavin pulls up a chair next to his old Prune partner Guggi. A bigmouth from the Golden Horde, a Dublin band, careens over and announces in a voice so loud that he must be wearing earplugs, "I saw you play when I was eleven! U2 opened and they were shite, but the Virgin Prunes were *brilliant!*"

Gavin and Guggi sip their drinks and do not acknowledge the compliment. After the loudmouth leaves, Gavin talks about the earliest days of the two brother bands (literally: each had an Evans brother on guitar). At the very first Virgin Prunes gig the band consisted of Gavin and Guggi backed by Adam, Edge, and Larry—in dresses. When U2 got a job that demanded they play for two hours, Gavin would come up and sing Ramone's songs and Bowie's "Suffragette City" so that Bono could rest his voice.

"Bill Graham said in 1980," Gavin reminds Guggi, "that U2 would eventually turn into the Virgin Prunes. And with Macphisto it's finally happened. It took thirteen years for Bono to get up the balls to put on lipstick." Guggi nods and Gavin declares, "On my next tour I'm going to come out carrying a white flag!"

Gavin starts singing "Sad," a song he and Bono wrote when they were seventeen. I tell him it's a good song, he should put it on his next album. Gavin says that won't happen; he won't even sing a Prunes song onstage. "The Virgin Prunes are like a first marriage that ended in divorce," he says. "I respect it but I can't return to it."

The stories continue till morning, getting taller as they go. There are stories from tonight, stories from last week, and stories from fifteen years ago, all flying around Lillie's Library like the stories Bono claims the great Irish writers told in this room.

I'm bearing in mind what Bono told me earlier in this week-long speaking tour: "Anthony Burgess said that Joyce had to leave Dublin to write *Ulysses*, 'cause if he'd stayed here he'd have *talked* it."

Among the fans who hover outside Bono's house is a girl who looks so much like him that she fooled Bono's own brother when he was driving by. The Principles refer to her as "the Bonette."

At lunchtime Sunday young U2 fans and neighborhood kids are perching on the walls across from Bono's house like stone monkeys, scrutinizing every car that pulls up and is waved through the forbidding electric gates. Bono's house, hidden behind high walls, is a pale mansion on the sea. It is big, but not absurdly big. It sits in a lush green hill that slopes down toward the ocean through bushes, gravel paths, and gardens full of blooming flowers. There is a children's playhouse almost hidden in the trees.

Ali got back from Ireland in time for Saturday's concert and she knew how to bring Bono home. The end-of-tour party for the Zoo crew is at their house. The sultan tent from the gig was lugged over here and set up on the tennis court and a fine buffet has been prepared. One hundred and forty guests wander in. You've met them all already.

I drop my jacket in one of the kids' bedrooms and bump into Larry and Jim Sheridan, the director of *My Left Foot* and *The Field*. Sheridan used to run the Project Arts Centre in Dublin, where U2 and the Virgin Prunes played. Now they're Dublin's leading lights. Sheridan's deep into his new movie, a controversial film called *In the Name of the Father* about an innocent family convicted by English courts of being IRA terrorists. Bono and Gavin are writing music for it. Sheridan asks Larry if he's interested in acting.

"I am actually," Larry says. "I'd like to try it because it's so unlike me. I'm not an extrovert at all. So I think it would be good for me. But it would have to be the right, very small, role, so if I was shite the director could say, 'You're shite' and I could say, 'Oh, okay, thanks,' and that would be it."

"Well, look," Sheridan says, "sometime you should come down and I'll get a video camera and write a few lines and we'll try it."

"I'd like that," Larry says.

"Have a laugh."

"Well, don't laugh too much," Larry deadpans. "I've got my pride!"

There's a running joke in U2 that Larry's too good-looking, he makes the rest of them look bad. The others always say that they should have been as smart as the Beatles, who fired handsome Pete Best as soon as they got signed. Bono and Edge have both been heard to say, "We needed a Ringo."

I see my pal Salman and we start talking about books and rock. I suggest that this party at this mansion on this sea sure reminds me of *The Great Gatsby*—and the fact that Ali has just put on a Prince tape makes me think that Gatsby is the role Prince was born to play. "Picture it: the Time or Sheila E. would have everybody dancing all over the lawn while Prince stands up in the window of his lonely palace, watching to see if Daisy shows up." Salman says he can't picture it.

Salman wanders off and I stand there on the back patio admiring Bono and Ali's house. Tom Freston asks what I think of it. "It'd make a hell of a funeral parlor," I suggest. One of my favorite stories about the impenetrable cells of U2 finance revolves around this house. Bear in mind that I'm telling the story the way I heard it from inside sources. When I asked U2 accountant Ossie Kilkenny to confirm it with a tape recorder running he claimed for the record that this account was all mixed up and out of context. Maybe it is, but I still like to believe it.

The story goes like this: The property next door to Bono and Ali's, consisting of a yard and a little gatehouse, was going up for auction.

Bono wanted to buy it so that no one could come in and, for example, put up an apartment building that would overlook his back garden. But he figured if he went out to bid for it himself the owner would see dollar signs and jack up the price. So Bono whispered word to his intimates that some false buyer should go to the auction and grab the property for Bono *secretly.* So tight was U2 secrecy, though, that somehow two different beards were sent to the auction, each unaware of the other and each with firm orders to spend whatever it took to get that gatehouse for Bono. Well, you don't have to have grown up watching TV sitcoms to know what happened. The two designated beards chased each other's bids through the roof. Bono ended up paying perhaps five times the value of the property.

Bono says that story is wildly exaggerated—but if people want to believe it, fine: "Never let the truth get in the way of a good story." I'm contemplating all this when Tom Freston comes up and teaches me a lesson about believing gossip. He says he heard that last night at the party in the hotel room after the party at the disco after the party in the tent after the final gig, Fintan tried to shave my head.

"Why is everybody saying that?" I ask him. I've been hearing this story since I got here. "I said I knew it was time to go when Fintan suggested he shave my head and I thought it was a good idea."

"What time did you get to bed?" Freston asks.

"Eleven this morning," I say. "Two hours ago. This week is wearing me down."

"What the hell did you find to do until eleven?" Freston asks.

"You wouldn't believe me," I tell him.

The truth is that after staying up all night Friday and then going over to the second Dublin gig Saturday afternoon, after a series of Zooropa tour finale parties, and after clearing out of the hotel one step ahead of Fintan's strop and razor at about 9 A.M. I found myself on St. Stephen's Green as it started raining and Sunday churchbells rang. I went into mass and sat down on a bench in the back and tried to recall when I'd last changed my socks.

The priest began his sermon, talking about how little time people give to God compared to how much time we give to the foolish distractions that get in the way. I thought, "That's true." He talked of shallow Hollywood values—who's got the biggest house, the best job. He said all that was trivial. I agreed. He said, "Maybe you'd rather hang around with celebrities than think about spending time with the less fortunate."

Uh-oh, I thought, *is he looking at me?*

"Why, just last night," he thundered, "down at the RDS"—uh-oh— "they had this big show. I could hear it here, so I can imagine how loud it was there! And people paid *25 pounds a ticket* for this . . . stupidity!" The priest bowed his head and said, "And my spies told me there were things in that show that were not fit for children *or* adults!"

I relate this near-death experience to Suzanne Doyle, who says, "if I'd been there I'd have cried."

Suzanne is sitting next to Edge, to whom she is reading travel orders. She has been assigned to escort Edge to Los Angeles tomorrow for the MTV Awards. "It's you and me," she says, "all the way to L.A."

"That'll be nice," Edge says. Then Suzanne tells him she's got a big stack of work for him to do on the long plane ride. Edge sinks lower in his seat as she ticks off the list ending with, "And by the time you land you're going to know all the lyrics to 'Numb'!" Edge groans. "You're going to have it down!" Edge puts his elbows on the table and his face in his hands.

Boy, I sure wouldn't want to be the passenger in front of Edge on that flight! If I had to sit on a plane from Ireland to California listening to an eleven-hour monotone recitation of "Numb" I'd chew off all my nails and start on the fingers of the person next to me.

Bono is eating his dinner with Rushdie at his left and Wim Wenders at his right. When I tell the great German director of *Until the End of the World* that my book is called *U2 at the End of the World* he looks at me with such sour discomfort that you'd think I told him I had a pet rat named Wim.

Later on I asked Bono what he thinks the connection is between U2 and Wenders, aside from the fact that the band keeps writing title songs for his movies. Bono says that in the 1980s U2 and Wenders were the two European artists devoted to getting a handle on America. "The monologue in *Paris, Texas* was a big influence on 'Running to Stand Still,' " Bono says. "You just have to be in my house to see that I share Wim's fascination with angels. His *Until the End of the World* is ostensibly about perception, vision, how we see. Blindness is the metaphor of that movie, as it is of 'Love Is Blindness.' Wim said a very important thing. He said he had lost his faith in pictures. It's an amazing statement for a filmmaker. In the end, Zoo TV is an image bonfire. Zoo TV is finally about the end of the idea of the Image and the wake of the imagination. Wim is plugged into that. That's where he's at and that's where we're at, so we're in synch."

Bono—and in fact all of Zoo TV—has been greatly influenced by Daniel Boorstin's 1962 book *The Image*, which popularized the notions of people who are famous only for being famous and of "pseudoevents" —phenomena such as press conferences and photo opportunities that exist only to be reported. U2's invasion of Sellafield fits Boorstin's criteria. I ask Bono what exists after the death of the image. He says, "Words. There is a part of me that says, 'I'm thirty-three, maybe I should start writing more, and focusing on words and language. Songs are still great vehicles for words. Granted, my voice is quite limited in comparison to other voices, but I can get to places that those other voices can't get to."

If Bono pursues this course, if he takes U2 in the direction Rushdie and his other literary friends hope he will take, then the whole Zoo TV experience will turn out to have been not the beginning of U2's future but the public funeral of U2's past. Admittedly, not even Lincoln had such a *long* funeral. But then, Lincoln wasn't as popular as U2.

"Bono is very needy," Rushdie says—and calls it an admirable trait. "He needs food for his mind all the time. I think that one of the reasons he may be interested in meeting people like me or like Wim Wenders or many of the other artists that are around here is that they give him food. I like that hunger in him because it means that he won't stand still. In a way, looking at the show it seems to me that it takes this kind of idea almost as far as it can go. So now what?"

I grab some lunch while pondering that and take a seat at a table next to Edge, who is sitting closer to Morleigh than you are to this page. That's funny, I think. The two of them have been getting chummier for the last month, but now they're rubbing each other's shoulders and laughing together like young lovers. Maybe Edge won't have to look so far to find out where he goes when he can't keep U2 working anymore.

42

Superstar Trailer Park

*the mtv awards/ switching cerebral hemispheres/ a man in
uniform/ "it looks like bono!"/ the pixies problem/ edge in
love/ the many different ways to be a rock star*

ALL I HAVE to do is make it across the lobby of the Sunset
Marquis hotel, pick up my room key, and get to bed without
seeing Edge or anyone else who will make me stay up all night.
I am determined to get some sleep. Since Bono's party ended in Dublin
in the early hours of Monday morning I have been in London, flown
back to New York, dealt with about two dozen crises at my office, and
tried to make up for lost time with my kids. Since landing in Los
Angeles two hours ago I have driven out to the Bel-Air hotel to pick up
credentials for tomorrow's MTV Video Music Awards show from Tom
Freston (who threw in an MTV watch "So you show up on time!"), and
made it over here to Hollywood. It is Wednesday evening. It is sixty
hours since I left Bono's house after the week of staying awake walking
and talking in Ireland. I am exhausted. I only have to cross the lobby
without running into anybody and I can sleep through the night with a
clear conscience.

As I pass the little bar to the left of the front door I look in and see
Edge sitting at a table with Peter Gabriel, Sinéad O'Connor, and Peter
Buck and Michael Stipe of R.E.M. So much for going to bed. I might
miss something. I get my key, drop my bag in my room, and head back
toward the bar. In the lobby I run into Keryn Kaplan, who is here
representing Principle America. Keryn says she's booked a big table at
an exclusive Japanese restaurant, so let's grab Edge and go. Keryn is
imploring a portable phone to hold that reservation, we are on our way.
I duck into the bathroom and Chris Robinson, the singer from the
Black Crowes, is at the urinal next to me. Hollywood may not have the

celebrity weight of Rushdie/Jagger/Wenders, but it is clearly going to try to win the big fame bake-off with sheer numbers.

In my sleep-deprived, semihallucinatory state I decide that between Germany and here I have switched the hemisphere of the brain with which I observe this circus. I have been going out on the road with rock bands since the late seventies; a lot of my friends are musicians; I thought I knew what it was like. But something Dennis Sheehan said to me a year ago turns out to be true: you don't know what it's like after a week on the road. It takes a lot longer than that to feel touring the way the musician and crew feel it.

When you go out with a band for only a few dates—no matter how well you know them—your internal compass is still fixed to the real world. So the band's world seems funny and out of whack. As a journalist, that oddness is what you focus on and bring back to readers who also live in the real world. But after a long time with the same band on the same tour, that perspective turns inside out. Eventually the tour world—in this case Zoo World—starts to seem natural and sensible, and the real world begins looking flat and black and white. Stopping into my office in New York yesterday I felt as if I was stepping into some bland old episode of *Father Knows Best*. When you get adjusted to tourworld, regular life appears very much like adult life did when you were a kid on summer vacation: "Wow, look at all those men with briefcases and ties going into offices to move paper around! Yuck! I'm going fishin'!"

I mentioned this to my friend Richard Lloyd, who plays guitar with the band Television, and he said, "Oh, yeah, you got it. On the road you don't know where you are, the name of the hotel, the name of the venue. You find yourself looking out one night and saying, 'Hey—how come everybody in the audience has black hair?' ' 'Cause we're in Japan.' 'Oh.' When Tom [Verlaine] and I were in Cincinnati we'd been up all night and in the morning decided to take a bus downtown. We got on with all the people going to work and just started laughing hysterically, that kind of laughter where you think you're going to suffocate, because to us they all looked like bug-eyed aliens. They looked like they were bolted to the bus seats. We knew that tomorrow we'd be in some other city but they would be on this bus again. And the next day and the next day and the next. That's part of why it's so hard to readjust when you come home to your family. It's not only that your body is used to the adrenaline charge of playing for an audience every night; your mind is used to constant stimulus. Every day you're seeing new places, eating new food, meeting new people, sleeping in a different room. It's hard for the brain to get used to absorbing so much and then have it all stop."

I was home in May for my daughter's school play. Keryn Kaplan (who, U2 connections aside, is a neighbor) brought over the final mix of *Zooropa*. I was listening to it while painting backdrops for the kindergarten production of *The Little Mermaid* with my kids, and it flipped me right out. To be pulled so fiercely back into the tour head while I was engaged with my children's world gave me vertigo. I understood then viscerally why it was so hard for Bono to leave his family to come back out for Ellen's farewell party last winter. Not because the Zoo World isn't fun, but because it *is* fun—and knowing it's out there is like seeing yourself leading another life in a parallel dimension.

Larry got annoyed with me one night when I said that being on tour feels natural because it allows people to revert to the state in which they spend the first five years of their lives: someone else feeds you, someone else picks you up and puts you where you're supposed to be, someone else pays the bills for you, and when you do a trick everybody applauds. Subconsciously, we are probably all in shock that it ever stopped being like that! Going on a big tour feels like a restoration of the natural order. Larry stopped just short of punching me in the nose, letting me know that he hates that old line. Far from being *babied,* he said, the sort of luxury U2 lives in is what is the necessary minimum requirement for the band to focus on carrying this monstrous creative/financial/logistical burden around the world for two years on their four backs. It's the same for any business executive jetting around doing big deals, Larry pointed out. It is not infantilism—it is clearing the decks of petty distractions in order to do a mammoth job.

I don't disagree with him, but neither do I think the two things are contradictory. I think that a side effect of having the decks cleared to undertake a mammoth, stressful job is the imposition of a sort of babying that is very, very seductive. Especially for those of us who are not behind the wheel, but riding in the backseat.

Keryn has rounded up Edge and other Irish refugees—Ned, Maurice, Suzanne—and organized a car to take us to the Japanese restaurant. When we get there an Asian woman is standing in the doorway waving at us to hurry, hurry or we'll lose our table. But stop. Who's this sitting alone at a table outside the place? It's Morleigh. Edge is surprised and delighted. Morleigh had to come home to Los Angeles after Bono's party to have a heart-to-heart with her boyfriend about the fact that she and Edge were falling for each other. I had the impression that Edge wasn't sure which way it was going to go, but I guess it's gone his way. Edge and Morleigh mumble to each other and study their shoes like schoolkids.

Well, this could be good news for the other three. If Edge gets a girlfriend maybe they can stop working for a while!

The next day, though, Edge has to do the work for all of them. Some smooth talker in the U2 camp convinced everyone else that the best way for U2 to perform at the MTV awards show would be for Edge to go there and sing "Numb" in person with the other three on videotape on big TV sets. (No doubt Tom Sawyer could have convinced Edge to whitewash his fence too.) The scene backstage at Universal Studios, where the show is being done, is chaos. It's ninety-five degrees and everyone's a star. There's Sharon Stone, Whoopi Goldberg, Keanu Reeves, Christian Slater, Sting, Sinéad, Gabriel, R.E.M., Arrested Development, the Red Hot Chili Peppers, Aerosmith, and on and on and on and on. Everybody knows everybody, but it's hard for people to keep straight if they know each other 'cause they've actually met before or because they've seen each other on talk shows.

Edge is given a trailer just outside the theater's back gate, in a long row of celebrity mobile homes. His next door neighbor is Pearl Jam. Eddie Vedder and his girlfriend Beth Liebling come out and wave like the folks down the block sayin' howdy. Actually the whole setup is a sort of Superstar Trailer Park. The longest limousine in the world pulls up in front of us—one of those comically extended Cadillacs you'd see in a movie parodying Texas—and Eddie says, "Who could that be? Who would come to this in a car like that?" We wait anxiously for the door to open and out hobbles Milton Berle, the ancient comedian who was America's first TV superstar forty years ago.

As soon as Uncle Miltie is ushered inside, along comes the Universal Studio tour, a train of oversize golf carts loaded with families in short pants who have just seen the shark from *Jaws* and the *Jurassic Park* display and are now being shown the freaks of rock & roll. Edge waves at the tourists, who stare blankly at him as they pass.

"They get to see you right after the dinosaurs," I observe.

"You mean Steven Tyler?" Eddie asks. Then he smiles and waves to the vacant tourists. When they are almost out of sight Eddie hurls the orange he's been eating at the trailer. Hits it too.

Flea from the Red Hot Chili Peppers comes running up in a baseball cap and an agitated state. "You gotta be honest with me," he says. "I just got a haircut and you gotta tell me how it looks." Flea pulls off his cap to reveal a new crew cut and a high forehead. "Nah, it looks fine," Eddie assures him. Flea seems relieved—he's about to go on TV. Then Eddie, smiling, adds, "Makes you look like Sting." Flea rushes off to get a mohawk—but not before Eddie's reminded him to wave to the next tour bus.

Pearl Jam goes in to rehearse just after R.E.M. finishes. Peter Buck watches from the empty auditorium and says, "If their new album is good, they're going to be the biggest band in the world."

Wading into the backstage celebrity throng is like going swimming through tides of ego, anxiety, power, and tension. There's the Spin Doctors, there's Soul Asylum, there's Janet Jackson, there's Nirvana, there's Madonna, there's the guy who plays Kramer on *Seinfeld.* I'm standing out back talking to Sinéad O'Connor when Kurt Cobain and Courtney Love breeze past looking health, happy, and wholesome. He is wearing a striped, long-sleeve T-shirt and jeans, she is wearing a white Marilyn Monroe dress and they are bouncing their baby daughter between them while every photographer in California snaps roll after roll of the happy couple. No doubt this will become the official Cobain family portrait. Sinéad, herself a young parent and herself the object of intense media condemnation, zips over to Courtney and starts asking about the baby. Pretty soon they're chatting about child rearing like two suburban moms in the A&P.

There is some adventure going on amid all this bonding too. Rapper Snoop Doggy Dogg is zigging and zagging through the backstage passes trying to stay one step ahead of Los Angeles cops, who want to arrest him for allegedly driving a Jeep from which his bodyguard shot and killed a probationer who had threatened Snoop. The police want to charge the rapper with being an accessory to murder. Snoop apparently hopes to fulfill his obligations to MTV before considering his debt to society.

Here comes Lyle Lovett, the great Texas singer/songwriter who I have not seen since he made headlines earlier this summer by running off and marrying movie star Julia Roberts. He says his life has turned pretty strange: paparazzi now camp out outside motels where he stays on tour in case she shows up. While we're talking an MTV associate producer comes up to Lyle's manager—ignoring Lyle himself who is standing right there—and says, "Listen, I know Lyle doesn't want to do this, but if when he goes up to the podium he could say, *Whew, a night without the old ball and chain,* it'd get such a laugh!" The producer smiles anxiously and nods his head vigorously. " 'Cause it's an industry crowd. *A night without the old ball and chain!*" Lyle stares away tight-lipped while his manager says he'll think about it.

There is a great rustling in the hall as security guards start hustling out the riffraff (meaning people like Lovett and Buck) because Madonna is about to rehearse her number and she must have privacy. She pulled the same sort of peer-offending stunt at Live Aid, demanding that all the other artists turn their backs when she walked through. For a famous exhibitionist, she picks funny times to be shy. Anyhow, once the other musicians have been shooed out, Madonna and her female dancers come onto the stage to rehearse their number and they are—for all intents and purposes—naked. I mean, I guess if you got close enough there might be some sort of pasties on some of those nipples, and I suppose a gynecologist could detect a slip of fabric between those butt cheeks, but it would be a purely technical distinction. They are not half-naked or semi-nude. They are, save for a thread here and a feather there, bare. When the music starts they all jump around like Madonna does and Madonna struts around like Madonna struts, and lip-synchs to a prerecorded track and then stalks off back to her trailer like the bare-assed reincarnation of Leona Helmsley.

Ol' Tom Freston had to do the dirty duty with Don Henley at the inaugural: he ain't going near this one! It falls on MTV president Judy McGrath to go to Madonna's trailer and broach the delicate subject of the network's uneasiness with nude dancers on television. Judy is stopped in the first room of the trailer by Madonna's brother, who says she should talk to him. Sure, Judy says, calm as a judge, here's the question: we need to know if Madonna and her dancers are planning to dress like that during the performance tonight, because if they are we need to let the cameramen know to shoot only Madonna's face. That gets a rise out of the Isadora Duncan of Danceteria! Madonna's voice comes from the back room like Medea with a rash saying she KNEW that would be MTV's reaction and YES they will wear clothes on the air. Judy says thank you to the disembodied voice and backs out of the trailer like Dorothy leaving the throne room of the great and powerful Oz.

The broadcast begins with Madonna and her dancers, dressed in modified tuxedos, doing their "Girlie Show" routine, which stripped of its nudity feels like the sort of Vegas number that used to open the *Jackie Gleason Show*. For all the credit she is given for being a step ahead of the trends, Madonna is starting to take on the aspect of a one-trick pony. When she appeared ten years ago, doing disco with provocative lyrics and great videos, Madonna seemed new and all the long-haired guitar bands seemed old. Now the wheel has spun the other way. If Madonna had come out tonight singing in front of a grunge band she might have stolen the show. But doing her variety number she just seems out-of-date, like one of those cabaret acts you used to have to sit through on TV before the Rolling Stones came on. One woman in the audience cries to her date, "She's still living in the 80s!"

Edge, by contrast, comes out looking like he's living in the 90s—the 2090s. He walks onstage in a blue military uniform, black shades, and beret. The whole band got these dress blues for the "Lemon" video; in fact, there are three little lemon insignias that declare Edge's high rank. He sits down in a chair facing the audience and intones "Numb" while TVs around him crackle with images and sound effects—including Bono's smirking face, which seems to be subliminally saying, "I'm watching this at home with my shoes off and you're stuck in Los Angeles, you sucker!" Edge finishes the song, the TVs go off, and he stands, turns, and walks offstage. It is a deliberately weird performance that goes over quite well. It is one more example of U2 distancing themselves from what the other bands are doing, and from what U2 is expected to do.

Neil Young joins Pearl Jam for a version of "Rockin' in the Free World" that runs overtime, wins the night's only standing ovation from the jaded industry crowd, and is—by wide acclaim—the high point of the show. (It is also the low point of the TV ratings.) Pearl Jam cleans up the awards portion of the evening, winning four trophies, including Video of the Year for "Jeremy." Eddie is not joking when he tells the audience that without music, he might have ended up like Jeremy in the video, shooting himself in front of the classroom. On a lighter note, he weighs MTV's moon-man trophy in his hand and observes, "It looks like Bono."

Bono is watching on his TV in Dublin, talking to Edge on the trailer phone. "What do you make of that?" he asks. Eddie is suddenly wondering the same thing. Coming backstage Eddie worries that he might have hurt Bono's feelings. He finds Edge and apologizes, asking if he can have Bono's phone number so he can call and make amends and telling Edge to look into his eyes and know how sincere he is.

"I just hung up with Bono," Edge replies, deadpan. "And, Eddie, he was crying."

Eddie and Edge stare intently into each other's eyes for a few moments—then they both start laughing.

MTV has hired out a big chunk of the Universal Studios lot for a postshow party. We go up there for a while, but it's too much. There are thousands of people and there are tents of food and a Roman circus atmosphere and ordinary people peering through the fences and legions of the famous and well-built pouring through the gates. Suzanne summons a limo and Edge and his entourage fall in and head across town to a restaurant where R.E.M. (who were great on the show in their first public performance in a couple of years) is hosting a small party. It is much more pleasant. In the outer room there's Natalie Merchant, T-Bone Burnett and Sam Phillips, Lindsey Buckingham, and—here's a funny scene—Roseanna Arquette is intensely comparing notes with Sinéad O'Connor while Peter Gabriel, who has dated both women, looks on nervously.

In the next room Edge secures a table at one side with some of the R.E.M. guys and such U2 familiars as Anton Corbijn (who is about to direct a Nirvana video) and Mark Pellington (one of the architects of Zoo TV, who won a video award tonight for directing Pearl Jam's "Jeremy"). Across the room is a table that includes Krist and Dave from Nirvana, Tanya Donelly of Belly, and Kim Deal—now of the Breeders since the Pixies broke up in acrimony and recriminations after their stint opening for U2 on the first American leg of Zoo TV, a year and a half ago. Courtney Love comes in wearing a big smile and the same white Marilyn dress she had on this afternoon. She looks like a million bucks. She is leading by the hand her husband, Kurt Cobain, who looks like about a dollar and a half. He is staring at nothing with glassy eyes. He looks so fragile that he and Courtney seem less like a couple than like a mom leading her tired little kid to bed. They settle in with Tanya, Kim, and the other Nirvanas.

Crossing the room toward that alternative table with smiles and greetings comes Bob Guccione, Jr., the editor/publisher of *Spin* magazine. Bob is my Greenwich Village neighbor, professional rival, and sometimes chum, which is more than U2 can say. Before *Achtung Baby* was released, Guccione pressed Paul McGuinness for a U2 interview and an advance copy of the album for *Spin* to review. McGuinness told Bono that Bob seemed like an okay chap and let's let him have the tape as long as he promises that *Spin* will run no review before the album is out. Bono hadn't trusted Guccione since *Spin* bought a secondhand interview with Edge and Adam from a British paper and then ran a picture of Bono on the cover. There's been other dubious stuff, too—*Spin* offered Amnesty International a chance to guest-edit an issue and then sent out a mailing to advertisers saying that the Amnesty issue would feature an exclusive interview with Bono. It didn't.

Nonetheless, Paul said, Guccione promises he'll honor our embargo, let's give him a copy of the album. Bono relented, *Spin* got an advance of *Achtung Baby*—and they broke the embargo and wrote about the album early! (Bad review too.) Bono said, "Aha, I told you so!" McGuinness called Bob and said, "How could you do this to me? You gave me your word!" And Bob said (so U2 claims), "Oh, you must have seen one of those issues that was stolen from the warehouse and put on sale early! I was shocked!"

Thus *Spin*'s chances of getting a U2 interview went down the crapper. (In fact, Bob said to me once that he figured U2 only gave interviews to my magazine, *Musician*, in order to hurt *Spin*. Which to me is like saying Yoko only married John to annoy Ringo.) But Bob was not deterred. *Spin* writer Jim Greer was dating Kim Deal, bassist of the Pixies, U2's opening act. He was going to a lot of the shows with Kim, and could write an inside–Zoo TV story *surreptitiously*. What emerged—in a *Spin* cover story headlined "U2 on Tour: The Story They Didn't Want You to Read"—was a bizarre article in which the writer and his unidentified girlfriend went from U2 show to U2 show, making nasty cracks about the band and observing how rotten they treated their opening act, the Pixies—who never got to meet any of them except Larry.

Well, when U2 found out about the article they hit the roof. Bono called a meeting with Deal in which he said it was keyhole peeking and she said that the whole gigantic Zoo extravaganza had gotten too far away from rock & roll, that bands and journalists should all hang out together and have some sort of equality. After some saber-rattling U2 decided to let the Pixies finish the tour, but Pixies leader Charles Thompson was furious with Deal about the whole thing. He said that U2 had treated the Pixies great and he couldn't imagine what Deal thought she had to complain about. No one would feel comfortable saying that the *Spin* story broke up the Pixies, but it was one contributing factor in the demise of a group no longer big enough to contain both Thompson and Deal.

And, I imagine, it was hard on the Pixies—a great band who were a big influence on Nirvana and a hundred other groups—to finally go out and play American arenas after years in clubs and not go over. Thompson launched a solo career under the name Frank Black, and Deal gave her full attention to the Breeders, who quickly got more popular than the Pixies had ever been. I was having dinner with Bob Guccione one night not too long after the dust settled, and he told me that *Spin* no longer had any interest in doing interviews with U2; he could not forgive them for what they did to the Pixies. Tonight the different camps stay on different sides of the room, with R.E.M. going easily from one side to the other.

U2 has also been pilloried in much of the American underground for their alleged part in the destruction of the parody group Negativland. I think it's a bum rap. In the weeks before *Achtung Baby* was released, when anticipation for the new U2 album was high, the satirical group Negativland released a twelve-inch vinyl single called "U2." It juxtaposed U2's "I Still Haven't Found What I'm Looking For" with a bootleg tape of U.S. radio personality Casey Kasem screwing up a scripted reading about the band and cursing out his staff for feeding him shit about this band "from England" that nobody gives a shit about. It was a very funny, naughty record. It also looked like a new U2 album. The LP-sized jacket had a huge red "U2" across the cover with the word "Negativland" in small type, like a title. It looked something like the cover of *War*. Island Records immediately hit Negativland and STS, the independent record label for which they recorded, with a lawsuit for illegal use of the U2 trademark and for releasing a record that U2 fans would buy, thinking it was the new U2 LP.

That was a real consideration. My friend Timothy White, the respected rock journalist and editor in chief of *Billboard*, picked up the parody disk at Tower Records thinking it was the new U2 album. If it fooled Tim, it could sure fool teenagers in the boondocks.

Anyhow, Negativland's label, STS, at first responded to the Island lawsuit as a great publicity opportunity. They launched a "Kill Bono" campaign and made public requests for U2 to play a benefit show for Negativland. But when it became clear that the court was going to rule that it was a copyright infringement, STS turned around and froze Negativland's royalties and insisted that the parody group pay all the damages. What followed was an increasingly ugly battle between Negativland and STS. Island Records president Chris Blackwell wrote to Negativland that U2 had asked him to back off, and he would, but he would not swallow the court costs. Those costs, and their own label's refusal to share the burden, bankrupted the parody group, who were meanwhile further sued and injuncted by Casey Kasem, who accused them of maliciously disparaging his wholesome image.

What a mess! At one point two members of Negativland even posed as journalists and got Edge on the phone, did half an interview with him, and then revealed their identities and begged him for money to help pay their legal bills. Edge laughed and said he'd think about it, but he did not cough up. The whole fiasco went down with almost no effect on or notice from U2 themselves. Island had the right to protect the trademark they paid so much money to license, and anyway, the Island lawsuit was curbed early on. Negativland themselves vacillated between being contrite and taking on the battered defensiveness of Lenny Bruce in his last days, railing against the injustice of copyright laws and saying that such laws should only be enforced on people whose *intentions* are bad. Not on artists.

Like the Pixies-*Spin* controversy, the Negativland brouhaha cast U2 as evil giants stomping on the little guys who get in their way. One editor of an alternative rock magazine told me with a straight face that he could not listen to *Achtung Baby* because "U2 are fascists." I said, "Oh, come on! They may be capitalists, they may believe in intellectual property rights, but if that makes them fascists, then so are we all." But he was adamant. He thinks U2 are literally Nazis. I find that sort of simplemindedness offensive on a dozen levels, but I'll tell you what— that editor is not stupid and he is not alone.

The day after the MTV awards everybody sleeps late and then limps around the Sunset Marquis like wounded soldiers. Well, almost everyone. The Irish actor Richard Harris is smiling and greeting all comers while strolling about in some kind of powder-blue pajamas (or lightweight leisure suit), cradling a white toy poodle and looking for a volunteer to join him at the bar. Eddie Vedder gives me two cassettes of Pearl Jam's unreleased second album—one for me and one for Edge, with hand-customized covers and personal notes. If Pearl Jam is about to ascend to the Biggest Band throne, they are doing it in a remarkably human way.

I bring Edge's tape to him at a breakfast table by the pool, where he and Morleigh are looking at maps and talking about driving out to the desert. I hope he's not planning to propose to her under the Joshua tree. The members of Nirvana wander by the pool, gather their belongings, and load them into a single car—a big old dad sedan, a Caprice or Impala. They drive off together looking like a high school band going to play at the big dance. There are a lot of different ways to be a rock star.

43

The Troubles

scandal rocks the U2 camp/ a trip to the gaultier show/ the gossip press/ "in the name of the father"/ catholics & protestants/ proposed: shakespeare was a lunatic/ falling into the television

"T HIS HAS BEEN a tough week for U2," Bono says wearily. He's smoking, drinking, and wearing two weeks' worth of beard. He has deep bags under his eyes. He's sitting at a small table in the restaurant of the Clarence Hotel, the Dublin property purchased by U2 a couple of years ago and into which they keep pouring money. Ali is sitting at a long table nearby talking gaily with Larry's girlfriend, Ann, director Jim Sheridan, and a half dozen other guests. Bono is off by himself, getting serious and stealing bites of my dessert while Ali's not looking.

The tough week began when the British tabloids ran stories about Adam Clayton's wild binge in a London hotel after a fight with Naomi. According to the report, Adam got wrecked and sent out for a succession of expensive prostitutes. The tabloids claimed that Adam had paid for the whores with his credit card, leaving a paper trail of ugly proof. Regine, U2's publicist, did not deny the story. She merely pointed out that Adam and Naomi had since reconciled.

The story shook the U2 camp, Naomi most of all. She was about to appear at the big Gaultier fashion show in Paris, which is a media zoo anyway, and this scandal added about sixteen tons of unneeded anxiety to the event. Bono, Ali, Larry, and Ann accompanied Adam to Paris and the fashion show in a public display of solidarity and the lovey-doveyness of the Adam-Naomi union.

Bono was overwhelmed by the hoopla attending the Gallic clothing circus. "It's bigger than rock & roll to them!" he says. "It's bigger than movies! There were models with chains, pierced nipples, the whole nine yards—and for some reason they all seemed to stop in front of *me*. Naomi stopped in front of me to wind me up. Christy Turlington stops, gives me a kiss, gives Ali a kiss. Now, you know there's been stories in the tabloids about me and Christy. So all the papers run pictures of Christy kissing me and don't mention that my wife was right there!" Bono shakes his head and chuckles. There has been gossip that he and Christy were having an affair ever since she started coming around with Adam and Naomi, and for a long time no one around U2 was very bothered by it. When Bono told his wife last summer that he would avoid hanging around with Christy so that the tabloids wouldn't get fed, Ali chastised Bono for it and told him that Christy is a lovely girl and if he lets the gossip press run his life, then he's a sap. "Don't miss the opportunity," Ali advised. But since the Adam scandal Bono is more concerned with setting the record right.

"You know, I had fun flirting with Christy, but I never had *an affair* with her! I wouldn't. After introducing these beautiful women to my wife they all lost interest in me! They're *her* friends now."

Bono glances across the room at Ali and then turns serious again. "And Adam is not a sleaze. Ask any of the women who work for us. Adam is not a sleazy guy. But when Adam bottoms out he goes way down. And that's what happened. He hurts no one but himself. But I'll tell you, if Adam gets in his car some night and kills himself or someone else, it won't be funny anymore. Then it won't be a joke. That is my fear. Adam is a good person. He is. He may have screwed up, but at heart he's good. Being with Naomi has been good for Adam because it's forced him to be the stable one in a relationship. Usually the woman has to look after Adam, but Naomi's so wild that Adam has had to become the responsible one."

Some more bad news today was that Martin Scorsese said no to directing the video for Bono and Sinatra doing, "I've Got You Under My Skin." They have to find a substitute quickly, as the video must be shot in California next week, when Bono is on the way to Australia to begin the final leg of the tour.

Gavin Friday joins us at about midnight. He is brain-burned from working night and day on the soundtrack to *In the Name of the Father*, Jim Sheridan's new movie. Bono and Gavin are doing the music. It is due on Saturday and this is Tuesday evening. Time is tight. It is equally tight for Sheridan, who is over at the next table eating dinner and trying to forget for a minute that he is supposed to have the movie finished by the weekend, and he's still working. He's just completed the editing and he still has to do the sound, including whatever music Bono and Gavin deliver. Vanessa Redgrave has convinced Sheridan to join his lead actor, Daniel Day-Lewis, and a group of other artists on a trip to Sarajevo. Were it a less noble commitment, Sheridan would have already blown it off, but he has given his promise to go protest the Bosnian slaughter. He'd just like to finish his movie first.

In the Name of the Father has already stoked tremendous controversy, especially in England. It is the story of the Guildford Four, a group of hippie layabouts who were framed by the British government for an IRA pub bombing in the 1970s. Day-Lewis plays Gerry Conlon, one of the accused. Tonight on the news there was a report on British anger at Sheridan's re-creation of the pub explosion, and the assumption that this was going to be a pro-IRA/anti-English movie.

Watching the TV news tonight—at Edge's parents' house—I had the feeling I often get with U2: that I had fallen into the television. In addition to the *Name of the Father* controversy, there was film of Naomi at the Paris fashion show, and a report about Salman Rushdie, another of whose publishers has just been shot by Islamic terrorists. After the news came Ali Hewson's Chernobyl documentary, "Black Wind, White Land" which was an effective and terrifying look at how the countryside around that disaster area has been ravaged and the people ruined since they became irradiated. Ali has been enormously uncomfortable this week with being made a public figure in the reviews of the show and in interviews she's done to promote it. She will not do any more. She has a new understanding of how the public praise and scorn constantly heaped on him sometimes blows the gaskets in her husband's head.

It's probably nuts for Bono to be trying to squeeze in this movie soundtrack with so much going on, but he and Gavin have known Sheridan since U2 and the Virgin Prunes played their first professional shows at Sheridan's Project Arts Centre. Part theater, part art gallery, the PAC was also home to aspiring young actors Gabriel Byrne, Stephen Rea, and Liam Neeson. When Sheridan's 1990 film *My Left Foot* set the movie world on its ear, Bono and Gavin liked to believe that Daniel Day-Lewis's Oscar-winning performance in that film was based at least a little on Sheridan's in-your-face, thinking-faster-than-he-can-get-the-words-out manner. Both musicians are convinced the director is a genius. As they work on the soundtrack Sheridan gives them musical instructions such as this: "Do you know the way when you're running from someone who's trying to kill you, his foot-beats behind you are louder than your own? Can you make it sound like that?"

Or: "That's jazz, isn't it? Do you know what jazz is? Jazz is a black man in a spotlight. Only the spotlight is the headlights of a police car and he's trying to lean out of it. That's why jazz leans out of the melody. So no one can say he stole it. Now, on this, can you lean farther?"

The incredible sensitivity in Britain to all matters related to the Irish Republican Army has made for some moments of black comedy too. On the train going up to Liverpool to shoot the pub bombing scene, Sheridan got into an argument with a crew member who wanted to delay filming the explosion for technical reasons. Finally Sheridan said loudly, "The bomb goes off at two! That's the plan we agreed to and we're sticking to it! The bomb goes off at two!" When he settled down he looked around the train and realized that the English passengers were all staring at him in fear and horror—they thought he was a real IRA terrorist.

The IRA and the troubles in Northern Ireland are swimming through Sheridan's mind when Bono and Gavin join him at the main dinner table. Sheridan wants to invite the families of the victims of the Guildford bombing to a private movie screening. Sheridan says the IRA kill randomly, but the Protestant Unionists kill with precision and logic: "Seven killed in IRA bombing. All right, we will go out this weekend and kill seven Catholics. Agreed." Sheridan says the Irish still think England is the master of the world. They don't know the USA has been running things for some time.

Bono says he thinks this comes from an Irish Catholic sense of deserved guilt. Ireland must *deserve* the lash England gives it. Bono, who understands evangelical thinking, says that Unionist Ian Paisley and his ilk have an apparent, evangelic logic behind their philosophy of retribution—but that it crumbles under real scrutiny because the Protestant-dominated Northerners had the opportunity for Home Rule and rejected it. Therefore, by evangelical logic, the initial rebellion was Protestant and theirs is the ultimate fault.

This is all interesting talk in a bar, but it has real consequences for people who live in Ireland. U2 has always rejected the violence on both sides in Northern Ireland. Although Bono waving a white flag onstage turned into a cartoon, it was originally in the context of an Irish kid saying, in "Sunday Bloody Sunday," that both sides had to lay down their arms and forget the past. It's a lot to ask of the Irish, for whom the past is often their most treasured possession. By calling for peace U2 was accused of ducking the issue. They clarified their position by announcing on the *Under a Blood Red Sky* version of "Sunday Bloody Sunday," "This song is *not* a rebel song." When that wasn't deemed clear enough, Bono took the literally life-threatening step of including in the film *Rattle and Hum* an onstage condemnation of Republican violence, filmed the night of the IRA's Enniskillen bombing:

"Let me tell you somthin.' I've had enough of Irish Americans who haven't been back to their country in twenty or thirty years comin' up to talk to me about the *resistance*, the revolution back home. And the *glory* of the revolution and the glory of dying for the revolution. FUCK THE REVOLUTION! They don't talk about the glory of killing for the revolution. What's the glory in taking a man from his bed and gunning him down in front of his wife and children? Where's the glory in that? Where's the glory in bombing a Remembrance Day parade of old-age pensioners, their medals taken out and polished up for the day? Where's the glory in that? To leave them dying or crippled for life or dead. Under the rubble of a revolution. That, the majority of the people in my country don't want. No more!"

It's a heartfelt sentiment, but as U2 are Protestants (even Larry, raised Catholic, embraced charismatic Christianity in his teens) it could be misinterpreted as pro-Unionist, which it is not. One of the evidences of Britain's colonization of Ireland is that it is still, for the most part, Protestant Irish who get ahead and succeed in the outside world. If a Catholic wants to be accepted as an artist or writer or musician outside of Ireland, he must first reject Catholicism. Many Irish Catholics would say that the inclination to do that has more to do with the insufferability of the Irish Catholic Church than it does with Protestant prejudices, but those two phenomena—the pressure from outside to abandon the Church and the Church's militant conservatism—form a blood knot that each side, in its obstinacy, yanks tighter.

The sad truth is that the Irish Catholics were screwed by the British Protestants as completely and unjustifiably as any race in history has been screwed by any other . . . but that cannot be undone now. What was lost can never be returned; it no longer exists. As Europe moves closer to unity the notion of England and Ireland continuing to fight over Ulster becomes anachronistic. Certainly the Northern Protestants have every right to wish not to be subjected to the laws of a state dominated by the Catholic Church, a state where, for example, divorce is still illegal. It seems inevitable that Ireland will finally be reunited with Dublin as the capital, but not as a Roman Catholic theocracy. And by the time that reunification comes and the Catholics declare victory, Ireland will have become Protestantized to the point where the differences won't much matter.

Anyway, the drinks are now flowing and the Dubliners are doing what they do best: talking. The specifics of *In the Name of the Father* have given way to a grand dissection of cinema, drama, and art itself—the usual subjects. Sheridan is insisting that in art there is one creative explosion and all that follows are variations on that. For example, he says to Bono, Elvis Presley was an explosion and all subsequent rock has been variations on Presley. *Oedipus Rex* was an explosion; *Hamlet,* for example, is a variation.

This leads Sheridan to insist that he's sure Shakespeare was insane and trying to impose order on his lunacy. That's too much for me. I remind Sheridan that Shakespeare's plots, *Hamlet* included, had been around for years as entertainment. Shakespeare imposed structure, poetry, and psychological insight on stories that may indeed have burst from some tribal or primal neurosis—but the neurosis wasn't Shakespeare's.

Bono declares, "Just as a nervous breakdown may be the sane response to insane circumstances—for example, combat—art may be a sort of safety response to violent stimulus. For example, the news."

What's really screwy is when the art you make in response to the news—be it *In the Name of the Father* or *Black Wind* or *The Satanic Verses*—ends up coming back to you as news again. I can't tell you how often since I joined U2's carnival I've gone home with too much information swimming through my brain, turned on the television to unwind, and come face-to-face with whoever or wherever I just left. They told me the future was interactive TV; I just didn't know I wouldn't be able to unplug it.

44

Meltheads

---

planning the triplecast/ allen ginsberg writes in the great book of ireland/ the cyberpunk rules/ how far U2 will go to get out of rehearsing/ bono & gavin captured by british soldiers dressed as flowerpots

A s U2 GEAR up for the final leg of their two years of touring, they have added one more burden to the pile of projects on their backs: the Triplecast. The idea is that while they are in Australia—and in *addition* to an international pay-per-view TV broadcast—they will film a concert that will be broadcast in January, through MTV, on three channels at the same time. Each channel will have at least a different angle, at most a different content, so the viewer can sit with his remote control and click between options.

Among those options are going to be people who have influenced U2 reacting to or commenting on or supplying amendments to the music. This afternoon Ned O'Hanlon has poet Allen Ginsberg over at Windmill Lane filming his "Cigarette Smoking Rag" to the rhythm of "Numb."

Ginsberg has made a big impression on Bono this trip. Ginsberg and Bono were the last of 140 poets, 120 artists, 9 composers, and one calligrapher to contribute to *The Great Book of Ireland*, an ambitious (some might say vainglorious) attempt to create a sort of sequel to the ancient Irish Book of Kells. (Hey, they wrote a sequel to *Gone with the Wind*, right?) A joint venture between Poetry Ireland and the charity Clashganna Mills Trust, the book is a huge bound volume of pages made from animal-skin parchment, kept in a wooden box made from a tree planted by W. B. Yeats. Animals, vegetables, and minerals are all lining up to get in on this project!

Among the contributors who each wrote or painted on a page were

Samuel Beckett, Seamus Heaney, Derek Mahon, Brendan Kennelly, Thomas Kinsella, and Ted Hughes. Now finished by Bono and Ginsberg, the weighty tome is to be sold to the first person who will cough up a million pounds for it. The money will go to charity and the book will go wherever the new owner wants—perhaps on tour, perhaps into seclusion, perhaps into some Nipponese bank vault.

So far this trip Ginsberg has ditched Van Morrison, who turned out to be a little too intense for the poet to handle, and challenged Bono to explain to him why he wants to believe in God and thus circumscribe his universe. Ginsberg told Gavin, "Bob Dylan and Van Morrison don't know who they are. Leonard Cohen does; he knows exactly who he is. I haven't figured out Bono."

"I wonder what he meant by that?" Bono asks.

"Maybe," I suggest, "it means Cohen still returns his phone calls and Dylan and Van don't."

Also in town to tape a spot for the Triplecast is cyberpunk author William Gibson. Gibson's view of a funky interactive future has been a big influence on Zoo TV, and Bono has been going back and forth about an offer to make his acting debut next year in the film *Johnny Mnemonic,* based on a Gibson story. The artist Robert Longo is going to direct. Other actors lined up are Ice-T and Henry Rollins. Bono is enticed by the possibility of mixing it up with his antagonist Rollins on-screen. Three pop stars in a science fiction movie by a first-time director from outside the film world: sounds like a recipe for disaster. Bono's been offered a stack of cinematic roles for U2's year off, including *Batman Forever.* He's waffling on whether to do any of them.

Gibson's futuristic fiction describes a world not unlike the one U2 inhabits now—a blur of intense, electronically enhanced intellectual stimulation and activities shooting from country to country in a jumble of languages and colliding cultures. Gibson's name for the darkest section of the twenty-first century technolopolis is "Night City," an overpopulated hot-wired extension of Joyce's Night-town.

After taping his Triplecast contribution, Gibson sits down with Bono and Edge to conduct an interview for *Details* magazine. "Part of what you do is like rock & roll glasnost," Gibson tells U2. "You've adopted this deliberate policy of *openness.*"

"We've got the media bonfire going," Bono says half-seriously. "The fireworks are lighting up our sky and we're just exploding the clichés whilst warming our hands on them. It's different when lightning is your business."

"There's myth and mystery," Edge adds, "and they are two completely different things. Although it's part of being a big group, I don't particularly like myth, but to me mystery is everything."

"At first, when you're reading stories about your life in the media," Bono says, "who you're supposedly sleeping with, how much money you're supposed to be making, what you had for breakfast—you feel violated. Then you start to realize that the person they're describing has very little to do with you and is in fact much more interesting than you are. . . . Your public image is interactive: people stick on arms, an extra leg; it's sort of a Robo-Bono thing."

Gibson observes: "This prefigures the truly digital pop figure, of course, who won't exist in any literal way. We already see that in quite a pure form in the *idoru* scene in Japan. These 'idol singers' are constructed from one girl's looks, another girl's voice, and a P.R. team to handle moments like these. . . ."

They talk about U2 abandoning their old save-the-world persona and Bono says, "In the '80s we had this real struggle: we felt that we had some kind of onus to literally save the planet, and though that's not a bad instinct, if you start walking like you're carrying the planet on your head, it's not a very *funky* walk."

At the Factory, rehearsals for the Pacific tour—Australia, New Zealand, and Japan—are under way. U2 is using this opportunity to actually work out arrangements of songs from the *Zooropa* album, a luxury they didn't have before the European tour. Only "Numb" and an acoustic, B-stage version of "Stay" got into the summer sets regularly (attempts to do "Babyface" ended in the Bono-straddling woman from the audience who so annoyed his dad).

Edge was the first one to arrive today, so he programmed the machines for the set. Now he's standing in front of the bank of sequencers and keyboards that will be stashed in underworld during the concerts, playing "Where the Streets Have No Name" and "Angel of Harlem" while his bandmates sprawl on the chairs in the next room delaying the start of another workday. Edge's guitar stops. He comes into the room and picks up the phone. He calls Morleigh in Los Angeles—eight time zones earlier—to ask if she'll be around next week when he stops on his way to Australia. When he gets off the phone he's as happy as a sixteen-year-old with a prom date. Then he glances around at his partners with a look that says, "Work," and they all struggle to their feet and file into the studio behind Edge like the cover of *Abbey Road.*

Bono, the last in line, drops out at the studio door to get himself a cup of tea and decides to put off work a little longer by holding forth on how Adam and Larry always put off work. "They'll do anything to get out of rehearsing," Bono says as the sound of the band beginning comes through the door. He sips his tea as the music turns into something unfamiliar, a jazzy 5/4 groove. Bono listens and says, "They'll write a new song just to get out of rehearsing!" Bono takes his time wandering in; in his absence U2 plays their set with Edge singing lead.

Joe O'Herlihy's behind the sound desk. I take a seat on an amp and enjoy the private concert. It's valuable to see U2 play in a room without any lights or videoscreens or hoopla; it's a reminder that along the way to becoming big stars U2 also became terrific players. Watching Adam's fingers I think that his slippery bass should not sound so full-bellied, but it does. Larry has the snap and precision of Charlie Watts. They're a great band from the bottom up. Bono stands off to the side, listening to Edge finish singing "New Year's Day" and then, as Edge begins to lead the band into "Satellite of Love," Bono steps forward and says, "We should do 'Dirty Day.' "

" 'Satellite' is just as important, in a way," Edge says. They do "Satellite" first and "Dirty Day" second, Bono's voice taking over for Edge's. Their vocal tone is very similar. U2 is figuring out how to approach "Dirty Day," "Lemon," and "Daddy's Gonna Pay for Your Crashed Car." Edge keeps playing with different sounds. When he discovers a sharp, grinding guitar tone he grins and says, "Whoa! Captain Beefheart!" He then proceeds to gnash at that sound until blood runs out of my ears.

Adam is standing near an artist's easel, on which he sometimes jots chord changes while he's learning a song. Facing the band is a chalkboard on which are listed various running-order options:

OPENER	B-STAGE	CONFESSIONAL
Zooropa	Satellite	Fanfare
Fly?	Dirty Day	Crashed Car
	Bullet	Lemon intro
		(Macphisto vibe)
		Lemon
		Phone Call
		With or Without You

When U2 plays "Crashed Car" Bono suddenly slinks across the room to the mike stand in hobble-legged Macphisto character. In his street clothes it looks pretty silly, but I notice that Edge is moving the same way, lurching and weaving, as if to give Bono encouragement and make sure he doesn't feel like he's out there alone. It is the sort of tiny gesture of solidarity you almost never see in rock bands, where the players like to maintain their cool while the lead singer makes a prat of himself. It's subtly generous, and typical of U2.

That song slides into "Lemon," which grooves along great until the end, when Bono signals the band to get quieter and quieter. They do, but when they actually stop playing it stops flat, with a clunk. "Fading down is fine," Edge says, "but we still don't know how to actually *end* it."

A break is called while Bono goes off to do an interview with an Australian TV show. When he emerges it's Edge's turn. Passing in the hall, Edge asks Bono how they are. Bono says they're very nice but they know nothing about music. Edge's eyes light up. "Oh, so we can make things up." He smiles. "I think I'll take them on a tour of the mixing board!"

I join Larry and Adam in the Factory lunchroom. They are ruminating on the latest international movements of the elusive Michael Jackson and ask what I've heard. I tell them that when Edge and I were in L.A. I met a couple of self-proclaimed Jackson insiders who said they knew all about the sort of terrible stuff Michael had been up to. But whenever I pressed them to be specific—"So you know for a fact he slept with little boys?"—they'd hem and haw and admit, *Well, no, I never saw that, but you could just tell something bad was going on over there.* Talk about the buzzards circling! What does it say about these people that they now claim to have been scandalized by what Jackson was up to, which only they knew about, but they did nothing to interfere with it? Hollywood puts the "hype" back in "hypocrisy."

We go on speculating for a while and then Adam and Larry look up and notice the crew leaving. They thought U2 had more playing ahead. "Edge already left," they are told. The two haircuts look at each other and laugh. "Well, that was a tough day," Larry says.

"Get my stuff ready!" Adam calls to no one. "Larry and I are going to rehearse!"

With U2's workday done, Bono heads over to his second job. He joins Gavin at STS—the studio where he did the Sinatra duet—to continue his work on the *Name of the Father* soundtrack. As is his lifetime habit, Bono arrives just in time for dinner. There is shepherd's pie on the STS stove and Gavin, his partner, Maurice Seezer, and the studio crew are wolfing it down while arguing about Northern Ireland, inspired less by the music they are working on than by the current news that the Hume-Adams initiative, a first-step proposal for peace in Northern Ireland, is moving forward faster than anyone expected. John Hume is a member of British Parliament from Ulster. Gerry Adams is the president of Sinn Fein, the political arm of the IRA. Such progress is a mixed blessing. The Belfast gangsters who use the Unionist or IRA flags as an excuse to make big money in extortion and protection have no desire to see their rackets disrupted by peace. Any real movement toward a settlement of the Irish Troubles is bound to set off more violence, as the thugs try to make sure the Catholics and Protestants keep hating each other. Peace would destroy their profits.

Over dinner some of the studio crew are maintaining that Ireland should relinquish its constitutional claims to the northern counties in return for a real peace settlement. Gavin says he would not go along with that. Seezer says, "They've already *got* it, Gavin."

Confronted by Gavin, most of the opinionated Irishmen at the table admit they've never even been to the North. Gavin tells how for one of the last Virgin Prunes shows they drove up to Belfast very early to get a sound check before opening for Siouxsie and the Banshees. En route they heard the announcement of the 1985 Anglo-Irish Agreement between Prime Ministers Fitzgerald and Thatcher. It was just a promise to *talk* about the situation, but it was not well-received among the British loyalists in Ulster. As the Prunes drove through Belfast they saw people in the streets burning Irish flags. The band didn't know what was going on. When they arrived at the gig the nervous club owner pulled them inside and said, "This is not a good night to put on a band of Republicans."

"We're not Republicans," Gavin said. "We're Irish!" The club owner said that was not a distinction worth mentioning to the angry gangs in the street. He told them not to try to go out to eat, he'd bring food in to them. That night the crowd tore the Prunes apart. They hurled bottles at them, and covered them in so much spit that Gavin had to finish the set with his coat on. After the set they had to crawl under their car to check for bombs.

Another time, Bono and Gavin were driving in the northern part of the Irish Republic, on their way to visit Guggi in jail (don't ask) and getting carried away with free-associating into a Walkman their plan to write a play called *Melthead*, about people who get in your ear and don't let go until your brain is running out of your skull. They were having such a good time drinking whiskey and being creative that they didn't notice they had accidentally driven across the border into Northern Ireland until a British soldier with a flowerpot on his head for camouflage leaped out of the tall grass screaming and waving a rifle at the car.

"Get out of the car!" he shouted, holding the rifle barrel in their faces. "Get out of the car!"

"Don't get out of the car!" Bono insisted under his breath.

"GET OUT OF THE CAR NOW!"

"Don't get out of the car!"

Slowly every flower in the meadow rose up to reveal itself attached to a British helmet. A squad of soldiers, rifles ready, moved out of the grass and surrounded the tipsy musicians. Gavin was ready to get out, Bono put his hand out to hold him in. The soldiers, fierce and shouting, fingers on triggers, moved in closer and closer and said . . .

"Good Lord, It's Bo-no!"

War was averted! The happy soldiers in their flower hats danced around the car like a scene out of *Fantasia* and asked for autographs.

Gavin recalls how as a child his father told him that Martin Luther was a Catholic who fell off his horse, hit his head, and came up with Lutheranism. Henry VIII was a syphilitic old reprobate who invented the Anglican Church so he could marry everyone he saw. There is a lull in the conversation and then one of the Irishmen around the table says,

"Well, your da was right." The others mumble agreement. Then they get up and head upstairs to go back to work.

Bono and Gavin take advantage of the sudden privacy to grab some pens and paper and finish the lyrics to the film's title song. Part of the track is a litany, like "Numb," listing flash points of Anglo-Irish culture. They need words for the rest. Bono stops writing and reads aloud "In the name of United and the BBC/ In the name of Georgie Best and LSD/ In the name of the Father and his wife the spirit," which I mishear as, "In the name of the father and his wife, despair." I tell him that's great and he corrects me. Bono likes to emphasize the idea of the Holy Spirit as feminine. He claims the Hebrew word for *God* meant "breasted one."

"The Holy Spirit is like a woman," Bono says seriously. "Undependable." He cracks into a smile. "Joke! Joke!" The rhythm on this track weaves back and forth between a Lambeg (Unionist military) drum and Irish bodhrans, a gut-level representation of the theme of the movie.

Gavin and Bono sit facing each other across the table, scratching away at their lyrics like two students taking a test. Bono eventually looks up and reads out, "There's peace in the sound of the silence spilling over." He asks for a better word for *silence* and lands on either *white* or *black*—something to represent blankness. Bono tries it with *white*, tries it with *black*, then tries, "There's peace in the sound of the white and the black spilling over." He thinks that's better. "I just got a shock," he says, "at the idea of death calling me." He looks for approval to Gavin who nods, perhaps considering that this close to deadline Death looks a lot like Jim Sheridan. The line is accepted.

Gavin asks, "Keep the doorway imagery in the second verse?"

Bono says, "Yes."

Bono starts remembering some of what he said in his Australian TV interview this afternoon and wonders if the tabloid press will take it out of context to hang him with. "I said the British left a cancer in Northern Ireland," Bono says. "The loyalists will hear that and say, 'Oh, a cancer, are we?' The interviewer said, 'Fachtna O'Ceallaigh called you the lard-assed godfather of Irish rock.' I said, 'This is not about what he said. It's about that he's a supporter of the provisional IRA and I'm not!' "

Gavin flinches. He tells Bono to forget the cancer bit; there's the quote that will cause him trouble. Fachtna O'Ceallaigh, an outspoken

Irish Republican, used to work for U2, used to manage Sinéad O'Connor, and has been one of U2's most quoted critics.

Which brings up another subject: they've got Sinéad coming in to sing and by singing to formalize a detente that has been blooming between the two opposing kingdoms of Irish rock since Sinéad split with Fachtna. While sticking an occasional forkful of pie into their mouths, Bono and Gavin switch to the lyrics of the next song, "You Made Me the Thief of Your Heart." Neither of them had been able to sing the song the way they heard it in their heads, so in a fit of pub-talk they decided they should ask Sinéad to come in and do it. Unlike most pub-talk, they followed through. She is arriving tomorrow. The sound-track has to be delivered within two days. They better get the song written.

They scribble for a minute more, passing one sheet of paper between them, then hand it to me and watch my reaction while I read it. I tell them I have trouble with one line: "I was a child to your dark star."

They nod. "That's the line that was buggin' us," Gavin says.

I ask if they might say the child of "your darkest part." They tell me no, that "part" is a bad word to sing. Bono says, "I was a child to you so far."

He explains that he liked the Dark Star because it's a reference to Lucifer, the rebellious child, and this is a song for a child who has murdered its father. I'm sure Bono and Gavin are conscious that the cadence of their lines ("You were a hard man/ No harder in this world") echoes Yeats's Irish patriot poem "Come Gather Round Me, Parnellites" ("For Parnell was a proud man/ No prouder trod the ground"). They're out to hit every hot spot in the Anglo-Irish psyche.

Bono and Gavin are grabbed by the inspiration that this soundtrack needs a fiddle playing the melodies of the Irish, U.K., and U.S. national anthems. They haul me upstairs and have me show Seezer the "Star-Spangled Banner," which none of them know. Pretty soon nine sweaty men are crammed into the tiny control booth, along with enough keyboards, synths, and pieces of outboard gear to cut a Rick Wakeman album. One of the engineers opens a window to let some air in, and Bono ends up standing in that window with his microphone, singing "In the Name of the Father." He's been rehearsing with U2 all day every day this week and he's having trouble catching his breath. To give himself a chance he adds little passing phrases that leave him time to breathe between longer lines.

A little after 11 P.M. I say good night and head downstairs to the empty street. It's cold. Winter has come to Dublin quick and early this year though it's not yet Halloween. The deserted street is filled with the sound of Bono's voice, singing from the open window on the third floor. A couple of bleary-eyed boys stumble by on their way home from the pub and pay no attention at all. I'm sure they think it's just another open window with a U2 record coming out of it, one of the thousand in this city. If they looked up they'd see Bono in the flesh, giving them a private concert. But they never look up.

45

Another Troy for Her to Burn

<hr>

the emperor's new clothes/ fachtna's version/ sex and politics/ sinéad o'connor scares the studio crew/ U2 as the justice league/ a moonlit journey over the halfpenny bridge

FACHTNA O'CEALLAIGH went to work for U2 in 1986. The band wanted someone to run the day-to-day operations of Mother Records, their altruistic label for young Irish bands. The idea of Mother was that it would release the first single by new bands, give them a leg up, and then set them free to sign deals with whoever they wanted with no strings attached. Island had agreed to distribute Mother and U2 wanted someone representing Mother stationed at the Island offices in London. Ossie Kilkenny, U2's accountant and McGuinness's sometime partner in extra-U2 businesses, suggested his friend Fachtna, one-time manager of the Boomtown Rats and lately unemployed. Fachtna barely knew U2 and he did not like their music, but he was glad for the job and impressed by the noble ideals of the little label.

Not long after settling into his new office at Island, Fachtna got another call from Ossie, asking him to look up a young Irish girl who had just arrived in London to record for Ensign Records, was having a hard time, and had few friends in England. Her name was Sinéad O'Connor and her claim to fame was having sung a song she cowrote with Edge on the soundtrack to a movie called *Captive*, which Edge had scored. Fachtna, twenty years older than Sinéad, called to say hello. He quickly got involved in trying to mediate her disputes with Ensign (a label that, like most, had passed on U2 in the olden days). Pretty soon Fachtna was managing Sinéad, helping her win the right to record her first album, *The Lion & the Cobra*, the way she wanted. Eventually Fachtna and Sinéad became lovers too.

As he was becoming immersed in Sinéad's life and career, Fachtna was finding his job at Mother more and more frustrating. Island Records had no motivation to work hard promoting one-off singles by bands who would then go and sign with other labels, even when the bands were as promising as Hothouse Flowers and Cactus World News. It began to gnaw at Fachtna that he had to deal with the frustrations of kids who would be discovered by a member of U2, promised a chance to make a record, and then pin all their hopes on Fachtna getting Island excited. What bugged him even more was that every step of every Mother project had to be approved by the convened U2. Singles that Fachtna felt should have been rushed out sat gathering dust while the jacket art chased the *Joshua Tree* tour around America, awaiting the day when U2 would sit down together, look at it, and sign off.

Fachtna shared his frustrations with Sinéad. Then he shared them with the world. "*Hot Press* did their annual yearbook in Dublin," Fachtna explains, "and in the course of a long interview I was asked about U2 and Mother Records, and with my great honesty I said that basically I despised U2 and the music they made and what they represented. I didn't find this a contradiction, but some of them found it a major contradiction. I always thought they had the capacity to accept criticism or accept somebody disliking them or their music. Kilkenny was telling me, 'Oh, they're really upset by what you said.'

"Then Sinéad gave an interview to a London magazine called *i-D* and described U2 as being, I think, 'bombastic.' I don't know whether it was the straw that broke the camel's back, but at the time they seemed to feel that this was part of some campaign by me against them. One thing led to another, it all escalated, and I got a letter from McGuinness some time in June saying, 'Thank you very much and bye-bye.' Which was fine as far as I was concerned, it wasn't the end of the world. Unfortunately the repercussions continued for a couple of years afterward. Sinéad seemed to take up the cudgels on my behalf. It became some issue between her and them and it was all very messy and uncomfortable for everybody."

Sinéad didn't just take up the cudgels; she took up the bazooka. As her first album was breaking, she blasted U2 from one end of the music press to the other, accusing them of hypocrisy, controlling the Dublin rock scene, and secretly owning *Hot Press* magazine, among other imaginative indictments. Some close to U2 figured she was just looking for publicity, making her bones by attacking the big guys.

"There were occasions when Sinéad would meet up with Bono and ask him honestly to tell her what happened from their point of view." Fachtna sighs. "Then she would come back to me and say, 'I must talk to you, you've been lying to me. Bono says this, this, and this and you said this, this, and this,' and they'd be two completely different stories. There was all this kind of stupidity and confusion going on. She was backstage at some show they did at Wembley and Ossie Kilkenny shouted across to her, 'What the fuck are you doing here? How dare you turn up here after the things you've been saying?' And then she came back to me saying, 'Oh, they really hate me.' It was distressing enough for her that the night after she got back from Wembley, having spoken to Bono for some considerable length of time, she rang me at about seven o'clock the next morning and said, 'Are you definitely coming in today? It's something very serious I need to talk to you about.' And when I did go down to the studio, she said, 'Now I want you to be totally truthful with me. The stories you've been telling me about what happened between U2 and yourself are not correct, are they?' And I was thinking, *What's going on here?* 'Of course they're correct, Sinéad. It's of no benefit to me to lie about U2. I couldn't care less really.'

"Then she said, 'Well, I sat down with Bono for a long time last night and he looked me straight in the eye and told me things different to what you had told me.' And my attitude was just, 'Sinéad, all I know is that I know. I'm not asking you to believe me, but I have told you what I believe the truth to be. It's up to you to figure it out.' "

Sinéad must have figured out that she believed Fachtna, 'cause her most vicious attacks on U2 followed the Wembley meeting with Bono.

"There were all kinds of emotional things that went on at the time that heightened it," Fachtna says. "Especially her need to express her independence of them. On her first tour in America the general perception was that somehow she'd been discovered by U2 and as a young emerging artist she didn't see that as anything to be. So the minute she would see, 'U2 Protégée Sinéad O'Connor' in some American publication, she'd start freaking out. You know the way she is: she's very intense about the idea of honesty and very often makes her own life very painful.

"As far as I know once she stopped . . . *employing me as her manager,* let's put it that way, she began to make her peace with U2. When I had this horrible split-up with Sinéad, among the things that she said to me was that I had manipulated her and used her in relation to this U2 business. My moment of honesty in answering a question in an interview caused me endless pain over the next few years. Caused Sinéad pain. I don't know whether it caused U2 pain or not. I doubt it very much.

"Any problem I have with U2 does not relate to that period of time," Fachtna says. "As I say, I was asked a question, I gave an honest answer, and I do despise them and the music they make, so I don't care about that. I do care about the fact that it became such a huge issue between Sinéad and them and clouded things and made some people think that she was using U2 to get publicity."

That leaves gaping the question of exactly what Fachtna's problem with U2—aside from not liking their music—was. He says he was upset that at a certain point they decided Mother should retain the publishing on one song by each artist they signed, but that seems like small potatoes, a justifiable attempt to keep a generous enterprise somewhere near the break-even line. As Bono told that Australian TV interviewer, Fachtna's real sore spot with U2 was that he is a self-professed Irish Republican and U2 ain't.

"The reason I despise them and hate them is because of the lies and rubbish they propagate about Ireland and the out-and-out British-supporting propaganda that they put forward around the world," Fachtna says. "The idea of some major rock star going around the world with a white flag in his hand and singing 'Sunday Bloody Sunday' and then saying, *This is not a rebel song* has some nerve, as far as I'm concerned, to exploit the pain and suffering of people in a part of . . . whether it's his own country or anybody else's. That's the problem I have with them."

"I'm sure Bono would say an artist has a right to talk about these issues," I say.

"An artist has the right to inform him or herself in the first place before they open their mouths," Fachtna snaps. "If they talk from the point of view of ignorance, well, then they'll get abused for their ignorance. If he wants to be taken seriously by the people that are fighting a war in Ireland and by the people who are dying left, right, and center, whether it's Loyalists or Republicans, he'll have serious conversations with them. He'd soon realize how utterly and totally and absolutely uninformed and ignorant he is. Take the time to go to Belfast or Derry and find out, or not even go there but meet up with people who are politically active in the war that goes on, from whatever side he cares to meet up with. He never chose to do that. He uses a major emotional tactic in order to look good.

"The information is all available to people if they choose to seek it. The younger Irish Americans are probably more informed about what goes on there than are the people in the south of Ireland who live a hundred miles down the road, because in Ireland we have out-and-out censorship on radio and TV of anybody connected with Sinn Fein. They can't speak, they can't appear on Irish television or Irish radio. Recently a book written by [Sinn Fein President] Gerry Adams called *The Streets,* a book of *fictional short stories,* none of which had a Republican content, couldn't even be advertised on TV because of the fact that it was written by Gerry Adams.

"In Britain there is the Broadcasting Act, which prevents members of Sinn Fein or anybody of that ilk from being interviewed on radio or TV. Pictures of Gerry Adams can appear, but they have to use an actor's voice to speak his words! I'd have much more respect for Bono if he was out there campaigning for the removal of censorship than I do when he turns around and calls the IRA fascists.

"It's not exclusive to U2. In the twenty-six counties in the so-called Republic of Ireland there is an amazing lack of interest, a complete and utter averting the eyes from what goes on a hundred miles away. And in some ways it's understandable because it's very painful. We're a relatively new nation from the beginning of this century who achieved some degree of freedom with an uprising and yet settled for less than what the uprising and rebellion had been about. And as a result of the civil war I know that my grandfather and my father couldn't get jobs because the government that was in power happened to disagree with what my family believed in. So there are all those undercurrents of old emotions. We can't turn a blind eye to them. We have to accept the responsibility and face the challenge of these things, not just the recent history but the seven hundred years of British oppression. We can't turn around and say, as I heard Bono say on television one time, 'Let's cast aside the baggage of history, let's start anew, let's look to the future rather than always looking back at the past.' We can't do that, it's unnatural. Unfortunately. We have to be informed by our past in order to face whatever challenge there is in the future and in order to look at ourselves and reexamine ourselves and reevaluate ourselves, our thoughts, our politics and opinions and how we deal with other people.

"My perspective on U2 or for that fact any creative person who comes out of Ireland is that I'm baffled that nobody writes about what's going on there. I'm completely, utterly, and totally baffled that none of the so-called superstars that have come from Ireland have addressed the issue in any way other than in a kind of a bland, platitudinous *Peace, man.* We all want peace! But let's take the next step. How are we going to go about it? That's the problem I have, and the way I've articulated it in the past may have been incorrect or offensive to those on the receiving end of it. I don't want to offend anybody, but it's so hard to express the Republican point of view in Ireland and in Britain when there's an avalanche of the anti-Republican point of view. It's very hard not to get angry and feel that people are exploiting a situation or are turning a blind eye to the truth.

"Somehow or another we've maneuvered ourselves into a position whereby we can live with the fact that there is murder and mayhem going on up the road but it's not affecting us directly so we're okay. We look outward to the rest of the world rather than inward to our own heart and soul. It's not just the English who have to learn an awful lot more about Ireland, it's the Irish themselves. Over the last ten years or so, through Sinéad and Van Morrison and Bono and other artists, this whole thing has grown about the mystical strange land that is Ireland. It's dangerously close to becoming a Walt Disney fantasy about roots, nature, literature, and spirits. It's like our grandparents' rosy, misty picture of Ireland with leprechauns and saints and scholars, this mythological place that exists on the fringes of Western Europe. It's not like that, obviously.

"In the last thirty years Ireland's been turned into a Third World country and economy. We provide slave labor for multinational companies who come in with huge government grants, big tax breaks, and then leave with their profits. And where are the young voices that are talking about these things?

"It's far too complex an issue for anybody, whether pop star or politician, to treat lightly. There are people dying left, right, and center, being assassinated, whether by gangs who are funded by the British Government or gangs operated by the IRA. One way or another there are people dying all the time and it's too easy an option to turn around and say the IRA are fascists or the British government are wrong or whatever. We can have all those opinions, but then it's, 'Okay, that's what you believe in. Now, what are we going to do about it?' And that's how we look forward rather than just name calling. It's too easy to condemn. We've had twenty-five years of condemnation and not one life has been saved as a result of it. I think it's time we dealt with reality as opposed to the self-gratification of turning around and just condemning people. And that's the problem I have in a nutshell. Plus I don't like their music, either."

He thinks about it and then declares, "I think I hate them far more than they would hate me. They have more important things on their mind than thinking about me. Whereas I have little to amuse me."

Let's throw a hand grenade into Mrs. Murphy's chowder. Let's go ask Larry, "Has U2 deliberately avoided making statements about the Irish political situation?"

"It's something that we've been criticized for," Larry says as if he doesn't understand why. "That's such a complex issue that to get politically involved is actually not right. However, Bono has always stood up, has been quoted on several occasions, saying violence is not the way. We've always said violence is not the answer, it's not going to solve anything. And Bono's reaction in *Rattle and Hum* ("Fuck the revolution!") was the biggest political statement you could make! There's no chance we're ever going to get involved in party politics. That is not what we are. We're not good at that. We are able to stand up and make a social statement that killing people is not the way to solve anything, be that the IRA, the PLO or whoever it is. We've never been silent on those issues."

"That will not satisfy the people who say Belfast is an occupied country," I tell him, "and to say *peace* to people in an occupied country is to tell them to accept being conquered."

"That's such a load of absolute bollocks!" Larry says. "I've never heard such crap in all my life! People in Northern Ireland who are striving for peace, people like John Hume, have never talked about using violence! He never said, 'How can you sit back and let the British do this to us and not take up arms!' He's never done that. Ever. So that's just complete rubbish."

"Fachtna O'Ceallaigh says U2 will not speak out against the British oppression," I say.

"That's just what I would expect from Factna O'Ceallaigh," Larry sneers.

After Sinéad and Fachtna split (a breakup that inspired much of her album *I Do Not Want What I Haven't Got*) she began trying to reconcile with U2. That was fine with Bono. I can't summarize the band's feelings about Sinéad now, because I don't think the four band members are of one mind (or, to be fair, spend a lot of time thinking about her), but I reckon if you averaged out their opinions you'd come up with the diagnosis that Sinéad is (a) something of a kook and (b) conscious of her ability to manipulate people and the press. "I will take a heart of flesh over a heart of stone," Bono says of Sinéad. "People boo her because they can see how she manipulates people. A part of me will always love her. She knows that and will use it to manipulate me. She's like a child in that way."

My own feelings are a little different (maybe I've been manipulated). I suspect that Sinéad is one of those people who explores everything, converts to a new idea quickly, proselytizes for her new idea like crazy, and then gets disillusioned and rejects it and moves on to something new. John Lennon was like that, and Lennon had a special gift for conveying his sincerity even as he contradicted himself and acted like a public fool. Maybe because he was so honest about everything he was going through, Lennon's audience treated him like a pal you make excuses for, rather than like a celebrity who's disillusioned them. Lennon's fans gave him tremendous leeway because he worked so hard to avoid *illusioning* them in the first place.

Sinéad is like Lennon in that she believes passionately in what she's saying at the moment, but does not cling to any belief past the point where she sees something that contradicts it. I think she is in that respect a pure soul, which makes her a valuable artist.

Since her second album, *I Do Not Want . . .* went to number one and sold six million copies, Sinéad has been in a tough spot. She was involved in a number of public controversies that made her millions of enemies among the sort of people who call in to radio talk shows. She refused to go onstage in New Jersey if the U.S. national anthem were played. That got her branded anti-American and led to Frank Sinatra threatening to kick her ass. She walked off the TV show *Saturday Night Live* because it was being hosted by Andrew Dice Clay, a comedian she accused of misogynism. She agreed to return to the show later, promising no bad behavior, and came out and tore up a photo of the pope. She said in a *Rolling Stone* interview that the woman raped by heavyweight champion Mike Tyson was a bitch who should have just shut up about it. Within a week of the last two incidents she went onstage at Madison Square Garden at a televised Bob Dylan tribute and was booed off. She perhaps encouraged the booing by refusing to begin her song. As the follow-up to *I Do Not Want . . .* she released an album of standards such as "Don't Cry for Me, Argentina" performed with an orchestra, which flopped. Maybe it was easier to offer that to all the people waiting for her to fail than if she'd given them an album of her own songs.

Apparently just after we last saw her—at the MTV awards in L.A.— Sinéad went back to the hotel room and took an overdose of sleeping pills. Peter Gabriel found her in time to call for help. If it was a genuine suicide attempt or a cry for help is something I doubt even Sinéad knows. Lately she's been lying low, sometimes showing up to sing with other people but neither recording nor performing under her own name. There is considerable nervousness at STS about how her session for "In the Name of the Father" will go . Gavin had to fight to use her, as some of the film's financial backers claimed that any association with Sinéad would hurt the movie in America. The fact that it is now Thursday night and the music is due by Saturday does not lighten the load.

When I arrive at the studio's dining room I feel like I've entered a combat hospital. The crew are all sitting on couches looking shell-shocked, like they don't want to go back upstairs. The door opens and Bono and Eno step out. Bono looks completely wasted. Exhaustion lines are running across his face. "It's really something," he says. "It's good you're here. Go up and listen."

I ascend the stairs a little spooked by the psychic fallout. But Sinéad's waiting at the top smiling. She gives me a hug and invites me in. Maybe I'm being manipulated, but I figure that most of the anxiety people like the crew downstairs bring to dealing with Sinéad is provided by their expectations, not by her behavior.

Not that I can't see how she freaked them out. The room is illumi-nated only by candles and she is singing to a doll (smiling at her on the other side of the microphone), which she introduces as "Sinéad." As soon as she arrived she unnerved the already jumpy crew by unpacking the candles, setting up a vase of flowers, ordering the lights off, and introducing them to her doll. She knows how to spook those superstitious Irish! No wonder they're hiding downstairs in the kitchen. They're probably afraid the doll's going to start singing any minute.

But look at it this way: Sinéad has walked into a very tough, potentially hostile situation and immediately gained control. She has asserted her territorial imperative as surely as if she had pissed in a circle, and she has established emotional control of the studio. I don't think that's a power game; I think it's probably necessary to enable her to forget the pressure and get straight to a mental point where she can find the inspiration to record the song without holding back.

Any argument about Sinéad O'Connor motives is made moot when she opens her mouth. She wails out Bono and Gavin's death song, "You Made Me the Thief of Your Heart" as if her own father's ghost were standing in front of her:

> I'll never wash these clothes, I want to keep the stain
> Your blood to me is precious, nor would I spill it in vain
> Your spirit sings though your lips never part
> Singing only to me, the thief of your heart

Sinéad plays Hamlet! Joni Mitchell once said that it's hard to switch from the purely emotional state necessary for good singing to the purely analytical state needed to adjudicate the recording of a performance; she said the quick flipping between the two demanded by the studio can give you the bends. Sinéad seems to have no problem. One minute she is pouring out Celtic soul, emoting like a banshee, and the next she happily stops to punch in a part or correct a bum note.

Gavin, exhausted and mentally submerged in the project, tells engineer Paul Barrett to stop turning off the tape as soon as Sinéad hits a bad note—it's embarrassing for a singer who's trying to dig into her soul to suddenly have the music click off and be left howling alone. Sinéad, though, doesn't seem to be bothered. She sings along powerfully, hits a flat note, and segues straight into the theme from *The Beverly Hillbillies*. The techs may be walking on eggshells, but in this world she's conjured Sinéad is completely confident. As hours pass and Sinéad sings beautifully, adding harmonies when she's finished the melody, it occurs to me that when I was a teenager listening to *Blonde on Blonde* or *Astral Weeks* on the floor in the dark with my head between the speakers, this is how I imagined records were made—with the smell of flowers and candlelight and breezes blowing through open windows.

Gavin is crouched in the producer's chair like Rodin's "Thinker." At 2:30 in the morning he announces, "Let's knock it on the head." The session's over, the song is complete. Sinéad picks up her flowers, blows out her candles, and stuffs her doll into a plastic bag. She puts on a ragged coat with a hood to disguise her famous face. When we get downstairs Gavin wants to call a cab. Sinéad says no, she'll walk home. I say I'll walk her. Gavin says let's all go. So we set out across Temple Bar, Sinéad clutching her bagged doll to her chest like a little kid. It's very cold out. Young couples are kissing in doorways. We cross the Halfpenny Bridge under a big autumn moon and stop into a shop for a steaming bag of chips to eat (and to keep our hands warm) along the rest of the way.

The discos are letting out. We pass gangs of frustrated teenage boys kicking parked cars and pissing against walls. We turn away from the crowded areas, up cobblestone streets. I ask Sinéad if she's filling up loads of cassettes with new songs and she says no, she needs to get her life together, to spend time with her little boy, and to try to figure out everything that's happened to her since she became famous.

"I love to sing," she says. "I'll always love to sing. But I'm not sure the rest of it is worth it."

"What's not worth it?" I ask. "The writing or the celebrity?"

"Everything that comes after it," she says with her eyes down, waving vaguely to indicate the whole big world beyond this little corner of Dublin. I suggest that she might well be right to not perform or make records or in any way be a public figure—but that she should not deny her gift. She should write songs even if all she does is put them in a shoe box in her closet.

We go along in silence for a while and then she says, "I never thought of that. I could do it without doing anything *with* it."

The rest of the walk is devoted to talk about kids, with Sinéad of the opinion that all the decisions you make—about where to live, what to do—are really about deciding what's best for your children. We reach Sinéad's door and say good night. Gavin and I sit down on the steps and eat our french fries and watch stray teenagers stumbling home, knocking over trash cans. Gavin says he is wasted from this soundtrack work, as Bono is.

"He sure is," I say. "Those lines in Bono's face look like they were painted on. I was down at the Factory this afternoon and U2 are working so hard these days they hardly get to play music."

"Meeting after meeting." Gavin nods.

"Yeah, it must be terribly frustrating."

"Their life is insane." Gavin says that tonight while he was working on the record, waiting for Bono, the studio phone rang and it was Winona Ryder, the actress friend of U2, calling from some phone booth in the Pacific Northwest where she was trying to track down a little girl who had been kidnapped from her home. She told Gavin to give Bono that message and then hung up. Gavin shook his head in burned-out wonder. "What is *that* about?" he asks. "Winona Ryder's looking for a kidnapped child somewhere near Seattle and she calls Bono in Dublin for help?" (Actually Winona was returning a call from Bono asking if he could help, but Gavin doesn't know that.)

"U2 used to be able to go out into the big world, float around among the celebrities and artists, and then come back to Dublin and resume normal lives," I say. "But now . . ."

"It's followed them back home," Gavin says. "That's right."

We watch two young drunks down the road trying unsuccessfully to commit some vandalism with a trash can chained to a fence. "Why don't they hurt themselves instead?" I ask.

"They will," Gavin answers. Finally they give up and stomp away.

"That bit with Adam in London was wild," Gavin says. "And we had the papers to tell us all about it. You know what the next big one the papers get hold of will be? Edge and Morleigh."

"Why would that make the papers?" I ask. "They're both single. She's a dancer and choreographer, he's a musician. Why would that be news?"

Gavin shakes his head and says, "Morleigh's great, she's a wonderful girl. But the papers won't care about who she really is or what she really does. The headline will be—"

"Oh. 'Edge Runs Off with Belly Dancer.'"

"That's it." Gavin nods. "That's all they'll need to know and all they'll *want* to know."

Gavin pulls himself up to his feet, dusts himself off, and says, "I'm completely knackered." He heads up the road, shooting to be home before dawn.

46

Rancho Mirage

sinatra sets some records/ bono's journey to the desert/ a swinging summit meeting/ a hasty retreat and relaxed reconciliation/ mud in yer eye and scotch in yer crotch

Bono's duet with Frank Sinatra on "I've Got You Under My Skin" has been chosen as the lead-off single from Sinatra's *Duets* album, which debuts on the *Billboard* charts at number two, kept out of the top spot by the simultaneous release of Pearl Jam's second album. Sinatra's previous LP in 1984, had peaked at number fifty-eight. His last album to hit the top ten was *That's Life* in 1967. With *Duets* Sinatra has charted records in seven different decades, a statistic no one else will beat unless Paul McCartney or the Rolling Stones can keep having hits until the 2030s. At seventy-seven Sinatra has also broken Louis Armstrong's record for being the *oldest* artist ever to have a top two record. Armstrong topped the chart with *Hello, Dolly!* when he was sixty-two.

Critics are tripping over their superlatives praising the album, especially the Sinatra-Bono duet. A long article by Stephen Holden on the front page of the *New York Times'* Sunday Arts & Leisure section begins, "The most remarkable moment in Frank Sinatra's 'Duets,' the new album that returns the 77-year-old singer to the mainstream of popular music with a startling force and authority, is a rendition of 'I've Got You Under My Skin' in which the Chairman of the Board is joined by Bono of U2. After Mr. Sinatra punches out the opening phrases of Cole Porter's standard, Bono slips into the song crooning the words, 'so deep in my heart you're really a part of me,' in a soft, sexy growl. From here the two singers, who sound as though they are sitting elbow to elbow in a bar comparing notes about love and life, trade the song back and forth, with the 33-year-old Irish rock star occasionally drawing back to interpolate high, plaintive vocal doodles around his companion's gruff assertions.

"The song hits a peak of passion when Bono exclaims, 'Don't you know, Blue Eyes, you never can win.' In a flash it conjures up a picture of a young man in the throes of romantic turmoil sharing his exhilaration and confusion with a tough, resilient father who has been through it all. With its mixture of sagacity and sexiness, 'I've Got You Under My Skin' is a stunning intergenerational collaboration that reveals how profoundly Mr. Sinatra has influenced younger singers, even rockers like Bono, who is a longtime Sinatra admirer."

Vanity Fair writer David McClintick goes even further in a seven-page appreciation of the album, praising the Bono-Frank collaboration and claiming, "*Frank Sinatra Duets* signals a late, dramatic, and unexpected surge in what already stands as the most extraordinary career in the history of popular culture, surpassing those of Bing Crosby, Elvis, Judy Garland, the Beatles, the Rolling Stones, Chaplin, Garbo, Brando, and all other contenders."

U2's old adversaries in the British music weeklies offer a contrary proposal. *Melody Maker* has photos of Bono and Sinatra on its cover, but snickers about Bono's contribution to the team-up: "It's debatable whether his posturing narcissistic over-delivery is (in contrast to Frank's clipped dry suggestion) entirely appropriate or plain ludicrous. Certainly he can't be accused of lacking the ego or presence to rise to the challenge."

New Musical Express is more reserved in its praise. "A crappier and more, well, insulting record would be hard to imagine," they declare. "Bono's mumbling take on 'I've Got You Under My Skin' confirms his covetable status as World's Most Pretentious Human Being."

The strangest critic, though, is Nixon-aide-turned-right-wing-political-columnist William Safire. On the op-ed page of the *New York Times* Safire attacks the method of recording *Duets* with a venom he usually reserves for progressive social causes. "Much as I despise Sinatra's bridgework between entertainment, casinos, and crime, I have always admired his artistry," Safire writes. He then says of *Duets*, "It's a disaster; his voice is shot. Not all the vocal technique and tricks of recording enhancement and propping up by other voices can make him sound other than the pitiful straining of an old man pretending to be the singer he is no longer. Unlike Garbo and Dietrich who refused to be photographed in their later years lest it spoil the public's memory of their beauty, Sinatra greedily diminishes his reputation."

Safire goes on to rail against the trickery of studio overdubbing that allows Sinatra to sing with people he was never in a room with: "When a performer's voice and image can not only be edited, echoed, refined, spliced, corrected and enhanced—but can be transported and combined with others not physically present—what is a performance? In our lust for technical brilliance, are we losing the integrity of individual talent?"

Other writers echo the accusation, although in the world of popular music the argument about the validity of creating in the recording studio what could not be created on a stage is usually considered to have been settled with *Sgt. Pepper*.

The TV comedy show *Saturday Night Live* weighs in with a sketch in which an impatient Sinatra bullies Bono in the recording studio. Comedian Adam Sandler plays Bono in Fly shades and a thick brogue, telling Sinatra (Phil Hartman) that he's written a song for them about technology and humanity. Sinatra cuts him off, calls for "I've Got You Under My Skin," and races through it while Bono struggles to keep up. Bono begs for a second take and Frank snaps, "I'm ninety-three, baby. When you're pushing a century, there is no *take two!* Get out, Bozo!"

All of this notoriety is having its desired effect. *Duets* is double platinum—the bestselling album of Frank Sinatra's career. Phil Ramone is giving interviews about it everywhere, usually working in some variation on the story of U2 going to see Sinatra in Vegas. I just saw Ramone on CNN. In today's version Frank looked at U2 and said, "Great guys—don't you think you could afford a better wardrobe?"

I'm sure not going to tell Bono that I have heard that when the Capitol Records executives first presented Sinatra with the list of people they had lined up for him to duet with, Frank flew into a rage. Apparently when Frank is in such a fury he often vents his spleen on his perennial opening act, Steve Lawrence. This particular day Lawrence answered the phone and could not make out what the hell Sinatra was shouting about. He asked his wife, Eydie Gorme, to see if she could calm him down. Eydie got on and said Frank, Frank, what is it? What's wrong?

Sinatra was shouting, *If these idiots think that at this point in my career I'm going to record a duet with Sonny Bono . . . !*

Steve and Eydie counseled Frank that maybe that wasn't the intended Bono.

Which makes it somewhat ironic that our Bono is to meet Frank Sinatra outside his wife Barbara Sinatra's Children's Clinic near Palm Springs, California—the city that elected Sonny Bono, former member of "& Cher," mayor. Mrs. Sinatra's clinic is next to Betty Ford's. Hey— if the wife of an appointed, two-year president of the U.S. should have her own hospital, why should the wife of "the most extraordinary career in the history of popular culture" have less?

Bono has arrived in the California desert to meet up with Sinatra to make the video for "I've Got You Under My Skin." After Martin Scorsese dropped out a number of names of great filmmakers was bandied about. It was decided that characters such as Robert Altman and Wim Wenders might send Frank right out the door. God knew what they'd get if they asked Coppola—and might Frank be offended by the *Godfather* association? I lobbied hard for Clint Eastwood, but I don't think Bono was ever convinced. Finally afraid that they were loading too much weight onto this fragile alliance, Bono asked Kevin Godley to come out and do it. At least with Kevin they have a relationship and he won't be bringing any ego games of his own to the summit.

Just before Bono left Ireland, Principle got a fax from EMI Japan congratulating the singer on recording a duet with Mr. Frank *Sinotta* of "I've Got You Under My Chicken."

Mr. and Mrs. Frank Sinatra arrive and bid Bono welcome. Barbara is wearing a red dress, which inspires Frank to declare, "Barbara! You look like a blood clot!" It's a standard Sinatra line, I've heard him use it onstage with Shirley MacLaine, but Bono and company laugh loudly.

Frank and Bono climb into the back of a limo and head down the highway, the film crew across from them getting shots of the two swingers hanging out in style. Sinatra, the total pro, tells Bono to open the car window to improve the lighting of the shot. They cruise along through Rancho Mirage, Sinatra telling Dean Martin stories, while the cameras whirl.

Bono knows that Sinatra's not going to lip-synch ("Frank doesn't know how to mime and his attitude is, he ain't learning now"), so the plan is to film Bono and Blue Eyes hanging out in a saloon, talking like a father and son. One of Frank's pals has a bar nearby, and that's where they're heading. Godley will shoot the two greeting each other at the door, ordering drinks, and having a heart to heart while "I've Got You Under My Skin" swings along beneath them.

They arrive at the bar, shake hands with a few people, and start filming. First take they come in, sit down, Bono gives Frank a first edition of a Yeats anthology, saying "I know you like a great lyric," and a bottle of Irish whiskey. Frank smiles. He knows this joint well but it looks weird to him today; there are no other customers, and the lamps are all too bright (the video crew has replaced the bulbs with high-watt movie lights). The crew has been told to stay in the shadows, out of Sinatra's sight lines. A message is relayed from Godley, hidden in the kitchen watching on a monitor, for Bono and Frank to do another take —come in, exchange the gifts, pick up drinks. Bono sees that Frank is getting twitchy. He looks upset. "What are we doing?" Sinatra demands.

"We're doing another take, Frank."

"What do ya mean, another take? For what?"

"For the video."

"What video?"

"For the duet."

"What duet?"

Frank's losing it. Bono is getting spooked. Someone says, "Hey, Frank, let's get a picture." Anton comes forward out of a dark corner and shoots a photograph of the two of them. Frank is startled and furious. "Who's this?" he demands.

One of Sinatra's people tries to calm him down. He tells him it's a photo for the owner of the bar, Frank's pal, to hang on the wall. "That bum!" Frank snaps. "After all I've done for him!" Frank seems disoriented now. "I've gotta go. I got a plane! I've gotta go!"

And with that, Frank Sinatra is gone.

Bono, Anton, and Kevin Godley are left in a saloon in Palm Springs, California, with their mouths hanging open. Godley will have to cobble together a video interspersing archival footage of Sinatra with Bono lip-synching his part, and a couple of bits from the back of the limo to at least show that the two of them have actually met. Bono fears that this means Frank Sinatra is never going to record "Two Shots of Happy."

A while later Bono speculates that Frank uses disorientation as an act to get out of awkward situations. "I don't think he's losing it, I think he knows what he's doing," Bono says. "So he gets out. And his excuse doesn't have to be logical." Bono gets a call from Barbara apologizing for Frank's hasty exit and inviting him over to the house that evening. Bono says sure, and he arrives to a night of whiskey drinking and storytelling with Sinatra and about six of his pals. Frank seems fine now, and completely in his element. Eventually Bono proposes a toast, stands up, raises his glass—and sings "Two Shots of Happy" for Frank and his cronies. Sinatra smiles as he listens. Bono decides that's going to have to be good enough.

Sinatra is a painter, and Bono thinks his stuff reveals a sensitive (he avoids using the word *feminine*) side contrary to the macho image. "Even his paintings are conflicted," Bono says. "He doesn't want to be sweet, tender, but he is." Bono stops to admire one painting and says, "That one has a jazz vibe."

Sinatra looks at him and says, "That one's called 'Jazz.'"

As the whiskey continues to flow and Bono's head spins, he begins to perceive that these old guys are drinking him under the table. Sunk in a chair, Bono watches dreamily as Sinatra pushes a switch and the wall opens to reveal a movie screen. An old film comes on and Bono falls asleep.

He awakes with horror. His pants are soaking wet. Oh, my God, Bono thinks, here I am watching a movie with Frank Sinatra and his friends in Frank Sinatra's house and I've pissed myself. This goes beyond shaming himself; this is shaming Ireland before Italy, this is shaming rock & roll before the big bands. Gingerly, Bono slips his hand down toward his crotch. The liquid is cold. Thank you, Lord! If it were urine it would be warm! Bono gropes around and finds an upturned whiskey tumbler next to his leg. Yes! He passed out and poured the liquor on himself! He didn't wet his pants! He won't have to commit hara-kiri.

Bono climbs to his feet. Sinatra and his chums are still watching the old movie, still knocking back the booze. Bono bids them good night. Frank tells him to come back tomorrow. The song-plugger in Bono figures that's a good idea—he'll come back tomorrow *with a pianist* and really sell Frank that tune! But he thinks better of it once he's out the door. He has to get back to L.A. and get on a plane for Australia. U2 is waiting. The Zoo tour—this next leg dubbed "Zoomerang"—is waiting. Bono will have to leave Frank Sinatra where he is, laughing with his sidekicks, bending his elbow, flickering in the light of an old movie.

47

Pressure Points

---

an understudy saves the big show/ an infestation of winged pests/ the sinking of the triplecast/ tiny tim as rorschach test/ larry's admonition against the aggrandizement of the lovey-dovey

I'M STARTING to develop a dim freshman's appreciation for how architecture reflects its environment. Just as the Olympic Stadium in Berlin seemed to have been designed to the strains of martial music and Viking drums, the football stadium in Sydney rolls up and down in big concrete waves, as if God knocked it off between designing high tide and palm trees. The sound may turn to mud up at the crests of these cement curves, but it sure looks idyllic.

The audience is wandering in slowly, filling up the field like migrating birds returning for the summer. In Dublin the winter's rolling down, in London the Christmas lights are being strung across Oxford Street, and in the United States the Thanksgiving dishes are being cleared, but here in Australia spring is turning into summer and vegetation is shooting up through every crack in the pavement. The whole city of Sydney seems to be blooming. There's not another continent where man's dominion over nature feels so shaky. If the human race came to an end on Monday, the flora and fauna would reclaim Australia by Wednesday afternoon.

Hard to believe amid so much bliss and pollen that U2 is falling apart backstage. All the tensions of the Zoo tour—the combined weight of pressure, politics, and sleep deprivation—are coming to a climax during this two-day stand in the city where all the men have blond ponytails and all the women wear halter tops. You know that scene in *The Treasure of the Sierra Madre* when Bogart and Tim Holt are competing to see which of them can stay awake longer so he can kill the other and steal the dough? There is some of that spirit in the U2 throne room today.

U2 have just canceled the plan to film the Sydney shows for the January triplecast—three versions of Zoo TV broadcast simultaneously on three different channels. This is the project for which Allen Ginsberg, William Gibson, and others filmed bits to interact with U2 songs for channel surfers. Triplecast planning has already eaten up many hours of U2's time and much of U2's money, but on the eve of the filming the band decided that the concept had not come together; if they go ahead it will look half-assed. So they pulled the plug—which got MTV (their partners in the project) steamed and means the loss of a huge paycheck that was supposed to make this Pacific tour really profitable.

Profits—there's another horror. The "spare no expense" largesse of Zoo TV has been haunting the band for a long time, but here in Australia it's turned ugly. In order to pay for the Pacific tour U2 had to demand big guarantees from concert promoters in Australia, New Zealand, and Japan. As the Biggest Band in the World they were in a position to squeeze the impressarios dry, but that doesn't make it pleasant. In the past the band was willing to share some risk with the local promoters and then share in the profit afterward, but this time the show was so big that there had to be money up front and lots of it. The promoters coughed up, but they tried to protect themselves by jacking ticket prices through the ceiling. U2 fans in Australia are being asked to cough up fifty (Australian) bucks a pop to sit in a football stadium, and a lot of them just can't afford it. There is public bitching from disk jockeys asking if U2 have gone greedy and the band keeps running into fans who tell them they couldn't afford to go to the concert 'cause it would have cost a week's pay.

Amid this general tension and recrimination, Bono and Edge are getting antsy that some of the concert routines have been repeated so long they are turning into pantomime. And wrapping all these other aggravations into a big, pulsating package of paranoia is the ulcer-inducing fact that tomorrow night's concert is to be broadcast live around the world as a pay-TV special, and tonight's show is the television crew's only shot at a rehearsal and run-through. Aside from needing it to pay the bills, the pay-per-view broadcast is U2's only real shot at promoting the songs from Zooropa, the new album that was almost ignored during the summer European tour. They have worked about half of the *Zooropa* songs into the show, but they don't sit as comfortably as the songs they replaced. At this moment no one would be too surprised if any or all of the four members of U2 disappeared into the bush and was never seen again.

Willie Williams, the affable production designer, has taken to telling everyone that this TV broadcast is the final exam, and once it's done U2 can treat New Zealand and Japan as a postprom party; the pressure will be off and they can play whatever they want. The band members appreciate hearing that, but it doesn't keep the blood vessels from standing out in their eyes.

And here comes a big new problem. Last night Adam fell off the wagon he's been riding since the British tabloid scandals of last August and today he did not turn up for sound check. As bad as things have ever gotten with Adam's dissenting lifestyle, that has never happened before. Drunk or sober, Adam's made the gig. This time he was too blitzed even to recognize crew members in the hotel elevator. I'm wondering if he's heard about the gossip in the British papers that Naomi has been seen around London with her old boyfriend Robert De Niro. At first I think, "We're in Australia! Of course he hasn't heard!" Then I realize that if I've heard, Adam's heard. When crap like that floats by there's always a dozen so-called friends who can't wait to point it out to you.

This is a bad night to be in U2. This is a bad night to be anywhere near U2. This is a bad night to know how to spell U2.

"Three more weeks of seeing your ugly face!" Larry announces as he plops his plate of sushi down next to me in the backstage cafeteria. I tell him I've just run into a pal of mine who recently eloped with a friend of U2's after a very quick courtship. Larry ain't the most sentimental Irishman in the best of times, and today he's feeling especially unromantic.

"What the hell is that marriage all about?" he asks.

"I think they're madly in love," I say.

"I'm sorry," Larry says, getting increasingly peeved at his inability to work his chopsticks and finally grabbing a fork to spear his dinner. "I'm a cynic about all that lovey-dovey stuff. A marriage is a partnership and you better look at it that way or you're in trouble! All that lovey-dovey business gets in the way." Larry says *lovey-dovey* as if he's describing a particularly unpleasant rectal disorder. "How's she gonna feel about him in a couple of years when he's pickin' his nose? Or when he's pickin' *her* nose?"

"Yeah, well," I say, "you better have a whole lot of that lovey-dovey stuff at the beginning to help carry you through the forty years of nose-picking."

"Fair enough," Larry says, and I ask him if he's still thinking about moving to New York for a while after the tour. He glances around to emphasize that what he's about to tell me is top secret and then confides, "I bought an apartment. I'm really excited." I ask where it is and he tells me, describes the building and I say, "Larry! My wife's sister lives in that building! I'll see you all the time!"

"Oh, fuck!" Larry cries. "I'm never going to get away from you! It's never going to end!"

Edge arrives, exasperated and mumbling curses. "I've been under the stage since sound check!" he tells Larry. That's over two hours. "Don't ever try to reprogram a string section while the support band is playing above your head!" He notices that we are sitting in front of a particularly gruesome mural of Bono and Edge, painted by the locals in tribute. It pretty much kills what's left of his appetite.

Edge is grumbling about impending disaster when Morleigh slips up behind him, puts her hands on his shoulders and, when he turns his head, plants a kiss on his lips. Edge's mood lightens at once. Pretty soon he's joking about the string of mechanical disasters that have befallen U2's high-tech operation here in the land of aboriginal sorcery.

Relaxing into his usual focused work-mode, Edge asks who Bono should telephone from the stage for the TV broadcast tomorrow. This is the last the world will see of Zoo TV—indeed it's the last the world will see of U2 for a while. They need a summing up. Maybe Macphisto should try to call President Clinton—then when he doesn't get through he can cry, "But I got him elected!" Edge considers the idea and then rejects it as too American. This has to be something that makes sense to viewers all over the world. Edge says that perhaps Bono, as Macphisto, should address the world audience, make a summing-up speech for Zoo TV. We start tossing out ideas for a speech that would combine the spirits of John F. Kennedy, Christ ascending from the apostles, and the Wizard of Oz preparing to board his balloon. Then Edge excuses himself to go get ready for the show.

I go out to watch B.A.D. and discover that the place is swarming with millions of tiny black flies. They're all over the hair and chairs and clothes of the audience. Everybody's scratching. I'm standing at the soundboard slapping bugs with the only other early guest, Tiny Tim. But he couldn't have brought *all* of them.

Just before showtime Dallas Schoo, Edge's guitar tech, gets a summons from the U2 dressing room. He enters to find himself face-to-face with Edge, Bono, Larry, and McGuinness, all looking as grim as a firing squad. They want Dallas's opinion. Adam will not be able to play the show tonight. What does Dallas think the options are? Dallas tells his bosses what they already know: they can't consider canceling because tonight is the only chance for the TV director and cameramen to block out the concert for tomorrow night's broadcast. With or without Adam Clayton on bass, U2 has to go on. Edge raises the theoretical possibility of Dallas playing guitar and Edge playing bass. But that's absurd and everybody knows it. Aside from the fact that the audience damn well expects to hear Edge on guitar when they shell out for a U2 ticket, the TV crew would only be confused by a run-through in which people were playing the wrong instruments. Somebody has to substitute for Adam, and the only candidate who could possibly be deputized in the next fifteen minutes is Adam's bass roadie, a quiet, skinny guy named Stuart Morgan.

"Dallas," Edge says, "you know Stuart. You play with him every day at sound check. You know he knows the songs. Can Stuart do the gig?" McGuinness puts down his drink and gives the guitar tech his full attention.

All eyes are on Dallas, who would rather be anywhere than here right now. He speaks carefully in his slow cowboy drawl: "Stuart can do it. He knows those songs. But you gotta keep eye contact with him, let him know when a bridge is coming up." The four bosses nod and thank Dallas. Then they send for Stuart to tell him he's been drafted.

"We have some bad news!" Bono tells the Sydney throng after the cheers for "Zoo Station" have subsided. "This is the first show we've ever played without Adam! Adam is very sick!" Bono's laying on the announcement with enough melodrama that I half expect him to drop to his knees and lead a prayer. Bono introduces Stuart (who is trying to become invisible in black shirts, pants, and a black cap pulled low over his eyes) as "Adam's mentor." The singer goes on to rouse the crowd by declaring, "We didn't want to cancel Sydney—'cause you'd get pissed off! And who knows when we're gonna get another blue sky day in *Sydneyyyyy!*"

As U2 plays, Edge cues Stuart in to every impending section change. Otherwise the understudy keeps his eyes locked with Larry's, who keeps the tempo together while Bono holds the attention of the audience. Even that is not easy tonight. During "New Year's Day" Bono's hand microphone dies, leaving Edge howling the background *aiii-ya*s over and over while Bono signals the roadies frantically with an outstretched arm. The roadies, misunderstanding the signal, run out and put a cup of water in Bono's hand. Finally his manic gesturing communicates and he is given a second mike—which he sings into and which turns out to also be dead. At this point any of our less brilliant rock stars might start weeping, stalk into the wings to fire people, or jump into the audience to beat someone up. Not Bono. He walks to the front lip of the stage, throws down the broken microphone, and starts howling out the words unamplified. Not that anyone in the stadium can hear him—he almost surely cannot hear himself over the gigantic amplification of the band— but the dramatic gesture creates a surge of excitement in the audience, who sing the missing words themselves while Bono stands there, out-stretched and glorious.

Watching with me at the soundboard are two delegates from MTV America, the young woman veejay who goes by the single name Kennedy and her young man producer. They were supposed to be here to take part in the triplecast, but when that plug was pulled by U2, Tom Freston let the kids go to Australia anyway. Kennedy, whose public persona is that of a wisecracking gal who might say anything, has never been out of America before. She just turned twenty-one and right now she is agog at the figure standing a few feet away from us.

"Tiny Tim is here!" she whispers.

"Who would give Tiny Tim bus fare," her boy producer sneers, "let alone airfare to Australia?"

This condescension really rubs me the wrong way, so I tell them a big lie: "Are you kidding? Tiny Tim is like God in Australia! He's the biggest American star down here!"

"Really?" Kennedy says.

"Like Jerry Lewis in France," the producer explains, as if he knew it all along.

Kennedy ponders this like Einstein looking for a unified field theory and then she shakes her head and says, "I just can't believe Australians think Tiny Tim is cool."

"Well," I say. "They can't believe we think Michael Hutchence is cool."

Kennedy considers this for a while and then asks, "Do you think Tiny Tim would be happy if I offered him a handjob?"

I tell her he'd be happy to be offered a handkerchief and turn my attention back to the stage. I'll tell you one guy who's profiting from the absence of Adam Clayton: Larry Mullen, Jr., At every point in the show where the video screens would normally cut to Adam they are showing Larry instead. He's getting all his own close-ups and Adam's too. The cameras are avoiding Stuart like a prostitute at a church picnic. Finally, during "Pride" there is a long shot of Stuart up on the screens. The concert's nearly over, he looks as relaxed as Gomer Pyle at the Mayberry filling station. At the end of the song Bono brings Stuart to the front of the stage and raises his hand in the air to the cheers of the crowd.

In his hotel room, a semiconscious Adam Clayton lies in bed and comes to a hard realization. Right now U2 is playing and he's not there. There have been plenty of times over the course of this tour when Adam has wanted to tell them all to fuck themselves and walk out, but he never imagined it feeling like this. Adam is caught in the dilemma that broke up the Beatles and a thousand lesser bands. It is almost impossibly hard for a successful, famous, wealthy man to have to be subjected to criticism about every aspect of himself—from the music he likes to the shoes he wears—from three childhood friends. It is almost insurmountably strange to reach a position of power and celebrity where everyone you come in contact with in the outside world kisses your ass, where you can make decisions to build a mansion or fly to Paris for dinner or have a tree moved because it's blocking your view, where you get whatever you want—except when it comes to the central thing you do. And there, in your own job and your own music, the very thing responsible for all this success and power, you have to compromise on *everything* with three other people. For Adam the petty humiliations have begun to overpower the familiar joy.

But tonight it's different. Somewhere right now U2 is playing and Adam is not with them. If he left U2, he would have to feel like this every night. It makes Adam admit something he has been denying: "I don't want to lose the band."

At the stadium the crowds are making their way through the parking lot, the liggers are filling the backstage hospitality rooms, Stuart is being toasted by the crew, and U2 are finishing their showers and getting to work. At I A.M. the top TV people, along with McGuinness, Ned and Maurice, Robbie Adams, and a few other insiders, are assembling to review the videotape of tonight's concert and plan, shot-by-shot, tomorrow's broadcast. They must also prepare an edit of tonight's concert to have ready to air if a rainstorm or other act of God should shut down tomorrow's show.

Edge is behind the TV monitor in the dressing room, reconnecting wires to repair some glitch. Bono, a towel wrapped around his neck, has a yellow legal pad in his lap and a pen in his hand. They roll the tape. There's a great opening crane shot of the crowd, the enormity of the stage. It's an exciting start. The prerecorded opening fanfare swells under the buzzing of the audience. . . . "Stop the tape!" Bono has an objection.

"There's too many *look how big this thing is* establishing shots," Bono says. "We're hitting the viewer over the head with it. He'll say, 'All right all right, it's big!' Also, the fanfare is mixed too low against the crowd noise."

They start the tape again. The first song, "Zoo Station," begins. Everyone watches, Bono is writing furiously. "Stop the tape!" The color was a little off on *this* shot, Bono explains, the angle on Edge was bad on *that* shot, the mix was wrong on *this* line. . . .

So it goes, shot by shot and line by line through a 140-minute concert. And no one raises an eyebrow, no one thinks it's unusual. The people in this room will work all night and not hesitate to argue over a camera angle or guitar mix until the sun returns to the Sydney sky. Eventually I slip out and find a roadie who's heading in the direction of the hotel. As he gives me a lift home he comments on U2's work ethic.

"They really bite the bullet and do the work," he says in a broad Australian accent. "Most bands wouldn't. They wouldn't sit up all night going over every inch of that. They sure wouldn't go on without their bassist on fifteen minutes' notice."

He's right. Bono—perhaps because he still thinks of himself as a kid getting away with having fun for a living—resents it whenever I mention how hard U2 works. He claims it's all inspiration and jumping in with their eyes closed. But when pushed far enough even he will admit that it requires a lot of labor to keep the machinery moving, even if the music itself comes freely. I'm reminded of something Lyle Lovett told me as his career moved up through both the music and movie industries. "The thing you find out as you go," Lovett said, "is that the people at the very top seem to be the ones who just *work harder* than anybody else."

It's true. It's a big secret too. 'Cause nobody wants to believe it.

48

To Confer, Converse, and
Otherwise Hobnob

macphisto's farewell address/ the veejay proposes date rape/ a frequent flyer causes panic in the aisles/ god blows on the soundman/ bono cuts off michael jackson's penis

"FRIENDS, FANS, followers. My time among you is almost at an end. No, no, don't be frightened. I must go back where I came from. The great glory that has been Zoo TV must ascend from among you and take its place among all the millions of other satellites shining in the sky. But don't fear. I will still be up there watching you all. Watching everything you do. You may not be able to see me. But I will be able to see you!

"I leave behind video cameras for all of you! Tape each other! Tape yourselves! Children, tape your parents. Parents, tape your wills." Bono holds up a video camera. "Take this, all of you, and watch it!"

Bono stops reading there and turns to McGuinness. "What do you think?"

McGuinness is laughing. "If you're going to be blasphemous, go for it!"

Bono looks uncomfortable. "Is that blasphemous?"

Bono's holed up in the band's trailer working on Macphisto's farewell speech for the international TV broadcast tonight. He's trying out lines, throwing out lines, putting in other people's lines and new lines of his own. Willie Williams comes in and out of the room, tossing in suggestions while I sit typing it all up on a laptop computer. Maurice is sitting next to me with a laptop of his own, writing Bono's opening speech, formalizing a version of what Bono's been saying every night at the start of the show: "Welcome to Zoo TV! We've got the latest in hardware, software, and menswear!"

Maurice always carries himself with a sort of Jack Benny deadpan resignation. He rolls his eyes at a lunatic world and then carries on with his job. Today his passive exasperation is exacerbated by the fact that when he got to Australia—after a twenty-hour plane ride from Dublin —U2 decided that there was some emergency video decision back home that could only be made by the Rosencrantz of Rogerson's Quay. So Maurice had to get back on the plane, return to Dublin, sort out the trouble, then turn right around and fly back to Australia. It's enough to knacker Lindbergh. Maurice figured he had the final flight beat, though. He borrowed a bottle of sleeping pills, planning to take one and use the last twenty-hour journey to catch up on all the rest he'd missed.

Turned out he didn't need them. The minute the plane took off he collapsed into a deep sleep without taking any medication. Somewhere along the way the flight attendant roused him to eat dinner. He passed out again with the fork in his hand. Each time the stewardess returned she tried to wake him and could not. She got worried. So did the people around him. Maurice was deep in his REM state, oblivious to the uproar. The stewardess went through his pockets and found . . . a bottle of sleeping pills! Now she was sure she had a suicide in the aisle seat. The captain came on and called for a doctor. A doctor jumped up. Maurice woke to the physician slapping him in the face, shouting, "How many did you take?" while attendants and passengers hovered over him like gargoyles. "HOW MANY DID YOU TAKE?"

"Huh? What?"

"WHY ARE YOU SLEEPING?"

"Because I'm tired, you fuckin' idiot!"

So nobody's pestering Maurice today. Let him get on with his work and leave him alone.

Bono keeps practicing the farewell speech. "To all the women of the world, I give you the dream of marrying a rock star! As close as your VCR, as intimate as the headphones on your Walkman. To all the men of the world, I give you the dream of marrying a supermodel! Just slip in the tape and watch. She's always perfect, she never changes, and when you're bored with her you can just turn her off."

"Nope," Bono announces. All that is out. I protest and he says, "Don't want to offend the in-laws." The events of last night are still a little too touchy to risk any intentions being misconstrued. Adam comes into the room, smiling but looking sheepish. He is not affecting any bluster or acting like last night's absence was no big deal. He's too honest for that. Too embarrassed too. How the band is dealing with Adam going AWOL is, for now, staying between themselves. But it is clearly not a subject that's going to go away quickly.

Bono keeps reading: "Now it's time for me to go, to confer, converse, and otherwise hobnob with my fellow celebrities. But I leave these three —the Scarecrow, the Tin Man, and the Edge—to rule in my place until such time as I return."

No, Bono, says, the reference to the other three has to go. It makes Macphisto too literally a part of U2. Bono's foot is swollen, bandaged, and wrapped in ice and towels. He fell and twisted it last night at the end of "Bullet the Blue Sky," reaggravating a sprain from an earlier show. He ignores the discomfort and plows ahead with his speech.

"America! I gave you Bill Clinton! Watch him!

"Frank Sinatra! I gave you MTV!

"Salman Rushdie! Is the price on your head too much to pay for so much airtime?

"People of Europe! When I found you, you were divided by culture, language, and history—as different as the channels on a dial. Now you are joined together on the same cable. You will never be separated again!

"People of Sarajevo—look on the bright side. There are those all over the world with food, heat, and security who never get to be on television like you are!

"Good-bye, Squidgy—I hope they give you Wales!

"Good-bye, all you neo-Nazis—I hope they give you Auschwitz!

"Good-bye, Michael—I hope you get your new penis. . . ."

Bono stops reading and looks at McGuinness, who is laughing and telling him to do it, go all the way. The papers have been full of wild speculation that Michael Jackson may be having his male member surgically altered to confound a description of its eccentricities given by the boy he allegedly molested. Talk about tampering with evidence! Willie Williams returns asking for a final copy of the speech to put on the video monitors. After a few more edits and revisions Bono hands over the text.

Most nerves are on edge tonight. There are photocopied notices stuck up all over the backstage, reading:

TO: ALL WHO SOMETIMES WATCH THE SHOW FROM INSIDE THE
BARRICADE AND OTHER PLACES YOU SHOULDN'T BE.

BECAUSE THESE SHOWS ARE BEING RECORDED AND BROADCAST, PLEASE DO
NOT GO INSIDE THE BARRICADE AREA TONIGHT OR TOMORROW NIGHT. IF
YOU ARE THERE, YOU WILL BE IN THE WAY AND ALSO IN CAMERA SHOT.

UNDERWORLD IS ALSO GOING TO BE A HIGH STRESS AREA. PLEASE KEEP
AWAY FROM ALL UNDERGROUND WORK AREAS.

ALSO, PLEASE DO NOT USE CELLULAR PHONES OR YOUR WALKIE-TALKIES
AROUND THE STAGE.

Out at the mixing board Joe O'Herlihy is struggling to compensate
for a strong wind that is blowing away the balance he spent the afternoon achieving. The soundman looks up with sad resignation and says,
"I work so hard to get the sound right and then God comes along and
blows it all away."

God has mercy on Joe that evening. During the concert that follows
everything goes as right as it went wrong last night. The general dynamic of the show is as it's been since the beginning of the tour: the
concert opens with the full barrage of Zoo TV effects and a string of
songs from *Achtung Baby*. But where those songs were brand-new and
somewhat unfamiliar in the spring of '92, by the fall of '93 they are
U2's greatest hits. "Numb," another hit, now comes during that high-
tech part of the set, before U2 walks out to the B stage to perform
acoustic songs, including "Stay." Upon returning to the main stage for
the U2 classic rock climax, they perform "Dirty Day" from the new
album.

It's the encore, Macphisto's part of the show, that has changed the
most since the band had a chance to stop, think, and figure out how to
play the *Zooropa* songs in Dublin. After the audience has been treated to
clips from the Video Confessional, Adam, Edge, and Larry return to the
stage wearing their blue "Lemon" uniforms. They look either like Sgt.
Pepper's military honor guard or bellhops at some posh Indian hotel.
They begin playing "Daddy's Gonna Pay For Your Crashed Car" and
the video screens fill up with Bono in a devilish red dressing room
backstage, applying the last bits of Macphisto's lipstick and preening in

the mirror. Helen and Nassim, the wardrobe assistants, are in black Zoo gear behind him, helping to dust him off and slip on his gold jacket. As he dresses, Macphisto picks up a hand mike and begins singing the song. He brushes his attendants aside and strolls toward the stage, singing to the camera as he goes. He walks out of the video screens onto the stage during the last verse, as fireworks explode, the Trabants above shiver, and cannons shoot Zoo dollars (with Macphisto's face on them) into the cheering crowd.

As the ovation subsides Bono begins Macphisto's farewell address. He is somewhat hunched over so he can read off a video monitor on the floor—which plays okay to the people watching on TV but is confusing for the audience here in the stadium. He delivers the line about Sarajevo, but when he gets to Salman Rushdie he gets spooked and says, "Salman Rushdie, I give you"—Bono looks around—"decibals!" No one knows what the hell that means. He talks on, delivering his soliloquy in Macphisto's upper-class British voice: "Good-bye, Squidgy, I hope they give you Wales." Applause from the crowd. "Good-bye, Michael . . ." Bono looks at the lines on the video monitor: *I hope you get your new penis.* He suddenly has a vision of Michael Jackson committing suicide. He freezes. He does not finish the thought. He skips ahead to, "Good-bye, all you neo-Nazis, I hope they give you Auschwitz," and the audience cheers.

Then Macphisto calls a Sydney cab company and asks for a taxi to take him home. The woman on the other end of the line hangs up on him and he looks heartbroken. He begins singing "Show me the way to go home" and the audience sings along. U2 kicks into "Lemon" and Macphisto slinks across the stage in the cloven-hoofed lurch that Bono and Edge worked out in their Dublin rehearsal room. It looks great. Bono's twisted ankle may torture him tomorrow, but tonight he is walking on two shots of showbiz, the greatest anesthetic of all.

Backstage afterward everyone feels great. Finals are over. U2 has a lot of friends in Sydney, including Edge's sister and her husband and Bono's brother-in-law (Ali's brother) and his family. There is a billiards tent set up near the band's dressing room, and it is there that they are chatting with their relations and playing pool when Eileen Long's walkie-talkie buzzes. Sheila Roche is calling from McGuinness's jam-packed hospitality room. "Eileen, would the band let Kennedy come in and say hello?"

"Who is Kennedy and why would the band want to meet him?"

"She's an MTV veejay. She came all the way from America."

Eileen approaches Edge, who is in the middle of a life-and-death pool tournament. He says sure, send her in. Kennedy appears wearing men's pajamas and says to Edge, "Hi, would you like to go on a date with me?" Edge is not sure what to say. She adds, "These are my real breasts!"

Kennedy explains that she wants to write a book about dates with famous men. Edge says, "If I take you out, you can't write about it."

Kennedy decides to try Larry. She tells him her dream would be to go on a date with both Larry Mullen, Jr., *and* Larry Mullen, Sr. Larry says Kennedy will have to call his girlfriend and explain it to her. I suggest Kennedy call her book "Dates with Greats." She says no, she has a catchier title: "Date Rape."

There is a rumor going around that McGuinness told Kennedy that Lou Reed has to sit in a film studio every single night waiting to broadcast his half of the "Satellite of Love" duet with Bono. The story is that she believed it, but it's pretty hard to tell around here who's leg is being pulled by whom.

49

Skin Diving

---

bono swipes a boat/ adam's hidden gifts/ a conga line forms at the gay bar/ a wager over underpants/ acquiring a postsexual perspective/ bono swipes a waitress/ bondi beach party

O N SUNDAY afternoon Polygram Australia has hired a small yacht to take U2 and forty guests on a four-hour tour of Sydney Harbor. Ali's brother's family, Edge's sister Jill and her husband, Tim, and many of the Principles pile onto the boat. Bono stops to sign autographs for kids on the dock. Adam heads straight below, finds a sleeping cabin, and goes to bed.

The rest of us chow down on a fancy buffet while the Sydney Opera House floats by the window and the radio playing in the background takes phone calls about last night's U2 pay-per-view. A caller from Carolina says he watched it on TV in the USA and the sound wasn't good enough—but he liked it when U2 "went out to the little stage and did an 'MTV Unplugged' thing." Bono and Larry, their plates in their laps, groan. The disk jockey asks the caller how he'd rate the concert on a scale of one to ten. "Seven and a half." Bono and Larry both flip him the V, the Irish bird.

Unfortunately the kid from Carolina may have had reason to complain. Word arrives of a major glitch in last night's broadcast—the first half hour of the concert was broadcast in mono rather than stereo in the USA. It probably did sound awful. Bono is stunned, and says evenly, "We gotta sue over that one."

Now, there's one thing you have to watch out for when you sail with Bono. He likes to steal boats. It's an eccentricity the roots of which I would not like to imagine, but when the urge overtakes him it can get anyone around him in hot water. He's been joyriding in swiped vessels since he was a kid, and as his prominence has grown so has his nautical kleptomania. Once he was drinking in the south of France with his friend Rene Castro (the artist who helped design U2's 1989 Love Town tour and painted some of the onstage Trabants, a former member of Allende's government and subsequent Chilean political prisoner) when they ran out of whiskey and wanted more. Bono, his caution compromised by drink, spotted a destroyer out in the harbor and said, "The U.S. Marines'll know me! They'll be glad to give us whiskey!" So he put on his pirate face, led Castro to the shore, and stole a rowboat.

They paddled out about a mile—even in their inebriated state the project was beginning to feel a little dubious—and came up against the side of the huge ship. Bono grabbed an oar and started banging on the hull, screaming, "Come on! We want whiskey!" They must have made some impression, because infrared lights flashed on and there was all kinds of shouting way up on the deck. Bono forced himself to focus enough to figure out that the shouting was not in English. They were banging on a French warship. The French have no sense of humor about stuff like that. Bono looked at his companion. Castro was wearing a P.L.O. T-shirt. Bono panicked. No telling what they'd be accused of. He told Castro to start rowing. Over his shoulder he could see the French lowering what looked like some kind of pursuit craft into the water.

This was not an isolated incident. Another time Bono convinced the English workers fixing up his house in France that it would be a blast if they hot-wired a motorboat and took it for a spin. A police boat pursued them, and though they hit the shore and split up, two of Bono's cohorts were caught and arrested. Bono had to go to the police station the next day and make a formal apology.

Hell, one time in Switzerland on a day not unlike today Bono leaped off a moving boat into the water. McGuinness freaked out and dove in after him, forever earning his 20 percent.

So it is with an impending sense of trouble that I go to the very back of the boat and find Bono and U2's Australian friend Libby stripping down to their underwear. Bono turns and dives into Sydney Harbor. His head bobs up a few yards away, spitting out the little cigar he had between his teeth and calling "Maurice! Come on!" Maurice, with his usual weary sigh, puts down his drink, says, "Back to work," takes off his clothes, and jumps into the water.

On the upper decks some of U2's guests are gathering to watch the show. Bono is swimming toward the cabin cruisers anchored in front of the fancy houses along this stretch of waterfront. Maurice is swimming along behind him. Bono climbs aboard one boat and furiously tries to get its engine to turn over. Maurice stays close, ready to throw himself in front of any bullet that might come Bono's way. Giving up on his first choice, Bono swims from boat to boat. Clearly he is not the commando in charge of jump starts. Despairing of getting a big boat going, he jumps back into the water and swims to a small private dock, where he swipes a dinghy and paddles. I can see a man coming out of one of the houses in the hill over the dock, looking down toward the water. I have visions of Bono being netted, gutted, and fried for dinner. The man on the hill returns inside, perhaps to call the cops, perhaps to get a shotgun. Bono and Maurice, unaware, paddle away.

Eventually Bono rows up to another dock and presents his stolen lifeboat to a gentleman named Herbie who is standing there staring at this dripping wet apparition in black underpants. Bono asks Herbie to please make sure the gentleman on the hill gets his boat back. Then he dives back into the harbor, Maurice still in escort, and swims back to our yacht. He takes off his soaking wet briefs, balls them up, tosses them overboard, saying, "And Mrs. Herbie asked for these."

Bono tells Ali's nephews that he hopes they've learned an important lesson today: "It's good to steal."

Eric Hausch, Bono's security man, has been watching all the action from the poop deck. No doubt he would have jumped in if Bono had been in danger, but he was not going to swim around like a moron as long as he had his charge in sight. Now, assured that the boss is back aboard and secure, Eric decides to have a little fun with his commander, Jerry Mele. Jerry is a recidivist practical joker, so Eric is delighted to see an opportunity to wind him up. He puts in a call to the hotel and gets the security chief on the line. Then Eric goes into his act: "Jerry! Bono dove off the boat and got hauled off to jail in just his underpants! He's got no money! He's got no I.D.! They think he's a boat thief! We gotta get down there and get him out!"

"Oh, shit! Shit! Who do I know down there? I gotta think! Shit!" Jerry is halfway out the door to the police station before Eric cracks up laughing and suffers an earful of curses, smiling the whole time.

*   *   *

A few hours later Bono is showered and sharp, sitting out on his balcony forty stories above Sydney Harbor, drinking Kahlúa and vodka and surveying the beautiful city spread out before him. Sinatra is singing "One for My Baby" in the background. The lights of Sydney are shining golden, the night sky is purple, and in the penthouse across the way a geisha in full costume is arranging her screens, expecting a visitor.

"I started writing the songs that became *Achtung Baby* in that building over there," Bono says, pointing to another tower. "You see that apartment tower across from it? There was a woman living there I use to watch when I'd come in at six, seven in the morning. She was overweight, had a punk haircut, and used to get home around the same time I did. I made up a whole life for her—that she ran a punk club, that her parents financed it for her. I started watching her through a telescope." He laughs and says, "We excuse a lot in the name of reconnaissance!"

He sips his White Russian. "One night I was watching her and I happened to look two windows above her. There was another woman with another telescope watching me! I was furious! I was so offended. I jumped up and called her a bitch and pulled the curtains shut."

We laugh and then sit in silence, studying the whole panorama. "You know," Bono says quietly, "most people in the world never get to see this."

An hour later Bono's in a Thai restaurant, with Adam's brother Sebastian, Edge, Morleigh, Edge's sister Jill and her husband, Tim. Tim, who grew up in the same neighborhood as the Evanses and Claytons, now works for Polygram here in Australia. As is bound to happen at such a reunion, childhood stories dominate the conversation. Sebastian says he remembers as a little boy jumping on Edge and beating on him as hard as he could, while Edge paid absolutely no attention. Tim says that he recalls being knocked hard on the head by Adam with a toy gun. Bono says that his great memory of the Clayton house is that it was the first place he ever ate spaghetti.

"They didn't serve spaghetti in my neighborhood," he says. He was having trouble figuring out how to wind it onto his fork when Mrs. Clayton said, "Oh, that's all right, Paul. It's okay to just cut it up into little pieces and eat it." Young Bono went happily about doing that, chomping away, when Mrs. Clayton noticed little Sebastian having the same problem and reprimanded, "Sebastian! Will you eat properly or do

I have to cut it up for you like a *baby*?" Bono's face turned bright red and fell into his napkin.

As the wine bottles are emptied everyone agrees that as a child Adam's great claim to fame was his virtuoso ability to fart at the perfect moment. As the English teacher was making his most poignant poetic point Adam would poot. Bono says that the year he sat next to Adam his English grade plummeted. Edge says that Adam's legendary status among his fellow schoolchildren was assured the time he let a big ripper in class and told the angry teacher, "I'm sorry, ma'am, it just slipped out of my bottom."

The plates are cleared and the party considers where to move next and settles on a gay club down the street. Edge's sister gets as far as the flaming Karaoke queens in the outer lounge and says it's time for Tim and her to call it a night. Bono plows farther into the club, coming to a huge barroom where homosexual men in wild costumes are dancing on the tables and across the bar. A man dressed in a buffalo head is spanking a fellow dressed as the pope with a very long feather.

Bono pauses to let Edge take his photo cuddling a sort of bison-headed Batman. A spontaneous chorus line is high-kicking to the Village People's "Go West," when who should I spot standing with his arms folded in the middle of the scene but that handsome heterosexual Larry Mullen—who I must say in this context bears more than a passing resemblance to one of those Macho Men the Village People so eloquently celebrated.

"Gay clubs are the best place for us to come to," Larry shouts in my ear above the music. "Nobody hassles us, there's not the asshole you find in other clubs who just has to get up and try to start something. They respect us and they're glad to have us. The gay community is always on the cutting edge in music. I'm proud that they like U2 and come to our concerts. They don't see in U2 that macho shit that's beneath so much rock. I have a lot of time for the gay community."

Boy George has gotten a lot of publicity in the British press by saying he's attracted to Larry. When he first went public with his crush in the mid-eighties ("I fancy the drummer in U2! Every time I hear Bono sing 'I still haven't found what I'm looking for,' I feel like shouting, 'Turn *around!*'") Larry was embarrassed. Now he says he has a whole different attitude. "I take it as a compliment!"

As more drinks are downed and the music gets louder U2 and their friends are drawn into the partying. Eventually a rumba line starts snaking around the room, everyone's hands on the butts of the person in front of them. As the line gets squeezed together a humping motion takes over, until the train of bodies looks like an orgy of caterpillars. Edge reaches back over the shoulders of the woman between them and strokes Larry's chest, which inspires another woman to lift up Larry's shirt and lick his torso. Larry lurches backward and the whole line collapses into a pigpile on the floor.

The members of U2 pick themselves up and agree it's time to go. Edge and Morleigh are going to go home, but Larry and Bono are up for finding another club. They head to a straight disco across the street. They are waved through the entry, escorted downstairs, and placed on a slightly elevated platform behind a velvet rope. A small, thin man in a floppy hat approaches the rope and Bono jumps up, waves him through, then gives him a big hug. It's a photographer friend of U2's from past trips to Australia who used to be a cross-dresser. Bono laughs and introduces him around and asks what's new. "Well, I'm HIV-positive."

Bono engages his friend in intense conversation while Larry orders drinks and studies the roomful of dancers, most of whom are studying Bono and Larry. It's hard to tell which side of this velvet rope represents the tourists and which side the monkeys, but we are all in the zoo. Over the next half hour a bizarre ritual unfolds. Women accumulate along the rope, displaying themselves for U2. They lick their lips, they bat their eyes, they gesture suggestively. Joni Mitchell once told me about going to the Playboy mansion with Warren Beatty and Jack Nicholson. She said that every bunny and centerfold who approached the two movie stars would stick out whatever part of her anatomy—breasts, butt—was most developed. I understand now that Joni was not exaggerating. Some of these women are sliding the velvet rope between their legs. Some are stoking the poles from which the rope is suspended. They are no longer looking at Bono and Larry like animals in a cage, they are looking at them like hamburger on a plate.

For the first time in my life I have some sympathy for Mick Jagger's defense of sexist Rolling Stones songs like "Stupid Girl." Jagger always said that when you're in the Stones' position you really do meet a lot of women like that. I figure it's an artist's job to rise above that level, but you know what? It would be very hard to objectify some of these writhing women more than they are objectifying themselves. When people make a commodity of their sexuality and throw it in your face it doesn't take very long—if you're not interested in taking advantage of the offer—to sink into a vaguely amused contempt. It's not right, it's not justified, but that seems to be what happens to a lot of rock stars. Maybe it happens to movie stars and politicians too. If people around you treat themselves like prostitutes, it's eventually easy to act like a pimp.

I made a note the first time I heard *Zooropa* all the way through that the album sounded to me "postsexual." Looking at that comment later I couldn't figure out what I had thought that meant. Now I remember! It ties in with Bono's comment back at the transvestite party in New York that he now knows how it feels to be a babe. Rock stars at U2's level are in the very strange position of knowing that if they feel like having sex with a beautiful woman, there are hundreds anxious to volunteer at any time. The rare men who have become big enough rock stars to find themselves in that unusual situation have in their songs either (a) ignored it, so as not to alienate an audience unable to identify with such circumstances (as with Springsteen) or (b) used it to peddle pin-up fantasies to adolescents (as with Aerosmith). But in fact, morality aside, a man liberated from the need to pursue sex may find himself with a very odd perspective on human behavior. Sex has lost much of its power over him. The attitude I sensed during that first listen to *Zooropa* was one where sex was no longer even a very interesting issue, as money ceases to be an issue for the very rich: the characters had moved on to other things. Now I'm thinking that it would be great if U2 or—even better —Mick Jagger came at the subject head-on: what does it mean to be a man and be sated? That would really be new ground for rock & roll, where most men are such prisoners of their pee-pees that they will not be able to think past it until they are dead.

A woman with very long legs in a very short miniskirt knows the fellow guarding U2's little podium, and she manages to get through the rope and starts dancing on the band's perifery—as if she just happened to be there and hadn't noticed any rock stars. She moves closer and closer to Bono, keeping her eyes fixed across the room. Finally she succeeds in catching his attention. He is not, however, lovestruck. He is floating in alcohol. He leans into my ear like Henry Higgins studying an anthropological curiosity.

"What color knickers do you think she's wearing?" he asks.

"Well," I say, "her bra's hanging out and it's black, so her underpants must be black."

"Hmmmm," Bono says with the detachment of a boozed-up professor. "I think she's the type to wear a black bra and white little-girl knickers."

"You're crazy."

"Ten bucks says I'm right."

"You're on."

Eric, Bono's faithful security man, is as always standing nonchalantly within Bono's sightlines. Bono waves for him to come over and whispers in his ear. Eric grins and studies the situation. He clears the drinks from a short glass coffee table in front of us, reaches out and takes the dancer by the hand, and suggests she climb up on it. She jumps at the chance and starts frugging before us, her head brushing the ceiling.

Bono gives Eric the thumbs-up and we lean forward to settle our bet. Just as we do a startlingly bright strobe flashes off in our faces. Someone has just shot a humiliating photo and blinded us in the process. We fall back rubbing our eyes while the dancer shimmies off the table and across the floor.

"I didn't see a thing!" Bono shouts in my ear. "Did you?"

"I still can't see anything," I say, Bono's face eclipsed by a floating purple blotch. "At least you were wearing those welder's glasses."

Eventually the dancer—who Bono correctly describes as amazonian, finishes shimmying and flops down between us. "Will you show us your underpants?" Bono asks.

She smiles and hikes up the dress to her hip, snapping a black strap. Bono hangs his head in defeat. "That's American dollars, Bono," I say.

He reaches in his pocket and hands me a fifty.

As we leave the club, feeling a little embarrassed, Bono says, "There's a peculiar thing that happens when you flirt sometimes. At the end of the night when a person realizes you *don't* want to sleep with them, it can hurt their feelings. But the next time they see you they decide they like you better for it."

No doubt that's true, but there are not girls like the waitress who serves us at the bar/disco/restaurant where we land next. She looks like a pixie, like Tinker Bell. She has short blond hair, almond eyes and pointed eyebrows, and she handles a roomful of noisy drunks with the relaxed detachment of the head nurse in a pediatric ward. We have lost

Larry Mullen in our travels, but we have found Fightin' Fintan Fitzgerald and it is his birthday! This is all the excuse Bono needs to keep the drinks flowing and plot some special birthday exercise. Several people we met at the last bar wander in, including the long-legged table dancer. It must be after 4 A.M., but from the yacht trip to Bono's balcony to the Adam Clayton Juvenile Flatulence Tribute Dinner to the gay bar to the loose-libido disco to this place, far too much alcohol has been ingested for anyone to care. Or for anyone to object when Bono slaps the table and cries, "Who's up for a swim?"

There is a little muttering, which Bono quiets by announcing, "It's Fintan's *birthday!* We must go swimming for *him!*"

What does it say about our mental state that this argument convinces everyone, including Fintan? Soon poor Eric has been sent to a nearby hotel to try to buy towels. He comes back in failure. Bono calls our pixie waitress over and asks if there are any towels here that we might borrow for a short trip to Bondi Beach. She shakes her head no. All right, Bono says, who needs towels! And we pour out of the cafe and into our car.

Suddenly our waitress comes chasing us out the door as if we skipped off on the check. She is carrying an armload of white tablecloths, which she dumps into the backseat. "They're not towels," she says, "but they're better than nothing."

Obviously this is the greatest woman in the world! Bono insists she come with us. "No, no," she laughs. "I can't."

"Yes!" everyone shouts. "It's Fintan's birthday!" and with that Bono hauls her into the car. Other customers are sitting at tables outside the restaurant applauding.

"No," she says. "I'll lose my job!"

"Yes!" Bono orders.

"Oh, who needs a job?" She smiles as the car takes off and the patrons back on the sidewalk cheer.

Bondi Beach is big; Bondi Beach is beautiful; Bondi Beach is bare; and at 4:30 in the morning Bondi Beach is bloody freezing. They say there's bad riptides out there—lots of warnings to the tourists about people drowning. We'd better send Fintan in first. Fintan is fearless. Within moments our birthday boy is in his birthday suit charging toward the ocean. He leaps into the surf and a moment later pops up like a cork and comes tearing out again.

Bono is like Sergeant Fury, always ready to take the lead. He howls naked down the sand and right into the sea, bobbing, diving, and calling for everyone to follow. Pretty soon everyone's in, splashing beneath the stars. The pixie waitress marches in as relaxed as if she were alone in her bathtub. A second car has followed us—the table dancer and her friends from the disco. Bono is body surfing on a big wave when she swoops up under him like a dolphin and breaks the water, startling him. Bono can hear Eric back on shore shouting, "Don't go out too far! There's an undertow! Don't go out too far!"

"Don't worry," the table dancer tells him. "I'm a lifeguard!"

A little later everyone's sitting in the sand, shivering in their table-cloths, watching the sun rise. The pixie waitress turns out to be a student of political science and is cross-examining Bono about some of his onstage political statements, which has him red-eyed and flabber-gasted as he stumbles to form intelligent replies. Meanwhile our dolphinlike Salome is gazing at Bono as if she fully expects to begin bearing his children and Fintan is trolling the beach looking for the lost Fly shades. "Found them!" Fintan calls, which means we can leave.

Bono stands up, wipes off some sand, and says so long. The kid-napped waitress says, "Not so fast." Uh-oh. "You pulled me out of work in the middle of my shift," she reminds Bono. "You're going to come back and explain it to my boss."

This woman is going to be president of Australia someday.

Our shoes are soggy, our seats are sandy, and the sky is sunny as we pull back up to the restaurant. The late-night customers at the tables outside have turned into a breakfast crowd and clearly the legend of the lost waitress has been a topic hotter than the pancakes. As Tinkerbell steps out of the car the diners clap and whistle. She left a barmaid, she's returning a legend.

She grabs Bono by the arm and hauls him toward the restaurant. Her boss comes out to meet her in the doorway. "Didn't you *used* to work here?" he says.

"I'd like you to meet Bono," she says evenly. "He can explain."

Bono looks around. A crowd had gathered to hear what he has to say. "There's a perfectly good explanation," Bono says, vamping while he tries to think of one. "See . . . we needed a lifeguard . . ."

He rambles on, spinning a long cock-and-bull story as the patrons applaud and call for the boss to forgive the waitress.

"Okay," the boss says, "you can have your job back." Cheers from the audience. She goes back inside to finish her shift, carrying an armload of damp tablecloths.

50

World AIDS Day

flight of the zoo crew/ bono's soul leaves his body/ wine tasting in new zealand/ the english-irish problem rears its head/ a meditation on rock stardom/ ascending mt. cavendish in a creaky gondola

THERE IS no Zoo plane to carry U2 from Australia to New Zealand or from New Zealand to Japan. The band and crew instead take commercial airlines, often buying up all the tickets on a flight. This means that U2 and the twenty or thirty Principles travel the Pacific air with many of the two hundred grips, riggers, carpenters, and other hard-core roadies who have had the better part of two years to perfect their airline etiquette. As our flight sits on the runway in Sydney waiting to take off for Christchurch, the flight attendant steps up to issue the safety instructions and realizes she is stewardess on the voyage of the damned.

"Please make sure your safety belts are buckled," she says, and two hundred seat belt buckles *clickclickclickclick* for thirty seconds. "The exits are located—" Four hundred arms flaps up in the air, mimicking her instructional gestures. She steels herself to continue. "In case of sudden loss of cabin pressure oxygen masks will descend." She dangles a plastic oxygen mask in front of her face and two hundred hands hold up two hundred dirty sneakers and dangle them by the shoestrings. "Place the oxygen mask over your face and breath normally." The roadies all hold their sneakers over their noses and inhale loudly. "To inflate the lifejacket—" Two hundred inflated airsickness bags pop at once. "There is a whistle to attract attention—" Everyone whistles. "Your safety card is in the seat pocket in front of you." Two hundred plastic safety cards are held aloft and flapped. "Please be careful when opening the overhead compartments, as objects may shift during flight." Two hundred little airline pillows go flying through the cabin. The stewardess retreats to the galley and the plane heads down the runway and into the wild blue yonder.

In the air David Guyer, Larry's security man and motorcycle partner, gets up, takes the flight attendant's microphone, and announces that he is going to present a trophy to Larry Mullen for covering 10,000 miles on his motorcycle during the course of this tour. Larry rode in every kind of weather, in every kind of terrain, David says. "He's got balls."

A cry comes from the roadies: "Show us your balls, Larry!"

Night falls while we're flying over the rugged terrain of New Zealand's north island. When we land in Christchurch, down toward the bottom of the south island, down toward the bottom of the world, it's dark and cold. A few reporters are waiting on the airport tarmac to interview U2. Edge and Bono step up and speak to them.

"We heard there's a few tickets free," Bono says. "We're very upset. Madonna's not coming. Michael Jackson's not coming. They only like you. We love you."

A reporter asks, "Can New Zealanders expect something different for their concerts?"

"The greatest show on Earth," Bono says evenly. He thanks them for coming and climbs into a waiting car.

Even though it's supposed to be the first day of summer, it's still mighty chilly this close to Antarctica, and tickets for U2's outdoor concert have not sold well. When the band was last here, in 1989, there was tremendous local interest in U2. A young Maori fan named Greg Carroll had been hired by the band in 1984 and taken on the road with them. When the tour ended Greg stayed on, relocating in Dublin and working for Bono. One day in 1986 Greg was out on Bono's motorcycle when he ran into Guggi on his. They decided to switch bikes for a laugh. Greg might not have been prepared for Guggi's more powerful machine. He took off down the road, straight toward a drunk driver who turned without signaling. He crashed the bike and was killed.

Bono and Larry accompanied Greg's body back to New Zealand and attended his Maori funeral. Bono wrote a song about the experience called "One Tree Hill" and dedicated the album on which it appeared, *The Joshua Tree*, to Greg. That song, and the story behind it, got great attention in New Zealand, and when U2 came through the next time they were treated like the pope. There was even what local papers called a riot outside their 1989 Christchurch concert, when a couple of thousand fans who could not get in clashed with police.

This time, though, U2 is just another foreign act with expensive tickets. When we get into town I see a gang of boys mocking the U2 posters stuck up on the walls and shouting, "Ah'm not buggin' ya, am I?" quoting Bono in *Rattle and Hum.* They laugh and stumble on down the road.

Bono's in a crappy mood as he checks into the Park Royal Hotel and heads toward his room. He turns on CNN and L. J. Ferentz, the tour's masseuse, comes in to rewrap his twisted ankle. Bono is pretty much oblivious to her ministrations. He is usually uncomfortable around masseuses. In California a Japanese back-rubber started screaming at him, threw him off the board, and pummeled him while screaming "Relax! Relax!" There are also New Age tendencies among many in the profession that are at odds with Bono's Christianity.

"They're often into *reading auras* and all and I have no time for it," he once told me. "Also, for some reason they always see a bright red aura around me and start freaking out. One woman started bowing to me and calling me Your Highness or something."

L. J. is a lot less pushy. But sensing how tense Bono is as she works on his ankle, she tries to sell him on a massage. He says no. "Okay then," she says, "I'll just do your polarities." Bono rolls his eyes. L. J. starts rattling her fingers rapidly across Bono's brow while he makes a show of concentrating on the television, which he knows offends masseuses.

Suddenly Bono experiences a great cosmic *whoosh* and is shocked to find himself floating out of his body, out of the hotel, and flying through the sky above the city. He does a couple of loop-de-loops and then executes a reentry, disembarking from his ectoplasmic spin back into his body in front of the TV. Bono is quite fascinated and a little shaken, but he refuses to admit to L. J. that he felt anything at all. After she leaves, though, he hooks up with Edge and Morleigh and tries to explain what happened.

"All of a sudden I'm out of my body and floating over Christchurch with L. J. hanging on to my ankle!" Bono sputters. "I didn't tell her—I don't want her coming up with any other ideas!"

"Admit it," Edge says. "You got a stiffy."

"No, no!" Bono protests.

"Was she typing on your forehead?" Edge asks.

Bono looks at him confused. Edge drums his fingers across Bono's brow. "Like that. Was L. J. taking dictation on your forehead?"

"Yes!" Bono says, "She called it *doing my polarities.*"

"She did that to me," Edge says, "and I had the same experience you did."

"She did it to me," Morleigh says, "and I started crying."

"Really?" Bono says. "That's quite amazing." He considers this new method of space travel for a minute and then announces, "But I'm still not admitting it to her!"

One of the reasons that tension and exhaustion have been amplified on this last leg of the tour is that the dates have been booked too far apart, not just by location but by time. U2 have stretches of up to five days between shows, which gives them too much time to get homesick, too much time for petty problems to swell to great proportion, too much time to get bored and too much time to get into trouble in attempting not to get bored. The band and most of the people around them are taking on the aspect of horses who have been ridden too long and wouldn't mind finding a low branch with which to dismount their riders so they can get back to the old salt lick.

In an effort to fill up one empty day in Christchurch, it has been arranged for U2 to drive out to the country to have lunch at a winery. Right after breakfast Bono and I climb into one car with Willie Williams, the production designer. Willie looks as if he's just seen a ghost. He is blue, somewhat spacey, given to staring off into the distance as we pull out of the hotel.

I stick in a homemade cassette and the car fills with Leonard Cohen singing "Hallelujah." Cohen sings, "They say I took the name in vain, but I don't even know the name," and Bono laughs. On the chorus Willie—who cannot sing—begins mournfully crooning along: "HALLE-LUJAH! HALLE-LUJAH!" Something odd is up with him all right.

Cohen ends and "Nightswimming" by R.E.M. comes on. "He's a lovely singer, isn't he?" Bono says of Michael Stipe. Stipe sings, "You cannot see me naked," and Bono says, "What is this song about?"

"In the song Stipe's looking at an old photograph," I say. "It's he and some friends ten years ago at a pond where they used to go skinny-dipping and make out. He's realizing that those days are gone forever. Because of AIDS, because they've all gotten older, and because he's now famous."

"He's in the wrong band," Bono says. "I'll never give up night swimming."

I see that Bono is squeezing Willie's hand, stroking his fingers. Willie must have gotten some awful news. I suppose he'll tell me when he's ready. Bono insists we stop and get ice-cream cones before we continue into the countryside. We pass a ski lift going up to a restaurant on top of Mt. Cavendish and promise we will stop there for a ride on the way home. The car has to stop once and wait for a herd of cows to clear the road, and then we wind around steep green hills rolling down to the bluest bays I've ever seen. The white settlers only arrived in New Zealand in the 1800s, and the country feels raw and unpolluted. The hills are volcanic—they shoot straight up at jagged angles, but they are covered with grass and trees, hedges and stone walls, grazing sheep and goats. There are palm trees next to fir trees. It reminds Bono of the west of Ireland, Willie of the coast of Scotland, me of western Maine. I imagine New Zealand reminds everyone of the prettiest place they know.

We arrive at the winery after another hour. Edge and Morleigh are already there. Edge is sampling different vintages and ordering some crates for U2's restaurant in Dublin ("The chardonnay has a certain je ne sais quoi"). There are wooden tables in a flowery grove out front, and the owners lay out a fantastic feast: salmon, ham, stir-fried vegetables, ripe tomatoes, and fresh bread hot from the oven. As we dig in a pair of cows are romping and gamboling in a paddock nearby.

"Oh, I hate to see cows playing tag," Edge says. "Makes you think the hamburger you're eating might have been playing kiss-and-run the day before."

Morleigh is arranging with the owner to borrow a pair of horses for a ride, and declining an offer of rifles. I am amazed by the whole bucolic setup and mention that while the British empire may have been brutal, they sure did lay some solid groundwork for future generations of tourists. The London-born Edge picks up on this: "Actually, it's never said—but if not for the British, Ireland would *have* no architecture."

"Well, we'll never know now, will we?" Bono snaps, suddenly a Dublin Irishman, his ears burning red in the presence of a Brit.

"Woooo!" Edge laughs. "Did you see that? Did you see how quick he turned!"

Everyone moves their attention back to the chow, but Edge does mention after a little while that St. Patrick was actually Welsh. Bono just lets it go by. The trees are filled with music—high three-note figures. Edge is impressed and asks the owner what is causing it.

"Those are bellbirds singing," the owner says in a thick New Zealand accent that sounds to us like . . .

"Billboards?" Edge says. "You have singing billboards?" Sometimes on this tour the differences between Irish, British, American, Canadian, Scottish, Welsh, Australian, New Zealand, Carribean, and Indian accents can build a Babel between English-speaking brethren. At the airport in Sydney, Edge went to buy cigarettes and was asked if he "wanted a ten." He thought he was being offered smokes in a tin. The I/E flip in this part of the world causes all sorts of confusion. If a New Zealander tells you the weather tomorrow will be *better*, you may hear that the weather will be *bitter*.

Adam arrives along with Eric, Bono's long-suffering security man, and Bret Alexander, the tour's travel coordinator, and surveys the orchard. Willie is wandering the groves, looking as if it's his last day on Earth. Eventually U2 pull themselves away from the winery, and continue down the coast in a little caravan, stopping around dusk in a seaside village called Akoroa Harbor. They get coffee in a restaurant on a pier and talk about what everybody's going to do when the tour is over. Bret says he and his family are going to build a house in Seattle and he may go to work for Pearl Jam.

More than a few of the job-hunting Zoo crew are hoping Pearl Jam tours next year, but Eddie Vedder is wavering. With the release of Pearl Jam's second album his face was plastered on the cover of *Time* magazine (without his cooperation—he would not give *Time* an interview) and his fame continued to explode in spite of his refusal to do any videos for the new album, which debuted at number one. Eddie is threatening, if people don't give him some room, to quit the superstar sweepstakes altogether and sell homemade tapes out of his house.

Something has really changed in the culture that is ripping apart the people who become rock stars. The last four singers raised to the pantheon—Axl Rose, Sinéad O'Connor, Kurt Cobain, and Eddie—have all been made publicly miserable by the process. Maybe it's the fact

that there's been an explosion of celebrity media in the last ten years—
People magazine, *Entertainment Weekly, Entertainment Tonight,* MTV, and all
the talk shows—that either was not there before or ignored rock before.
Or maybe it's the spread of the notion that any rock musician who gets
popular must be doing something wrong, must be a sellout. That's a
complete reversal of the ethic that ruled from Elvis to the Beatles to U2
—that you wanted your band to be the biggest thing in the world and
reach as many people as possible.

Some fans come up looking for photos and autographs. Bono, Edge,
and Adam oblige, but it's a signal to start heading back to Christchurch.
It's getting dark out.

As we ride through the twilight with Willie and Eric, Bono continues
to brood about the nature of celebrity. The writer Charles M. Young
has a theory, I tell him, that the reason rock stars get so obsessed with
critics is because unlike most people, rock stars control 99 percent of
what happens in their lives. So they become obsessed with the 1 percent
they can't control. It infuriates them that some little gnat in the newspaper is allowed to mock them or say they stink. They want to respond to
the gnat with a cannon.

"I think that's a very smart insight," Bono says. "I've felt that in
myself. Ali recently went through it for the first time with her
Chernobyl film. She got some good reviews and some bad reviews, she
felt she wasn't quoted quite accurately once or twice, and now she won't
have anything to do with it. She's been nominated for Irish Woman of
the Year but she refuses to take part, refuses even to have her photo
taken for it."

We ride along in silence and then Bono says, "It's too bad that
comedian is making fun of Eddie Vedder now." Bono's referring to
Howard Stern, an American disk jockey and TV personality who's been
doing a routine about how when Pearl Jam first appeared Eddie Vedder
was a happy, smiley guy and now that he's a big star he's morose and
doesn't want to be famous. "I know what Eddie's going through," Bono
says.

"Sure," I say. "He's shocked to realize that everything he says is being
written down, recorded, and held up for dissection."

"When that happens," Bono says, "it makes you very self-conscious
and serious. That's what happened to us in the mid-eighties. You

become the Serious Men. Now we've spent three years confusing the issue so much that hopefully people won't be sure *who* we are.

"Just in the last week the red light has gone on in my head. I know U2's been in people's faces too much. We have to stop right now. We've done two albums, two years of touring. I didn't know the Sinatra duet would turn into such a big thing. Roger Daltrey just asked me to sing with him at Carnegie Hall on a show called 'Daltrey Sings Townshend.' I'd like to pay my respects to Townshend, but I said no. We considered recording a version of 'Jean Genie' in Tokyo for a tribute to Bowie. *Ziggy Stardust* and *Aladdin Sane* were big influences on U2 and should be acknowledged. But I said no. The red light went on with *Rattle and Hum* and I ignored it. This time I won't."

A huge full moon has risen over the hills, and we look out to see that we are passing Mt. Cavendish and the ski lift we promised ourselves a ride on this morning. We pull into a parking lot at the base and climb out of the car. The ski lift ferries diners up to a restaurant at the pinnacle. Empty gondolas clank down the slope, make a turn at the bottom, and then ascend again. The sign says they stopped serving ten minutes ago. The sign also says no more than three to a car. But the four of us—Bono, Willie, Eric, and me—decide to take a chance and jump in.

It seems like a bad idea almost immediately. As we climb higher and higher over jagged rocks the gondola lurches and rattles in the wind. Eric talks about his days as a fireman, having to go through the debris of a terrible plane crash picking up eyeballs and human brains. The moon has gone behind a black cloud. The cables overhead groan. I'm saying a Hail Mary and thinking of the old joke about the musician who dies and goes to heaven. He meets Jimi Hendrix, Elvis Presley, John Lennon—and then he sees Bono flying by. "Hey," the musician says, "I didn't know Bono was dead!" "He's not," Elvis replies. "That's God—He likes to pretend He's Bono."

We arrive at the Ridge Restaurant all feeling a little nearer to heaven. The innkeeper takes pity and agrees to serve us dinner. Willie's mood seems to have lightened a little, but whatever bad news he received still has command of his attention. We fall into a discussion about immortality.

"I didn't have Sunday school on my back," Bono says of his own upbringing. Then, of U2's spiritual conversion he explains, "We had something far stronger—a bright white light. It was *too* hot. But it will never leave us. And it made the Sunday school notion of God seem *squeaky.* Squeaky clean."

Among themselves U2 refer to no smoking/no drinking/no dancing Christians as "Squeakies." In the early days of their conversion, though, they were pretty upright themselves. They realized that they could replace "Him" in songs about God with "You" and they would work as love songs. Later on sex became a metaphor, and they then realized that that metaphor was all through the Bible—it all came down to *faithfulness.* And in U2's current work, from "Love Is Blindness" to "The Wanderer," it still does.

Cardiff, Wales, is a hotbed of evangelical enthusiasm. When U2 arrived there last summer on their way to London they knew they'd be facing stiff judgment. Every night at the end of the concert, during the instrumental coda to "Love Is Blindness," Bono brings a woman up onto the B stage to waltz with him while the band plays out the song. Although it look elegaic in the dim blue light, he is often whispering orders ("Shut up, calm down, listen to the music, listen to the music") in the ears of hysterical partners and holding them steady to keep them from leaping up and down, tearing off a souvenir, or waving to their buddies. Well, in Cardiff he reached out to a woman who, while they slow danced, was giving him the twice-born third degree about this Macphisto nonsense. "What are you doing?" she demanded while wiping the Macphisto makeup off his face. *"What are you doing?"*

Bono understood he had solicited a squeaky. "It's Ecclesiastes," he whispered while waltzing her around romantically for the crowd. She didn't buy it, she was angry. "Did you ever read *The Screwtape Letters?*" Bono asked her. She said she had. *The Screwtape Letters* by the Christian writer C. S. Lewis pretends to be a series of instructions about how to corrupt mortals sent by a senior devil to a young demon-in-training. Lewis described his devil this way: "Screwtape's outlook is like a photographic negative; his whites are our blacks and whatever he welcomes we ought to dread." While waltzing with the angry evangelical Bono invoked Screwtape and told her, "That's what this is."

"Oh." She thought about it and then nodded, put her arm on his shoulder, and gave in to the dance.

"It took U2 fifteen years to get from Psalms to Ecclesiastes." Bono sighs. "And it's only one book!"

When we get back to the bottom of the mountain a few kids are waiting with cameras and autograph pads. Eric, Willie, and I step aside to let Bono pose and the kids say, *No, no, no! Please! The whole group!* We try to explain that we are not the other members of U2, but they will not believe it. So we give up and pose. "You know, Larry," I say to Eric, "I don't usually let myself be photographed without my hat."

The kids thank us profusely, one boy saying, "My best friend loves U2—without a photo he would never believe I met you!"

"You just show him that picture, kid," I say. "He'll know if you really met U2."

Back in Christchurch at midnight we head to a bar called Americano. Larry Mullen's there, as are a number of people from the tour. Eileen Long from Principle comes in—she's been searching everywhere for Bono. He's supposed to get on the phone to Dublin radio to take part in World AIDS Awareness Day. She drags Bono off by the ear. Willie and I go up to the bar and order drinks.

"This has been the longest day of my life," Willie says. "I got a call this morning from my friend in California. He went in for a routine checkup and found out he's HIV-positive."

I don't know what to say. Willie smiles, letting me off the hook. "That's why I've been sort of preoccupied all day. I told Bono, but I don't want everyone to know. I don't want people treating me differently."

Willie leans on the bar and stares into midair. "It means nothing, I know. Scientists are working round the clock to find a cure." He takes a drink and says quietly, "He hasn't told his mother yet."

"Are your parents alive, Willie?" I ask.

"No, neither of them."

"Mine either. You know, in life you have this little window—maybe ten years—between when the older people you love finish dying and your own generation starts. It feels like that window is closing."

We drink to long life and better days. I show Willie pictures of my kids and he says they're beautiful; he shows me a photo of his friend and realizes that I'm not sure what I'm supposed to say, so he laughs and says, "If you go for that type!"

It's the middle of the night here in New Zealand, but Bono is on the phone to Ireland, where it's afternoon. He is reading on the radio from Oscar Wilde's "Requiescat":

Coffin-board, heavy stone,
Lie on her breast,
I vex my heart alone,
She is at rest.

Peace, peace, she cannot hear
Lyre or sonnet,
All my life's buried here
Heap earth upon it.

Willie and I are in the bar, drinking a toast to World AIDS Day, here at the end of the world.

51

Adam Agonistes

---

clayton at the crossroads/ a visit to the wonderbar/ bono does an art deal/ an aztec experience/ larry mullen: frugal or tightwad?/ sunrise over one tree hill

O H, SAY, can you set your internal clock to this: it is late November, so your body is prepared to start sprouting extra fur and layers of protective fat. But here in New Zealand it is the first day of summer and although it was a shock to go from the early winter of Ireland to the nose-peeling heat of Australia, you got the hang of it. The Christmas decorations going up were overruled by the post-ozone sunburns. Christchurch, however, is as close as you're ever likely to be dragged to the South Pole and as the brave fans huddle under blankets and cheer through frosty breath at U2's outdoor concert to-night, Christchurch is freezing.

The band are playing well, but they are moving around far more than usual to keep from icing over. "I've never been so cold onstage!" Larry says when he ducks behind the curtain to warm himself during Bono and Edge's "Satellite" duet. He chats for a while and then says in an upper-class voice, "Will you excuse me for a moment? I'm in the middle of something," and turns and lands back on his drum stool for the kick into "Dirty Day."

Adam is taking the temperature more stoically—he is simply adding another item of clothing every ten or fifteen minutes, like the Madonna of the Bizzaro World. He starts the concert in a T-shirt, he ends in overcoat, wool hat pulled down to his nose, and fingerless gloves.

I'm no fool. I head down to the warmth of underworld, where the crew are brewing hot toddys behind the guitar tuner and passing around a bottle of brandy. At one point a pudgy roadie attaches himself to the outside of the Plexiglas window of Dallas's little guitar shop like the gremlin on the airplane window in *Twilight Zone* and begs to come in where it's warm. Sitting down here rubbing hands together and passing the bottle while the mighty amps of a rock concert blast above our heads is like huddling in a little Vermont cabin while a blizzard rages outside.

After the show Bono and Larry head to Americano, but word has spread that U2 have been going there and the place is full of U2 fans in U2 T-shirts. The band members are led to a corner with couches facing each other and sit down while Eric and David stand at parade rest, forming a human fence between U2 and the kids, who line up staring at them as if it were feeding time at Sea World. It is impossible to relax, so the group heads off to a campy club by the docks called Wonderbar, full of Italian sailors, old drunks, and weirdos. Bono loves it immediately, Larry starts shooting pool, and over the course of the next couple of hours McGuinness, Sebastian, and Zoo deejay Paul Oakenfold all show up there. A neckless man with a spherical head shoved into a trapezoid torso sticks his face in Bono's and tells him he was a pal of Greg Carroll's. They chat for a minute and the neckless man goes back to the bar, but he returns every half hour or so to make the same announcement. An old sunken-cheeked sea dog with coal-black eyes presses up and begs Bono to bring him along to Tokyo. A sixtyish stevedore with a white chin beard down to his clavicle leans across the table into Bono's nose and sings Irish songs. Nothing unusual, Bono keeps drinking and talking.

A thin, doe-eyed young woman in a cape and beret comes up and tells Bono she's a painter and her studio's nearby, would he like to come over. He looks at his watch and says, sorry, it's 3:30 and he has an early flight, but if she has color Xeroxes of her stuff she could leave them at his hotel in the morning. The next day at breakfast Bono comes down waving the Xeroxes. He really likes them. He just bought two of her paintings and is having them shipped home to Dublin. He shows me the copies. One is a nude, clearly an art-school model, dappled in impressionist reds. The other is a sketch for a painting called "Spilled Milk" of a big-eyed figure curled up and flipping out, a little like "The Scream." That Bono is a soft touch.

On the plane up to Auckland, at the top of New Zealand's north island and back in the tropical heat wave, the flight attendants have been warned about the Zoo crew. They announce, "In case of sudden loss of cabin pressure your shoes will descend." It is a wobbly flight. Edge sits engrossed in some technical magazine for electrical engineers. Adam asks Larry if he's closed the deal on his apartment in New York. Larry says he hasn't signed the papers. Adam has heard about a great house in London and hopes to run over and see it on the way home to Ireland, after Japan. He tells Larry the price and Larry, ever vigilant, warns him of the potential for spending much more in repairs and modifications.

I mention to Paul McGuinness that *Forbes* or one of those magazines that lists the highest-paid entertainers had put Bono in one position, Edge somewhere beneath him, Adam down below Edge, and Larry not on the chart at all—pretty funny considering that they have a long tradition of splitting their income equally.

"The truth is," McGuinness says, "Bono is always broke, while Larry still has his First Communion money." (It sometimes causes a little sore feeling that when Edge and Bono are off working on songs for U2, Adam and Larry have free time to grow their fortunes.)

Adam and Larry ask Paul how he enjoyed a Madonna concert he flew off to see in Australia while they were cooling their heels in Christchurch. Paul says it was good, maybe not big enough for a football stadium, but she's a real star and a far better dancer than he'd ever appreciated. He says she stopped the show at one point to talk about two friends who had died of AIDS. "Ah," Adam says. "Her *Sarajevo Moment.*"

On the bus into Auckland we pass One Tree Hill, lonely and majestic as U2 mythology would imply but closer to superhighways and urban sprawl than one would expect, just as U2's "One Tree Hill" comes on the bus radio. (Here's a better one: when we were driving back to Christchurch on World AIDS Day we were listening to Elvis Costello's new album and a song came on called "Rocking Horse Road." I said, "You know, that song was written about a street Costello got lost on somewhere in New Zealand." The driver said, "Rockin' Horse Road? Why, that's it right over there." We were passing it. Spooky, huh? I'm going to put on "Abraham, Martin, and John" down here and see who shows up.)

If Christchurch was twenty or thirty years in the past, Auckland is a generation in the future. It's a shining, seaside city full of new buildings and prosperity. There are Japanese signs next to the English signs everywhere, and Japanese tourists and immigrants mingling among the

Anglos. The Japanese are more welcome here than in Australia, which still has a lot of bitter World War II memories, so there is plenty of Japanese investment. There is also, both here and in Australia, tons of money being moved from Hong Kong before the British lease expires and the Communist Chinese take over in 1997.

(Communism may be dead in Europe and Russia, but it's mutated into something particularly ugly in the Far East. As long as the Chinese are willing to kick in their tribute to capitalism—which in their case means exporting goods made with slave labor and giving George Bush's family the Chinese golf course concession—the West doesn't much care how brutally they oppress their people. The Western rationale is that the men who rule China are all about ninety-nine years old and will be dead soon and places like Hong Kong will inoculate the Chinese virus with a healthy shot of free market vaccine. Maybe so, but I think the Chinese dictators have realized that a little capitalism does not mean they have to kick in *political* freedom. The same old pigs who rolled over the demonstrators in Tiananmen Square could spill a lot of blood in Hong Kong, and as long as they don't screw up the cash flow there's no indication the Western powers will much care.)

As soon as we get settled in the hotel I go down the hall to Adam's room for a heart-to-heart. The missed gig in Sydney is still looming in the air. The band has been nervous about Adam's love for getting crocked for a long time, but after the tabloid scandal with the hookers last summer it became too big to be left to Adam's discretion. He stayed on the wagon from that point till this, but he fell off in Sydney with a crash heard around the world. Now he knows he's got to either commit to cleaning up completely, with outside help if that's what it takes, or walk away from the band. The other guys have made it clear that they will break up U2 before they will lose a member to rock star excess. To submit to that tragic and stupid cliché would pretty much ruin everything else U2 has stood for.

Although he's put on his usual all's-well face this week, Adam's been in a steel-cage death match with his demons, wishing the tour would hurry up and end so he can get his life back. He is torn between wanting to run away from music and into the good life with Naomi and wanting to turn away from all that flash and high life and spend the year-off studying music. Right now rock & roll represents the bars of Adam's prison and he wants out. "I'm empty, completely empty," he says. "We really need to take time off, to go live without thinking about music." When I tell him that those are the exact words Bono's been using he is surprised, he says he didn't know Bono felt that way.

"I feel like we have really got something out of our system," Adam says. "I think we have become the group that we always wanted to become. That in itself inevitably brings you to yet another border in your life and I suppose it means that we really are free to let our imaginations run wild in terms of what we could be now. We've got to the point where we may well be the greatest group in the world. Now what do you do with it?

"I'd love to say I feel like we can kick back and rest a bit and do a few guest appearances on other people's work, but that isn't really satisfying. It's the ongoing U2 work that's important. I don't even want to think what that could be. In the same way that when we started *Achtung Baby* we had to acknowledge what had happened in music during that three- or four-year period, I'm sure we will have to react to whatever happens next. Live work, I could not even imagine what we could do now. I don't know if we will feel the necessity for live work. We might just want to get the records out and enjoy time with our families and creative time. We could think about recording two or three records and fringe projects and then think about touring as we get to the end of this decade. I personally feel it would be very hard to beat Zoo TV, and I wouldn't want to do another two-year tour. What is more rewarding is actually creating the music. Playing concerts is great to a certain point. Although getting big is a challenge and being successful is nice, it doesn't really give you the fuel that you need."

I suggest that over the course of the long journey from Hansa to here, Adam and Edge have both stepped into the spotlight that used to be only Bono's—the place where you're famous even to people who don't follow music. Only Larry has managed to retain (it's silly to say *anonymity* when he's world famous) a separation from a general showbiz sort of celebrity.

"Larry's always been noticed 'cause he's the pretty one," Adam says. "He's honed that character down in a way that he can feel comfortable in public as he didn't used to. And that's enough. His very silence speaks louder than anything else.

"It is going to be especially different for Larry and myself. Bono and Edge have a different mindset which allows them to work at a fairly manic pace and they like that. Maybe I'll get to like it, I'm not sure if I do. I suppose it's a psychological issue in many ways. I don't feel psychologically prepared for that, I like the anonymity of being able to seek out things and reel them back to my life and then be able to create from that. I don't like the culture where you are *reacting* and that is a large part of the way the culture has become. As communciation speeds up, art becomes much more a reaction than an intellectual process, and I prefer it as an intellectual process.

"I find celebrity-dom, being a personality, a Hollywoodization. People in Hollywood seek it knowing that their gig may be getting up and being very funny or being on TV or reading the news, but they're very good at saying, 'If you're not paying me I'm not going to be funny, I'm not going to do what you want, this is my life.' As Irish people we're not used to being that cold about it, that blunt about it. I find it hard to come back to Dublin and realize that Irish people now expect me to be that man, they expect you to always be Hollywood in that you're always performing for them and, secondly, willing to hand out if not the secrets of your success certainly the *rewards* of your success. And that's hard to live with. I'm not running away from Dublin; I just don't feel it's inspiring to me at the moment."

I observe that the change in Dublin's attitude toward U2 that was so apparent last summer seems to have all happened in the last year or two; for the first ten years of the band's success, Dublin was cool about it.

"Definitely." Adam nods. "Up to the release of *Achtung Baby* and maybe even up until the summer stadium tour of America it felt as if we were a hardworking rock & roll band. Then the criticism of the band turned to carte blanche acceptance of what we were doing and we were hailed for taking risks, reinventing ourselves, changing the world, being on the cutting edge. Plus the costumes that we had and the ease with which our celebrity friendships suddenly started to become noticed. Obviously the models were a new addition, but we'd met big models before. We got into that situation where the tabloid press has a stupid gossipy fantastical story to print regularly."

I ask Adam if he's ready to talk about his own summer tabloid scandal.

"I don't really want to be quoted on it because I don't really know enough about what happened or where Naomi and I are at in a way that I can share with the public. Suffice to say that after a number of years of having difficulties, this year has been a very, very difficult year. I do love Naomi and certain things have got in the way of that, which are my problems that I have to deal with. Anymore than that I can't really go into at the moment 'cause I'm not sure myself. But it has been a watershed year and there are certain things that I do have to face. I hope very much that I can deal with being in U2 and going out with Naomi and the lifestyle that it seems to thrust on me. Or that I allow. I have to sort that out."

Let's talk about your missing the gig the other night. That was something new.

A look of pain crosses Adam's face and he says, "It was a moment where I had to face a lot of things I hadn't really been facing and realize if I was going to be able to go on and be a useful member of this band —and indeed a husband—I had to beat alcohol. I had to realize that every fuckup of mine, every problem over the last ten years that hasn't been quite so serious as that night, has been related to alcohol abuse. So I'm kind of glad I finally had to confront it."

I tell Adam that I don't want to in any way diminish a tough decision, but he's not crawling up the wallpaper or sucking fluid from the radiator. He seems likely to be able to make that adjustment.

"I hadn't had a drink this whole tour until Friday," he says. "When you actually shift in the brain and say, 'You've got a problem with alcohol,' and accept it, you look back over a lot of things and realize that drink was the problem. And I don't want that future. I don't feel like it's 'Poor me, oh, what a terrible problem.' I feel it's a life-changing decision. And maybe I'll slip up. But I think for me and the bottle—it's over."

Flipping through my list of happy topics, I ask if it bugs him that U2 has worked for so hard for so long and done so well—and is still coming home from the tour with very little profit.

"It does, yeah, 'cause it has been a lot of work. It was a lot of work before the tour even started. It was a lot of work making *Achtung Baby* and *Zooropa* and while I know we had to do things much as we did in order for people to take notice, I think to do a second stadium tour over a two-year period that at the end of the day just paid the bills is quite a significant decision to have taken. And we did take it. It seems to me that financially we'll be in much the same position we were in before we started recording *Achtung Baby*. I don't know if it was a mistake. Ask me in five years. While I'm not obsessed by the financial element it would have been nice if there were at the end a financial freedom there. And I don't think there is."

The whole time we're talking, Adam's TV is on. It's showing *Let it Be*, the documentary about the disintegrating Beatles. When it gets to the scene where an angry George Harrison tells a bossy Paul McCartney, "Just tell me what you want me to play and I'll play it, or if you want I won't play at all," the parallel is a little too close for comfort.

The show in Auckland is the last outdoor concert of the tour; the two nights in Japan will be inside the Tokyo Dome. The venue is beautiful, in a field that rises up into steep hillsides where people can perch. When U2 arrive they are honored with a traditional Maori greeting dance by tribesmen in full costume. During sound check Edge remembers that the last time U2 was here, in 1989, they came up with the music that became "Acrobat" during sound check at this venue.

During the concert I decide to climb up one of the hills overlooking the stage and watch from there. It is a tough climb! I grab on to clumps of grass to haul myself up around hundreds of tight clusters of people watching the concert with the rapt attention of Brando's jungle army in *Apocalypse Now.*

When I get to the top I look down at what seems like a massive tribal gathering. I feel like some ancient Native American peeking over the ridge at a forbidden Aztec ritual. U2 is playing "Bullet the Blue Sky," the most powerful song in the set, and forty thousand pulsing people are laid out in front of Bono, bathed in waves of red light, while he stands, feet far apart at the edge of the stage, singing, "See the face of fear running scared in the valley below!"

Looking down into the valley below, this gives me the willies. When the red and yellow smoke billows up around him at the end of "Running to Stand Still" it looks like he's about to either sacrifice a virgin or elect a pontiff, and at the end of the night the star maps that fill the TV screens during "Love Is Blindness" become indistinguishable from the stars filling the night sky overhead.

Back at the hotel, at 2:30 in the morning, Bono announces to every straggler that it's time to go out and look for some fun. Kerrie Anne Quinn, one of the Principle reps on the road with U2, says she could get in dutch with Dennis Sheehan if she takes off with Bono. Bono says he'll write her a note of excuse for Dennis. Edge pipes in, "The only valid excuses are those signed by Larry." A van coming back from the venue is unloading outside. It seems like it would be a really good time to test the mettle of the U2 security staff. So several of us sneak outside and when the driver steps out of the van, jump in. I slide behind the steering wheel—which is on the right, not where I'm used to it being, and floor it out of the hotel, weaving down the wrong side of the road while Edge stands in the hotel doorway laughing and Jerry rips at his hair and yells at Eric for letting Bono escape.

I like driving on the other side of the road; it reminds me of how driving felt when I had just gotten my learner's permit and was intensely in touch with the potential of every automobile on the street to kill you, especially the one you're driving. Once the laughter over ditching security and the local driver dies down, though, it occurs to all of us that without them we have no idea how to get anywhere. We drive around for a long time, following promises of obscure dockside after-hours joints out of the downtown and down to the waterfront, but we can't find anything swinging in Auckland until we head back downtown, ditch the van, and take to the streets.

Down one alley of cafés and nightclubs Bono bumps into someone he's met before, a mysterious young woman under a cape and cloak with a face like a Botticelli angel. Bono says she lives among the street people here but no one ever touches her, she passes through them like a saint. She has no home because she doesn't need one; she works all week in an office, stays up Monday through Thursday nights in the cabarets and cafés, and then spends all weekend sleeping on the beach. The remarkable thing about Bono is not that he knows people like this wherever he goes, it's that he always manages to wander into them again when he's in town. At about 5 A.M. we're in a smoke-filled pool hall and I say I'm going to bed, we've got to be up in just a few hours for our flight to Tokyo. Bono says, "Bill! No! We're going *out* soon!"

The magic mick is as good as his word. He leads an entourage out of the pool hall and across town to One Tree Hill, where everyone jumps the fences, climbs to the top of the hill, and watches the sun come up. On the way back down morning has broken and church bells are ringing in the town, so Bono leads his procession to mass. "The stained glass windows," he whispers, "are more articulate than the sermon."

Is it any wonder that no one feels very peppy at the airport, waiting for the all-day flight out to Tokyo and back into winter? Production coordinator Tim Buckley surveys the ragged-out faces in the departure lounge and announces, "If we took all the broken parts here and put them together we might get one human being!"

52

Penny-Wise

---

sore feelings above the pacific ocean/ tensions in the inner circle/ when adam and paul used to hunt as a pair/ this is not a band like most bands/ adam smith vs. the workers in the vineyard

A DAM'S LOST NIGHT in Australia brought close to the surface a tension that has been boiling under the surface of U2 all during this two-year tour. It revolves around the sort of argument that outsiders never hear about and that the people closest to the band catch only in glimpses, because it is an argument between the family—Adam, Bono, Edge, Larry, and Paul.

From the start of Paul McGuinness's association with U2, the four musicians and the manager agreed to share everything they made equally. "That was something I recommended right at the beginning," McGuinness explains. "It was pretty academic. There wasn't going to be any money for the first four or five years, so why fall out over what was undoubtedly going to be very little money? After the first wave of deals ended and were being renegotiated it seemed natural to them to continue, though by then the alternative was pretty clear. They have simply continued to operate that way ever since."

Now, on the surface such sharing is not so uncommon in the music business. It is not unusual for a manager to get 20 percent, and for the members of a band to divide the rest. As U2 were a four-piece, all five principals ended up with an equal cut. It is unusual that the members of the group also elected to split the songwriting credits and royalties equally—but not unprecedented. The Clash did it that way before U2, and R.E.M. afterward.

Songwriting money, these groups realized, is a big source of the tension that breaks bands apart. There is as much money to be made from royalties on songs as there is from record sales, and it comes in a lot quicker. That's why Pete Townshend, who wrote almost all the Who songs, was much richer than his bandmates. That's why Sting had to let Andy Summers and Stewart Copeland get some of their (mediocre) songs on Police albums. That's why Lennon and McCartney and Jagger and Richards formed publishing partnerships; it kept the two strongest members of the band equal and then kept their bandmates' songs at bay.

All money generated by U2—from record royalties to T-shirt sales —was split evenly between the five people. That's how they set it up at the beginning, that's what they stuck to, and it served them well for years.

Bono points out that hard feelings begin in a collective such as U2 because the partners who contribute less get as much as the partners who contribute more. There is no penalty if one member fails to do his share, though the guilt can be corrosive. Larry agrees but raises an equally crucial point: the partners who want to spend all the collective's money dip equally into everybody's wallets. Since in U2 the ones who contribute the most creatively are also the ones most likely to want to do the most expensive tour in rock history and refuse all commercial sponsorship and spend two years of hard work doing something that eats up almost all the profits, the five partners do end up in some sort of balance.

But it is unlike the balance in almost every other business partnership. During the difficult making of *Achtung Baby*, the fact that McGuinness was not a member of the band gave him what was perceived as an unfair advantage: he got an equal share of all the money that the band generated, but while they were in some miserable studio or distant stage generating it he could be off working on outside investments and projects that he did not have to share with U2.

Paul defended himself by pointing out that if anyone wanted to say he did not contribute as much to U2 as Bono did, fine—he would not argue, he would take a smaller percentage than Bono. But in that case let's evaluate how much *everyone* contributes and talk about constructing a sliding scale, which would put McGuinness somewhere beneath Bono but above Adam.

"Obviously Bono makes the biggest sacrifice," Paul says as the airplane moves across the South Pacific, "in that the conventional calculation of songwriting is that fifty percent goes to the lyric and fifty percent goes to the music. Since Bono writes all the lyrics and certainly a quarter of the music, that would give him under a normal regime 62.5 percent of the publishing income. He doesn't do that. But it is kind of up to him. This is, in a way, the thing that makes U2 work. It's foolish to call something a democratic structure if you've got officers and men. They have successfully avoided that confrontation. Obviously it remains under review."

Paul's management deal with U2 expired around the time the Zoo TV tour was starting, and they agreed to put aside the arguments about changing the five people's equity structure until after the whole two-year marathon was over. Now it's almost done, and these tensions are bubbling up. Adam's missed gig in Australia reminded all of them that there was still at least one fight ahead. I suggest that missing the show in Australia may have been a blessing in disguise if Adam got a look at the ghost of Christmas future and decided to change his ways.

"Yes," Paul says. "Obviously he's got a problem and it never surfaced quite as spectacularly as that before. I'm really glad it was resolved the way it was. But it's something that we have to think a lot about next year. I don't know what's going to happen." Paul pauses for a moment and then says firmly, "It's not up to *him* anymore."

I ask if it's fair to say that Bono, Edge, and Larry form a sort of irreducible core, and that Paul and Adam, separately and together, move in and out of that core depending on what else is going on in their lives. Paul says, yes, that's fair to say. I ask, then, if when there are conflicts between Paul and the band, it serves his interests to have Adam pushed away, or if Adam might move closer to the other three if there were a band conflict with Paul.

McGuinness doesn't like where this is going. "I don't see it that way," he says. "I don't see it happening. Adam has, to some extent, removed himself over the last while from a responsibility for the band. But I haven't noticed what you describe.

"There's been a very natural process over the years of growing up," Paul says. "We're ten years apart in age, they and I, and at the beginning they really knew very little about the world. Now they are five years older than I was when I started managing them. That enforced contact over that many years does produce a certain amount of irritation. We've all got quite good at staying out of each other's way, though we still genuinely enjoy each other's company." The manager looks at me firmly and says, "It is also a business relationship. And there's nothing wrong with that."

It's a business relationship that reflects the deep and sometimes conflicted feelings these five people have for each other. Adam was once the band member closest to Paul, and has, over the last ten years, moved farther and farther away from him. Both of them are way too proud, too tough, and too ancestrally British to ever admit it, but I can't help thinking that Paul may feel a little abandoned by Adam, and Adam—when he gets defensive—resents in Paul the qualities that he has worked hardest to erase in himself.

First, understand how much they shared. Adam was U2's manager until he recruited Paul to take over. Paul and Adam were both English kids in Ireland, sons of R.A.F. pilots, rebels who had rejected the family expectations held out for them but who retained British social graces and a British notion of sophistication. They pretended to be worldly, and eventually they were. In all those things they stood apart from Bono, Edge, and Larry, who were naive, parochial, style-unconscious, and—eventually—charismatic Christians.

Although U2 maintained publicly that the *October*-era evangelization of Bono, Edge, and Larry caused no great rift with Adam and Paul, of course it did. It scared them to death. To protect themselves Adam and Paul made a deal that the two of them would always back each other in arguments with the three believers. That way neither of them could get pushed out. That pact held from the time of *October* through *War* and *The Unforgettable Fire.* It was only after the *Unforgettable Fire* tour that Adam went to Paul and said he no longer felt comfortable being Paul's proxy in U2.

By that time, too, the others' Christianity had lost its beetle-eating fanaticism and Adam found himself moving closer to their spiritual beliefs. In the internal war between Adam the hobnobbing businessman and Adam the artist, the artist won.

When they made their pact in 1981, Adam says, "Paul and I still felt that we had a role within the music, whether or not U2 succeeded. In those days we hunted as a pair. Paul and I would do the record company things, we'd do the journalist things, we'd be visible, we'd have a profile, and we'd know what was going on. After the *Unforgettable Fire* tour I realized that my position was actually becoming destructive to the band's position. I felt Paul's wishes for what the band should do were not necessarily the best decisions *artistically* and that the band needed my support artistically, and by then spiritually as well. Certainly I needed to listen to that voice more, and I felt at that stage I had more in common with the three guys. Whereas up to that point I felt I had a bit more in common with Paul, background-wise and the way I saw things business-wise.

"So that did change and that was tough on all of us. It was certainly tough on me and Paul to separate that way. But we'd started to move in different worlds. His world was much more grown-up schmoozing, much more dinner parties and lunches. I couldn't do those things and contribute to the band, 'cause so much of those things are about telling stories *against* the band, really. They're about stories people in bands shouldn't say about each other. Maybe managers can say, 'Well, of course, the reason Bono wrote that lyric was such and such . . .' That's not something I could do by then. I had to protect the mystery of the band, and I couldn't do that as Paul's sidekick.

"I don't feel Paul protects Bono's persona. He's too willing to expose Bono as a nice guy and oversimplify him. You don't see that happen with Prince. Paul likes to believe it's all done with mirrors and wires. He doesn't like to acknowledge the hard work. Instead of saying, 'That was hard, Bono had to put himself through hoops to get it,' he'll say, 'Oh, Bono just wanted to look cool.' By saying that, he takes away from Bono. It implies he *needs* this stuff to look cool."

Then, unknowingly echoing Paul saying "It's not up to him [Adam] anymore," Adam says, "We still, amongst ourselves, have to readdress Paul's situation."

Maybe all business is ultimately personal. When Paul points a finger at Adam now, it's not just a maneuver to keep the band from aligning against him. There's a lot of emotional history behind it. This is not a crafty businessman trying to play four boys against each other; these are five smart men who know the game and each other very well. Though he's less likely to expound on it than, say, Bono, Paul McGuinness got into this world as much from emotion and personal belief as the band did, and he still responds to suggestions that push him away from the band in a very personal way. Of course, he may mask his emotional response in an argument that sounds like cold business strategy. In his ability to intellectually rationalize a gut reaction he is like Bono. And of course, in that he would rather swallow snot than let on how much such slights hurt him he is very much like Adam.

Adam says, "I think Paul suffered from exactly the same thing we had all suffered from [while making *Achtung Baby*]. He wasn't around for the recording of the album. He doesn't really know what went on with that record. Up till that point, when we were struggling with *Joshua Tree* and with the movie, he had been pretty much a fifth member in the shit that he had to take." Adam adds sarcastically, "*Everyone's* a fifth member when it's going well. After that point he kind of left the cosmos. He'd been to Hollywood. He came back to Dublin as an impressario, he was moving in political circles, he was getting involved in setting up a TV station. He was in mogul mode. He's come back from that, but I don't think he's back in the studio with us or on tour with us. He still has a good life in my opinion and hasn't had to take the knocks and scrapes that we've all taken over the last three years. In my opinion."

But, I ask, is that not the natural way it should be between a manager and a grown-up, experienced band? Maybe the early relationship was unnaturally close.

"Yeah, it is fair enough," Adam says sharply. "I'm not saying that it is healthy for him to be back in that fifth member role. You asked me to describe what happened to the relationship; I think that is what the relationship has become. I think we instruct him far more now and rely less on his ability to have a creative vision of the music."

Paul says, "I've always rejected that moniker: *fifth member of the band.* I'm not a member of the band! There are four members of the band and what I do is something completely different. I'm obviously very proud of what I do, but it's not the same as what they do."

Paul's perspective is probably that he is a manager who commissions 20 percent of the income of each of his four clients. How those four clients divide up the 80 percent they retain is entirely up to them—but if they work out a deal that pays some of them less than others it should have no bearing on his commission. Larry and Adam might argue that very few bands in U2's superstar position continue to pay their manager 20 percent. Paul has kept that deal because he was there for them in the beginning, and because he has passed on the chance to augment his earnings by taking on other clients—but if Larry and Adam are willing to recut the pie, Paul must be willing to do the same.

Adam and Larry have allowed that they would, in principle, accept something like a 30/20/30/20 split of the band's money (after Paul's commission) for *Achtung Baby* and *Zooropa*, rather than the usual 25 percent each. This in acknowledgment of Edge and Bono's greater contributions to those two records. Next album they will sit down and cut the pie again, reflecting how hard each of them works. The four members of U2 have appointed the great and powerful Ossie to judge how much of *Achtung Baby* and *Zooropa* each of them should take home. At this point U2 do not themselves know exactly what the split will be.

During the long flight from New Zealand to Japan I go over and sit down next to Edge and say, "Suppose a year from now the band regroups and Adam or Paul or both of them are not there. Can you see U2 going on?"

"Yes," he says immediately. "But not in the same way. I think the members of the band are creative people and I can't see us stifling or stopping that creative instinct, so I would say that we would continue in some way. But I don't think it could be the same and I don't think we would just carry on as if nothing had happened. There would have to be some kind of difference of approach. But yeah, we would carry on."

Edge's face softens and he adds, "It's not *likely*, but I guess anything's possible." Edge figures Adam's dive in Australia was "a kind of emotional convulsion," a signal to the band that he needed a hand. "We're still *friends*," Edge says. "This is not a band like most bands. We're still very close. We still care a lot about each other. There is a lot of support for each other and a lot of leeway and a lot of understanding. I like to think that it would be difficult for one of us to really get off the wall and really go out there without the others realizing it and being there to do something about it. Obviously it's not up to me what the other guys do in their private time, but I think you can make it hard for somebody to fuck themselves up, you can be the squeaky wheel, you can just tell him the truth, which a lot of people never get."

I remind Edge of Larry's perspective about the crisis that shook U2 during the making of *Achtung Baby*. He said that ultimately the four of them realized that the band grew out of friendship, and the friendships were more important than the band.

"If we'd accepted that the friendships were over," Edge says, "I think it probably would have been just a matter of time until the band came to an end. It would have taken all the fun out of it and the strength, the belief. You can't do something like this for two years unless you have a very strong feeling about what you're trying to do and that everyone's along for the ride. So much of what we do is trust, you know. The difference between this band and what happened with the Beatles and the Stones is that for whatever reason we never got to that point where everyone is trying to protect themselves and their position in a kind of paranoid way, because they feel threatened that someone else is going to steal their credit or their glory or their royalties or whatever it is.

"Because there is a lot of trust we can kind of relax on certain levels. Like, I feel okay about letting things go. If I've put together a piece of music from scratch and done all the writing, I'm not looking for every last bit of credit, because I feel there's a sort of understanding and there's a balance there. It irons out a lot of those problems. You don't get that paranoid, protectionist, itchy competitiveness if you are all friends. It's when the friendships start to go and the trust goes that all that stuff happens. I think it's the beginning of the end of bands, and that's never kicked in with U2. It probably came closest to it around that time, but we managed to stop it.

"I'm not saying it could never happen. It's very hard to deal with things like credit sometimes. It's sort of tough being the guitar player in a band with a singer like Bono, because he's such a media magnet that if you didn't have a lot of confidence about what you were about and where you stood within the group, you might start to feel, *Hold on a second—I'm being overlooked here.* Ultimately I don't have a problem. I know that being the guitar player is an important thing. It's never ever going to get the same credit or response that being the singer is. That's just the way life is. I'm cool about that.

"We never wanted to get into a situation where we were crediting every little thing," Edge says, " 'cause that just becomes laborious and, again, causes a lot of friction and misunderstanding and confusion. This production credit (on *Zooropa*) was some way of describing my role in the process, which varies over a huge range of different responsibilities from lyric editor to Bono—sitting there and bouncing ideas off him and vice versa—to taking responsibility for developing a lot of the music, either from scratch or taking what are essentially jams and trying to put them into some shape or form—to just the general production work which tends to mean just a lot more *worrying* than anyone else. But some of what I do really isn't production, some of what I do is just being a songwriter. It has not seemed like an appropriate thing to start apportioning credit in that area, 'cause it does vary a lot. Some songs I take most of the musical responsibility for, some I'm just one of the members of the band. It's not the same as the lyrics, where basically Bono takes on the responsibility and writes ninety-eight percent of the lyrics and you can clearly say that's the way it happens. It's not an option to carve it all up. In order for this thing to survive you've got to have that trust."

Preserving that trust is important to everyone in U2. Bono has been talking excitedly to all the inner circle about what a blessing it was that in Sydney, Adam had to face his devil in such a dramatic way, has admitted his problem and resolved to stop drinking. Bono's position is, the storm is over.

"Adam's back!" Bono announced more than once in the last week. "It's great! Some artists become dull when they stop drinking or drugging, but Adam's not one of them. He's his old self. He loses none of his rubber band shooting, water gun squirting, public disrobing spirit when he doesn't drink."

And maybe it is as simple—though surely not as easy—as that. Maybe what I've witnessed is an extreme example of how the immediate family of U2 lets its members stray so far and then yanks them back. In fact, I wonder if even the threats of reduced equity are really tough-love discipline, a way to say to any of the five, "There's a price for letting the family down." My analysis is interupted by a sharp pain across my right ear. I turn and look over the airplane seat and see a laughing Adam Clayton several rows back, shooting rubber bands.

53

Tokyo Overload

---

discovering japan/ kato's rebellion/ investigating the hostess trade/ larry encounters an ardent fan/ snake-handling is not an inherited skill/ sunrise like a nosebleed

T HE PACIFIC is a big ocean, especially when you're stuck on a plane full of sleep-deprived roadhogs beginning the last fevered week of their two year marathon. How long have we been in the air from Auckland to Tokyo? Ten hours? Twelve hours? Long enough to get on a flight in New York, go to Ireland, do a jig, and get back to New York. Too long. I have been reading this week's *Time* magazine cover story about the emergence of the Pacific Rim as the future of global commerce, culture, and civilization. (On the flight from Australia to New Zealand last week we were treated to *Rising Sun,* in which Sean Connery outwits the unscrupulous Japanese businessmen who are taking over the world. Stage manager Tim Buckley cried, "This isn't in-flight entertainment. It's a pre-Tokyo instructional video!")

At dinnertime all the Zoo people are herded out of the plane at the Narita airport like dispeptic bison and steered through Japanese customs. There is confusion, arguments with the passport officials, changing of lanes and direction. As U2 pass through the processing and head toward their waiting cars flashbulbs pop, TV cameras hum, and screaming Asian kids run around them like moons in orbit yelling, "Adam! Adam!"

On the long ride to Tokyo everyone is jet-lagged and shell-shocked and the landscape—initially as mundane as any suburban ring road—turns surreal. The first strange sight is the magic castle tower of Japanese Disneyland, but it's once we start negotiating the on-ramps, off-ramps and elevated highways of downtown Tokyo that things become completely dislocated. See, the science fiction film *Blade Runner* is not a projection of the future, it is a documentary about Tokyo today. I live in New York City, my office is in a skyscraper overlooking Times Square —I should not be shook by a big neon-lit urban center. But driving exhausted through Tokyo, I feel like Jethro Bodine on Krypton. There seem to be buildings made of Lego next to structures made of tinfoil next to gigantic, shining sushi knives. And whenever we come to a place in the highway where we can see any sort of horizon, the black silouettes in the distance have blinking red-lit roofs, like Christmas decorations. Like, come to think of it, the Zoo TV stage.

Electric signs cover whole sides of skyscrapers; they seem to go upward forever, blinking and swirling the whole way. In this culture we are illiterate; the symbols and slogans flashing on and off are meaningless shapes to us. The buildings our cars slip between are not just enormous, they are packed together. Instead of celebrating height, as the freestanding towers of Manhattan or Chicago do, they exude density. In New York the skyscrapers have enough space between them that their effect is to make you say, "Wow, are they big!" In Tokyo the jam-packed buildings make you say, "Wow, am I small!"

As we circle down a highway ramp toward our hotel Bono points out a building that looks like a concrete beehive. Each egg-shaped bump, he says, is a little sleeping pod with a porthole. Japanese businessmen rent them as places to crash in the city, when they work too late to make the journey home. They are like the cabins on a submarine. They are like the sleep "coffins" in William Gibson's *Neuromancer*. Remember the wild side of Gibson's Tokyo is called Night City, a hot-wired version of Nighttown.

Eventually we arrive at a Four Seasons Hotel in a Japanese garden and collect our room keys. Everyone who wants to go out is to meet up in the hospitality suite in an hour. I get to my room, drop my suitcase, and head to the can. I am impressed to discover a toilet worthy of Darth Vader in a small water closet off the bathroom. It has an armrest on which are knobs, buttons, and gauges with Japanese labels. The only English instruction is hanging on the wall: "Important—do not try to operate this automatic toilet without first being seated." (It is hung where you would not normally see it unless seated already.) Well, that convinces me not to put my butt anywhere near that toilet seat until I figure out what this contraption can do. What if there's an enema button? Or a suction switch? I lift the seat, lean forward cautiously and

—ready to jump back if something explodes—hit the nearest knob. A stream of water shoots out of the bowl and squirts me in the eye. I have found the "bidet" option. I clean up and go to meet the others. Four of my fellow travelers admit to having done exactly the same thing. Perhaps our Japanese hosts are watching us through one-way mirrors, laughing.

While people gather in the hospitality room the TV is switched to CNN—the one constant in all our travels—and the news summary adds to the general feeling of psychic overload. The little kidnapped girl Winona Ryder was searching for has been found dead. The peace movement in Northern Ireland may have been derailed by the killing of a group of Catholics in Belfast. Princess Diana, distraught at her harassment by the gossip press, tearfully announces she is stepping down from public life. The Serb shelling of a Sarajevo market results in heavy casualties. President Clinton is being assailed by American Muslims for meeting with Salman Rushdie. Michael Jackson, responding to a plea from his mother, says he will return to the U.S. to fight the charges being leveled against him. The neo-Nazis who bombed the homes of the Turks in Germany have been sentenced to life in prison. And the builders of the Channel Tunnel that will connect Britain to Europe have officially handed over the keys to the operators. Paul McGuinness arrives with the news that U2's "Lemon" is number one on the dance charts. It doesn't seem like such a big deal.

Everyone is tired. Everyone's nerves are on edge. Everyone wants to cram as much as possible into the last week of the tour. Tonight the Zoo zeitgeist is zeroing in on a fish market/restaurant in Kabuki-cho that Regine Moylett's brother—who lives in Tokyo—recommended. Our Japanese guides and drivers do not think it is a good idea, that is a bad part of town, but Bono insists and off everyone goes, with a carload of twitchy local "guides" following behind. They have been provided by the concert promoter, and U2 are sure they are not here to serve the band as much as to control them.

Rolling though Tokyo, Bono says quietly, "The strangest thing has happened. I really miss my dog. That's never happened to me before. You know, on a long tour you do hear people saying they miss their pets. I never have. But last night I started really missing my dog. It's very odd." He stares for a long time out the car window and then says, distracted but dead serious, " 'Cause I don't *have* a dog."

The sulking drivers find the fish market. Edge and Morleigh are here with some Japanese friends of hers. Adam and Sebastian pull up with McGuinness and Sheila. The carload of local minders screeches up and they tumble out like the Keystone Kops. Bono is appalled to see that they are all wearing dark plastic rain macs with "U2" emblazoned in huge white letters on the back. He makes them take them off.

The party makes their way up to the room above the fish market where there are tables set up for dinner. I tell Bono that our pal Hal Willner is in town working on an album for a Japanese record company. I called his hotel and he said he'd be up for going out at around midnight. Bono says great, it's almost twelve now. He tells Eric to go collect Hal and bring him here. Eric objects. He is here to provide security—he does not want to leave Bono's body unguarded in a tough part of town while he runs errands. Bono makes it an order. Eric makes him promise not to leave till he gets back.

Within the hour Eric delivers Hal, as rumpled and heavy-eyed in Tokyo as he is at home in New York. When he's not producing eccentric records Hal has a day job supplying the background music on the TV show *Saturday Night Live.* He does not want to lose that gig, so he contorts his recording schedule around the show. That means that he left New York for Tokyo after *SNL* finished on Sunday morning. He will work in Tokyo for three days without sleep, get on a plane out of Japan on Wednesday, get off the plane in New York on Thursday, and head straight back to the TV studio for the intensive work up till Saturday night. Hal's mental condition is right on U2's whacked-out wavelength!

Finishing a fine fish meal, Bono decides it's time to investigate some of the hoochie-coochie parlors up and down the street outside. You don't have to speak Japanese to get the message from the flashing photos of strippers and the friendly goons in the doorways waving invitingly. Adam, Sebastian, and McGuinness head across the street to check out the first one and as soon as our driver sees that Bono, Eric, Hal, and I intend to do the same he goes nuts, insisting that we have to let him drive us there. Bono says, no, no—we're just going across the road, but the driver says in half-English, half-Japanese something about him getting in big trouble if we walk over, please get in and let him drive us.

We shrug and get in the car and he hits the gas like Steve McQueen and starts barreling across town in the other direction, chattering into his car phone the whole way. "No, no!" Bono yells. "We want to go to the places back there! We left our friends behind! Turn around!" But there's no stopping Kato. It is a quick lesson to jettison Western notions about the employer/employee relationship. Around here everyone plays by the house rules, and the house rules outrank free will.

Kato drops us in front of a club called "One-Eyed Jacks," named after the whorehouse in *Twin Peaks*. Bono hesitates before going down the stairs. "One drink," he says. "Then we go back to find the others." He plunges down a long flight of steps and tries to turn right into a room where women in bondage gear are gyrating on a raised stage, only to run into the stiff arm of a big bouncer who directs him to turn around and head through a different door. He does, coming into a room filled with gambling tables, chips, dice, and money. That's it, we're out of here. As he starts up the stairs the same bouncer grabs him and says, okay, okay, you can go watch the girls.

The girls are dancing on a raised platform with seats around it, in which Asian businessmen sit leering and lapping it up. We settle down at the far end of the great oval, in front of the bar. Most of these young women are Caucasian. That must be why the driver brought us here. We get our drinks and several pretty girls in lingerie who I at first mistake for barmaids come over and start asking questions, making small talk, and blocking our view of the show. They are hostesses, and they a big part of the attraction of these places. Their job is to chat up the men and hustle drinks. Some might be prostitutes, but not all. Their assignment is to provide the company of pretty women for the men who patronize these joints. Bono and I pump them for stories while Hal sits with his elbow on the bar and his head in his hand, gazing off into space, and Eric stands behind us, watching for trouble.

A blond American who says she's twenty but looks seventeen explains that many of the girls are Australian, a good number American, some European. They come to Tokyo with the promise of modeling jobs ("The elephant man could model in Japan," an Asian girl laughs), but when those jobs don't pay enough to survive in this overpriced city, they fall into hostessing. Some fall farther. A girl from New Zealand points to the Asian businessmen ogling the go-go girls and says, "We give 'em *ego* massages!"

A redheaded hostess who looks like Ann-Margret starts doing the watusi like this is *Viva Las Vegas* and Bono is Elvis. She pushes her big breasts under his nose and shakes, making it hard for Bono to keep up his cross-examination of the others. She is the only one to whom he is not polite, with whom he refuses to talk, but that just makes her push harder. So he says it's time to go. The blond American girl says she gets off work at 4, and she and the others will be going to an after-hours place. She gives us the name. We say we might see her there and head back to the car.

After some car phone calls and walkie-talkie talk we find Edge and Morleigh and her friends in a quiet bar not far away, and join them for a civilized drink. Edge says that David Morales, who did the dance remix of "Lemon," is deejaying at a disco called Yello tonight and he and Morleigh are heading there. U2 has never met Morales. Bono tells Edge, "We'll meet you there in a while," and heads back outside.

Crossing town we pass through an area where lights are flashing, people are jumping, cars are swerving, and there's U2 security chief Jerry Mele shouting and laughing on the sidewalk as he heads back into a disco. Jerry, Larry Mullen, and David Guyer are hours deep into a tour of hidden Tokyo. They told their driver not to take them to any tourist places, "Take us where you'd go!" When the driver resisted they threatened to lock him in the trunk and drive the car themselves. Having his guests' intentions explained to him so clearly helped the Japanese guide's sense of direction considerably. Larry and the security boys have seen things that should turn an infidel to stone. Now, stoked up on a high-grade combination of sake, beer, and vodka, the three horsemen are swimming in Asian beauties. When Larry goes to the john a sexy woman jumps in after him, locks the door, and insists he make love to her right now. The ever-continent Larry squeezes around her, unlocks the hatch, and stumbles back into the club, with her shouting after him, "I always get what I want!"

Somehow Bono, Eric, and I find our way to the disco where David Morales is deejaying, where a lot of people from the tour have landed. "Lemon" is playing. Instead of dancing free-form with individual partners all over the room, almost all of the Japanese kids are dancing in neat rows, facing the deejay—like old ladies at a wedding doing the Hully Gully. It looks like a morning calisthenics class.

Bono is shown to a private VIP room upstairs where Edge and Paul McGuinness are deep in their cups and a nostalgic reverie about the early days of U2. They say that they used to have a song called "Pete the Chop" (no relation to the later track, "Whatever Happened to Pete the

Chop?") that was their surefire hit single. They were holding it in reserve in case U2 ever got into real trouble and it looked like they might be dropped. They never had to use it. They marvel at how much freedom the band was given by Island Records, right from the start, and lament for the ten thousanth time not listening to the label about that cover photo on *October*. "What a horrible picture! Adam's coat! Arrrggghhh!"

Bono and Edge decide they better go down and meet Morales. They pass through the crowd and climb up into the deejay booth, where Edge becomes so fascinated with the mixing and scratching skills on display that he decides he is going to stand behind Morales for a couple of hours and study. Morleigh thinks that's a good reason for her to head back to the hotel, and Edge asks Scott, his security man, to take her. The bodyguards hate it when the band members order them to leave them unprotected in weird places, but Edge insists.

On the way up the stairs that lead out of the club I bump into Fightin' Fintan Fitzgerald, who has taken on the half-cracked late-night demeanor that earned him his nickname. The most radical barber since Sweeney Todd, Fintan decides that this is the moment to lecture Hal and me on our haircuts. I suggest he can regain control of himself by calmly singing the entire *Bob Dylan at Budakon* album with me, starting with "Mr. Tambourine Man."

Fintan reels back and shouts, "You old hippies! Bob Dylan is dead! Don't you get it, you hippies? Bob Dylan is dead!" Fintan's eyes seem to be glowing. (I figure this is the sort of detail that will cause some people to disbelieve my reporting, so I grab Fintan by the shoulders and study his eyes. They *are* glowing—luminous purple. It seems to be a strange reaction of his pupils to the ultaviolet lights in this hallway.) I catch up to Bono and Eric on the stairs and say, "Boy, Fintan's wild tonight."

"Fintan's an asshole!" Eric shouts. "His behavior puts himself and other people in danger and I'm sick of it!" The security man is at the end of his U2-frayed rope. It is hard enough to protect Bono when he keeps wanting to go to the most dangerous places, run through doors marked Do Not Enter, and ignore the warnings of the local guides provided to protect him. But what makes it even worse are trouble-lovers like Fintan providing Bono with companionship and encouragement as he goes. Eric has been on edge ever since Bono sent him away from his post tonight to collect Hal. He says he's sorry, he didn't mean to be rude, but I get the message.

That doesn't mean I won't ignore it, though! I've heard stories from U2 of the first time they came to Tokyo, ten years ago, and of a hotel bar that was the hangout for Western fashion models in Japan. It was the first place where U2 was assaulted by throngs of beautiful women who wanted to have sex with them, and it blew their born-again minds. I tell Bono it sounds like a place we ought to check out—for historical research—and he says he's heard it's fallen out of favor. Nonetheless, he agrees to stop there for one drink. It's sad, though. The old casbah is dead and nearly deserted. The only people in the once-hopping saloon are a couple of tired-looking middle-aged women and Terence Trent D'Arby.

So we continue to search for the after-hours place our new hostess friends from One-Eyed Jacks told us about. It's well after 4 A.M. now, the hostesses should be there. We keep stopping revelers on the streets and following their cross-lingual directions until one punk kid points to a door down an alley and says, *that's it.* We ride a warehouse elevator as the sound of music gets louder, the doors open, and people are partying like a Prince video. The smell of poppers is in the air, motivating women who have worked (and drunk) all night to keep jumping. The women from One-Eyed Jacks greet Bono and his pals like lost brothers and the management clears a table for us (except for one unconscious Japanese man who they don't want to move).

It's a small room with a large bar in the middle and booths along the walls. The small dance floor is crowded. Inevitably, they put on a U2 tape. The Ann-Margret girl from One-Eyed Jack's sees Bono and follows him around the room, bumbing her breasts into him until he finally tells her to go away, he's not interested. She reels back, rejected, and shouts in my ear, "I love that man! And tonight he broke my heart!" I point to Eric, standing guard by the door, and say, "You see that good-looking guy over there? Did you see *The Bodyguard?* Kevin Costner based his character on him. That's who you want to meet."

The blond American hostess joins me and I ask her to tell me the stories of all the people in the room. She laughs and starts reeling them off. She points to a sexy woman in a minidress playing with the necktie of a Westerner. "That girl there? The blonde making out with the American businessman? She just met him tonight, but she's gonna go home with him, because she misses the States and she's lonely in Tokyo and she hasn't been with anybody in a few weeks.

"That good-looking Kiwi guy is a gigolo. He brings home a different woman every night. One local Japanese lady bought him a motor bike. Not because of his smile—let me put it that way.

"That really pretty girl had a sister who was two years older and even more beautiful. She's spent her whole life competing with her. Every guy her sister slept with, she had to sleep with too. Her sister became a model, so she came here to model. She never catches up."

She points out a handsome man who looks half Asian and half Caucasian. "He's a really good guy, he lives downstairs from me, but he has to sleep with every woman he meets. Now he's finally met a woman he really loves and he's being faithful to her, but the bad news is that she has a husband.

"See that older woman over there? She's been a hostess for *seven years!* Is that unbelievable? Can you imagine somebody that old still hostessing?" She pauses in amazement and explains, "She's *twenty-five!*"

Another hostess joins us and listens in on the tutorial. "You have to totally depersonalize the men," the American girl says. "Almost laugh at them."

Her friend adds, "You have to understand, for Japanese men hostessing is the fast-food version of geisha."

The people on the dance floor are hopping to "Who's Gonna Ride Your Wild Horses." I go back to the table and sit down next to Bono. A hard-looking character comes over with a wide smile and makes a big deal out of putting two glasses filled with some radioactive orange liquid down in front of us. He makes it clear that this is an honor and a treat and we must drink up. Bono and Eric share a glance and Eric (switching to wine-tasting duties) smells the drink, dips his pinkie into and tastes a drop, and then hands it back to Bono, whispering in his ear as he does. A moment later Bono raises the empty glass in salute to the man who bought it for us. Well, I figure, when in Gomorrah . . . and I gulp mine down and raise my glass to the guy too.

"Did you drink that?" Bono asks, appalled.

"Sure," I say. "Eric thought it was safe for you to drink, right?"

"He did not!" Bono says. "He said it was spiked with something. I dumped it under the table and then held up the empty glass!"

"Oh, hell," I say. "Like Tokyo wasn't psychedelic enough already."

When the room finally shuts down, just before dawn, the girls say there's another bar that will still be serving. It's called Juice. We go out to the alley, where I try to decide if my drink was drugged: I look around and see an electric city, giant faces on video screens across the sides of buildings, pinwheel lights rolling up and down spires into the sky. Nope, that's Tokyo. While Eric is trying to organize the car, Bono leads a jailbreak. Eric looks up to realize that the worst has happened—his charge is gone. As Bono legs it around the corner Eric's voice is shouting into a car phone: "Jerry! Number one has run off down the street! Number one has run off down the street!"

Bono is never unguarded for long, though. A few alleys away he is recognized by some Japanese party girls. "Where are you going?" they ask the gaijin rock star.

"I dunno," Bono says. "Where are *you* guys goin'?"

They offer to lead the way to Juice. Juice is a weird white room with tables shaped like teeth. It's like stepping inside a denture. There are only two customers in the joint: a Japanese woman engaged in an intense discussion about the meaning of love with an Irishman. Why . . . it's philosophizin' Fintan Fitzgerald.

"Oh, hi," Fintan says in greeting. "How did you guys find this place?" This really is Eric's worst nightmare: Bono unguarded and on the loose with Fintan in charge of directions. When Juice locks up, around 7:30 A.M., the women ask if Bono and his friends want to continue the party at their place. It's morning now, everything is foggy, all sense of direction has long departed. Tokyo looked like *Blade Runner* from the cars, but up close it is clearly *Blue Velvet*. Once home, the girls—who seem to have been on speed to start with—start smoking heroin to calm down. Bono waves it away, crawls onto a mat, and closes his eyes. One of the girls offers to have sex with him. He says no, thank you, and loses consciousness.

He wakes at nine to the alarming sensation of something slippery crawling up his leg. *He told her he wasn't interested!* He looks down and comes eyeball to eyeball with a python that is slithering across his belly. He is in a hallucinatory dream state, more confused than scared.

He stares at the snake. He does not move. Then he hears Fintan's voice: "My mudda worked in a zoo. I'm used to snakes." And with that Fintan scoops the python off Bono and wraps it around his own neck. Plucky though he may be, U2's haberdasher is no snake-charmer. The python unleashes a cascade of piss and shit all over Fintan. The Japanese party girl who owns the python screams as a startled Fintan does a snake-dance Salome never imagined.

Bono regains his senses enough to figure out that this place is trouble, but it is Fintan—the much-maligned Fintan—who steps in as security. He hoists Bono up by the arm and says, "Let's get out of here." Fintan organizes the company's escape, secures a taxi, and finds the Four Seasons' Hotel. Bono buys breakfast and broods. This has got to stop, this band has got to get off the road and back home. "I know I've pushed it too far," he mumbles. "I could have been arrested surrounded by prostitutes and heroin in some Yakuza crack den. Okay, I wasn't taking part—but try telling that to the judge!"

I don't think Bono's ever written a lyric he can't occupy, from the boy watching the hearse come for his mother in "Tomorrow" to the power-hungry hustler in "Desire," but right now I am certain that his most-perfect self-portrait is the holy fool in "Tryin' to Throw Your Arms Around the World," the guy who just cannot give up on the night and go home until the night has more than given up on him. Bono has finally reached the far end of Nighttown, and he's ready to crawl back to Ali and his house by the sea.

"I know it's right, though," Bono says of his spiritual ledge-walking. "It's Ecclesiastes."

At 1 P.M. Larry strolls down the corridor looking for breakfast, wearing just a white hotel bathrobe and calling, "GOOD MORNING, VIETNAM!" He joins the four security men who are drinking coffee and checking off last night's log-in sheet. Adam returned to the hotel at 3 A.M., Edge at 5, Larry at 6, Bono at 10. The Final Week Iron Man Nightlife Marathon is under way.

54

Judo

U2 stops the traffic/ shootout in the noodle factory/ electric stained glass windows/ making the yakuza blink/ bono in the city of the dead/ hal willner goes disco

BONO, EDGE, AND PAUL spend one midweek afternoon Christmas shopping for their kids in the toy stores of Tokyo. I'll tell you, all the elves at the North Pole could not keep these endless shelves stocked. For a non-Christian nation Japan seems to have embraced the extrareligious iconography of Christmas with an enthusiasm worthy of Toys-R-Us. There are great blinking electric Santas and luminous neon reindeer flashing and glowing across the skyline and phonetic recreations of Western holiday carols blaring out of the speakers of every store. Forgive me for wading into the cesspool of ethnic stereotypes, but until you've been subjected to a tinny version of "Lockin' alound the Clistmas Tlee" while trying to compute in your head the price of Japanese Barbie dolls, you don't know what *yellow peril* means.

Edge's enthusiasm for trying out all the laser target pistols makes me doubt he's buying them for his daughters. Once you get into one of the toy stores you could stay for a year, but trying to get away is tough. The problem is, again, the Goebbels-like enthusiasm for order and routine that guides U2's Japanese guides and chauffeurs. Today's party has two cars, two drivers, and plans to shop for a while, go to a particular restaurant for lunch (*Spaghetti* is the cuisine craze sweeping Tokyo, by the way. Sick of noodles—try something continental!), and then return to the hotel. Bono is considering taking one of the cars back to the hotel early and leaving the rest of us the other. So when we climb in for what was going to be a fairly long trip to the international house of spaghetti, he tells the driver there's been a change of plans. Forget going across town to the restaurant of record; we will just grab a quick bite anywhere close by, and then Bono will take one of the cars back to the Four Seasons.

OH, NO, HE WON'T. Our driver blows a mental carburetor at this deviation from the schedule. He stops the car sideways in the middle of the traffic and jumps out, squawking simultaneously into his portable phone to his unseen master and to the driver of the other car, who has also bailed out and is equally beside himself that the natural order has been breached. Bono, not known for his ability to stay out of any argument, jumps out and jumps in, throwing a multilingual Tower of Babel patina onto the proceedings, while gridlocked motorists fume and honk in the cars around us. . . . Hey—I just realized something spooky; they're actually not honking. Far more horrible, they're getting out and joining in the jittery lamentations.

The Buddha alone knows what mesh of strings has to be pulled or what the long-term repercussions for the economic stability of the West might be, but finally Bono is allowed to change his plans and take a car home ahead of schedule.

On the way back to the hotel an icy winter rain begins. The funny thing is that in spite of all the hassles, Bono is falling in love with Tokyo. He thinks it's the epitome of the ideas behind Zoo TV: embracing the contradictions between the hidden side, the nightlife, the depth of respect for ancient traditions and rituals, and the amazing twenty first-century technology. These people splash electricity across their buildings like paint. Bono's pet phrase for the Zoo philosophy has been judo, jujitsu: using your enemy's strength against him. It's how the band reconciled their embrace of all the tools—commercialism, glamour, stardom, ostentation—to which U2's music and beliefs had previously stood in opposition. Art students might suss this stuff by sophomore year, but U2 are artists by instinct, not training. It took them a decade to figure it out.

U2's next job is a photo shoot with Anton, who flew in last night, just in time for Bono to take him back to Kabuki-cho. After walking around scouting locations for a while, Bono, Adam, Eric, and Anton picked a noodle joint at random, walked up the stairs, sat down and ordered dinner. Halfway through the meal sirens, screaming, and gunshots erupted outside. The police, in full combat gear, were raiding the noodle place next door, apparently a front for some illegal activity.

"That wasn't an arrest!" Bono said as the cops withdrew. "That was an army invading a foreign country!"

Today's photo shoot begins in the same tough area, with Bono posing as if breaking into one of five black Bentleys lined up, he insists, since their Yakuza owners were dragged off by the cops last night. Bono may be getting ahead of the fact checkers here, but he certainly is succeeding in making U2's latest translator—code name: Oddjob— nervous. While Anton's shooting, another limousine comes down the narrow street and starts trying to nudge us out of the way. Black hat bodyguard David Guyer responds by violently smashing the umbrella he's holding over the car and shouting, "How do you like that, asshole?" Oddjob's ready to keel over. A couple of slick, mean-looking Japanese men lean out the window and lock eyes with David, shouting threats. He stands there silently daring them. They blink and drive away.

Eric, the white hat, wishes David wouldn't do that. David's a world-class martial artist, but Eric thinks he still has to internalize the turn-the-other cheek teachings of spiritual master Jerry Mele.

It's a little after four, getting dark. The rain has let up and all the neon is coming on. Bono is seduced and excited by what he calls the "fireworks in the architecture." He pulls me aside in front of a porno parlor and says mischievously, "Bill, I'm having an epiphany. We must make the next album here! At the end of a tour you get clues what the next stage should be." I have to swear not to tell Edge or Adam, who if they got wind of this suggestion at this point would hang Bono from a lamppost while shouting *Sic semper tyrannis.* While those two intellectuals are distracted, Bono puts the bug in Larry's ear and Larry says okay. It's like Bosnia all over again!

U2 pose for photographs in front of the symbols decorating the front of a sex shop. "All this beautiful script," Bono says with a sigh, "and it probably says 'Pussy.'" The owner of the porno shop comes screaming out the door, shooing Anton and his camera away while U2 laugh and Oddjob, the only one who can understand what the angry man is shouting, turns white and says we must get away fast, Yakuza protection!

As we walk through rows of flashing electric arcades and massage parlors and fast-food machines and sex shows, Bono says, "Well, you asked for it. Here it is. U2 at the end of the world."

We hike through the hallucinogenic landscape as the neighborhood gets nicer and we finally come out into a great park surrounded by flashing skyscrapers that makes Times Square look puny by comparison. It is Alta Square, named—as far as I can understand from our guide— for a TV and recording studio that overlooks it. That sounds backward to me—surely the studio was named for the area, not the other way around; but then I suppose that if Times Square and Herald Square are named for the newspapers published there, shouldn't that tradition be extended to newer media too?

"I expected a lot," Bono says, staring at the neon explosions, "but I didn't expect this!" Beneath the lights, in the park in the middle of the square, there is what seems to be a big communist rally going on. It's a photo-op for sure, and Anton shoots U2 walking back and forth with the red banners and podium-pounding speakers in the background.

"They have no religion in Tokyo," Bono says, waving an arm at the electric signs. "Only the oldest go to church. So these are their stained glass windows."

A little, round-faced Japanese fellow keeps genuflecting to U2, saying "Bono, Bono! Edge, Edge! Bono, Bono!" Anton's next location is the Shinjuku train station. There is a wave of screaming from teenage girls as U2 plows into the rush-hour mob. It really is chaos. Anton shoots the band walking through the station, waiting on the platforms, and even stepping onto a train. (When the doors close and the train pulls out, Anton is left behind. Needless to say we jump out at the next station, run over to the opposite track, and are very grateful when we land back where we started.) Bono maneuvers his way through the mob on the platform, calling, "Purgatory now boarding on Track 7! Last train for Hades—Track 2!

"What I'll remember is voices," Bono shouts over the nonstop loudspeaker making train announcements. "The voices of the traffic over the voices of the loudspeakers over the voices of the carols! All of these voices on top of each other."

Off the train, commuters converge on Bono, with pens and paper and cameras. One guy yanks off his Walkman and places it on Bono's head. It's playing "Even Better than the Real Thing." Larry stands off to one side laughing at Bono, the international diplomat, bowing and shaking hands, bowing and shaking hands. Anton, well over six feet tall, wades in above the little rock stars and their little fans, snapping away.

As we leave the station Bono says, "Mind you, it's a very advanced civilization where people wear face masks when they have colds." That's true, but in an island country so desperately overcrowded it is probably also a tough necessity. Just as the strict adherence to order and structure and rules is. There're just too many people to accommodate the sort of independence and, I guess, self-centeredness that Westerners assume to be a birthright. Lately it seems as if every week another new disease, or a new vaccine-resistant strain of an old one, pops up in another urban area. That's the end of the world I'm worried about: one in which we cram so many humans into the subway that nature decides to thin us out like a fat herd in tick season.

Riding back to the hotel Bono says that the three most amazing cities he's been to are Tokyo, Mexico City, and Cairo. I ask why Cairo and he tells me about the City of the Dead, an area where the people live in open graves. He and Ali found it during their journeys in Africa. The impoverished citizens of the City of the Dead live in pits where, years ago, wealthy Egyptians were buried in graves like cupboards. Bono explains that the population of this necropolis "take the refuse of the city, collect it all at night, and take it back to the City of the Dead. Precious things, tin and silver, anything with piping. They use it, they store it, and they burn all that they can't use so the City of the Dead is covered with black smoke, the children have soot on their faces. It is beyond *The Road Warrior*. It is very dangerous to go there.

"They work with the tin, they are in my opinion related to the Irish tinkers. That name means tin-ker, they used to sharpen the shears and make pots. Nowadays they joyride and they dismantle cars. Metal is the key. The metallurgists in the City of the Dead and the Irish tinkers are the same thing. They're nomadic people and I'm sure they are remnants of the alchemists."

Bono says that Arabic chanting with its bent blues notes, its pentatonic scale, is the brother of the mournful Gaelic singing heard in the west of Ireland. He's sure that in antiquity Ireland and North Africa connected and shared influence through their mutual trade with Spain. He says that the nautical maps of the ancient Phoenicians are, by today's standards, tipped sideways, with our east at the top, so that what's now Ireland, Spain, and Morrocco are lined up together at the center and given great prominence, while England and France are drawn as obscure hinterlands. As with his theory that rap and hip-hop connect American blacks back to Africa, Bono finds the trade routes that the history books leave out.

We pull back up to the hotel and run upstairs to ablute ourselves before hurrying back down to a big hotel function room where Phonogram Nippon has laid on a Japanese banquet that would make a glutton weep with gratitude. Lovely handmaids in traditional kimonos float through the room with serving trays like foot-bound seraphim, offering marinated pork, spiced chicken, steamed shrimp, baisted lobster, and beef so succulent it would make a carnivore of Morrisey, a meat eater of Linda McCartney, a cannibal of a cow. The Zoologists, sated for days on fast food and room service, nearly moan for joy with every mouthful. It being a traditional Japanese feast, there are no chairs—we are expected to sit cross-legged at dining tables raised just a foot or so above the floor. After a few awkward moments of contemplating the yoga position, the sophisticated Westerners opt for sitting on the edges of the tables with their plates in their laps.

The Asian Phonogram executives ignore any breaches with perfect manners and grace. They make warm speeches of greeting and give large wrapped gifts to Paul, Regine, Sheila, and the band. McGuinness and Bono get up and make courteous acceptance speeches. Paul thanks the Japanese executives for all their hard work on behalf of U2's recent albums and this tour and says that for Zoo TV's melding of art and technology to succeed in Japan probably means more than anywhere else. Bono says that he likes Tokyo so much he hasn't slept since he arrived.

The Principles open their presents: carving-board clocks with chopsticks for hands and twelve different sorts of plastic sushi where the numbers should be. "Hey, Paul," I say, "It's quarter to salmon!" The Japanese, at least, are too courteous to groan. Anton points to Bono, engaged in intense discussion with two of the record executives, and says that what's really remarkable about Bono is that he can talk with wealthy foreign businessmen and with hookers in the red-light district and be equally interested in each.

Everyone wanders around the room, chatting with the hosts, listening to another traditionally garbed woman playing the koto, a sort of sitar, and stuffing desserts in their pockets. It's hard to reconcile this elaborate gentility with the decadence we slogged through last night—until I drop my expectations and consider that this is exactly the sort of discrepancy

I live with every day of my life. At home in New York I am used to stepping over an unconscious junkie on my way out of a black-tie charity fundraiser in an elegant museum around the corner from a porno parlor. Same in London or Los Angeles or Berlin. Why be surprised to see equivalent cultural hypocrisy in Japan? It, too, is full of Earthlings.

When the banquet breaks up we head off to pick up our man Willner at his hotel and jump back into the nocturnal hoopla. Bono, Eric, Nassim, and I meet Hal in the bar of his hotel. God knows what Willner's Japanese employers make of his sleep-deprived, deteriorating state. He is looking a lot like the picture of Dorian Gray. (I myself have been covering the mirrors with bath mats since Sydney.) We might stay sitting in the dark corners of this quiet lounge all night, but someone recognizes the Englishmen at the next table as Deep Purple (they're big in Japan) and we decide to split before they want to jam.

We go back to the car and end up leaping out at some restaurant that looks inviting but where we get chased from room to room and table to table by frantic orientals whose manner suggests that each time we sit down we are committing some awful atrocity we cannot comprehend. Finally the owner (how the hell do I know if he's the owner? Maybe he's the janitor's shell-shocked cousin) shoos us down into a corner stall in the basement where we sit down on mats around a low table and—*look out*—now some Asian adrenaline-case is hopping on one foot, yanking at his shoe and sputtering what is clearly an order to get our boots off. We do so and he collects them and takes them away for God knows what wicked ritual.

"I can only take this humility thing so far," Bono says sharply. "Pretty soon he's gonna get a bare Irish foot in the side of his head."

After another fifteen minutes of antic condemnations in an Eastern tongue, we give up, climb the stairs back to the street, and set off in search of more nightclubs, speakeasys, and tattoo parlors. Paul Oakenfold, the Zoo deejay since B.P. was cast out of Eden, is spinning the forty-fives tonight at some disco in town, but we do not know where. It is an indication of how far out of normalcy everyone around U2 has become that it was assumed we could just dump ourselves in the middle of the biggest metropolis in the world, where none of us speak or read the language, and find our friend without instructions. And we were right! Bono, with his divine gift for bumping into people he knows everywhere on earth, recognizes a young woman coming down the alley and shouts, "Yoko!"

"Bono! Hi!"

"Do you know where Paul Oakenfold's playing?"

She sure does and she can show us! We are soon underground, in a big frantic disco with films of naked women's privates flickering on the wall while U2's "Lemon" pipes out of the loudspeakers and the Tokyo subculture shakes its booty. There are lots of Zoo people here already, dancing, drinking, and sweating up a storm. Pretty soon we all join in, except for Willner, who stands slouching on the sidelines in four layers of shirts and coats grumbling about the idiocy of the disco beat. He is subjected to the further indignity of becoming a human coatrack for the rest of his party as they stink up the ballroom. After a half hour or so Hal cracks under the esthetic assault of a rhythm than never changes and hurls himself onto the dance floor, doing the monkey with the sunken eyes and miserable expression Richard Nixon would have worn had he ever done a guest spot on *Soul Train*.

After quitting that bacchanal (and losing Nassim to better dancers), Bono, Eric, Hal, and I return to some of the gin mills we visited before, as well as some that were I to describe them could get even casual readers of this book excommunicated. At 5 A.M. we are tramping the back alleys with nothing to guide us but the name of an after-after-hours club that was given to us by Mick Jones of B.A.D. We follow the instructions of stray pipe-heads and whoremasters and finally come to the payoff. The club sits on the fifth floor of a sort of decayed office building that appears to be made of stucco. To get to the barroom we've got to climb a staircase that cuts back and forth up the outside of the building. We start trudging, pulling our coats tight against the freezing December wind and wondering what this waterfall we're walking against is made of. It's not water—it seems to be beer, running down the steps around our shoes as we haul ourselves up to the second landing, the third landing, the fourth landing—ascending against the current.

When we get to the fifth floor, where the club is, the flood has not abated, so we stick our heads around to the sixth floor landing and are more than a little appalled to see that it was not beer we had just waded through, but urine. The men's room is overflowing and the drunken patrons are hanging out their snorkels and pissing down the stairs.

Inside, though, the club is pulsating with the darkened vibe of the kind of dancing and drug den I thought only existed on *Dragnet*. It is so dark that you can only see the people within five or ten feet of you, which is fine. As my eyes adjust I can make out women in bras and half-slips dancing on tables and tripping over chairs. Occasionally I catch a glimpse of one of the One-Eyed-Jacks hostesses shimmying through a strobe light. They are our pals now! Every time for the past few days I have tried to go to my room and sleep I have had the ringing phone to remind me that Bono gave them all my name and hotel room number and told them to call me to get tickets for the U2 concerts.

We grab seats behind some sort of table or shelf not far from the door and settle in. I notice several women sitting on the window ledge, holding beers and looking at Bono. One of them, a very pretty, almost fragile-looking young hippie girl, comes over and starts talking to me. She is English. Both her articulate language and perfect bone structure would seem more at home at a country club in Devonshire than here. But she's another wandering spirit. She looks sixteen and says she's twenty-six. She says she lives in the Himalayas and comes down to Tokyo for three months at a time to work as a hostess when she runs out of money. Then she goes back up to the mountains.

She grabs my arm and points to Bono. "I used to put on his records and masturbate to his poster on my wall when I was fourteen," she says. "I don't like his music anymore, though. He sold out and I grew up."

55

Bono at Bottom

---

rejecting the brown rice position/ the future of the zoo tv network/ getting lost and missing sound check/ bono is left stripped and unconscious/ U2 plays a stinker/ god isn't dead, nietzsche is

"LOOK AT THAT," Bono says, pointing up from the tranquil Japanese garden where we are sitting this morning to the top floors of the hotel. Larry and Edge have each come to the windows of their rooms, one a floor above the other, and without knowing it have each stood in the same way at their windows, surveying the landscape with the same expression (the one Ben Cartwright wore while looking out across the Ponderosa at the opening of *Bonanza*) and mannerisms, and then turned away.

"We've reached the end of this thing," I say to Bono. "You're out of steam, you've exhausted the spark that set this off three years ago. Fair enough?"

"Yup, I think so," Bono says. "Until we came to Tokyo!"

"Now you're renewed?"

"No, we're not renewed—redirected. I don't want to play more shows or anything like that, but I could stay here for a while. There's something that's catching my interest here that I don't know quite what it is. Maybe it's just the obvious, the high-tech art-and-people collision. I don't know if it's just that, but I think there's maybe other stuff here that I wouldn't mind rooting through."

"At the beginning of this ride you talked about challenging the age and embracing the age. And you were saying last night that maybe you had succeeded in both."

"I wasn't really commenting on whether we'd succeeded or failed, but that we were confirmed about our instincts that the idea of counterculture, the way it used to be in the sixties, that number is up. And I'm interested in these more Asian ideas, which we playfully call judo, that you use the energy of what's going against you—and by that I just mean popular culture, commerce, science—to defend yourself. Rather than *resistance*, in the hippie or punk sense of the word. You try to walk through it, rather than walk away from it. As opposed to the old ideas of dropping out and forming your own garden of eden—the sort of brown-rice position.

"That's where the TV stations come in. Let's take Zoo TV and turn it into a TV network. To see that go on into another field could be interesting. It becomes an extension of that idea. And why not?"

The proposed Zoo TV network, in conjuction with MTV and paid for by Polygram and some other investors, is snowballing into reality with the same sort of "If it can be done, we should do it" momentum that led to the creation of nuclear reactors, quad sound, and the Frankenstein monster. Everyone around U2 seems to have a different idea, though, of what it should be. Bono sees it as a window for the world to the films of Kenneth Anger and Wim Wenders, avant-garde music, progressive theater, philosophical talk shows, and semisurreal home shopping. McGuinness thinks it's a chance for U2 to make a whole lot of dough using other people's money. Edge is cautiously optimistic, Larry is cautiously pessimistic, and Adam says that while he has no doubt U2 could come up with a channel that *he* would enjoy watching, he's not sure that qualifies them to become network executives. I suggest to Bono that—as long as they're not risking their own money—the only real *why not* is the added demands and pressure it would put on the four band members.

"Yeah," Bono sighs. "And that's what we have to weigh up. That might be a reason why we wouldn't do it. The biggest threat to the group at present is the complexity of the running of our organization. That's the biggest threat. Our musical life is suffering as a result of it. And even though we can't get away with clichés like 'That's not important, it's the music that's important,' there is some truth that people who manage themselves lose that. There are a lot of examples. So we've got to be very careful. One of the signposts that we have at the moment is the idea of 'simplifying,' and then there's this other one. And I really don't know which way we're gonna go. Should we go further into the morass of options and permutations and combinations, or should we actually simplify?"

"Well," I say, taking a firm stand on both sides of the issue, "it might be possible to do both, but it would demand you four giving up the scrutiny that you put on everything that goes out under your name."

"Right," Bono says. "That's right. Brian Eno brought up the metaphor of Warhol's Factory, which is not too removed. Warhol brought in a lot of people, and he was just the arrowhead of all that energy. But you could argue that at a certain point maybe he released too much control."

You sure could. Bono and I went to a Warhol exhibit in Australia that gave me the shakes—it was like being trapped with someone you'd gotten sick of years before, showing you home movies of people you tried to avoid. One man's creative laboratory is another man's license to wank. "This sort of project puts another pressure on the band," I tell Bono, "because the four individuals may not have the same interest in it. It seems to me that one of things that Adam's struggling to resolve is the degree to which he wants to *have* to be involved in all these things."

"Yeah," Bono says. "That is a complex question because in one part it is an observation and a decision about the quality of life that he wants to have, but in another way it's a defensive position from a person whose energy had been eaten up elsewhere. It's so hard here, because nobody wants to fall behind, and when you are a cooperative, and when by and large you don't get paid more for working harder, you feel you can't fall behind, because it threatens the whole thing. This is what I don't have any answers for. But we're all in this one, Adam's not the only one. I'm thinking about it. I'm thinking about whether I'd like to completely withdraw from megastructures to more of a micro point of view. I think it was you that said, 'Sinatra took fifty years to get the phrasing right.' That comment rattled around my head for a while, and I thought, I've got this voice that gets so little attention. I have a point of view as an artist and an ability to write that is so undeveloped, that gets so little time. You've been there. You've seen me as the air traffic controller writing out of the sky, asking the cleaning lady, anyone who walks by for advice about lyrics. Now, that's partly strategy; it's not *just* the fact that it receives so little attention. But there are so many others areas. Performance! The ability to perform is innate, but in me it's so undeveloped. What if I had a chance to *think* about it, work it? On this tour I've been sticking to a script that was written very quickly, because you don't get a chance in this kind of thing to rewrite. It's like trying to rewrite a movie on the set. You can do it, but you'll pay a very high price. You might make a lot of bad decisions."

It is pretty remarkable that in all matters relating to U2, the parts that the public focuses on—Bono's part: the lyrics, the singing, what he does on stage—are added at the very end—after the music is written, after the backing track is recorded, after the set is designed and the costumes are tailored and the song lists are taped to the monitors.

"In the eighties," Bono says, "when I'd tell people, 'You don't understand. We're just scraping the top of this thing,' they'd always think it was modesty. But it was quite accurate. It wasn't any kind of forecast of great things to come; this was just pure frustration. 'What would happen if we could all play in time?' 'What would happen if we got a chance to songwrite?' And so whenever there'd be these quantum leaps those people would say, 'I didn't think they could do it.'"

We wander out of the garden and into the backstreets of Tokyo, talking all the way. As we slip between clotheslines in a back alley Bono says of U2, "Our evolution is back to front. It's completely arseways. And maybe one of the ways the group might progress is through simplification. I don't know. Maybe that's the way. I know people haven't got the energy for anything new right now. And that's why I didn't even mention Tokyo to them. There'd be a collective nervous breakdown. I don't even want them to think about things like that. And it may be me that gets us into trouble, if you like, gets us into these places, but I need them to get us *out* of those places. We really need each other. That's the other thing. If we end up doing the Zoo TV network I'm gonna need Larry there going, 'This is a wank! Who is this guy?'

"So I don't know." Bono sighs, looking at the fork in the road with the same ambivalence that confronted Dorothy, the Scarecrow, and Robert Frost. "Something in me would love to write a song, and you know, *try it in a few different keys.* Which still has never happened."

A motorist collides with a man on a bicycle, sending him sprawling and hurling Nipponese curses as Bono stops in the street to admire a Japanese car, an RVR open gear.

"I keep having rows with people who are very annoyed by Japanese design," he says. "I find the contours really a clue to the future. Just the way in the seventies everyone pooh-poohed their bikes, and by the eighties they reigned supreme, I think the same will happen in the nineties with cars." Time to trade in the Trabant for a Toyota.

We find a spaghetti joint and order lunch.

"There's something that might not be represented fairly in the book if you don't talk about it," I tell Bono as we twirl our pasta with a confidence that would make Mrs. Clayton proud. "The fact that your faith is still intact. You've done so much work against the image of U2 as the pious men on the mountaintop that a reader could have the impression that the faith of the members had become very much like standard American Episcopalianism: 'We believe in Jesus on Christmas, but it's not going to affect our day-to-day lives and if you really want, the minister will baptize your cat.' Want to address that?"

Bono makes a face that suggests that either the spaghetti stinks or the question does. "It's a nicely freeing position to be in to have nobody expecting it from us," he says.

"We've found different ways of expressing it, and recognized the power of the media to manipulate such signs. Maybe we just have to sort of draw our fish in the sand. It's there for people who are interested. It shouldn't be there for people who aren't."

"Do you think that you, Larry, and Edge are still on the same wavelength in your beliefs?"

"What about Adam?" Bono says quickly. "Adam's the same. I mean, nobody is exactly the same, but Adam's a believer. I think that the spirit will more and more become the important thing over the next ten years, when it becomes clear that God isn't dead, Nietzsche is."

We pay our bill and begin walking back to the hotel, each of us assuming the other knows where we're going and only gradually realizing that we're completely lost. We try asking directions and get vague gestures in conflicting directions. We decide that if we wander long enough we'll stumble across it. Bono does not figure that U2 going home from their two-year night on the town means any end of interesting subject matter. "People may feel dead, but they're not actually dead," he says. "I'm ready to actually start examining that much more scary topic of the kitchen, and domesticity, and real life."

Hey, there's the hotel! I recognize it by the cordon of kids with cameras and autograph books. As we approach the fans they squeal and bob and Bono smiles. "I've had no sleep the last week. I had a great time, I needed to let off some steam, and you know . . . I actually have had it. I don't want any more." (The wardrobe people have taken to staking out Bono's room and when he briefly shows up to pass out on his bed they go in, strip him, and take his clothes away to wash without waking him.)

As Bono signs her book one of the Japanese girls asks, "Are you okay, do you have a cold?"

I tell her, "No, he always looks like that."

"No, he doesn't!" she insists.

In the lobby we learn we are in big trouble. Everyone departed for the gig long ago, except for Eric, who stayed behind to wait for Bono. Not only had we lost ourselves in Tokyo, we'd lost track of time and forgotten that the show here is an hour earlier than usual—U2 has to be on stage at 8. So there's some panic as Bono is thrown into a car and raced to the gig. It's been a confusing tour anyway—Christchurch and Aukland were the only two successive shows on this whole leg that were in the same time zone.

The Tokyo Dome is a big white egg. Inside it has a weird, packed-in-Styrofoam blandness. It is like being inside a Ping-Pong ball. The rows and rows of folding chairs are lined up with wide aisles between each section, and a wide chasm between the front row and the stage. Bono has missed sound check; he barely has time to get dressed before U2 goes onstage. The high-tech awesomeness of the Zoo TV stage and towers is seriously curtailed by being placed inside. It doesn't matter if the ceiling is ten stories high; the very fact that there is a ceiling hurts the stage's cityscape effect.

But nothing hurts as much as the fact that Bono's working at half-speed and the band is experiencing a feast of malfunctions, the worst of which is when Edge's guitar vanishes on "Even Better than the Real Thing," leaving Bono to try vamping with improvised words over a bass-and-drum version of the song, hoping Edge will come back. The Japanese audience has a reputation for being the most subdued in the world. They might be, but they are still clearly having fun in their conservative way. Bono tries to get things jumping. He cries out, "Tokyo! The capital of Zoo TV!" and kicks in a little restrained stage diving, swimming across the rows along the path to the B stage. They get a big charge out of that, and that section of the audience, at least, remains goosed and standing afterward. But overall it's pretty dull, and it's not the audience's fault. U2 is dragging ass tonight.

Standing next to me at the soundboard, McGuinness leans over and says, "Well, sooner or later you had to see a real stinker."

Bono is exhausted and a little contrite afterward. "I think I spent all the energy that should have gone into that gig talking to you this afternoon," he says. "I left that show in the Japanese garden."

56

Fin de Siecle

the bomb japan scandal/ U2's promoter banzais madonna's/ t-shirts save the day/ larry takes stock/ the 157th and final zoo tv concert/ the secret of the universe

U2 HAS A FEW misunderstandings to sort out with the Japanese. The biggest is a report, widely circulated in Japan, that during the American leg of the tour the Zoo TV screens lit up with the message BOMB JAPAN NOW. An Atlanta newspaper reporter said he saw it, and he wrote it, and while it was no big deal to readers in Atlanta it was a hell of a big stink in Tokyo. The polite teenage girls who wait in the hotel lobby all day with their U2 albums like to come up and ask questions about the band of any Anglo who passes, and one of the most popular is, "Do they really hate Japan?"

What U2 has been unable to make clear is that while it's possible that those three words—*bomb, Japan,* and *now*—might have shown up in rapid sequence one time, it was not intended and there is no way to check. During "The Fly" all the screens around Bono flash hundreds of random words at high speed in random sequence. Those three words are all in the file, so they might have come up together, but given that each word flashes for a fraction of a second it's equally possible that the reporter saw those three amid a barrage and his brain connected them into a sentence that didn't really exist. There's no way to tell and it's a waste of time guessing, but since U2 is unable to issue a flat denial, the bomb-sensitive Japanese are touchy about the band these days. It just goes to show: give a monkey a typewriter and he'll eventually offend some national sensibility.

In addition to those hard feelings there's bad blood with the local promoter who is putting on the Zoo TV concerts here. As I explained back in Australia, one of the mean side effects of the enormous expense of this tour is that U2 had to demand big guarantees from promoters who wanted to book them. Some bands—the Rolling Stones, for example—do that as a matter of course, but in the past U2 operated by sharing more of the risk with promoters. This time McGuinness had to tell local bookers to pony up the big bucks up front. This led to some promoters trying to cover their asses by jacking up the ticket prices, which at some shows led to unsold seats.

The Friday show at the forty-five-thousand seat Tokyo Dome is packed, but Thursday was not even close. The promoter is angry that McGuinness will not consider giving back some of the advance and sharing the loss. McGuinness's attitude is that this whole week of the tour and journey to Japan has been added just to accommodate these two concerts, and it would be unfair to his clients to now tell them they are not going to be paid for it.

The situation is especially touchy because the promoter battled like a ninja for U2 when their dates were threatened, when the Tokyo Dome, which promotes some events in-house, made a deal with Madonna to come and play for five nights. The Dome wanted to take back one or both of the nights promised to U2 to accommodate the Material Girl, and since it's their house they might very well have done it. U2's promoter hit the roof and hurled a samurai curse at the backsliders: "If you break your word to me about this I will destroy you, even if in doing so I must destroy myself!"

The Tokyo Dome freaked. McGuinness got an angry call from Madonna's people saying, "*Your* Tokyo promoter has threatened to kill *our* Tokyo promoter!"

McGuinness said, more or less, "Good for him." (McGuinness also says that the threat was symbolic, a demonstration of determination.) U2 got their dates. Madonna has to play around them. But the promoter who was willing to go kamikaze for U2 is now so bitter that he won't even come to the shows.

This week it's possible to look at the final figures for the two years of heavy work. U2 has landed in the black, but not by a wide margin. What saved them from being wiped out was the garment industry. "We grossed $30 million in T-shirt sales," McGuinness says. "Without those we'd be fucked."

Backstage at the Tokyo Dome, someone (I daresay Willie) has lined the corridors with 157 pieces of paper, each with the name and number of one of the 157 dates on this two-year tour and attached messages, photos, and phrases. This memory lane wallpaper runs up and down stairs, in and out of the lunchroom, and around every backstage corner, listing concerts from Lakeland, Florida, to this air-conditioned beach ball. The final stretch includes:

"118 Berlin. Get your balls out of the bunker!"

"138 Glasgow." A photo of Fintan onto which someone has drawn an ax, cleaving his head in half and the caption, "Would you trust a bald hairdresser?"

"143 Wembley. Babes of rock." Photos of the Principle women.

"146 Dublin. You need *how* many tickets?"

"152 Sydney. Bass? What bass? Stu TV. Stuart rocks! Sturopa!"

"156 Tokyo. "Real Thing—nice rap version, guys."

I follow the paper trail into the lunchroom, where I find Edge sitting at a dinner table backstage, practicing Motown-type hand twirls and gestures. "I think this is where U2's future lies," he says. "Choreography. Four Tops type stuff." Edge says he can tell U2 is drained when they get together to play sound checks: "The ideas have really dried up lately."

He says he's looking forward to getting away from the circus for a while, having a chance to input again. He's also concerned with figuring out how to fit the guitar into the music's future. "Things are looking extremely tough for the guitar at the moment," he says. "Except as a retro instrument. Synth guitars just sound like cheap synths. But I don't want to give up on the guitar, on that great vitality." His gaze drifts off into the air, mentally subdividing God-knows-what complex equation.

It turns out he's wondering if right now Larry is finding the fan letter Edge left lying conspicuously in the dressing room. The letter tells Edge that he is "the best-looking member of U2. Bono has a big nose and

Larry looks like an inflatable doll." Edge got the note in Australia and he plans to keep leaving it out until Larry notices it.

"Bass players attract the weirdest fans," Edge says. "I tend to get the bespectacled M.I.T. students. Bono gets the poets. And Larry, unfortunately, gets the girls." Edge sighs and repeats the old saw: "We should have gotten a Ringo."

The Beautiful Boy himself enters the cafeteria, showing no signs of having yet seen himself described as inflatable. Edge gets up to collect his mash note for next time, and I sit down with Larry for a last-minute talk before the last-ever Zoo show begins.

I ask him if he has any regrets that the band has worked so hard for so long and played to so many people—and is coming out of it with millions of dollars less than if they had staged a simpler show.

"In comparison to a lot of people in our position we don't make a lot of money," Larry concedes. "We've chosen instead to retain our dignity and also to give ourselves more time making music. By putting on a show like this we're not making any money, but that's irrelevant. It broadens our base so next time round we can do what we want, we can make more music. In the end it's investing in our future. Not in our future financially, in our future musically—'cause at the end of the day that's what it's all about. We've all made enough money to live for the rest of our lives quite comfortably. That's enough money.

"The biggest responsibility out of all this is the fact that you employ a lot of people and you are responsible for them, responsible to make sure they're taken care of. People's livelihoods are depending on you. I don't like that responsibilty too much, but that comes with the territory."

Larry is still the only other band member to whom Bono has dared broach the idea of returning to Tokyo to make the next album. I ask how he feels about the idea and he says, "I could deal with it. It's a very difficult place, a very different place. It's one of the strangest places I've been. There's a funny atmosphere here. I'm not sure on a spirtiual level how I feel about it. However"—he smiles—"I'm on for the ride, I'm up for it. If it'll help make a great record, if it'll help Bono be inspired and if it'll make the band be a better band, I'm there."

I suggest that one of the advantages might be that if you're in a weird enough environment you can do what comes naturally and it will come out sounding fresh. I remind him what Adam and Flood said while making Zooropa—that if U2 just go into a room and play, it wll sound like the old U2, so now everything has to be stopped and thought about because of a conscious band decision to explore new ground. True?

"I think it *was* true," Larry says. "I think we've discovered how to marry electronics to what U2 do. There's nothing different; it's using the technology to help you do better what you do. The idea of the four of us going into a room and playing together doesn't interest me anymore. I'd much prefer to have some electronic drum machines, something I can play off. 'Cause I play better like that! I never thought I'd think so, but I play better playing against stuff and being inspired by things like that. After ten years, four people in a room is not as inspiring as it was. You've got to break new ground. That's what we're trying to do and I think that's really healthy.

"I've come through my own learning process. It was very difficult during *Achtung Baby.* When we got that out of the way I found a real sense of peace within myself. I'm very sure about what I'm doing, very sure about what I want. I've reached a stage in my life where I'm happy to do this! I want it more than anything else and I'm prepared to do whatever's necessary to make it happen. I recommitted myself to the band."

One Zoo insider told me that Larry has said that during the band's year off he is going to go off and "become a great fucking drummer," and he plans to bring Adam along with him if he has to drag him by the boots. Over the last couple of years Larry has quietly taken on the role of Adam's cop and conscience. It's a touchy subject, but I ask Larry to comment on the chances of Adam and him both spending a year studying music in New York.

"It is a touchy subject," Larry says, " 'cause it's to do with Adam on a personal level. My preference would be for Adam to come along with me and take responsibility for his position—which is bass player in the band—but hold a lot more weight than that. I prefer that he would choose to fight for all that. However, he's got different things that he's got to cope with. He's got different difficulties with being successful. Different people cope in different ways."

I mention the time in Berlin when Adam took off his bass and said to Bono, *just tell me what you want me to play and I'll play it—or if you want to play it, go ahead.*

"It's disappointing that Adam maybe feels like that sometimes,"

Larry says slowly. "However, although we're a band, people have got to choose their own way and do whatever is necessary to get them through that tour or that night or that record. And if saying, 'Look, just show me the line and I'll play it,' is the option he wants to take, that's his choice. It's not *my* choice. *I'm* not going to let go that easy for anybody. I couldn't take it! I actually just couldn't take it. I am not that."

I warn Larry that I'm going to try to tag him with the shot Bono ducked yesterday: discussing the band members' ongoing religious faith.

"It's a very difficult question," Larry says cautiously. "Very, very difficult. It was always a personal thing and within the band we always had very differing views on where we were going as individuals. On a personal level, I haven't lost my faith at all. I don't practice it in the same way I did when I was younger, but I haven't lost sight of the fundamentals of it. There are many people out there who would disagree and say, 'Well, how can you do this and how can you consider yourself that?'

"There have never been any rules applied to my faith. My faith is a personal thing. I'm sure there are things that you can get away with"— he smiles—"like in anything else, and there's no doubt that we push it to the edge, to the very edge. And occasionally we fall off the other end. But I never felt that my job as a musician was to sing gospel or to proselytize. I've always felt that I'm a musician in a band and I've been given a gift. And I believe that gift is from God. I don't believe it's from anywhere else. And if at any stage I abuse that, I think I'll know. That will be time to stop. I do think it's important."

It's time for U2 to play. As the house lights go down I make my way out to watch the concert. Among the guests at the unusually crowded soundboard are Madonna, much of her band and crew, Terence Trent D'Arby, and Simon LeBon of Duran Duran.

Tonight, the final show, Bono will not accept anything less than a great concert. That last night stunk chews at his conscience, that this is the last time U2 will ever mount Zoo TV on stage bites the nails of his ambition. The band does come out playing well, but you can spot the foreigners in the audience because they're the only ones who stand up and dance. The Japanese fans remain politely in their seats. This time Bono's not going to take that. The man with the white flag never accepted "cultural differences" as any sort of excuse. If the Fly can't get them going, he'll try something else. During "Until the End of the

World" he runs to the end of the B stage, implores the crowd to their feet, reaches out to slap their hands. He is making eye contact, making physical contact, making heart contact. And as I watch him I am overwhelmed with the feeling that I am seeing someone I used to know. *I recognize this guy!* I remember him from the clubs when U2 first came around! This is the kid who will do anything to get through to the audience, whether it's climbing the scaffolding or diving off the balcony. There is no Fly now, no Macphisto, no public mask. There's only Bono, praying through his microphone, infecting everyone he touches with his spastic enthusiasm, winning over the doubters as he won over cynics in every new wave club from Dublin to California in the early eighties. I'd almost forgotten about this nut; I didn't realize I'd missed him.

Anton's on his belly like a snake, slithering down the ramp to the B stage to shoot Bono whipping up the confused, excited, standing, *dancing* audience. He's got one foot off the B stage and he's leaning over the kids' heads, exhorting them to rise while Jerry Mele hangs on to the back of his belt to keep him from tumbling off. Then Bono looks out at the panorama of faces filling the Dome and he slaps Jerry's hand away, leaping off the stage and into the crowd. Now the kids start loosening up! Like an alcoholic taking one little nip after a long layoff, the old stage-diving Bono is back in the house. During "Where the Streets Have No Name" he always runs out to the end of the ramp on Adam's side of the stage. Tonight Bono keeps going, launching himself off the end of the ramp and into the startled crowd. He comes to his feet running, racing into them, trying to get across.

The security men take off after Bono. The fans he passes begin to climb up as he goes by, getting the idea of it, clapping, dancing a little. Because they still can't bring themselves to step out into the aisles, Bono has a wide-open path and he keeps going, all the way to the outer rim of the floor, running along the circumference singing into his radio mike as fans caged off on the sides by fences charge forward, leaping onto the mesh and trying to climb over or stick their fingers through as Bono races by. Now, as he approaches the back of the hall, even the fans on the floor are losing their inhibitions. They start jumping up, some even running toward him. The Japanese security guards are beside themselves —they are running, too, trying to wave people back, get them to sit down.

The security team is racing along, pacing Bono. Jerry—his adrenaline surging, his arm flung forward like Johnny Unitas, his eyes darting around looking for danger—*starts to have a Vietnam flashback.* He and his commander and his junior officer are running, running, and people are screaming and shouting and Asians are charging, running toward them and away from them and some of them, the audience, are his friends he has to protect, and others, the angry security guards, he has to avoid or stop from hurting the nice ones and Jerry's sweating hard and trying to keep his eye on Bono, keep the situation under control and keep telling himself *this is not Vietnam!*

As they come down the homestretch toward the stage, Bono is drenched with sweat, his heart flipping, pushing with all his might to keep running. The kids are going wild now behind and in front of him, charging out into the aisles to touch him or run beside him, the whole hall cheering. Eric cannot believe Bono's ability to find an opening and dash through it a second before it closes; Eric feels like they're running over hills with no idea what's coming up but the ground under their feet collapsing the second they step off it. Bono makes it to the edge of the stage, where the band is still cranking out "Streets" and thinks, "I'll never be able to climb back up there," when he feels Jerry, Eric, and David lifting him, other arms helping and then he's back on the stage, the mike in his hand, climbing up to his feet and into the spotlight and singing. And the whole place knows who he really is now. And the whole place knows they are like him. They are shouting "You too!" "You too!" "You too!"

After the concert there is plenty of well-wishing and wine-toasting. Madonna has split without saying good night, but her band and D'Arby and LeBon all come back to congratulate U2. Jerry is regaling Bono with a description of his 'Nam flashback during the big run. "I'll tell ya, boss"—Jerry smiles, shaking his head—"if there'd been *trees* I'd have taken somebody out!" Nobody's seen Adam or Fintan for a while. A door opens and the bassist emerges with a fully shaved head. Fintan follows with a gleam in his eye and proceeds to sit down next to one of the One-Eyed Jacks hostesses. "You've got to drink a lot of sake to get drunk," she observes when she sees what he's having. "I fully intend to," Fintan replies.

After an hour or two of back-scratching it's time to go to the hotel. As Bono walks up the ramp from the back door of the Tokyo Dome to the waiting tour bus, a scream goes up from fans being held behind a rope and one young man clutching a U2 tour book zips under the rope and comes tearing toward Bono. It is startling, and I don't blame Oddjob, the Japanese guide, for karate-chopping the guy in the throat, so that his legs shoot forward and he sits down sharply on his ass. But Bono is furious. He screams at Oddjob and then picks the intruder up, makes sure he's okay, and spends five minutes talking to him and signing his tour book while the kids behind the rope get more and more frantic and the security guards more nervous.

Back at the hotel, the End of Tour party is weary and restrained. A suite at the hotel has been hired and people drift in and out all night, sipping drinks and munching snacks and chatting. Adam sits in the corner in a bathrobe looking as comfortable as if this were his front parlor. The first batch of flights back to Europe and America are at dawn, so a lot of people plan to stay up till then and sleep on the plane. Bono is one of them. But at about 3 he says he's going down to his room for a minute to make a call, and falls asleep on his bed.

One by one the other U2s drift away from the shindig. Fintan puts on one of his endless supply of dance tapes. (Fintan's influence on U2's taste cannot be overestimated. There must be twenty or thirty people anxious to tell the world how this or that Zoo TV/*Achtung Baby*/*Zooropa* idea came from them. Fintan's a bigger influence than all of them put together, but you'll never hear that from Fintan.)

Some of the hostesses from One-Eyed Jacks are here, too, ordering endless sake from room service and exchanging sensitive glances with the security squad. Paul McGuinness departs with an invitation to call him anytime and "ask me the really tough questions."

The last star standing is Larry Mullen. At about 4 A.M. the most private member of U2 turns and tells me the Secret of the Universe: "Nobody in U2 understands it. None of us understands where this music comes from. If one of us wrote a book about the band he wouldn't be able to explain it. *We don't know.* You asked me earlier about our faith." He raises his eyes to indicate heaven without saying it out loud and says, "I have to believe that is where it comes from. And we do dance right along the edge of how far we can go away from that. And sometimes we go too far."

The question that started this journey was, "How far are you gonna go before you lose your way back home?" These jokers have gone all the way to the ends of the world, danced with their doubts and tested their temptations, and never did get completely lost. From here on I know they will have the confidence to go anywhere their imaginations take them.

57

Aftershocks

*burning promises on the beach/ into the earthquake zone/
inducting bob marley/ the corrioles effect/ the charge of the
capitol gang/ bono's promise to the young people*

G ETTING HOME a week before Christmas turns out to be a
blessing. The members of U2—pretty much everyone else
aboard the Zoo train, too—get off their planes and find
themselves thrown right into the middle of last-minute shopping, gift
wrapping, tree decorating, and decking the halls. There is the holiday
rush of rituals, victuals, and visitors, after which the post-Christmas
decompression sucks up a lot of the posttour decompression. One of
the Christmas gifts waiting for Bono is from Rancho Mirage. It is
"Jazz," the Frank Sinatra painting he admired at Sinatra's home.

On New Year's Eve, four years after the night the old U2 told their
hometown audience they were going away to dream it up again, Bono
and Ali and some of their close friends light a bonfire on the beach in
Ireland, write down everything they want to let go of, and throw them
into the flames. It's a Japanese ritual and Bono says, "It's a really good
omen, a good way to start the year."

There is still plenty of winding down to do and loose ends to bind.
In the Name of the Father has its debut in Dublin. The film is another
critical smash for Jim Sheridan, earning a fresh pile of Oscar nomina-
tions, including one as Best Director. Bono, Ali, and Paul go to Los
Angeles for the Golden Globes, where Bono and Gavin's music is up for
an award. Bono is not used to the sort of hoopla Hollywood rolls out
(although he does stick up for Irish fashion by showing up at the black-
tie event in a Hawaiian shirt). They have arrived during the aftershocks
of a major earthquake that has Californians jumpy and depressed. The

city has been hit in quick succession by riots, floods, fires, and now earthquakes that seem to never end. The L.A. dream is over.

Lined up on the way into the awards are about a hundred yards of TV crews and another hundred yards of photographers. Bono thinks he's supposed to stop and give an interview to each TV camera, so he does, finally getting to the end where an old lady admonishes him that he skipped Argentine TV back at the start of the line. Bono goes back to talk to Argentina and the other crews applaud. When he gets inside, talked-out, he asks Daniel Day-Lewis how many of the TV interviews he did. The actor shrugs and says, "Oh, one." Bono says, "Thanks for telling me!"

Bono and Gavin's "In the Name of the Father" loses Best Song to Bruce Springsteen's "Streets of Philadelphia." While in Los Angeles, Bono, Ali, and Paul hook up with Bill Carter, who just pulled off a New Year's Day Sarajevo broadcast on MTV Europe. Bill got back to the States and settled into a beach house in Santa Monica to attempt to calm down and get his blood pressure back to *Homo sapiens* levels after his year of grief and gunfire. He was there for one day when he woke up with the room shaking, thought it was shelling, then thought, *No, I'm home, it must be me shaking.* Then three bookcases, a toolbox, and a computer fell over on him and he got the message. "I came through a war in Sarajevo without a scratch," he says, "and was finally wounded in an earthquake in Santa Monica."

T-Bone Burnett, who slept through the earthquake, says he's been worried that I might not know he was joking when he said Bono was a heretic, and he'd hate for me to put that in the book.

"I don't know what you're talking about, T-Bone," I reply. "I don't remember you saying that Bono was a heretic. But now I will certainly have to put it in the book."

T-Bone says that he's decided U2 are a lot like Aimee Semple McPherson, the miracle-working evangelist and supercelebrity of 1920s America. She healed the lame and made the blind see. She rode motorcycles in her church and became fascinated by the world of Hollywood. She'd disappear with Tallulah Bankhead. Finally she began to think it was *her* power that was healing people and not God's. I think it's safe to say that T-Bone has a lot more faith in U2 than to think they'll end up like Sister Aimee, but he is enough of an ethical forest ranger to want to warn them of the temptation.

Back in New York, Sheila Roche comes through town to pack up her belongings and move back to Ireland, where she is going to be overseeing the management of P. J. Harvey. Adam and Larry are making ready their uptown pads. Bono skis in amidst blizzards and ice storms that are freezing North America from Canada to Tennessee to make a speech inducting Bob Marley into the Rock & Roll Hall of Fame.

"I know claiming Bob Marley is Irish might be a little difficult here tonight," he tells the ponytailed power brokers in the audience, "but bear with me. Jamaica and Ireland have a lot in common. Naomi Campbell, Chris Blackwell, Guinness, a fondness for little green leaves —the weed, religion, the philosophy of procrastination—don't put off till tomorrow what you can put off till the day after. Unless, of course, it's freedom.

"We are both islands. We are both colonies. We share a common yoke: the struggle for identity, the struggle for independence, the vulnerable and uncertain future that's left behind when the jackboot of empire is finally retreated. The roots, the getting up, the standing up, and the hard bit—the staying up. In such a struggle, an often violent struggle, the voice of Bob Marley was the voice of reason. There were love songs that you could admit listening to, songs of hurt, hard but healing. Tuff gong. Songs of freedom where that word meant something again. Redemption songs. A sexy revolution where Jah is Jehovah on street level. Not over his people but with his people. Not just stylin'—jammin'. Down the line from Ethiopia where it all began for the Rastaman.

"I spent some time in Ethiopia with my wife, Ali, and everywhere we went we saw Bob Marley's face. There he was, dressed to hustle God. 'Let my people go,' an ancient plea. Prayers catching fire in Mozambique, Nigeria, Lebanon, Alabama, Detroit, New York, Notting Hill, Belfast. Dr. King in dreads, a Third- and First-World superstar.

"Mental slavery ends where imagination begins. Here was this new music, rocking out of the shantytowns. Lolling, loping rhythms, telling it like it was, like it is, like it ever shall be. Skanking, ska, bluebeat, rock steady, reggae, dub, and now ragga. And all of this from a man who drove three BMWs. BMW—Bob Marley and the Wailers—that was his excuse!

"Rock & roll loves its juvenilia, its caricatures, its cartoons. The protest singer, the gospel singer, the sex god, your more mature messiah types. We love the extremes and we're expected to choose. The mud of the blues or the oxygen of gospel. The hellhounds on our trail or the bands of angels. Well, Bob Marley didn't choose, or walk down the middle. He raced to the edges, embracing all extremes, creating a oneness. His oneness. One love. He wanted everything at the same time and he was everything at the same time. Prophet, soul rebel, Rastaman, herbsman, wildman, natural mystic man, lady's man, Island man, family man, Rita's man, soccer man, showman, shaman, human, Jamaican.

"The spirit of Bob and the spirit of Jah lives on in his son, Ziggy, and his lover, Rita Marley. I'm proud to welcome Bob Marley into the Hall of Fame. Amen!"

It's a beautiful speech, and no doubt it tells us as much about Bono's aspirations for himself as it does his vision of Bob Marley. Bono goes home to Ireland after that. The faxes imploring him to act in the movie *Johnny Mnemonic* are piling up like pancakes on a slow day at IHOP, and Warner Bros. is offering to write a Macphisto-like character into *Batman Forever.* He has been invited to give a speech bestowing on Frank Sinatra a lifetime achievement Grammy. Finally making his choices based on conservation of energy, Bono says no to the movies and yes to the speech.

In March, with snow still up to New York's filthy belly button, Bono, Ali, and Paul again hit Manhattan. First stop is a Rock the Vote party MTV is throwing to celebrate itself and to honor R.E.M. for their efforts in voter registration. Clinton's small, sharp-looking, thirty-two-year-old Senior Policy Advisor George Stephanopoulos leads those representing the White House at the hoedown, which is held at a nightclub in Times Square. Jeff Pollack makes a speech, Tom Freston makes a speech. Michael Stipe shows up with a shaved head and his mother. Bono and various Principles are given a table in a little alcove overlooking the festivities, right next to Sting, and a couple of Roman draperies down from R.E.M.

When Bono and Stipe huddle to talk there quickly develops, as inevitably as it does when two weather fronts come together, a vortex spiraling out from their epicenter. Lesser pop deities, management associates, record execs, MTV personnel, freeloaders and eavesdroppers circle around the great men in expanding spirals of attendant schmooze. I look out across this widening gyre and see a tall, stern figure plowing through the rings with the sort of fierce determination that always brings to mind the cry, "Half a league, half a league, half a league on!"

Imagine my surprise when I see that this invader is an old fellow who was a priest in the Rhode Island of my youth, who later went on to suck up to President Nixon during the Watergate crisis, offering absolution for the president's sins before Gerry Ford ever thought of it and vying to become the Catholic Billy Graham during that fall of that White House of Usher.

Later this same ambitious padre ran for Congress from Rhode Island as a Republican and was thumped. He went over the hill from the priesthood, got married, and was next spotted as the host of an obnoxious but very popular TV show called *The McLaughlin Group* in which the former Father presides over a howling pack of political commentators who verbally groin-kick each other in their drooling haste to spew invective on all statesmen, politicians, and public figures—but especially leftists—from coast to coast on Sunday mornings. The old priest still has a pulpit! So famous that *Saturday Night Live* regularly parodies him, the post-frocked broadcaster is called John McLaughlin. Not the Mahavishnu. After knocking through the crowd around Bono and Stipe, he finally elbows aside the last small woman in his path, raises his chins, casts down his eyes imperiously on Bono, and shouts with the amplified voice of the hard-of-hearing, "That's not Stephanopoulos!" After which outburst he turns and stalks away.

Well, now my interest is piqued. I leave Bono, Stipe, and Sting and follow McLaughlin into a side room, where R.E.M. has arranged to have an exhibition of photos and paintings by HIV-infected artists. I come up next to the turn-collar, point to a photograph of a man displaying an engorged penis, and ask, "What do you make of that one, Mr. McLaughlin?" He peers over his spectacles, studies the picture, and then says loudly, "Mapplethorpe!"

"It is not," I tell him. "That's my doorman."

I go back to Bono, who is being told by Stephanopoulos that it looks as if the Clinton White House made a big mistake allowing Sinn Fein president Gerry Adams into the United States recently. It was a gamble that if Adams was treated as a diplomat rather than a terrorist the IRA might reciprocate with a serious peace initiative in Northern Ireland. But nothing happened and all the Americans accomplished was to get the British angry. Bono tells Stephanopoulos not to give up yet; Adams was cheered as a peacemaker during that trip. Bono says that a man can develop a taste for that sort of applause—Adams may decide he likes the sound of it and come through with a peace initiative yet.

Stephanopoulos goes up to the podium and makes a speech about the political vitality of *the young people*. He must use that horrible phrase three or four times. "When he says *the young people*," I ask Bono, "does he mean us or does he mean the really *young* people? It always gives me the creeps when I hear people in their early thirties talking about *the young people today*."

Bono doesn't say anything, but as he heads out the door a TV crew grabs him for an interview and he says it's a great event but he just wishes they'd lay off the "young people" baloney. That makes me feel good. But not as good as the next night when Bono shambles onstage at the Grammys to pick up *Zooropa*'s award for Best Alternative Album. After a few nods to the alternative and college charts he looks at his feet as if his mind's gone blank, mumbles, "What else . . ." scratches his nose and then comes up smiling to say to the live TV audience, "I think I'd like to give a message to the young people of America. And that is: We shall continue to abuse our position and fuck up the mainstream."

Suddenly TV censors are panicking and phones are ringing and doors are slamming and lights are flashing like in an old James Thurber cartoon. A cry goes out: "Did you hear what Bono said on live network television?"

Yes, I did. He said *young people*.

58

The City That Doesn't Sleep

---

the big bang of pop/ cutting off the capo/ more news from sarajevo/ irishmen in new york/ adam sets a few things straight/ what's the word?

BONO CLAIMS he doesn't know what all the excitement is about. He said *fuck* on live TV? Big deal, he says it every day. He makes the rather legalistic point that he said *fuck up*, not *fuck* as in "intercourse." I appreciate his sentiment but I think he's being a little insincere, implying his expletive was a thoughtless slip of the tongue. For the biggest band in the world to win the Alternative Award could get U2 mocked by the gatekeepers of the sacred alternative subculture. It's like a few years ago, when the Grammys named Jethro Tull Best Heavy Metal Band. It wasn't Tull's fault, but they took the backlash. So I suspect that Bono wanted to make some gesture to make it clear that he was not the Grammy's housebroken puppy, politely swiping a statue that should have been conferred on Nirvana or Sugar or Pavement. (False humility aside, though, Bono feels strongly that if *alternative* means the music and not the fashion movement, *Zooropa* deserves the award more than any of the seventies-leaning grunge bands do.)

Anyhow, the big event, and the only reason Bono is standing in the wings of Radio City Music Hall tonight, is ahead. Last week Bono read me big chunks of his Sinatra induction speech and said he couldn't come up with anything good. I told him he was nuts—the speech he had written was exceptional, all he had to do was go out and read it. Bono was wary that the Grammy people might try to tone it down, but the only real compromise he had to make was to take out a reference to Sinatra as the *capo di tutti capi*, the *Godfather* designation for "boss of all bosses."

Bono's loose lips in his own acceptance speech may be attributable to the fact that when he got to the hall this afternoon he went to the dressing room to see Sinatra and the two crooners started knocking back whiskey together.

"What are we doin' here?" Frank demanded.

"Hey, don't complain to me about comin' from Palm Springs," Bono told him. "I came in from Dublin!" Bono figures Frank likes the cockiness. I figure one of them ought to figure out that Dublin and Palm Springs are about the same distance from New York.

When Bono returns to the stage to make his speech honoring Frank, the TV censors may be poised over their bleep buttons, but what comes out is prose so perfect it makes you think that Rushdie is right about Bono's literary gifts:

"Frank never did like rock & roll," Bono begins, and the crowd laughs. "He's not crazy about guys wearing earrings either"—more laughter—"but he doesn't hold it against me, and anyway, the feeling is not mutual. Rock & roll people love Frank Sinatra because Frank Sinatra has got what we want: swagger and attitude. He's big on attitude. Serious attitude. Bad attitude. Frank's the chairman of the bad." The crowd laughs.

"Rock & roll plays at being tough, but this guy, well, he's the boss. The boss of bosses. The man. The big bang of pop. I'm not gonna mess with him. Are you?

"Who's this guy that every city in America wants to claim as their own? This painter who lives in the desert? This first-rate first-take actor. This singer who makes other men poets, boxing clever with every word, talking like America—fast, straight up, in headlines, comin' through with the big shtick, the aside, the quiet complement, good cop/bad cop all in the same breath. You know his story 'cause it's your story. Frank walks like America—cocksure.

"It's 1945 and the U.S. cavalry are trying to get their asses out of Europe but they never really do. They're part of another kind of invasion: American Forces Radio broadcasting a music that'll curl the stiff upper lip of England and the rest of the world. Paving the way for rock & roll with jazz, Duke Ellington, the big bands, Tommy Dorsey, and right out in front—Frank Sinatra. His voice as tight as a fist, opening at the end of a bar, not on the beat—over it, playing with it, splitting it. Like a jazz man, like Miles Davis, turning on the right phrase in the right song, which is where he lives, where he lets go, where he reveals himself. His songs are his home and he lets you in.

"But you know, to sing like that you've got to have lost a couple of fights. To know tenderness and romance you've got to have had your heart broken. People say Frank Sinatra hasn't talked to the press. They want to know how he is, what's on his mind. But you know, Sinatra's out there more nights than most punk bands selling his story through the songs, telling and articulate in the choice of those songs. Private thoughts on a public address system. Generous.

"This is the conundrum of Frank Sinatra. Left and right brain hardly talkin', boxer and painter, actor and singer, lover and father, band man and loner, troubleshooter and troublemaker. The champ who would rather show you his scars than his medals. He may be putty in Barbara's hands, but I'm not gonna mess with him. Are you?

"Ladies and gentlemen, are you prepared to welcome a man heavier than the Empire State? More connected than the Twin Towers? As recognizable as the Statue of Liberty? And living proof that God is a Catholic!" Now the laughter and cheers begin building into huge applause that continues as Bono shouts, "Will you welcome the king of New York City—Francis Albert Sinatra!"

Sinatra comes onstage to a chandelier-shaking standing ovation from the audience, and he is clearly, powerfully moved. Bono shakes his hand, backs off, and then is told to run back and give him his award. Finally the clapping dies down and Sinatra, teary-eyed, speaks. "That's the best welcome"—he chokes up—"I ever had." The applause begins again.

What happens next is almost unprecedented in the forty-five-year career of America's biggest and most guarded star; Frank Sinatra starts to really open up, to talk unguardedly: "Ladies and gentlemen, I'm delighted to see you all and I hope that we do this again—I'm not leaving you yet—but we do it again from time to time and I get to see you and get to know some of you. It's important to me. Very important."

They start clapping again and Sinatra cracks, "This is more applause than Dean heard in his whole career." The crowd laughs and Sinatra says, "He used to keep one guy in the audience to keep it going all the time."

Sure, he rambles a bit. Some people think he's tipsy from the whiskey, those closest to him might be scared that he's going to float out of his head the way he did at the video shoot last fall. But for people watching at home the effect of seeing a very human, loquacious Frank Sinatra speaking so openly is at least compelling, if not downright riveting.

Backstage, though, it's pandemonium. The panicking powers are trying to shove Bono out onstage to give Frank the hook and Bono is digging in his heels and whispering, "No way! Let him talk! No!" After four minutes of Sinatra, the TV director cues the band to start playing and the cameras to pull back to a long shot and the network to cut to a commercial.

The audience in the hall is shocked as Sinatra is abruptly drowned out by the fanfare and announcer's voice. Sinatra is confused. Bono walks out, puts his arm on Sinatra's shoulder and says, "Time to go, Frank." And the two singers walk off stage.

If the phones lit up with complaints about Bono's obscenity, they are igniting with outrage over the insult to Sinatra. When host Gary Shandling returns he announces, "Before I go on I think you'll join me in going on record that Mr. Sinatra should have finished his speech." The clapped-out crowd pound their palms until shards of skin fly onto the sleeves of French tuxedos and blood splashes onto their ermine and pearls. (Well, that's not true, but I'm running out of ways to describe "applauding with gusto.")

The best commentary comes from the next musical performer. Sinatra fan Billy Joel stops his song cold in the middle, smirks at the TV camera, studies his wristwatch and says, "Valuable advertising time going by . . . Valuable advertising time going by . . . Dollars . . . Dollars . . . Dollars." Then he kicks back in. Somewhere in this building a TV director is sliding under the door like a Chinese menu.

The Grammy Awards ceremony is only a prelude to the elephantine parties that the record companies throw at New York's most expensive restaurants afterward. The labels spend the sort of money that could sign and record a hundred young bands, trying to top each other with ice sculptures, endless feasts, orchestras, tankers of booze, and the most lavish parties of the year at the ritziest joints. Grammy night is an excuse for schnorrers in tuxes to run from "21" to the Rockefeller Center skating rink to the Museum of Modern Art to the Four Seasons to the Met in a Manhattan high-life spree that would have wilted Fred Astaire's tails.

My wife and I have ridden Bono and Ali's wake to the best table in the Rainbow Room (right next to Sting's! That cat is inevitable) and are contemplating cutting a rug to the big band when McGuinness looms up and points at his watch and says to Bono, "Frank is waiting for you at the restaurant. He wants to give you a gift."

So Bono follows Paul to a car to a restaurant where the Chairman of the Board gives his duet partner a fancy wristwatch with the inscription, "To Bono—Thanks—Frank A. Sinatra." Later Bono says that he wasn't sure if Frank might be offended by his speech, but he *liked* it. Bono, almost whispering, mentions what millions of TV viewers know, that Sinatra was moved to tears by Bono's tribute. "That's as good as it gets," Bono says, "for me."

I say, "Bono, that's as good as it gets for anybody."

The night after the Grammys I have dinner with Bono and Ali downtown, where the glitz is less ritzy but you can find meatloaf on the menu. He says that Regine has sent him the London newspapers, full of headlines such as "Bono Shocks States" because he swore on TV. The papers in Ireland, meanwhile, are berating him for public *smoking*, dooming impressionable young people to lung cancer. The American press generally sneers at his obscenity but praises the Sinatra induction speech. In the *L.A. Times,* television critic Howard Rosenberg calls it "the first time that truly memorable prose was lavished on a winner." Robert Hilburn, pop music critic for the same paper, calls it "probably the best introduction Sinatra ever got."

The main topic in all the papers, though, is the astonishing decision to cut to a commercial in the middle of Sinatra's acceptance speech. Mike Greene, the president of the Recording Industry Association of America, is widely hooted at for saying that the request came from Sinatra's own people, but Bono says he suspects that's true. He reckons that Frank's handlers were so nervous that he might slip up or drift too far astray that they jumped the gun. That they knew Frank and Bono had been backstage probably didn't help them relax.

And speaking of booze, Bono says Adam still hasn't touched a drop since Sydney. "It's too bad for Adam he can't have a drink anymore," Bono says, "but the world won't miss it. Unlike some people, who get straight and then get so boring that you feel like telling them, 'Just say yes!' "

When we get home from dinner I turn on the TV and Jay Leno is making jokes about Bono's obscenity offending Axl Rose, and "Three things you don't want to do if you hope to live a long life—don't smoke, don't eat meat, and don't cut off Frank Sinatra!"

On the Conan O'Brien show the host asks if the audience watched the Grammys and then says, "Bono beat Sting for an award. For most pretentious person with only one name!"

Edge, meanwhile, has been spending a lot of time with Morleigh in L.A. How remarkable that after the long emotional journey Edge began at the start of the Zoo TV experience, he actually came out at the other end with a new hand to hold. He pushed himself and U2 past all their old limits and traveled to the ends of the earth to fall in love with someone he'd known the whole time.

By the time the snow melts, Paul McGuinness has arrived in New York to attend the T. J. Martell dinner, the music industry's collective charity, and spend a week negotiating details of the proposed Zoo TV network with MTV. Every year the Martell Foundation honors some music biz bigwig as Humanitarian of the Year, and this time it's MTV boss Tom Freston—a tremendously deserving recipient, but also, as McGuinness points out—a sure bonanza of thousand-dollar-a-pop tickets, as every record company has to kiss MTV's ass. The entertainment is Eric Clapton, who plays an all-blues set, tracing the music from Robert Johnson to Muddy Waters and previewing his next album in the process.

There is a lot of back-and-forth between Principle and MTV over how to launch Zoo TV. Freston summed it up in his usual style—with a funny quip that contains a hard truth: "Gee, everybody wants their own TV network these days. Maybe as a prerequisite to getting your own network you should first have to try coming up with one good hour of programming a week."

Now both parties are leaning toward trying out the Zoo TV concept with a weekly show and seeing how that works. When asked my opinion (and nobody has to ask me twice) I suggest that one hour could only be a distortion of what a whole Zoo TV network would be like. Better to experiment with Zoo TV as an overnight show—say, midnight to 5 A.M.—on VH1, MTV's boring sister channel. (Another Freston line: "What should we do with VH1? It's like I have this great beachfront property and I got a shack sittin' on it!" He's lining up new management to reinvent the channel.)

Meanwhile Adam and Larry, both settled into their Manhattan apartments, adjust to life as musicians in New York. They spend a week playing together on Nanci Griffith recording sessions. Larry starts music lessons, commuting up to Boston to work with a drum teacher, and Adam plays on an album by Little Steven Van Zandt. Adam calls one afternoon and suggests we get together that evening. I pick a restaurant in the West Village. Coming out of the Seventh Avenue subway at Sheridan Square, Adam asks the first person he sees for directions. That first person is Lou Reed. Adam feels right at home.

At dinner I ask how the Zoo TV/MTV negotiations are proceeding and Adam says, "I'm staying away from it. I had to decide if I was going to use this period to become more of a businessman or more of a musician. I've chosen music. I had my first singing lesson ever today. The funny thing is, I can do it! And I met a guy there who gives bass lessons, so I made a date to start with him. Then I'm going to try to learn about computers."

Adam says he and Naomi have split for good, but the press doesn't know it so they're not going to say anything. He's a single man living in New York and he loves it. He says he's gotten back something he didn't know he'd lost—the alertness of being aware of everything going on on the street around him. He says it was buried under a self-awareness of *I am a rock star/Those people are looking at me/Here comes a photographer.* Here in New York he can see and feel the bigger picture, and it feels great.

I am reminded of Larry's words the last night in Japan, that the way for Adam and him to contribute as much as anyone else as U2 continued to evolve was to go out and work and learn new things to bring back to the band. ("Don't give the impression that I'm doing this to keep up with Bono or Edge or anyone else," Larry warned me. "I'm doing this for myself.") That's how Larry was going to spend 1994, and he hoped Adam would choose to join him. It is great, six months later, to see that Adam has and Adam loves it. He drinks water all night, he's skinny as a skeleton, his hair has grown back in its natural brown and is now startlingly balanced by a long, Russian-looking goatee. Adam looks like he should be making bombs with Mr. Molotov or writing *Crime and Punishment* by candlelight.

I tell him I got a postcard today from Willie Williams—he's back on the road with Bryan Adams and talking to R.E.M. about enlisting for their next tour. Adam says Suzanne Doyle is doing great working for

MTV in London. I tell Adam that Bill Carter landed in New York this week and has moved into an apartment in the Village that he found through Vanessa Redgrave—one of the many connections he made through his U2-backed "Miss Sarajevo" documentary.

Carter just completed a reporting assignment in Bosnia for MTV and *Rolling Stone.* As always, he was full of new stories about the lunacy of that war. I tell Adam he's got to hear this one: the parents of a friend of Bill's had lived for years in an apartment on the outskirts of Sarajevo and refused to leave. The mother was a Muslim, the father Serbian, and they sort of kidded themselves that his being a Serb might spare them from the Chetniks. Most of the other tenants had fled the building, though one woman—a teacher of retarded children—remained a couple of floors below them.

One day the old couple hears screaming and shouting in the street. They look out and see that a Serbian tank has pulled up outside, and four jibbering Serbian soldiers are climbing out and running into their building. This, they figure, is it. So for an hour they sit on the couch, hugging each other, talking about their long life together, and saying good-bye. They can hear the soldiers shouting downstairs, in the apartment of the teacher. Then, to their amazement, the voices move outside again, the tank starts up, and the soldiers drive away. They are beside themselves with relief, but figure they'd better go check on their neighbor. They go down to the special ed teacher's apartment, knock on the door and ask if she's okay. Oh, sure, she says, that was four of my students returning for a visit.

Four retarded kids in a tank! There are places on this planet where fiction cannot take you.

Oh, and I was watching some TV talk show today and the guest was Pete Best, the Beatle drummer deposed by Ringo. The interviewer asked him if any other band had ever come along who had what the Beatles had, and he said he thought only U2.

After dinner Adam wants to talk about how I'm going to write about the proposed restructuring of the deals between the four members of U2 and Paul McGuinness that was such a touchy subject by the end of the tour. He says that things have calmed down a lot.

"I think whether Paul's interests at the end of the day are musical is still in the balance for him," Adam says carefully. "I don't know where he gets his new energy from, his new blood. He seems to enjoy the corporate and the political world, and that's a great thing for us—for him to operate so well in those particular worlds. But as a fifth member to a partnership, it's not as good as it could be."

So will Paul be asked to accept a reduction from his equal fifth of U2?

"I think that's impossible to say at this point," Adam says, "and I don't think it's fair to allude to *that* as being the discussion. The roles and imbalances are a more important thing to address than the equity. If one accepts the point of view that it is the corporate, political, business world that Paul is best at, well, nobody's been in this position before! Maybe that's what he should be encouraged to go and do. Make Zoo TV into the Zoo TV Corporation, that sort of thing. It's only when we've sorted those things out that any rearrangement will be able to be thought about or discussed.

"But I'm now thinking it's not a choice of this or that. It's 'Look at the situation and see how to make the picture work for you.' These problems are resolvable. These are *growing* things, I'm not as negative as I may have once been about them. It's only as I start to learn more about other people's business that I realize the uniqueness of our own situation. Not that our own situation should be hidden because of that. I think it should be *revealed* because of it."

I couldn't agree more. The world, especially the music world, should understand U2's collectivist approach. They should understand the generosity Bono, particularly, displayed in agreeing that everything the band generated would be split equally between the four musicians and the manager. Is the system fair? Of course not, not in the way capitalism understands fairness. But it is fair according to the New Testament parable of the workers in the vineyard, in which Jesus taught that as long as one man is paid fairly, it does him no injustice if a man who does less is paid the same.

It was this all-for-one belief that allowed U2 to grow together as musicians and as people. It encouraged an environment in which if one person fell behind, the others helped bring him along. No one in U2 could profit from anyone else's loss.

And if now, fifteen years down the line, the contributions of Bono and Edge have outpaced those of the others—or if the extra *time* Bono and Edge put in entitles them to some extra compensation—honesty demands that they all consider how to make things equal again. But it is to their great credit as people that rather than recut the pie to reflect recent contributions, they have decided to see if Adam and Larry can each in his own way expand what he does to make the whole thing equal again. Paul is involved in a similar enterprise.

Faced with a partner who was not generating as much revenue as others, most multimillion dollar corporations would say, "You should accept less." U2 says, "You should add more." So far everyone's rising to the challenge.

And at the risk of making this read like an inspirational book for boys, it is satisfying to see both Paul and Adam turn away from the pursuits that were separating them from U2 and bring that energy and interest back home. God knows there was a real chance that Adam was going to opt for the easy life of a millionaire playboy, jet-setting around with the world's most glamorous women on his arm. Instead he's playing sessions and taking lessons. And Paul seems to have decided that if he could get involved in TV projects that competed with his time for U2, he could just as well get involved in setting up a channel *for* U2. He is putting all of his considerable business creativity back into the service of the band.

Adam and Paul still have a lot in common, including carrying themselves as sophisticated and unsentimental men of the world. They don't like to let on that they love U2 as much as anybody.

Adam says that U2 will reconvene in six months to decide what they will do next. Adam says that the next U2 album could be a rock & roll record (that would start off from the rock songs left off *Zooropa*), or it could be a high-tech computer album (as Edge said that last night in Japan, the future's not looking bright for the old guitar) or it could be an Irish album, lyric-based and inspired by that metaphysical, linguistically promiscuous Wildean/Yeatsean/Joycean/Beckettean/Van Morrisonean gift of gab tradition with which Bono feels such kinship.

Adam, though, is starting to evolve a different idea. He sees the future in a black woman named Me'Shell Ndgeocello, who combines a post hip-hop sensibility with a sense of seventies roots funk. He sees a point at which the rap-jazz fusion movement will find common ground with the pop audience that's gotten tired of Madonna and Prince. There seems to be a new community forming in New York: a dreadlocked, politically conscious and poetry-conscious crowd that listened to rap as kids and is now looking backward to Curtis Mayfield and Gil Scott-Heron and forward to some new hybrid—a sensibility that allows for crack musicianship alongside machines and amateurism, that would let rap move past the dead-end of gangsta without denying the harshness of ghetto life.

Adam's right on top of it. He's been checking out the atmosphere around the soul club the Cooler, discovering the Brooklyn scene that has grown up in the last ten years around Spike Lee and the M-base musicians, and listening to Me'Shell and old Stevie Wonder back to back. He loves what he's learning, and he is sending tapes of the stuff to Bono, hoping to pull Bono away from what Adam worries will be too literary an approach to the next U2 music. He says that on the next U2 album, instead of Larry playing drums with the band and then overdubbing conga or shakers, wouldn't it be great to start with the band playing with congas or some such looser percussion, and then overdub as much drum as was necessary. Of course, he shrugs, ultimately the songs will dictate the approach. But he's going to keep mailing these tapes to Bono, hoping it sinks in.

We end up heading down to S.O.B.'s to see Gil Scott-Heron, the man who wrote "The Revolution Will Not Be Televised" and who Adam is considering recommending to Mother Records. Scott-Heron, the spiritual godfather of Disposable Heroes and a ton of other socially incisive black music, can no longer raise the roof the way he could twenty years ago, but there is one enormously emotional moment in his show, when he dedicates his 1975 antiapartheid song "Johannesburg" to Nelson Mandela—who became the first black president of South Africa yesterday. That such a day would ever come seemed beyond imagining when the song was recorded. Hell, it was beyond imagining when Bono sang on Little Steven's protest song "Sun City" in 1985—when Mandela was twenty years in prison.

And maybe, maybe for just the length of Gil Scott-Heron's song tonight, we could consider that we might all have, in these last few years, dodged the bullet. Maybe we got those Fatima warnings in time and the apocalypse was averted. If ten years ago some prophet had predicted that the Berlin Wall would fall and all the Soviet states be set free, that apartheid would crumble, that the political prisoners Václav Havel and Lech Walesa and Nelson Mandela would be not only released from jail *but become presidents of their countries*, we would have said it sounds like a golden age.

Instead we've come to a crossroad, with an age of miracles over one horizon and chaos across the other. Maybe in twenty years we'll look back at this as the last moment of peace before *everybody* got nuclear weapons. At this moment of change, in these last days of the tortured twentieth century, no one's naive enough to expect the joyful moments to stay forever. So it is important that we grab them and celebrate them for as long as they last. Even if it's only the length of a single song.

59

Scoring

---

time returns to its normal shape/ going to the world cup/ an outpouring of gaelic emotion and beer/ edge passes up a chance to meet the girl of his dreams/ italian restaurants and irish bars

"I T'S MY BIRTHDAY," Paul McGuinness says in June in the swanky bar of a Manhattan hotel. Everyone raises their glasses to toast him. "I'm forty-three." I point out to Edge that it was a year ago that U2 played at the Olympic Stadium in Berlin and we toasted Paul's birthday on the plane back to Dublin. It was two years ago this week that U2 landed at Sellafield, three years since *Achtung Baby* came together in Dublin. Edge's jaw drops another notch with each anniversary I tick off. Time was elastic during the Zoo tour. During the two years on the road time stretched, snapped, shrank, and stretched again as U2 flew outside the calendar. In the six months since the tour ended in Japan, time has returned to its usual pace.

Tom Freston is here. He and McGuinness are continuing development of the Zoo TV network. The idea is becoming simpler—a hip movie channel with a few home shopping bells and whistles. Freston figures that it will be the nineties TV equivalent of all those campus repertory cinemas that showed *King of Hearts, The Harder They Come,* and *Harold and Maude* every weekend in the 1970s; it will be alternative television. Freston is exhausted—he has spent the last year on airplanes, overseeing MTV's international expansion. He has been to China three times recently. The Chinese government got so annoyed at the subversive programming being beamed in from Hong Kong that they outlawed satellite dishes and sent troops to smash up any they could find. Freston has been meeting with the communists about replacing the outlawed MTV Asia with a nice state-controlled MTV of their own. ("We have no human rights policy at MTV," he joked. "If they want to make videos using slave labor, that's fine with us.")

The Zoo TV discussions are only an excuse for McGuinness, his eight-year-old son, Max, and half the Principles to be in New York. The real occasion is the World Cup soccer match between Ireland and Italy at Giants Stadium on Saturday. It is the first time the football championships have been played in the United States and the sheer existential perfection of those two icons of ethnicity facing off within shouting distance of Ellis Island has made this match the hottest of World Cup tickets. Ireland, which has never won a game in World Cup competition, is not given much of a chance against Roberto Baggio and his mighty azzurri—but, as every Hibernian flying into New York this weekend will tell you, the Irish team recently handed the Germans an unprecedented defeat in their home stadium, and they upset the Swiss in pre-Cup play. A tie with Italy would be considered a victory, and would allow the Irish to move ahead with fists aloft and off-key singing.

New York is suffering under a railroad strike and a week-long 95-degree heat wave, made worse by oppressive humidity and thick haze. There is some sad muttering that this weather will be too much for the poor Irish team. Americans are hanging by their TVs following the bizarre case of O. J. Simpson, the legendary gridiron hero who is being pursued by police for the grisly murder of his ex-wife and a male friend. But the city is aswamp with green jerseys and Dublin accents, all of whom have only one kind of football in mind.

Edge is among them. He called me to say he was in town and was staying at Adam's place. "Adam's pad!" I said. "Boy, there must be glamorous women calling there twenty-four hours a day! Gina Lollobrigida! Raquel Welch!"

"Yeah!" said Edge. "I can't wait to get off the phone to see which of them calls next!" We meet for dinner that night with Ned ("Call Me Rosencrantz") O'Hanlon, in for the game from Dublin, and Suzanne Doyle, in from London where she has been living since going to work for MTV Europe. Over dinner there flows a lot of nostalgia, exaggerations, and shocked expressions as people fill each other in about who on the tour was having affairs with whom. There are also toasts made to Ned whose Dreamchaser has produced two of the six documentaries shortlisted from a couple of hundred submissions for the upcoming International Monitor Awards in Washington, D.C. The two

Dreamchaser nominees are Bill Carter's "Miss Sarajevo" and "Black Wind, White Land," Ali Hewson's Chernobyl documentary.

All through the meal, and afterward as we visit a couple of clubs, New Yorkers recognize Edge and send him drinks, ask for autographs, shake his hand, and tell him they are rooting for Ireland in the World Cup. Morleigh has gone off to direct a dance project overseas, so Edge is on his own. He says he's been enjoying his first real break in the fifteen years since U2 started on the road. He's been traveling a lot and working with Philips on an interactive computer "magazine."

I think Edge is onto something there; it seems that the Internet and other computer bulletin boards have taken on the air of mystery, of being part of a secret world, which rock & roll used to have when it was hard to find, when a kid had to lie in bed and fiddle with the radio dial to pull in some crazy music that he'd never heard before. I never thought I'd say this, but there is more of a sense of community in the computer world, in cyberspace, these days than there is in rock & roll. One of the amazing properties such secret communities have is the ability to imbue even the hardware they use with a piece of that mystery. Jimi Hendrix made the Stratocaster an object of beauty and magic for one generation of kids. Who's to say that someone won't make a computer look the same way to the next?

Edge, though, only wants to hear about a controversy that made a small blip in the American media last week, before being overwhelmed by the O. J. Simpson story. The television talk show host Phil Donahue made an agreement with a condemned man to broadcast the man's execution on his TV program. Conservatives successfully opposed the measure, on the grounds that if the American public saw executions on TV they might turn against capital punishment. (Fat chance! They'd probably demand boiling in oil and *Drawing and Quartering with the Rich and Famous.*) The debate ended when the potential guest star was executed. Off-camera. Edge finds this latest development in ratings-grabbing an astonishment. He wants to know if the whole culture has gone media mad.

I tell him that I recently took a friend's advice and rented Paddy Chayefsky's 1976 satirical film *Network.* My pal was right—it's all come true. *Network* predicted a culture in which the race for ratings would turn Americans into a swarm of demagogue-following, reality-program-addicted, violence-watching video junkies. At the end of the movie the hero, an old television newsman being put out to pasture, makes a speech to his Infotainment-happy successor that could have been printed on the Zoo TV screens:

> "You're television incarnate, Diana—indifferent to suffering, insensitive to joy. All of life is reduced to the common rubble of banality. War, murder, death is the same to you as bottles of beer. And the daily business of life is a corrupt comedy. You even shatter the sensations of time and space into split seconds, instant replays. You're madness, Diana. Everything you touch dies with you."

At the climax of the movie a televised assassination (paid for by the network) is run on one TV screen next to other screens filled with ads for cereal, soda pop, and the friendly skies. Edge says he doesn't know the movie. I tell him he's lived it. At the bar across the restaurant patrons are watching live helicopter transmissions of O. J. Simpson's car fleeing from the L.A. police.

The next day Ossie Kilkenny stands like Santa Claus in the lobby of the Ritz-Carlton hotel, handing out tickets to a Giants Stadium skybox and directing about forty friends and freeloaders into waiting cars and vans. Larry Mullen and Joe O'Herlihy want no part of such nonsense; they go off to sit by themselves close to the soccer field and watch Ireland battle Italy unimpeded by social interactivity.

Given the oppressive heat, even the skybox is pretty humid, but there is an appropriate corned beef and lasagna buffet and great emotion for the Gaelic/Garlic contest. As soon as the match begins one guest starts screeching, "Come on, ye boys in green!" at the top of her lungs and does not stop even as those around her recoil, pop aspirin, and plug their ears.

To an American the greatest thing about soccer is that it is played without time-outs or breaks. No commercials! Just two forty-five-minute halves, which in this heat demands superhuman stamina. Early in the game Irish midfielder Ray Houghton makes a long cross into the middle of the Italian defense. He intercepts a Marco Baresi header near the penalty area, swerves, and bangs a left-footed shot over the head of startled Italian goalkeeper Gianluca Pagliuca to score for Ireland.

Pandemonium explodes among the Irish in the packed stadium and among the Irish in our box. Everyone's screaming, hugging, jumping, almost weeping. I have to duck to avoid being kissed by Ossie Kilkenny. In soccer a single goal can mean the whole game, and the Irish immediately switch to a completely defensive strategy to make sure that happens. A couple of times Italian star Baggio makes fierce runs at the Irish goal—and the mood in our box becomes like that in the cabin of a crashing airliner. But the goal shots miss and elation explodes again. During half-time I ask Edge if it feels odd to look down at this stadium and realize he's played here too. He says it does—it looks a lot bigger from the stage—but it makes him feel even more connected to the Irish team. McGuinness is wearing one of the souvenirs on sale to celebrate the glory of Ireland: green Bono fly shades.

(One of the stories going around is that Bono, who is in London with Gavin today, was stopped by a TV reporter who in an attempt to trip him up asked if Ireland's most famous rock star could name three members of Ireland's beloved football team. Bono finessed the pharisee by saying, "Joyce, Synge, and Beckett.")

The Green hold the Blues at bay in the second half, and when the whistle blows giving Ireland its first win over Italy since they first met in 1926, well, New Year's Eve 2000 will have to go a long way to match the frenzy. Edge has been shaking a can of beer for about five minutes so that when victory is declared he can spray the whole box. Soon the Guinness is cascading like Vesuvius. "You have no idea what this means!" Edge tells me. "You have no idea!"

The hugging and spraying and weeping and laughing continues for a long, long time. Finally the guests of McGuinness and Kilkenny begin moving toward the parking lot. Larry and Joe have not turned up, but I am told not to worry about them: "Larry is probably in the *shower* with the team. We won't see them for a while!"

The mood of Irish ecstasy is best summed up by one beer-pickled son of St. Patrick, who I come across in the filthy, urine-splashed men's toilet, stumbling around the slippery floor as if in the presence of the Beatific Vision, exclaiming, "This is heaven! There is a God! This is heaven!"

Passing through the parking lot Edge keeps collecting ecstatic Irishmen who have no way of getting back to the city and offering them rides. There's Shane from Cafe Sin-e! There's Paul Brady! Ossie is appalled by Edge's generosity; we kept only two ten-seat minivans and we now have forty-eight passengers. Sweat-soaked, beer-drenched, glory-crazed Irishmen pile in on top of each other. Edge himself ends up sitting in the tiny crack between the seat and the door. "What are you doing down there, Edge?" Ossie calls halfway to New York. Edge's voice comes back, "I'm looking over the books, Ossie!"

The accountant has a portable phone and much of the ride is taken up with calling people in Dublin for trans-Atlantic shouting and screaming. Ned calls his better half, Anne-Louise, who is with Sheila and Chanty. They hold their phone out the window so we can hear the sound of every car horn in Dublin honking, and people dancing in the streets.

The gussied-up, furred-and-tuxedoed guests of the Ritz-Carlton Hotel look horrified when these two van-loads of soaking Celts dislodge onto the sidewalk in front of them and tumble into the bar of the fancy hotel. It is quickly decided that the best place to go for dinner after such a glorious triumph over Italy is to an Italian restaurant—and nobody's to take off their sweaty green shirts and green hats. I call Carmine's, the best Italian restaurant I know, and try to convince them to do something they will never do: accept a Saturday night dinner reservation for fourteen on one hour's notice. I finally get the manager on the phone and explain that I have a group of important Irish dignitaries who wish to experience the finest restaurant in New York. He gives in.

Oddly enough, we turn out to not be the only Irish dignitaries who thought it would be fun to come to celebrate at an Italian restaurant. Half of Dublin is in Carmine's when we get there. There are old soccer heroes at the bar, obnoxious drunken Irishmen singing football songs at the tables, and looks of incredulity from the regular patrons out for a night of theater and fine dining. Hooligan, after all, is an Irish name. Inevitably many of these people come by to jawbone with Paul, Edge, and the others. And just as inevitably, other drunks and groupies see that as an invitation to careen over to our table and pester Edge.

One very beautiful, very plastered woman lands next to Edge and begins throwing her arm around him, nuzzling him and flirting.

"What do you play in U2?" she asks him.

"There's no easy answer to that," he mumbles.

"Are you married? Divorced? Married but living apart?"

"I don't want to talk about it."

She proceeds to do her imitation of Edge singing "Numb" and

laughs loud at what a bad voice he has! (She's dissin' the Edge—other diners start ducking under the table.)

"What's your real name?" she asks.

"David Evans."

"I'm going to call you Dave."

"Suit yourself."

"Hello, Dave Evans."

I decide to step in. "You know," I tell her as Edge shoots daggers at me from his eyes, "the whole world loves the man called the Edge—but he's been waiting all his life for the gal who'll fall in love with simple Dave."

"Is that true?" she asks, almost crawling into his ear. "Is that what you want, Dave?"

"I just want to be loved for who I really am."

"And who are you really, Dave Evans?"

"A BIG FAMOUS MEGA RICH ROCK STAR!"

That pretty much puts the kibosh on that romance. Bono once told me that the difference between Edge and him is that if Bono sees a woman he is attracted to, he will go up and try to find out everything about her, hopefully coming across something that will assure him she and he could never get along (the trouble starts, he said, if that doesn't happen). It is the same impulse to face whatever frightens him that led a kid scared of heights to climb bridges and walk along high railings. By contrast, if Edge is attracted to a woman, he will get up and leave before he is led into temptation. I tell you this only by way of illuminating two different approaches to maintaining fidelity for all you married folks out there. I don't mean to suggest that Edge was attracted to this woman; I think he wanted to ditch her in spite of the fact that he was not attracted to her.

Edge, Ned, and I head out of the restaurant, Edge signing autographs and posing for pictures the whole way. We get a cab down to the Village, figuring we'll start celebrating our Irishness at Sin-e. But when we get there the crowd in the pub is spilling out onto the sidewalk. We buy drinks and wander down the crowded street with them. At the end of the block is another club, not quite so crowded, where a band is playing some insane Irish/Brazilian crossover and people in green hats are dancing on chairs. It looks good, so we go in and run straight into Suzanne Doyle and her retinue of revelers.

We stay there, swinging from the light fixtures, till about 3 in the morning. Then Edge, Ned, and I wander up Second Avenue looking for a quiet place for a nightcap. We find an almost empty bar and order a round. A band has finished packing up their equipment, and two tipsy women are on the stage telling Kurt Cobain jokes in the one remaining microphone.

"What was the last thing that went through Kurt Cobain's mind when he shot himself? His teeth!"

We turn around and tell them to shut up. One of them stumbles over to where we are and sticks a cigarette in her mouth looking for a light. She doesn't get it. She doesn't leave, either. She stares at Edge for a long time and says, "Are you famous? You're not . . . No, you couldn't be. Are you? I mean, I'm not impressed by celebrities. I don't care. And I mean, I don't even *like* U2."

It's all downhill from there! She stumbles on back and forth for a while, saying she likes "One," but "You're not that Edge, right? You're not *the* Edge from U2, right?"

"No," I tell her. "This is *Irving* Edge."

Edge, splendid in his green soccer jersey, says it's time to go home. "This day has done everything it can for us," he announces. "This day owes us nothing."

60

The Rest Is Easy

All God wants is a willing heart and for us to call out to Him

I N NOVEMBER of 1994 U2 are together again, in a small studio near Ladbroke Grove in London, finding out how all their parts fit together after a year away from each other. Adam came in and started programming keyboards. Larry played complicated drum patterns that impressed Bono. ("I'm less surprised that he *can* play that way than that he wants to," Bono cracks.) As they did with *Rattle and Hum* and *Zooropa* and so disastrously did not with *Achtung Baby*—the band is trying to ease into making their next album without taking on the full pressure of BEGINNING U2'S NEXT STAGE. They will not officially begin a new U2 album until the spring of 1995. But for now they will spend a couple of weeks working with Eno on improvisations that they will perhaps peddle as a motion picture soundtrack. (They have been screening rough cuts of upcoming movies, looking for the right one.)

Eno goads the band into all sorts of exercises, such as switching instruments. Edge is playing a lot of bass and Bono some impressively Edge-like guitar. During one jam with Bono on drums, guitarist Larry comes up with a surf riff inspired by the current movie *Pulp Fiction* that knocks everyone out. Bono says that one of the great things about such experimentation is that sometimes a complete song springs full grown to life in the midst of it: "A real Elvis Presley song appeared the other night. I figure we've got about eighty pieces altogether." He pauses a beat and adds, "Of course, fifty of them are awful, but still . . ."

Still, that leaves a lot of interesting material. Bono points out, quite accurately, that Tokyo is popping up all over the improvisations. "I thought we'd have to go back to Japan to get that spirit," he says. "But it's with us." Maybe it's just the group flashing back to the last time they played together, but it is startling almost a full year later to hear that sense of Tokyo overload coming out of the music U2 is making. A jam called "Tokyo Fast Bass" ducks and weaves with the barely organized frenzy of the Alta train station. "Fleet Click" staggers like those nights in the neon back alleys, but what's impressive is that, unlike almost every rhythm track I've ever heard a rock band cook up, it does not suggest any limitation on what could sit on top of it. The piece could go anywhere.

Some of the improvs get silly—on one experiment Edge, Adam, and Bono play a dark, F sharp minor pattern a little like the Velvet Underground's "Ocean" while Eno has Larry play a happy Japanese jingle on the keyboard in C major. Eno calls the result "Black and White"— because three of the band are playing all black key notes and Larry's playing all white keys. It's a clever notion, but it still sounds terrible. U2 isn't worried; they're having fun and making music no one's ever heard before while Eno runs loony animated shorts and bits of old movies on a TV monitor to keep them inspired.

During dinner one night Edge announces that this is not even a U2 session—this is Bono, Edge, Larry, Adam, and Eno. He says this five-man group has an entirely different dynamic than the four-man U2 and deserves a different name. He votes for "Babel." Also at dinner—at a funky restaurant called All Saints—is the singer Neneh Cherry and several of her collaborators. U2 invited them down to put their own spin on a bass-powered track that has been around since the Hansa sessions four years ago. During the making of Zooropa it emerged again, picking up lyrics along the lines of "Power in the wires/Power in the satellite/Power in communication." After dinner Bono gets the waiter to put a new version of the song on the restaurant's cassette player and he, Neneh, and Neneh's friend Andrea scat over it at the table, throwing out ideas for words and melodies. Bono suggests they turn the notion of power on its head. Soon they are singing "Power in submission/power in letting go" and listing all the things one should strip away to make it through the needle's eye: badges, color, skin, backstage passes.

Long after midnight the party—which has expanded to include Fintan, Regine, Anton, and lots of other Zoo veterans—takes mercy on the weary waiters and moves on across Notting Hill to the hip underground club called the Globe—immortalized in song by B.A.D. There is a wide halo around the full moon along the way, and no room at all in the club when we get there. Inside are more Zoo vets, along with punks, rastas, mad old men staring into smoky space, and chess players ignoring the blaring hip-hop. Larry, bleary from hard work and wine, elects to go home to bed. Edge takes off with his brother, Dick. Dennis Sheehan assumes a watchful position by the front door. Bono grabs a spot by the crowded bar and dances in place with Neneh while passing drinks to all who draw near. Adam, sober for a year this week, laughs and shakes hands with old friends and regards the whole scene with easygoing delight.

After an hour or so—close to 3 A.M.—I wave good night above the music and head outside. A few things about U2 seem clearer to me now than they did in the middle of the Zoo TV tour. One is how much being on the road and in the spotlight for months affects everyone's personality, and how different they all are now that they've had a year off duty. Bono in particular is much more thoughtful, much more likely to see all the sides of an issue. He recently asked that in writing of our travels I not portray him "leaping up on the table to make pronouncements while waving a sword," which is fair enough—when he's off the road he does not act like that. And I think it's a little hard for him to believe that when he's on the road he sometimes does.

Bono's hair has grown out in its natural light brown after two years of being dyed black, and his pointed beard is flecked at the chin with a bit of white. Edge jokes that he resembles Buffalo Bill. I would have said Custer. He is now nothing like the Fly, but the Fly is who he was once and who he will be again. Watching U2 in the first steps of firing up the whole machine, I am struck by how hard it must be for each of them to come back—not to the band but to who each of them is when the band is together. These are four smart, worldly, and self-sufficient men who must spend half their lives fitting into roles based on who they were as teenagers. For one of them to grow, they all have to grow. Otherwise the formula doesn't work. But you know that—this, after all, is where we came in.

During their time off, Larry fell victim to the curse that hits many people when they move to New York: because it is possible in Manhattan to work all the time, that's what he did. He learned a lot about music and freed himself up as a drummer in ways that he wants to continue to explore. But Larry wonders where his vacation went—he hardly ever socialized or relaxed.

Adam worked hard, too, but found time to have fun. A few weeks ago I ran into him with some friends at a club in New York and was reminded of what a remarkable character he is. One of Adam's friends said to me that years ago he had to make a speech taking an unpopular political position at an Irish university. He was quite nervous, and when he got up to the podium he looked down and saw Adam sitting in the front row, giving him moral support. That, he said, is the sort of thing Adam does all the time in a hundred different ways. He never asks for special consideration for himself, but when he spots someone who seems to be uncomfortable or having a bad time Adam slips in and makes sure they feel welcome. Adam seems to specialize in letting people know they're not alone.

By ducking off to America, Adam and Larry did manage to avoid some dismal Dublin duties—including the ongoing efforts to redesign the Clarence, the hotel that U2 bought. Bono and Edge ended up enduring long meetings during which they would sometimes look at each other and say, "Are we really sitting here arguing about *forks?*" During one such conference Bono insisted everyone address each other by new names. Edge, for example, was "Mr. Comfort."

Bigger fish were also fried. The Zoo TV network seems destined to take to the American airwaves in two-hour blocks, leaping from channel to channel as it goes. And although nothing in the movie business is ever fixed until it is filmed, it seems likely that *The Million Dollar Hotel* will be made after all—by Wim Wenders.

This is a remarkable world U2 have built for themselves, a world that takes in what happens outside (last week President Clinton was given a stinging rebuke in the U.S. midterm elections—both houses of Congress went Republican for the first time in our lives. Today Irish Prime Minister Albert Reynolds was forced to resign) but carries on under its own rules. U2 imagined their own world and then they created it.

When they began, four teenagers who could barely sing or play, U2 thought they would be a world-beating rock & roll band in the tradition of the Beatles, the Stones, and the Who. They thought this against absurd odds and overwhelming evidence to the contrary. And they were right. They believed, and their belief was rewarded a hundredfold. Why would they stop believing now?

I talked to Bono's father about this side of the son he refuses to call Bono, and a real paternal pride began to crack through the hard surface of the old Dub: "I remember one day distinctly saying to him, 'I hope you appreciate that this could be very transient. In six months you could be a has-been.' From what I know of the rock & roll and entertainment business, that's what happens. You're up today and gone tomorrow. He said to me, 'Dad, if we were to be gone tomorrow, I would accept it all. I'm quite prepared.'

"Now, whether he is or he isn't, I don't know. I think the last couple of years have been a change. I remember when they started off. . . . I could give you an idea, I have a letter he wrote to me."

And with that, Bob Hewson went off to search for something he'd been saving since 1980. He rummaged around for a while and came back into his parlor with a handwritten letter of several pages in a yellow envelope. He sat back down in his chair and unfolded it with a care that, were he not such a gruff character, could almost be called sentimental.

"This is when they started off," he explained. "Very early. Might give you an insight. He doesn't even know I have this bloody letter.

" 'Hello, Father . . .

" 'Just a letter to let you know your son is well and at least learned how to write at school. I started this letter in a hotel in Birmingham. . . . It's a bit of a mess. It's hard to know why people would want to live in a place like this. Even the houses look like small biscuit tins. Anyway we're here, another stop on the motorway. I'm looking forward to tonight's concert as the tour goes on. The band are getting tighter and tighter. The nights at the Marquee are very successful. Each Monday the crowd gets bigger and bigger, a situation that hasn't occurred in the Marquee on a Monday night for a long time. We did three encores last week. The single sold a thousand copies and for the first time we are getting daytime radio play on Radio One. We have four deejays behind us now. It is only a matter of time. We did two radio sessions as well. That means we go to a BBC studio and did three songs for radio. . . . .

" 'Paul McGuinness is in America at the moment planning our moves over there. We now have a rough schedule of what we're doing for the next year.' "

Bob laughed and said, "One of the dates here he says, 'November twelfth—Start the second leg of the Battle of Britain.' "

He flipped over to the next page and then read: " 'So as you can see, what was once a dream is now very real. But understand that underneath the gloss there is a lot of hard work ahead, and I hope a lot of fun. I miss home, you, Alison Stewart, sausages, and even the occasional disagreement.

" 'You should be aware that at the moment three of the group are committed Christians. That means offering each day up to God, meeting in the morning for prayers, readings, and letting God work in our lives. This gives us our strength and a joy that does not depend on drink or drugs. This strength will, I believe, be the quality that will take us to the top of the music business. I hope our lives will be a testament to the people who follow us, and to the music business where never before have so many lost and sorrowful people gathered in one place pretending they're having a good time. It is our ambition to make more than good music.

" 'I know that you must find this a ludicrous ambition, but compared to the task of getting ourselves from where we were to where we are, the rest is easy.

" 'Being older and wiser I know you must find it hard to accept what I'm saying. But all God wants is a willing heart and for us to call out to Him. Being young and troublesome can be an advantage in that you start questioning things around you. The Bible says seek and ye shall find, knock and the door will be opened. As people grow older they can grow cynical. They stop asking questions. . . . .

" 'I don't think you have stopped asking questions. Neither do I expect you to believe I have all the answers. I haven't and I keep making mistakes. . . . But I am trying and God is great. Anyway, as you can see, I'm having a good time.' "

Bob Hewson stopped reading and carefully refolded the letter. "I haven't a date on that but it's a good many years ago," he said. "It's what I was talking about earlier; they had this thing where they were committed Christians. They believed in what they were doing and they presented this image, particularly, to the American public. And I think that, perhaps, has been lost in the transition between then and now. I believe it's a bad thing."

I told Bob that perhaps U2 had not lost their sense of God's plan for them. Nothing they've done has contradicted their early faith, though they may have become less obvious in professing it, and yeah, even walked a long way into the shadows to see if they could find their way back to the light.

Bob shrugged. "You mentioned God's plan," he said. "There's something I'd forgotten that my sister-in-law reminded me of recently. Years ago, before either of the boys were born, my wife and I went down to Sligo for a week. She went to a fortune-teller and the fortune-teller told my wife that she would have two children and one of them would have the initial P and he would be famous in whatever life he took up. Isn't that extraordinary? I'd forgotten about this for years and my sister-in-law reminded me of it a few months ago."

I said that maybe Bono's mother remembered and gave Paul a little extra encouragement. Bob thought that was baloney. "Nah," he snorted. "that would be pushing it a bit. In fact, one of my regrets is that she never lived to see this. But maybe she's still looking down at him." He shrugged. "We don't know."

He sat and looked out his window at the silver Irish sea. I figured it was time for me to hit the road. Then Bob said, "I remember when he was about three, only a toddler. He was out in the back garden. He went over to a flower with a bee. He put out his finger, lifted the bee up, talked to the bee, and put it back again. He probably doesn't remember it, I don't think I ever mentioned it, but I can remember to this day the horror of my wife and myself. He could go from flower to flower picking up bees and never get stung."

Bono's father looked off, as if he were watching his exasperating child in the garden again, and he said, "Amazing, isn't it?"

Acknowledgments

Ellen Darst brought me into U2's world in 1980 and worked at keeping me there forever after. Thank you, Ellen. Special thanks also to everyone who made me feel at home on the road: the sultry Sheila Roche, the lovely Suzanne Doyle, dependable Dallas Schoo, unflappable Regine Moylett, steady Dennis Sheehan, balanced Joe O'Herlihy, Soulful Willie Williams, Fightin' Fintan Fitzgerald, Mysterious Morleigh Steinberg, and the Rosencrantz and Guildenstern of Windmill Lane—Ned O'Hanlon and Maurice Linnane.

Thanks also to those night owls Ossie Kilkenny, Eilenn Long, Bret and Theresa Alexander, Bill Carter, Nassim Khalifa, Helen Campbell, Ian Flooks, Anton Corbijn, Sharon Blankson, Tim Buckley, Kerry Anne Quinn, Bob Koch, Laura Jean Ferentz, Paul Oakenfold, Des Broadbery, and the security squad—Jerry Mele, Eric Hausch, David Guyer, Darrel Ives, Tim Ross, and L. Scott Nichols.

In Dublin—thanks for the help and hospitality to Garvin and Gwenda Evans, Dick Evans, Ali Hewson, Bob Hewson, Sebastian Clayton, Mr. & Mrs. Gavin Friday, Flood, Brian Eno, Willie Mannion, B. P. Fallon, Derek Rowan (Guggi), Fachtna O'Ceallaigh, Jim Sheridan, Sinéad O'Connor, Paul Barrett, Lindsey Sheehan, Candida Bottaci, Sandra Long, Barbara Galavan, and everyone at Principle. A special genuflection in the direction of Anne-Louise Kelly, without whom none of this would be possible and I'm sure she often wished it weren't.

In the USA—thanks first to my old pals Keryn Kaplan and Dan Russell. And to Susie Smith, Catherine Owens, Tom Freston, Judy McGrath, Jeff Jones, Jeff Pollack, Carter Allen, Phil Joanou, Jimmy

Iovine, Peter Buck, Hyacinth Amero, Nathan Brackett, George Regis, Nancy Sullivan, Ina Meibach, Rick Dobbis, Dennis Fine, Cameron Crowe, Holly Peters, Bess Dulany, Barbara Skydel, Frank Barsalona, Sue and Kevin Godley, Holly George-Warren and all at *Rolling Stone* Press, Paul Wasserman, Brian O'Neal, Richard Lloyd, Heather M. Beckel, the Glide Memorial United Methodist Church, Billy Graham Ministries, Rhonda Markowitz, Michael Shore, Al Dunstan, and the inimitable Hal Willner. I owe an enormous debt to everyone at *Musician* magazine, especially Mark Rowland.

Please give a big hand to our guest stars—R.E.M.! Naomi Campbell! Christy Turlington! Bruce Springsteen! Axl Rose! Salman Rushdie (such a nice guy that after the first hour I forgot about trying to collect the reward)! Gary Oldman! Lou Reed! Peter Gabriel! Pearl Jam! Mick Jagger! Bob Dylan! Van Morrison! Sting! Frank Sinatra! John Lydon! Randy Newman! Aimee Mann! Robbie Robertson! Let's all get together and do a charity concert.

Thanks for the good advice—T-Bone Burnett & Sam Phillips, Elvis Costello & Cait O'Riordan, Jeff Rosen, Jim Stein, Lavinia Trevor, Thom Duffy, John Telfer, Ed Bicknell & Mark Knopfler. Thanks to Betsy Bundschuh for getting it from the get-go.

All the reporting and interviews in this book are my own, except where I cite another source in the text. Fred Schruers was kind enough to ask Dan Lanois some questions for me when he interviewed Dan for *Musician.* Thanks, Fred. My work on the chapter about the coming changes in communications technology led to my asking Fred Goodman to write a story on that subject for *Musician.* Goodman's reporting, in turn, gave me new information, which I used in the book. How's that for a snake eating its tail? I swiped Bono's exclamation on hearing Clinton had been elected from an article by Paul Du Noyer in *Q* magazine.

Adam Clayton, Bono, Edge, Larry Mullen, and Paul McGuinness have a reputation for exerting tight control over media access to U2. It is not, by and large, a bum rap. But when I approached them about cooperating with this book they agreed to give me unlimited access to the band and their organization and asked for nothing in return—no manuscript approval, no financial remuneration, no controls of any kind. My experience writing about well-known people is that you cannot predict what they will like and what will get them angry. It seems very unlikely that I could write a whole book about U2 and not cause some hard feelings. That is the nature of biography; it's the nature of journalism and criticism. I am very grateful to them for letting me get so close.

Larry Mullen told me at the outset of this project that he was comfortable with it because U2 had been introduced to me in 1980 as a journalist and, however friendly we'd become, that had remained our relationship. There was no question between us about confidences being betrayed or motives being questioned. If they said or did something in front of me, it was fair game. During the months I traveled with U2 they were extraordinarily open and generous with me, but we both knew that if they didn't want something to get into print they should keep it away from me.

There must have been occasions when U2 regretted that I was around, but they never tried to get me to bury something. They took the best attitude anyone can take with a working writer: "I knew he was a scorpion when I put him on my back."

I've thought a lot about why a band with nothing to gain let me so far in, and I think the answer is in an interview I did with Bono ten years ago. He said, "I would aspire to being a soul singer," and he explained, "A singer becomes a soul singer when he decides to reveal rather than conceal." For all the sunglasses and photo-approval and image-shaping that they have learned since then, U2 still believe in their hearts that the truth will justify and set them free. They still reveal everything when they play their songs. They are soul singers now.

Bill Flanagan
New York, January 1995

Index